INTERNATIONAL FINANCIAL MARKETS

SECOND EDITION

INTERNATIONAL FINANCIAL MARKETS

SECOND EDITION

J. Orlin Grabbe
formerly of the Wharton School of the University of Pennsylvania

Elsevier
New York • Amsterdam • London • Tokyo

Cover photograph courtesy of Citicorp.

Elsevier Science Publishing Co., Inc.
655 Avenue of the Americas
New York, New York 10010

Sole distributors outside the United States and Canada:

Elsevier Science Publishers B.V.
P.O. Box 211, 1000 AE Amsterdam, The Netherlands

Library of Congress Cataloging-in-Publication Data

Grabbe, J. Orlin.
    International financial markets / J. Orlin Grabbe.—2nd ed.
        p.   cm.
    Includes bibliographical references (p.   ) and index.
    ISBN 0-444-01598-1 (hardcover : acid-free paper)
        1. Foreign exchange. 2. Euro-bond market. 3. Euro-dollar market.
    4. Currency question—Europe.   I. Title.
HG3851.G64   1991
332.4′5—dc20   91-3584
                                                                        CIP

Current printing (last digit):

10   9   8   7   6   5   4   3   2   1

Manufactured in the United States of America

CONTENTS

PREFACE   vii

READER'S INTRODUCTION   xi

PART I HISTORY OF THE INTERNATIONAL FINANCIAL SYSTEM, 1944—1990   **1**

CHAPTER 1 THE RISE AND FALL OF BRETTON WOODS   3

2 GLOBALIZATION AND THE GROWTH OF DERIVATIVES   27

PART II FOREIGN EXCHANGE MARKETS   **63**

CHAPTER 3 INTRODUCTION TO THE FOREIGN EXCHANGE MARKET   65

4 FORWARDS, SWAPS, AND INTEREST PARITY   83

5 FOREIGN CURRENCY FUTURES   99

6 FOREIGN CURRENCY OPTIONS   121

PART III THE DETERMINATION OF EXCHANGE RATES   **175**

CHAPTER 7 EXPECTATIONS, INFORMATION, AND EXCHANGE RATE SPECULATION   177

8 PURCHASING POWER PARITY   189

9 FOREIGN EXCHANGE RATES AND THE
BALANCE OF PAYMENTS   205

10 FOREIGN EXCHANGE FORECASTING   221

11 PORTFOLIO CHOICE AND FOREIGN EXCHANGE   231

PART IV **EUROCURRENCY MARKETS**   **245**

CHAPTER 12 EUROBANKING AND EUROCURRENCY CENTERS   247

13 DEPOSIT DEALING AND THE TERM STRUCTURE
OF EUROCURRENCY RATES   261

14 EUROCURRENCY FUTURES AND OPTIONS   271

15 SYNDICATED EUROCREDITS   287

PART V **INTERNATIONAL BOND MARKETS**   **299**

CHAPTER 16 INTRODUCTION TO THE INTERNATIONAL
BOND MARKETS   301

17 NEW ISSUE PROCEDURES IN THE
EUROBOND MARKET   317

18 EUROBOND VALUATION AND HEDGING   329

19 INTEREST RATE AND CURRENCY SWAPS   347

20 PRICING OPTION FEATURES IN
INTERNATIONAL BONDS   367

SELECTED BIBLIOGRAPHY   381
GLOSSARY   389
INDEX   403

PREFACE

This book, an introduction to international financial markets for students in an MBA program, should also be of interest to undergraduates and could serve as supplementary reading in doctoral courses. The subject matter—the international financial markets for foreign exchange, eurocurrencies, and international bonds—is a neglected topic. Standard economics courses, although labeled "international finance," are really courses in open-economy macroeconomics whose principal focus is optimal monetary and fiscal policy in an open economy. These courses seem to imply that government policy is the major issue of importance in international finance, a point of view that may not be convincing to someone envisioning a career in investment or commercial banking or international trade and investment. In addition, in these courses financial markets are often so stylized that an average student with a practical orientation may be tempted into mental segmentation: he or she comes to believe that there is economic theory and there is the real world, and never shall the twain meet. My own point of view is that optimal monetary and fiscal policy is appropriate subject matter for the standard *macroeconomics* course but does not need to be covered twice. There are no open and closed economies—only open and closed economists. If the macroeconomics instructor has never heard of imports, exports, or foreign exchange, that problem should be remedied at the source.

Many descriptive institutional accounts of the international financial markets are also available, but these sometimes suffer from too much institutional detail and not enough theory. The beginning student needs to grasp the basic dynamic structure of a market (which is what theory tries to get at) before he or she can easily stockpile a great many real-world facts. Without a proper organizing framework, the student is in much the same position as those international bureaucrats of the 1960s of whom it was said, "They could not see the Bretton Woods for the Bretton trees."

In between these two extremes are standard financial management courses oriented toward multinational corporations or international banking. Such courses discuss international financial markets in connection with other management issues, but their scope is too broad for a proper treatment of financial markets *as markets*. For example, it would be desirable for a student already to have acquired an understanding of the interbank market in foreign exchange, an empirical feel for the nature or magnitude of FX risk, and an understanding of how to hedge with FX forwards, futures, and options before approaching the management question of how an operational FX risk-control system should or should not be organized.

This book attempts to delineate the basic rules of the game in each of the three major international financial markets and to convey to the student an intuitive feel for market dynamics. It is designed to precede logically courses devoted to the individual management issues faced, respectively, by multinational corporations, commercial banks, investment banks, and central banks or finance ministries. The material of this book should thus comprise an introductory course in international finance that can then be followed by standard courses in multinational corporate finance, open-economy macroeconomics, or international banking. The book will not only be of interest to international managers generally but also has immediate relevance for students desiring to participate in such market activities as FX trading, bond syndication, or eurodollar creation.

Since the text is a blend of theory and institutions, some sacrifice of detail in both areas has been necessary, and my guiding principle has been to select that which is of the greatest practical use. Of course, what is of most use is a matter for individual judgment; this book represents mine. For example, while I have included a discussion of risk-return tradeoffs in connection with international capital flows, I have not devoted space to the international capital-asset pricing model because I believe its extreme assumptions preclude its practical usefulness.

The student is assumed to have had, as academic prerequisites, an introductory course in economics (covering both macroeconomics and microeconomics) and an introductory course in statistics. No calculus is used in the text except for the integral of the normal distribution, and technical discussions are conducted at an intuitive level. The level of mathematical treatment varies from topic to topic. This is intentional and is based on value-added considerations. For example, the European Monetary System is treated in detail in Chapter 2 because it is a living institution that exerts a daily influence on European exchange rates. By contrast, no equations are used to describe the Bretton Woods system, which is primarily of historical interest. As another example, the mathematics of option pricing has proved to be of great practical importance, so Chapter 6 is somewhat more technical than other chapters. As an aid to the student, the more technical paragraphs that can be skipped without loss of continuity begin with an open square ($\square$) and end with a solid square ($\blacksquare$).

Most of the material in this book is based on multiple sources, with some of the most helpful published references listed in the bibliography. In addition, I am grateful for useful information provided by individuals at the following institutions: Bankers Trust Company; Chemical Bank; Credit Lyonnais; Drexel, Burnham, Lambert; European Inter-American Finance (Eurinam); Euroclear Clearance System, Ltd.; the Federal Reserve Board; FX Systems

Inc.; Goldman Sachs; the International Monetary Fund; the International Money Market of the Chicago Mercantile Exchange; Irving Trust Co.; Merrill Lynch; the Ministry of Finance of Japan; the Ministry of Finance of Mexico; Morgan Guaranty Trust Co.; the Philadelphia Stock Exchange; Salomon Brothers; and the World Bank.

A Note on the Second Edition
The first edition of this book found a place in bank training programs around the world, as well as in 60 business schools. It is hoped this updated edition will help maintain the book's usefulness. The principal revisions or additions are in Chapters 2, 6, and 12 to 20. The previous chapter 15, on money creation in the eurodollar market, has been dropped. Its replacement is a chapter devoted to eurocurrency futures and options, which appears as chapter 14 in this edition.

J. Orlin Grabbe

READER'S INTRODUCTION

International finance exists because individual sovereign states exist. Without different states that have different currencies and different policies governing financial assets denominated in those currencies there would only be domestic finance. For the immediate future, however, there seems little danger that the division of the world into domestic and foreign, Greek and barbarian, will disappear.

This book is concerned with the three major international financial markets—the foreign exchange market, the eurocurrency market, and the international bond market—and is oriented to those who may wish to participate in these markets. For market participants, the existence of diverse policy regimes is a fact of nature; devoting excessive amounts of time to the question of why different countries have different policies is comparable to extended preoccupation with the question of why different consumers have different tastes or why different investors have different risk preferences. The focus of attention here is thus on market action in an environment of which government is a part, an approach different from the widespread one that takes market behavior as given and concentrates on the manipulation of markets through government policy.

The foreign exchange, eurocurrency, and international bond markets are each treated in four aspects: historical, institutional, economic, and empirical. Each type of information has its place in understanding the operation of international financial markets. The existence of institutions such as the International Monetary Fund or currency arrangements like the European Monetary System is most easily understood in a historical context. While institutional features (what FX traders do, how eurobonds are cleared in the secondary market, where eurobanks are located) will change over time, they are not nearly so arbitrary as often thought, and at any rate represent the machine through which the ghost of theory operates. Clarification of the underlying economic principles governing international finance is the heart of this book and the basis on which it is organized. I have focused on the

conceptual insights of theory as applied to markets—and avoided the method-
ological debates with which the academic literature is preoccupied—on the
assumption that most readers are interested in achieving professional success
in a market rather than an academic environment. An acquaintance with some
empirical evidence—about purchasing-power parity, or transactions costs in
the international bond market, or the performance of FX forecasters—is also
important for understanding international financial markets.

Since the historical material is easier to grasp when told as a continuous
story, it is collected and presented chronologically in Part I. Part I also serves
as a general introduction to and overview of the rest of the book and should
not, under any circumstances, be omitted. Chapter 1 covers the background of
the Bretton Woods agreement, the rise of the eurocurrency markets, the gold
politics of the 1960s, and the breakdown of Bretton Woods at the beginning of
the 1970s. Chapter 2 looks at successor currency arrangements (including the
European Monetary System), developments in the eurocurrency and international bond markets, the background of the debt crisis, and the arrival of Japan
on the international financial stage. In addition to illustrating the interaction
between economics and politics, Part I also introduces a number of basic
economic concepts in historical context. Chapter 1, for example, examines the
effects of central bank intervention in the FX and gold markets, explains what
eurocurrencies are, and illustrates the policy requirements of a fixed exchange
rate system.

Part II covers the basic forms of foreign exchange contracts: spot, forward,
futures, and option. Chapter 3 introduces the concept of the market-maker,
surveys interbank currency trading in a free market, and looks at the effects of
exchange controls. Chapter 4 explains forward and swap FX contracts and
their relation to eurocurrency interest rates through the interest parity theorem. Chapter 5 looks at organized currency futures trading, compares futures
and forward contracts, and explains futures hedging. Chapter 6 explains what
FX option contracts are, how they may be used as FX insurance, and how to
price them in relation to other financial assets.

After finishing Parts I and II, the reader may proceed directly to any one of
Parts III, IV, or V, since these three sections are essentially independent of
one another. The chapters within a part should, however, be read in the order
presented.

Part III builds a framework for understanding why exchange rates change
and how such changes relate to economic decision-making. Chapter 7 looks at
foreign currency speculation in terms of a trader's expectations and information. Chapter 8 examines commodity arbitrage in international markets and
examines the requirements for different versions of purchasing power parity to
hold. Chapter 9 relates FX determination to a broader spectrum of economic
forces, including not only trade in commodities but also consumption and
savings and central bank intervention. It explains the basic structure of a
"balance of payments" flow of funds statement and looks at some empirical
evidence pertaining to central bank informational superiority. Chapter 10 in-
terprets FX forecasting as the formal process of generating expectations and
looks at the empirical evidence on forecasting performance in light of the
Model Theorem introduced in Chapter 7. Chapter 11 then looks at risk-return

tradeoffs in a portfolio context, given forecast-generated expectations and the associated uncertainty.

Part IV is devoted to the eurocurrency market. Chapter 12 describes the market in terms of the major features of a typical eurobank balance sheet and gives some additional material on eurobanking centers and the Basle risk-based capital requirements. Chapter 13 focuses on the interbank market. It relates the market risks in borrowing and lending to the term structure of eurocurrency interest rates and forward rate agreements (FRAs). Chapter 14 looks at eurocurrency futures, relates the futures strip to FRAs, and explains the pricing of eurodollar options, as well as caps, floors, and collars. Chapter 15 covers the formation of eurocredit syndicates, and more recent developments such as loan participations, debt swaps, revolving underwriting facilities, and eurocommercial paper.

The international bond markets are the subject of Part V. Chapter 16 distinguishes between the eurobond and foreign bond markets and describes major features of leading markets. Procedures followed in bringing a new eurobond to market are explained in Chapter 17. Chapter 18 considers secondary eurobond trading and clearing, the valuation of eurobonds in relation to other assets, and hedging with bond futures. Interest rate and currency swaps, and related contracts like swaptions, bridge the capital and money markets, so it was natural to include them in Part V as Chapter 19. Chapter 20 extends the options analysis of Chapters 6, 14, and 19, examining option features in international bonds.

Paragraphs set off by open (□) and solid (■) squares are fairly technical and may be skipped on the first reading without loss of continuity.

Numerical examples are dispersed throughout the book. Readers should make certain they understand each example as it is encountered before proceeding with the text. In most cases, this will involve working through the steps with pencil and paper. Further numerical problems are provided at the ends of chapters.

Readers are also encouraged to supplement the text with a steady diet of current news relating to international finance. Some useful sources in this regard include the daily newspapers *The Wall Street Journal* and the London *Financial Times*, the weekly newsmagazine *The Economist*, the monthly *Euromoney*, and the *Annual Report* of the Bank for International Settlements.

HISTORY OF THE INTERNATIONAL FINANCIAL SYSTEM, 1944-1990

THE RISE AND FALL OF BRETTON WOODS

BRETTON WOODS

The end of the Second World War can be taken as year zero for the current system of international finance. There wasn't much in the way of foreign exchange or international bond trading in 1945 and another decade would pass before eurocurrency markets were created. The depression of the 1930s, followed by the war, had vastly diminished commercial trade, the international exchange of currencies, and cross-border lending and borrowing. Left were only memories of what the system had once been, along with competing visions of what could and should be resurrected from the rubble. Revival, it was generally agreed, entailed new institutions and political agreements. Certainly not much thought was given to the enormous progress in information technology and telecommunications that had come about during the war and would later have a profound impact on international financial practice.

Reconstruction of the postwar financial system began with the Bretton Woods agreement that emerged from the International Monetary and Financial Conference of the United and Associated Nations in July 1944 at Bretton Woods, New Hampshire. Bretton Woods is a tiny ski village in the White Mountains whose notable features are the world's longest cog railway and the mammoth Mount Washington Resort Hotel—which, situated at the foot of the Presidential range, is an ideal setting for a conference. The 1944 agreement, setting out the major parameters of the postwar system, represented an unusual degree of advance planning. The establishment of a beachhead on Normandy by Allied forces under General Dwight Eisenhower had taken place only the month before, and even the outcome of the war with Germany could not yet be predicted with total certainty.

But there was a deep-rooted reason for the timing of the Bretton Woods debate about postwar finances. Many at the conference were convinced that, by making advance preparations for the peace, they could avoid the mistakes associated with the aftermath of the Great War of 1914–1919. They had concluded that the primary reason they were at war—once again with Germany—was that, although the Allies had won the earlier war, they had mismanaged the peace. This mismanagement, they felt, had resulted from the squabbling among the great powers, who had yielded to the political sentiments of the moment and had shown a lack of foresight in the economic provisions of the peace negotiations of 1919. Bretton Woods was part of an attempt to avoid a repetition of the same mistakes when the war with Hitler was over.

American and British rivalry was another factor that underlay the early planning. Although forty-four nations signed the Bretton Woods agreement, it was primarily the United States and Great Britain who negotiated the terms, each intent on persuading everyone else to adopt its particular vision of postwar monetary arrangements. The two principal individuals involved in the negotiations were Harry Dexter White, representing the United States, and John Maynard Keynes, representing Great Britain.

The chain of events leading to Bretton Woods had started in 1940. German propaganda broadcasts were describing a "New Order," the National Socialist vision of how the world would be organized financially and economically in the future, under German leadership. Such propaganda can be effective in two senses. By being first to propose a plan you get people thinking your way: you structure the debate. Second, such a plan implied Germany was so sure of winning the war that it could get on with planning the next stage. Such confidence invited neutral third parties to join a winning team. In November 1940, the British Ministry of Information asked John Maynard Keynes, the noted British economist, to prepare counterpropaganda broadcasts, which required Keynes to give some thought to financial organization after the war. Aside from the propaganda needs of the moment (Winston Churchill said that "in wartime, truth is so precious that she should always be attended by a bodyguard of lies"), both Keynes and British government officials were determined that, whatever plans were made, they could not afford to repeat the miscalculations associated with the Treaty of Versailles that had ended World War I.

In fact, Keynes had first become famous in 1919 with his international bestseller *The Economic Consequences of the Peace*. The official representative of the British Empire to the Supreme Economic Council that set out the terms of German reparations, Keynes had resigned in protest and had written a book explaining why. He had argued that the primary policy objective of the Allies should be the stabilization of central Europe, not the imposition of unpayable reparations on Germany. Europe was in a dangerously chaotic political condition following the collapse of the Austro-Hungarian Empire, he had said, and the terms of the Versailles treaty would aggravate the situation and play into the hands of the extreme elements.

In warfare, the spoils traditionally go to the victor. The modern interpretation of this principle meant that the loser in the war reimbursed the victor for costs associated with conducting the war. This reimbursement was referred to as *reparations*. Germany had exacted reparations from France after the Franco-Prussian War of 1870–1871, for example. And in Article 231 of the Treaty of Versailles (signed on June 28, 1919) Germany and its allies were named the aggressors in the recent war and were held responsible for all loss and damage suffered by the Allies. But it seemed obvious, at least to Keynes, that the degree of international interdependence had now increased to the point that it was no longer necessarily in one's own self-interest to demand from the loser payment in gold and goods. He sounded the ominous warning that the "Carthaginian peace is not *practically* right or possible. . . . You cannot restore Central Europe to 1870 without setting up such strains in the European structure and letting loose human and spiritual forces as . . . will overwhelm not only you and your 'guarantees,' but your institutions and the existing order of your society."

Whether for the reasons Keynes set out or for others, events did not follow the course anticipated by most members of the Versailles Peace Conference in 1919, and by 1940 officials in both the British and the U.S. treasuries viewed Versailles as an administrative disaster. The treaty had been followed in Germany by the hyperinflation of 1920–1923 that had effectively undermined the power of the German middle class, with its moderating political influence, by destroying the real value of middle-class savings—which had been generally kept in the form of financial assets. The extent of the inflation can be seen in the exchange value of the mark, which was about 14 per U.S. dollar at the end of the war in 1919. When the inflation ended on November 20, 1923, the exchange rate was 4 *trillion* marks per U.S. dollar. (That same day the president of the Reichsbank—the German central bank—died of a heart attack, raising an interesting question of cause and effect.) Hitler's famous Munich beer-hall putsch occurred in November 1923, at the height of the inflation, and later the National Socialists were able effectively to exploit popular resentment over the terms of the treaty.

In 1941, Keynes was sent to Washington as a representative of Churchill and the Chancellor of the Exchequer to settle the terms of Lend-Lease aid that Britain would receive from the United States. As part of the conditions for receiving the ultimate $30 billion in aid, the British were pressured to commit themselves to postwar arrangements as foreseen by the United States. While not in much of a bargaining position, the British did press for their objectives. They did not want to surrender the reserve currency status of the pound sterling. They took it for granted (as did the United States) that exchange rates should be fixed. In this context, they assumed that Britain would have a persistent tendency to import more from the United States than it exported to the United States and thought that this factor, combined with the British goal of full employment, would require various types of import restrictions, barter arrangements, and capital controls. Keynes, in fact, approved of the methods practiced by Hjalmar Schacht—the German "financial wizard" who had brought about the termination of the German hyperinflation and later served as Hitler's economic minister—which involved economic units directly bartering (trading) one type of good for another without the use of currency.

On the U.S. side, Secretary of the Treasury Henry Morgenthau gave Harry Dexter White the task, in December 1941, of thinking about future international money arrangements. White's views were already on record in an earlier study he had done in 1934 for Jacob Viner at the Treasury. It had stressed the need for fixed exchange rates, international cooperation, and settlement in gold as the basis for the international financial system. White's report to Morgenthau, making similar proposals, formed the basis for the Bretton

Woods agreement. The White report also proposed an Inter-Allied (later a United Nations) Stabilization Fund to stabilize exchange rates and remove exchange controls and an Inter-Allied (later United Nations) Bank to provide capital for economic reconstruction. These two proposals came to fruition as the present-day International Monetary Fund (IMF) and the International Bank for Reconstruction and Development (World Bank).

The views of other U.S. officials were also important in setting the tone of the Bretton Woods negotiations. Secretary of State Cordell Hull believed that the fundamental causes of the two world wars lay in economic discrimination and trade warfare. Specifically he had in mind the trade and exchange controls (bilateral arrangements) of Nazi Germany and the imperial preference system practiced by Britain (by which members or former members of the British Empire were accorded special trade status). An internal State Department paper in 1939 had even proposed a trade agreement with Germany as a way to avoid war. Overall, the Americans wanted a postwar system in which trade could expand. William Clayton, the assistant secretary of state for economic affairs, said: "We need markets—big markets—around the world in which to buy and sell." The free trade concerns would finally lead in 1947 to the General Agreement on Trade and Tariffs (GATT), by which member nations would generally agree to accord no special trade status to any one member that was not accorded to all. The concern over exchange controls was incorporated in the articles of agreement of the International Monetary Fund. Members were pledged to work for the removal of all such controls.

In the State Department the view prevailed that the United States should remove itself from its historical isolation and play a leading role in a new world order in which it was thought power politics would be absent. According to Harry Dexter White, "it was expected that the early post-war world would witness a degree of unity and good-will in international political relationships among the victorious allies [including Russia] never before reached in peacetime. It was expected that the world would move rapidly . . . toward 'One World.' . . . No influential person, as far as I can remember, expressed the expectation or the fear that international relations would worsen during those years." International institutions like the International Monetary Fund and the World Bank, with willing U.S. participation, were a step in the direction of this one, united world.

Finally, a strong antibanking perspective led Secretary of the Treasury Morgenthau to throw his support to the new international financial institutions. At the Bretton Woods conference he predicted that the establishment of the IMF and the World Bank would "drive the usurious money lenders from the temple of international finance." Morgenthau's view contrasted with U.S. private-sector sentiment, which was not greatly exercised over usurious moneylenders but rather saw the proposed institutions as a covert scheme to subsidize debtor nations.

The main points of the postwar system evolving from the Bretton Woods agreement that are important for our purposes can be summarized as follows:

1. A new institution, The International Monetary Fund (IMF), would be established in Washington, D.C. Its purpose would be to lend foreign exchange to any member whose supply of foreign exchange had become

scarce. This lending would not be automatic, but would be conditional on the member's pursuit of economic policies consistent with the other points of the agreement, a determination that would be made by the IMF.

2. The U.S. dollar (and, de facto, the British pound) would be designated as reserve currencies, and other nations would maintain their foreign exchange reserves principally in the form of dollars or pounds.

3. Each Fund member would establish a *par value* for its currency, and maintain the exchange rate for its currency within *1 percent* of par value. In practice, since the principal reserve currency would be the U.S. dollar, this meant that other countries would peg their currencies to the U.S. dollar, and—once convertibility was restored—would buy and sell U.S. dollars to keep market exchange rates within the 1 percent band around par value. The United States, meanwhile, separately agreed to buy gold from or sell gold to foreign official monetary authorities at $35 per ounce in settlement of international financial transactions. The U.S. dollar was thus pegged to gold, and any other currency pegged to the dollar was indirectly pegged to gold at a price determined by its par value.

4. A Fund member could change its par value only with Fund approval and only if the country's balance of payments was in "fundamental disequilibrium." The meaning of fundamental disequilibrium was left unspecified, but everyone understood that par value changes were not to be used as a matter of course to adjust economic imbalances.

5. After a postwar transition period, currencies were to become convertible. That meant, to anyone who was not a lawyer, currencies could be freely bought and sold for other foreign currencies. Restrictions were to be removed, and hopefully eliminated. So, in order to keep market exchange rates within 1 percent of par value, central banks and exchange authorities would have to build up a stock of dollar reserves with which to intervene in the foreign exchange market.

6. The Fund would get gold and currencies to lend through "subscription." That is, countries would have to make a payment (subscription) of gold and currency to the IMF in order to become a member. Subscription quotas were assigned according to a member's size and resources. Payment of the quota normally was 25 percent in gold and 75 percent in the member's own currency. Those with bigger quotas had to pay more but also got more voting rights regarding Fund decisions.

FIXING THE PRICE OF FOREIGN EXCHANGE AND GOLD

The Bretton Woods agreement committed member countries to peg exchange rates—or rather to keep them within a plus or minus 1 percent margin around a declared par value. What does it mean to fix the price (the exchange value) of something? If no trading other than with official authorities is allowed (as where a currency is "inconvertible"), then fixing the price is easy. The central bank or exchange authority simply says the price is S, say S = 4 German marks per 1 U.S. dollar, and no one can say differently. If you want to trade German marks for dollars, you have to deal with the central bank, and you have to trade at central bank prices. The central bank may in fact even refuse to trade with you, but it can still claim that the exchange rate is fixed. If, however, free trade is allowed, fixing the price requires a great deal more. The price can be fixed only by altering either the supply of or the demand for the asset. For example, if you wanted to fix the price of gold at $35 per ounce, you could only do so by being willing and able to supply unlimited amounts of gold to the market to drive the price back down to $35 per ounce whenever there would otherwise be excess demand at that price, or to purchase unlimited amounts of gold from the market to drive the price back up to $35 per ounce whenever there would otherwise be excess supply at that price.

In order to peg the price of gold you would thus need two things: a large stock of gold to supply to the market whenever there is a tendency for the market price of gold to go up, and a large stock of dollars with which to purchase gold whenever there is a tendency for the market price of gold to go down. The same is true if the central bank wants to peg the exchange value of the domestic currency with respect to a foreign currency. If the German central bank wants to peg the exchange rate at DM4 = U.S.$1, it has to have a stock of deutschemarks and a stock of dollars. The deutschemarks are no problem—the central bank can always create more of them at will. But dollars are a problem to the German central bank. If there is excess demand for dollars, perhaps because at the pegged exchange rate dollars are too cheap (the central bank is selling them for DM4 when it should be selling them for, say, DM5), the central bank may run out of dollars and will no longer be able to maintain the peg. Dollars in this case are the German central bank's reserves, so we may summarize by saying: If the central bank or exchange authority sets an exchange rate that undervalues foreign currency—that is, overvalues domestic currency—the central bank will lose reserves. Conversely, if the pegged rate overvalues foreign currency, the central bank will gain reserves.

If a central bank is *losing* reserves, there is an excess demand for foreign currency (an excess supply of domestic currency) at the rate at which the central bank is pegging. In this case, the country is said to be running a *balance of payments deficit*. If a central bank (or exchange authority) is *gaining* reserves, there is an excess supply of foreign currency (an excess demand for domestic currency) at the rate at which the central bank is pegging. In the second case, the country is said to be running a *balance of payments surplus*.

We will explore the concept of balance of payments in Chapter 9. It should be obvious from the preceding paragraph, however, that if the central bank is not pegging or otherwise making any attempt to influence the market value of its currency, it will not have either a surplus or a deficit on the balance of payments except as an accounting artifice. This qualification is used because creative accountants can always jerry-rig a "deficit" or a "surplus" by calculating the balance in an arbitrary way. Such engineering deficits or surpluses may have no importance, however, except as political entertainment.

As an additional part of the Bretton Woods agreement, the United States committed itself to trade gold with foreign officials at a fixed price of $35 per ounce. In a sense, this was a commitment to peg the market price of gold, because if the private market price of gold differed from the official price—if, for example, the private market price were $37 per ounce—a foreign central bank would have an incentive to buy from the United States at $35 per ounce and sell on the private market at $37 per ounce. So the U.S. commitment meant that the United States needed, in principle, a large stock of gold to sell whenever the private market price rose above $35. Gold the United States had aplenty: by war's end in 1945 the United States had about 60 percent of the total world stock.

The U.S. commitment to peg the price of gold had other implications. Suppose that gold would always at any time trade for the same amount of other real goods—wheat, steel, bananas. In such a situation, the price of gold would by synonymous with *purchasing power*. You could always trade an ounce of gold for a predetermined bundle of other commodities. The U.S. commitment to buy and sell gold for $35 per ounce would then mean that the purchasing power of the dollar would have to be maintained at a constant level; there could be no inflation in the United States. In addition, if other countries did not alter the par value of their currencies in terms of the U.S. dollar, their currencies would also have fixed purchasing power, and there could be no inflation in these countries either.

It will, of course, not work exactly that way in practice. The relative price of gold in terms of wheat, steel, and bananas will change over time depending on relative supply and demand in each of those commodity markets. Thus, the price of gold will at best only roughly approximate purchasing power. In addition, the 1 percent margins around par value for exchange rates will allow some additional variation in the gold value of other countries' currencies. Finally, in case of "fundamental disequilibrium," a country might be allowed to change its par value from time to time, which would also alter its currency's gold value.

But even when we grant all these modifications, it is still safe to summarize: *The Bretton Woods agreement, if adhered to, precluded sustained inflation on the part of member nations.* The values of other currencies were pegged to the dollar, which was pegged to gold. On the other hand, if the requirement that the dollar be pegged to gold were dropped and only the requirement that the par values of other currencies be maintained with respect to the dollar kept, a different implication would emerge. The implication, without the dollar-gold peg, would be that the United States and other countries would in the long run have to have the same rate of inflation or deflation. (For further details see Chapter 8.)

THE COLD WAR, THE MARSHALL PLAN, AND EUROPEAN INTEGRATION

The Bretton Woods agreement committed member nations to restore the convertibility of their currencies as soon as possible, and there was no reason free trade in foreign exchange could not have begun immediately. Without government controls or threats of punishment, a foreign exchange market would automatically emerge through the voluntary association of buyers and sellers. (Some trade in foreign exchange would take place anyway, despite controls. Such trading, defined as illegal by the government, is referred to as the black market or parallel market. Parallel markets exist whenever government exchange or other restrictions create a divergence between the market value of a currency and the government's declared official value. In recent decades, parallel markets have been widespread throughout Latin America, Eastern Europe, and certain countries of the Middle East.)

Most governments at the end of the war, however, were not inclined to allow free trading in their currencies. If private citizens were allowed free access to foreign exchange, they would use it as they desired. Governments, however, wanted prior access to foreign exchange so they could spend it on what *they* wanted: to import food, to import materials considered essential for reconstruction, to buy military equipment, or to reward companies who politically supported the current regime. In addition, many governments had preconceived ideas of what exchange rates ought to be. Back in 1925, Great Britain had set the exchange rate for the pound sterling at £1 = $4.86, the pre–Great War rate, "so the pound could look the dollar in the face" (meaning that British government officials could look American government officials in the face and pretend that the world of 1925 was not different from the world of 1910.) And, in the new postwar years of the late 1940s, if free trading were allowed in its currency, a government would either have to set a par value that represented market equilibrium or find itself continuously intervening in order to maintain an artificial price.

When governments got around to restoring convertibility as planned under the Bretton Woods agreement, they would need a supply of dollars with which to do exchange intervention. And that, they felt, was the key missing ingredient: *There was a shortage of dollar reserves with which to intervene in the exchange market.* As Hendrik Houthakker, a later member of the U.S. Council of Economic Advisors, was to say: "You can't play poker unless all the participants have at least some chips." The Cold War would eventually assure European nations enough dollar chips to play the intervention game.

The U.S. Congress had agreed only reluctantly to fund the American contribution to the new IMF, and there was a great deal of skepticism in the private sector concerning an increased international role for the United States. Domestic support for a traditional U.S. isolationist stance began to erode, however, as tensions between the Soviet Union and the other nations allied against Nazi Germany—the United States, Britain, and France—increased following the war. In the United States, the overriding foreign policy concern became that of stopping the spread of communism internationally. An early expression of this policy was the European Recovery Program (Marshall Plan) proposed by Secretary of State Marshall at the Harvard commencement in 1947. The idea was to supply capital to European economies to enable them to rebuild and to become capable military allies of the United States against the Soviet Union. The Organization for European Economic Cooperation (OEEC), later reorganized as the Organization for Economic Cooperation and Development (OECD), was set up to administer Marshall Plan aid. The Soviet Union responded by forming an Eastern European equivalent, the Council for Mutual Economic Assistance (COMECON).

The opening rounds of the Cold War arrived in connection with currency reform in occupied Germany. In 1945, the American army had brought with it to Germany occupation reichsmarks printed in the United States. The Soviets had also been given printing plates for the currency, and the millions of reichsmarks printed in Russia were used to extract, in a matter of weeks, several hundred million dollars worth of goods from the American and British occupation zones. The Soviet paper was then declared unacceptable in Western zones. The payment of troops in reichsmarks was discontinued, and cigarettes became the de facto medium of exchange and store of value in Germany, Lucky Strikes reaching at one point a price of $2300 a carton. Currency reform, planned under the name Operation Bird Dog, involved the replacement of the old reichsmarks with new deutschemarks (DM) printed in Washington at an exchange ratio of 1000 reichsmarks = 65 DM. The new currency would be legal tender in the Western zones, and its supply would be outside Soviet control. The Soviet Union viewed this as a part of an overall American plan to set up a separate West German government that would be ideologically opposed to the Soviets. On the day the new currency was to go into circulation in Berlin's Western zones, the Soviet military blockaded the city.

With the Berlin blockade of 1948, the successful communist revolution under Mao Tse-tung in China in 1949, and the outbreak of the Korean War in 1950, the mood of the U.S. Congress and the country changed to one of support for effecting a real financial transfer from the United States to Western Europe.

Initially, foreign trade was carried out in Europe through a set of clearing accounts. Under an arrangement called the European Payments Union, member countries kept track of all their payments deficits and surpluses with other member countries. The monthly net deficit or surplus of a particular country with all other member countries combined was considered a deficit or surplus of the union. At the end of each month, each country settled its net position with respect to the union in terms of U.S. dollars, gold, or credits. Credits were any amounts not settled in dollars or gold and could be accumulated only up to a specified limit. Calculation of the monthly surplus or deficit among countries took place at fixed exchange rates. Thus member countries could maintain the fiction that they were adhering to the Bretton Woods system of par values.

Throughout the 1950s, European governments, who never felt they had enough dollar reserves, made frequent reference to a "dollar shortage." In one sense, there actually was not a dollar shortage, since dollars would have always been available at *some* exchange rate, though not necessarily at the rate countries were willing to pay. A better phrase would have been "capital shortage," since capital goods were really the issue. The demand for dollars was equivalent to a demand for imports and raw materials to rebuild the European industrial base. "Hard currencies," such as the U.S. and Canadian dollars, could be spent anywhere in the world for such goods, while (because of exchange controls and other restrictions) so-called soft currencies had to be spent in the country in which they were earned. The reduction of the European capital shortage through Marshall Plan aid made it possible for European nations to build up foreign exchange reserves. While the total amount of Marshall Plan aid constituted only about 4 percent of European gross national product (GNP), it made up about 40 percent of European receipts of hard currency.

In addition to receiving aid, European countries were encouraged by the United States to liberalize trade among themselves. Official support was given to the ideas of individuals like Jean Monnet and Robert Shuman, who wanted to bring about a united Europe and to so integrate the economies of Germany and France that the two countries could never go to war again. "There will be no peace in Europe if States reestablish themselves on the basis of national sovereignty, with all that this implies by way of prestige politics and economic protectionism,'' Monnet had written in 1943. The European Coal and Steel Community, with Jean Monnet as its head, was formed in 1952, and in 1958, the European Economic Community (abbreviated EEC but frequently referred to as the Common Market) went into operation. The goal of the Common Market was to create a free trade area among member nations with free movement of labor and capital. It also entailed, however, the erection of common tariff barriers against the rest of the world. The political motivation for this economic organization was emphasized by a president of the EEC commission: ''We are not in business at all; we are in politics.''

European nations were officially encouraged by the United States to expand their exports to the dollar area even while maintaining restrictions on U.S. goods, and to use part of the earnings to build up dollar exchange reserves. As a consequence, between the end of 1949 and the end of 1959, U.S. liabilities to foreign monetary authorities rose from $3.1 billion to $10.1 billion. Toward the end of the 1950s, European authorities felt they had enough dollar reserves both to allow trade in their currencies and to defend their chosen par values, and at the end of 1958, current account convertibility was restored for the major European currencies. Current account convertibility meant that foreign exchange could be freely bought and sold provided its use was associated with international trade in goods and services. But there were still restrictions that applied when the intended use of the foreign exchange was to purchase foreign financial assets or to make equity investments. (Free trade in currencies for the latter purpose is called capital account convertibility.) Current acount convertibility for the Japanese yen was not restored until 1964. (Japan is discussed in Chapter 2.)

Thus, almost fifteen years after the Bretton Woods agreement, foreign exchange markets were once again in operation in the Western world.

DOLLAR RESTRICTIONS AND THE ORIGINS OF THE EURODOLLAR MARKET

After the return to European convertibility, it was discovered that there was no longer any dollar shortage. Par values of roughly the market equilibrium values had been chosen. The deutschemark price of dollars had been set too high, however. The dollar was overvalued and the deutschemark undervalued, so the Bundesbank, the German central bank, continued to accumulate dollars (Germany continued to run a balance of payments surplus).

With a dollar shortage no longer a problem, European countries began to add up the total stock of U.S. dollars in foreign official hands and compare them to the total U.S. gold supply. They began to realize that the United States could no longer keep its part of the Bretton Woods agreement to convert dollars into gold at $35 per ounce. By 1960 total foreign dollar claims on the United States were greater than the total value of the U.S. gold stock when gold was valued at $35 per ounce. If all foreign official dollars were turned in for gold at the same time, U.S. gold would run short. The United States would either have to turn away dollar-holders or increase the dollar price of gold. (An increase in the dollar price of gold was referred to as a devaluation of the dollar.)

The right to exchange dollars for gold had become roughly equivalent to the right to exchange the money in a checking account for cash. Anyone has the right to convert his or her checking account into cash. But if everyone tries to exercise this right at once, the bank will eventually run out of cash, since a bank's vault cash amount is much smaller than its checking-account liabilities. Now, in one sense, it did not make a material economic difference whether the United States could convert dollars to gold or not. As long as the purchasing power of the dollar remained constant, dollar-holders would suffer no economic loss, and if they really wanted gold they could always buy it in the private market. Moreover, even if there were dollar inflation, as long as official reserve holders were paid an interest rate sufficient to compensate them for inflation and in addition pay them a competitive real return, they had no basis to complain that holding dollars involved an opportunity cost on their part.

There were, however, problems of perception. First, suppose that the price of gold had a tendency to rise above $35 per ounce in the private market. This could happen because there was dollar inflation, so that prices in general—including the price of gold—would rise. Or there could be an increase in the value of gold relative to other goods. If the increase were due to inflation, then Germany, for example, might not be happy, because Germany could argue that the Bretton Woods agreement was implicitly an agreement by the United States to maintain a stable price level. (Memories of the 1920s hyperinflation have since given Germany a strong noninflationary stance.) If there was inflation in the United States, then—since the mark was pegged to the dollar—there would be inflation in Germany. Secondly, if the market price of gold rose above $35 per ounce, whether due to inflation or to an increase in the relative price of gold, even official dollar-holders might be tempted to switch from dollars to gold in order to enjoy a capital gain if the official U.S. dollar price of gold were later altered also. Finally, as we shall see, the French president de Gaulle made an issue out of gold purely on principle.

The inability to convert dollars into gold at $35 per ounce was therefore treated as a political problem by the U.S. administration. It became concerned about the private market price of gold (discussed further in the following section) and about the statistical measure of the U.S. balance of payments. The growing U.S. liabilities to foreign official agencies—obligations that could be converted into gold—reflected the deficit on the U.S. balance of payments, which was matched by a European surplus. American President Kennedy said he feared only two things: nuclear war and a deficit in the balance of payments. Nuclear war could wipe out all of one's assets. A deficit in the balance of payments could—in the context of German and French complaints—be used as a basis for domestic politicians to charge the administration with economic mismanagement and could act as an impediment to the Kennedy administration's plan to construct an Atlantic Alliance against the Soviet Union.

One solution to the "problem" of the U.S. balance of payments deficit would have been to allow the prices of major foreign currencies with respect to the U.S. dollar to rise. This action would have decreased the demand for those currencies: equivalently, it would have decreased the supply of dollars to foreigners. However, many felt that the dollar, as the central reserve currency, should not be allowed to devalue generally with respect to other currencies (and thus to devalue with respect to gold). They felt that the dollar ought to be a riskless asset. Another solution might have been to take no action at all, since it was not clear there was a problem. The accumulation of dollars by foreign official agencies was, after all, voluntary, and if they desired to continue to add dollars to their reserves, the United States would have to run a deficit to supply those reserves. But this fact was also ignored. Instead, the concern over the deficit led to a series of credit restrictions and capital controls under Presidents John Kennedy and Lyndon Johnson.

On July 18, 1963, Kennedy proposed an Interest Equalization Tax (IET) on American purchases of foreign securities. This tax raised the cost to foreign borrowers who came to New York to issue bonds in the Yankee bond market. Bond coupons would have to be raised to compensate bond-buyers for the withholding tax they would have to pay the U.S. government. The naive idea of the tax was to keep dollars out of foreign hands, so outsiders would not have any dollars with which to demand gold. (This tax created a reason for issuing eurobonds denominated in dollars. Such bonds would be issued internationally, in foreign capital markets, and would be free of the tax; see Chapter 16.) In February 1965, the IET was extended to apply to loans with a maturity of one to three years when these loans were made by U.S. banks and other financial institutions to designated foreign borrowers.

In February 1965, the U.S. voluntary Foreign Credit Restraint Program (FCRP) was also instituted. (It was "voluntary" in the sense that the government would not interfere in bank lending activity as long as the banks obeyed the general guidelines of the FCRP anyway). This program involved the setting of quotas—maximal amounts—on lending by U.S. banks to U.S. multinationals involved in foreign direct investment. On January 1, 1968, these controls were made legally mandatory. This set of controls gave companies an incentive to borrow dollars from sources not subject to these quotas.

The effect of the IET and FCRP was to give a strong impetus to the rate of growth of a new international money market that had slowly begun to emerge: the eurodollar market. In order to make clear what was involved, a slight digression from the historical sequence will be useful. An up-to-date definition of a eurodollar is "a dollar-denominated deposit in a bank outside the United States or in International Banking Facilities in the United States." (International Banking Facilities did not yet exist in the 1960s but were created beginning December 1981 and will be discussed in Chapter 12). The typical eurodollar deposit is a thirty- or ninety-day time deposit. The principal characteristic that makes it a "euro" deposit is the location of the bank giving the deposit, not the ownership of the bank or the funds. For example, if a U.S. corporation owns a dollar deposit at the Cayman Islands branch of a U.S. bank, the deposit is a eurodollar deposit because it is a deposit in a bank outside the United States. It is irrelevant whether the Cayman Islands bank is or is not a U.S. bank, and it is irrelevant whether the deposit is owned by a foreigner or a U.S. citizen. If a German corporation owns a dollar deposit in a New York bank, the deposit is *not* a eurodollar deposit, because the bank is not located outside the United States.

Similarly, a eurocurrency is a foreign-currency-denominated deposit in a bank outside the country where the currency is issued as legal tender. For example, a deutschemark-denominated deposit in a bank in Luxembourg is a eurodeutschemark deposit. As of 1990, there were fifteen eurocurrencies regularly traded in London. The dollar accounted for 60 percent of the total euromarket's gross liabilities and the deutschemark for another 14 percent.

A eurodollar is created this way. Suppose a U.S. company transfers $1 million from a U.S. domestic bank to a eurobank. This eurobank may, for example, be a branch of the U.S. bank in London or Nassau, or it may be a foreign bank. The company wires funds from the U.S. bank to the eurobank. The eurobank now owns a deposit at the U.S. bank. In return, the company is issued a time deposit at the eurobank. The $1 million transfer would show up on the books of the two banks as follows:

U.S. Domestic Bank		Eurobank	
Assets	Liabilities	Assets	Liabilities
	− $1 million deposit of U.S. company	+ $1 million deposit at U.S. domestic bank	+ $1 million deposit of U.S. company
	+ $1 million deposit of Eurobank		

Dollar liabilities of U.S. domestic banks have not altered in the slightest by this transaction. All that has changed at this point is that *ownership* of the $1 million deposit has been transferred from the U.S. company to the eurobank. The company may have been moved to transfer its deposit to the eurobank by the offer of a higher interest rate on deposits. The eurobank in turn can afford to pay higher interest only if it can loan out the deposit acquired at the U.S. domestic bank at an interest rate sufficiently higher than its deposit rate to obtain an acceptable profit margin. The U.S. domestic bank, meanwhile, is indifferent as to whether its liability is to a U.S. company or to a eurobank, except in the sense that there are legal distinctions (such as reserve requirement differences) among deposit-holders. Prior to May 1969, for example, there was no reserve requirement if the deposit-holder was a foreign branch of the U.S. domestic bank.

If the eurobank now makes a $1 million loan to Party Z, where Party Z may be another eurobank or a corporate customer, the accounting changes that take place are:

U.S. Domestic Bank		Eurobank		Party Z	
Assets	Liabilities	Assets	Liabilities	Assets	Liabilities
	− $1 million deposit of Eurobank	− $1 million deposit at U.S. domestic bank		+ $1 million deposit at U.S. domestic bank	+ $1 million debt to Eurobank
	+ $1 million deposit of Party Z	+ $1 million loan to Party Z			

The Eurobank makes the loan, in effect, by writing a check on its account at the U.S. domestic bank. The net result is that the $1 million deposit at the U.S.

domestic bank again undergoes a transfer of ownership. But there has been no change in U.S. domestic bank liabilities.

Eurobanks acquire ownership of demand deposits at commercial banks and loan out these same demand deposits. Whether U.S. domestic bank liabilities are affected by eurobank activity depends on the structure of reserve requirements. If all deposit (or similar) liabilities of U.S. domestic banks are treated uniformly according to reserve requirements, eurobank activity cannot affect the quantity of total U.S. domestic bank liabilities. But if, for example, foreign branch banks have a smaller reserve requirement, an increase in the ownership share of U.S. domestic bank liabilities by foreign branch banks will free up reserves and will—under conditions of excess loan demand—expand total U.S. domestic bank liabilities.

Returning now to our main story, the eurodollar market had emerged shortly before the general return to European currency convertibility and had come about this way. International financial practice had established the British pound sterling as a reserve currency along with the dollar. During the 1950s, the par value was set as £1 = $2.80. As a result of the Suez crisis in 1956, during which Egyptian president Gamal Abdel Nasser's nationalization of the canal was followed by a joint British-French-Israeli attack on Egypt, there was a run on the British pound as pound-holders switched from pounds to dollars. The Bank of England had difficulty maintaining the market price at the lower range of the 1 percent band, $2.7720/£. The U.S. Federal Reserve was itself a seller of pounds, and, as a way of pressuring Britain to withdraw from Egypt, the United States blocked British attempts to borrow from the IMF. One consequence of the sterling crisis was the Bank of England's prohibition of external sterling loans, the notion being that if foreigners did not have sterling they could not put pressure on the exchange rate by trading sterling for dollars.

However, one group of financial institutions, London overseas and merchant banks, made their living in part by arranging sterling financing for international trade. Trade between India and Nigeria, for example, was usually denominated in sterling, as opposed to the currencies of either of these two countries. These London institutions had the choice of closing shop or finding some other way to provide international trade financing. Their solution was to open a market in U.S. dollars. By offering to take in dollar deposits at competitive interest rates, they could acquire dollars to lend. (Bank of England prohibitions said nothing about dollars.) The idea that financial institutions in one country would open up a deposit market denominated in the currency of another country was considered a practice so strange that only merchant bankers would engage in it and in its early years was referred to as the Merchant Bank's Market. When a journalist for the *Financial Times,* Paul Einzig, discovered the market's existence, he was asked not to write about it.

The eurodollar market turned out to be a spectacular financial innovation, and as with any successful invention, all sorts of people later claimed to have thought of it first. What was *new* about the new market was that it was a market for *both deposits and loans* denominated in a foreign currency. The simple fact that these banks offered foreign currency deposits was not new: banks in Vienna and Berlin had commonly done this prior to World War II. Later, in the early 1950s, when currencies in Europe were generally inconvertible, Italian banks took in dollars in a small way to make loans to local businessmen. But this was viewed as a temporary expedient and did not endure. During the early years of the Cold War, the Soviet Union began to fear expropriation of its dollar deposits in New York and so switched ownership of these deposits to Soviet-controlled banks like the Moscow Narodny in London and the Banque Commerciale pour l'Europe du Nord in Paris. It was felt that the United States would not expropriate deposits owned by a British or a French bank. These banks in turn issued dollar deposits to the Soviet Union. Although this practice would later give rise to the rumor that Russians created the eurodollar market, the two banks were simply holding dollars in trust and did not get involved in dollar-lending until the later emergence of the Merchant Bank's Market in 1957.

There is no reason a specialty market in dollars could not have arisen in London without the artificial help of official regulatory restrictions. British banks might, for example, have specialized knowledge of financing trade in former parts of the British Empire that New York did not and might enjoy a comparative advantage of financing in dollars even given the fact that British banks would, in turn, have to hold and lend deposits in New York. Nevertheless, it is historically clear that regulatory restrictions were enormously important in inspiring the rapid growth of the market.

First of all, there were supply restrictions that hindered the ability of some to borrow dollars in New York. The Interest Equalization Tax and the Foreign Credit Restraint Program increased the interest cost, and placed limits on the amount, of bank loans available to foreigners and to U.S. companies investing abroad. Thus, for dollar loans many had little choice but to turn to the euro-dollar market.

Second, there were demand restrictions that reduced the attractiveness of New York as a place to lend dollars by placing deposits with New York banks. In particular, the Federal Reserve's Regulation Q placed an interest ceiling on the amount U.S. banks could pay on bank deposits. Of course, such a ceiling is irrelevant if it is not binding—if market interest rates are lower than the ceiling. But, as seen in Figure 1.1, in 1966 and again in 1968–1969, market interest rates rose above Regulation Q ceiling rates—eurodollar deposits in the latter case paying as much as 500 basis points more.

As market interest rates rose above Regulation Q ceilings in 1966, money center banks experienced disintermediation: funds were switched out of time deposits and into Treasury bills and commercial paper, assets for which there were no interest ceilings. Banks with eurobank branches were better able to maintain their deposit base, since eurobank branches could pay market interest rates and relend the funds to headquarters. With a repetition of disinter-mediation in 1968–1969, many banks looked to open up eurobranches as a temporary solution to their funding problem but were hindered by the $500,000 minimum capital investment required to open a branch in London. A change in Federal Reserve regulations enabled them to open so-called shell branches in the Caribbean. Although such branches were legally established in a foreign country, a branch was really operated as a separate set of books in New York. The Cayman Islands branch of a major New York bank might, for example, be nothing more than a fellow named Bill with a desk and a telephone next to the foreign exchange traders in the New York bank's trading room. During 1969,

FIGURE 1.1
Short-term interest rates compared to Regulation Q ceiling rate. [*Source:* Bank for International Settlements, *Annual Report* (1970).]

forty U.S. banks opened branches, referred to as "Nassau shells," in the Bahamas. For a small investment of capital, U.S. banks could offer competitive rates of interest on deposits through eurobank branches in Nassau.

THE POLITICS OF GOLD AND THE SDR

In addition to the various restrictions referred to above, the United States joined with the central banks of the Common Market countries as well as with Great Britain and Switzerland to intervene in the private market for gold in the fall of 1960. If the private market price did not rise above $35 per ounce, it was felt, the Bretton Woods price was de facto the correct price, and in addition no one could complain if dollars were not exchangeable for gold. This coordinated intervention, which involved maintaining the gold price within a narrow range around $35 per ounce, became formalized a year later as the *gold pool*. Since London was the center of world gold trading, the pool was managed by the Bank of England, which intervened in the private market via the daily gold price fixing at N. M. Rothschild. In order to see how this worked, we now turn to a brief description of the gold market and once again depart slightly from a strictly chronological sequence.

In its current form, the London gold price fixing takes place twice each business day, at 10:30 A.M. and 3:00 P.M. in the "fixing room" of the merchant banking firm of N. M. Rothschild. Five individuals, one each from five major gold-trading firms, are involved in the fixing. The firms represented are Mocatta & Goldsmid, a trading arm of Standard Chartered Bank; Sharps Pixley, a broker owned by the merchant bank Kleinwort Benson; N. M. Rothschild & Sons, whose representative acts as the auctioneer; Mase-Westpac, a bullion subsidiary of Westpac Bank; and Samuel Montagu, a merchant banking subsidiary of Midland Bank. Each representative at the fixing keeps an open phone line to his firm's trading room. Each trading room in turn has buy and sell orders, at various prices, from customers located all over the world. In addition, there are customers with no existing buy or sell orders who keep an open line to a trading room in touch with the fixing and who may decide to buy or sell depending on what price is announced. The N. M. Rothschild representative announces a price at which trading will begin. Each of the five individuals then confers with his trading room, and the trading room tallies up supply and demand—in terms of 400-ounce bars—from orders originating around the world. In a few minutes, each firm has determined if it is a net buyer or seller of gold. If there is excess supply or demand a new price is announced, but no orders are filled until an equilibrium price is determined. The equilibrium price, at which supply equals demand, is referred to as the "fixing price." The A.M. and P.M. fixing prices are published daily in major newspapers.

Even though immediately before and after a fixing gold trading will continue at prices that may vary from the fixing price, the fixing price is an important benchmark in the gold market because much of the daily trading volume goes through at the fixing price. Hence some central banks value their gold at an average of daily fixing prices, and industrial customers often have contracts with their suppliers written in terms of the fixing price. Since a fixing price represents temporary equilibrium for a large volume of trading, it may be subject to less "noise" than are trading prices at other times of the day. Usually the equilibrium fixing price is found rapidly, but sometimes it takes twenty to thirty tries. Once in October 1979, with supply and demand fluctuating rapidly from moment to moment, the afternoon fixing in London lasted an hour and thirty-nine minutes.

The practice of fixing the gold price began in 1919. It continued until 1939, when the London gold market was closed as a result of war. The market was reopened in 1954. When the central bank gold pool began officially in 1961, the Bank of England—as agent for the pool—maintained an open phone line with N. M. Rothschild during the morning fixing (there was as yet no afternoon fixing). If it appeared that a fixing price would be established that was above $35.20 or below $34.80, the Bank of England (as agent) became a seller or buyer of gold in an amount sufficient to ensure that the fixing price remained within the prescribed bands.

While the gold pool held down the private market price of gold, gold politics took a new turn in the international arena. While it was actually Germany that was running the greatest surplus and accumulating dollar reserves in the early 1960s, it was France under the leadership of Charles de Gaulle that made the most noise about it. During World War II, in conversations with Jean Monnet, de Gaulle had supported the notion of a united Europe—but a Europe, he insisted, under the leadership of France. After the war, France had opposed the American plan for German rearmament even in the context of European defense. France had been induced to agree, however, through Marshall Plan aid, which France was not inclined to refuse after it became embroiled in the Indo-China War. But now, in the 1960s, de Gaulle's vision of France as a leading world power led him to withdraw from NATO because NATO was a U.S.-dominated military alliance. It also led him to oppose Bretton Woods, because the international monetary system was organized with the U.S. dollar as a reserve currency.

In the early 1960s there was, however, no realistic alternative to the dollar as a reserve asset, if one wanted to keep reserves in a form that both would bear interest and could be traded internationally. Official dollar-reserve holders not only were made exempt from the interest ceilings of Regulation Q for their deposits in New York but also began as a regular practice to hold dollars in the eurodollar market. Prior to 1965, central banks were the largest suppliers of dollars to the euromarket. Thus reserve holders received a competitive return on their dollar assets, and the United States gained no special benefit from the use of the dollar as a reserve asset.

Nevertheless, de Gaulle's stance on gold made domestic political sense, and in February 1965, in a well-publicized speech, he said: "We hold as necessary that international exchange be established . . . on an indisputable monetary base that does not carry the mark of any particular country. What base? In truth, one does not see how in this respect it can have any criterion, any standard, other than gold. Eh! Yes, gold, which does not change in nature, which is made indifferently into bars, ingots and coins, which does not have any nationality, which is held eternally and universally. . . ." By the "mark of any particular country" he had in mind the United States, which announced the Foreign Credit Restraint Program about a week later, in part as a direct response to de Gaulle's speech. France stepped up its purchases of gold from the U.S. Treasury and in June 1967, when the Arab-Israeli Six-Day War led to a large increase in the demand for gold, withdrew from the gold pool.

Then in November 1967, the British pound sterling was devalued from $2.80 to $2.40. Those holding sterling reserves took a 14.3 percent capital loss in dollar terms. This raised the question of the exchange rate of the other reserve assets: if the dollar was devalued with respect to gold, a capital gain in dollar terms could be made by holding gold. Therefore demand for gold rose and, as it did, gold pool sales in the private market to hold down the price were so large that month that the U.S. Air Force made an emergency airlift of gold from Fort Knox to London, and the floor of the weighing room at the Bank of England collapsed from the accumulated tonnage of gold bars.

In March 1968, the effort to control the private market price of gold was abandoned. A *two-tier* system began: official transactions in gold were insulated from the free market price. Central banks would trade gold among themselves at $35 per ounce but would not trade with the private market. The private market could trade at the equilibrium market price and there would be no official intervention. The price immediately jumped to $43 per ounce, but by the end of 1969 it was back at $35. The two-tier system would be abandoned in November 1973, after the emergence of floating exchange rates and the de facto dissolution of the Bretton Woods agreement. By then the price had reached $100 per ounce.

When the gold pool was disbanded and the two-tier system began in March 1968, there was a two-week period during which the London gold market was forceably closed by British authorities. A number of important changes took place during those two weeks. South Africa as a country is the single largest supplier of gold and had for years marketed the sale of its gold through London, with the Bank of England acting as agent for the South African Reserve Bank. With the breakdown of the gold pool, South Africa was no longer assured of steady central bank demand, and—with the London market temporarily closed—the three major Swiss banks (Swiss Bank Corporation, Swiss Credit Bank, and Union Bank of Switzerland) formed their own gold pool and persuaded South Africa to market through Zurich. In 1972, the second major country supplier of gold, the Soviet Union, also began to market through Zurich. In 1921, V. I. Lenin had written, "sell [gold] at the highest price, buy goods with it at the lowest price." Since the Soviet ruble was not convertible, the Soviet Union used gold sales as one major source of its earnings of Western currencies, and in the 1950s and 1960s sold gold through the Moscow Narodny in London (the same bank that provided dollar cover for the Soviets during the early days of the Cold War). In Zurich, the Soviet Union dealt gold via the Wozchod Handelsbank, a subsidiary of the Soviet Foreign Trade Bank, the Vneshtorgbank. (In March 1985, the Soviet Union announced that the Wozchod would be closed because of gold-trading losses and would be replaced with a branch office of the Vneshtorgbank. The branch office, unlike the Wozchod, would not be required to publish information concerning operations.)

London, in order to stay competitive, has since become more of a gold-trading center than a distribution center. When the London market reopened in March 1968 after the two-week "holiday," a second daily fixing (the 3:00 P.M. fixing) was added in order to overlap with U.S. trading hours, and the fixing price was switched to U.S. dollar terms from pound sterling terms. In more recent years, London's role as a trading center has also been challenged by the Comex gold futures market in New York.

During the early years of the gold pool, it came to be believed that there was a deficiency of international reserves and that more reserves had to be created by legal fiat to enable reserve-holders to diversify out of the U.S. dollar and gold. In retrospect, this was a curious view of the world. The form in which reserves are held will ultimately always be determined on the basis of international competition. People will hold their wealth in the form of a particular asset only if they want to. If they do not have an economic incentive to desire a particular asset, no legal document will alter that fact. A particular currency will be attractive as a reserve asset if these four criteria exist: (1) an absence of exchange controls so people can spend, transfer, or exchange their reserves denominated in that currency when and where they want them; (2) an absence of applicable credit controls and taxes that would prevent assets denominated in the currency from bearing a competitive rate of return relative to other available assets; (3) political stability, in the sense that there is a lack of substantial risk that points (1) and (2) will change within or between government regimes; (4) a currency that is in sufficient use internationally to limit the costs of making transactions. These four points explain why, for example, the Swiss but not the French franc has been traditionally used as an international reserve asset.

Many felt that formal agreement on a new international reserve asset was nevertheless needed, if only to reduce political tension. And while France wanted to replace the dollar as a reserve asset, other nations were looking instead for a replacement for gold. The decision was made by the Group of Ten (ten OECD nations with most of the voting rights in the IMF) to create an artificial reserve asset that would be traded among central banks in settlement of reserves. The asset would be kept on the books of the IMF and would be called a Special Drawing Right (SDR). In fact it was a new reserve asset, a type of artificial or "paper gold," but it was called a drawing right by concession to the French, who did not want it called a reserve asset.

The SDR was approved in July 1969, and the first "allocation" (creation) of SDRs was made in January 1970. Overnight, countries gained more reserves at the IMF, because the IMF added new numbers to its accounts and called these numbers SDRs. The timing of the allocation was especially maladroit. In the previous four years the United States had been in the process of financing the Great Society domestic social programs of the Johnson administration as well as a war in Vietnam, and the world was being flooded with more reserves than it wanted at the going price of dollars for deutschemarks, yen, or gold. In the 1965 *Economic Report of the President,* Johnson wrote, in reference to his Great Society Program and the Vietnam War: "The Federal Reserve must be free to accommodate the expansion in 1965 and the years beyond 1965." U.S. money supply (M1) growth, which had averaged 2.2 percent per year during the 1950s, inched upward slightly during the Kennedy years (2.9 percent per year for 1961–1963) but changed materially under the Johnson administration. The growth rate of M1 averaged 4.6 percent per year over 1964–1967, then rose to 7.7 percent in 1968. Under the Nixon administration that followed, money growth initially slowed to 3.2 percent in 1969 and 5.2 percent in 1970, then accelerated to 7.1 percent for 1971–1973. The latter three years would encompass the breakdown of Bretton Woods.

THE BREAKDOWN OF BRETTON WOODS

In order to succeed, a regime of fixed exchange rates (and under Bretton Woods, rates for the major currencies were fixed in terms of their par values, which could not be casually altered) requires coordinated economic policies, particularly monetary policies. If two different currencies trade at a fixed exchange rate and one currency is undervalued with respect to the other, the undervalued currency will be in excess demand. By the end of the 1960s both the deutschemark and the yen had become undervalued with respect to the U.S. dollar. Therefore the countries concerned (Germany and Japan) had two choices: either increase the supplies of their currencies to meet the excess demand or adjust the exchange values of their currencies upward enough to eliminate the excess demand.

As long as either country intervened in the market to maintain the par value of its currency with respect to the U.S. dollar, an increased supply of the domestic currency would take place automatically. To see why this is so, take the case of Germany. In order to keep the DM from increasing in value with respect to the U.S. dollar, the Bundesbank would have to intervene in the foreign exchange market to buy dollars. It would buy dollars by selling DM.

The operation would increase the supply of DM in the market, driving down DM's relative value, and increase the demand for the dollar, driving up the dollar's relative value.

Any time the central bank intervenes in any market to buy or sell something, it potentially changes the domestic money supply. If the central bank buys assets such as government bonds or foreign exchange, it does so by writing a check on itself. Central bank assets go up: the central bank now owns the bonds or the foreign exchange. But central bank liabilities go up also, since the check represents a central bank liability. The seller of the bonds or foreign exchange or other asset will deposit the central bank's check, in payment for the value of the assets, in an account at a commercial bank. The commercial bank will in turn deposit the check in its account at the central bank. The commercial bank will now have more reserves, in the form of a deposit at the central bank. The bank can use the reserves to make more loans, and the money supply will expand by a multiple of the initial reserve increase.

A typical central bank balance sheet follows. Central banks have two general types of assets: domestic and foreign. Domestic assets are things like government bonds and direct loans to the commercial banking system. In some countries they have included corporate stock and direct loans to private industry. Foreign assets are things like gold, SDRs, and foreign exchange.

Central Bank

Assets	Liabilities
Domestic assets	High-powered money
Foreign assets	

Central bank liabilities make up the monetary base, or "high-powered money." In the case of the Federal Reserve in the United States, the two principal components of this liability are currency in circulation (printed money and coins) and commercial bank checking accounts (federal funds). Either component can serve as reserves of commercial banks. Checking accounts at the Federal Reserve are automatically reserves, and currency can serve as bank reserves if it is held in a bank's vault ("cash in the vault").

Different banking systems differ in detail but generally have a similar structure. Consider now the Bundesbank, the German central bank, intervening in the foreign exchange market to buy up $1 billion, at a fixed exchange rate of DM4 = $1. The transaction would show up on the books of the Bundesbank as follows:

Bundesbank

Assets	Liabilities
+ DM4 billion in foreign assets	+ DM4 billion in reserves of banking system

The foreign exchange intervention automatically increases the monetary base in Germany by DM4 billion. Eventually the money supply in Germany will increase by a multiple of this amount. The total increase in the German money supply will depend on the size of the money multiplier in Germany. If the money (M1) multiplier were 2.5, then the M1 money supply in Germany would eventually rise by (DM4 billion)(2.5) = DM10 billion.

Is there anything the German authorities can do to prevent the money-supply increase? Essentially not as long as they attempt to maintain the fixed exchange rate. There is, however, an operation referred to as sterilization. Sterilization refers to the practice of offsetting any impact on the monetary base caused by foreign exchange intervention, by making reverse transactions in terms of domestic assets. For example, if the money base went up by DM4 billion because the central bank bought dollars in the foreign exchange market, a sterilization operation would involve selling DM4 billion worth of domestic assets to reduce central bank liabilities by an equal and offsetting amount. If the Bundesbank sold domestic assets, these would be paid for by checks drawn on the commercial banking system and reserves would disappear as the commercial banks' checking accounts were debited at the central bank.

However, the Bundesbank could not simultaneously engage in complete sterilization (a complete offset) and also maintain the fixed exchange rate. If there was no change in the supply of DM, the DM would continue to be undervalued with respect to the dollar, and foreign exchange traders would continue to exchange dollars for DM. During the course of 1971, the Bundesbank intervened so much that the German high-powered money base would have increased by 42 percent from foreign exchange intervention alone. About half this increase was offset by sterilization, but, even so, the increase in the money base—and eventually the money supply—by more than 20 percent in one year was enormous by German standards. The breakdown of the Bretton Woods system began that year.

It came about this way. From the end of World War II to about 1965, U.S. domestic monetary and fiscal policies were conducted in such a way as to be noninflationary. As world trade expanded during this period, the relative importance of Germany and Japan grew, so that by the end of the 1960s it was unreasonable to expect any system of international finance to endure without a consensus at least among the United States, Germany, and Japan. But after 1965, U.S. economic policy began to conflict with policies desired by Germany and Japan. In particular, the United States began a strong expansion, and moderate inflation, as a result of the Vietnam War and the Great Society program.

When it became obvious that the DM and yen were undervalued with respect to the dollar, the United States urged these two nations to revalue their currencies upward. Germany and Japan argued that the United States should revise its economic policy to be consistent with those in Germany and Japan as well as with previous U.S. policy. They wanted the United States to curb money-supply growth, tighten credit, and cut government spending. In the ensuing stalemate, the U.S. policy essentially followed the recommendations of a task force chaired by Gottfried Haberler. This was a policy of officially doing nothing and was commonly referred to as a policy of ''benign neglect.'' If Germany and Japan chose to intervene to maintain their chosen par values, so be it. They would be allowed to accumulate dollar reserves until such time as they decided to change the par values of their currencies. That was the only alternative if the United States would not willingly change its policy. It was clearly understood at the time that a unilateral action on the part of the United States to devalue the dollar by increasing the dollar price of gold would be matched by similar European devaluations.

In April 1971, the Bundesbank took in $3 billion through foreign exchange intervention. On May 4 it took in $1 billion in the course of the day. On May 5 the Bundesbank took in $1 billion during the first hour of trading, then suspended intervention in the foreign exchange market. The DM was allowed to float upward. On August 15 the U.S. president, Nixon, suspended the convertibility of the dollar into gold and announced a 10 percent tax on imports. The tax was temporary and was intended to signal the magnitude by which the United States thought the par values of the major European and Japanese currencies should be changed.

An attempt was made to keep the Bretton Woods system going by a revised agreement, the Smithsonian agreement, reached at the Smithsonian Institution in Washington on December 17–18, 1971. Called by President Nixon "the most important monetary agreement in the history of the world," it lasted only slightly more than a year, but beyond the 1972 U.S. presidential election. At the Smithsonian Institution the Group of Ten agreed on a realignment of currencies, an increase in the official price of gold to $38 per ounce, and expanded exchange rate bands of 2.25 percent around their new par values.

Over the period February 5–9, 1973, history repeated itself, with the Bundesbank taking in $5 billion in foreign exchange intervention. On February 12, exchange markets were closed in Europe and Japan, and the United States announced a 10 percent devaluation of the dollar. European countries and Japan allowed their currencies to float and, over the next month, a de facto regime of floating exchange rates began. The floating rate system has persisted to the present, with none of the five most widely traded currencies (the dollar, the DM, the British pound, the Japanese yen, the Swiss franc) in any way officially fixed in exchange value with respect to the others. (In October 1990 the DM and the British pound were nominally linked in the European Monetary System.) With the breakdown of Bretton Woods, there began a slow dismantling of the array of controls that had been erected in its name. Over 1973–1974, for example, the Interest Equalization Tax, the Foreign Credit Restraint Program, and the two-tier system for gold were all discarded.

The U.S. inflationary process, mild as it was by later standards, had a profound impact, via the Bretton Woods regime of par values, on other industrial countries. Economist Ronald McKinnon notes "the remarkable loss of monetary control among the major industrial economies concurrently in the last years of the fixed exchange rate regime. Taking ten industrial countries combined, their aggregate money supply grew about 12 percent per annum in the 1971–1973 period as compared to a little over 7 percent per annum in the preceding ten years." The stage was set for the inflationary seventies.

PROBLEMS FOR CHAPTER 1

1. Suppose that free trading is allowed in both the Belgian franc and the French franc, but that the French and Belgian central banks peg their currencies with respect to

each other at an exchange rate that undervalues the French franc relative to the Belgian franc. Which central bank will gain foreign exchange reserves? Which central bank will lose foreign exchange reserves?

2. The central bank of Surlandia pegs the peso to the U.S. dollar at a price of Ps.150/$. The market exchange rate is Ps.180/$. Will the central bank of Surlandia gain or lose dollar reserves?

3. Which of the following items would be defined as eurodollars: German-owned dollar deposits in a New York bank; any deposit in a branch of a U.S. bank located in Zurich; a dollar deposit in the Los Angeles branch of the Bank of Tokyo; U.S. Treasury bills owned by the Saudi Arabian Monetary Authority; dollar deposits in London banks owned by French exporters?

4. A company in Houston transfers $10 million to a eurobank in Panama, writing a check on Texas Commerce Bank. The bank in Panama deposits the check in Chemical Bank, New York, and subsequently loans $8 million to a eurobank in Nassau. Show the accounting changes that take place on the balance sheets of Texas Commerce Bank and the Panamanian eurobank.

5. Suppose the Bundesbank intervenes in the foreign exchange market and sells dollars. How does this affect the German monetary base?

6. The Federal Reserve sells 24 million ounces of gold at $35 an ounce, buys $2.38 billion worth of Treasury bills, and sells DM2.2 billion at an average exchange rate of DM3.90/$. What is the net change in the U.S. monetary base from these operations? If the U.S. money (M1) multiplier is 2.58, what will be the net change in the U.S. money supply?

7. Suppose the Federal Reserve were required to buy gold from, or sell gold to, *anyone* at a fixed price of $35 per ounce. Assume that the gold market is currently in equilibrium at that level. Explain why inflation in the United States would then automatically lead to a decrease in the U.S. money supply, assuming that changes in the price of gold accurately reflected changes in the purchasing power of the dollar.

2

GLOBALIZATION AND THE GROWTH OF DERIVATIVES

With the breakdown of Bretton Woods in 1973, the world had become suddenly smaller. Central banks had long enjoyed a monopoly over national money supplies, which they had manipulated as whim dictated. Now they found themselves competing to maintain the values of their respective currencies in an international marketplace. The same was true in the eurocurrency and international bond markets. When regulatory burdens regarding taxes, quotas, or exchange and interest controls became overly severe in one location, money and capital markets shifted to other regulatory environments. Regulators had to compete to maintain their nations' shares of the business of international finance.

The inflationary pressures that put an end to Bretton Woods continued throughout the 1970s. Inflation-related borrowing by energy, natural resource, and real estate sectors in both developed and developing countries became the norm, as oil producers, agricultural farmers, mining companies, and owners of commercial and residential real estate saw the value of their assets increase relative to the value of financial assets. But what made sense in the inflationary '70s (borrowing at fixed interest rates to buy assets whose market prices appreciated with inflation) did not make sense in the disinflationary '80s, and in 1982, a global debt crisis emerged due to the overextended borrowing of these same economic units.

The 1980s were years of deregulation, liberalized capital markets, and generally falling inflation rates. Bank profit margins fell due to increased competition and nonperforming loans, even while bank regulators pressured banks to increase capital ratios. A worldwide boom in equities began in 1982 and continued throughout the decade (though slowed by the 1987 Wall Street crash), ending only in 1990 with the collapse of the Tokyo stock market.

By the 1990s, the international financial arena had come full circle. The economic collapse of countries formerly behind the Iron Curtain, followed by the opening of Eastern Europe and the unification of the two Germanys, had created an enormous demand for an international flow of capital to build modern, efficient economies. While European Community optimists looked forward to complete economic unification by the end of 1992, real interest rates were on the rise: worldwide demand for investment was supplied from a savings pool increasingly depleted by government consumption. Meanwhile, toward the end of 1990, war-related U.S. propaganda broadcasts, like those of Germany fifty years earlier, were proclaiming a "new world order." A new order was indeed emerging, but it was driven more by technology and economic cycles than by the political visions of the Trilateral Commission.

DEVELOPMENTS IN EXCHANGE MARKETS

New risks had entered the world of currency trading. The decline, rise, and decline again of the foreign exchange value of the U.S. dollar from 1973 to 1990 took place in a market with daily turnover exceeding $100 billion each business day by 1980, and $650 billion by 1990. In the final years of Bretton Woods, foreign exchange traders had become accustomed to taking large speculative positions against central banks at times when central banks intervened to maintain exchange rates at levels traders did not see as representing market equilibrium. If central banks stopped their intervention and rates were allowed to adjust, then traders made a speculative profit. If central banks continued to intervene and were able to maintain the fixed rate, traders did not make a profit, but there was little risk at such times of rates going in the other direction with a resulting loss. After March 1973, however, with the central banks of Europe and Japan committed to no specific prices for their currencies with respect to the U.S. dollar, it had become more risky to take speculative positions. Traders who took such positions did so against other traders, and it was a sure thing that someone would prove to be wrong. This was dramatized in 1974 when two large banks—Bankhaus I. D. Herstatt in Cologne and Franklin National in New York—failed as a result of foreign exchange losses.

Central banks of industrial countries did, however, continue to intervene in currency markets in a discretionary fashion whenever officials felt exchange rates ought to be different from their prevailing market levels. This was called "managed" or "dirty" floating.(Such intervention, as we will see in Chapter 9, has remained an important source of profit for traders.) Not only has central bank intervention remained widespread, but capital controls have also been temporarily imposed from time to time to influence the direction taken by rates in the foreign exchange market. In early 1978, for example, during a period when there were large shifts out of dollar assets and into assets denominated in DM, Swiss francs, and Japanese yen, the Swiss National Bank imposed negative interest rates on deposits held by foreigners and also prohibited foreign purchase of stocks and bonds. The Bundesbank placed a 100 percent reserve requirement on foreign deposits at German commercial banks. Japan took similar measures.

One of the more dramatic examples of exchange manipulation was the Carter package of November 1, 1978, under the administration of U.S. President Jimmy Carter. Thirty billion dollars' worth of foreign currencies were gathered for potential foreign exchange intervention in support of the U.S. dollar: $15 billion in new Federal Reserve swap lines with other central banks, $10 billion through the issue of foreign-currency-denominated bonds in foreign markets ("Carter bonds"), $3 billion from IMF borrowing, and $2 billion through the sale of SDRs. In addition, increased reserve requirements were placed on large-denomination time deposits at U.S. commercial banks, and the U.S. Treasury (which had begun to sell off its holdings of gold) announced that sales would rise to 1.5 million ounces annually. This package, however, had only little effect on the value of the dollar as measured by Morgan Guaranty's trade-weighted average of the dollar's nominal exchange rate with respect to fifteen other currencies. Based on an index of 100 in October 1978, the index stood at 101.7 in October 1980.

By contrast, exchange intervention operations were essentially suspended altogether under the following U.S. administration of Ronald Reagan. But the dollar rose sharply against foreign currencies beginning in 1981. The index rose to 116.9 by October 1981. In March 1985, it stood at 156.6. The 1984 *Economic Report of the President* attributed the rise of the dollar to portfolio shifts from other foreign currency assets into the dollar—a result of decreased expectations of U.S. inflation, an increase in U.S. real interest rates relative to real interest rates elsewhere, and increased political risk in Latin America and Europe. Even though the U.S. current account deficit in 1984 supplied foreigners with a net total of about $100 billion in U.S. assets, demand for dollar assets remained greater than the supply at exchange rates prevailing in early 1985. Consequently, the price of the dollar continued to be driven up, hitting a thirteen-year high of DM3.47 per dollar in late February.

The dollar then depreciated until September 1985, reaching a level of around DM2.85/$, at which time it was noted, in the Plaza Agreement (named for the G-5 members—the United States, the United Kingdom, Germany, France, and Japan—meeting in the Plaza Hotel in New York) that the "U.S. current account deficit, together with other factors, is now contributing to protectionist pressures which, if not resisted, could lead to mutually destructive retaliation with serious damage to the world economy. . ." and that "some further orderly appreciation of the main non-dollar currencies against the dollar is desirable." Central banks accordingly leaned with the wind, selling dollars, and the dollar continued to depreciate. Later, at the Louvre Accord in Paris in February 1987, with the dollar at DM1.83/$, six of the G-7 members (including Canada but with Italy boycotting the meeting) agreed "to cooperate closely to foster stability of exchange rates around current levels."

The Louvre Accord was followed by three years of unprecedented exchange intervention without, however, noticeable impact on exchange rate fluctuations. Toward the end of 1990, the DM stood at DM1.47/$, a postwar high. The commitment to maintain the status quo nevertheless served to attract foreign capital investment into countries with high interest rates, since investors appeared to believe intervention would prevent exchange rate depreciation from offsetting high returns, even in cases where the high rates of interest stemmed from inflation.

The mood in Europe for further European integration alternated between mild enthusiasm and disinterest throughout the 1970s. United States support was decidedly cooler, for reasons such as those listed in a report prepared for the U.S. national security advisor, Henry Kissinger: "In the long run we could be confronted by an 'expanded Europe' comprising a Common Market of at least ten full members, associated memberships for the EFTA [European Free

Trade Area] neutrals, and preferential trade arrangements with at least the Mediterranean and most of Africa. This bloc will account for about half of world trade, compared with our 15%; it will hold monetary reserves approaching twice our own; and it will even be able to outvote us in the international economic organizations.'' In March 1979, the member nations of the European Economic Community began operation of the European Monetary System (EMS), a cooperative arrangement linking together EEC member currencies and discussed later in the chapter.

When the principal industrial countries allowed their currencies to float beginning in March 1973, the International Monetary Fund took the position that such floating was illegal, since it was in violation of the Bretton Woods agreement as amended in the Smithsonian agreement. The currencies and countries involved were, however, those playing a major role in international finance. As a consequence, the IMF came to be increasingly viewed as an irrelevant institution, having little to do with daily international financial practice. Then, in a meeting in Jamaica in 1976, the IMF articles were formally amended to say that countries could choose their own exchange regimes. The Jamaica agreement canonized what was already fact and was of little help in restoring the primary relic of Bretton Woods—the IMF itself—as a forum for international financial coordination. However, following the second oil shock in 1979, the IMF strongly reentered the financial scene as a dispenser of macroeconomic advice to international debtor nations. Since most countries of the world—particularly developing countries—maintained fixed exchange rates, the IMF continued to supply balance of payments loans. In the early 1980s, the IMF concentrated its balance of payments lending to the same group of countries dealt with by the World Bank, which had fulfilled its role in reconstruction finance by 1960 and found its raison d'être in making development and project loans to countries with low per capita incomes. IMF lending was conditional on countries following macroeconomic policies the IMF deemed suitable (referred to as *conditionality*), a fact used by private international banks as a basis for their own lending. Commercial banks with large loans outstanding to developing countries were willing to reschedule existing debt only if a country first accepted an IMF program of macroeconomic adjustment. The acceptance of an IMF program was viewed by banks as increasing the probability that the loans would eventually be repaid.

Even though the most widely traded currencies—the U.S. dollar, the DM, the British pound, the Japanese yen, and the Swiss franc—do not now trade within a range of any agreed par values, except for a loose linkage of the DM with the pound, a majority of countries worldwide still set par values for their currencies in one form or another. A classification of recent practices is given in Table 2.1. As of 1990, many countries pegged the value of their currencies with respect to either the U.S. dollar (Nicaragua), the French franc (Chad), or the SDR (Iran). A number of Latin American countries maintained exchange rates fixed in terms of the U.S. dollar but devalued their currencies at regular intervals by fixed amounts or according to a set of economic indicators. These scheduled monthly or daily devaluations are referred to as minidevaluations. When an unscheduled devaluation takes place, it is termed a maxidevaluation. Other countries (such as Sweden) peg to a portfolio of foreign currencies. The currencies of the European Monetary System are pegged with respect to each other. The currencies of the Soviet Union and much of Eastern Europe are not classified in Table 2.1, but these currencies were not generally convertible.

The demise of fixed exchange rates for the widely traded currencies brought a change in the IMF's definition of its artificial reserve asset, the SDR. In 1974, the SDR was redefined in terms of a basket of sixteen currencies. The composition of the sixteen currencies was altered slightly in 1978. In 1981, the SDR was defined as a basket of five currencies: the U.S. dollar, the German mark, the French franc, the British pound sterling, and the Japanese yen:

SDR1 = $.54 + DM.46 + FF.74 + ¥34 + £.071

In 1986, the SDR was redefined as:

SDR1 = $.452 + DM.527 + FF1.02 + ¥33.4 + £.0893.

The smaller basket was intended to promote the use of the SDR in the private sector, but in the 1980s little enthusiasm was shown outside the offices of the IMF. A number of regional organizations, however, now use the SDR as their unit of account, and a small market in SDR bank deposits has developed. In connection with the SDR, the IMF has promoted the idea of a "substitution account." This involves a scheme by which the IMF would issue SDR claims to member nations in return for their voluntary deposit of U.S. dollars with the IMF. The purpose of this scheme is to promote the role of the SDR as a reserve asset and, allegedly, to allow central banks to shift out of dollars without affecting exchange rates. Support for this scheme on the part of members holding dollar reserves dwindled in 1981 and afterward as the dollar's value rose in foreign exchange markets.

Gold, the principal international reserve asset outside the dollar, was another issue. As part of the Jamaica agreement in 1976, IMF members agreed to demote the role of gold, but few central banks have subsequently followed up this agreement in practice (see Chapter 11 for a further discussion of the changing pattern of international reserve assets). One associated change that did come about, however, affected the private gold market in the United States. On January 2, 1975, after forty years of prohibition, U.S. citizens were allowed to purchase gold bullion legally. The Comex in New York subsequently became an important center for the trading of gold futures.

DEVELOPMENTS IN THE EUROCURRENCY MARKETS

As interest rates rose toward the end of the Bretton Woods years, thereby creating losses for banks funding fixed-rate loans with short-term deposits, eurocurrency lending began to take the form of rollover credits in 1969. The lending rate in a rollover credit was tied to the bank's cost of funds (usually LIBOR, the London Interbank Offered Rate) and included a built-in spread or profit margin. Later, when the debt crisis emerged in the 1980s, lending became increasingly "securitized" through the use of loan participations, revolving underwriting facilities, and eurocommercial paper. By removing loans from, or avoiding placing loans on, their balance sheets, banks could earn fees while conserving on capital. Domestic markets saw a similar development of secondary loan markets in the form of fungible, tradeable securities—such as

TABLE 2.1
Currency Arrangements as of March 31, 1990.[1]

Pegged					Flexibility Limited vis-à-vis a Single Currency or Group of Currencies		More Flexible		
Single Currency			Currency Composite		Single Currency[2]	Cooperative Arrangements[3]	Adjusted According to a Set of Indicators	Other Managed Floating	Independently Floating
U.S. Dollar[4]	French Franc	Other	SDR	Other					
Afghanistan[4]	Benin	Bhutan (Indian rupee)	Burundi	Algeria	Bahrain[5]	Belgium	Chile[4,9]	China[4]	Argentina
Angola	Burkina Faso	Kiribati (Australian dollar)	Iran, Islamic Republic of[4]	Austria	Qatar[5]	Denmark	Colombia	Costa Rica[4]	Australia
Antigua and Barbuda	Cameroon	Lesotho[4] (South African rand)	Libyan Arab Jamahiriya[6]	Bangladesh[4]	Saudi Arabia[5]	France	Madagascar	Ecuador[4]	Bolivia
Bahamas, The[4]	Central African Republic	Swaziland (South African rand)	Myanmar	Botswana	United Arab Emirates[5]	Germany, Federal Republic of	Portugal	Egypt[4]	Brazil
Barbados	Chad		Rwanda	Cape Verde		Ireland		El Salvador[4]	Canada
Belize	Comoros		Seychelles	Cyprus		Italy		Greece	Gambia, The
Djibouti	Congo		Zambia[4]	Fiji		Luxembourg		Guinea	Ghana[4]
Dominica	Côte d'Ivoire			Finland[7]		Netherlands		Guinea Bissau	Guatemala
Dominican Republic	Equatorial Guinea			Hungary		Spain		Honduras[4]	Japan
Ethiopia	Gabon			Iceland[8]				India[10]	Lebanon
Grenada	Mali	Tonga (Australian dollar)		Israel[9]				Indonesia	Maldives
Guyana[4]	Niger			Jordan				Korea	New Zealand
Haiti	Senegal			Kenya				Lao People's Democratic Republic	Nigeria
Iraq	Togo			Kuwait				Mauritania	Paraguay
Jamaica				Malawi				Mexico[4]	Philippines
Liberia[4]				Malaysia[8]				Morocco	South Africa[4]
Nicaragua[4]				Malta				Pakistan	United Kingdom
Oman				Mauritius				Singapore	United States
Panama				Mozambique				Sri Lanka	Uruguay
Peru[4]				Nepal				Tunisia	Venezuela
				Norway[8]					Zaire
				Papua New Guinea					

St. Kitts and Nevis	Poland[4]	Turkey
St. Lucia	Romania	Viet Nam
St. Vincent and The Grenadines	Sao Tome and Principe	Yugoslavia[11]
Sierra Leone		
Sudan[4]	Solomon Islands	
	Somalia	
Suriname	Sweden[12]	
Syrian Arab Republic[4]	Tanzania	
Trinidad and Tobago	Thailand	
Yemen Arab Republic[13]		
Yemen, People's Democratic Republic of	Uganda	
	Vanuatu	
	Western Samoa	
	Zimbabwe	

Source: IMF, *Annual Report*, 1990.

[1] Cambodia is not classified.

[2] In all cases listed in this column, the U.S. dollar was the currency against which exchange rates showed limited flexibility.

[3] This category consists of countries participating in the exchange rate mechanism of the European Monetary System. In each case, the exchange rate is maintained within a margin of 2.25 percent around the bilateral central rates against other participating currencies, with the exception of Spain in which case the exchange rate is maintained within a margin of 6 percent.

[4] Member maintains exchange arrangements involving more than one exchange market. The arrangement shown is that maintained in the major market.

[5] Exchange rates are determined on the basis of a fixed relationship to the SDR, within margins of up to ∓ 7.25 percent. However, because of the maintenance of a relatively stable relationship with the U.S. dollar, these margins are not always observed.

[6] The exchange rate is maintained within margins of ∓ 7.5 percent.

[7] The exchange rate is maintained within margins of ∓ 3.0 percent.

[8] The exchange rate is maintained within margins of ∓ 2.25 percent.

[9] The exchange rate is maintained within margins of ∓ 5.0 percent.

[10] The exchange rate is maintained within margins of ∓ 5.0 percent on either side of a weighted composite of the currencies of the main trading partners.

[11] Member maintains a fixed relationship of Din7 = DM1.

[12] The exchange rate is maintained within margins of ∓ 1.5 percent.

[13] In June 1990, the Executive Board of the Fund, following the merger of the Yemen Arab Republic and the People's Democratic Republic of Yemen, concluded that the Republic of Yemen is a single member of the Fund.

collateralized mortgage obligations—backed with nonfungible, nontradeable loan assets.

In the old days—at least as recalled by nostalgic bankers—commercial banking was a simple activity governed by the 3-5-3 rule: take in money at 3 percent, lend it out at 5 percent, and drive home at 3 P.M. No longer. The principal development in international financial markets in the 1980s was the growth of exchange and over-the-counter trading of derivative products—futures, options, FRAs, and interest rate and currency swaps. Increased central bank emphasis in the early 1980s on capital "adequacy" and loan loss provisions for developing country loans put pressure on banks worldwide to minimize their use of capital. Banks responded by turning to off-balance sheet items like financial futures and options, interest rate swaps, and forward rate agreements to handle the funding gaps in their balance sheets. (See Table 2.2.)

The key reference rates in the eurodollar market became the forward rates for three-month LIBOR embedded in eurodollar futures prices at the IMM in Chicago. By September 1990, open interest in eurodollar futures at the IMM was 750,000 contracts, representing a face amount of $750 billion. Eurodollar futures prices also determined the rates paid on FRAs, or forward rate agreements, which are cash-settled, interbank-traded forward contracts on interest rates, as well as the market rates for one-year interest rate swaps (an exchange of a one-year fixed interest payment for four floating payments based on three-month LIBOR).

The market for syndicated eurocredits—large sovereign and corporate loans that were the norm in the eurocurrency market up until the Mexican debt moratorium of August 1982—experienced a revival in the late 1980s related to activity in mergers and acquisitions. By the end of the decade, 80 percent of syndicated lending went to corporate borrowers, especially in the United States and the United Kingdom.

TABLE 2.2
Worldwide Trade in Futures and Options

	Turnover in Millions of Contracts				Open Interest ($ billions)
	1986	1987	1988	1989	End 1989
Short-Term Interest Rate Futures	16.4	29.4	33.7	70.2	1002.5
three-month eurodollars	12.4	23.7	25.2	46.8	671.9
Long-Term Interest Rate Futures	74.6	116.3	122.6	130.6	196.5
U.S. Treasury bond	54.1	68.4	72.4	71.3	31.5
10-year Japanese government	9.4	18.4	18.8	19.1	129.1
Currency Futures	19.7	20.8	22.1	27.5	15.7
Interest Rate Options	22.2	29.3	31.3	41.5	388.3
Currency Options	13.0	18.2	18.2	20.7	44.3

Source: BIS, *Annual Report,* 1990.

DEVELOPMENTS IN THE INTERNATIONAL BOND MARKETS

The U.S. Interest Equalization Tax in 1963 inspired the first eurobond, a dollar-denominated bond lead-managed by the British merchant bank S. G. Warburg and issued in London on behalf of the Italian Autostrada. Though valued in U.S. currency, the eurobond issue was not registered under U.S. securities laws or distributed to U.S. investors. The yearly volume of new eurobond issues then grew from less than $150 million in 1963 to more than $3 billion by1968. As the amounts outstanding grew, eurobonds were increasingly traded in a secondary market. A desire to standardize trading practices resulted in the formation of the Association of International Bond Dealers (AIBD) in 1969. The costs of trading dropped when facilities were developed for clearing eurobonds and foreign bonds against payment through book-entry transactions. Euroclear was founded in Brussels in 1968 by Morgan Guaranty, and Cedel was founded in 1970 in Luxembourg by a group of European banks.

Innovation was prompted by changing economic conditions. When a rise in interest rates in 1970 created problems for fixed-rate eurobonds, the first floating-rate note (FRN)—a ten-year eurobond that paid a LIBOR-based interest rate reset at six-month intervals—was brought to market by Bankers Trust International and S. G. Warburg. Later, in the euphoria that accompanied the drop in interest rates after 1982, even perpetual floating-rate notes (ones with no maturity) were issued. But after a crisis in the FRN market in late 1986, equity-related eurobonds supplanted FRNs as the second most important eurobond category. (In 1989 equity-related eurobonds amounted to $85.2 billion, versus $23.4 billion for FRNs and $150.1 billion in straight fixed-rate issues.)

Equity-related issues were largely a Japanese phenomenon. The Tokyo stock market boom enabled Japanese companies to issue dollar eurobonds with attached warrants that allowed the bearer to purchase company stock at a fixed price. The companies traded off the value of the warrants for lower bond coupon rates (less than 4 percent). In addition, the companies believed, the owners of the warrants would later exercise them and purchase newly issued company shares, and the cash received by the company could be used to pay off maturing bonds. Japanese banks had similarly issued Swiss-franc-denominated bonds convertible into bank equity, which would increase banks' capital ratios if conversion took place. But by September 1990, the Tokyo stock market crash had left $125 billion of the $140 billion of outstanding warrants "out of the money." That meant that $125 billion of maturing bonds would probably have to be refinanced—not with equity, but in part with bank loans, on which interest rates at that time exceeded 8 percent in Tokyo. Japanese banks would likewise have to look for other sources of capital.

During the 1980s, profits among investment banks and securities firms were increasingly squeezed. In the United States, the securities industry's pretax return on equity dropped from 49 percent in 1980 to 7 percent in 1989. This was partly a result of deregulation. Fixed commissions on stockbroking were eliminated in the United States on May 1, 1975 ("May Day"), and (along with those on government bonds) in London in October 1986 ("Big Bang"). The erosion of the Glass-Steagall Act brought U.S. commercial banks into the competitive arena: in 1989, for example, U.S. commercial banks were allowed to underwrite corporate debt.

Size became more important. Tradition and prudence had provided for the underwriting risk in a eurobond issue to be shared among a number of banks. But toward the end of the 1970s, a form of underwriting called the "bought deal" came into play. In a bought deal there was one lead manager who guaranteed to the borrower the terms of the offering prior to its announcement. Only a bank with a large capital base could handle the risks involved. Shelf registration motivated a similar tendency in domestic underwritings. The share of industry capital of the top ten U.S. securities firms increased from 33 percent to 61 percent between 1973 and 1989, according to the Securities Industry Association. During the final year of the period, 90 percent of bond issues in the United States were underwritten by a single firm, compared to just 1 percent in 1980.

Only in one bond category had spreads failed to narrow, namely in high-yield or "junk" bonds. This new market for financing medium-sized companies previously denied access to the bond markets was mostly the creation of Michael Milken, an employee of the investment bank Drexel Burnham Lambert. Later, junk bonds were controversially introduced into mergers and acquisitions, and made Drexel Burnham Lambert in 1986 the most profitable investment bank in the United States, even after compensating Milken $500 million for his activities. Milken became the key financier for a takeover technique called leveraged buyouts, which involved issuing debt partly secured by the assets and cash flow of the target company, and then using the debt proceeds to obtain control of the company by purchasing its stock. (Junk bonds comprised the unsecured or "mezzanine" part of the debt issue.) First Drexel (which declared bankruptcy in 1990), and later Milken, became the targets of government prosecution stemming from alleged violations of securities laws.

FROM THE SNAKE TO THE EUROPEAN MONETARY SYSTEM

In the Smithsonian agreement, signed in December 1971, it had been decided to widen the plus-or-minus 1 percent bands of the Bretton Woods agreement to plus or minus 2.25 percent. However, the members of the European Economic Community decided to keep their currencies within narower margins with respect to each other. Recall that at the time of the formation of the European Economic Community (the Common Market) in 1958, the eventual goal had been economic unification as a prelude to political unification. By 1970 many trade restrictions between community members had been removed, and a new goal of monetary unification by 1980 was set. The Werner Plan, developed by a group of experts headed by Pierre Werner of Luxembourg, called for smaller margins of fluctuation between European currencies and exchange market intervention in local currencies rather than the dollar as steps toward eventual monetary unification. To maintain these narrow margins, community members would have to coordinate monetary policies. The ultimate stage of coordination would be a single policy with a single EEC currency.

Thus, following the Smithsonian agreement, the EEC decided on narrower bands of plus or minus 1.125 percent for community members. Because of the

visual appearance of a time graph giving changes in the value of EEC currencies with respect to the U.S. dollar, the arrangement was referred to as the
"snake in the tunnel." The snake was EEC currencies, which moved closely
together with respect to third currencies such as the dollar, while the tunnel
was formed by non-EEC currencies, which moved in the larger Smithsonian
band of plus or minus 2.25 percent. The snake arrangement commenced in
April 1972.

With the beginning of floating exchange rates in March 1973, European
countries continued the joint float of their respective currencies. Since non-
EEC currencies no longer traded in any fixed range with respect to each other,
the joint EEC float was referred to as the "snake in the lake." The snake
arrangement was not terribly successful after the movement to floating rates,
however, because there was no strong commitment on the part of member
countries to undertake the coordination of monetary and other economic
policies necessary to make the arrangement work. France, for example,
dropped out of the snake in January 1974, joined again in July 1975, and
dropped out again in March 1976. Nevertheless, a small core of currencies
remained in a joint float around the DM up to 1979, when the European
Monetary System (EMS) was formed.

The EMS was proposed by Helmut Schmidt at the European Community
summit meeting in Copenhagen in April 1978. Although some sentiment was
expressed that the United States and Japan did not worry sufficiently about
currency fluctuations, the primary motive for the formation of the EMS was
really political: the proposal represented a joint effort by Germany and France
to revive the movement toward European unification. The unification movement had fizzled out, and working on monetary union appeared to be a good
way to get it going again. So, on March 13, 1979, a new "zone of monetary
stability" in Europe was born. Seven of the community members had jointly
floated their six currencies from January to March, and the EMS began officially when France joined in March. Following are the main points of the
original EMS agreement.

1. Under the terms of the original agreement in 1979, the snake was to be
   enlarged to include all European Community member currencies. Great
   Britain, however, decided not to participate. It did not become a member of
   the parity grid system (2, next) until October 1990, even though the pound
   was included in the definition of the ECU (3, next). That left eight countries
   and seven currencies (since the Luxembourg franc is equivalent to the
   Belgian franc by a long-standing agreement between the central banks of
   those two countries). Greece subsequently became a member of the European Economic Community, but—like Britain—did not become a member of the exchange rate mechanism. The Greek drachma was, however,
   included in the definition of the ECU beginning in September 1984. The
   Spanish peseta and Portugese escudo were added in September 1989.
2. A parity grid system would be established. The parity grid would be a
   system of fixed par values, much like the Bretton Woods system although
   with fewer currencies and bigger bands around par. Each currency within
   the European Monetary System would have a declared par value with
   respect to each other currency in the system. A given currency would be

allowed to deviate a maximum of plus or minus 2.25 percent from its par value with respect to any other currency, except for the Italian lira, which would be allowed a range of plus or minus 6 percent. (The Spanish peseta was added with a 6 percent range in 1989, and in 1990 the lira range was reduced to 2.25 percent. The pound was added with a 6 percent range in October 1990.) The parity grid as it originally existed on March 13, 1979, is illustrated in Table 2.3. The middle number in a cell is the par value, and the upper and lower numbers present the allowable range for market exchange rates. For example, the par value for the DM and French franc (FF) was originally set at DM1 = FF2.3095 (equivalently, FF1 = DM.432995). The upper limit for the DM was DM1 = FF2.3621 (equivalently, the lower limit for the FF was FF1 = DM.42335). The lower limit for the DM was DM1 = FF2.2581 (equivalently, the upper limit for the FF was FF1 = DM.44285).

When a currency is at its upper or lower intervention point with respect to the parity grid, the central banks of *both* countries are obligated to intervene in the foreign exchange market to keep market exchange rates within the range allowed by the upper and lower bands. The intervention is "no-fault" under the parity grid system: each country is required to intervene to keep market exchange rates within the upper and lower grid values, irrespective of how it may feel about the other country's economic policies.

TABLE 2.3
The Original Parity Grid, March 13, 1979

	DM	FF	BF	IL	DK	DG	IP
DM		2.3621	16.074	485.576	2.8866	1.10835	.269937
		2.3095	15.7164	457.314	2.82237	1.0837	.263932
		2.2581	15.3665	430.698	2.7596	1.0596	.25806
FF	.44285		6.96	210.252	1.24985	.4799	.116881
	.432995		6.80512	198.015	1.22207	.469235	.114281
	.42335		6.65375	186.49	1.1949	.4588	.111739
BF	.06508	.15029		30.8961	.183665	.07052	.0171755
	.0636227	.146948		29.0979	.179581	.0689531	.0167934
	.06221	.14368		27.4044	.175585	.06742	.0164198
IL	.002322	.005362	.03649		.006553	.002516	.000612801
	.00218668	.00505013	.0343668		.0061716	.0023697	.000577135
	.002059	.004756	.032365		.005813	.00223175	.000543545
DK	.36235	.8369	5.695	172.045		.3927	.0956424
	.354313	.818286	5.56852	162.033		.383967	.0935147
	.34645	.8001	5.4445	152.605		.375425	.0914343
DG	.94375	2.1796	14.8325	448.074	2.66365		.249089
	.922767	2.13113	14.5026	421.995	2.60439		.243548
	.90225	2.0838	14.18	397.434	2.54645		.23813
IP	3.875	8.9495	60.9020	1839.78	10.9365	4.1195	
	3.78886	8.75034	59.5471	1732.7	10.6935	4.10597	
	3.705	8.5555	58.2225	1631.85	10.4555	4.0145	

DM = deutschemark; FF = French franc; BF = Belgian franc; IL = Italian lira; DK = Danish krone; DG = Dutch guilder; IP = Irish pound.

Technically, the par values in the parity grid are calculated by first defining a par value for each currency with respect to the ECU. (The ECU will be explained shortly. For now just think of it as another currency.) These par values defined in terms of the ECU are called ECU *central rates*. The ECU central rates are used to calculate the bilateral par values. For example, if the ECU central rates for the DM and the FF are ECU1 = DM4 and ECU1 = FF12, this implies a bilateral par value of DM1 = FF3. The ECU central rates used to calculate the parity grid are published daily in the *Financial Times* of London. When there is a "devaluation" or a "revaluation" in the EMS, a new set of ECU central rates is picked. The new ECU central rates then give rise to a new parity grid.

The device used to calculate the par values in the parity grid is irrelevant, however, since par values could just as easily be defined from scratch. In particular, the operation of the parity grid does not depend in any way on the ECU.

EXAMPLE 2.1

Here are the ECU central rates giving rise to the par values in the parity grid of Table 2.3:

ECU1 = DM2.51064
ECU1 = FF5.79831
ECU1 = DG2.72077
ECU1 = BF39.4582
ECU1 = IL1148.15
ECU1 = DK7.08592
ECU1 = IP.662638

For example, since ECU1 = DK7.08592 and ECU1 = IP.662638, we obtain IP1 = DK(7.08592/.662638) = DK10.6935. Alternatively, DK1 = IP1/(10.6935) = IP.0935147. And so on. As an example of a devaluation of the French franc in the EMS, we might reassign the ECU central rate for the French franc to be ECU1 = FF5.92884 instead of ECU1 = 5.79831. This reassignment would give rise to a new set of bilateral par values in the parity grid, and—at these new par values—the French franc would buy smaller amounts of all other EMS currencies. Notice that "devaluation" in this case would refer to a change in the ECU central rate: a change in a number written down on paper. The market exchange rate for the French franc might or might not depreciate, depending on whether the new upper and lower bands implied central bank intervention to alter the market rate or whether the change in the ECU central rate caused market participants to change their demand for, or supply of, French francs.

After par values are determined, the next task is to calculate upper and lower intervention points around each parity grid par value. The allowable market exchange rate ranges above and below par are usually referred to as "2.25 percent" bands (or "6 percent" bands originally for lira). However, because of a mathematical relationship known as Jensen's inequality, the upper and lower intervention points cannot be calculated literally by adding or subtracting 2.25 percent (or 6 percent). Instead, the upper (lower) intervention points are obtained by multiplying (dividing) the par values by

1.022753 except for the Italian lira, where the par value is multiplied (divided) by 1.061798.

□

To see why, consider the exchange rate of DM for FF. Suppose a par value of FF4 = DM1 is chosen. Rewriting this exchange rate in terms of the FF, we have FF1 = DM.2500. If we then calculate plus-or-minus 2.25 percent upper and lower limit points, we get that (.0225) (4) = .0900 is to be added to, and subtracted from, the par value of 4, while (.0225) (.2500) = .005625 is to be added to, and subtracted from, the par value of .2500:

	FF per DM	DM per FF
Upper	4.0900	.255625
Par	4	.2500
Lower	3.9100	.244375

Examination of these numbers shows that even though 4 is the reciprocal of .2500, it is *not* true that 4.0900 is the reciprocal of .244375, nor is 3.9100 the reciprocal of .255625. Therefore, whether central banks are obligated to intervene may depend on which of the two currencies they use to calculate the upper or lower intervention points. This is obviously absurd: the same answer should be obtained independently of whether calculation is done in terms of DM or in terms of FF.   ■

□

To get around this paradox, suppose we choose a number X by which we will first multiply, then divide, the par value P to get the upper and lower bands. If we do the calculation this way, the paradox goes away: the upper and lower bands in terms of one currency are the reciprocals of the lower and upper bands of the other currency. If P represents the number of FF per DM at par, our table would read, after multiplying and dividing the par values by X:

	FF per DM	DM per FF
Upper	XP	X/P
Par	P	$1/P$
Lower	P/X	$1/XP$

As we see, XP is the reciprocal of $1/XP$, and P/X is the reciprocal of X/P. The next step then is to calculate the value of X in such a way that we get a total range of 4.5 percent around the par value (just as we would get by taking plus or minus 2.25 percent of par). That is, we want

$$XP - P/X = .045\ P,$$

which implies

$$X^2 - .045X - 1 = 0.$$

Solving for X, we get $X = 1.022753$. Therefore the par value is alternatively multiplied and divided by 1.022753 to get the upper and lower intervention points. For the Italian lira or (later) for the Spanish peseta or the British pound, the total range is 12 percent or .12. Substituting .12 for .045 in the above equation and solving again for X, we get $X = 1.061798$. There are special rules as to whether a fraction is to be rounded up or down after the multiplication or division. These need not concern us here.   ■

EXAMPLE 2.2

Referring again to Table 2.3, we see that the par value for the DM with respect to the FF is DM1 = FF2.3095. If we multiply and divide the par value of FF2.3095 by 1.022753, we get the upper and lower limits of DM1 = FF2.3621 and DM1 = FF2.2581. Similarly, the par value for the DM against the Italian lira is DM1 = IL457.314. If we multiply and divide IL457.314 by 1.061798, we get the upper and lower limits of DM1 = IL485.576 and DM1 = IL430.698.

---

3. Germany had insisted on the parity grid system because it had viewed the purpose of the EMS as a way of imposing monetary discipline on member countries. However, other nations, in particular the United Kingdom and France, wanted a system organized according to the concept of community average, where average behavior would be considered good and "divergent" behavior bad. Either too little or too much inflation could be divergent behavior, for example, if the European Community average was moderate inflation.

The concept of average behavior was used as the basis for the divergence indicator system. The divergence indicator system differs in purpose and in practice from the parity grid system. The divergence indicator system is intended to deal with the old Bretton Woods question of who has to alter economic policies in order to maintain a fixed exchange rate. Bretton Woods broke down when the United States, on one hand, and Germany and Japan, on the other, disagreed on whose economic policy should be altered to conform to the other's. So the EMS set up a finger-pointing system, the divergence indicator system, which is supposed to answer the question of who is conducting economic policy that conflicts with everyone else's. For example, if both France and Germany are intervening in the foreign exchange market under the parity grid system to keep the French franc from falling in market value with respect to the DM, this could happen because French monetary policy is too expansionary or because German monetary policy is not expansionary enough. Hopefully, in such a case, the divergence indicator will pick out one of the two countries as having a divergent policy. If a country is divergent, then it is expected to adjust such things as money supply growth and the size of its government deficit to bring its macroeconomic policies in line with other EEC member countries.

Here is how the divergence indicator system works. First, an artificial currency, the European Currency Unit (ECU) was defined as a basket, or portfolio, of member currencies. The composition of the ECU as set in 1979 was:

ECU1 = DM.828 + FF1.15 + £.0885 + DG.286 + IL109
       + BF3.66 + LF.14 + DK.217 + IP.00759

where LF = Luxembourg franc (equivalent to the Belgian franc), and the other currencies are those listed in Table 2.3. In September 1984, the composition of the basket was altered to include the Greek drachma (GD):

ECU1 = DM.719 + FF1.31 + £.0878 + DG.256 + IL140
       + BF3.71 + LF.14 + DK.219 + IP.00871 + GD1.15

In September 1989, the Spanish peseta (SP) and Portuguese escudo (PE) were added:

ECU1 = DM.6242 + FF1.332 + £.08784 + DG.2198 + IL151.8
       + BF3.301 + LF.13 + DK.1976 + IP.008552
       + GD1.44 + SP6.885 + PE1.393.

The ECU defines the "community average."

Given the portfolio definition of the ECU, the *market* value of the ECU in terms of, say, the U.S. dollar would depend on the U.S. dollar price of each of the component currencies in the ECU. Suppose market exchange rates were these:

Foreign Currency	U.S. Dollar Price of Foreign Currency
DM	.3998
FF	.1415
£	1.7125
DG	.3663
IL	.00071
BF,LF	.02
DK	.1134
IP	1.3650
GD	.0095

Then the market value of the ECU, using the September 1984 definition, would be (adding together the weights for the BF and LF):

ECU1 = DM.719 ($.3998/DM) + FF1.31 ($.1415/FF)
       + £.0878 ($1.7125/£) + DG.256 ($.3663/DG)
       + IL140 ($.00071/IL) + BF3.85 ($.02/BF)
       + DK.219 ($.1134/DK) + IP.00871 ($1.3650/IP)
       + GD1.15 ($.0095/GD)
     = $.9410.

In this example, the market value of the ECU in terms of a common measuring unit, the U.S. dollar, is ECU1 = $.9410. If we compare this value to the market value of a member currency in terms of the U.S. dollar, we get the ECU market exchange rate for that currency. For example, since DM1 = $.3998 in the foreign exchange market, and ECU1 = $.9410 in the foreign exchange market, we get that the number of DM per ECU is ECU1 = DM(.9410/.3998) = DM2.3537. In the divergence indicator system, this ECU *market* value is compared to the ECU central rate (the rate written down on paper that is used to calculate the parity grid values). For example, suppose the ECU central rate were ECU1 = DM2.3324:

ECU central rate: ECU1 = DM2.3324
ECU market rate: ECU1 = DM2.3537. *> central rate*

Clearly, for the hypothetical market, exchange rates above the DM would have diverged somewhat from its central value. The percentage movement in the DM from the central rate would be (DM2.3537/DM2.3324 − 1) × 100 = .913 percent. The DM would have depreciated in the foreign exchange market with respect to the ECU. The DM would have become less valuable.

EXAMPLE 2.3

In Table 2.4 we see the European monetary system as reported in the *Financial Times* for October 24, 1990. The first column lists the ECU central rates used to determine the parity grid par values. These central rates were the ones in force in October 1990. The second column ("Currency amounts against ECU Oct. 23") gives the ECU *market* value of each currency as calculated using market exchange rates on October 23, 1990. The third column ("Percent change from central rate") is calculated from the first two columns. For example, for the Spanish peseta we have (129.207/133.631 − 1) × 100 = −3.31 percent.

TABLE 2.4
The European Monetary System as Reported in the *Financial Times*

		EMS European Currency Unit Rates			
	ECU Central Rates	Currency Amounts Against ECU, Oct. 23	% Change from Central Rate	% Spread vs. Weakest Narrow Band Currency	Divergence Indicator
Spanish Peseta	133.631	129.207	−3.31	3.77	58
French Franc	6.89509	6.89760	0.04	0.30	2
Belgian Franc	42.4032	42.4240	0.05	0.28	1
Sterling	0.696904	0.697472	0.08	0.25	−2
Irish Punt	0.767417	0.768532	0.15	0.19	−3
German D-Mark ..	2.05586	2.06051	0.23	0.11	−9
Danish Krone	7.84195	7.86189	0.25	0.08	−8
Dutch Guilder	2.31643	2.32259	0.27	0.07	−9
Italian Lira	1538.24	1543.34	0.33	0.00	−12

Source: Financial Times, October 24, 1990
ECU central rates set by the European Commission. Currencies are in descending relative strength. Percentage changes are for ECU; a positive change denotes a weak currency. Divergence shows the ratio between two spreads; the percentage difference between the actual market and ECU central rates for a currency, and the maximum permitted percentage deviation of the currency's market rate from its ECU central rate.
Adjustment calculated by *Financial Times*.

How much movement of a currency's ECU market value away from the currency's ECU central value is too much under the divergence indicator? Two further steps are required to answer this question. First, an adjustment to the calculated amount of divergence is made in order to strip out the effects of the Portuguese escudo and the Greek drachma (which are not in the grid, but are in the ECU), and to deal with the fact that the Spanish peseta and British pound have a wider band around par than do other currencies. Second, this adjusted percentage market divergence of a currency is compared to another number, the "maximum divergence." If the adjusted divergence approaches the maximum divergence, the country is supposed to take action to bring its economic policy into conformity with the European Community average. In Table 2.4, column 5 ("Divergence indicator") gives the ratio in percent of adjusted market divergence to the maximum divergence for each currency. We see that movement from the ECU central rate by the Spanish peseta is 58 percent of its allowable range in that direction. If the maximum is approached (i.e., if the divergence indicator approaches 100), Spain will have to bring its economic policies in line with the community average.

☐

Calculation of the maximum divergence as well as the adjusted market divergence is somewhat complicated. To calculate the maximum divergence, we first have to calculate the *weight* of each of the component currencies in the ECU, *using ECU central rates*. To get a currency's weight, simply divide the amount of a currency in the formal definition of the ECU by the ECU central rate for the currency. For example, the amount of the DM in the ECU in the 1989 portfolio definition was DM.6242. Table 2.4 shows that the ECU central rate on October 23, 1990, for the DM was ECU1 = DM2.05586. This implies a weight (w) for the DM of $w = (.6242/2.05586) = .3036$. The DM, at the ECU central rates prevailing on October 23, 1990, made up 30.36 percent of the value of the ECU.

Each of the currencies in the ECU has its own weight, and the sum of the weights of the component currencies is 1. Since the Portuguese escudo and the Greek drachma are two of the ECU's component currencies, they too have weights. Even though neither currency is part of the parity grid, each is assigned an ECU central value like other currencies, and these ECU central values are used to calculate the weights for the escudo and the drachma.

Under the parity grid, a currency can diverge approximately (but not exactly, as we saw above) 2.25 percent against other currencies, except for the peseta and pound (approximately 6 percent) and the escudo and drachma (which are not in the grid). But in the divergence indicator calculations, it is initially pretended that all currencies, including pound, peseta, escudo, and drachma, are only allowed an exact 2.25 percent divergence. Thus a currency can diverge 2.25 percent (.0225) against all other currencies, but even so a currency cannot diverge against itself. Since its divergence against itself is zero, the maximum possible divergence against the ECU is .0225 $[1 - w(i)]$ where $w(i)$ is the weight of the currency in the ECU. This is the idea behind the following definition.

Define a *maximum divergence M(i)* for each currency *i*, using the weight *w(i)* of the currency in the ECU, where the weight is calculated using ECU central rates:

$M(i) = .0225 [1 - w(i)]$, if currency *i* is not pound or peseta.
$M(i) = .0600 [1 - w(i)]$, if currency *i* is pound or peseta.

After the influence of a currency's own weight is eliminated (by multiplying by $1 - w(i)$), and if we ignore complications rising from peseta, escudo, pound, and drachma, a maximum percentage divergence of 2.25 is possible if the currency is not pound or peseta, or 6 percent for pound and peseta.

EXAMPLE 2.4

Referring to Table 2.4, we can calculate the maximum divergence for the DM against the ECU for October 23, 1990. Since the amount of the DM in the 1989 portfolio definition of the ECU was DM.6242, we calculate the weight of the DM as $w = (.6242/2.05586) = .3036$. The maximum divergence M is then $M = (.0225)[1 - .3036] = .0157 = 1.57$ percent. For the Spanish peseta, the weight is $w = (6.885/133.631) = .0515 = 5.15$ percent. The maximum divergence for the Spanish peseta is $M = (.0600)[1 - .0515] = .0569 = 5.69$ percent.

The values for the maximum divergence remain the same as long as the ECU central values (and definition of the ECU) remain the same. At times when there has been a devaluation or revaluation in the EMS and new ECU central values assigned, the values for the maximum divergence have changed correspondingly.

Now, it may seem at this point that all that is left to do is compare the ECU central rate for each currency with the ECU market rate for that currency and see if they differ by more than the maximum divergence. That is, we would just compare column 3 and the maximum divergence. However, one more necessary calculation involves an adjustment to column 3. Remember that when we defined the maximum divergence we pretended that the pound, peseta, escudo, and drachma were only allowed a 2.25 percent margin around par in the parity grid. But since Portugal and Greece do not participate in the exchange rate mechanism, and since the margins for the pound and peseta are really 6.0 percent, in the foreign exchange market these currencies can move freely outside the pretended range. So the final adjustment is to strip out the effects of market movements of these currencies that are greater than 2.25 percent from the ECU central rate. We start by finding the weakest currency in the system (the one that has depreciated the most from its ECU central rate).

In Table 2.4 the weakest currency is the Italian lira. Column 3 notes that the lira has depreciated by .33 percent from its ECU central rate. Then column 4 compares the movement of each currency in the system away from its central rate *relative* to the movement of the lira from the lira's central rate. For example, for the DM we have:

$(2.05586/2.06051)/(1538.24/1543.34) - 1 = .00105 = .11$ percent.

Of all the currencies listed in column 4, only the Spanish peseta has exceeded the limit of 2.25 percent (+ or −). Thus we calculate an adjustment factor for the movement of the peseta outside the 2.25 percent bands. We do this by taking the difference between the peseta's divergence against the weakest currency, the lira, and 2.25, and multiplying the result by the peseta's weight in the ECU. This gives

$$(3.77 - 2.25)(.0515) = .0782 \text{ percent.}$$

This number is subtracted from each of the numbers in column 3 for all currencies other than the pound and peseta. This yields the adjusted divergences. We then take the ratio of the adjusted divergence to the maximum divergence for each currency, which yields column 5 of Table 2.4:

	div	adj div	max div	div indicator
Peseta	−3.3106	−3.3106	5.691	58.17
French franc	.0364	−.0418	1.815	2.30
Belgian franc	.0491	−.0291	2.075	1.40
Pound	.0815	.0815	5.246	−1.55
Punt	.1453	.0671	2.225	−3.02
Deutschemark	.2262	.1480	1.567	−9.45
Krone	.2543	.1761	2.193	−8.03
Guilder	.2659	.1878	2.037	−9.22
Lira	.3315	.2534	2.028	−12.50

Since the peseta is not adjusted, the divergence as a percentage of maximum allowable divergence is $-100(-3.3106/5.691) = 58.17$. For the DM, the calculation is $-100(.1480/1.567) = -9.45$. And so on. Calculated this way, if the divergence indicator is greater than 100, the currency has appreciated too much; if less than −100, the currency has depreciated too much. ∎

4. A final provision of the EMS agreement was that member countries would buy into a credit fund with 20 percent of their dollars, gold, and other reserves. In return they would be issued ECUs to be used for central bank settlement and would also have borrowing privileges to obtain foreign exchange for intervention. This "fund" was really just a set of books kept at the Bank for International Settlements (BIS) in Basel, Switzerland. The portion of a central bank's gold and other reserves that has been "turned over" to the fund through book-entry transfers really remains safe and sound in the central bank's own vault.

This, then, is the cumbersome system of the EMS. Has it been a success? The answer depends on what one means by success. Initially, countries such as Germany and France did little to coordinate economic policies, even though their central banks generally maintained exchange rates within the ranges permitted by the parity grid. A combination of relatively fixed exchange rates with divergent inflation rates in the early 1980s may have resulted in distortions in international trade through unnecessary changes in real exchange rates (discussed in Chapter 8). As a result of this lack of policy coordination, the ECU central rate for the DM was changed by 5.5 percent on October 5, 1981, by 4.25 percent on June 14, 1982, and by 5.5 percent on March 21, 1983, the changes reflecting an increase in the value of the DM. The corresponding ECU percentage changes for the French franc on those dates were −3 percent, −5.75 percent, −2.5 percent. For example, the combination of a 5.5 percent increase in the ECU value of the DM on March 21, 1983, along with a −2.5 percent change in the ECU value of the French franc resulted in a net change of roughly 8 percent in the bilateral par value of the DM against the FF in the parity grid. On paper, at the par value, the DM bought 8 percent more FF after the realignment. In all, ECU central rates were realigned eight times from 1979 to July 1985. In the last realignment, the Italian lira was devalued by 6 percent, while the other participating EMS currencies were revalued upward by 2 percent, following a fall in the lira from IL1840/U.S. $ to IL2200/U.S. $ on July 19, 1985. (See problem 11 at the end of this chapter.)

In the next five years, there were four more realignments: on April 7 and August 24, 1986; January 12, 1987; and January 8, 1990. In the realignment of August 24, 1986, the Irish punt was devalued 8 percent. The Italian lira was devalued 3.7 percent on January 8, 1990, at the time its bands were narrowed from 6 percent to 2.25 percent. Overall, the exchange rate mechanism may have served as a modest brake on the inflationary tendencies of the Banque de France and Banca d'Italia (Fratianni, 1988).

The ECU has become an important unit used to denominate trade between Common Market countries. ECU-denominated bond issues and syndicated loans are common, and there has developed a liquid ECU interbank deposit market formed by more than a thousand banks in thirty countries. By 1985, ECU traveler's checks and credit cards were available, and more than 200 European banks offered ECU-denominated checking accounts. The market's further development was initially hindered by Bundesbank opposition to the use of the ECU in Germany. It was not clear that business contracts stated in terms of the ECU were legally binding under German commercial law. The German ban on ECU-denominated bank deposits was, however, lifted in 1987.

Developments in the European Community (EC) continued to dominate those in the EMS. The drive toward European unification was scheduled to culminate in 1992 with 330 million Europeans obtaining the freedom to do business or reside in any of the twelve member states of the EC. The original Treaty of Rome had called for ''the free movement of persons, services, and capital'' by December 31, 1969, and—almost twenty years past the deadline— an amendment (the Single European Act) called for the same freedoms by December 31, 1992. This time, closer to schedule, financial harmonization was given a boost with the abolition of intra-EC capital controls. This allowed investment capital to seek out the country with the lowest tax and regulatory burdens, putting pressure on those members at variance with the community average.

THE INTERNATIONAL DEBT CRISIS

In the mid-1970s and again after 1982, the ''debt crisis'' was a prominent financial market preoccupation, originally in the eurocurrency markets, but eventually spilling over into domestic markets as well. Of particular relevance was debt owed by borrowers in developing countries to commercial banks in industrial countries. During the period extending from the end of 1973 to the end of 1982, debt of non-OPEC developing countries owed to banks in the United States, Canada, Western Europe, and Japan (BIS reporting banks) increased by $215 billion, according to BIS data. This total growth in bank debt was approximately twice the growth in nominal GNP of non-OPEC LDCs and more than two times the growth in their exports. Bank debt as a proportion of exports rose from 60 percent to 130 percent. This dramatic increase in non-OPEC LDC bank debt (accompanied also by an increase in other types of debt) was only in part associated with an increase in the price of energy. More importantly, bank debt growth represented a significant expansion in non-energy-related public sector deficits financed by foreign borrowing and a major shift from equity to debt financing in the non-OPEC LDC private and state enterprise sectors.

We can divide up this time period into OPEC I (1973–1978) and OPEC II (1979–1982). The embargo by the Organization of Petroleum Exporting Countries (OPEC) that followed the Egyptian attack on Israel in October 1973 saw the price of Saudi Arabian light crude rise from $1.73 per barrel to $10. Over the next year, the nominal price increased to $12. Afterward, however, while the nominal price continued to rise, the real price (the price adjusted for purchasing power) fell and continued to fall until 1979. With the Iranian revolution in 1979 (OPEC II), the real price of oil rose again, the nominal price going to $30 a barrel, then higher. Only in 1982 did the nominal price begin a significant drift downward.

Prior to the first round of oil price increases, non-OPEC LDCs had run modest current account deficits financed mostly through official capital transfers, direct investment, and import finance. With a rise in oil costs, many nations (such as Brazil) decided as a matter of deliberate policy to continue their pace of energy consumption through international borrowing. Others, such as Mexico and Nigeria, used the presence of oil reserves as the basis for new social and "development" programs. Since there was neither a large domestic savings base nor a significant capital market in any of these countries, government deficits were financed either by borrowing in foreign capital markets, thus increasing foreign debt, or by selling bonds to the central bank, which vastly increased the high-powered monetary base. Large money supply increases were accompanied by significant inflation and—because exchange rates were fixed and only adjusted at government discretion—the domestic currency in many cases became significantly overvalued. As a result, export sectors became increasingly noncompetitive while import sectors were subsidized by access to artificially cheap foreign exchange. Deterioration in the balance of trade from currency overvaluation made it increasingly difficult to generate foreign exchange to repay foreign debts independently of other facts mentioned below.

Over the 1974–1978 period the OPEC countries ran an accumulated current account surplus of $179.1 billion, according to IMF data. That means that, in terms of goods and services, OPEC countries sold more than they purchased by $179.1 billion. When a country runs a current account surplus, it accumulates wealth in the form of financial assets: bank deposits, Treasury bills, and other types of IOUs. The mirror image of OPEC's surplus is the rest of the world, which—if the numbers are measured correctly (and they usually are not)—had an equivalent deficit. If the numbers are to be believed, the non-OPEC LDCs had an accumulated deficit over the 1974–1978 period of $187.4 billion (see Table 2.5). That is, much of the OPEC surplus translated directly into a non-OPEC LDC deficit. Thus, the accumulation of financial assets by OPEC countries was mirrored by an accumulation of foreign debt by non-OPEC developing countries.

The largest single category of asset accumulation by OPEC countries was in the form of eurocurrency deposits. According to Bank of England estimates, net OPEC eurodeposits over the 1974–1978 period were about $64 billion. Eurobanks accumulated OPEC assets and made loans on the basis of these assets. Now, there is no reason these loans necessarily had to go to any particular category of borrower. It is conceivable, for example, that eurobank lending could have gone exclusively to U.S. or French companies. However, as it turned out, eurobanks played a direct role in the "recycling" process. Gross medium-term euroborrowing by non-OPEC LDCs was about $63 billion over the 1974–1978 period. Thus, eurobanks acted to channel the financial savings of OPEC directly to non-OPEC LDCs, during the OPEC I period.

The "Erdman scenario" presented by Paul Erdman in his novel *The Crash of '79,* a book that appeared in 1976 and was widely read by policymakers, went like this: OPEC accumulates a lot of short-term deposits in eurobanks. Banks turn these short-term deposits into longer-term loans to developing countries on a rollover basis. Then one day there is a run on eurobanks when OPEC funds are switched from eurodeposits to other types of assets. Banks try to call in their loans, but the developing countries cannot pay. The international financial system collapses. "Do you really think it could happen?" U.S. Vice-President Nelson Rockefeller reportedly asked Erdman. The Erdman scenario never came about. An OPEC run on eurodollar assets was fairly implausible because OPEC assets were being managed by people trained in the top U.S. and U.K. business schools. A massive switch into other currencies would drive down the exchange value of the dollar, with a resulting capital loss on OPEC assets. In addition, a run on particular banks conducted in such a way as to lead to widespread bank failures would also threaten OPEC's accumulated financial wealth. Finally, as the most important factor, non-OPEC LDCs were able to repay their debts without any great difficulty during the OPEC I period.

The real burden of non-OPEC LDC debt was steadily eroded over the 1974–1978 period because nominal interest rates on borrowing failed to keep pace with the rise in inflation. As a result, the great "recycling problem" was solved under OPEC I without protracted adjustments in economic policy in developing countries. The average dollar borrowing rate over the 1974–1978 period was roughly zero in real terms. Much of the lending had been made at a margin above the six-month London Interbank Offer Rate (LIBOR), the market rate at which banks lend eurodollars to each other in London. Interest rates would be fixed at the beginning of each six-month period, then changed at the beginning of the next period, according to the prevailing LIBOR rate. Average six-month LIBOR for the U.S. dollar during 1974–1978 was 8.3 percent. The average dollar inflation rate was about 8.0 percent, giving an ex-post real interest rate of .3 percent (see Table 2.6). The existence of low real borrowing rates is further seen when the nominal eurodollar borrowing rate is compared,

TABLE 2.5
Current Account Balances of OPEC and Non-OPEC LDCs During the First and Second Oil Shocks

	1973	1974	1975	1976	1977	1978	1979	1980	1981	1982	1983
Current account (billions of U.S.$)											
OPEC:	6.7	68.3	35.4	40.3	29.4	5.7	62.3	110.3	52.0	−13.5	−18.4
Non-OPEC LDCs:	−11.3	−37.0	−46.3	−32.6	−29.6	−41.9	−62.1	−87.7	−108.3	−86.1	−52.1
Increase in official reserves by non-OPEC LDCS (billions of U.S.$)	10.4	2.7	−1.7	13.0	11.2	16.5	11.7	6.7	3.7	−4.1	10.1
Price index of non-oil primary commodities exported by non-OPEC LDCs (percentage change per year)	51.2	30.3	−17.8	17.0	25.4	−7.2	14.4	9.7	−15.2	−13.4	9.1

Source: IMF, *World Economic Outlook* (data prior to 1977 are taken from 1983 volume; subsequent data are taken from 1985 volume).

TABLE 2.6
Real Borrowing Rates and Real Growth Rates for Selected Borrowing Countries

	1974–1978 (%)	1979 (%)	1980 (%)	1981 (%)	1982 (%)
Average six-month LIBOR (U.S.$)	8.3	12.1	14.3	17.2	13.0
U.S.$ inflation (CPI)	8.0	13.2	12.4	8.9	6.0
Real dollar rate of interest	.3	−1.1	1.9	8.3	7.0
Real growth in GNP					
Mexico	5.5		8.7		4.5
Brazil	7.0		7.4		−1.7
Argentina	1.4		4.3		−6.0
Chile	3.3		7.9		−2.6
Colombia	5.6		4.5		3.0
Ecuador	6.8		4.9		2.9
Peru	2.0		3.5		2.3
Venezuela*	6.1		−0.2		0
Indonesia*	7.0		7.5		6.3
Korea	10.4		0.1		6.0
Malaysia	7.1		8.6		5.2
Phillipines	6.3		5.9		3.2
Taiwan	9.0		7.3		4.7
Thailand	10.3		5.9		6.3

* OPEC member.
Source: Morgan Guaranty, *World Financial Markets.*

not with inflation, but with the rate of growth of non-OPEC LDC export prices (see Figure 2.1 and Table 2.5). The rapid growth in export prices meant that the burden of foreign interest payments on debt used to finance exports was falling continuously over this period. (A similar situation existed in the U.S. domestic market, where the appreciation in real estate, energy, and farm product prices outran interest payments on mortgages and energy and farm loans.) This propitious state of affairs, from a borrower's standpoint, allowed non-OPEC LDCs to accumulate a considerable proportion of borrowings in the form of foreign exchange reserves. (See Table 2.5 for the years 1976–1978.)

Some significant changes in the outlook for further debt increases had taken place by 1979, however. The variable interest rate portion of the debt (such as that based on LIBOR) had gone up, leaving debtors more vulnerable to a sudden increase in short-term real interest rates. And by the end of 1979, 52 percent of non-OPEC LDC debt to BIS-reporting banks was concentrated in the MBA countries (Mexico, Brazil, and Argentina), leaving lending banks with a relatively nondiversified international loan portfolio. With the second major round of oil-price increases in 1979, apparently remembering the relative ease in which the first oil shock had been endured, major developing countries like Brazil and Mexico not only continued the previous pace of borrowing but expanded it considerably—Mexico expecting ever-increasing oil revenues, while Brazil faced increased payments for imported oil. Greater borrowing implied, of course, greater lending, showing that borrowers' repayment as-

*6-month annualized rates of change of 3-month moving averages

FIGURE 2.1
Growth in non-OPEC LDC export prices compared to eurodollar borrowing rate, 1973–1983. [*Source:* BIS, *Fifty-Third Annual Report.*]

sumptions were shared also by the headquarters offices of lending banks. (A clear shift in bank lending assumptions did not emerge until the announcement of a ninety-day debt moratorium by Mexico on August 20, 1982.) The role of the euromarkets continued to be important under OPEC II, as under OPEC I, with eurocurrency bank credits to non-OPEC LDCs totaling $113 billion from the beginning of 1979 to mid-1982, according to Morgan Guaranty data. Branches and subsidiaries, as well as head offices, of U.S. banks played a particularly important role. By 1982, total outstanding loans made by the nine largest U.S. banks to borrowers in the three MBA countries alone exceeded 100 percent of the aggregate paid-in capital and reserves of those nine banks.

Not only was the pace of borrowing initially much greater than before, it coincided with a major shift in the pattern of real interest rates. In the first two years of OPEC II, 1978–1980, real-dollar borrowing rates remained at zero but rose dramatically afterward, as seen in Table 2.6. The worldwide economic slump among industrial countries over the period (real GNP growth fell from about 4 percent in 1978 to 0 in 1982) resulted also in a sharp drop in demand for non-OPEC LDC exports, with a consequent drop in non-OPEC LDC export revenues and real growth rates. Standard development models suggest that if a country's foreign borrowing is used for productive investment, then the country's foreign debt will stabilize at some fraction of GNP as long as the country's real growth rate exceeds its real borrowing rate. But Table 2.6 shows that after 1980, real-dollar borrowing rates had come to exceed real growth rates in many developing countries. Complicating the picture was the fact that borrowing was sometimes used to finance consumption or nonproductive prestige investment projects or was funneled into inefficient state enterprises, and thus had little potential to generate a sufficient return to repay the debt. Further complications were introduced by bizarre political developments, such as the decision of Argentina's military government to go to war over the Falklands/Malvinas Islands in April 1982 during a period of negative real GNP growth, and Lopez-Portillo's compounding of a crisis of confidence in the Mexican financial system by nationalizing Mexican banks following the debt moratorium announced in August 1982.

Thus, not only were developing countries not aided by an inflationary erosion of their debt burden accompanied by rapidly increasing export prices as happened in the mid-1970s, but in the early 1980s they faced real interest rates that were as much above the historical norm as the 1970s' real interest rates had been below the norm. In the year following the Mexican crisis of August 1982, some thirty countries entered rescheduling agreements with commercial banks, and policymakers in the United States and other major lending countries worried greatly about the possible consequences of widespread defaults on both the international and domestic financial systems. Relations among debtor countries, international banks, the IMF, and industrial country governments took on the characteristics of a complex game of strategy. We can briefly summarize the players and their roles as follows.

Lending Banks

By 1983, most lending banks viewed the amount and pace of lending from 1979 to mid-1982 as excessive and a mistake of judgment on their part, regardless of the amount of time they spent justifying themselves in public. But now they had to make the best of the situation. To cut off all lending immediately would ensure that bank lending exposure did not increase and also promised to bring about an economic and political crisis in borrowing countries of sufficient magnitude to ensure that little of the debt already outstanding would ever be repaid. That would leave the major banks technically bankrupt, which was not a possibility they could contentedly contemplate, and at any rate appeared to be a suboptimal solution. Therefore, they were willing to lend even more, because they calculated that to do so would increase the total risk-adjusted expected return on lending. The probability of the lending banks being repaid was not independent of the lending behavior of the banks themselves. However, the probability of banks being repaid was not independent of the behavior of borrowing countries either. To ensure that borrowing countries adjusted their economic policies in ways the banks considered appropriate, they made both new lending and rescheduling of existing debt contingent on borrowing countries' acceptance of an IMF program of macroeconomic adjustment.

Borrowing Country Governments

The governments of borrowing countries did not want IMF programs. In the first place, they didn't like other people telling them what to do. IMF lending was based on conditionality, and the IMF would not lend unless the country agreed to certain criteria with respect to government deficits, growth of the money supply, wage increases, price inflation, and exchange rates. In the second place, to admit the need for an IMF program could suggest that the current government was economically incompetent. This meant that, at best, IMF programs could only be accepted after—and not immediately before— governmental elections. But the amount of funds the IMF itself had to lend was puny. Borrowing country governments did not consider the magnitude of IMF loans worth the IMF hassle. Rather, they would only countenance an IMF program because that was the only way they would get money from commercial banks.

As an alternative, borrowing country governments could simply refuse to pay their debts (as one Harvard economist recommended). That way they wouldn't need to deal with the IMF or the banks, and they could keep the foreign exchange that would otherwise be spent on debt payments. This, however, was not an attractive option. Foreign banks would no longer lend, and foreign countries would embargo trade in the goods of the debt-repudiating country. Repudiation might prove politically popular at home for a time. But sentiment would change when import credits and imports dried up and export markets were closed. A few countries (including Argentina, which Walter Wriston, the Citibank chairman, suggested *was* the debt crisis) were essentially self-sufficient, but there would be little joy in having all of one's foreign assets seized by banks in the industrial countries. In addition, in the absence of borrowing, the curtailment of certain domestic programs would be much more severe than would be the case if an IMF program were accepted along with additional credit. So the best policy appeared to be to negotiate with the banks and the IMF but to try to arrange things so that the banks and the IMF took as much of local dissatisfaction as possible while the government took as little as possible. The government strategy would be to nurture the image that it was "standing firm" against the banks and the IMF and getting as many "concessions" as possible. Of course, changes would still have to be made. But if, for example, the IMF insisted that the government deficit be cut and that the government elected remove food subsidies in place of a reduction in military expenditures as a way of meeting the IMF requirement, the reduction in food subsidies could be announced as part of the IMF program. The IMF was responsible—not the government, which had done its best. But this strategy, too, was dangerous. It ran the risk of making any negotiation appear as government collaboration with the enemy. A graffito on a wall in Brazil alleged that IMF (abbreviated FMI, in Portuguese) stood for *fome* (hunger), *morte* (death), and *imperialismo*. Was not a government that accepted an IMF program guilty of the same things?

The IMF

The IMF was subject to the normal bureaucratic imperative to increase its role in world affairs. With the breakdown of Bretton Woods, no one was certain what the function of the IMF was, and no one seemed to care. Henry Morgenthau had thought the IMF would "drive the usurious money-lenders from the temple of international finance," but in the mid-1970s the IMF found itself very much on the outside, looking in, while the international banks recycled the OPEC surplus. The new offices on 19th Street in Washington were filled with people, but not—apparently—with purpose. Then came OPEC II. The desire of the commercial banks to involve the IMF in rescheduling gave the IMF new leverage in the affairs of member nations. And it exercised this leverage in accordance with its charter. The banks and the public often seemed to view the IMF as an international aid agency. It was not. It was set up to make balance of payments loans, and its programs were designed to improve the current account balance.

In pursuing its policies, the IMF faced criticism beyond simple developing-country resentment. The focus of IMF programs did not appear to meet the objective of a long-run solution to the borrowing countries' debt problem. It seemed to be clear that repayment of non-OPEC LDC debt could only be brought about in the long run by the pursuit of policies that promoted real growth in those countries. IMF programs had certainly led to dramatic improvement in the trade balances of, for example, the MBA countries during 1982 and 1983. The current account deficit of $30.4 billion in 1981 fell to $5.9 billion in 1983. But this improvement had come largely by cutting imports. Such a policy was not sustainable, because the reduction in raw material stocks and spare parts had brought investment to a standstill in certain sectors. In addition, since many borrowing countries traded with each other, a reduction in imports automatically entailed a reduction in the exports of their trading partners. An IMF program that might be good for one country did not appear to make much sense when simultaneously applied to thirty.

Industrial Countries

United States policy was of particular relevance. Even though commercial banks would be the major lenders to non-OPEC LDCs, by 1983 the IMF needed more funds even to do the limited lending associated with the acceptance of its programs. That meant more funds for the IMF had to be supplied by member countries, and the United States was to make the largest contribution ($8.4 billion). While an increased contribution was supported by the administration of Ronald Reagan, the funds had to be approved by Congress, which in turn was simultaneously concerned with the interests of U.S. banks and with U.S. voter preferences. The mood of Congress was to punish the banks, for they had sinned. Congress might be willing to vote more funds for the IMF, but not without a bit of bank-bashing first. Did not banks, who had used the hard-earned savings of American workers to fund jungle boondoggles, need more oversight? The IMF was not popular either. The Black Caucus did not like the IMF because it had made balance of payments loans to South Africa. Conservatives did not like the IMF because it had made loans to communist countries in Eastern Europe. Libertarians viewed the IMF quota increase as a scheme to bail out bank stockholders. (The U.S. contribution to the IMF was eventually approved in early 1984.)

The "Baker Plan," announced by U.S. Treasury Secretary James Baker in 1985, asked commercial banks to lend another $20 billion to indebted nations, and asked multilateral development banks to increase their lending by 50 percent. To improve the climate for economic growth (it was claimed), the lending would be tied to indebted-country market-oriented economic reforms, overseen by the World Bank. The United States supported a $74.8 billion general capital increase for the World Bank for that purpose. The World Bank, unfortunately, particularly under the presidency of Robert McNamara (1968–1981), had devoted itself not to economic growth but rather to subsidizing failed political systems and statist economic intervention. Examples included the "monopoly marketing boards that systematically create and aggravate food shortages throughout Africa by seizing farmers' crops at below market prices" (Bandow, 1989). After 1981, the World Bank changed its rhetorical focus, but policy continued pretty much as before.

An additional objective of the Baker Plan was to encourage capital inflows by improving the indebted-country investment climate. Citizens of these countries, fearing government confiscation or negative returns, had transferred their savings elsewhere. The five largest Latin American debtor nations may have experienced outflows of $101 billion in private sector assets between 1979 and 1984 (study cited in *Economic Report of the President,* 1990).

Meanwhile, the fifteen heavily indebted countries potentially impacted by the Baker Plan experienced little improvement from 1982 to 1987. Their combined current account deficit fell from $50.1 billion in 1982 to $7.6 billion in 1987. But this improvement came almost entirely from a reduction of imports of goods and services of $41.1 billion. Export earnings remained unchanged (BIS, *Annual Report,* 1988).

The 1989 "Brady Initiative" of Treasury Secretary Nicholas Brady continued to emphasize economic reform—with reference to public sector deficits, price controls, and trade protection—and asked commercial banks to forgive debt as a way of rewarding compliant countries and creating a climate for sustained economic growth. (It was, however, the use—not just existence—of debt that implied low economic growth: Malaysia and South Korea had high growth rates despite high debt levels in the 1980s.) The amount of debt forgiveness was related to the size of the discounts at which developing-country debt traded in secondary markets, which gave the same countries an incentive to manipulate the size of the discount. By the beginning of 1990, three agreements (with respect to Mexico, the Philippines, and Costa Rica) had been negotiated under Brady Initiative auspices.

Although, as noted above, large commercial banks in the United States initially increased their exposures to developing countries, by the end of 1988

TABLE 2.7
Changes in Reported Exposures of Groups of U.S. Banks to non-OPEC Developing Countries

	6/82–12/85 ($ billions)	12/85–12/88 ($ billions)	6/82–12/88 (%)
Top nine banks	.89	−11.55	−17.3
Next thirteen banks	−1.73	− 6.62	−40.7
All other banks	−1.74	− 8.21	−50.0
Total	−2.58	−26.38	−28.4

Source: Economic Report of the President, 1990.

the top nine banks had reduced loans by $10.7 billion (17 percent) (see Table 2.7) and U.S. banks overall by $29.0 billion (28 percent).

THE OPENING OF JAPANESE FINANCIAL MARKETS

Outside the United States, the country with the largest bond and stock markets and banking and thrift sectors is Japan. One of the most significant international financial developments of the 1980s has been the gradual opening of these markets to the outside world. Some background history will give perspective to this trend.

U.S. occupation policy after World War II in Japan followed a course similar to that in Europe. The initial emphasis under General Douglas MacArthur in Japan was with demilitarization and political reform. But after 1948 the focus shifted to the economy, both because economic stability and prosperity were considered a necessary prerequisite to make the Japanese reforms work and because economic growth promised to reduce the costs of U.S. occupation. In Germany, the original occupation plan had been for de-industrialization and the breaking up of "dangerous concentrations of economic power" (JCS 1067), but this plan was soon replaced with the operating assumption that an "orderly and prosperous Europe requires the economic contribution of a stable and productive Germany" (JCS 1779). Similarly in Japan, MacArthur's preoccupation with breaking up the *zaibatsu* (major industrial or financial groupings characterized by joint decision making) was de-emphasized, and rein was given to those who could make the economy work. Versailles formed a backdrop in Japan as it had in Europe. The Japanese peace treaty was negotiated by John Foster Dulles from the U.S. side and Shigeru Yoshida from the Japanese. Both had served in a diplomatic capacity at Versailles in 1919, and both were convinced that the vindictive terms of the 1919 peace treaty with Germany had been partly responsible for the later war of Adolf Hitler and General Tojo Hideki.

The financial legacy of the occupation was a semimarket economy involving heavy government regulation. Foreign exchange transactions were strictly controlled. Interest rates on bank deposits were fixed by law in an attempt to channel the flow of private savings, and hence bank credit, into those economic sectors favored by government policy. Special long-term credit banks, which made loans to industry, were given the exclusive banking right to finance themselves by issuing long-maturity bonds. Although private non-financial corporations also had the right to issue bonds, the latter companies were effectively denied access to the bond market by the requirement that bond issues be collaterized with company assets. As a result, a significant corporate bond market in Japan did not develop. A further and much later consequence was that Japanese companies would begin to make increasing use of the eurobond and foreign bond markets in the 1970s.

Article 65 of the Securities and Exchange Law erected a division between commercial and investment banking. It prohibited banks from underwriting bond issues or trading corporate stock. This article was patterned after the Glass-Steagall Act (1933) in the United States.

Despite these and other impediments to the development of financial markets, the *potential* importance of Japan as an international financial center grew because of the expanding economy and domestic savings base. American involvement was important to Japanese growth in the beginning. U.S. assistance to Japan over the 1945–1952 period amounted to about 4 percent of Japan's GNP and 15 percent of Japan's imports. The Korean War (1950–1953) which followed brought an economic boom to the country, with U.S. military procurements from Japan reaching 7 percent of Japan's GNP in 1953. Real gross domestic product growth of over 9 percent per year continued to 1965, when the Vietnam War (1965–1972) brought another economic boom. Japan became a member of GATT in 1955 and the IMF in 1964. By 1980, Japan was not only the world's second largest economy after the United States as measured by GNP (ignoring fraudulent data for the Soviet Union) but also the third largest trading nation (after the United States and West Germany) as measured by the dollar value of exports. As in the United States, however, the export sector was a smaller fraction of the overall domestic economy than in other trading nations. Exports as a percentage of GNP were 10 percent for the United States and 15 percent for Japan, as compared to 20 percent for France, 28 percent for the United Kingdom and West Germany, and 57 percent for the Netherlands.

Nevertheless, Japan treated trade with special importance, not only because exports formed a major share of certain industries (like automobiles, electronic goods), but also because Japan imported most of its raw materials. This included most of its oil and about half the caloric value of its food. This export/import dependence focused attention on the U.S. dollar/Japanese yen exchange rate, since on the one hand the United States was Japan's most important export destination (so that a rise in the real value of the yen against the dollar was considered by Japanese exporters to be threatening) and, on the other hand, crucial imports such as oil were also priced in dollars (so that a fall in the exchange value of the yen against the dollar raised the price of oil in domestic currency terms). Major shocks to the Japanese economy in the 1970s revolved around these simple relationships. Of particular note were the "Nixon shock" of 1971 (the revaluation of the yen upward by 16.9 percent against the U.S. dollar), the U.S. embargo on soybean exports in 1973, and the unanticipated oil-price increases in 1973 and 1979. The initial Japanese policy reaction to the supply-related increases in the prices of food and energy in 1973 was to strongly expand aggregate demand. Significant additional price inflation was the principal result. The rate of growth of the GNP deflator, which had averaged 4.7 percent in the previous ten years (1963–1972) rose to 11.7 percent in 1973 and 20.6 percent in 1974. Overall, the yearly inflation rate during the OPEC I period (1974–1978) was 8.9 percent. The same type of expansionary policy was not repeated during the OPEC II period (1979–1982), and the yearly rate of Japanese inflation only averaged 2.5 percent.

In the late 1960s, as the DM and the yen became undervalued with respect to the U.S. dollar, official Japanese policy seemed to prefer the situation, since at that time the price of imported oil was low anyway, and the undervalued yen gave a stimulus to exports. According to Hendrik Houthakker, the Japanese "were happy with their undervalued currency which gave them a tremendous volume of exports. The Japanese were (and perhaps are) great believers in 'export-led growth'; the large growth in their exports meant a high rate of growth for the country as a whole. It was a dubious proposition because they were in effect giving some of their exports away. The imports they got in return were not commensurate with the value of those exports." After the breakdown of Bretton Woods, on the other hand, there was no official Japanese attempt to undervalue the yen, though some company executives in inefficient U.S. industries such as automobiles and steel would sometimes suggest otherwise. Rather, the Bank of Japan pursued a policy of "leaning against the wind"— intervening to slow the pace of yen appreciation against the dollar in years like 1978, while intervening to slow the pace of yen depreciation against the dollar in years like 1982.

The feeling of yen undervaluation became particularly strong after 1980, when an increasing Japanese current account surplus was accompanied by an increasing U.S. current account deficit. This feeling was based in part on a misconception, since a Japanese current account surplus was not of itself evidence of an undervalued yen. Rather, the current account surplus was partly the simple consequence of the high Japanese savings rate. In a world of capital (savings) mobility, the Japanese would save in part through a net acquisition of foreign financial assets. This would require Japan to run a current account surplus (sell more than it purchased) as a way of generating a net yearly flow of savings in the form of foreign IOUs.

Nevertheless, it was not clear how much the high Japanese savings rate represented a genuine difference in preferences and how much was inspired by policy. Some of the factors contributing to the high savings rate included tax-exempt savings deposits available from the postal savings system, minimal provisions for social security, and limited availability of mortgages and consumer credit.

Capital controls were another issue. With the demise of Bretton Woods, the United States, Germany, and the United Kingdom worked gradually to relax constraints on the movements of capital. But Japan maintained strict controls both on the inflow of capital (direct or portfolio investment in Japanese assets by foreigners) and on the outflow of capital (the acquisition of foreign assets by Japanese citizens). An exception to the inflow prohibition was that Japanese companies were allowed to issue foreign-currency-denominated bonds (such as U.S. dollar eurobonds) after December 1973. However, foreigners were barred from membership in the Tokyo Stock Exchange, and foreign securities and insurance companies were not allowed to compete with domestic firms. Foreign banks could make foreign currency loans to Japanese business but faced restrictions on conducting local currency (yen) business, as they were restricted in their ability to borrow in the domestic (yen) money market or to engage in currency swaps to hedge their exchange risk if they borrowed in external money markets (currency swaps are explained in Chapter 4). Japanese citizens had only a limited right to exchange the yen or to borrow and lend foreign currencies. The maintenance of capital controls overall impeded the growth of Tokyo as an international financial center and gave an artificial advantage to regional financial centers such as Singapore and Hong Kong.

In recent years, a number of factors have worked toward financial market deregulation. The structure of interest rate ceilings has been undermined since 1975 by Japanese budget deficits and a growing supply of government debt that is traded in a secondary market. The increased supply of government debt has tended to drive up market interest rates on the debt, which in turn has competed with bank deposits and put pressure on banks to raise deposit interest rates above government-imposed ceilings. Restrictions on capital inflows began to be loosened in 1979, as the dollar price of oil rose and the dollar also appreciated slightly against the yen. In May of that year foreigners were given access to the *gensaki* market. (This is a market similar to the U.S. repo market, which involves the sale and subsequent repurchase of government securities. The interest rate on a transaction is determined by the difference between the purchase price and the resale price of the securities. If the borrower turns the securities over to the lender for the short-term life of the loan, the loan is virtually risk-free.) Later in the year a market in bank CDs was created and foreigners were allowed to participate.

The admission of foreign capital inflows was initially justified by the authorities as a move to strengthen the value of the yen by allowing foreigners to diversify their portfolios into yen-denominated assets. Increased foreign demand for the yen would bring about a yen appreciation until a new exchange rate level representing portfolio equilibrium ws reached. However, with the Foreign Exchange and Foreign Trade Control Law of 1980, Japanese official restrictions on capital outflows began to be relaxed also. And as a result of the rise in U.S. real interest rates after 1980, the outflow of Japanese capital into dollar-denominated assets was larger than inflows into yen-denominated assets. The net shift into dollar assets acted to strengthen the dollar against the yen.

In 1981, a new banking law allowed Japanese banks to sell government bonds to the public for the first time. In response to the entry into securities dealing by the banks, the brokerage firms eventually acquired the right to set up money market funds. Since money market funds allowed small savers to obtain market interest rates, ceilings on bank deposit rates became increasingly ineffective.

In May 1984, the U.S. Treasury and the Japanese Ministry of Finance concluded negotiations on a program to "internationalize the yen." Even though Japan had the second largest economy in the noncommunist world, as a result of years of capital controls the yen was little used in international transactions or as a reserve asset. (At the end of 1983, according to IMF data, 69.1 percent of world official foreign exchange reserves were denominated in the U.S. dollar, 11.9 percent in the DM, and only 4.2 percent in the Japanese yen.) The points agreed to between Japan and the United States included further measures to liberalize capital movements, promote Japanese domestic deregulation, and improve foreign access to Japanese domestic markets. The agreement also sought to promote increased international use of the yen by encouraging the growth of the euroyen market and greater use of the yen in trade finance. (As of 1982, 40 percent of Japanese exports were yen-denominated, but only 3 percent of Japanese imports.)

The pace of opening of Japanese financial markets since the 1984 agreement has been slow, but nevertheless real. The newly created euroyen market has continued to exert competitive pressure to further deregulate the domestic market, just as the eurodollar market once acted to make obsolete U.S. deposit ceilings and capital controls. The parallel existence of free and regulated markets for yen implies that financial wealth will increasingly flow through the more efficient channel. The less efficient channel will have to change to survive.

TABLE 2.8
International Bank Assets and Liabilities by Nationality

	End 1985		End 1989	
	Assets	Liabilities	Assets	Liabilities
	(U.S. $ billions)		(U.S. $ billions)	
Japanese banks	707.0	672.5	1967.2	1924.7
U.S. banks	593.3	555.2	727.4	742.4
French banks	245.2	248.9	432.1	458.0
German banks	191.0	157.4	435.8	329.3
UK banks	191.0	200.8	247.3	308.7
Other banks	786.2	779.8	1329.4	1336.8
Total	2713.7	2614.6	5139.2	5099.9

Source: BIS, *Annual Report,* 1990.

By 1990, Japanese banks (including branches of Japanese banks based in London and elsewhere) were the leaders in international banking, followed by U.S., French, and German banks. (In Table 2.8, "international" assets and liabilities include not only eurocurrency assets and liabilities but also domestic currency loans to foreigners.)

PROBLEMS FOR CHAPTER 2

1. Using the information given in the table below, calculate the bilateral par values among the DM, the French franc, and the Italian lira, as well as the upper and lower intervention points in the parity grid. What do these points imply about central bank behavior?

EMS European Currency Unit Rates

	ECU Central Rates	Currency Amounts Against ECU, Dec 10	% Change from Central Rate	% Spread vs. Weakest Currency	Divergence Indicator
Spanish peseta ...	133.631	130.803	−2.12	4.28	37
Deutschemark	2.05586	2.04073	−0.74	2.83	44
Dutch guilder	2.31643	2.30198	−0.62	2.71	28
Belgian franc	42.4032	42.3009	−0.24	2.32	9
Irish punt	0.767417	0.766278	−0.15	2.22	4
Italian lira	1538.24	1540.84	0.17	1.90	−11
Danish krone	7.84195	7.86304	0.27	1.80	−15
French franc	6.89509	6.93360	0.56	1.51	−33
Sterling	0.696904	0.711350	2.07	0.00	−40

ECU central rates set by the European Commission. Currencies are in descending relative strength. Percentage changes are for ECU; a positive change denotes a weak currency. Divergence shows the ratio between two spreads: the percentage difference between the actual market and ECU central rates for a currency, and the maximum permitted percentage deviation of the currency's market rate from its ECU central rate.
Adjustment calculated by *Financial Times*.

2. How is column 2 ("Currency amounts against ECU") derived? In what sense is it a measure of a currency's "average" value?

3. Show how column 3 ("Percent change from central rate") is derived from columns 1 and 2. In what sense does column 3 measure a country's departure from the "community average"?

4. Why does column 4 differ from column 3?

5. Explain the significance of column 5 for the operation of the divergence indicator. When does column 5 indicate the need for a change in a country's economic policy?

6. Derive the weight of the Dutch guilder in the ECU (measured at ECU central rates) using the September 1989 definition of the ECU and the information in column 1.

7. What is the relation between a currency's weight and the size of its divergence limit?

8. Using information given in the table, determine the following *market* exchange rates for the date given: French franc/DM and Italian lira/Belgian franc.

9. Suppose the French franc price of the ECU (the FF "ECU central rate") is increased by 5 percent (i.e., the FF is "devalued" by 5 percent). What are the new par values for the currencies given in Problem 1?

10. Suppose that it were desired to change the upper and lower bands to plus or minus 5 percent for all currencies. Solve for the number that would then be used to determine the upper and lower intervention points around par in the parity grid.

11. On July 20, 1985, financial newspapers announced that the Italian lira was "devalued by 6 percent" in the EMS, while other participating currencies were "revalued upward by 2 percent." Below are the EMS central rates before and after this realignment:

Currency	Currency/ECU before	Currency/ECU after
Irish punt	.72569	.724578
French franc	6.87456	6.86402
Danish krone	8.14104	8.12857
Dutch guilder	2.52595	2.52208
DM	2.24184	2.2384
Belgian franc	44.9008	44.832
Luxembourg franc	44.9008	44.832
Italian lira	1403.49	1520.6
British pound	.585992	.555312
Greek drachma	87.4813	100.719

Verify that the Italian lira/DM par value has changed by approximately 8 percent. Compare the percentage change in the DM/Italian lira par value. How do these percentage changes compare to the actual percentage changes in the ECU central rates?

FOREIGN EXCHANGE MARKETS

INTRODUCTION TO THE FOREIGN EXCHANGE MARKET

The foreign exchange market is the world's largest market. At the beginning of the 1990s, daily turnover amounted to about $650 billion per day (BIS, February 1990). Most of the trading takes place in just a few currencies—the U.S. dollar ($), German mark (DM), Japanese yen (¥), British pound sterling (£), Swiss franc (SF), Canadian dollar (Can$), French franc (FF), Australian dollar (Aus$), Netherlands (Dutch) guilder (DG), Belgian franc (BF), and Italian lira (IL). Participants in the market include importers, who may pay for goods invoiced in foreign currencies; exporters, who may have foreign currency sales; portfolio managers, who may buy or sell foreign currency assets and receive foreign currency dividends or interest payments; central banks, who may conduct exchange intervention; foreign currency brokers, who earn a profit by matching buy and sell orders; and commercial banks, who may be borrowing in multiple currencies, servicing their own or their customers' needs, and whose traders make the foreign exchange market through continual interbank trading.

The foreign exchange market is an over-the-counter market. That is, there is no one physical location where traders get together to exchange currencies. Rather, traders are located in the offices of major commercial banks around the world and communicate using computer terminals, telephones, telexes, and other information channels. If a foreign exchange (FX) trader in a bank in New York deals dollars for pounds with an FX trader in London, the traders will, over the phone, agree on a price. Each trader will then enter the trade in the bank's computer or other record system, and then get on with the business of trading. The mechanics of actually transferring the currencies are not the traders' concern, so a trade takes a few seconds at most. Later, however, the two banks will send each other confirmation messages concerning the details of the trade, and will make arrangements for *settlement* of the traders' contract. The bank in New York will turn over a dollar deposit (at some New York bank) to the bank in London, and the bank in London will turn over a pound deposit (at some London bank) to the bank in New York. This exchange of currencies will take place entirely in the form of an exchange of electronic messages. The messages will be sent through established communications networks.

The most important communications network for international financial market transactions is the Society for Worldwide Interbank Financial Tele-communication (SWIFT), a Belgian not-for-profit cooperative. This system for transferring foreign exchange deposits and loans began actual operation in May 1977 and by 1990 connected 3000 banks and securities industry partici-pants in sixty-seven countries and carried an average of 1.1 million messages per day. SWIFT messages are transmitted from country to country via central, interconnected operating centers located in Brussels, Amsterdam, and Cul-peper, Virginia. These three operating centers are in turn connected by inter-national data-transmission lines to regional processors in most member countries. Banks in an individual country use the available national commu-nication facilities to send messages to the regional processor. A bank in Lon-don, for example, will access SWIFT by sending messages to a regional processing center in the north of London. The message will be received by a bank in New York via the SWIFT operating center in Culpeper, Virginia. Locally in New York, 140 banks settle foreign exchange and eurodollar trans-actions through the Clearing House Interbank Payments System (CHIPS), which in 1989 processed a daily average of 146,000 transactions with a total daily average value of $760.8 billion. Foreign exchange transactions were 73 percent of total CHIPS messages (55 percent of total dollar value).

The FX market is almost a twenty-four-hour market, since as one center closes another is still trading. Business hours overlap around the world. When it is 3:00 P.M. in Tokyo it is 2:00 P.M. in Hong Kong. When it is 3:00 P.M. in Hong Kong, it is 1:00 P.M. in Singapore. When it is 3:00 P.M. in Singapore, it is noon in Bahrain. When it is 3:00 P.M. in Bahrain, it is noon in Frankfurt and Zurich and 11:00 A.M. in London. When it is 3:00 P.M. in London, it is 10:00 A.M. in New York. When it is 3:00 P.M. in New York, it is noon in Los Angeles. When it is 3:00 P.M. in Los Angeles, it is 9:00 A.M. the next day in Sydney, Australia. The major foreign exchange trading centers are in London, New York, and Tokyo, where about 60 percent of FX trading takes place. Another 20 percent takes place in Zurich, Singapore, and Hong Kong. The market is busiest in the early morning, New York time, when banks in London and New York are simultaneously open and trading. The working life of a trader is not necessarily limited to banking hours, however. Senior traders may have Reuters and Telerate monitors installed at home so they can keep track of foreign exchange and news developments around the clock and adjust their foreign exchange positions accordingly. They may expect phone calls from foreign offices of their bank at midnight or 4 A.M.

MARKETMAKERS VERSUS WALRASIAN AUCTIONEERS

What do FX traders do? Of course they buy and sell currencies. But, more important, they create prices. The creation of prices is no trivial feat, and before explaining how it takes place in the FX market it will be helpful to simplify by describing the simplest case of price creation. It involves a one-room market with a Walrasian auctioneer.

In the nineteenth century, the French economist Léon Walras told the following story about how market equilibrium prices are determined. Suppose you get all the buyers and sellers of a particular commodity—wheat, for example—in a single room. One individual will serve as an auctioneer. The auctioneer will start off by announcing an arbitrary price, say $3.00 per bushel. At that price, each trader will decide whether to be a buyer of wheat or a seller of wheat. If the trader views wheat as cheap at the $3.00 price, he or she will want to buy. If the trader views $3.00-a-bushel wheat as expensive, he or she will want to sell. Each trader writes down on a slip of paper the amount desired to buy or to sell at $3.00, and gives the slip to the auctioneer. The auctioneer will tally the total amount of wheat supplied at that price and the total amount demanded. If the two amounts are equal, the market is in equilibrium, and suppliers deliver wheat to the buyers, who pay them $3.00 per bushel. If, however, the two amounts are not equal at $3.00, the rules of the game say that no trading takes place. Instead, a new price is announced. If there is more wheat supplied than demanded ("excess supply") at $3.00, the price is too high, so a new price less than $3.00 is announced. If there is excess demand at $3.00, the price is too low, so a new price greater than $3.00 is announced. Eventually, through this process, a price at which supply exactly equals demand will be found. To summarize the story: The Walrasian auctioneer announces prices, excess (positive or negative) demand is tabulated, and trading takes place when and only when the equilibrium price has been established. We have already seen one real-world example of a Walrasian market in Chapter 1: the twice-daily fixing of the price of gold at the London merchant banking firm of N. M. Rothschild.

Let's now contrast this simple process by which a single market equilibrium price is determined in a Walrasian market with the more complex system of price creation in an over-the-counter speculative market such as the foreign exchange market. This more complex process makes the job of an FX trader correspondingly more difficult. There are at least three important aspects that distinguish the foreign exchange market from a simple Walrasian market.

1. There are two prices, not one, that are announced—a bid price at which a trader is willing to buy, and an offer or asked price at which a trader is willing to sell. The difference between the two prices is referred to as the *bid/asked (or bid/offer) spread*. Traders in the major money center banks around the world who deal in two-way prices, for both buying and selling, are referred to as marketmakers. Whether you want to buy or to sell, they will quote a price at which they are willing to take the other side of your transaction. They create the market by creating bid and asked prices and dealing at those prices.

   Marketmakers differ conceptually from brokers, who are individuals who simply match up buy and sell orders from two different parties. If every time a corporation wanted to sell U.S. dollars and buy Dutch guilders, there would be simultaneously available a corporation that wanted to buy U.S. dollars and sell Dutch guilders, the market could easily be handled by foreign exchange brokers. There would be no need for marketmakers. But in a real-world continuous auction market, buy and sell orders do not match at all points in time. Marketmakers make possible the immediate execution of orders from ultimate buyers and sellers of foreign exchange because marketmakers are willing to take the other side of the transaction themselves.

2. By contrast to the single Walrasian auctioneer, there are dozens of marketmakers, all of whom simultaneously announce bid and offer prices at which they will exchange two currencies. And since any particular trader in a particular bank will have difficulty keeping track of all the bid and asked prices concurrently announced by all other traders, there will normally be a dispersion of bid and asked prices throughout the foreign exchange market, and even simultaneous trades may take place at different exchange rates.

3. The concept of a single overall "equilibrium" market price is only a convenient simplifying fiction. A particular marketmaker is usually concerned only with equilibrium as viewed from his or her own vantage point. To see what is involved, suppose a trader buys deutschemarks for $.6550/DM and sells them for $.6560/DM. The difference in the prices (the bid/asked spread) is $.001/DM. If (a) the trader is able to buy and sell equal amounts of DM at these prices, and (b) the trader has a large volume of trade, then the trader will make a large profit and go home that night a happy person. The trader will earn an amount equal to the size of the bid/asked spread multiplied by the day's volume measured as the number of units of DM that have been both bought and sold. In this example, if the trader both buys and sells DM50,000,000 with a spread of $.001/DM, then the profit would be $(\$.001/DM)(DM50,000,000) = \$50,000$.

But here is the trader's problem. At any moment the trader may find that the number of times he is "hit" on the bid side is different from the number of times he is hit on the offer side. He is selling more of a particular currency than he is buying, or buying more than he is selling. The trader is then no longer living off the bid/asked spread: The trader is acquiring a long or short position in a foreign currency and becomes subject to the risk of exchange rate movements. He becomes a net speculator. If he wishes to avoid a speculative position, he has to keep moving his bid and asked prices up and down in response to the relative frequency at which he gets hit on either side. Moreover, even if the relative frequency of hits is the same, the volume may be too low if his bid/asked spread is being undercut by other marketmakers. The size of the spread is then another variable that must be adjusted. The marketmaker's profit on the bid/asked spread is thus compensation for the opportunity cost of the marketmaker's time as well as for the exposure of the bank's capital to the risk of equilibrium price fluctuations (Stigler, 1961).

Now, some countries do have a daily "fixing" for their currencies, where a price will be fixed once a day by representatives of commercial banks and the central bank. They meet at a central location such as a stock exchange and follow a process similar to the gold-price fixing. These fixings do represent Walrasian auctions. But the volume of trade is small, so that the fixing price has limited relevance to the overall market, except as a benchmark price for certain small dealers. There are daily fixings in Japan, Germany, France, Italy, the Scandinavian countries, and Belgium.

It has been estimated that there are 200 marketmaking banks worldwide. Much of their trading takes place by *direct dealing,* in which marketmakers call each other to ask for two-way prices, while the rest takes place through *brokers.* A survey of New York banks in 1983 showed 42 percent direct dealing, while 58 percent went through brokers (Andrews, 1984). Brokers charge a fee for matching up buyers and sellers. A bank dealing through a broker typically quotes only a bid or an asked price, and the broker—who may have open phone lines to 100 or 200 banks—will see if anyone wants to take the other side of the transaction. The broker will facilitate the process by quoting at the outset indicative bid/asked prices that he or she will attempt to make firm by finding a matching party to a dealer's bid or offer. In contrast to direct dealing, a bank dealing through a broker keeps its identity confidential until just prior to the consummation of the transaction.

Worldwide, about 85 percent of all FX trading is between marketmakers (BIS, February 1990). Less than 15 percent is commercial business: FX purchases and sales by companies engaged in trade, by tourists, and so on. That most trading involves marketmakers is a crucial detail when we come to the question of exchange rate determination (in Part III). Factors such as trade balances, relative prices, and so on are irrelevant to exchange rate movements in the short run, except to the extent they influence the actions of interbank traders. Suppose, for example, that all traders simultaneously came to the conclusion that the DM will drop in value with respect to the dollar and consequently began selling DM for dollars. If 85 percent of the market is selling DM, the value of the DM will fall relative to the dollar. Similarly, if 85 percent of the market is ignoring relative price levels, it will be difficult to prove them wrong in the short run, because the 15 percent of commercial-trade-related business is small compared to the interbank market. To summarize: *Day-to-day exchange rate movements hinge on the activity of interbank traders. Their actions and expectations are decisive. Any variable used as a basis for decision making by traders is important in the short run, while other variables may be irrelevant.*

The fact that most trading takes place between marketmakers also has important implications for speculative gains and losses. Foreign exchange traders as a whole are able to make a profit because they provide a basic service to the final users of the market: exporters, importers, portfolio managers, and tourists. The fact that marketmakers deal with each other keeps the market liquid and helps keep the prices announced by various marketmakers from diverging greatly from marketmaker to marketmaker. But if marketmakers, in addition, accumulate long or short positions in a currency and make speculative gains or losses, they do so principally with respect to other marketmakers. That is, speculation in the FX market is potentially a zero-sum game: One trader's speculative gain will be another trader's speculative loss. This is potentially true, but not true in fact, because of central bank intervention. If central banks intervene, speculation will become a positive-sum game to FX traders viewed as a group if central banks make net speculative losses. (That is, FX traders *as a group* can earn a net speculative profit.) Similarly, speculation will become a negative-sum game to FX traders as a group if central banks make net exchange gains from intervention, while speculation will remain a zero-sum game if central banks make no net profit or loss.

THE MECHANICS OF CURRENCY TRADING

Ninety percent of trading of convertible currencies take place with respect to the U.S. dollar (BIS, February 1990). For example, both the £ and the DM will be traded with prices quoted vis-à-vis the U.S. dollar. If a commercial customer asked for a DM price in terms of the £, this cross rate will be determined from the two dollar rates (see the following example). There are two major reasons for quoting most exchange rates against a common currency (a "vehicle currency"). The first has to do with information complexity. If each currency were traded directly against each other currency, it would involve an enormous number of dealing markets. For ten currencies there would be forty-five exchange rates.

□

The first currency would have an exchange rate against the other nine currencies. The second currency would have eight additional exchange rates (since the exchange rate against the first currency has already been counted). And so on, giving a total of $9 + 8 + 7 + 6 + 5 + 4 + 3 + 2 + 1 = 45$ exchange rates. For n currencies there would similarly be $n(n - 1)/2$ bilateral exchange rates.   ■

A second reason for quoting all exchange rates against a common currency is to avoid the possibility of *triangular arbitrage*. If all currencies were traded against each other directly, the exchange rate of the dollar against the pound compared with the exchange rate of the pound against the DM would imply an exchange rate of the dollar against the DM. If this implied exchange rate differed from the direct dollar/DM exchange rate by an amount sufficient to cover the costs of the transactions, there would be a profit available by buying at one of the dollar/DM exchange rates and selling at the other. By contrast, when all cross rates are *derived* from the rates of the two currencies with respect to the dollar, there is only one available cross rate and no possibility of arbitrage.

There do exist, however, banks that specialize in giving cross rates. Since the bid/asked spread of a normal cross-rate quotation incorporates both bid/asked spreads from the two currencies quoted with respect to the dollar, there is room for banks to specialize and undercut the size of the total spread, provided they have enough cross-rate business to make it profitable.

If the quoted price is the dollar price of a unit of foreign exchange (or, restated, the number of dollars per unit of foreign exchange), then the quotation is said to be in *American* (or *direct*) terms. Examples of quotations in American terms include:

$1.55 = £1 $.40 = DM1 $.50 = SF1 $.0044 = ¥1

If the quoted price is the foreign currency price of a dollar (or, restated, the number of units of foreign currency per one U.S. dollar), then the quotation is said to be in *European* (or *indirect* or *reciprocal*) terms. Examples of quotations in European terms include:

$$£.645 = \$1 \quad DM2.5 = \$1 \quad SF2.00 = \$1 \quad ¥227 = \$1$$

In the interbank market, European terms are used for all currency quotations except for the British pound, the Irish punt, and the Australian and New Zealand dollars, with American terms being used for the latter currencies. (Thus, one would quote DM2.5 = $1, but $1.55 = £1.) Currency quotations are generally in American terms, however, in the markets for FX futures and options on futures. (FX futures and options are discussed in Chapters 5 and 6.)

Three general types of transactions take place in the FX market: spot, forward, and swap. *Spot* transactions involve an agreement on price today, with *settlement* (actual delivery of currency for currency) usually two business days later. When, however, currencies whose home countries are in the same time zone are traded, such as the U.S. dollar for the Canadian dollar, or the U.S. dollar for the Mexican peso, settlement is typically one business day later. Further detail on settlement dates is covered below. *Forward* transactions involve an agreement on price today for settlement at some date in the future (beyond the normal time lag for spot settlement). Frequently traded forward maturities are for one or two weeks, or one through twelve months. Odd maturity dates may be negotiated, however, and large banks will give forward quotations for major currencies out to five or ten years.

Sometimes a forward transaction is called an *outright forward* to emphasize that no spot transaction is involved. Outright forward transactions usually take place between a bank and a commercial customer. For example, Exxon may have a scheduled payment of £25,000,000 in eight months and may buy that amount of British pounds forward today. No money will change hands now. The forward contract will simply lock in the price at which the transaction will take place between Exxon and Exxon's bank eight months from now. By contrast, transactions involving forward exchange in the interbank market usually take the form of swap transactions. A swap is the sale of a foreign currency with a simultaneous agreement to repurchase it at some date in the future, or the purchase of a foreign currency with an agreement to resell it at some date in the future. For example, Citibank might buy DM2,500,000 from Deutsche Bank for $1,000,000, with a simultaneous agreement to sell the DM back in six months for $1,050,000. In a swap transaction, it is the difference between the sale price and the repurchase price (and not their absolute magnitudes) that is important. This difference is called the *swap rate* (see Chapter 4 for further details). It was estimated in 1983 that 65 percent of trading by New York banks was in the spot market, 33 percent in the swap market, and 2 percent in the market for outright forwards (Andrews, 1984).

As covered earlier, all foreign exchange trading involves two prices, a bid or buying price and an asked (offered) or selling price. However, all transactions also involve two currencies, so it is essential to keep straight which currency you have in mind. If you bid for DM with dollars, that is the same as offering dollars for DM. Thus, whether an exchange rate represents a "bid" price or an "offered" price depends on which currency you use for reference. The following example explores this in detail and establishes the convention for quoting exchange rates in this book.

EXAMPLE 3.1

bid   *ask*

A trader quotes the DM against the dollar at a bid/offer price of

DM2.3697/2.3725 per $1

It is natural to think of the small number, DM2.3697, as the bid price, and the large number, DM2.3725, as the offer price. Question: Bid and offer for what? The DM? Answer: DM2.3697 is the bid price *for the U.S. dollar*, while DM2.3725 is the offer (or asked) price for the U.S. dollar. In order to keep this straight, keep in mind the trader's objective: to make money. The trader will make money by giving away as few DM as possible when he purchases dollars (hence his bid for the dollar is DM2.3697), while acquiring as many DM as possible when he sells dollars (hence he offers to sell $1 for DM2.3725).

For a rate quoted in American terms, we may again refer to the smaller number as the bid price, but in this case it would be the bid price for the foreign currency. For the bid/offer price of $1.5525/$1.5535 per £1, $1.5525 is the bid price for the pound (offer price for the dollar), while $1.5535 is the offer price for the pound (bid price for the dollar).

No fees are charged in ordinary foreign exchange transactions. Rather, *transactions costs* relate to the size of the bid/offer spread. For a standard FX contract of $1 million traded against FX, the typical cost (the spread multiplied by $1 million) of the transaction might be $200 for Canadian dollar trades, or $500 for the DM, ¥, or SF. For cross rates, however, the bid/asked spread enters twice, so that typical transactions costs may be larger. The calculation of cross rates is shown in the following example.

EXAMPLE 3.2

A bank is currently quoting the following two exchange rates with respect to the dollar:

DM2.3697/2.3725 per $1 $1.5525/1.5535 per £1

What DM per £ cross rate would the bank quote if asked? The way to answer this question is *conceptually* to engage in two transactions with respect to the U.S. dollar. First consider the bank's bid rate for £s. In order to buy £s with DM, conceptually one would first buy $ with DM, then buy £s with $. The trader would choose the most advantageous price with each transaction. The trader will get the most dollars for DM by dealing at the DM2.3697/$ price and will get the most £s for dollars by dealing at the $1.5525/£ price. Hence, the bid price for £s would be:

(DM2.3697/$)($1.5525/£) = DM3.6789/£.

Similarly, in order to sell £s for DM, one would first sell £s for $, then sell $ for DM. Choosing the most advantageous price at each point from the trader's perspective, we get the price at which £s are offered as:

($1.5535/£)(DM2.3725/$) = DM3.6857/£.

This gives a bid/offer quotation for the £ of DM3.6789/3.6857 = £1. Competition from other banks may well force the trader to deal at a narrower spread than DM.0068/£. But the bid/offer quotation calculated here will avoid arbitrage.

THE RISK FROM AN OPEN POSITION IN FOREIGN EXCHANGE

An FX trader is a probability manager. Suppose that an FX trader intentionally or unintentionally adjusts his or her bid and asked prices in such a way that the trader is hit unequally on the bid and asked sides. Because the trader's purchases and sales of a foreign currency are not equalized, the trader begins to build up a net short or long position. (A short position is involved if the amount sold is greater than the amount purchased, while a long position is involved if the amount purchased is greater). Having a net long or short position can be very risky, as the following example illustrates.

EXAMPLE 3.3

A trader in a bank that is concerned with dollar profits is short DM15,000,000. The current exchange rate is DM2.500 = $1, so that the bank's liability is $6,000,000. If the exchange rate were suddenly to jump to DM2.600 = $1 (that is, if the DM were to depreciate in value with respect to the dollar), the bank's liability would fall to $5,769,230.77. The trader might receive a large bonus. But if the exchange rate were to jump to DM2.400 = $1 (that is, if the DM were to appreciate in value with respect to the dollar), the bank's liability would increase to $6,250,000. The trader might be fired. Because of exchange rate risk, most banks set *position limits* which are the maximum net FX exposure traders can have at any one time. A typical position limit for an experienced trader might be $35,000,000 in FX exposure during the trading day, or $7,000,000 in FX exposure carried overnight. Daily exchange rate movements of the size (4 percent) used in this example are rare. On the other hand, 1 percent daily movements are common.

It is important to have some empirical estimate of the risk involved in holding open positions in foreign exchange. Let today's spot rate be $S(t)$, while the spot rate one day later is $S(t + 1)$. The daily proportional change ΔS in the spot rate is:

$$\Delta S = \frac{[S(t + 1) - S(t)]}{S(t)}.$$

In many instances the expected value of ΔS can be taken as zero for all practical purposes. Even so, there may be wide variations around this expected value. That is, there is risk that the change in the exchange rate will be different from what is anticipated. One measure of foreign exchange risk is the standard deviation (SD) of ΔS. Below are standard deviations of ΔS, where S is the dollar price of the given foreign currency for days in the calendar year 1981. In the second column is the corresponding change in the dollar value of foreign currency with an initial value of $1,000,000, given a change in the spot exchange rate over a one-day period equal in size to one standard deviation:

SD of ΔS in 1981	Equivalent Change in Value of an Initial $1,000,000
DM.00868	$ 8,680
SF.01120	$11,200
¥.00823	$ 8,230
£.00850	$ 8,500

What do these numbers mean? We can give a simple interpretation in terms of probability. Assume that the values for ΔS are drawings from a normal distribution with mean zero and with the standard deviations just given. (This is not an entirely valid assumption empirically, but will be close enough for our purposes.) Recall that for a normal distribution, we can expect that the values of our drawings will fall within plus or minus one standard deviation around the mean about 68 percent of the time, within plus or minus two SDs about 95 percent of the time, and within plus or minus three SDs about 99 percent of the time. For example, since a change in the dollar/Swiss franc exchange rate in an amount equal to one SD is $11,200, we can expect that over the course of a day our foreign currency—which had an initial value of $1,000,000—will have an ending value in the range of $988,800 to $1,011,200 with a probability of 68 percentage. The following is a summary based on the SD rate of the dollar price of Swiss francs:

Range in Terms of SD	Probability for Drawings from a Normal Distribution	Change in Value of SF Position
±1	.6826	±$11,200
±2	.9544	±$22,400
±3	.9974	±$33,600

A trader operating on a .2 percent ($2000) profit margin might find this degree of exchange risk large indeed. In about 32 percent of the cases, the change in the value of the position from foreign exchange rate changes over a day's time would be more than five times as large as the entire profit margin. This exchange rate change could work to the trader's advantage, increasing the profit, but it could just as easily go the other way.

☐

The normal probability distribution will be used for illustration throughout this book. The intention is that the reader learn to think in terms of probability, and it is the author's belief that the introduction of multiple distributions will get in the way of this objective. However, it is well established that daily proportional exchange rate changes are too "leptokurtic" to represent drawings from a normal distribution. That is, by reference to the normal distribution, they have (1) a greater proportion of very small deviations from the mean; (2) a greater proportion of very large deviations from the mean; but (3) a smaller proportion of intermediate deviations from the mean. Imagine two erratic drivers driving along a highway. The mean location of each is on the center line. Let the normal distribution represent the proportion of time the first spends on each part of the highway. If the second driver has a leptokurtic distribution, this second driver spends relatively more time close to the center line and relatively more time driving in the ditch than does the first, but spends proportionately less time driving on the shoulders.

Leptokurtosis as measured in empirical samples of exchange rates may be the result of a time-varying scale parameter (such as a standard deviation that changes over time), in which case ΔS may be normal once an adjustment for scale changes has been made. Or ΔS may be drawn from the class of infinite-variance stable distributions (with or without time-varying scale), as has been suggested by Cornell and Dietrich (1978); MacFarland, Pettit, and Sung (1982); So (1987); and Westerfield (1977). An infinite-variance stable distribution might result from the fact that information arrives in "lumps." If ΔS had a normal distribution, the total price change over a period of time would be the result of a large number of very small changes. But in an infinite-variance stable market, the total price change would more likely be the result of a few very large changes (Mandelbrot, 1963), which could result from the lumpy arrival of information that affects the market exchange rate.   ■

SETTLEMENT DATES

Settlement of a spot or forward contract always takes place by giving the other party a bank deposit denominated in the relevant currency. If the relevant currency is DM, then a DM deposit in a German bank is transferred to the other party. If the relevant currency is the $, then a $ deposit in a U.S. bank is transferred to the other party. The location of the bank corresponds to the currency's home country: the *settlement location*. The two parties trading currencies can themselves be physically located in an area different from that of the currency they trade. This is referred to as the *dealing location*. For example, two banks in London can trade DM. The dealing location is the United Kingdom but the settlement location would be Germany.

The first principle involved in settlement dates is that if banks in the settlement location are not open, no settlement can be made. If banks in Germany are not open on a particular day, then a transfer of DM deposits cannot take place on that date.

A spot *settlement date* is usually *two business days after the trading date* for either the European currencies or the yen traded against the U.S. dollar. (The time gap results from the practical problems associated with confirming and clearing the trades through the appropriate channels, such as SWIFT and CHIPS.) Thus, if a London bank sells DM to a New York bank for dollars, then two business days later the London bank will turn over a DM deposit in Germany to the New York bank, while the New York bank will turn over a dollar deposit in the United States to the London bank. The "compensated value" principle says that settlement of both sides of an FX contract will take place on the same working day. This principle is intended to reduce credit risk and is followed in all FX trading except for some Middle Eastern currencies. (The latter exception is due to the fact that Islamic banks are closed on Friday but open on Saturday and Sunday. So for a U.S. dollar–Saudi riyal trade on Wednesday, for example, dollars will normally be delivered at a U.S. bank on Friday but riyals will be delivered at a Saudi bank on Saturday.)

But what is meant by "two business days after"? This is easily answered if the two banks that are trading have the same holidays. For example, both London and New York banks are closed on Saturday and Sunday, so if spot trading between a New York and a London bank takes place Friday, two business days later is Tuesday. Thus, spot settlement would be Tuesday if banks in the settlement location are also open. However, if the DM was being traded and Tuesday was a holiday in Germany, settlement would have to be postponed until Wednesday. Also, if Tuesday were a holiday in either New York or London, settlement would also be put off until Wednesday. Finally, there is the question of Monday. What if, say, Monday is a holiday in New York, but not in London? Then "two business days" later, for a trade on Friday, would be Wednesday in New York but Tuesday in London. On which of the two dates would settlement take place? The answer is that normally (in the absence of special arrangements) the value date (settlement date) of the bank making the market is applied. Thus, if the New York bank called the London bank, the London bank's value date (Tuesday) would be applied, while if the London bank called New York, the New York bank's value date (Wednesday) would be applied.

For U.S. dollar trades against the Canadian dollar and the Mexican peso, settlement is one day later. The shorter time to settlement stems from the fact that most trading takes place in the United States, so that both the dealing banks and the settlement banks are in similar time zones.

One- through twelve-month *forward* maturities follow a simple pattern. To determine the one-month (or "30-day") forward settlement date for forward trading that takes place today, first determine the spot settlement date. Then go to *the same day of the month, one month forward.* For example, if the spot settlement date for a trade taking place on June 21 is June 23, then the one-month forward settlement date would be July 23.

What if, in the previous example, July 23 is a holiday in the dealing center, or the banks are not open in the settlement location? Answer: Move the date forward to the first suitable day. However, a rule followed in the market is that you can never move the date forward into the next month (into August, in our example). If you hit the end of the month, then you go backward to the first suitable settlement date.

A final rule for forward maturity dates is the "end-end" rule. If the spot value date takes place on the last business day of the current month, then all forward value dates are also for the last business day of the appropriate month. For example, if the spot value date for trades made today is March 28 and this is the last business day in March, then a two-month forward contract traded today will mature on the last business day of May. If the last business day is May 31, then May 31 (not May 28) is the value date.

These rules will sometimes cause bunching of forward maturity dates, as the following example shows.

EXAMPLE 3.4

Exchange is traded one month forward on Monday, January 26; Tuesday, January 27; and Wednesday, January 28. The corresponding spot settlement dates are, respectively, Wednesday, January 28; Thursday, January 29; and Friday, January 30. What are the one-month forward settlement dates? The one-month forward value date would be the same in all three cases. First, going forward one month from January 28, we get February 28. But February 28 would be a Saturday, so we go backward to Friday, February 27, and this would be the settlement date if February 27 were a business day for both banks; otherwise, the last business day in February. Similarly, going forward one month from January 29 and January 30 would take us to the last business day in February, since we cannot have a March settlement date for one-month forward trades in January.

EXCHANGE CONTROLS

Most countries of the world set a price (or a small range of prices) at which their currencies can be traded for a foreign currency. This price usually represents a *political equilibrium:* The price is chosen so as to benefit one economic group while penalizing another. The principles involved can be stated simply: *If the domestic currency price is chosen so as to undervalue foreign currency, then the price acts to subsidize buyers of foreign exchange and to tax sellers of foreign exchange. If the domestic currency price is chosen so as to overvalue foreign currency, then the price acts to subsidize sellers of foreign exchange and to tax buyers of foreign exchange.*

Suppose that in an ordinary market, where the price adjusts to equate the supply of a foreign currency with the demand for that currency, a particular exchange rate would be 85 pesos = 1 dollar. The local government, however, sets the exchange rate at 39 pesos = 1 dollar. What are the consequences? Assuming that the dollar is the foreign currency in this case, the exchange rate chosen *undervalues* foreign exchange. It treats the dollar as though it were worth only 39 pesos, whereas in normal market equilibrium the dollar would be worth 85 pesos. One consequence is that buyers of dollars are subsidized. Buyers of dollars can get them at the cheap price of 39 pesos instead of the normal price of 85 pesos. One group of dollar-buyers will be *importers* of dollar-priced goods. To buy dollar goods, they will first exchange pesos for dollars. A good with a price of $1 would normally cost 85 pesos, but they are able to buy it for 39 pesos. As a consequence, imports of dollar goods are likely to soar. Other buyers of dollars will be tourists who travel to the dollar's home country. The local government will in effect pay travelers 85 − 39 = 46 pesos per dollar to take a vacation.

Dollar-sellers, however, are penalized by a tax. In ordinary circumstances, they would be able to sell each dollar for 85 pesos. However, at the chosen exchange rate they are only able to get 39 pesos. One group of dollar-sellers will be exporters of goods to the dollar's home country. They will receive dollars for goods sold and will then sell dollars for pesos in order to pay local wages and other costs. Since the local government extracts 85 − 39 = 46 pesos directly from each dollar's worth of goods sold, exporters may soon find themselves going broke. Exports will drop.

Initially, the local government may find the exchange control scheme entirely workable. The tax of 46 pesos on dollar-sellers can be used to pay the subsidy of 46 pesos to dollar-buyers. But this will not last for long. Soon the government's supply of foreign exchange will disappear. First, consider dollar-sellers such as exporters. Exporters will try to get back the 46 pesos they are paying to the government. One way might be to raise the dollar price of their goods sold in the dollar's home country. But this may be self-defeating; raising the dollar price of goods sold may result in fewer sales. If the markets in which they sell their goods in the dollar's home country are characterized by perfect competition, an increase in the dollar price of the exporter's goods will result in sales falling to zero. In general, the feasibility of raising prices depends on the elasticity of demand for their product, and only in rare circumstances would they be able to significantly reduce the 46-peso tax by increasing the foreign-currency price of their goods.

As another alternative, they may decide to leave the dollar proceeds from the sales of foreign goods deposited in foreign banks. They may hope that the exchange rate will be changed later (say to 70 pesos = 1 dollar), which would reduce the size of the tax on selling dollars to the local government. In the meantime, they may attempt to pay local wage and other costs through local borrowing. The local government, seeing its inflow of cheap dollars drying up, will likely respond by passing a law that says companies must repatriate the proceeds from foreign sales immediately. To attempt to enforce this law, the government will require companies to keep and turn in elaborate records to the government concerning foreign sales and the management of foreign currency funds.

Meanwhile, the government will have found that a reduction in the supply of foreign exchange did not bring about a reduction in the demand. Rather, long lines of people who wish to buy dollars at 39 pesos each will have formed at the central bank. The government will not have enough dollars to go around at that price, so it will begin to ration foreign exchange. Travelers will be allowed a maximum number of dollars they can buy per year. To keep track of who has purchased foreign exchange and who has not, the government will have to keep careful records, and buyers of foreign exchange will have to fill out elaborate forms. Importers of goods may be required to obtain a license before they can buy dollars at the cheap 39-peso rate. There may be a long waiting period before a license is granted, and the actual permission to purchase dollars will be subject to "legitimate need." Importers who import goods the government favors will be granted a license, while others will be turned away. Importers who support the current regime politically will almost certainly be found to have needs more legitimate than those who oppose the current regime or those who fail to show support by making the appropriate political contributions. Government officials in charge of licenses may be offered (or may demand) side payments in return for their services.

Since many people who want dollars, and who are not able to get them from the government, would be willing to pay more than 39 pesos per dollar, a black or parallel market will develop. Those willing to pay more than 39 pesos per dollar will get together with those who want to sell dollars but who want to sell them for more than 39 pesos per dollar. Travelers returning from vacation in the dollar's home country will sell dollars on the black market. Word will spread that dollars may be exchanged for pesos at a better rate at offices of travel agents, or in the back room of the Casa del Gallo, or in taxicabs, or on the sidewalk in front of the local bank. Local companies may also sell their export proceeds on the black market, but they will have a more difficult time escaping detection than will individuals. And, of course, there will be those who deal in foreign exchange but who were not able to deal with the government in the first place because their trade is declared illegal. It may be illegal to buy foreign TVs, to export wheat, to buy or sell cocaine, or to purchase Bibles or foreign books. Importers or exporters of these goods and services will also buy and sell on the parallel market.

The black market in Brazil is so well organized that the cruzeiro/U.S. dollar black market exchange rate is reported daily in major newspapers. The premium paid for the dollar on the black market rises and falls with dollar inflows and outflows associated with tourist trade at the time of the Festival, with seasonal smuggling of grain, and with expectations of maxidevaluations of the cruzeiro. In one Central American country in early 1984, citizens could take out a local currency loan at their bank, buy the maximum number of U.S. dollars that the government permitted, sell part of the dollars at a higher price on the black market—enough to repay their local currency loan from the bank—and have enough dollars left over to purchase a round-trip airline ticket to the United States. The level at which the exchange rate was fixed not only subsidized travel to the United States, it also discouraged any capital inflows into the country. In Mexico in 1984 the central bank faced shortages of foreign exchange because it was maintaining an exchange rate for the Mexican peso that overvalued the peso with respect to the U.S. dollar. In one attempt to acquire artificially cheap U.S. dollars, the government told foreign auto companies that their exports from Mexico would have to match their imports into Mexico. Since the companies concerned needed to import parts before they had finished cars to sell, they had to close automotive assembly plants. Then, in order to generate a sufficient volume of exports that would then allow them to import parts, the auto companies turned to the export of local commodities like horsemeat, chickpeas, and coffee. Prior to 1990, tourists to East Germany from West Germany were required to change a small amount of West German marks to East German marks as the price of an entrance ticket to the country. The official exchange rate was 1 West German mark = 1 East German mark. The black market rate in 1985 was 1 West German mark = 17 East German marks. Thus tourists were led to subsidize the East German government by giving up their West German marks at an artificially low price. Foreign exchange control regulations in France once filled four published volumes. The services of lawyers who knew these regulations by heart were much in demand. After the Iranian Revolution under the Ayatollah Khomeini, the former head of the central bank was sentenced to death for maintaining an "incorrect" exchange rate for the Iranian rial with respect to the U.S. dollar. (In a humanitarian gesture, the sentence was later commuted to life imprisonment.)

There can be little doubt that exchange controls usually stem from political motives, and seldom—if ever—have any net positive benefit to *both* the buyers and the sellers of foreign exchange. Instead, controls impose deadweight costs to all users of the foreign exchange market. And it is usually fixed exchange rates, or fixed par values, that lead to exchange controls, because governments that fix exchange rates seldom pursue economic policies consistent with the chosen rate. Although economists have contributed a great deal of literature to a debate on "fixed versus flexible" exchange rates, this analysis (as important as it may be) seems to have had little impact either way on the political process that results in the selection of an official trading value for the local currency. When in the 1920s Winston Churchill set the dollar/pound rate at $4.86 = £1, so "the pound can look the dollar in the face," the decision was not based on a simple economic cost-benefit analysis. And today, when countries claim they have imposed exchange controls for "balance of payments reasons," the explanation is circular, since it is generally the existence of fixed prices and exchange and other controls that created the payments "imbalance" in the first place (see Chapter 9).

Fixed exchange rates frequently also lead to capital controls. In many Latin American countries today, domestic interest rates are fixed and there is in addition high inflation, so the inflation-adjusted (real) return to domestic deposits or interest-bearing securities is negative. Holders of deposits or other assets would normally switch to foreign currency deposits in order to escape the inflation tax, so governments legally prohibit or restrict the ownership of foreign deposits or securities. In such cases, governments consider (correctly) that the purchase of foreign currency securities is a vote against their domestic economic policies. Having created a climate in which their own citizens will not voluntarily hold the domestic currency, governments then resort to controls as an attempt to force people to hold and use it anyway. Occasionally, however, a country will impose controls to make its currency *less* attractive. Switzerland at one time even set negative interest rates on foreign-owned Swiss-franc-denominated assets in order to discourage foreign purchases.

The use of *multiple exchange rates* is similarly related to a political decision to favor certain transactions over others. Often a distinction is made between current account transactions (those involving goods and services) and capital account transactions (those involving only the exchange of financial assets). The best-known example is the system in Belgium, where one exchange rate ("the commercial franc") is freely determined in the market, and exchange purchased at this rate may be used for transactions in goods and services. A slightly different rate ("the financial franc") must be used to purchase foreign securities. Venezuela in 1984 had a three-tier system in which U.S. dollars for debt repayments could be purchased at a low bolivar price, U.S. dollars from oil sales were exchanged at a somewhat higher bolivar price, while most other transactions took place at a still higher number of bolivars per U.S. dollar.

□

Some of the economic effects of exchange controls are explored in Bank of England (1981), Culbertson (1977), and Krueger (1966). An annual listing of controls in force in IMF member countries can be found in the IMF's *Annual Report on Exchange Arrangements and Exchange Restrictions*.   ■

PROBLEMS FOR CHAPTER 3

1. If you could reorganize the foreign exchange market, which currency would you choose as the vehicle currency? What advantages would there be in using this currency? What problems?

2. How many bilateral exchange rates can be created using twenty currencies?

3. If the U.S. dollar price of the Japanese yen is $.0042, what is the Japanese yen price of the U.S. dollar?

4. Consider the following bid/asked prices: DM4.085 − 4.095/£. Which is the asked price for the pound sterling? Which is the bid price for the DM?

5. A bank quotes bid/asked rates of SF2.5110 − 2.5140/$ and ¥245 − 246/$. What ¥/SF bid and asked cross rates would the bank quote?

6. A bank is currently quoting spot rates of DM3.2446 − 3.2456/$ and BF65.30 − 65.40/$. What would be the bank's bid price for the Belgian franc in terms of DM?

7. At the end of the day, an FX trader has a net FX position totaling $45 million. If the expected proportional overnight exchange rate change is zero with a standard deviation of .6 percent, what is the probability distribution of the position's dollar

value on the next day? (Assume a normal probability distribution and state the values corresponding to plus or minus 1, 2, and 3 standard deviations, along with the corresponding probabilities.)

8. Refer to today's calendar and assume that a spot trade of dollars for pounds takes place between a New York bank and a London bank. Assume there are no special banking holidays. Determine the spot settlement date, the one-month forward settlement date, and the two-month forward settlement date. Is the length in days of the two-month forward contract exactly twice the length of the one-month forward contract?

9. Comment on the following news item, which appeared in the *Wall Street Journal* on March 7, 1984:

The black-market rate for U.S. dollars in Brazil rose sharply last week. Dealers said the rate jumped to 1600 Brazilian cruzeiros for $1, or about 30 percent above the official exchange rate. A week earlier, the black-market rate was only 13 percent above the official rate. The jump was surprising because it came just ahead of the long carnival weekend, which lasts from Saturday through today. In previous years, the spread between the black-market and official rates often narrowed before the carnival as foreign tourists brought in dollars. On Monday, Brazil made a small devaluation of the cruzeiro, the 13th this year. The official rate is 1225 to the dollar for buyers and 1231 for sellers.

10. Comment on the following news item, which appeared in the *Wall Street Journal* on March 7, 1985:

Pressured by high inflation and the strong U.S. dollar, Mexico said it will devalue the peso at a faster rate and implement export policies designed to right its economic recovery. Beginning yesterday, the dollar was raised against the Mexico peso by 21 centavos a day, rather than 17 centavos. There are 100 centavos in a peso. The change means that the controlled peso rate, used for most imports and exports, will fall about 27 percent annually against the dollar, contrasted with a projected decline of 23 percent at the old pace. . . .

Exporters have complained that, because inflation boosts their costs, an earlier increase in the peso devaluation rate in December wasn't enough to keep their goods competitive in foreign markets. Exporters say they have especially had problems competing with European exporters because European currencies have fallen faster against the dollar than the peso.

4

FORWARDS, SWAPS, AND INTEREST PARITY

FORWARD RATE QUOTATIONS

As noted in the preceding chapter, forward exchange is traded in the interbank market in connection with spot exchange. Although banks will quote "outright forwards" (that is, forward prices quoted without reference to the spot rate) to their corporate customers, marketmaking banks trade among themselves in the form of swaps, which involves both a spot and a forward contract. Thus, forward rates are always quoted by reference to spot rates. (There is a special type of swap, a "forward-forward" swap, that involves trading one forward contract for another forward contract of different maturity. However, in this case each of the forward rates involved has been determined by reference to the spot rate, so that the existence of this type of swap does not provide an exception to the rule that forward rates are determined in reference to spot rates.)

If the value of a foreign currency (in terms of the domestic currency) is greater forward than it is spot, the foreign currency is said to be at a *premium* (which implies that the domestic currency is at a forward *discount*). If the forward value of a foreign currency is less than the spot value, then the foreign currency is at a *discount* (which implies that the domestic currency is at a *premium*). For example, if the spot DM is DM2.4370 = $1 and the one-month forward DM is DM2.4320 = $1, then the one-month forward DM is at a premium. The one-month forward DM is at a premium here because the forward DM is more valuable. It takes fewer DM (namely, DM2.4320) to buy $1 forward than it takes to buy $1 spot. By the same criterion, the forward dollar is at a discount in this example because the forward dollar buys fewer DM (namely, DM2.4320) than does the spot dollar (DM2.4370).

Because forward exchange is traded at a premium or discount to spot exchange in the interbank market, forward rates are quoted in terms of the premium or discount that is to be added to the spot rate. Since two numbers (the bid price and the asked price) are quoted in the spot market, discounts or premiums are quoted as two numbers: one number to be added to or subtracted from the bid price and one number to be added to or subtracted from the offered price. For example, a forward premium for the one-month forward DM might be 30/20. Then if the spot DM is quoted as DM2.4273/90, the one-month forward DM would be DM2.4243/70. In this case, .0030 ("30") is subtracted from 2.4273 to give 2.4243, and .0020 ("20") is subtracted from 2.4290 to give 2.4270.

How would one know to *subtract* 30/20 instead of adding in this example? To keep the calculations straight, keep in mind that the bid/asked spread will always widen as we go forward. By subtracting in this case, we got a wider spread on one-month forward exchange (DM2.4270 − DM2.4243 = .0027) than on spot exchange (DM2.4290 − DM2.4273 = .0017). If we had added 30/20, the spread on forward exchange would have narrowed to .0007. An alternative way to keep the calculations straight is to note that 30/20 has the form "large number/small number" while, say, 30/40 would have the form "small number/large number." Then follow the rule to *subtract* if the form is "large number/small number" but *add* if the form is "small number/large number."

EXAMPLE 4.1

An FX trader quotes the spot DM against the U.S. dollar as 2.5005/10 and one-month forward margins as 100/95. What are the one-month outright forward rates? Answer: Since 100/95 has the form large number/small numer, the margins should be subtracted to yield an outright forward rate of DM2.4905/15. The one-month forward DM is at a premium (the dollar is at a discount). On the other hand, if the quotation had been 95/100, then the margins would have been added to yield DM2.5100/110.

INTEREST PARITY

What determines whether a foreign currency will be quoted at a premium or discount with respect to the domestic currency? The answer lies in interest rates, and the relationship between spot and forward exchange can be summarized in the form of an arbitrage condition called interest parity. *By "arbitrage" we mean the simultaneous buying and selling (or borrowing and lending) of two commodities or assets in such a way that the action locks in a sure, known profit.* The calculation of this profit in no way depends on the outcome of random events or on people's expectations. (There is, however, usually a presumption that people will honor their contracts. That is, when we use the term *arbitrage* we will be excluding the possibility that random events determine the profit outcome, given that there is no risk of default on contracts.)

The interest parity theorem is an arbitrage condition relating the discount or premium on forward exchange to the term structure of interest rates on financial assets denominated in the two currencies involved in an exchange rate. In particular, if interest rates are *higher* in the domestic country than in the foreign country, then the foreign country's currency will be selling at a *premium* in the forward market, while if interest rates are *lower* in the domestic country, then the foreign currency will be selling at a *discount* in the forward market. For example, if interest rates are higher in the United States than Germany, then the forward DM will cost more U.S. dollars than will the spot DM. The forward DM will be at a premium and the forward dollar at a discount. If interest rates are higher in the United Kingdom than in the United States, then the forward £ will cost fewer dollars than will the spot £. The forward £ will be at a discount and the forward dollar at a premium.

Before getting to the arbitrage strategy that brings about interest parity, we should explore a few market conventions about how interest rates are quoted. In particular, for reasons mentioned later, we will be especially concerned with interest rates on eurocurrency deposits. Eurocurrency interest rates, like all interest rates, are always quoted at a yearly rate. Thus if a 30-day rate of "8 percent" is quoted, that does not literally mean 8 percent over the 30-day period. The 8 percent is a "yearly" rate with the year in question a 360-day year. A 30-day rate of "8 percent" means that, for a $1 deposit, at the end of 30 days one will receive $(1 + .08(30/360)) = $1.006667 back. That is, one adjusts the "yearly" interest rate by changing it to a decimal and then multiplying by the fraction of a 360-day year involved in the time period of the deposit. (*Note:* You do it this way because that is the agreed meaning of "8 percent" in the market. You are not free to make up your own interpretation. That means, for example, that if you take $1.08 to the power $\frac{1}{12}$ and get $1.0064, your answer is wrong.)

The 360-day year applies to most eurocurrencies. Notable exceptions, however, are the British pound and the Australian dollar, which use 365-day years. Therefore "8 percent" paid on a eurosterling deposit for 30 days would, for an initial deposit of £1, yield

£(1 + .08(30/365)) = £1.006575

at maturity.

Eurocurrency deposits are traded over the phone, just like foreign exchange, with a bid/offer spread (the bid price being the rate one will pay on deposits and the offer price being the rate one charges on loans). Settlement dates mostly follow the same conventions as in the FX market except for the end-end rule. For example, if one-month DM deposits are traded today, the deposit is actually made (at the interest rate agreed today) on the settlement date for spot DM. The DM deposit will mature on the same date as does a one-month forward DM contract traded today, provided settlement is not the last trade day of the month.

Now we are ready for the interest parity theorem. We will need some notation. At first we will simplify, and ignore the difference in bid and offer prices. That is, we will assume there is only one price quotation for spot exchange, for forward exchange, and for interest rates. After we have derived the theorem under these simplifying assumptions and seen some examples, we will then redo it taking into account bid and offer prices. Let $S(t)$ be the *domestic currency price of spot foreign exchange* at time t. For example, if the domestic currency is taken to be the dollar, and the foreign currency is the DM, then we might have $S(t) = $.40/DM. Thus, $S(t)$ is in "American" terms if we take the dollar as our domestic currency. But if we take the DM for our domestic currency, then $S(t)$ would be in European terms. We can treat any currency as the domestic currency just as long as we are consistent. Let $F(t,T)$ be the *domestic currency price of forward exchange* at time t, for a contract that matures at time $t + T$. Let i and i^* be the yearly rates of interest paid on eurocurrency deposits denominated in the domestic (i) or foreign (i^*) currency. The maturity of the deposits is chosen to coincide with the maturity of the forward contract. Notice that matching maturities here is no problem, since eurocurrency deposits have settlement dates that usually correspond to those for forward contracts. We will assume for the following calculation that i and i^* are for a 360-day year.

Consider a trader with access to the interbank market in foreign exchange and eurocurrency deposits. At time t, this trader can borrow one unit of the domestic currency at an interest rate i, for which he will to repay $1 + i(T/360)$ at time $t + T$:

Time t	Time $t + T$
Borrow 1 unit domestic currency	Repay $1 + i(T/360)$ units of domestic currency

With one unit of domestic currency in hand at time t, the trader can buy $1/S(t)$ units of foreign currency. If this amount is placed on deposit, he will receive $[1/S(t)][1 + i^*(T/360)]$ back at time $t + T$. This amount of foreign currency will, however, have an uncertain value in domestic currency terms. So to lock in a domestic currency value now he can sell this amount forward at the forward rate $F(t,T)$. The domestic currency value of the amount sold forward is therefore $[1/S(t)][1 + i^*(T/360)] \, F(t,T)$. To summarize:

Time t	Time $t + T$
Purchase $[1/S(t)]$ units of foreign currency; sell forward $[1/S(t)][1 + i^*(T/360)]$ units of foreign currency at forward rate $F(t,T)$	Deposit matures and pays $[1/S(t)][1 + i^*(T/360)]$ units of foreign currency; deliver this amount of foreign currency in fulfillment of forward contract, receiving $[1/S(t)][1 + i^*(T/360)] \, F(t,T)$ units of domestic currency

Notice that the trader has put up no money in the process of making these transactions. Therefore, if the investment in foreign currency deposits, after covering through the forward market, yielded an amount greater than that which the trader would have to repay on his loan, the trader would make a riskless profit, having used none of the trader's own capital. And in the contrary case, if the investment in foreign currency deposits, after covering through the forward market, yielded an amount less than the trader would have to repay on his loan, the trader could reverse this procedure (by borrowing foreign currency) and also make a riskless profit using only borrowed money. Either way, the trader would realize he had hold of a money machine, and would keep repeating the process as long as the market kept giving him a free profit. Other traders would have a similar idea, so their volume of trading would cause prices to adjust in such a way that a free, riskless profit was no longer available.

To summarize, in economic equilibrium (an absence of free profit opportunities like those just covered) we must have equality between the rate of return on domestic assets and covered foreign assets:

$$1 + i(T/360) = [1/S(t)][1 + i*(T/360)]F(t,T)$$

Or, rearranging this equation,

$$F(t,T) = S(t) \frac{[1 + i(T/360)]}{[1 + i*(T/360)]} \tag{4.1}$$

The last equation is the famous interest parity "theorem." It relates the forward exchange rate to the spot exchange rate and the interest rates on eurodeposits denominated in the domestic (i) and foreign ($i*$) currencies. Notice that if i is greater than $i*$ (the domestic interest rate is higher than the foreign interest rate), then the domestic currency price of forward exchange [$F(t,T)$] will be higher than the domestic currency price of spot exchange [$S(t)$]. Foreign currency would be at a forward premium and domestic currency at a forward discount. Finally, notice that 360 appears in the equation because a 360-day year is assumed as the basis for the interest rate quotation. If one currency were quoted on the basis of a 365-day year, however, 365 should be substituted adjacent to the relevant interest rate.

EXAMPLE 4.2

Let the spot rate $S(t) = \$.40000/DM$ and the one-year forward rate $F(t,T) = \$.42026/DM$. Assume that the forward contract will mature in $T = 365$ days from the spot value date. Let the rates on eurodollar deposits and euro-DM deposits be, respectively, $i = 11.3$ percent and $i* = 6.0$ percent. Then, comparing the return on domestic borrowing with the return on covered foreign lending,

$$1 + i(T/360) = 1 + .113(365/360) = \$1.114569.$$
$$[1/S(t)][1 + i*(T/360)]F(t,T) = (1/.40)[1 + .06(365/360)](.42026) = \$1.114565.$$

For each dollar borrowed domestically, a trader would have to repay $1.114569. The return from using the $1 to buy spot foreign exchange, placing the deposit at the foreign rate of interest, and selling the total return forward would be $1.114565. These two amounts are so close that it would in all probability not be worth anyone's time trying to exploit the difference. So in this case, interest parity can be said to hold. In fact, as we will see when we look at the realistic case involving both bid and offer prices, the two sides of the transaction can differ by a good bit more than they do here, and still there may be no profit opportunity.

INTEREST PARITY AND SWAPS

How do interbank swaps relate to the interest parity theorem? There are several parts to the answer. First, referring back to the interest parity formula, we see that it gives the forward rate as a function of the spot rate. Therefore the swap rate should be the difference between $F(t,T)$, as given by the formula, and the spot rate $S(t)$. That is, the swap rate $F(t,T) - S(t)$ should have the value:

$$F(t,T) - S(t) = S(t) \left(\frac{1 + i(T/360)}{1 + i^*(T/360)} - 1 \right)$$

$$= S(t) \left(\frac{(i - i^*)(T/360)}{1 + i^*(T/360)} \right) \tag{4.2}$$

To see what this implies in practice, consider the situation of a commercial bank. Suppose the bank assigns a group of traders to do arbitrage between the spot and forward markets in the way described in deriving the interest parity theorem. If the traders do the task correctly, soon there will be no arbitrage opportunities left and the traders will serve no useful purpose. That is, they will put themselves out of a job if they do their job of arbitraging well; thus the bank may not consider it a good idea to assign a lot of people to do covered interest arbitrage.

Neither, on the other hand, does the bank want to give money away by quoting prices inconsistently, whereby other banks can arbitrage against it. Even if the bank does not think it will find long-lasting arbitrage opportunities, it still may worry that other banks will and that it will be a source of arbitrage profit to the benefit of other banks. How can the first bank ensure that this never happens? Answer: Quote forward rates according to the interest parity theorem. This is, in fact, what essentially all marketmaking banks do. They use the interest parity theorem to calculate the swap rate, as in (4.2).

This, of course, does not mean there will *never* be an arbitrage opportunity. The first qualification comes from the fact that because there are many traders in the market, there is always a spectrum of spot exchange rates being quoted simultaneously throughout the foreign exchange market. These spot prices are not the same, so the forward rates derived from them will not be exactly the same across banks at any one time either. Second, the size of the discount or the premium on forward exchange relates to eurocurrency interest rates on the domestic and foreign currencies. These interest rates may not be quite the same as seen by different traders at any point in time in the market, so the size of the discount or premium quoted on forward exchange will vary from trader to trader.

Why should the trader be looking at eurocurrency interest rates as opposed to some other set of rates? There are many reasons. Recall from the history in Chapter 1 that the eurocurrency market grew out of the Merchant Banks' Market of the late 1950s. At that time, eurocurrency dealing was done in foreign exchange trading rooms by foreign exchange traders. Therefore, conventions in the eurodeposits market such as settlement and maturity dates were chosen to correspond to foreign exchange conventions. A trader could thus arbitrage using eurocurrency deposits and never have to worry about the deposits maturing on a different day than the forward contract. Moreover, eurocurrencies corresponded precisely to that set of money market instruments that could be freely traded internationally, usually without controls, taxes, and other restrictions. Thus an arbitrage could be done in the simple manner described by the interest parity theorem, without incurring so many additional transactions costs as to rule out any possible profit opportunity.

Therefore, a bank will quote its swap rate using eurocurrency rates as reference rates in the interest parity formula. For some currencies with forward markets, however, eurocurrency rates do not exist. As of 1985, for example, there were functioning interbank forward markets for about twenty-one currencies but eurocurrency rates for only fifteen of them. In cases where no relevant euromarket exists, or exists but is too thin to be really useful, then some money market instrument other than eurocurrency deposits may be relevant.

Here is an example of how banks use swaps to manage outright forward exposures incurred in dealing with corporate customers.

EXAMPLE 4.3

A company buys £1 million six months forward from a bank. The bank selling the £1 million has done an "outright forward" deal with the company. The bank now has a foreign exchange exposure in that it is short (it has sold) £1 million. To cover this exposure, the bank will *buy* £1 million forward. This purchase forward, if done in the interbank market, must be done in the form of a swap, so the bank will do a swap involving a *spot sale and forward purchase* of £1 million. After doing the swap, the bank has now matched its forward commitments. But it is now short (it has sold) £1 million spot. So to even out its spot position, the bank does a separate spot purchase of £1 million. To summarize:

Company	Bank
Purchases £1 million in the forward market	Sells £1 million as an "outright forward"
	Does a swap in which it buys £1 million
	forward and sells £1 million spot
	Purchases £1 million spot

DIVERGENCES FROM INTEREST PARITY

Let's now consider some examples where interest parity does not hold. We will see how to use the interest parity relation to detect arbitrage opportunities and to compare hedging costs. (We will continue to simplify in this section by ignoring bid/asked prices.)

EXAMPLE 4.4

Suppose an interbank trader noticed the following market prices:

$S(t) = \$.40/DM$, $F(t,T) = \$.42/DM$ for $T = 360$ days, $i = 10\%$, and $i^* = 6.0\%$.

Is there an arbitrage opportunity available? A quick way to check for arbitrage possibilities is to calculate both sides of the interest parity theorem. Since interest rates do not have to be adjusted (since $360/360 = 1$), the trader observes:

$$F = \$.42/DM \qquad S\frac{(1 + i)}{(1 + i^*)} = \$.40/DM \frac{(1.10)}{(1.06)} = \$.41509/DM.$$

The actual forward rate, $.42/DM, is larger than the synthetic forward rate ($.41509/DM) calculated from the other side of the equation. Following the principle "buy low, sell high," the trader will want to sell forward because forward exchange is overvalued by relation to spot exchange and the two interest rates. That is, the actual forward rate is overvalued by reference to the synthetic forward rate. She will end up selling forward, if she borrows the dollar, buys DM, and sells DM forward. Hence *she will borrow the dollar and undertake an interbank swap.* A typical transaction size will be $1 million, but it is simpler to think in terms of $1. She will borrow $1, buy 1/.40 = DM2.5, and place the DM at 6 percent interest to yield DM2.65 in 360 days. Meanwhile, she has sold the DM2.65 forward for (DM2.65)($.42/DM) = $1.113. She will pay off her $1 loan with $1.10, so that her net gain is $.013. For a $1 million transaction, the profit would be $13,000. (Profit of this magnitude would be enormous and would occur rarely, if ever, on a single transaction in the interbank market.)

Let's now consider a corporation. Because the relevant interest rates seen in the interbank market are eurocurrency rates, while the relevant interest rates as seen by a corporation may be something else, interest parity may not hold for the corporation, even if it does in the interbank market. That does not mean that the corporation is necessarily in a position to do arbitrage; probably it will not be since the corporation would have to deal at larger spreads than will the bank. But the corporation may be in a position to alter its hedging costs.

EXAMPLE 4.5

A U.S. importer of machinery must pay DM2 million in 6 months (180 days). The company's borrowing rate for dollars is 10 percent, while its lending rate for DM is 5.5 percent. The company is quoted a bank rate of $.3752/DM for spot exchange, and $.3900/DM for six-months forward exchange (180 days). The company wishes to lock in the dollar cost of the DM2 million now, and has decided to use a forward hedge or a money market equivalent. Given the prices faced by the company, which should it use?

To hedge through the forward market, the company will buy forward DM 2 million at a cost of (DM2 million)($.3900/DM) = $780,000 to be paid in 180 days.

To use a money market equivalent, the company calculates the amount of DM it needs now, which, if placed on deposit, will yield DM2 million in 180 days. The interest over 180 days would be (180/360)(.055) = .0275, so the company will need to deposit DM2 million/1.0275 = DM1,946,472. The dollars the company would need now to buy this amount of DM is (DM1,946,472)($.3752/DM) = $730,316.30. So the company will need to borrow $730,316.30 in order to buy DM, and it will pay back its loan in the amount of ($730,316.30)(1.05) = $766,832.12, as interest in the amount of (180/360)(.10) = .05 will be paid on each dollar borrowed.

The money market equivalent is cheaper by $780,000 − $766,832.12 = $13,167.88. The only reason the two hedging procedures give different numbers is that interest parity in this case doesn't hold at interest rates that are relevant to the company.

INTEREST PARITY WITH BID/ASKED SPREADS

Let's now turn to the realistic case where all prices are quoted with bid/asked spreads. We will need slightly different notation. Let $Sb(t)$ and $Sa(t)$ be, respectively, the bid and asked domestic currency prices of spot exchange. Let

$Fb(t,T)$ and $Fa(t,T)$ be the bid and asked domestic currency prices of forward exchange. And let ib, ib^* and ia, ia^* be the bid and asked interest rates on eurodeposits denominated in the domestic and the foreign (*) currency. Again, assume a 360-day year as the basis for the interest quotations although a 365-day year should be substituted if relevant.

Consider now a trader in the interbank market. The trader will have to buy or borrow at the other party's asked price while he will sell or lend at the bid price. If the trader wishes to do arbitrage, there are two approaches to take: borrow domestic currency or borrow foreign currency. Let's consider each case in turn.

BORROW DOMESTIC CURRENCY

The trader can borrow $1/[1 + ia(T/360)]$ units of domestic currency at time t, and repay 1 unit at time $t + T$. Using the borrowed domestic currency, he can engage in a swap to buy spot foreign currency and sell the currency forward, meanwhile placing the foreign currency at the foreign rate of interest. This would yield, in terms of domestic currency:

$$(1/[1 + ia(T/360)])([1/Sa(t)][1 + ib^*(T/360)]Fb(t,T)).$$

For this procedure, to yield no profit, which is the requirement for economic equilibrium, it must be the case that it gives an amount less than or equal to the 1 unit of domestic currency that must be repaid on the loan:

$$(1/[1 + ia(T/360)])([1/Sa(t)][1 + i^*b(T/360)]Fb(t,T)) \leq 1.$$

Rewriting, we get

$$Fb(t,T) \leq Sa(t) \frac{1 + ia(T/360)}{1 + ib^*(T/360)}. \tag{4.3}$$

So, to eliminate arbitrage, the forward bid price must be less than the spot asked price multiplied by the ratio of one plus the domestic asked interest divided by one plus the foreign bid interest.

BORROW FOREIGN CURRENCY

The trader can borrow $1/[1 + ia^*(T/360)]$ units of foreign currency at time t and repay 1 unit of foreign currency at time $t + T$. With the foreign currency, he or she can buy spot domestic currency, place it at the domestic interest rate, and sell it forward. This will yield a foreign currency amount of

$$(1/[1 + ia^*(T/360)])(Sb(t)[1 + ib(T/360)][1/Fa(t,T)]),$$

which must, in economic equilibrium, be less than or equal to the one unit of foreign currency that must be repaid. From this inequality, we get

$$Fa(t,T) \geq Sb(t) \frac{1 + ib(T/360)}{1 + ia^*(T/360)}. \tag{4.4}$$

To avoid arbitrage, the market prices must be such that the forward asked price is greater than or equal to the spot bid price multiplied by one plus the domestic bid interest divided by one plus the foreign asked interest.

Conditions:

$$Fb(t,T) \leq Sa(t) \ \frac{1 + ia(T/360)}{1 + ib^*(T/360)} = Y$$

$$Fa(t,T) \geq Sb(t) \ \frac{1 + ib(T/360)}{1 + ia^*(T/360)} = X$$

$Fb(t,T) \leq Y$

Range of
forward rate $F(t,T)$

$Fa(t,T) \geq X$

FIGURE 4.1
Constraints on forward exchange rate to avoid covered interest arbitrage. Allowable
ranges for Fb, Fa (conditional on $Fb < Fa$) are shown.

Notice that *both* conditions must hold simultaneously at all times, else the
market will be offering a riskless profit to the trader. These relationships are
illustrated in Figure 4.1.

EXAMPLE 4.6

Suppose, at market prices, we have the spot price of DM at \$.4428 − .4438/DM, while the
one-month forward rate (with $T = 30$ days) is \$.4450 − .4460/DM. The rate on one-
month euro-DM deposits is $5\frac{7}{8}$–6 percent, while the rate on one-month eurodollar deposits
is $10\frac{11}{16}$–$10\frac{13}{16}$ percent. Is there an arbitrage possibility?

If a trader borrows dollars, he will borrow \$1/[1 + (.10$\frac{13}{16}$)(30/360)] and repay \$1. If he
buys spot DM, places them at the DM interest rate, and sells forward, he will obtain

(\$1/[1 + (.10$\frac{13}{16}$)(30/360)])([1/\$.4438/DM][1 + (.05$\frac{7}{8}$)(30/360)][\$.4450/DM])
= \$.9986.

Therefore there is no arbitrage opportunity. For each \$1 the trader would have to repay he
would receive \$.9986 in return. This is a losing proposition.

If a trader borrows DM, he will borrow DM1/[1 + .06(30/360)] and repay DM1. If he
now buys spot dollars and places them at the dollar interest rate, and sells forward, he will
obtain

(DM1/[1 + .06(30/360)])([\$.4428/DM][1 + (.10$\frac{11}{16}$)(30/360)][1/\$.4460/DM])
= DM.9966.

Again, there is no arbitrage profit available this way. For each DM1 the trader would have
to repay on his loan, he would receive only DM.9966 in return.

In Example 4.6, there was no arbitrage possibility in the interbank market.
That does not mean, however, that a corporation will necessarily be indifferent
to hedging costs at the rates given. We see this in Example 4.7.

EXAMPLE 4.7

Consider a corporation not set up for arbitrage but large enough to have access to the interbank market. The corporation is buying DM to make payment 30 days hence. The prices are those in Example 4.6. There are two obvious routes the corporation can take to have DM on hand to make payment in 30 days. The corporation can set aside an amount in dollars for 30 days, meanwhile receiving interest, and sell the dollars forward for DM. For each $1 set aside this way, it will receive

$$\$1[1 + (.10\tfrac{11}{16})(30/360)](1/\$.4460/DM) = DM2.2621.$$

Alternatively, the company can take $1, buy spot DM, and place these at interest for 30 days. This will yield DM in the amount of

$$\$1(1/\$.4438/DM)[1 + (.05\tfrac{7}{8})(30/360)] = DM2.2643.$$

Thus the second route will yield more DM per dollar. For each $1 million, the company will receive an additional DM2200 by following the second procedure.

□

The range within which the forward rate can move without covered interest arbitrage possibilities is explored empirically in Frenkel and Levich (1975, 1977). The narrower range illustrated in Example 4.7 for corporations choosing the least-cost method of obtaining foreign currency is discussed in Deardorff (1979) and Bahmani-Oskooee and Das (1985). ■

INTEREST PARITY AND THE COST OF INFORMATION

Examples 4.5 and 4.7 illustrate an important principle. Some companies may pay more than they need to by dealing through the forward market. Even given the fact that on average interest parity will hold in the interbank market—because of the method of forward rate quotation—it does not follow that currency or hedging costs will be the same whether undertaken through the forward market or the spot market in connection with the money markets. A simple difference in costs of twenty-five basis points would amount to $25,000 on the purchase or sale of $10 million. Presumably corporate treasurers are not so highly compensated that it would fail to be worth a few minutes of their time to do the simple calculation necessary for comparing two equivalent hedging methods.

If the interest parity relation holds exactly, there is no advantage in choosing a money market hedge over a forward hedge, or vice versa. But interest parity may not hold when rates relevant to the corporation are used, and sometimes the money market hedge will be more advantageous. Does this mean the market is inefficient? Not necessarily, because of the costs of information. If a company were continually dealing in the interbank market, borrowing and lending and buying and selling currencies, the prices at which it made transactions would be immediately transmitted as information throughout the market, and any riskless arbitrage opportunities would be quickly eliminated. But a company such as the one in our hedging example may not do continuous dealing. It may only come to the market occasionally. Suppose we take the price at which spot exchange is available to the company as given and the rate at which the company can borrow the domestic currency as given. Now assume the company goes to the market and asks for a quotation on forward exchange and also asks for a quotation on the rate for lending a foreign currency. If the market quotes one rate on forward exchange, then there is one and only one lending rate that is consistent with this forward rate without interest parity being violated. But, likely as not, the two rates quoted will not be entirely consistent. The market is not inefficient, however, unless this difference is big enough to pay someone in the market a normal level of profit to collect and exploit the information concerning differences in quotations to companies. From a specific company's own point of view, however, it is virtually costless to compare hedging costs using the rates quoted to it. For an individual company's decision to be efficient, the company must choose the least-cost hedging method.

FORWARD MARKETS AND INTEREST RATES: HISTORICAL BACKGROUND

While forward contracts have existed for thousands of years, forward markets are a more recent innovation. FX forward markets in their modern form have, however, existed at least since the 1880s. On the Vienna stock exchange at that time, one could make forward contracts for the German mark for one-, three-, four-, and six-months' delivery. In Berlin, there were forward markets for the Austrian gulden and the Russian ruble, while a smaller forward market for the German mark existed in St. Petersberg. The Russian ruble in particular was subject to considerable fluctuations in value. British importers and exporters of that era insisted that trade contracts with Russia be denominated in the pound sterling. German traders were able to gain a competitive advantage by their willingness to denominate trade in terms of the Russian ruble. The Berlin forward market in the ruble had an essential part in their risk-exposure management (Schulze-Gaevernitz, 1899).

Later in the 1890s, the emergence of forward markets in the pound sterling and French franc in Berlin and Vienna led to some aggressive interest arbitrage between those two cities and London and Paris. The existence of such an operation as interest arbitrage was considered a trade secret, however, and was jealously guarded (Einsig, 1937, p. 42).

It was another thirty years before an extended public exposition of the interest parity relation was given. This account appeared in the *Manchester Guardian Reconstruction Supplement* on April 20, 1922, and was written by an economist named John Maynard Keynes. Keynes' article was expanded into a book, *A Tract on Monetary Reform* (1923), which described the postwar forward markets in detail. Keynes cited some dramatic examples of profitable interest arbitrage despite the fact that large bid/asked spreads were common in the forward market.

Keynes' lucid exposition of forward contracts and interest parity did not prevent economists from treating forward markets as an institutional development devoid of any major theoretical interest. When Paul Einsig published his *Theory of Forward Exchange* fifteen years later, in 1937, he complained: "Whatever may be the reason, Forward Exchange is one of the neglected branches of financial literature. The majority of economists avoid the subject if they can; the majority of bankers leave it to their Foreign Exchange dealers; as for the general public, they regard Forward Exchange as something deeply mysterious and infinitely complicated, like Relativity, and consider it futile even to try to understand the workings of the system." Einsig himself produced long charts comparing the forward premium to "parities" involving various interest rates. He calculated "discount rate" parity, "bank rate" parity, and "call money rate" parity.

If we jump ahead another thirty-five years, to 1972, the confusion over the relevant interest rates had disappeared. In the late 1950s the dealing of eurocurrency deposits had grown up in foreign exchange trading rooms, and settlement dates and procedures followed those for foreign exchange. The costs (as embodied in bid/asked spreads) of doing interest arbitrage using eurocurrency deposits were very small. Not only was the interest parity relation well understood, but it had also acquired increasing relevance as transactions costs fell, because the range of possible forward quotations was correspondingly narrowed. Soon banks dropped the pretense of maintaining a separate forward market and simply quoted the swap rate using the interest parity relation. Even if they were not engaged in interest arbitrage, it was not worth taking the risk that some *other* bank might be.

□

Since the reemergence of foreign exchange markets at the end of the 1950s, economists have conducted numerous "tests" of the interest parity "theorem." The usefulness or importance of many of these tests is unclear. Typically the discount or premium on forward exchange—usually measured without taking into account bid/asked spreads—was compared to an interest differential—again measured without bid/asked spreads. The assets whose interest rates were used in the tests might mature on different dates from the spot or forward exchange contracts or might have different credit risk or tax characteristics. Moreover, the tests were usually done with observational data on interest rates that were collected at times of the day different from the exchange rate data.

Since the interest parity relation is an arbitrage relation, the real empirical question was whether there were unexploited, essentially riskless profit opportunities. This question is difficult to answer on the basis of statistical tests. Profit is measured after the payment of transactions costs, which include the bid/asked spread omitted in the tests. The tests did not consider taxes, which become important (Levy, 1977) if, say, gains on forward contracts are taxed at a capital gains rate while interest rate gains are taxed as ordinary income. Political risk—the threat of capital or exchange controls—becomes important if arbitrage takes place across national borders (Aliber, 1973). Apparently riskless opportunities as shown in the data may simply indicate periods of high political risk. Of a more subtle nature, the tests involved regressions that measure "average" deviations from interest parity. Such an average measure is misleading because deviations may be large enough for profit opportunities yet zero on average, or too small for profit opportunities but nonzero on average (Frenkel and Levich, 1975).

Because eurocurrency deposits mature when forward contracts do, have similar credit risks, and face a similar absence of taxes and capital controls, tests using eurocurrency rates have generally found that any deviations from interest parity were sufficiently small as to be ascribable to transactions costs [see Aliber (1973), Frenkel and Levich (1975, 1977), and Herring and Marston (1976)]. Given that traders now use interest parity and eurocurrency rates to set the forward rate, it is not surprising that interest parity holds well when tested with eurocurrency data.   ∎

FORWARD CONTRACTS AND DUAL-CURRENCY BONDS

FX forward contracts show up in many different contexts. One important example is that of *dual-currency* bonds. A dual-currency bond is one that is purchased in terms of one currency—with coupon interest paid in that same currency—but is redeemed in terms of another currency. An example of a dual-currency bond was the issue led by the Swiss Bank Soditic for First City Financial in July 1985. Each bond could be purchased for its full face value of SF5000. Interest on the bonds is paid in Swiss francs. But when the bonds mature, at the end of ten years, the bond principal will be repaid in the amount of $2800.

At the time of issue, this bond could be viewed as the combination of (1) an ordinary ten-year Swiss franc bond that would repay principal in the amount of SF5000, plus (2) a ten-year forward contract to buy $2800 at SF1.7857/$. The reason is simple. As a dual-currency bond, the bond repays $2800. Alternatively, if one had a regular bond that repaid SF5000, plus the forward contract, one would have to give up the SF5000 in payment for the $2800 that would be received on the forward contract, since ($2800)(SF1.7857/$) = SF5000 (except for minor round-off error). In either case, one would end up with $2800.

Viewing a dual-currency bond as the sum of an ordinary bond and a forward contract helps elucidate the nature of the exchange risk involved. With a forward contract, one has locked in an exchange rate. For the dual-currency bond above, the locked-in exchange rate is SF1.7857/$. When a forward contract to purchase foreign currency matures, one will have an opportunity gain if the market price of foreign currency is higher than the price embodied in the contract. One will have an opportunity loss if the market price is lower. In the above example of a dual-currency bond, the holders of the bond will enjoy an exchange gain if the Swiss franc price of the dollar is higher than SF1.7857 at bond maturity in 1995, but suffer an exchange loss if the Swiss franc price of the dollar is lower than SF1.7857.

The motives for issuing such bonds are as various as the motives for using FX forward contracts in general. The chief reason a company might issue a dual-currency bond rather than issuing an ordinary bond and then taking out a forward contract is that the FX forward market provided by banks may not extend out to ten years. (For more on this, see Chapter 19.) In some cases there is a risk/return trade-off, as dual-currency issues often pay higher coupons than the equivalent single-currency issue (*Financial Times,* July 12, 1985). The pattern of a company's cash flows may be such that repayment in a different currency is less risky from the company's point of view. In order to obtain this risk reduction, the company is willing to give up some earnings now in the form of higher coupon payments.

PROBLEMS FOR CHAPTER 4

1. Calculate the settlement day, as well as the maturity date, for a three-month eurodollar deposit traded on the first Wednesday in September of the current year.

2. A bank's spot quotation is ¥244.95 − ¥245.15/$. If the three-month forward yen is quoted as 3.12 − 3.07, what is the actual three-month forward exchange rate?

3. A bank sells a company DM2,500,000 three months forward. What would be the customary way for the bank to cover its forward DM exposure?

4. A bank is currently quoting one-month forward rates of $1.2410 − 1.2425/£ and $1.0185 − 1.0200/Irish pound. What is the bank's one-month forward asked price for the Irish pound in terms of the British pound?

5. Consider two ninety-two-day eurodeposits, one denominated in the U.S. dollar and the other denominated in the pound sterling. Each pays interest at a yearly rate of $9\frac{7}{8}$ percent. Calculate the actual amount of interest paid on each deposit over the ninety-two days.

6. The interest rate on three-month (eighty-nine-day) eurodollar deposits is $11\frac{7}{16}$–$11\frac{9}{16}$ percent (bid/asked), while that on three-month euro-DM deposits is $5\frac{5}{16}$–$5\frac{7}{16}$ percent. Spot exchange is available at DM3.0215 − 3.0280/$ while three-month forward is available at DM2.9852 − 2.9910/$. Is there an arbitrage opportunity from borrowing either DM or dollars? If so, explain the steps that would be taken to exploit the arbitrage opportunity. What profit would be obtained from 1,000,000 units of currency? At what point in time would this profit be realized?

7. A company has a known cash payment of SF50,000,000 to be made to a Swiss supplier in 100 days. The company wishes to fix or lock in the nominal dollar price of this payment using currently available rates. The spot rate available to the company is SF2.50/$, the forward rate for maturity in 100 days is SF2.465/$, and the company faces a dollar interest rate of 12 percent and a SF interest rate of 6 percent. Given this information, what is the smallest dollar price on its SF 50,000,000 that the company can lock in with certainty? Explain the procedure the company will follow to obtain this price.

FOREIGN CURRENCY FUTURES

INTRODUCTION

FX futures contracts are different from the FX forward contracts covered in Chapter 4. It is important not to get futures and forwards confused, since futures involve a different type of contract from forwards.

The first important thing to realize about foreign currency futures is that when you have a futures contract, you do *not* own foreign exchange. A futures contract instead represents a pure *bet on the direction of price (exchange rate) movement of the underlying currency*. What this means is that the futures price is not a monetary amount you pay to anyone. Rather, the futures price is the variable about which you are betting. You can bet either that the price will go up or that it will go down. If you *buy* a futures contract, (go *long*) and the futures price goes up, you make money. If the futures price goes down, you lose money. Thus if your total FX portfolio consisted of a *long* position in FX futures, you would be betting that the price would go *up*. If you *sell* a futures contract (go *short*) and the futures price goes down, you make money. If the futures price goes up, you lose money. Thus if your total FX portfolio consisted of a *short* position in FX futures, you would be betting that the price would go *down*.

Futures trading in countries such as the United States takes place only on government-regulated exchanges. Buyers or sellers of futures contracts place orders through brokers or exchange members. These orders are communicated to the exchange floor and then transferred to a trading pit, where the price (or prices) for a given number of contracts will be negotiated by open outcry between floor brokers or traders. A futures trade will result in a futures contract with two sides—someone going long at the negotiated price and someone going short at that same price. Thus, if there were no transactions costs, futures trading would represent a zero-sum game: What one side will win will exactly match what the other side will lose. The futures price itself will change minute by minute. The futures price is a market price that adjusts to bring about equilibrium between the number of long positions and the number of short positions. If more people want to go long than want to go short at the current futures price, the futures price will be driven up until an equilibrium between desired short and long positions is reached. If desired short positions are greater than desired long positions at the current futures price, the price will be driven down. The number of two-sided futures bets in existence at any time is called the *open interest*.

Many publications, written by people who really know better, state that a "futures contract is a binding agreement to buy or sell an underlying asset at a specified date in the future." Such a definition is not only technically false, it is also misleading. A futures contract is really a binding agreement to pay up your bet on a daily basis, for every day the market is open and your bet is still in effect. There may be, however, certain specified dates on which, *if your bet is still in force at that time,* you will be legally obligated to acquire (if long) or deliver (if short) the underlying asset on whose price you are betting. For foreign currency futures, these dates correspond to the last trade dates covered below. If you stop an FX futures bet prior to the end of trading on the last trade date, you are never obligated to buy or to deliver anything. The way to stop a bet is to reverse whatever you did to get into it. If you are long a contract, then going short the same contract (at the same exchange) will kill the bet. If you are short, then going long will kill the bet. (Killing a bet results in a reduction in open interest.)

The size of the bet you take by opening a futures contract is governed by the face amount of the contract. If you have gone *long* a futures contract at a price $P(0)$, then at the end of the day there will be a positive or negative cash flow to your futures account in the amount of

$$[P(1) - P(0)] \times \text{Face value of contract},$$

where $P(1)$ is the settlement price at the end of the trading day. The next business day the cash flow to your account will be

$$[P(2) - P(1)] \times \text{Face value of contract},$$

where $P(2)$ is the next day's settlement price. If you go short, the cash flows are the reverse of those just shown. For example, suppose a £62,500 futures contract is opened during Day 1 at a negotiated price of $1.4500/£ and the settlement prices at the end of Day 1 and Day 2 are

Opening price	$1.4500/£
Settlement price, Day 1	$1.4460/£
Settlement price, Day 2	$1.4510/£,

then the respective cash flows for long and short positions in a single contract opened at $1.4500/£ are

Long	Short
($1.4460/£ − $1.4500/£) × £62,500 = − $250	+ $250
($1.4510/£ − $1.4460/£) × £62,500 = + $312.50	− $312.50

On Day 1, the long side will lose $250 while the short side will gain $250 on each contract. On Day 2, the long position gains $312.50 and the short position loses $312.50 on each contract.

It is important to realize that these cash flows take place every business day. If you win money, you can withdraw your winnings immediately. If you lose, you pay up immediately. But how can you be sure that the loser will pay up immediately, or even at all? The way this is taken care of is that the brokerage firm will require a certain amount of cash to be deposited with it as a security bond. The brokerage firm will in turn post margin with a *clearing house,* which will then guarantee both sides of the futures contract against default by the other party. The amount per contract you have to deposit with the broker is called *margin.* If the money won on a particular day leaves the account balance above the required margin, the surplus cash can be withdrawn immediately. If the money lost leaves the account balance below the required margin, more cash must be added. Margin requirements and the clearing house are discussed more fully later.

THE IMM

The most important place where FX futures contracts are traded is at the International Money Market (IMM) of the Chicago Mercantile Exchange. At this and other exchanges FX futures contracts are for standardized foreign currency amounts, terminate at standardized times (last trade dates), and have minimum allowable price moves (called "ticks") between trades. The available contracts in 1990 were as follows:

Contract	Face amount	Minimum price move	
British pound	62,500	$.0002	($12.50)
Deutschemark	125,000	$.0001	($12.50)
Swiss franc	125,000	$.0001	($12.50)
Japanese yen	12,500,000	.0001¢	($12.50)
Canadian dollar	100,000	$.0001	($10.00)
French franc	250,000	.005¢	($12.50)
Australian dollar	100,000	$.0001	($10.00)
ECU	125,000	$.0001	($12.50)

For some types of futures contracts there are also maximum allowable daily price movements ("limit moves") up or down from the previous day's settlement price. The IMM removed all daily price limits on currency futures in February 1985, but later reinstated them.

FX futures prices at the IMM are quoted in American terms—the U.S. dollar price of a unit of foreign exchange. Contracts are traded on a standard three-month cycle of March, June, September, and December. The month during which a contract expires is referred to as the *spot month.*

The process of actually turning over a foreign currency bank deposit in return for a dollar deposit is referred to as delivery. Delivery takes place on the third Wednesday of the spot month at the IMM or, if that is not a business day, the next business day. Trading in a contract ends two business days prior to the delivery day. If a futures bet is still in effect at the end of trading on the last trade date, then the long side of the FX futures contract has acquired the obligation to pay U.S. dollars for the face amount of foreign currency involved in the contract, at an exchange rate given by the last trading day's settlement price. The short side has the obligation to deliver the amount of foreign currency specified in the contract. The transfer of U.S. dollars for foreign currency (delivery) between the long and short positions then takes place two days later on the delivery date, according to procedures set by the exchange.

REGULATION AND GUARANTEES

Futures trading at the IMM and elsewhere in the United States is regulated by the Commodities Futures Trading Commission (CFTC), a regulatory body created by Congress in 1974. The CFTC assigns legal constraints on the type of business one may conduct. Futures commission merchants (who accept margin payments) and other associated persons (who do not) are authorized to solicit and accept orders from the public. Futures commission merchants may or may not be members of a clearinghouse. Clearing members are those exchange members who hold accounts at a clearinghouse. The clearinghouse guarantees both the long and short sides of a futures contract against the risk of default by the opposite party. The clearinghouse, in effect, takes the short side of every long futures position and the long side of every short futures position. This guarantee, however, applies only to futures contracts made by customers of clearing member firms, and then only after transactions have been registered and confirmed by the clearinghouse and margin on the transactions has been received from clearing members. Futures commission merchants who are not clearing members must have their trades cleared by a clearing member. Such a nonmember firm will then have its own contracts guaranteed by the clearinghouse (since the firm is a customer of a clearing member). But customers of the nonclearing member firm will still face default risk.

A customer's order is transmitted to the exchange floor by the futures commission merchant, who acts as the customer's agent. There a floor broker—an exchange member who acts as agent for the clearinghouse—will attempt to complete the trade by open outcry in the trading pit. The trade may be completed either with another floor broker or with a floor trader. A floor trader is an exchange member or nominee who trades for his or her own account. Floor traders may take speculative futures positions, or they may act as marketmakers, similar to marketmakers in the interbank FX market; this is discussed more fully later. Floor traders must have their trades cleared by a futures commission merchant who is a clearing member. Finally, there is a category of *broker-traders* or dual traders who trade both for their own and for customer accounts.

MARGIN REQUIREMENTS

The amount of margin required on an FX futures contract is related to the volatility of price movement of the underlying currency, and hence to the probability distribution of daily losses or gains. Margin requirements on the

Swiss franc, whose price is highly variable with respect to the U.S. dollar, are greater than margin requirements on the Canadian dollar, whose U.S. dollar price shows lower variability. Margins are negotiable, and therefore will vary from broker to broker. However, there is a *minimum margin* for each contract that will hold throughout the market, a minimum given by the margin the clearinghouse charges clearing members. Clearing members are required to set margins for their customers that are not less than the margins the clearing members have to hold with the clearinghouse. There is nothing, however, to prevent clearing members as well as brokerage firms (futures commission merchants) who are not clearing members from requiring higher margins, and most of them do so.

In the United States, a distinction is made between *initial* margin, which is the amount of money that must be deposited when a contract is opened, and *maintenance* margin, which is the minimum level to which the margin is allowed to fall (if there are losses after opening the contract) before additional money must be added to the account. If the balance in the account falls below the maintenance level, additional money called *variation margin* must be added to the account to restore the account balance to the initial margin level. Initial and maintenance margin required in July 1990 for IMM contracts by one brokerage firm were as follows:

Contract	Initial	Maintenance
British pound	$2800	$2100
Deutschemark	$1800	$1400
Japanese yen	$2700	$2000
Swiss franc	$2700	$2000
Canadian dollar	$1000	$ 800
Australian dollar	$2000	$1500

Because price movements on currency futures contracts are sometimes more volatile during spot months, margin requirements may go up. (For the currencies just listed, however, the required margins as of July 1990 for the brokerage firm were the same during spot months.) Margin requirements will similarly be altered if general market conditions change.

To the extent margin is posted in cash, there is an opportunity cost involved, because the cash could otherwise be held in the form of an interest-bearing asset. Generally, in the United States, initial margin can be posted in the form of interest-bearing obligations of the federal government or letters of credit issued by an approved bank. Hence there need be no interest lost on initial margin deposited with a futures commission merchant. However, variation margin must usually be paid in cash. Remember that people with positive cash flows (the winning side of the daily price bets) will generally be withdrawing their cash to put it into interest-bearing accounts (or spend it on something suitable). Hence if the clearing firm did not require the losers to pay up in cash, the firm would have to pay the winners from its own cash holdings.

Actually, it is slightly more complicated than the preceding paragraph suggests. Generally only a part of initial margin can be posted in the form of Treasury bills. One firm, for example, will allow 90 percent margin in the form of T-bills and 10 percent in cash, if the T-bills have face values totaling $25,000 or more, but for smaller face amounts, 40 percent of the initial margin must be posted in cash. Then if the cash position falls below the initial level, a "T-bill call" results, and the customer has three days to restore the cash to the initial level. If the cash level falls below zero, then a "cash call" ensues and the initial cash margin level must be restored the same day.

As an additional transaction cost to the public user of the futures markets, there is a brokerage fee associated with each futures contract. Such fees are usually quoted round turn, covering both the opening and the closing of a futures position. The round turn commission is charged at the time the contract is closed. As of July 1990, a round turn commission for public customers was typically about $30 per futures contract at discount brokerage firms.

FUTURES CONTRACTS COMPARED TO FORWARD CONTRACTS

There are a number of differences between a *forward* contract as used in the interbank market for foreign exchange and a *futures* contract as traded on exchanges like the IMM. The most important difference is the daily cash flows ("marking to market") that take place on a futures contract. In a forward contract, by contrast, no money will change hands until the contract expires. Then, on expiration day, currencies will be traded at the prearranged price, the forward price. The absence of daily cash flows in a forward contract is an important economic distinction.

The change in value of a futures contract represents today's cash flow, while the change in value of a forward contract represents a cash flow that will take place at some date in the future. Thus the two values can be compared only after an interest adjustment.

EXAMPLE 5.1

Today the price of September SF futures goes from $.7107/SF to $.7150/SF. Meanwhile, the price of a two-month ($T=61$ days) forward contract goes from $.7104/SF to $.7145/SF. What are the relative value changes in the two cases?

Assume the two-month euro-SF rate is 9.1875%. The futures price change represents today's cash flow, so the change in present value is

$$\Delta V = (\$.7150/SF - \$.7107/SF) \times \text{(contract size)}.$$

The forward price represents a cash flow that will take place in 61 days, so the change in present value is

$$\Delta V = \frac{1}{1 + .091875(61/360)} (\$.7150/SF - \$.7107/SF) \times \text{(contract size)}.$$

The reader should not be misled, however, into thinking that real-world forward contracts never involve any cash flow prior to maturity. There is potential credit risk in the corporate and the interbank market just like there is in the futures market. If a bank enters into a forward contract (via a swap) with another marketmaking bank, this credit risk may be considered small enough for nothing more to be involved in the forward contract than the verbal agreement on price. But if a corporation is involved, the corporation's line of credit at the bank will usually be reduced by the amount of the forward contract, provided the corporation has such a line of credit. If the company does not have a line of credit, usually a deposit of about 5 percent of the amount of the forward contract must be made with the bank. This insures the bank against the loss that might be incurred if the company defaulted on the forward contract and the bank had to replace it at a less attractive exchange rate.

Leaving aside these minor qualifications, however, it is easy to see intuitively why a simple purchase of a futures contract is different from a simple purchase of a forward contract. Suppose you buy September British pound futures for $1.50 per pound. You have decided to take delivery on the contract, so on the third Wednesday in September you will receive £62,500 for which you will have to pay a dollar price determined by the settlement price on the expiration day (which will occur two business days prior to the third Wednesday). During the meantime, the dollar price of the pound may have gone up or it may have gone down. In either case, your positive or negative cash flow will be such that it just offsets any change in the pound price from $1.50. For example, if the price has gone to $1.60, you have to pay $0.10 more for each pound than the $1.50 at which you opened the contract. However, you will have made $0.10 net on your futures bet because you were long the contract; the $0.10 offsets the difference between $1.50 and $1.60. Similarly, if the price had gone to $1.40, you would get the pounds at a cheaper price of $1.40, but in the meantime you will have lost $0.10 per pound on futures because you were long the contract and the price went down. So the net cost is still $1.50 per pound. However, *because the time pattern of cash flows was different in the two cases, your opportunity cost was different*. In the first case, you had generally positive cash flows. These cash flows could have been reinvested and earned interest. In the second case, you had negative cash flows. You had to forego interest by putting up more variation margin during the life of the contract. In the first case, you earned interest on the $0.10/£ positive cash flow, while in the second case you lost interest on the $0.10/£ negative cash flow. The cash flow in the first case is an *average* positive cash flow of $0.05 per pound, so that the dollar amount of interest earned would be about $0.05 per pound multiplied by the rate of interest and by the face amount of the contract. For example, for a £62,500 contract and 12 percent interest for one year, the interest earned would be roughly

$$(£62,500) \ (\$.05/£) \ (.12) = \$375.$$

A forward contract would not have earned this amount of interest. In the second case, the negative cash flow on the futures contract would entail a loss of interest. Again, this loss would not be present in a forward contract.

The above example shows an intrinsic difference between forwards and futures to the purchaser of a contract. It does not automatically follow from that discussion, however, that forwards and futures will have different *prices*. Nevertheless, it can be shown as a theoretical proposition that futures prices ought in general to be different from forward prices. This difference in prices should result from the random unpredictable behavior of interest rates. The behavior of interest rates is crucial, for it can also be shown as a theoretical proposition that *if interest rates were nonstochastic, then the forward price and the futures price should be equal*. That is, if interest rates were either constant or else predictable with certainty, there exists an arbitrage strategy that would yield the arbitrager a sure profit if the market were quoting a particular futures price differently from the equivalent forward price. Hence the cash flow distinction between forwards and futures would not be sufficient by itself to make their prices differ. [This arbitrage strategy is not important for our purposes, so will not be covered here, but a description can be found in Cox, Ingersoll, and Ross (1981).] But it can be shown, conversely, that when interest rates are stochastic (as they are in the real world), forward and futures prices should differ by an amount whose magnitude depends on the covariance between futures price movements and interest rate movements.

If the covariance between spot prices of an asset and default-free discount bonds is less (greater) than the variance of bond prices, then futures prices will be greater (less) than forward prices. Is this covariance important in practice for FX futures and FX forwards? Apparently not. For the few currencies in which futures markets exist, FX futures prices rarely differ from FX forward prices by an amount even as large as twice the bid/asked spread in the inter-bank forward market. [See Cornell and Reinganum (1981).]

There are a number of other more obvious, though less important differences between FX forward contracts and FX futures contracts. *Forward* contracts are usually traded in standardized amounts equivalent to $1 or $2 or $3 million. However, any amount is negotiable. *Futures* contracts traded on an exchange are completely standardized, so it is only possible to take a position in the futures market that is a multiple of the size of one standardized contract. *Forward* contracts are mostly traded for maturities of one week, two weeks, and one through twelve months. But again, any maturity can be negotiated, and major banks will give quotations out to five years for the major currencies. *Futures* contracts expire at standardized intervals. In practice, for currency futures that means in March, June, September, and December at the IMM. What this implies is that you will seldom, if ever, use the futures market as a way of actually acquiring or selling foreign exchange, since you could only do so on four dates during the year. The real purpose of futures is for hedging and speculation.

Forward contracts are traded over the counter: Banks and brokers can be located anywhere and deal with each other over the phone. FX futures are traded on the market floor of the IMM, the Tokyo International Financial Futures Exchange (TIFFE), the Sydney Futures Exchange, the New Zealand Futures Exchange, the MidAmerica Commodities Exchange, the New York Cotton Exchange (which trades a U.S. Dollar Index, as well as an ECU/U.S. dollar contract), the Stockholm Options Market, and the Singapore International Monetary Exchange (SIMEX).

Forward contracts are contracts made directly between two parties, and there is no secondary market. To reverse a forward position, you would have to make a separate additional forward contract. Unless this happens to be with the same bank, the first contract will not kill the second: You will still have two contracts to deal with, and there may be credit risk on both contracts. *Futures* contracts are netted out through a clearinghouse, so that the clearinghouse stands on the other side of every contract cleared through it. Moreover, as long as you are dealing through a single exchange, you are only responsible for *net* positions. If you go long a futures contract and then go short the same contract, the second cancels the first. (The IMM and SIMEX have, in addition, an arrangement that allows one to net a futures position between the two exchanges.)

Forward contracts have no daily price limit. That is, that forward contracts were traded at $1.50 yesterday does not imply anything about today's price, which could differ from $1.50 by an arbitrarily large amount. *Futures* contracts, as explained previously, may have daily price limits set by the exchange. *Forward* contracts in the interbank market have a delivery rate of about 90 percent. In the futures market, delivery is made or taken on less than 5 percent of FX contracts. The forward market is self-regulated. Forward contracts are subject, however, to the ordinary laws of contracts and taxation. In the United States, futures trading is regulated by the Commodity Futures Trading Commission.

EXCHANGE TRADING AND MARKETMAKING

Orders to buy or sell futures contracts take the form of either limit orders—orders to buy or sell at prestated prices—or market orders—orders to buy at the prevailing level of offers in the trading pit or to sell at the prevailing level of bids. An example of a limit bid order might be "Buy 2 DM futures at $.5323/DM or lower." An example of a market order might be "Buy 2 DM futures at the market." The market order would then be filled with the purchase of 2 DM futures contracts at the lowest available offered price prevailing in the trading pit. Limit orders provide liquidity to the market because they enable others to take the opposite side of the futures contract at the price embodied in the limit order. Market orders, by contrast, consume liquidity. Market orders to sell will fill some of the limit bid orders existing in the pit, while market orders to buy will fill some of the existing limit offer orders.

Futures trading is governed by a number of rules intended to ensure that orders will be executed in such a fashion as to produce a single market price determined on the basis of competition among floor brokers and traders. All bids and offers must be announced publicly. The highest bid price takes precedence over all other bid prices, and the lowest offer price takes precedence over all other offered prices. These rules are intended to ensure that the sale of a futures contract will take place at the highest price currently bid, while the purchase of a futures contract will take place at the lowest price currently offered.

As a result, the spectrum of prices at which trades simultaneously take place in the interbank FX market is mostly eliminated in the FX futures market. In addition, since most major banks also deal in the FX futures market and are able continually to observe FX futures prices, the existence of a single price quotation in the futures market acts as a common information variable that helps standardize price quotations in the interbank markets for spot and forward exchange. It was estimated that in 1983 roughly one-tenth of total FX dealing by New York banks involved the IMM (Andrews, 1984).

Like the interbank market, the futures market has marketmakers and bid/asked spreads. Floor traders may, at their option, provide marketmaking services by quoting two-way prices. Traders who perform these services are called "scalpers." By contrast to the interbank market, where an FX market-maker is in continuous contact only with a limited number of other market participants, all marketmaking in the futures markets is concentrated in the trading pit. Since only one price may prevail in the market at any one time, a marketmaker will be constantly tempted to raise his or her bid price above that of other marketmakers, or to lower his or her offered price, in order to capture more business. As a result it is difficult to determine the actual size of the effective bid/offered spread (the spread at which trades actually take place). But the effective spread will generally be smaller than the average bid/offered spread quoted by marketmakers.

□

Roll (1984) has suggested the following measure of the effective bid/asked spread in an efficient market. Let $cov[\Delta Z, \Delta Z(-1)]$ represent the average covariance of successive price changes on a futures contract (the "first order serial covariance" in statistical terminology). These successive price changes have a negative correlation because of trading across the bid/asked spread. This fact was used by Roll to derive a measure of the effective spread ("spr"), which in percentage terms is

$$\text{spr} = 200\sqrt{-cov[\Delta Z, \Delta Z(-1)]}. \qquad\blacksquare$$

As in the interbank market, marketmakers quote a bid/asked spread around an equilibrium market value. As supply and demand conditions change, the market equilibrium futures price changes. Marketmakers who are not inter-ested in taking positions on the direction of futures price movements must be adroit in adjusting their bid and offered price so as to buy and sell equal numbers of futures contracts and to keep their net futures positions as close to zero as possible. In a study of scalper behavior on the New York Futures Exchange, Silber (1984) found that a representative scalper held a net long or short futures position for an average time of less than two minutes. In addition, he found that the net profit per traded contract was significantly less than the value of the bid/asked spread. That is, the effective bid/asked spread was much smaller than the quoted spread.

HEDGING WITH FUTURES

The idea of hedging with futures is simple. You have a fixed position in an underlying asset or liability. For example, you have accounts receivable de-nominated in British pounds. There is exchange risk: The dollar value of the accounts receivable will drop if the British pound loses value with respect to the dollar. To hedge this risk, you take out a side bet in the futures market. *The futures bet must be chosen in such a way that whenever the underlying asset loses value, the futures bet generates a positive cash flow.* Because you have an underlying *long* position in pounds, to offset you should go *short* pound futures. (If you had an underlying short position in pounds, then to offset you would go long pound futures.) If the pound loses value in dollar terms, you will make money on your short futures position, which will offset the loss in value of your accounts receivable.

By the same criterion, if the value of the pound increases in dollar terms, the short futures position will generate a cash flow loss, which will offset the gain in value of your accounts receivable. So by hedging you avoid exchange rate loss, but also give up the possibility of exchange rate gain. This is the nature of hedging. It assumes you would prefer $10 million for sure rather than a fifty-fifty bet that would give you $20 million with probability .5 and $0 with probability .5. Restated, it assumes you are (or your company is) risk-averse. (By definition, risk aversion is the preference for a sure amount of wealth over a bet involving the same mathematical expectation. Hence risk aversion is one justification for hedging. A different justification for hedging in terms of ruin probabilities is given at the end of this chapter. This alternative interpretation relies on the practical assumption of limited capital and does not require risk aversion in order for hedging to be a desirable activity.)

In order to be hedged perfectly in dollar (or local currency) terms, the value of the futures position must change one-for-one (but with the opposite sign) with the value of the underlying position being hedged. Assuming that the amount of foreign currency involved in your futures bet exactly matches the amount of foreign currency involved in the underlying position, a perfect hedge requires that the futures price move one-for-one with the spot or cash price of the underlying currency.

To see why, let ΔS represent the change in the spot dollar (or local currency) price of foreign exchange, while ΔZ represents the change in the futures price. Let the total portfolio consist of one unit of cash or spot foreign currency held long that is hedged with one unit of foreign currency futures held short. The change in the value of the total portfolio, ΔV, can then be represented as

$$\Delta V = \Delta S - \Delta Z.$$

As long as $\Delta S = \Delta Z$ (the change in the spot price equals the change in the futures price), we have $\Delta V = 0$ (no change in total portfolio value). The same would obviously also be true for a portfolio of arbitrary size, or for a short spot position hedged with a long position in futures.

The difference between the spot or cash price and the futures price is called the basis. That is,

Basis = Spot price − Futures price = $S - Z$.

If the movement in the spot price and the futures price is one-for-one, the basis is constant. When you hedge with futures, there is always a risk that the movement in the spot and futures prices will not be one-for-one. This is referred to as *basis risk*. Hedging with futures will never eliminate exchange risk entirely. There will always be basis risk. Basis risk, however, is normally much smaller than would be the open position without the futures bet.

EXAMPLE 5.2

You are long a £62,500 asset and you go short one futures contract to offset this. The spot rate is $1.1545/£, and you go short at a futures price of $1.1620/£. One month later the spot price is $1.1350 and the futures price is $1.1460. The basis has changed, so the hedge has not been perfect.

	Spot Price	Basis	Futures Price
Beginning price	$1.1545	−.0075	$1.1620
One month later	$1.1350	−.0110	$1.1460

Loss in value of   Cash flow from futures
   spot asset: $1218.75   contract: $1000

The net loss is

$1218.75 − $1000 = $218.75.

An alternative way to do the calculation is to observe that the change in the basis is

−.0110 − (−.0075) = −.0035.

This yields a net cash flow of

−$.0035/£(£62,500) = −$218.75.

The hedge was not perfect, but the loss of $218.75 was much smaller than the unhedged loss of $1218.75.

In terms of the notation just used, here we have

$$\Delta S = \$1.1350 - \$1.1545 = -\$.0195$$

while

$$\Delta Z = \$1.1460 - \$1.1620 = -\$.0160.$$

Thus

$$\Delta V = \Delta S - \Delta Z = (-\$.0195) - (-\$.0160) = -\$.0035.$$

The change in portfolio value per foreign currency unit is −$.0035. The total change is

$$62,500(-\$.0035) = -\$218.75.$$

It should be clear from this example that *the ability to set up a good hedge depends on finding a futures contract whose price movement has a high degree of correlation with the underlying asset being hedged.* If the current time is February and you are hedging spot pounds with March pound futures, the movement in the two prices should be very close. But if the current time is February and you are hedging spot Danish krone with March deutschemark futures (an example of cross-hedging), there will be more risk involved because the correlation between price movements in spot krone and March DM futures will not be as high as the correlation between price movements in spot pounds and March pound futures.

In practice, no futures hedge is perfect. There is always some risk that the actual value of a position hedged with futures will change with movements in the spot exchange rate. However, the amount of risk—in the sense of the variation in dollar (or local currency) value of the underlying position—can usually be reduced with an appropriately chosen futures hedge.

☐

There is a simple way to estimate the risk on a position that is hedged with an equal amount of currency futures. Recall from statistics that for two random variables x and y, the variance ("var") of $u = x - y$ is

$$\text{var}(u) = \text{var}(x) + \text{var}(y) - 2\,\text{cov}(x,y)$$

where $\text{cov}(x,y)$ denotes the covariance of x and y. Let $x = \Delta S$ represent the change in the dollar (or local currency) spot or cash price of one unit of foreign currency, while $y = \Delta Z$ represents the change in price of one unit of foreign currency futures. The risk of the hedged position compared to the unhedged underlying position can be gotten by comparing the square root of var($u = \Delta V$) to the square root of var(x):

$$\text{Hedged risk as \% open risk} = \sqrt{\frac{\text{var}(u)}{\text{var}(x)}}\ 100.$$

EXAMPLE 5.3

Suppose that x and y have the same variance and a correlation ("corr") of .95. Then, since $\text{cov}(x,y) = \text{corr}(x,y)\,\sqrt{\text{var}(x)}\,\sqrt{\text{var}(y)} = .95\,\sqrt{\text{var}(x)}\,\sqrt{\text{var}(x)}$, we get that

$$\text{var}(u) = \text{var}(x) + \text{var}(x) - 2(.95)\,\sqrt{\text{var}(x)}\,\sqrt{\text{var}(x)} = .1\,\text{var}(x).$$

Therefore

$$\text{Hedged risk as \% open risk} = \sqrt{\frac{.1\,\text{var}(x)}{\text{var}(x)}}\ 100 = 31.6\%.$$

That is, given a correlation of .95 between changes in the futures price and changes in the spot price, and assuming that the two price changes have equal variance, hedging a currency position with an equal amount of currency futures will result in a position with risk reduced to 31.6 percent of its original value.

■

The hedging procedure considered thus far has involved the matching of a currency asset or liability with an offsetting futures position of equal currency amount. The hedge assumed an expected (though not a certain) one-for-one price movement between spot prices and futures prices. For some practical purposes this approximation will suffice. In general, however, movements in spot and futures prices cannot be expected to be one-for-one even if the spot position and futures hedge involve the same currency. The amount of the futures hedge should be adjusted to compensate for this fact. This point is explored in the following two sections.

THE RELATION OF FUTURES PRICES TO SPOT (CASH) PRICES

Previously we noted that if interest rates were nonstochastic there should be no difference between futures and forward prices. And even though interest rates are in fact stochastic, the empirical evidence cited indicated little difference between FX forward prices and FX futures prices. In Chapter 4, we saw that forward exchange rates were related to spot exchange rates by the interest parity theorem, where the relevant interest rates were eurocurrency rates. This implies, then, that FX futures prices are related to spot (or cash) prices by interest parity.

Let the price of a futures contract at time t for delivery at time $t + T$ be denoted $Z(t,T)$. If, as an empirical matter, FX futures prices do not differ materially from FX forward prices, we then have by the interest parity condition (ignoring bid/asked spreads):

$$Z(t,T) = b \ S(t)$$

where

$$b = \frac{1 + i(T/360)}{1 + i^*(T/360)}.$$

Note that as $T \to 0$ (the contract matures), we have $b \to 1$, and thus $Z(t,T) \to S(t)$. That is, the futures price converges to the spot price at maturity. This is as it should be. On the final trading day for an FX futures contract, for example, one has two alternative ways to get foreign exchange: Buy spot foreign exchange in the interbank market or buy an FX futures contract and take delivery. In either case, the foreign exchange will actually be delivered two days later. Thus, on the final trading day, simple arbitrage between the spot and futures markets will ensure that the prices are the same on that day.

This fact should be kept in mind in making hedging decisions. Price movements between the spot rate and the futures rate cannot be the same over the *entire* life of the contract if the prices themselves are not the same when a position is opened. For example, if spot DM is $.3552/DM and the December DM futures price is $.3576/DM when a position is opened, and if the spot (and futures) price on the last day of trading in December is $.3665/DM, the spot price will have moved by

$$\$.3665 - \$.3552 = \$.0113,$$

while the futures price will have moved by

$$\$.3665 - \$.3576 = \$.0089.$$

The relation between movements in the futures price and movements in the spot price prior to maturity is given in the equation above by b, which is referred to as the futures delta. The delta b can be greater than, or less than, 1. If b is greater than 1, the futures price will move more than the spot price.

Hence, the hedge should involve a smaller amount of currency futures than the actual amount of underlying currency being hedged. If b is less than 1, the futures price moves less than the spot price, so a greater amount of currency futures is needed to form the hedge. It is easy to see that for each unit of an underlying currency you are long, you should go short $1/b$ units in futures of the same currency. For each currency unit you are short, you should go long $1/b$ units in futures of the same currency.

To see why this is true, first note that by interest parity

$$\Delta Z(t,T) = b\Delta S(t).$$

If you are long one unit spot and short $1/b$ futures, your position can be represented as

$$S(t) - (1/b) Z(t,T).$$

So for a change in the spot rate, the change in the value of your position will be

$$\Delta S(t) - (1/b) \Delta Z(t,T) = \Delta S(t) - (1/b) b\Delta S(t) = 0,$$

provided that the interest parity relation holds perfectly.

Note, however, that even if we assume that interest parity holds perfectly, the amount of the hedge must be adjusted over time, because b, the futures delta, is a function of time. As the contract matures, $b \rightarrow 1$, a process referred to in the futures markets as *convergence*. As contracts mature, the futures price converges to the spot price. Simultaneously, the futures hedge must be continually adjusted because the futures delta is changing.

EXAMPLE 5.4

Suppose the spot rate is $.3645/DM, while the futures price is $.3733. The futures delta in this case is $b = 1.024$, indicating that you should go short $1/b = .9764$ in DM futures for each DM1 in the underlying position being hedged. Of course, you cannot go long or short a piece of a futures contract. However, if you are hedging a long position of DM5,000,000, which is equivalent to 40 IMM futures contracts $(40 \times DM125,000 = DM5,000,000)$, this calculation indicates you should go short 39 IMM DM futures contracts, as $(40)(.9764) \cong 39$.

□

CALCULATING THE RISK IN A DELTA HEDGE

When the futures contract is denominated in the same currency as the asset being hedged, we can use interest parity to get the futures delta b. For cross-hedging, such as a U.S. dollar/Danish krone position being hedged with U.S. dollar/DM futures, the concept of the futures delta is still meaningful. For cross-hedging, we similarly define the futures delta as a number b that gives the best linear relationship between changes in the spot price and changes in the futures price:

$$\Delta Z = b \Delta S.$$

For a cross-hedge, however, the futures delta b is not determined by interest parity. Consequently, b must be estimated using historical data.

In either case—whether b is derived from interest parity or from historical data—the futures hedge will not be perfect. How can you estimate the risk or variance of a delta hedge?

First, suppose that you use historical data to estimate the futures delta by means of a simple regression equation. Such an equation might involve regressing y and on x, where y is measured by weekly changes in the futures price, and x is measured as weekly changes in the spot price of the underlying asset being hedged. Assuming x and y have zero means, we can write the regression equation as

$$y = b\,x + e,$$

where b is the futures delta being estimated, and e is an error term. From statistics, we know that the least-squares estimate of b, $\hat{b}$, will have the value $\hat{b} = \text{cov}(x,y)/\text{var}(x)$. For example, we might have $\hat{b} = .8$. Given $\hat{b}$, the hedging rule is the same as above: For each unit of currency asset held long, sell short $1/\hat{b}$ units of currency futures. For each change x in the spot or cash price, you would then expect to see a change $\hat{b}\,x + \hat{e}$ in the futures price, where $\hat{e}$ results from the fact that your equation will not hold exactly. The expected value of $\hat{e}$ should be zero. Then, as prices change, the change u in the value of your portfolio, for each unit of foreign currency hedged with futures, would be

$$
\begin{aligned}
u &= x - (1/\hat{b})\,y \\
&= x - (1/\hat{b})(\hat{b}\,x + \hat{e}) \\
&= -(1/\hat{b})\hat{e}.
\end{aligned}
$$

Thus if the error term $\hat{e}$ is zero, the change in the value of your portfolio is zero, and you are perfectly hedged. However, the error term will in general not be zero. The variance of the portfolio position can be easily calculated. It is

$$\frac{\text{var}(\hat{e})}{\hat{b}^2}$$

so that the hedged risk as a proportion of open risk is

$$\text{Hedged risk as \% open risk} = \sqrt{\frac{\text{var}(\hat{e})}{\hat{b}^2\,\text{var}(x)}}\; 100.$$

EXAMPLE 5.5

Dutch guilders are being hedged using DM futures. Let x be weekly changes in the spot dollar price of the Dutch guilder, and let y be weekly changes in the dollar price of DM futures (for a particular delivery date). Suppose the regression equation gave the result

$$y = 1.26x.$$

This equation implies that for each unit of Dutch guilders held long, one should be short $1/1.26 = .79$ units of DM in futures. The risk of the hedged position depends on var(x) and on var(e). The future values of $\hat{e}$ cannot now be known, but their variance can be estimated from the variance of the residuals in the regression. For example, suppose that in the data sample used to estimate the above equation, var(x) = 6.28, while var(e) = 1.03. Then the hedged risk as a percentage of the unhedged risk can be estimated as

$$100 \times \sqrt{1.03/[(1.26)^2(6.28)]} = 32.14\%.$$

This estimate of the reduction in risk relies, of course, on the estimate of b, which is derived on the basis of past history. It will not be a reliable guide if historical relationships change in a material way.

■

A final qualification that should be made is that the above risk calculations assume you can buy futures in arbitrary amounts. But, as noted previously, you have to use futures in minimum amounts of £62,500, DM125,000, and the like. Thus the hedged risk in the calculation just shown only applies to the portion of your portfolio that can be matched with multiples of standardized futures contract amounts. Anything left over is unhedged and faces ordinary foreign exchange risk.

EXCHANGE FOR PHYSICALS (EFP)

The EFP market is a market for trading futures contracts outside exchange hours. Prices for FX futures in the EFP market are determined by interest parity from the spot market, which trades almost continuously. Such trading is allowed in the United States by Section 4c(a) of the Commodity Exchange Act. Conceptually, an EFP involves (1) the long and short sides of a futures contract closing out their respective positions at an agreed price, and (2) simultaneously making the reverse transaction in the spot (physical) market. That is, each party does one side of a spot/futures swap. As noted in Chapter 4, forward exchange is traded this way in the interbank market. But here the swap involves a futures contract instead of a forward contract. The previously long side of the futures contract goes short (leaving a net futures position of zero) and buys spot. The previously short side of the futures contract goes long (leaving a net futures position of zero) and sells spot.

Any futures broker can arrange for such trades. Obviously if two parties can do an EFP, it is also possible for three parties. Party A, a customer of a futures commission merchant (party B), sells futures to B and (unknown to A) buys spot from B. At this point, B has bought futures and sold spot. Then B sells futures to party C, also a customer, and (unknown to C) buys spot from C. The spot sale and purchase offset, at some fictitious price, leaving B flat in the spot market. As a marketmaker, B earns the difference between the two futures prices in the transactions with A and C. The key point here is that the customer doesn't have to engage in a spot transaction in order to offset a futures contract in the EFP market.

FX RISK MANAGEMENT AND THE GAMBLER'S RUIN PROBLEM

Many people assume that the futures price represents a fair bet. That is, they assume that the probability of an upward movement in the futures price is equal to the probability of a downward movement, and hence the mathematical expectation of a gain or loss is zero. They use the analogy of flipping a fair coin. If you bet $1 on the outcome of the flip, the probability of your winning $1 is one-half, while the probability of losing $1 is also one-half. Your expected gain or loss is zero. For the same reason, they conclude, futures gains and futures losses will tend to offset each other in the long run.

There is a hidden fallacy in such reasoning. Taking open positions in foreign exchange (whether in the futures market or just in accounts payable) is not analogous to a single flip of a coin. Rather, the correct analogy is that of a *repeated series of coin flips with a stochastic termination point*. Why? Because of limited capital. Suppose you are flipping a coin with a friend and betting $1 on the outcome of each flip. At some point either you or your friend will have a run of bad luck and will lose several dollars in succession. If one player has run out of money, the game will come to an end. The same is true in the futures market. If you have a string of losses on a futures position, you will have to post more margin. If at some point you cannot post the required margin, you will have to close out the contract. You are forced out of the game, and thus you cannot win back what you lost. In a similar way in 1974, Franklin National and Bankhaus I. D. Herstatt had a string of losses on their interbank foreign exchange positions. They did not break even in the long run because there was no long run. They went broke in the intermediate run. This phenomenon is referred to in probability theory as the gambler's ruin problem [see Feller (1968), chap. 14].

The gambler's ruin problem will be explored further in Chapter 7, where we will see that even if an FX futures price represented a "fair" bet when viewed as a single flip of the coin, when viewed as a series of flips with a stochastic ending point the odds are different. The probabilities of the game then depend on the relative amounts of capital held by the different players. This fact is important for FX risk management in general. Any company with foreign currency exposure is in a position to make or lose money when the exchange rate moves. Even if the probability of an upward move in the exchange rate were equal to the probability of a downward move, it would not generally be true that a company will in the long run make neither exchange rate gains nor exchange rate losses. Instead, because the company has limited capital, the odds are stacked against it if it plays against the market. Thus, if any company has a large foreign currency exposure, the existence of a significant ruin probability would constitute a strong argument for hedging away at least some portion of the risk.

MARGIN MANAGEMENT

Cash flows on futures contracts take place daily but the same may not be true for the underlying asset being hedged. A practical problem in cash management involves the amount to be deposited to meet daily variation margin calls. A manager may want to deposit the minimum necessary cash subject to a given small probability the cash will be exhausted over some time horizon.

The probability P of exhaustion (using up all the cash on deposit) may be calculated as

$$P = 2[1 - N(w)], \text{ where}$$

$$w = D/(V \times K \times \sqrt{T}).$$

In this formula, D is the amount of cash on deposit for each futures contract ($D \geq 0$). V is the standard deviation of daily changes (ΔZ) in the price of the futures contract. V is multiplied by K, the value of 1 futures contract, in order to translate the standard deviation into monetary terms. The result is then multiplied by $\sqrt{T}$, where T is the number of trading days over which the calculation is made. That is, the formula expresses the amount of cash D in terms of the number of "betting units" given by $V \times K \times \sqrt{T}$. Assuming daily price changes have a normal distribution leads to the formula just shown, where $N(.)$ is the cumulative distribution function for a standardized normal variant.

EXAMPLE 5.6

A manager with a position in DM futures wants to keep enough cash on hand so as to avoid with 95 percent probability posting additional variation margin more often than once a week (five trading days). The standard deviation of daily U.S. dollar price changes in the DM future is $V = .0040$, and the value of one DM futures contract at an assumed spot rate of $1/DM is ($1)(125,000) = $125,000$. Hence

$$w = D/(.0040 \times 125,000 \times \sqrt{5}) = D/1118.$$

The manager wants to choose D such that exhaustion occurs not more than 5 percent of the time, so $P = 1 - .95 = .05$. Hence w must be determined such that

$$.05 = 2[1 - N(w)].$$

Therefore $N(w) = .975$. From a normal distribution table we observe that

$$w = 1.96.$$

Hence $D/1118 = 1.96$ or $D = \$2191$. The manager should keep about $2191 deposited for each DM futures contract to meet variation margin calls, in addition to the sums of cash or securities or letters of credit already on deposit as maintenance margin.

ECONOMIC FUNCTIONS OF FX FUTURES MARKETS

The services provided by FX futures are not unlike those provided by FX forward contracts. Such contracts allow for long and short positions. If two hedgers are on either side of the contract, each views his or her own risk as reduced: The gain is the perceived advantage of an increase in price certainty. The success of futures markets depends on a hedging base (Working, 1953). But the market could not function if there were only hedgers. The reason is that the risks that are being hedged are endemic to the economy: The outcome of economic decisions made today depends on the uncertain course of events, prices, and currency exchange values in the future. This risk cannot be eliminated from the economy; it can only be transferred. Traders in futures markets are risk selectors, who choose the particular type of risk they are willing to bear (Gray, 1976). In futures and forward markets, the transfer of risk is from hedgers to speculators. Speculators assume the risks that hedgers prefer to avoid. We will see in Chapter 11, however, that there is no reason to expect this risk transfer ever to be complete. That is, speculators may be increasing their risk exposure through futures contracts while hedgers are reducing risk. But both will have some optimal risk/return trade-off, and as a result—provided there is uncertainty in the economy—everyone will face some risk.

In many cases the opposite sides of a futures contract will be held by two speculators: The contract increases the risk exposure of each. But this too has a useful economic purpose—price discovery. If two speculators are on opposite sides of a contract, this is probably due to different expectations, so the futures price will in part represent an expectational equilibrium. Some speculators may spend considerable time and money in acquiring and processing information about the economy and about future exchange rates. By position-taking in the futures market, they cause futures prices to reflect this information about potential supply and demand. In the case of exchange rates, however, the price discovery role is already played by the much larger interbank market. Nevertheless, the FX futures market would appear to have a secondary value to interbank marketmakers since the joint participation by many banks in the futures market causes the FX futures price to represent the temporary equilibrium price in this segment of the larger market.

PROBLEMS FOR CHAPTER 5

1. Determine the last day of trading as well as the settlement day for IMM DM futures for March of the current year.

2. At the beginning of the week, you buy seven British pound IMM futures contracts, and two days later sell four Canadian dollar IMM futures contracts. As a result of your transactions, open interest has increased by eleven contracts. The brokerage fee is $26 per round turn. What is the total brokerage fee actually paid so far?

3. Check the futures page in today's *Wall Street Journal,* and calculate the gain or loss on a short position of one contract in each of the listed currencies.

4. On February 8, you go long one IMM DM contract at an opening price of $.3423. There is an initial margin of $1500 and a maintenance margin of $1200. The settlement prices for February 8, 9, and 10 are $.3393, $.3441, and $.3496, respectively. On February 11, you close out the contract at a price of $.3483. Round turn commission was $28.56. Calculate the daily cash flows on your account, assuming that the beginning balance was $1500 and there were no cash additions or withdrawals other than the cash flows from gains or losses on the futures position or from additional required variation margin.

5. Explain why U.S. futures contracts can be said to involve a *fixed* amount of foreign currency, but a *variable* amount of U.S. dollars. Consider now the case of a Japanese company using U.S. futures contracts to hedge against a change in value of the U.S. dollar. In what way will the number of futures contracts chosen to hedge $1,000,000 change as the dollar/yen exchange rate changes?

6. On June 15, a UK firm is planning to import computers worth $5 million from the United States on September 3. The firm decides to hedge its position using IMM futures contracts. The spot rate is $1.3139/£; the September IMM futures price is $1.3080/£. The firm chooses an amount of futures contracts that matches as closely as possible, at the current exchange rate, its $5 million position. Later, on September 3, the spot rate is $1.2590/£, while the September futures price is $1.2550/£. Calculate the net gain or loss, in terms of £s, of the hedged position as of

September 3. (Ignore any interest rate opportunity gain or loss from the time pattern of cash flows.)

7. In the preceding problem, what was the change in the basis? How did this affect the net gain or loss on the hedged position?

8. A Philadelphia importer goes short one DM in futures for each DM in accounts receivable. The change in the dollar price of DM futures over a selected time interval has a variance of .40, while the change in the dollar price of each DM in receivables has a variance of .45. These two variables have a correlation coefficient of .93. Estimate the importer's hedged risk as a percentage of the risk inherent in the underlying long position in DM accounts receivable.

9. In what way does the level of interest rates affect the amount of FX futures used in a delta hedge?

10. A regression reveals the following recent relationship between changes in the $A/\$$ futures price and the $B/\$$ spot rate:

$$\Delta A/\$ = .79 \ \Delta B/\$.$$

In the sample data used

$$\text{var}(\Delta A/\$) = .012, \ \text{var}(\Delta B/\$) = .009,$$

while the variance of the residual in the regression was .001. A dollar-based company with a short position in currency B takes an offsetting $A/\$$ futures contract, using the above equation to establish a delta hedge. Estimate the risk inherent in the company's hedged position as compared to the risk of the original position.

FOREIGN CURRENCY OPTIONS

Options are a unique type of financial contract that have a throwaway feature. They give you the right, but not the obligation, to do something. You only use the contract if you want to. This contrasts with forward contracts, which obligate you to make a transaction at the preagreed price even if the market has changed and you would rather not. Options normally also differ from futures in that there are no daily cash flows ("marking to market") on the long side of an option. (Futures-style options, explained later, are exceptions.) In any case, potential loss on a long position in an option is limited if the price moves in the wrong direction. It is this limited-loss feature that distinguishes options from forward and futures contracts.

Options are usually classified according to whether they are options to buy (calls) or options to sell (puts), and according to whether they can be used only on a specific date (European) or at any time prior to a specific date (American). The terms "European" and "American" refer to *types* of options and have nothing to do with the geographical location of trading or the manner in which exchange rates are quoted. We will divide foreign currency options into three further categories: options on spot exchange, options on foreign currency futures, and futures-style options. The last category comprises both futures-style options on spot and futures-style options on futures.

OPTIONS ON SPOT EXCHANGE

An *American call on spot* is a contract between a buyer and a writer whereby the call buyer pays a price (the "premium") to the writer in order to acquire the right, but not the obligation, to purchase a given amount ("size") of one currency from the writer at a purchase price (the "exercise" or "strike" price) stated in terms of a second currency, on or before a stated date (the "expiration" or "maturity" date). For example, a call option on the British pound might give one the right to purchase £31,250 at $1.50/£ on or at any time before the Saturday prior to the third Wednesday in December 1995.

An *American put on spot* is similar, except that it gives the right to sell a given amount of currency. For example, a put option on the yen might give one the right to sell ¥100,000,000 at ¥150/$ on or before June 13. American-style options on spot exchange are traded over the counter and at the Philadelphia Stock Exchange (PHLX). For exchange-traded options, a clearinghouse or clearing corporation guarantees performance of all option contracts by becoming the writer to every customer who is a buyer and the buyer to every customer who is a writer.

A *European* option differs from an American option in that it may be exercised (used) only on the expiration date. If the call option in the penultimate paragraph were European, then it could be exercised only on, but not prior to, the Saturday prior to the third Wednesday in December 1995. If the put option in the preceding paragraph were European, it could be exercised only on June 13. European-style options on spot exchange are traded over the counter, as well as at the PHLX.

There are two sides to every option contract. There is the *buyer* of the option, who *purchases the right* either to buy (call) or sell (put) the asset contained in the option contract, and there is the *writer* of the option, who *sells the right* either to buy or sell the asset contained in the option contract. The buyer of an option on spot pays the price (or *premium*) of the option up front, and subsequently has the right to exercise or not to exercise the option contract. For example, the buyer might pay $86,000 to purchase a put that allows the buyer to sell SF25,000,000 at a strike price of $.50/SF. The other side of the put contract is the writer who sells this right. The writer receives the $86,000 premium the buyer pays. Then if the buyer decides to exercise the right to sell SF25,000,000, the writer has to purchase the SF25,000,000 at $.50/Swiss franc from the buyer of the put option. The buyer might be, for example, a U.S. company and the writer a U.S. bank. If the bank writes the put to the company, and then the company exercises its right to sell Swiss francs at the strike price of $.50/SF, the bank has to accept the SF25,000,000 and pay the company $12,500,000 in return.

OPTIONS ON FOREIGN CURRENCY FUTURES

Options on FX futures contracts are somewhat different from options on spot foreign exchange. A *call on futures* is a contract between a buyer and a writer whereby the call buyer pays a price (the premium) to the writer in order to acquire the right, but not the obligation, to go long an exchange-traded FX futures contract at an opening price (the strike price) stated in terms of a second currency. If the buyer of a call on futures exercises his or her right to go long a futures contract, the writer of the option must go short the futures contract. A *put on futures* similarly gives the right to establish a *short* position in an FX futures contract at a price given by the exercise price of the option. If the buyer of a put on futures exercises his or her right to go short a futures contract, the writer of the option must go long the futures contract. For reasons given later, all currently traded options on FX futures contracts are American in type, and can be exercised on any business day prior to expiration. For example, if you have an American call on September DM futures with a strike price of $.62/DM and the current futures price is $.6323/DM, exercising the option will give you a long position of one September DM futures contract at an opening futures price of $.62/DM. Since the current futures price is $.6323/DM, the value of this futures position is

$.6323/DM − $.62/DM = $.0123/DM.

This profit can be realized immediately by closing out the futures position (going short to offset), or by withdrawing the cash from the account (if futures margin requirements are otherwise already met). Options on IMM foreign currency futures are traded at the Chicago Mercantile Exchange (CME).

FUTURES-STYLE OPTIONS

A *futures-style call on spot* is a contract between a buyer and a writer whereby the call buyer agrees to pay a daily cash flow to the writer in an amount equal to any decrease in the market value of the call, the call writer agrees to pay a daily cash flow to the buyer in an amount equal to any increase in the market value of the call, and in addition the writer gives the call buyer the right, but not the obligation, to purchase a given amount (size) of one currency from the writer at a purchase price (strike price) stated in terms of a second currency. A *futures-style put on spot* is similar, except the value in question is the put value, and a put gives the right to sell. A futures-style option is like a futures contract in one respect: A futures-style option represents a bet on the direction of price change of the option contract. A buyer of a futures-style call goes long the call price, while the writer of the call goes short the call price. On any day that the price of the call goes up, the buyer makes money, while the writer loses money. On any day that the price of the call goes down, the buyer loses money, while the writer makes money. In a similar fashion, a buyer of a put option goes long the put price, while the writer goes short the put price. But a futures-style option is unlike a futures contract in that the long side of the option position can exercise the option either on any business day (if American) or at option expiration (if European). American futures-style options on spot exchange were once traded at the London International Financial Futures Exchange (LIFFE).

Both the buyer and the writer of a futures-style option (call or put) post margin, just as is done with an ordinary futures contract. The margin is a security bond that ensures that the loser pays up each day. The option price itself is not paid to anyone; it is just the variable about which the long and short sides are betting. The price of the option is *marked to market* daily. If money has been lost, more margin must be posted. If money has been gained, any excess over required margin may be withdrawn. For example, suppose a firm "buys" (goes long) a futures-style put option on £25,000 at a strike price of $1.35/£. Suppose the option price at that time is $.0265/£, for a total value of

£25,000($.0265/£) = $662.50

If the option price subsequently moves to $.0375/£, for a total value of

£25,000($.0375/£) = $937.50,

then the put buyer has a positive cash flow of

$937.50 − $662.50 = $275,

while the put writer has a negative cash flow of the same amount. The difference in this case between the futures-style option and an option on spot or futures is that the buyer of an option on spot or futures would have paid the initial option premium ($662.50) up front, whereas the "buyer" of a futures-style option does not pay the option premium but simply posts margin. The buyer of an option on spot or futures does not have a further cash flow until the option is either sold or exercised. But cash flows take place daily on both the long and short sides of a futures-style option.

At this point a short summary of the basic option definitions might be useful:

1. There are two sides to each option contract—the buyer who obtains the option right to exercise, and the writer who issues this right.
2. From the buyer's perspective, a call is an option to buy or go long, while a put is an option to sell or go short.
3. From the writer's perspective, a call is an obligation to sell or go short (if the call buyer exercises), while a put is an obligation to buy or go long (if the put buyer exercises).
4. An option on spot involves an up-front cash payment of the premium from the buyer to the writer, and in addition a subsequent exchange of currencies if the buyer exercises the option.
5. An option on futures involves an up-front cash payment of the premium from the buyer to the writer, and in addition a subsequent futures position in which the buyer and writer are on opposite sides if the buyer exercises the option.
6. A futures-style option does not involve an up-front payment between the buyer and the writer. Instead the buyer goes long the option premium and the writer goes short the option premium, and there is a daily cash flow between buyer and writer in a manner similar to a futures contract. The futures-style option is not purely a futures contract on the option premium, however. The option buyer has the right to exercise the option into the underlying asset (whether spot currency or an FX futures contract).
7. Any of these options can be American or European. The option is European if it can only be exercised on the final day, the expiration day. An American option can also be exercised on any business day prior to expiration.

THE FOREIGN CURRENCY OPTIONS MARKET

As of September 1990, the market for foreign currency options consisted of an interbank market centered in London, New York, and Tokyo, and exchange-based markets centered in Philadelphia (the PHLX) and Chicago (the CME). As Table 6.1 indicates, outside the latter two cities, the only exchange-traded option with significant volume was a guilder option on the dollar at the European Options Exchange (EOE). Total open interest in FX options for both the interbank market and the different exchanges was estimated by the Bank for International Settlements (BIS) as $44.3 billion at the end of 1989. Turnover during 1989 was around 20.7 million contracts of varying amounts.

Exchange options in the United States are traded in standardized sizes that generally relate to the foreign currency amounts in the IMM's FX futures contracts (described in Chapter 5). Each CME FX option represents the right to go long or short a single IMM FX futures contract.

TABLE 6.1
Principal Exchange-Traded FX Options Contracts in 1990

Contract	Exchange	Volume, Jan.–June 1990	Open Interest June 1990
Option on 1 DM future	CME	1,635,026	112,218
Option on 1 ¥ future	CME	1,371,811	85,796
Option on 1 £ future	CME	185,264	18,614
Option on DM62,500 spot	PHLX	2,702,504	244,910
Option on ¥6.25 million spot	PHLX	1,448,450	176,935
Option on £31,500 spot	PHLX	312,833	48,831
Option on A$100,000 spot	PHLX	153,306	18,391
Option on C$50,000 spot	PHLX	308,747	67,192
Option on ECU 62,500 spot	PHLX	1,826	303
Option on SF62,500 spot	PHLX	304,035	52,286
Guilder option on $10,000 spot	EOE	86,973	8,828

Source: Futures and Options World, September 1990.

PHLX options are on spot amounts of one-half the size of IMM futures contracts. (That is, PHLX options on the British pound, DM, Swiss franc, Japanese yen, and Canadian dollar are, respectively, options on £31,250; DM62,500; SF62,500; ¥6,250,000; and Can$50,000.)

The expiration dates of most exchange FX options contracts are likewise set to correspond to the March, June, September, December delivery dates on IMM FX futures. PHLX FX options, for example, are opened with terms to maturity of one, three, six, and twelve months. As a consequence, option contracts expiring in March, June, September, December, and, in addition, the two nearby months not part of this cycle, are always trading.

As we saw in Chapter 5, IMM futures contracts for a particular month expire on the second business day prior to the third Wednesday. CME FX options expire on the second Friday prior to the third Wednesday. PHLX FX options expire approximately a week later, on the Saturday prior to the third Wednesday. This usually means that the last day of FX options trading at the PHLX will be on a Friday, since no trading takes place on Saturday. The last day of IMM FX futures trading will then be the following Monday. Settlement for any options exercised on the last trade day at the PHLX takes place on the third Wednesday, corresponding to the IMM futures settlement date (if the month is a futures settlement month).

Each of the exchanges trades options with standardized strike price intervals, in addition to standardized expiration dates and currency amounts. The exercise price of an option at the PHLX or CME is stated as the price in U.S. cents of a unit of foreign currency. ("Foreign" here means foreign by reference to the dollar.)

Over-the-counter options, by contrast, can be tailor-made as to amount, maturity, and exercise price. The currency amount involved in over-the-counter options is usually much larger than exchange-traded options (typically involving a minimum of $1,000,000 or so of foreign currency) and over-the-counter options have been written on a larger variety of currencies—including some currencies in which there is little spot or forward trading. The interbank FX options market is closely related to the exchange market. Commercial banks, investment banks, and brokerage houses write over-the-counter options to companies, but do little direct interbank trading with each other. Instead, to manage their risk by keeping short and long options positions in rough balance, the banks rely on foreign currency option brokers, such as Exco International, Bierbaum-Martin, and Butler Treasury Services. These brokers match buy and sell orders between banks. In addition, both the banks and the brokers regularly buy and sell FX options on the available exchanges. In effect, they create tailor-made interbank options by buying and selling standardized exchange options contracts and repackaging them to the user's specification.

As with exchange-traded futures contracts, exchange-traded options are registered with a clearinghouse that guarantees both the long and short sides of puts and calls. FX options contracts at the CME are guaranteed by the Chicago Mercantile Exchange Clearing House, while PHLX contracts are guaranteed by the Options Clearing Corporation (OCC), the clearinghouse for all options traded on U.S. securities exchanges. Once an FX option has been exercised, there is a time gap before the currency exchange takes place (for options on spot) or the futures position is established (for options on futures). Exercise of an option at the CME is effective the next business day, while exercise is effective four business days later at the PHLX. OTC options usually settle two business days after exercise.

FX OPTIONS AS FOREIGN CURRENCY INSURANCE

We now turn to the use of FX options in hedging from the point of view of an option buyer. For the moment, we will simply treat options as contracts that are available to the buyer or the writer at a market-determined price, without concerning ourselves with the separate question of what the fair value (fair to both the buyer and writer) of an FX option is. Questions concerning FX option pricing will be dealt with in later sections.

For the purpose of hedging, foreign currency options can be viewed as exchange rate insurance. Consider how insurance works in general. Suppose you buy fire insurance on a $100,000 house. You insure the house for its full value of $100,000, and the insurance is good for one year. If, by the end of the year, your house has not been damaged by fire, the insurance will have proved worthless. You throw away the unused insurance policy. Your total cost has been the cost of the insurance premium. On the other hand, suppose that fire does $40,000 worth of damage to your house. In this case, you have a $40,000 loss. But the insurance policy pays off the difference between the amount of the insurance ($100,000) and the current value of the insured asset ($60,000), making up exactly the amount of your loss ($40,000). Thus your total loss is zero, except again for the insurance premium, which you pay in any case.

An option works in the same way. Suppose you buy a put option on the value of a house. In particular, suppose the strike price of the put is $100,000. That is, it gives you the right to sell the house for $100,000. You buy an American put (so that it can be used at any time), and it expires in one year. If the market value of the house stays at $100,000 or greater for the year, there would be no advantage in exercising the put. Thus the put would expire worthless. You would throw it away rather than use it to your disadvantage.

But if, because of fire or for some other reason, the value of the house dropped to $60,000, you could exercise the put and sell the house for $100,000. The put has then served as insurance. It paid off the difference between the strike price ($100,000) and the current value of the house ($60,000), thus making up the entire loss in value ($40,000). In any case, whether or not the house lost value, you pay the cost of the put. The price paid for an option is (conveniently) referred to in the options market as the premium and is analogous to an insurance premium. Overall, then, the put serves as an insurance policy. (Or, as some prefer to say, insurance itself is just a put option.)

Let's extend the analogy to deductible insurance. Suppose that, instead of insuring your house for $100,000, you insured it for $80,000. In this case if your house is damaged by fire, you will have to bear the loss of the first $20,000. On the other hand, the insurance premium on $80,000 will be less than the premium on $100,000, so that you may be willing to trade off the greater risk of loss in the case of fire with the lower fixed cost of the insurance premium. In the same way, if you purchased a put option on the house with a strike price of $80,000 instead of a strike price of $100,000, the premium (purchase price) of the put would be lower. But the insurance level of the put will be lower, because it will only pay to exercise the put if the value of the house falls below $80,000. Thus, buying a put option with a strike price that is lower than the current market value of the asset involved is like buying deductible insurance. Whether you like deductible insurance depends on your attitude to trading off lower insurance premiums with the risk of greater loss in the event disaster strikes.

Both foreign currency options on spot and foreign currency options on futures can be considered types of insurance against adverse exchange rate movements. Options on spot represent insurance bought or written on the spot rate, while options on futures represent insurance bought or written on the futures price. Futures-style options are slightly different. No insurance premium is paid or received for futures-style options. Rather, the buyer goes long the value of the insurance policy while the writer goes short. If the value of the policy goes up, this added value automatically accrues to the option buyer as a daily cash flow, without the need to make a claim (to exercise or sell the option). On the other hand, if the value of the policy goes down, this loss of policy value is automatically reflected in a loss on the margin account.

An individual with foreign currency to sell can use put options on spot to establish a floor price on the domestic currency value of the foreign currency. For example, a put option on DM1 with an exercise price of $.40/DM will ensure that, in the event the value of the DM falls below $.40/DM, the DM1 can be sold for $.40/DM anyway. If the put option costs $.01/DM, this floor price can be roughly approximated as

$$\$.40/DM - \$.01/DM = \$.39/DM,$$

or the strike price minus the premium. That is, if the option is used, you will be able to sell the DM1 for the $.40/DM strike price, but in the meantime you have paid a premium of $.01/DM. Deducting the cost of the premium leaves $.39/DM as the floor price established by the purchase of the put. (This ignores fees and interest rate adjustments. A more exact calculation is shown in the following example.)

Similarly, an individual who has to buy foreign currency at some point in the future can use call options on spot to establish a ceiling price on the domestic currency amount that will have to be paid to purchase the foreign exchange. For example, a call option on 1 DM with an exercise price of $.40/DM will ensure that, in the event the value of the DM rises above $.40/DM, the 1 DM can be bought for $.40/DM anyway. If the call option costs $.01/DM, this ceiling price can be approximated as

$.40/DM + $.01/DM = $.41/DM,

or the strike price plus the premium. To summarize these two important points involving FX puts and calls:

1. Foreign currency *put* options on spot can be used as insurance to establish a *floor price on the domestic currency value* of foreign exchange. This floor price is approximately

    Floor price = Exercise price of put − Put premium.

2. Foreign currency *call* options on spot can be used as insurance to establish a *ceiling price on the domestic currency cost* of foreign exchange. This ceiling price is approximately

    Ceiling price = Exercise price of call + Call premium.

These calculations are only approximate for essentially two reasons. First, the exercise price and the premium of the option on spot cannot be added directly without an interest rate adjustment. The premium will be paid now, up front, but the exercise price (if the option is eventually exercised) will be paid later. The time difference involved in the two payment amounts implies that one of the two should be adjusted by an interest rate factor. Second, there may be brokerage or other expenses associated with the purchase of an option, and there may be an additional fee if the option is exercised. The two examples below illustrate the insurance feature of FX options on spot and show how to calculate floor and ceiling values when some additional transactions costs are included.

EXAMPLE 6.1

A U.S. importer will have a net cash outflow of £250,000 in payment for goods bought. The payment date is not known with certainty, but should occur in late November. On September 16 the importer locks in a ceiling purchase for pounds by buying eight PHLX calls on the pound, with a striking price of $1.50/£ and an expiration date in December. The option premium on that date is $.0220/£. There is a brokerage commission of $4 per option contract. Thus the total cost of the eight contracts is:

8(£31,250)($.0220/£) + 8($4) = $5532.

Measured from today's viewpoint, the importer has essentially assured that the purchase price for pounds will not be greater than

$5532/£250,000 + $1.50/£ = $.02213/£ + $1.50/£ = $1.52213/£.

Notice here that the add factor $.02213/£ is larger than the option premium of $.0220/£ by $.00013/£, which represents the dollar brokerage cost per pound.

The number $1.52213/£ is the importer's ceiling price. The importer is assured he will not pay more than this, but he could pay less. The price the importer will actually pay will depend on the spot price on the November payment date. To illustrate this, we can consider two scenarios for the spot rate.

Case A

The spot rate on the November payment date is $1.46/£. The importer would not use the call options but would buy pounds spot for the cheaper rate of $1.46. He or she would then sell the eight calls for whatever market value they had remaining. Assuming a brokerage fee of $4 per contract for the sale, the options would be sold as long as their remaining market value was greater than $4 per option. The total cost per pound will have turned out to be

$1.46 + $.02213 − (Sale value of options − $32)/250,000.

If the resale value is not greater than $32, then the total cost per pound is

$1.46 + $.02213 = $1.48213.

The $.02213/£ that was the original cost of the premium and brokerage fee turned out in this case to be an unnecessary expense.

Now, to be strictly correct, a further adjustment to the calculation should be made. Namely, the $1.46 and $.02213 represent cash flows at two different times. Thus, if x is the amount of interest paid per dollar over the September 16 to November time period, the proper calculation is

$1.46 + $.02213(1 + x) − (Sale value of options − $32)/250,000.

Case B

The spot rate on the November payment date is $1.55/£. The importer can either exercise his options or sell them for their market value. Assume the importer sells them at a current market value of $.055 and pays $32 total in brokerage commissions on the sale of eight option contracts. The importer then buys the pounds in the spot market for $1.55/£. The total cost is, before adding the premium and commission costs paid in September:

($1.55/£)(£250,000) − ($.055)(£250,000 + 8($4) = $373,782

or

$373,782/£250,000 = $1.49513/£.

Adding in the premium and commission costs paid back in September, the total cost is

$1.49513/£ + $.02213(1 + x)/£.

If the importer chooses instead to exercise the option, the calculations will be similar except that the brokerage fee will be replaced by an exercise fee.

EXAMPLE 6.2

A Japanese company wants to lock in a minimum yen value of $50 million, this amount to be sold between July 1 and December 31. Since the company wishes to sell dollars and get yen, the company will buy a put option on dollars, with an exercise price stated in terms of yen. (Or, what is the same thing, the company will buy a call option on yen, with an exercise price stated in terms of dollars.) Suppose the company buys from its bank a put on $50,000,000 with a strike price of ¥230/$. The put is American, in that it can be used at any time prior to expiration. However, there is no resale value to the option. The company pays a premium of ¥4/$. In this case, assume there are no additional fees in dealing with the bank. Approximately, then, the Japanese company has established a floor value for its dollars at ¥230/$ − ¥4/$ = ¥226/$. Again, we can consider two scenarios, one in which the yen falls in value to ¥245/$ and the other in which the yen rises in value to ¥215/$.

Case A

The yen falls to ¥245/$. In this case the company will not exercise the option to sell dollars for yen at ¥230/$, since the company can do better than this in the exchange market. The company will have obtained a net value of

$$¥245/\$ − ¥4(1 + x)/\$,$$

where x is the opportunity cost of yen borrowing and reflects the fact that the ¥4 premium is paid up front. If the opportunity cost is 5 percent per year for one-half year, then $x = .025$, so the company will have obtained a net value of ¥245 − ¥4(1.025) = ¥240.9 for each U.S. dollar.

Case B

The yen rises to ¥215/$. The company will exercise the put and sell each U.S. dollar for ¥230/$. The company will obtain, net,

$$¥230/\$ − ¥4(1 + x)/\$,$$

or about ¥226/$. This is ¥11 better than would have been available in the FX market and reflects a case where the "insurance" paid off.

WRITING FOREIGN CURRENCY OPTIONS

The writer of a foreign currency option on spot or futures is in a different position from the buyer of one of these options. The buyer pays the premium up front and afterward can choose to exercise the option or not. The buyer is not a source of credit risk once the premium has been paid. The writer *is* a source of credit risk, however, because the writer has promised either to sell or to buy foreign currency if the buyer exercises his option. The writer could default on the promise to sell foreign currency if the writer did not have sufficient foreign currency available, or could default on the promise to buy foreign currency if the writer did not have sufficient domestic currency available. If the option is written by a bank, this risk of default is small. But if the option is written by a company, the bank may require the company to post margin or other security as a hedge against default risk. For exchange-traded options, as noted previously, the relevant clearinghouse guarantees fulfillment of both sides of the option contract. The clearinghouse covers its own risk, however, by requiring the writer of an option to post margin. At the PHLX, for example, the Options Clearing Corporation will allow a writer to meet margin requirements by having the actual foreign currency or U.S. dollars on deposit, by obtaining an irrevocable letter of credit from a suitable bank, or by posting cash margin. If cash margin is posted, the required deposit is the current market value of the option plus 4 percent of the value of the underlying foreign currency. This requirement is reduced by any amount the option is out of the money, to a minimum requirement of the premium plus .75 percent of the value of the underlying foreign currency. These percentages can be changed by the exchanges based on currency volatility. Thus, as the market value of the option changes, the margin requirement will change. So an option writer faces daily cash flows associated with changing margin requirements.

Other exchanges have similar requirements for option writers. The CME allows margins to be calculated on a net basis for accounts holding both CME FX futures options and IMM FX futures. That is, the amount of margin is based on one's total futures and futures options portfolio. The risk of an option writer at the CME is the risk of being exercised and consequently the risk of acquiring a short position (for call writers) or a long position (for put writers) in IMM futures. Hence the amount of margin the writer is required to post is related to the amount of margin required on an IMM FX futures contract. The exact calculation of margins at the CME relies on the concept of an option delta, which will be explained later in this chapter.

From the point of view of a company or individual, writing options is a form of risk-exposure management of importance equal to that of buying options. It may make perfectly good sense for a company to *sell* foreign currency insurance in the form of writing FX calls or puts. The choice of strike price on a written option reflects a straightforward trade-off. For reasons explained later, FX call options with a lower strike price will be more valuable than those with a higher strike price. Hence the premiums the option writer will receive are correspondingly larger. However, the probability that the written calls will be exercised by the buyer is also higher for calls with a lower strike price than for those with a higher strike. Hence the larger premiums received reflect greater risk taking on the part of the insurance seller (the option writer).

The following example will illustrate this risk/return trade-off for the case of an oil company that chooses to become an option writer.

EXAMPLE 6.3

Isis, a U.S.-based oil company, has a large foreign currency exposure in the form of a Canadian dollar cash flow from Canadian operations. The risk to Isis is that the Canadian dollar will depreciate against the U.S. dollar in such a way that Isis' total U.S. dollar revenues will fall.

Isis chooses to reduce its long position in Canadian dollars by writing Canadian dollar call options with a U.S. dollar strike. The particular option strategy chosen is one of "fully covered call writing," which involves writing call options with a face amount equal to the anticipated Canadian dollar cash flow over the period of maturity of the options. By writing options, Isis will receive an immediate U.S. dollar cash flow representing the market value of the options written. This cash flow will increase Isis' total U.S. dollar return in the event the Canadian dollar depreciates against the U.S. dollar, remains unchanged against the U.S. dollar, or appreciates only slightly against the U.S. dollar.

To implement its strategy, Isis will write Canadian dollar call options involving an amount of currency that matches its anticipated cash flow prior to the maturity of the options. This strategy will involve only a minimal amount of management of the option position. At the extreme, Isis could simply allow the options to expire or to be exercised. In either case, Isis walks away with the full amount of the option premium. If the U.S. dollar value of the Canadian dollar remains unchanged, the option premium received is simply additional profit. If the value of the Canadian dollar falls, the premium received on the written option will offset part or all of the opportunity loss on the underlying Canadian dollar position. If the value of the Canadian dollar rises sharply, Isis will only participate in this increased value up to a ceiling level, where the ceiling level is a function of the exercise price of the option written.

In short, the payoff to Isis' strategy will depend both on exchange rate movements and on the selection of the strike price of the written options. To illustrate Isis' strategy, consider an anticipated cash flow of Can$300,000,000 over the next 180 days. Assume that Isis writes PHLX options with a six-month expiration. Assume also that the current spot rate is $.75/Can$, while the six-month forward rate is $.7447/Can$. For this level of spot rate, logical strike price choices for the calls might be $.74, $.75, or $.76. For the illustration, we will assume that Isis pays a brokerage fee of $4 per written option and will let the hypothetical market values of the options be those listed below.

Strike Price	Option Value	No. of Options (PHLX)	U.S. $ Credit from Written Options	Brokerage Fees
74	$598.50	6000	$3,591,000	$24,000
75	$325.00	6000	$1,950,000	$24,000
76	$156.50	6000	$ 939,000	$24,000

The payoff to the total position will depend on the "terminal" value of the spot rate S ($/Can$) as well as the choice of strike price. The terminal spot rate is the market spot rate at the expiration date of the options. If the options are exercised, assume an additional clearing corporation fee of $35 per option, or a total fee of $210,000 for 6000 contracts. The value of the total long Canadian dollar plus short option position will be:

Strike Price	Spot Rate			
	$S < 74$	$74 < S < 75$	$75 < S < 76$	$76 < S$
74	S(Can$300 m.) + $3,567,000	$225,357,000	$225,357,000	$225,357,000
75	S(Can$300 m.) + $1,926,000	S(Can$300 m.) + $1,926,000	$226,716,000	$226,716,000
76	S(Can$300 m.) + $915,000	S(Can$300 m.) + $915,000	S(Can$300 m.) + $915,000	$228,705,000

As illustrated above, *the lower the strike price chosen, the better the protection against a depreciating Canadian dollar. On the other hand, a lower strike price corresponding limits profitability if the Canadian dollar appreciates.* The optimal decision will turn out to be, after the fact, a function of the terminal spot exchange rate. Table 6.2 summarizes the optimal decision for all possible values of the spot exchange rate, given our assumptions. The assumptions are that the company either maintains an open long position of Can$300,000,000 or (in addition) writes 6000 PHLX calls with 180-day maturity. Possible strike prices are $.76/Can$, $.75/Can$, $.74/Can$. Here the terminal spot rate is the market exchange rate when the options expire. It is assumed the company pays a brokerage fee of $4 per option contract and an additional fee of $35 per option to the clearing corporation if the options are exercised.

TABLE 6.2
Optimal Decision under Isis' Strategy, as a Function of the
(Now Unknown) Terminal Spot Rate*

Terminal Spot Rate (U.S. Cents/Can$)	Optimal Decision
$S > 76.235$	Hold long currency only
$75.267 < S < 76.235$	Write options with 76 strike
$74.477 < S < 75.267$	Write options with 75 strike
$S < 74.477$	Write options with 74 strike

* Current spot rate is $.75/Can$.

There are some additional points worth noting for Isis' strategy. Because of the large fee ($35) assumed to be charged by the clearing corporation if the options are exercised, it might be less expensive for Isis to buy back the options (and pay a brokerage fee of $4) in the event the options were in danger of being exercised. In addition, it is assumed that Isis will have the Canadian dollars on hand if the options are exercised. This would not be the case if actual Canadian dollar revenues were less than anticipated. In that event, the options would need to be repurchased prior to expiration.

Each of the three choices of strike price will have a different payoff, depending on the movement in the exchange rate. But Isis' expectation regarding the exchange rate is not the only relevant criterion for choosing a risk-management strategy. The possible variation in the underlying position should also be considered. Below are the maximal and minimal payoffs for each of the call-writing choices, compared to the unhedged position and a forward market hedge:

Strategy	Maximal Value	Minimal Value
Unhedged long position	None	Zero
Sell forward	$223,410,000	$223,410,000
Strategy A, 76 strike	$228,705,000	Unhedged minimum plus $915,000
Strategy A, 75 strike	$226,716,000	Unhedged minimum plus $1,926,000
Strategy A, 74 strike	$225,357,000	Unhedged minimum plus $3,567,000

SOME ELEMENTARY PRINCIPLES OF FX OPTION PRICING

In this section we will look at some basic principles of pricing FX options. These principles will enable us to narrow down the possible range of FX option values in terms of the values of other assets. Some more advanced principles, as well as exact pricing formulas, are given in the following sections.

First, here is some notation that will be used below. Let $C(t)$ and $P(t)$ denote the domestic currency prices of, respectively, American call and American put options on one unit of *spot* foreign exchange. The reason for looking at option prices on *one* unit of foreign exchange is simple. If $C(t)$ is the dollar price of an American call on DM1, then the dollar price of an American call on DM1000 is $1000 C(t)$, the dollar price of an American put on DM79681 is $79681 P(t)$, and so on. So it is convenient to think in terms of an option on one unit of foreign exchange. Similarly, let $c(t)$ and $p(t)$ denote the domestic currency prices, respectively, of a European call and a European put on one unit of spot foreign exchange.

In a similar way, let $C^*(t)$, $P^*(t)$, $c^*(t)$, $p^*(t)$ denote the prices of American and European calls and puts on one unit of FX *futures*. And let $C^{**}(t)$, $P^{**}(t)$, $c^{**}(t)$, $p^{**}(t)$ denote the prices of *futures-style* American and European FX calls and puts.

The exercise price of an option will be indicated by X. The current time will be t, and the option will be assumed to expire in T days from the present—at time $t + T$. The current spot exchange rate (the domestic currency price of a unit of foreign currency) will be designated as $S(t)$, and $Z(t)$ will be the current futures price. The maturity of the futures contract will be left unspecified, as the futures contract may or may not expire at the same time the option on the future expires. Finally, let $B(t,T)$ be the current price of a discount (or "zero-coupon") bond that matures at time $t + T$ and pays one unit of *domestic* currency at maturity. That is, $B(t,T)$ is expressed as a fraction of its maturity value. $B(t,T)$ is inversely related to the interest yield on the security. For example, if $B(t,T) = \$.95$ then, since at maturity the bond will have a value of $1, the interest yield over the time period T will be

$$1/.95 - 1 = .05263.$$

If T is 360 days, then .05263 corresponds to a yearly interest rate of 5.263 percent. But if T is 180 days, the corresponding money market interest rate would be

$$i = .05263(360/180) = .10526$$

or 10.526 percent.

An alternative way to think of $B(t,T)$ is that it is just the discount factor corresponding to the interest rate i, where i is quoted at a yearly rate:

$$B(t,T) = 1/[1 + i(T/360)].$$

Thus for $i = .10526$ and $T = 180$ days,

$$B(t,T) = \$1/[1 + i(180/360)] = \$.95.$$

A similar variable will be $B^*(t,T)$, where $B^*(t,T)$ is the price at time t of a discount bond that pays one unit of *foreign currency* at time $t + T$. For example, we might have

$$B^*(t,T) = DM.975.$$

Principle 1

An option is a limited liability contract to the option buyer. If you own an option, you can exercise it but you do not have to. You can always throw it away. That means that the value of an option you own can only go to zero, where zero corresponds to the case you throw the option away rather than exercise it or sell it. Hence, expressing this fact mathematically,

$$
\begin{array}{ll}
C(t),\ C^*(t),\ \text{and}\ C^{**}(t) \geq 0. & P(t),\ P^*(t),\ \text{and}\ P^{**}(t) \geq 0. \\
c(t),\ c^*(t),\ \text{and}\ c^{**}(t) \geq 0. & p(t),\ p^*(t),\ \text{and}\ p^{**}(t) \geq 0.
\end{array}
\tag{6.1}
$$

The owner of an option would never sell the option for a negative amount. The price can go down, but cannot become less than zero. (Notice, however, that for a futures-style [**] option, the change in the option price can generate both positive and negative cash flows for the buyer, even though the option price itself must remain positive.)

Principle 2

At the *expiration date*, an American or a European call option on spot will be worth either its immediate exercise value or zero, whichever is higher. Since call options allow you to buy one unit of foreign exchange for a domestic currency amount X, and the value of the unit of spot exchange on the maturity date, day $t + T$, will be that day's spot market price, $S(t + T)$, the immediate exercise value is $S(t + T) - X$. Thus

$$C(t + T) = \text{maximum } [0, S(t + T) - X]$$
$$c(t + T) = \text{maximum } [0, S(t + T) - X]. \tag{6.2}$$

For example, the dollar value of a European call option on DM1, with an exercise price of \$.40/DM and expiration on a day when the spot exchange rate is \$.42/DM, is maximum (0, \$.42 − \$.40) = \$.02. A corresponding European call on DM10,000,000 would have a value of DM10,000,000 (\$.02/DM) = \$200,000.

Notice that similar relations hold for calls on futures, $C^*(t)$ and $c^*(t)$, if we substitute the futures price $Z(t)$ for the spot price $S(t)$. Moreover, if the futures contract expires on the same date as the option, on that day $Z = S$ and hence $Z - X = S - X$, so the equations are identical to (6.2). In general, however, as is the case at the IMM, the options and the futures may expire on different dates. Hence the general relation is

$$C^*(t + T) = \text{maximum } [0, Z(t + T) - X]$$
$$c^*(t + T) = \text{maximum } [0, Z(t + T) - X]. \tag{6.3}$$

For futures-style calls $C^{**}(t)$ and $c^{**}(t)$, the relation is similar to (6.2) if they are futures-style calls on spot or (6.3) if they are futures-style calls on futures.

Principle 3

At the expiration date, an American or European put option on spot will be worth either its immediate exercise value or zero, whichever is higher. Since a put gives one the right to sell one unit of foreign exchange for a domestic currency amount of X, while the market price of the unit of spot exchange at expiration is $S(t + T)$, the immediate exercise value of the put is $X - S(t + T)$. Thus

$$P(t + T) = \text{maximum } [0, X - S(t + T)]$$
$$p(t + T) = \text{maximum } [0, X - S(t + T)]. \tag{6.4}$$

For example, the value of an American put option on £1, with an exercise price of \$1.50/£ and expiring when the spot exchange rate is \$1.41/£, would be maximum (0, \$1.50 − \$1.41) = \$.09. If it expires when the spot exchange rate is \$1.51/£, the put's value would be maximum (0, \$1.50 − \$1.51) = \$0.

Similarly, for put options on futures

$$P^*(t + T) = \text{maximum } [0, X - Z(t + T)]$$
$$p^*(t + T) = \text{maximum } [0, X - Z(t + T)].$$
                                                                                            (6.5)

Futures-style puts $P^{**}(t)$ and $p^{**}(t)$ obey equations similar to (6.4) if they are puts on spot exchange but (6.5) if they are puts on FX futures.

Principle 4

At all times prior to expiration, an American option has a value that is at least as large as its immediate exercise value. This holds true for both American puts and American calls because an American option can be exercised at any time, so that by exercising it one can force an option to have a value at least as large as its immediate exercise value. But, at all times prior to expiration, an American option has a value that is also at least as large as the corresponding European option. This is due to the fact that one chose to wait until maturity to exercise an American option. One can simply treat it like a European option. Combining these relationships, we have, for time $t < T$,

$$C(t) \geq \text{maximum } [c(t), S(t) - X]$$
$$P(t) \geq \text{maximum } [p(t), X - S(t)].$$
$$C^*(t) \geq \text{maximum } [c^*(t), Z(t) - X]$$
$$P^*(t) \geq \text{maximum } [p^*(t), X - Z(t)].$$
                                                                                            (6.6)

For example, if a European FX call option on 1 French franc had a value of \$.02, and $S(t) = \$.125$ and $X = \$.101$, then

$$C(t) \geq \text{maximum } (\$.02, \$.125 - \$.101) = \$.024.$$

This example illustrates the advantage of an American FX option. Sometimes European FX calls will have a value less than $S(t) - X$, but not American FX calls.

American futures-style options $C^{**}(t)$ and $P^{**}(t)$ obey relations similar to the first two equations of (6.6) if they are on spot but similar to the second two equations if they are on futures.

Principle 5

Given two American options on the same amounts of the same currency and with the same domestic currency exercise price, the one with the longer term to maturity has a value at least as large as the one with the shorter term to maturity. For example, consider a nine-month option and a six-month option. If you had a nine-month option, you could always choose to exercise it during the first six months. Therefore it could be used as a six-month option. But if not, the option is still good for an additional three months. The additional three months could never hurt the holder of the option. Thus the nine-month American option would have a value at least as great as the six-month American option. The same does not hold true for European FX options, however. A nine-month European option could not be exercised at the end of six months even if one wanted to. Under certain circumstances a nine-month European FX option (either call or put) can have a value that is less than a six-month

European FX option (an example is given later). This distinction between American and European options holds true for FX options on spot, FX options on futures, and futures-style FX options on spot. (See later for futures-style FX options on futures.)

Principle 6

Given two call options identical in every way except that one has a larger exercise price, the call option with the larger exercise price will have a value less than or equal to the one with the smaller exercise price. The opposite holds for put options. Given two put options identical in every way except that one has a larger exercise price, the put option with the larger exercise price has a value greater than or equal to the one with the smaller exercise price. It is easy to see why. With a higher exercise price, a call is less valuable because it obligates you to pay more domestic currency for a unit of foreign exchange. But with a higher exercise price, a put is more valuable because it gives you the right to sell foreign exchange at the higher exercise rate. These relations hold for FX options on spot, FX options on futures, and futures-style options. For example, given two six-month call options on the spot Swiss franc, one with an exercise price of $X = \$.50/SF$ has a value larger than one with $X = \$.55/SF$. But for the corresponding puts on the Swiss franc, the put with $X = \$.55/SF$ has a larger value than the put with $X = \$.50/SF$.

Principle 7

An FX call option on foreign currency can be considered an FX put option on the domestic currency. Similarly, an FX put option on a foreign currency can be considered an FX call option on the domestic currency. These relations follow from the fact that an exchange rate has two sides. For example, a call option on DM100,000,000 with an exercise price of SF.80/DM gives one the right to buy DM100,000,000 for SF80,000,000. Restated, this option gives one the right to sell SF80,000,000, for which one receives in return DM100,000,000. Thus it is a put option on SF80,000,000 with an exercise price of DM1.25/SF. As another example, the PHLX American put option on ¥6,250,000, with an exercise price of $.0042/¥, is simultaneously an American call option on $26,250, with an exercise price of ¥238.095/$.

Principle 8

Consider a European option on futures where the futures contract under consideration expires at the same time as the option. Since the futures contract expires when the option does, at option maturity the futures price will be equal to the spot price: $Z(t + T) = S(t + T)$. And since the option is European, it can only be exercised at maturity, in which case the option gives the right to buy (if a call) or sell (if a put) $Z(t + T)$ in exchange for the exercise price X. Compare this to a European option on spot. It also gives the right to buy (if a call) or sell (if a put) $S(t + T)$—which is the same as $Z(t + T)$—in return for the exercise price X. The European option on spot and European option on futures give the purchaser exactly the same privileges. Hence, *for an FX futures contract expiring at the same time as the option, a European option on FX futures has the same value as the equivalent European FX option on spot exchange.* That is,

$$c(t) = c^*(t)$$
$$p(t) = p^*(t). \tag{6.7}$$

This value equivalent between European options on spot and European options on futures does not apply to American options, however. The reason is simple: If an American option on FX futures is exercised prior to expiration, it has the value $Z(t) - X$, while an American FX option has the value $S(t) - X$ if exercised. Since $Z(t)$ will generally differ from $S(t)$ by an amount determined by interest parity (as we saw in Chapter 5), the two options will not have the same value. The "boundary constraints" differ, and thus the probability of early exercise differs between the two American options.

Principle 9

Consider futures-style options as compared to ordinary options on spot or futures. The special characteristic of the futures-style option is that the buyer of the option does not have to pay the option premium up front. Therefore the buyer does not forgo, and the writer does not receive, any interest on the money that would otherwise be needed to pay the option premium. (The buyer must post margin, but there will be no loss of interest as long as the buyer can post margin in the form of interest-bearing securities.) Except for this special feature of no forgone interest, the futures-style option on spot gives the buyer the same privileges as an option on spot, and the futures-style option on futures gives the buyer the same privileges as an option on futures. Therefore the value of the futures-style option is the same as the value of an ordinary option, once an adjustment for interest has been made. Restated, *the payoff of a futures-style option is not discounted.* Since the discount factor for any payoff at option expiration is the price of a domestic discount bond $B(t,T)$, we obtain the following equations for European calls and puts:

$$c(t) = B(t,T)\, c^{**}(t)$$
$$p(t) = B(t,T)\, p^{**}(t). \tag{6.8}$$

For two American options (one ordinary, the other futures-style) the relationship is more complex, because there is no single discount factor that relates the payoff boundaries between the two options.

All of the preceding principles (1 through 9) have been stated assuming no transactions costs. In practice, the relations will hold within a margin of error given by the relevant costs of making the transaction. These include bid/asked spreads and brokerage or exchange fees.

There are several important terms frequently used in connection with options. A call option on spot (futures) is said to be *in the money* if the current spot rate (futures price) is higher than the option exercise price. It is said to be *out of the money* if the current spot rate (futures price) is less than the exercise price, while it is *at the money* if the current spot rate (futures price) is equal to the exercise price. A put option on spot (futures) is said to be in the money if the current spot rate (futures price) is less than the exercise price; it is out of the money if the current spot rate (futures price) is greater than the exercise price; and it is at the money otherwise. Similar terminology is applied to futures-style options. The terminology comes from the fact that in-the-money options would have a positive value if they were exercised immediately (if American) or if they could be exercised immediately (if European).

Sometimes the terms "intrinsic value" and "time value" are used. The intrinsic value is the amount the option is in the money, while the time value is the option premium minus the intrinsic value. For example, if the spot rate is $.41/SF, a call with a strike price of $.40/SF and a premium of $.03/SF would have an intrinsic value of $.01/SF (since it is $.41/SF − $.40/SF = $.01/SF in the money) and a time value of $.02/SF. A put with a strike price of $.40/SF and a premium of $.01/SF would have an intrinsic value of zero and a time value of $.01/SF. These two terms, while widely used, are somewhat misleading, so we will not use them further here. The reason they are misleading is that the value of the option in excess of its immediate exercise value is not just a function of the time to maturity. This excess is also a function of the exchange rate volatility and the domestic and foreign interest rates.

☐

MORE ADVANCED PRINCIPLES OF FX OPTION PRICING

This section gives some further conditions that must be satisfied by the market prices of FX call and put options in order to avoid arbitrage. Since these relations will involve our keeping track of several variables simultaneously, call and put prices will be written as general functions of several option characteristics. For example, in the previous section a European call on spot exchange at time t was denoted as "$c(t)$." In this section, the more general form "$c(S(t),X,t,T)$" will sometimes be used. This notation simply reminds us that the European option price is a function of the spot rate $S(t)$, the exercise price X, and the term to maturity T. One new variable that will be used in this section is $F(t,T)$, which—as we saw in Chapter 4—denotes the price of forward exchange at time t, where the forward contract matures at time $t + T$. The notation will be simplified in cases where the meaning is clear.

Principle 10

Consider the following two portfolio strategies undertaken at time t when the spot exchange rate is $S(t)$:

Strategy A: 1. Purchase for $c(S(t),X,t,T)$ a European call option, with an exercise price of X and that expires in T units of time, on one unit of spot exchange.
2. Purchase X domestic currency discount bonds, which mature in T units of time, at the current price $B(t,T)$.
Total Domestic Currency Investment: $c + XB$.

Strategy B: 1. Purchase one foreign discount bond, which matures in T units of time, at a domestic currency price of $S(t)B^*(t,T)$.
Total Domestic Currency Investment: SB^*.

At time $t + T$, the spot exchange rate $S(t + T)$ will either be less than X or greater than or equal to X. The bonds will have values, in their respective currencies, of

$B(t + T,0) = 1, B^*(t + T,0) = 1.$

The call option will have a value

$c(S(t + T), X,T,0) = \max [0,S(t + T) - X].$

Therefore:

	Value of Strategy A	Value of Strategy B
$S(t + T) < X$	X	$S(t + T)$
$S(t + T) \geq X$	$S(t + T)$	$S(t + T)$

In either case, the payoff to strategy A will always be as good as or better than the payoff to strategy B. Hence the cost of A must, in economic equilibrium, be at least as great as that of B. Thus

$c + XB \geq SB^*$ or $c \geq SB^* - XB.$

Since an American call must be at least as valuable as its European counterpart (because it has all the same features plus the additional one that it can be exercised at any time), we get

$$C(S(t),X,t,T) \geq c(S(t),X,t,T) \geq S(t)B^*(t,T) - XB(t,T). \qquad (6.9)$$

For example, if 360-day eurodollar deposits have an interest rate of 11.11 percent $[B(t,T) = 1/1.1111 = 0.9]$, 360-day euro-SF deposits have an interest rate of 5.26 percent $[B^*(t,T) = 1/1.10526 = 0.95]$, and the spot rate $S(t) = \$.55/SF$, then a 360-day American option on one Swiss franc with an exercise price of $X = \$.50/SF$ will have the value

$$C(.55, .50, t, 360) \geq c(.55, .50, t, 360) \geq (.55)(.95) - (.50)(.9) = \$.0725.$$

Since an American option can be exercised at any time and must have a value at least as large as its immediate exercise value, we get the stronger inequality

$$C(S(t),X,t,T) \geq \max [S(t) - X, S(t)B^*(t,T) - XB(t,T)]. \qquad (6.10)$$

Notice that, depending on the bond prices B and B^*, sometimes $S - X$ will be greater than $SB^* - XB$, and sometimes $S - X$ will be smaller. This shows that the American call on spot has a constraint,

$C(t) \geq S - X,$

that is not subsumed in any constraint that applies also to the European call on spot. As a consequence, American calls will have values greater than European calls as long as there is a positive probability that this additional constraint will be binding.

Similar reasoning shows that for European and American puts on spot:

$$p(S(t),X,t,T) \geq XB(t,T) - S(t)B^*(t,T) \qquad (6.11)$$
$$P(S(t),X,t,T) \geq \max [X - S(t),XB(t,T) - S(t)B^*(t,T)]. \qquad (6.12)$$

Principle 11

The interest parity relation of Chapter 4 may be rewritten using the notation of this chapter as

$$F(t,T) = S(t) \frac{B^*(t,T)}{B(t,T)}. \qquad (6.13)$$

Substituting for $S(t)B^*(t,T)$ in equation (6.9), we obtain the relation

$$C(S(t),X,t,T) \geq c(S(t),X,t,T) \geq B(t,T)[F(t,T) - X]. \qquad (6.14)$$

A call option on one unit of spot exchange must have a value at least as great as the discounted difference between the forward exchange rate and the exercise price. The intuition is clear if we consider the case $F > X$. An owner of a European call can sell foreign currency forward for $F(t,T)$, even though the purchase price will be X. Thus such an option has a value at least as large as this difference, $F - X$, once it is discounted to the present.

Similarly, we have for puts

$$P(S(t),X,t,T) \geq p(S(t),X,t,T) \geq B(t,T)[X - F(t,T)]. \qquad (6.15)$$

Now consider futures-style options on either spot or futures. Combining the relations (6.7) and (6.8) in the previous section with (6.14) and (6.15), we get

$$C^{**}(S(t),X,t,T) \geq c^{**}(S(t),X,t,T) \geq [F(t,T) - X] \qquad (6.16)$$
$$P^{**}(S(t),X,t,T) \geq p^{**}(S(t),X,t,T) \geq [X - F(t,T)]. \qquad (6.17)$$

Principle 12

Here we derive a direct relation between the prices of European calls on spot and European puts on spot. Consider the following two portfolio strategies:

Strategy A: 1. Buy, at a domestic currency price of $p(S(t),X,t,T)$, a put option on one unit of foreign currency with exercise price X.

Strategy B: 1. Issue a foreign-currency-denominated discount bond at $B^*(t,T)$ and sell the foreign currency for $S(t)B^*(t,T)$.

2. Buy X domestic discount bonds at a price of $B(t,T)$ each for a total domestic currency amount $XB(t,T)$.

3. Buy, at a domestic currency price of $c(S(t),X,t,T)$, a European call option on one unit of foreign currency with an exercise price of X.

Total Domestic Currency Investment: $c - SB^* + XB$.

At time $t + T$ the spot exchange rate $S(t + T)$ will be such that either

$$S(t + T) < X \text{ or } S(t + T) \geq X.$$

In each case, since

$$p(S(t + T), X, T, 0) = \max[0, X - S(t + T)],$$

the strategies will have the payoffs:

	Value of Strategy A	Value of Strategy B
$S(t + T) < X$	$X - S(t + T)$	$X - S(t + T)$
$S(t + T) \geq X$	0	0

Since each strategy gives the same payoff, each must cost the same in economic equilibrium. Hence

$$p(S(t),X,t,T) = c(S(t),X,t,T) - S(t)B^*(t,T) + XB(t,T). \tag{6.18}$$

Thus *the price of a European put on spot is totally determined by the price of the corresponding European call, the spot exchange rate, and the prices of discount bonds denominated in the two currencies.* Equation (6.18) is a put-to-call conversion equation for European FX options on spot.

Principle 13

Using the interest parity relation (6.13), and substituting into equation (6.18), we obtain

$$p(S(t),X,t,T) = c(S(t),X,t,T) + B(t,T)[X - F(t,T)]. \tag{6.19}$$

The price of a European FX put differs from the price of the corresponding call by a factor that represents the discounted difference between the exercise price and the forward exchange rate.

Combining the relations of (6.8) with (6.19), we obtain a similar put-to-call conversion equation for futures-style European FX calls and puts as:

$$p^{**}(S(t),X,t,T) = c^{**}(S(t),X,t,T) + [X - F(t,T)]. \tag{6.20}$$

The prices of European futures-style puts and calls on spot or futures differ by the difference between the exercise price and the forward exchange rate. ■

PRICING MODELS FOR FX OPTIONS

Option-pricing models price options through arbitrage relationships. Think, for the sake of analogy, of the interest parity equation. The interest parity equation gives the forward rate as a function of the spot rate and two euro-currency interest rates. It shows that there cannot be four independent markets for spot exchange, forward exchange, and domestic and foreign currency eurodeposits. Once you specify three of these variables, the other can be solved for by interest parity. Given the spot rate and the two interest rates, you can solve the equation for a synthetic forward rate. If this synthetic forward rate is different from the market forward rate (by more than a margin of error allowed by transactions costs), a profit opportunity is available. Arbitrage will eliminate riskless profit opportunities and will thus tend to equalize the forward rate derived from the equation with the market forward rate.

Option-pricing models are derived using the same principle. A synthetic option is created using other market assets. The value of these assets is then the value of the option. In particular, *a European FX option on spot can be created synthetically by a portfolio consisting of eurocurrency deposits (or bonds) denominated in both the domestic and foreign currencies*. The cash flows involved in this portfolio will exactly duplicate the cash flows involved in a European FX option on spot. Keeping our previous notation, let $B(t,T)$ and $B^*(t,T)$ be the prices of discount bonds denominated in the domestic and foreign currency, respectively. To convert the value of the foreign bond into domestic currency terms, it must be multiplied by the spot exchange rate, so the domestic currency value of the foreign bond would be $S(t)B^*(t,T)$. The assertion that a European FX call option on spot can be created synthetically using domestic and foreign bonds can be written as:

$$c(t) = a[S(t)B^*(t,T)] + b[B(t,T)], \qquad (6.21)$$

where a and b are the amounts of the foreign and domestic bonds, respectively, in the portfolio.

It remains only to specify the exact values of a and b. It turns out that a and b are themselves functions of five variables: $S(t)$, $B^*(t,T)$, $B(t,T)$, T, and v, where v is related to the variation of the forward rate. Since most of these variables are changing with time, the values of a and b change with the passage of time. That is, *the portfolio of domestic and foreign currency assets must be adjusted continuously*. As a practical matter, this latter requirement is very strict, since real-world transactions costs would make it costly to continuously adjust such a portfolio. That means, as a practical matter, that it would be difficult to duplicate closely a European FX option synthetically. This fact has two implications: (1) Transactions costs will allow a proportionately larger range of prices at which a European FX option can trade without arbitrage possibilities than would be the case for an FX forward rate; (2) the creation of an FX options market serves a real economic need, since transactions costs make it difficult to create synthetic FX options using other market instruments (Ross, 1976).

To derive a European FX option-pricing formula, we must make some assumptions about the distribution of asset prices. The main assumption made for the formulas presented here is that the logarithmic change in the forward rate, $ln[F(t + u, T - u)] - ln[F(t,T)]$, is a normally distributed random variable with mean $m\,u$ and a variance $v^2\,u$. That is, both the mean and the variance are proportional to the passage of time u. Hence, there is a mean drift m per unit time, and a variance rate v^2 per unit time. (The variable v, which is the standard deviation rate per square root of unit time, is commonly referred to as *volatility* by options market participants.) Similar assumptions are made for logarithmic changes in bond prices:

$$ln[B(t + u, T - u)] - ln[B(t,T)]$$

and

$$ln[B^*(t + u, T - u)] - ln[B^*(t,T)].$$

With these probability assumptions, it is shown in Grabbe (1983) that the portfolio proportions a and b in (6.21) have the values $a = N(d1)$, and $b = -X N(d2)$, where X is the option strike, and $N(d1)$ and $N(d2)$ are the cumulative normal distribution evaluated at $d1$ and $d2$, respectively:

$$c(t) = S(t)B^*(t,T) N(d1) - XB(t,T) N(d2), \tag{6.22}$$

where

$$d1 = \frac{ln(SB^*/XB) + .5 \, v^2 T}{v \sqrt{T}}$$

$$d2 = \frac{ln(SB^*/XB) - .5 \, v^2 T}{v \sqrt{T}}$$

and

$$N(d) = \frac{1}{\sqrt{2\pi}} \int_{-\infty}^{d} \exp(-x^2/2) \, dx.$$

The expressions "v^2T" and "$v\sqrt{T}$" are unit-free. That is, if T is measured in days, then v^2 must be the daily variance rate. If T is measured in years, then v^2 must be the yearly variance rate. Commonly calculated values for v usually assume that T is measured in years.

EXAMPLE 6.4

The mechanics of the formula can be illustrated making the following data assumptions:

$$
\begin{array}{ll}
S(t) = \$1.5449/£ & B(t,T) = .99465 \\
X = \$1.50/£ & B^*(t,T) = .99315 \\
T = .05833 & v = .15705.
\end{array}
$$

The intermediate formula variables may be calculated as:

$$ln(SB^*/XB) = ln((1.5449)(.99315)/[(1.50)(.99465)]) = .027985$$

$$v\sqrt{T} = (.15705)(\sqrt{.05833}) = .03793$$

$$.5v^2T = .5(.15705)^2(.05833) = .0007193$$

$$d1 = \frac{(.027985) + (.0007193)}{.03793} = .7567$$

$$d2 = \frac{(.027985) - (.0007193)}{.03793} = .7188$$

$$N(d1) = .7754$$

$$N(d2) = .76387$$

$$c(t) = SB^* \, N(d1) - XB \, N(d2)$$

$$= (\$1.5449/£)(.99315)(.7754) - (\$1.50/£)(.99465)(.76387)$$

$$= \$.05/£.$$

TABLE 6.3
Values of European FX Calls on Spot*

	3 mo.	6 mo.	9 mo.	3 mo.	6 mo.	9 mo.	3 mo.	6 mo.	9 mo.
					$v = .10$				
B	.97	.94	.91	.98	.96	.94	.99	.98	.97
B*	.97	.94	.91	.97	.94	.91	.97	.94	.91
1.55	6.07	6.94	7.55	4.99	5.07	4.98	4.03	3.55	3.08
1.60	3.10	4.24	5.03	2.38	2.88	3.07	1.78	1.86	1.74
1.65	1.30	2.36	3.15	0.92	1.47	1.77	0.63	0.88	0.92
B	.97	.94	.91	.98	.96	.94	.99	.98	.97
B*	.98	.96	.94	.98	.96	.94	.98	.96	.94
1.55	7.31	9.29	11.03	6.13	7.09	7.80	5.05	5.21	5.22
1.60	3.98	6.08	7.87	3.13	4.33	5.19	2.41	2.96	3.22
1.65	1.80	3.64	5.32	1.31	2.41	3.26	0.93	1.52	1.86
B	.97	.94	.91	.98	.96	.94	.99	.98	.97
B*	.99	.98	.97	.99	.98	.97	.99	.98	.97
1.55	8.64	11.93	15.02	7.37	9.44	11.27	6.19	7.23	8.05
1.60	4.98	8.26	11.34	4.01	6.16	8.02	3.16	4.42	5.36
1.65	2.42	5.30	8.18	1.81	3.69	5.41	1.32	2.46	3.36

* Entries in the table are prices, in U.S. cents, of a European call option on one British pound, with the designated standard deviation rate (v), strike price ($1.55, $1.60, $1.65), time to maturity (3 months, 6 months, 9 months), and domestic (B) and foreign ($B*$) bond prices, when the spot rate is $1.60 per pound.

Some sample European call option values are given in Table 6.3, for a spot rate of $S(t) = \$1.60/\pounds$. The value of v is assumed to be $v = .10$ per year; maturities are for three, six, and nine months with various sets of domestic and foreign bond prices; and strike prices are $\$1.55/\pounds$, $\$1.60/\pounds$, and $\$1.65/\pounds$. Diagonal cells in the table illustrate that a lower level of interest rates (higher level of bond prices) yields higher cell values when the term structure is the same in both the domestic and foreign countries. Cells below the diagonal show that call values are an increasing function of the positive difference of domestic over foreign interest rates. Cells above the diagonal demonstrate that call prices are a decreasing function of the positive difference of foreign over domestic interest rates. They also show that the European FX call on spot can have an ambiguous time derivative. For $X = \$1.55$,

$$B \in \{.99, .98, .97\}, B* \in \{.97, .94, .91\},$$

for example, the value of the option decreases from 4.03 cents for a three-month term to maturity to 3.08 cents for a nine-month term to maturity.

The formula for the European put can be derived from (6.22) and the put-call conversion equation (6.18) as

$$p(t) = XB(t,T)[1 - N(d2)] - S(t)B*(t,T)[1 - N(d1)]. \tag{6.23}$$

Equations (6.22) and (6.23) can also be written in a form that contains the forward exchange rate. To do this, simply substitute $F(t,T)B(t,T)$ for the expression $S(t)B^*(t,T)$ in equations (6.22) and (6.23), since from the interest parity relation (6.13), we have

$$F(t,T)B(t,T) = S(t)B^*(t,T).$$

Note that as a result of (6.7), equations (6.22) and (6.23) also serve to price European options on futures, provided the futures price and forward rate for option expiration can be treated as equivalent.

For futures-style European options on spot, we have from (6.8) combined with (6.22), (6.23), and (6.13):

$$c^{**}(t) = F(t,T)N(d1) - XN(d2) \qquad (6.24)$$
$$p^{**}(t) = X[1 - N(d2)] - F(t,T)[1 - N(d1)]. \qquad (6.25)$$

□

A more exact statement of the probability assumptions used to derive the pricing equations above is that log S, log B, and log B^* are assumed to follow Wiener-Levy processes. These assumptions imply that log changes in exchange rates and bond prices have normal distributions. (A similar assumption for stock prices was made by Black and Scholes (1973) in deriving their famous equation for pricing European options on non-dividend-paying stock.) If the FX option price is assumed to be twice-continuously differentiable in these variables, then stochastic calculus may be used to construct a riskless hedge portfolio using the option, the domestic currency bond, and the foreign currency bond. As shown in Grabbe (1983), the construction of the hedge results in a partial differential equation whose solution is the option price. A slightly different equation is derived in Garman and Kohlhagen (1983), since they assume that bond prices (interest rates) are constant. The Garman-Kohlhagen pricing equations are similar to (6.22) and (6.23), except that with constant interest rates, the volatility parameter v becomes the volatility of the spot rate instead of that of the forward rate.

As noted in Chapter 3, it is well known that log changes in exchange rates are leptokurtic, which implies that the normal distribution is at best an approximation to the true empirical distribution. An alternative probability assumption that allows for leptokurtosis is made by McCulloch (1987), who derives an FX option-pricing formula assuming that log S has an infinite-variance stable distribution. McCulloch's formulation, however, requires an additional purchasing-power parity assumption.   ■

AMERICAN FX OPTION PRICING

The European FX pricing model gives a *minimum* price for American FX options as a consequence of equation (6.6), but American options will generally have higher prices. Unfortunately there is no known simple, closed-form pricing equation for American FX options generally. However, there are algorithms for getting the right answer, so American options are easily priced on the computer. The lack of a simple equation, however, makes it difficult to summarize the characteristics of the pricing formula easily, except for perpetual FX options.

The difference between American and European FX options is that American options can be exercised on any business day. Thus any variable that would influence the holder of an American option to exercise it prior to expiration increases the value of the American option relative to a European option. The chief influence in this regard is interest rates. In particular, higher foreign interest rates relative to domestic rates increase the probability that American FX calls will be exercised prior to expiration and decrease the probability that American FX puts will be exercised early. As a consequence, the higher foreign interest rates above domestic interest rates, the greater will be the differential between American FX call prices and European FX call prices and the smaller the differential between American FX put prices and European FX put prices. On the other hand, the higher domestic interest rates above foreign interest rates, the greater will be the differential between American FX put prices and European FX put prices and the smaller the differential between American FX call prices and European FX call prices. (A numerical example is given in the following section.)

The American boundary conditions in Table 6.4 can be used to tell us if a particular type of American call has a value strictly greater than the corresponding European call. The arguments for puts are similar, so we will confine the discussion here to calls. If exercised, the value of an American call option is exactly equal to the difference between the underlying asset price and the exercise price. Thus, an American call would never be exercised early if this immediate exercise value were less than the value of the corresponding European call.

For the future-style option on futures, we note that

$$FN(d1) - XN(d2) \geq F - X. \tag{6.26}$$

An exercised futures-style option on futures has a value of $F - X$, which is never greater than the European value. The value of early exercise is thus zero, and the American futures-style option on futures has the same value as the European equivalent, as noted in Table 6.5.

In the remaining cases the early-exercise boundary constraint can be strictly greater than the European value. If B, $B^* < 1$ (interest rates are positive), then for *some value* of S sufficiently large,

$$S - X > B[FN(d1) - XN(d2)], \text{ some } S, \tag{6.27}$$

TABLE 6.4
Boundary Constraints on American Calls

	European Value	American Boundary Constraint
Option on Spot	$B[FN(d1) - XN(d2)]$	$\geq B[FN(d1) - XN(d2)]$ $\geq S - X$
Option on Futures	$B[FN(d1) - XN(d2)]$	$\geq B[FN(d1) - XN(d2)]$ $\geq F - X$
Futures-style Option on Spot	$FN(d1) - XN(d2)$	$\geq FN(d1) - XN(d2)$ $\geq S - X$
Futures-style Option on Futures	$FN(d1) - XN(d2)$	$\geq FN(d1) - XN(d2)$ $\geq F - X$

TABLE 6.5
Value Relationships Among FX Options. [*Note:* Values for similar options only (both options are calls or both puts; same strike price; same *Date of Expiration*). The futures contract is assumed to expire at the same time as the option. When applying these relationships to traded options, keep in mind that CME options expire a week earlier than PHLX options.]

while for *some value* of F sufficiently large,

$$F - X > B[FN(d1) - XN(d2)], \text{ some } F. \tag{6.28}$$

Hence there is a *positive probability of early exercise*. This positive probability gives the American call a value strictly greater than the corresponding European call, both for calls on spot ($C > c$) and calls on futures ($C^* > c^*$).

The remaining relationships shown in Table 6.5 for American FX options may be obtained as follows. For $B < 1$, the inequality

$$FN(d1) - XN(d2) > B[FN(d1) - XN(d2)] \tag{6.29}$$

gives the American futures-style option on spot a value greater than the American option on spot, and gives the American futures-style option on futures a value greater than the American option on futures.

The fact that either

$$F - X \geq S - X \qquad \text{or} \qquad F - X \leq S - X \tag{6.30}$$

is possible makes the value relationship between American calls on spot and American calls on futures ambiguous. Whether the boundary constraint on one of the options is subsumed in that for the other depends on whether the forward rate is at a premium or a discount. If interest rates are constant, then in the event $S - X > F - X$, the call on spot will be more valuable ($C > C^*$), while if $F - X > S - X$, the call on futures will be more valuable ($C^* > C$).

The same conclusions are not possible if interest rates are stochastic, because there is then a positive probability that the forward rate may move from a premium to a discount or from a discount to a premium.

Equations 6.26 and 6.29 show that a futures-style option on spot has a value, for $B < 1$, greater than that of an option on futures. The futures-style option on spot has the additional constraint that it must at all times be $\geq S - X$, yielding (for stochastic interest rates) the results that the American futures-style option on spot is more valuable than the corresponding European option, and also more valuable than the American futures-style option on futures.

Further results on pricing American FX options may be found in the appendix to this chapter.

SOME OPTION CONCEPTS FOR HEDGING AND RISK MANAGEMENT

This section introduces some basic option concepts—the option delta, gamma, theta, elasticity, and lambda. Each of these variables will be illustrated by reference to Table 6.6, which gives comparative American and European call and put values for FX options on spot, options on FX futures, and futures-style FX options on spot. The underlying price assumptions for the spot rate,

TABLE 6.6
Comparison of Options on Spot, Options on Futures, and Futures-Style Options*

	Value	Delta	Gamma	Theta	Elasticity	Lambda
Option on spot						
Call						
European	1.069	.540	.159	−.007	17.58	.069
American	1.072	.540	.160	−.007	17.52	.069
Put						
European	.869	−.447	.159	−.003	−17.92	.069
American	.915	−.479	.180	−.004	−18.23	.068
Option on futures						
Call						
European	1.069	.540	.159	−.007	17.58	.069
American	1.079	.539	.159	−.005	17.58	.069
Put						
European	.869	−.447	.159	−.003	−17.92	.069
American	.876	−.445	.159	−.005	−17.91	.069
Futures-style option on spot						
Call						
European	1.096	.553	.163	−.008	17.58	.070
American	1.098	.552	.164	−.008	17.51	.070
Put						
European	.890	−.458	.163	−.003	−17.92	.070
American	.928	−.483	.179	−.004	−18.12	.070

Source: Author's calculations.

* *Assumptions:* Current spot rate = 34.82; Exercise price of option = 35; Days to option expiration = 93; Eurocurrency rate on domestic currency = 9.47%; Eurocurrency rate on foreign currency = 5.125%; Yearly standard deviation rate = .14; Current futures price determined by interest parity.

interest rates, exercise price, term-to-maturity, and volatility are listed below Table 6.6. The futures contract embodied in the option on futures is assumed to expire at the same time the option expires, and the futures price is assumed to be related to the spot rate by interest parity. (The rates listed in the table imply a futures price of 35.20573.) The European values given in the table were generated by the European pricing formulas just presented. The American values were calculated by a numerical technique that uses a binomial approximation to the normal distribution.

Value

For the sake of concreteness, we may think of the spot rate as being the price of the DM in terms of U.S. cents. Thus the spot rate is 34.82 cents per DM, while the strike price is 35 cents per DM. An option value generated by a pricing formula will appear in the same units used to measure the spot rate and exercise price. So the option values listed in Table 6.6 under the column heading "Value" are in terms of U.S. cents. For example, the value of the European call on one unit of spot DM is 1.069 cents.

Several characteristics of the relative option values should be noted. First, all the American options have values larger than their European counterparts. This will always be true for American FX options, just as long as neither interest rate is zero. (If the rate on domestic currency were zero, then American and European FX puts would have the same value. If the rate on foreign currency were zero, then the American and European calls would have the same value.) Second, each of the futures-style options on spot has a value larger than the corresponding option on spot. (For example, the value of the futures-style American put on spot is .928, versus .915 for the American put on spot.) This is a consequence of Principle 9. An option on spot is the discounted value of the corresponding futures-style option on spot. Hence, for a positive discount rate, the value of the ordinary option is always smaller than the value of the futures-style option. Third, the value of a European option on futures is equal to the value of the corresponding European option on spot. (For example, both puts have values of .869.) This is an illustration of equation (6.7). Finally, the value of the American call on futures is greater than the value of the American call on spot (1.079 versus 1.072), but the value of the American put on futures is less than the value of the American put on spot (.876 versus .915). This reflects the fact that the FX futures price is at a premium. If the FX futures price were at a discount, then the relative prices between the option on spot and the option on futures would be reversed on both the call and the put.

Delta

The option delta measures the amount the option price changes relative to a small increase in the spot rate (for options on spot) or futures price (for options on futures). The option price change is always less in absolute magnitude than the price change in the spot or futures. Hence an option delta always has an absolute value between 0 and 1. For example, for the American put option on spot, the delta value is given as $-.479$. This delta value implies that if the spot rate increases by .1 cent (from 34.82 to 34.92), the option value will increase by $(.1)(-.479) = -.0479$ cents (from .915 to .8671).

In Chapter 5, we looked at delta-hedging with futures contracts. Option deltas may be similarly used for delta-hedging between options and spot exchange, options and futures, or just between options. For example, the delta on the American call on futures is .539. This indicates that if one is long 1 IMM DM futures contract and short 1 IMM DM option on futures, the net delta of the position (per DM) is

$$1 - .539 = .461.$$

That is, the total position is equivalent to a long position in .461 IMM DM futures contracts. Since there are DM125,000 in a futures contract, the net position is equivalent to a long position in future DM of (.461)(DM125,000) = DM57,625. As a second example, if one is long 2 IMM DM futures contracts, and short 4 IMM DM call options on futures, the net delta is

$$2 - 4(.539) = -.156.$$

This total position is equivalent to a short position in .156 IMM DM futures contracts. As a final example, suppose one is long ten PHLX European calls on spot DM and also long twelve PHLX European puts on spot DM. The net delta is

$$10(.540) + 12(-.447) = .036 \text{ (per DM)}.$$

Since a PHLX DM option represents DM62,500, the net position is equivalent to a long position in spot DM of (.036)(DM62,500) = DM2250.

Because the net delta of a position represents the equivalent long or short position in foreign currency, it is a measure of one's total portfolio risk. For that reason, the IMM uses delta factors as a basis for margin requirements. Hedgers use delta factors to determine their actual FX exposure. It should be emphasized, however, that the delta value is only valid for small changes in the spot rate (or futures price), because the delta value itself changes with a change in the underlying price. This implies an additional source of risk once one has established a desired delta position. Suppose, for example, that one has a net delta position of zero. One is then said to be *delta-neutral*. For small changes in the spot rate, the change in the value of the position will be zero. One is fully hedged for small exchange rate fluctuations. Marketmakers who do large amounts of trading relative to their capital often attempt to remain delta-neutral. But there is still risk involved, because the net delta will itself change for any significant change in the spot rate.

Gamma

The option gamma measures the amount the option delta changes relative to a small increase in the spot rate (for options on spot) or futures prices (for options on futures). It is thus a measure of the risk inherent in a delta-neutral hedge. If the gamma is positive, then the delta will increase with an increase in the underlying price and decrease with a decrease in the underlying price. If the original delta were zero while the gamma was positive, then a rising price would result in a positive delta position. A falling price would result in a negative delta position. This is a very desirable state of affairs, because one would like to have a positive delta (net long position) if prices are rising but a negative delta (net short position) if prices are falling. Hence marketmakers who attempt to maintain a delta-neutral position can control their risk by maintaining a positive gamma position also.

Consider the American option on spot. The delta is .540 and the gamma is .160. If the spot rate increased by 1 cent (from 34.82 to 35.82), the gamma of .160 indicates that the delta will increase from approximately

.540 to .540 + .160 = .700.

Suppose that one were initially long a PHLX DM call option on DM62,500. The initial delta of .540 indicates that being long 1 PHLX DM call is equivalent to a long position in (.540)(DM62,500) = DM33,750. But this equivalent long position would be increasing with the spot rate, and at a spot rate of 35.82 would represent a long position of approximately

(.700)(DM62,500) = DM43,750.

All of the options have a positive gamma. This is viewed from the long side of the option. The gamma is negative to the option writer. Suppose one is long one PHLX American call on spot DM and short one PHLX American put on spot DM. The net delta (per DM in the option contract) would be

.540 − (−.479) = 1.019,

while the net gamma would be

.160 − (.180) = −.020.

The net delta for DM62,500 is

(1.019)(DM62,500) = DM63,687.5.

The net gamma for DM62,500 is

(−.020)(DM62,500) = −DM1250.

The small negative value for gamma here indicates that there will be only a small negative change in net delta as the spot rate moves. If the spot rate goes up, the net delta will fall, but only slightly. If the spot rate goes down, the net delta will rise, but only slightly.

Using gammas can be tricky because a gamma is not unit-free. For example, if the spot rate and exercise price in Table 6.6 were measured in U.S. dollar terms ($.3482 instead of 34.82 cents, and $.35 instead of 35 cents), all of the gammas would be multiplied by 100. That is, dividing the spot rate and exercise price by 100 multiplies the gamma value by 100. But the meaning of gamma has not changed in any way.

Theta

The option theta is a measure of the change in an option value with the passage of time. For example, the futures-style American call on spot has a theta of −.008. This indicates that if the option maturity goes from ninety-three days to ninety-two days while none of the other variables listed at the bottom of Table 6.6 changes, the value of the option will fall by .008 cents per unit of foreign currency. That is, the option value will go from 1.098 to 1.098 + (−.008) = 1.090 cents. Notice that to the buyer (long side) the option theta is always negative: The value of the option premium decays with time. The theta value is of great interest to people who write options. The reduction in the option value with the passage of time accrues as income to the option writer. A higher theta value implies a higher income stream.

For example, suppose one has written ten futures-style American calls on DM, each on DM125,000. Then the daily cash flow to the option writer— assuming no other variable changes—would be (10)(.008)(125,000) = 10,000 cents, or $100 per day.

Elasticity

The elasticity of an option represents the percentage change in the option premium for a 1 percent increase in the underlying price. For example, the elasticity of the American put on spot of -18.23 indicates that if the spot rate increases by 1 percent (from 34.82 to (1.01)(34.82) = 35.1682), the option value will decrease by approximately 18.23 percent (from .915 to .748). As a second example, if the futures price increases by 1 percent, the value of the American call on futures will increase by 17.58 percent.

Lambda

The option lambda represents the change in the option value for a unit increase in volatility. The unit used here is an increment of .01 to the volatility. For example, the lambda value for the European put on spot is .069. This indicates that if the volatility (yearly standard deviation rate) goes from .14 to .14 + .01 = .15, the option premium will increase by .069 cents (from .869 to .938). Call and put lambdas on otherwise similar European options are always equal, but call and put lambdas on similar American options can differ.

The sensitivity of the option price to the volatility is of great importance in the market for FX options. The pricing equations used above were derived under the assumption that the volatility v is a known variable. However, in the real world this is not true. One can calculate the yearly standard deviation rate over some recent time period from historical data, but one can't be sure that the actual value of v over the life of the option will be exactly the same. So any option position involves a risk that the assumed value for volatility will not be correct. So, unless one is extremely adroit in forecasting volatility, the only way to reduce volatility risk is to reduce the net lambda of the option position. For example, suppose one bought the European call on spot and wrote the American call on spot. The lambda for each option is .069, so the net lambda is .069 − .069 = 0. The net lambda of zero indicates that the value of the position should not change even if the volatility v changes. Thus there is little volatility risk in this position.

□

The concepts in this section are based on the partial derivatives of the option price with respect to the underlying variables that determine it. The delta is the partial derivative of the option price with respect to the spot rate (or futures price, for options on futures). The gamma is the second partial derivative of the option price with respect to the spot rate (or futures price, for options on futures). That is, the gamma is the partial derivative of the delta with respect to the spot rate (or futures price, for options on futures). The theta is the partial derivative of the option price with respect to time. The lambda is the partial derivative of the option price with respect to the volatility. The elasticity is calculated as the delta multiplied by the (spot rate/option value) [or (futures price/option value) for options on futures].   ∎

IMPLIED VOLATILITY

The implied volatility is that unique value of the volatility v that generates a model price of an option that is identical with an observed market price of the option—given market observations on the spot rate and the domestic and foreign interest rates, and given the strike price and term-to-maturity of the option. The way implied volatility is calculated in practice is that an arbitrary starting value for v (say $v = .12$ or 12 percent) is used to generate a model price (MOD) of the option. MOD is then compared with the observed market price (MAR). If MOD > MAR, then the value for v needs to be decreased (since the MOD price always decreases with decreasing v). If MOD < MAR, then the value for v needs to be increased. When MOD = MAR (or the difference in the two is less than some predefined small number, the "convergence criterion"), the final value of v is the implied volatility.

The chief reason for looking at implied volatility is that it is the only real way to get a handle on whether an option is underpriced or overpriced. For example, one may feel that option prices are "lower" or "higher" than they were last week, but how can one be sure? The spot rate may have changed, and the maturity of the options has also changed. So there is no reason that the same option should be priced the same as it was last week. The question is: Has the price of the option changed *after adjustment for changes in other market factors* such as the spot rate and term-to-maturity. The answer is no if implied volatility has not changed, and yes if implied volatility has changed. The same concept would apply to comparing two options with different strike prices: How can I know if one is overpriced relative to another? The answer hinges on whether they have the same implied volatility. Since they are both options on the same underlying currency, they should presumably have the same implied volatility if correctly priced relative to each other.

The calculated implied volatility (which generates a MOD value equal to the MAR value) is totally dependent on the option-pricing model used. If the model is irrelevant, then the implied volatility will also be irrelevant. For an extreme example, suppose the model for the call price (C) were

$$C = 100v - 3.$$

If a value of $C = 7$ is inserted into this equation, the solution will yield an implied volatility of $v = .10$, because

$$100(.10) - 3 = 7.$$

This implied volatility value is meaningless, however, because the option model is meaningless. For example, one can input a foreign currency option price into a stock option model and solve the stock option model backward to generate an implied volatility. This implied volatility would not be useful because the option model is incorrect. Similarly, a market price of an American FX option can be inserted into a European FX model. The resulting implied volatility will be too high, not necessarily because the American FX option is overpriced in the market but rather because the European FX model will normally generate smaller values for the options and thus compensate for the higher American price by returning a higher volatility.

Taken at face value, a correctly measured implied volatility represents an estimate of the actual volatility of the underlying currency over the life of the option. Thus, whether a given volatility is too "high" or "low" in absolute terms is partly a matter of forecasting judgment. One would expect implied volatilities to resemble recent historical actual volatilities (annual standard deviation rates) of the underlying currency. There is a very subtle issue involved here. Option-pricing models are universally derived on the assumption that the value for v over the life of the option is known in advance. Most people accept that this is not really true—they know v is probably a random variable—but letting v be stochastic in the model derivation makes the mathematics so messy as to be usually beyond solution. So they use models derived on the basis of a known v and then fudge by inserting continually updated v estimates. This uncertainty in the true value for v results in practice in implied volatilities being on average larger than the actual volatilities of the underlying currency.

MARKETMAKING IN FX OPTIONS

The environment for marketmaking in exchange FX options differs from that of the OTC trader, but the principles are the same. A floor trader works off pricing sheets. In the morning, sheets are run using implied volatilities based on night option trading, as well as current eurocurrency interest rates and swap rates from the interbank trade in eurodeposits and foreign exchange. A pricing sheet, such as the partial one shown in Table 6.7, shows the theoretical values for options of different strikes and maturities. Prices and deltas are calculated for a range of spot rates, say at ten-point (.0010) intervals. If exchange rates are extremely volatile and move outside the sheet ranges, new sheets will need to be run during the trading day. The lambda value shown at the right side of the sheet is used to update volatility estimates. If, for example, there is excess demand for calls and puts (buying of straddles) at current prices, the trader may decide his or her volatility value is too low, and take the prices in a row on

TABLE 6.7
Partial Pricing Sheet for Exchange Options

		March Calls (U.S. cent prices)					
					Swap Rate .06		
	Spot	53.50	53.60	53.70	53.80	53.90	Lambda/Theta
Strike 54	Call	.05	.08	.12	.16	.21	.02/−.01
	Delta	.30	.33	.36	.40	.46	
	Put	.49	.42	.36	.30	.25	.02/−.01
	Delta	.68	.66	.62	.58	.52	

the sheet up half a volatility percentage (by one-half the lambda value). The theta shows the option erosion over one day, and toward the end of the day the trader will quote prices reduced by the theta value, or on Friday by a three-day theta.

Suppose an order to sell 100 March 54 calls reaches the floor. The trader looks up at a display screen on the floor and sees the current futures price is 53.84. But the trader is trading options on spot, so subtracting the swap rate of .06 means the current spot rate is 53.78. The trader's sheet price for a spot of 53.80 is .16, so ideally he or she would like to buy at .14 and sell at .18. But competition from other traders means the best our trader can do is buy at a price of .15 and sell at .17. So he bids for 100 March 54 calls at .15. The bid is hit (he buys the options). He then looks at the call delta on the sheet, and sees it is .40. So the trader immediately hedges by selling .40(100) = 40 option-sized lots in the spot market. In this case, each option is worth 62,500 foreign currency units, so he sells 2.5 million units of the foreign currency in the spot market.

After a while, an order to buy 100 March calls reaches the floor. The trader calculates that the spot rate is now at 53.60, and the option has decreased in value to .08. At a theoretical value of .08, the trader will bid at .07 and offer at .09, so he offers to sell a 100 lot for .09. His offer is lifted (he makes the sale). He is now flat options (the buy and sale orders cancel out), so he buys back the 2.5 million units of spot currency previously sold. In the meantime, the spot rate has moved from 53.60 to 53.62.

At this point the trader, even though dealing at a spread, has purchased 100 calls at .15 and sold them at .09. Has he lost money? No, because of his spot hedge. The spot hedge makes (53.78 − 53.62) × 2.5 million = 400,000 cents or $4000. The 100 lot option trade makes (.09 − .15) × 100 × 62,500 = −375,000 or −$3750. So the net profit is $250, excluding fees and overhead.

Notice that the trader's spread of .02 implies a net profit of .02 × 100 × 62,500 = 125,000 cents or $1250. But his spot hedge was sold at 53.78 instead of 53.80, and repurchased at 53.62 instead of 53.60, for a loss of .04 × 2.5 million = 100,000 cents or $1000. So in this case the trader only captured 20 percent of the bid/offered spread.

The OTC trader, by contrast, will be quoting prices for, and buying and selling, nonstandardized options, so he will make his calculations on an option-by-option basis, using a computer-based option calculator. The trader may also use pricing sheets to keep track of exchange option values. Eventually the OTC trader will buy and sell so many different options at different strikes and maturities that his brain will turn to mush if he tries to juggle these in his head. But—not to worry—he makes decisions based on the analytical statistics of his total portfolio. The same is true for the serious exchange marketmaker.

Table 6.8 shows the current options-related FX portfolio of an OTC trader. He has a current delta of "2081" or DM2,081,000. The portfolio is essentially, but not quite, delta-neutral. He can become delta-neutral by selling DM 2,081,000 in the spot market. At that point, he would no longer be long or short foreign currency for tiny changes in the spot rate. But this wouldn't mean he could leave for vacation in Cannes. A delta-neutral portfolio is not really equivalent to a zero position in spot exchange. Rather, it represents a *gamma/ theta trade-off*.

TABLE 6.8
Risk Analysis of an FX Option Portfolio (Thousands)

	Spot Movements				
	−2%	−1%	+0%	+1%	+2%
Delta:	315,229	178,579	2081	−134,601	−266,004
Gamma:	317,310	180,660		−136,684	−268,085

	Time Horizon		
	1 Day	1 Week	1 Month
Theta:	−114	−838	−3,951

	Volatility Risk	
	−20%	+20%
Change in P/L:	−3,186	+3,264

	Interest Risk	
	−100 BP	+100 BP
Change in P/L:	+140	−118

	Profit/Loss Change for Spot Movements Versus Horizon Dates						
Date	−4%	−2%	−1%	0	+1%	+2%	+4%
1/15	6,792	1,826	471	0	344	1,354	5,061
1/22	6,003	924	−432	−838	−398	733	4,712
2/14	3,231	−2,466	−3,840	−3,951	−3,052	−1,353	3,748
3/16	−123	−8,763	−10,891	−9,062	−6,337	−3,318	3,327
4/15	−1,240	−10,013	−12,164	−10,350	−7,918	−4,256	3,247

In this case, the trader is long gamma and consequently his or her theta is negative. If exchange rates move in either direction fast enough, the trader makes money. But if nothing happens, or if something happens but not soon enough, he loses money from the erosion in value of his long option position.

To see this, first look at what happens to the delta of his position from a spot movement of +2%: The delta goes from DM2,081,000 to −DM266,004,000, for a gamma (change in delta) of −DM268,085,000. The "+2%" is in this case a spot movement from DM1.9140/$ to DM1.95228/$, or 2% in DM terms. Thus, the delta becomes negative as the DM depreciates, so the position will make money in dollar terms. Similarly, an appreciation of the DM (spot movement of −2%) is associated with a gamma of DM317,310,000. The position becomes net long (gains a positive delta) with the appreciation, so again a profit is made in dollar terms.

The long gamma position implies the trader has a net long option position, which can only be held at the expense of daily erosion. This is shown by the portfolio theta: If the spot rate doesn't move, the position loses $114,000 in the course of a day. In a month, the loss amounts to $3,951,000.

Thus, whether the trader wins or loses on this position depends not on the direction of spot movement but on the extent and rapidity of change in either direction. This is summarized at the bottom of Table 6.8, showing that if the spot rate doesn't move, the position loses $10,350,000 in three months. If the spot rate goes down 4 percent in one month, the position gains $3,231,000. But if it takes three months for the spot rate to go down this much, the position loses $1,240,000.

In addition to being long gamma, the net long option position is long volatility. If the volatility curve across option maturities goes up by 20 percent, the position makes $3,264,000. (For example, if option volatilities—standard deviations—are 10 percent or .10 across maturities, then an increase of "20%" here means the curve goes from 10 percent to (1.20)10 percent = 12 percent. A decrease of "20%" would take the curve to (1 − .20)10 percent = 8 percent.) If the curve goes down by a similar amount, the position loses $3,186,000. There is not too much the trader can do about volatility risk, except sell some straddles. But this will get rid of his long gamma position also.

The position also has interest rate risk, losing $118,000 if U.S. interest rates rise by 100 basis points, and gaining $140,000 if U.S. interest rates fall by that amount. This risk can be essentially hedged away, as explained in Chapter 14, by selling 50 IMM eurodollar futures. If interest rates rise by 100 basis points, the futures position will gain $50 \times $2500 = $125,000$. So the net gain will be $125,000 − $118,000 = $7,000. If interest rates fall by 100 basis points, the futures position loses $125,000. So the net gain will be $140,000 − $125,000 = $15,000. Thus, if the trader sells 50 eurodollar futures, he ends up with a long gamma position in interest rates also.

In calculating the gamma/theta trade-off from a risk analysis like that in Table 6.8, one should remember to properly measure the thetas and spot deltas of futures and forwards as well as options. From Chapter 5 we know that the futures price is determined from interest parity, so the *delta of a future* from (6.13) is B^*/B. This number will be greater than 1.0 if domestic interest rates are higher than foreign interest rates (B is smaller than B^*). The delta of a forward is different from that of a future. The forward represents a cash flow that takes place at the maturity of the forward, so this cash flow must be discounted to the present by multiplying by the discount bond price B. Hence the *delta of a forward* is $B(B^*/B) = B^*$. This number will always be less than 1.0 as long as foreign interest rates are positive. Over time, the futures and forwards converge to spot, so they have thetas that are negative if the foreign currency is at a premium but positive thetas if the foreign currency is at a discount.

RANGE FORWARDS AND CYLINDER OPTIONS

Let S^* be the spot rate at some date in the future. Consider a contract between a buyer and a seller under whose terms the buyer will be required to purchase foreign currency and pay a domestic currency price of $X1$ if $S^* \geq X1$, S^* if $X1 > S^* > X2$, or $X2$ if $X2 \geq S^*$. Such a contract is termed a *range forward* contract. The investment banking firm of Salomon Brothers began offering range forward contracts in 1985. It is easy to show that the purchase of a range forward with a maximum price of $X1$ and a minimum price of $X2$ is equivalent to buying a European call on spot and selling a European put on spot, where the strike price on the call is above that on the put.

Consider an option portfolio that consists of a long position in a European call on spot $c(t,X1)$ and a short position in a European put on spot $p(t,X2)$, where the option strike prices $X1$ and $X2$ are chosen in such a way that, at the current forward rate F,

$$X1 > F > X2$$

and

$$c(t,X1) = p(t,X2).$$

The current value of the position is $c - p = 0$, while at expiration, for a spot rate of S^*, the value will be

	Value of Long Call	Value of Short Put	Total Cost of FX
$S^* \geqslant X1$	$S^* - X1$	0	$X1$
$X1 > S^* > X2$	0	0	S^*
$X2 \geqslant S^*$	0	$-[X2 - S^*]$	$X2$

For spot values between $X1$ and $X2$, the holder of this option position will be required to pay the expiration spot rate S^* in order to receive foreign exchange, since the value of the two options will be zero. Otherwise, the holder will exercise the call and pay a maximum of $X1$ or else have the put exercised against the position and be required to pay a price of $X2$ for the exchange received. Since the option position has the same payoff as a range forward, we may summarize:

Long range forward with upper price $X1$ and lower price $X2$
$\quad = \quad$ Long European call with strike $X1$
$\quad + \quad$ Short European put with strike $X2$.

The seller of the range forward contract must choose $X1$ and $X2$ so that the value of the call and put are equal, and hence there will be no premium payment for the range forward contract. (When dealing at a spread, the marketmaker will sell a range forward at a zero price with $X1$ and $X2$ chosen so that the net value to the buyer is slightly negative.) What if the strikes $X1$, $X2$ are chosen in such a way that the values of the call and put are not equal? One then has a *cylinder option*, as marketed by Citibank and others. The difference between range forwards and cylinders is that in a range forward the buyer chooses one of the strike prices, and the bank then calculates the second one to equate the values of the call and the put. In a cylinder option the buyer specifies both strikes and then either pays or receives the net value difference between the two options.

OTHER FORWARD OPTIONS

In the previous section we saw that a range forward may be written as $c(X1) - p(X2)$. If $X1 = X2$, we have an ordinary forward. *A participating forward* may be written as

$$c(X) - kp(X) = 0 \qquad (6.31)$$

where $0 < k < 1$. In this type of forward contract, the buyer pays a maximum of X for spot exchange, because if the spot rate is above X at the time of forward settlement, the call would expire in the money. The cost of spot exchange would then be $S - c(X) = S - (S - X) = X$. But if the spot rate is below X at forward expiration, the cost is $S - (-kp(X)) = S + k(X - S) = kX + (1 - k)S$. The buyer pays an effective rate that lies *between* X and S. For example, if $k = .5$, $S = \$.80/Aus\$$ and $X = \$.82/Aus\$$, then the buyer pays $\$.81/Aus\$$.

Note from (6.19) that if $X = F$, the current forward rate, then $c(X) - p(X) = 0$. Hence $c(X) - kp(X) > 0$. For a given k, X must then be increased to reduce the value of (6.31) to zero, which implies that the bank must set the strike above the current forward rate in a participating forward.

A *conditional forward* is a contract that combines a forward contract and a put option. The put premium is added to the cost of the forward. The option buyer chooses a strike $X2$ representing the buyer's ceiling rate. The bank then chooses a strike $X1$ such that $X1 + p(X1) = X2$. The value of the conditional forward may then be written as

$$c(X2) - p(X2) + Bp(X1). \tag{6.32}$$

Note that if $X1 = F$, then by (6.19), $c(X2) - p(X2) = B(F - X2) = -Bp(X1)$, so the cost of the conditional forward is zero. But if $X1 \neq F$, there will be a positive or negative value.

The payoffs to the conditional forward at expiration are

Case	Value of Conditional Forward	Cost of Foreign Exchange
$S > X2$	$S - X2$	$X2$
$X2 > S > X1$	$S - X2$	$X2$
$S < X1$	$X1 - X2$	$S + (X2 - X1)$

One never pays more than $X2$ on this contract. But if $S < X1$, then since $X2 - X1 = p(X1)$, one pays the current spot rate plus the put premium.

AVERAGE-RATE (ASIAN) FX OPTIONS

An *average-rate option* is an option that pays off, at option maturity, the difference between the option strike price and the average rate A over the life of the option. If a call, the payoff is $\max(0, A-X)$, or if a put, $\max(0, X-A)$. At the time the option is written, the option buyer and writer agree on the notional FX amount of the option, the option premium, the option strike price, a public source of spot exchange rate quotations, and a sampling interval for observing the spot rate. The average exchange rate is then calculated from these observations. The value of the option payoff (if any) at maturity is usually settled between the buyer and writer in terms of the domestic currency. That is, the treatment is similar to a cash-settled index option, where the average spot rate serves as the index.

An intuitive understanding for the appeal of average-rate options can be obtained by considering a company that will make foreign sales in the amount of ¥100 per day for the coming year. Under one management style, the company covers this nominal exchange exposure by selling ¥100 forward for each day of the coming year. The total domestic currency value of these sales will be ¥100, times the number of days, times today's average forward rate, where the forward rates in the average mature on each day of the coming year. Under another management style, the company converts yen sales to the domestic currency at the spot rate prevailing when the sales occur. The total domestic currency value of these sales will be ¥100, times the number of days, times next year's actual average spot rate. These two management styles result in the same amount of domestic currency only if the realized average spot rate is equal to the average forward rate.

An average-rate option bridges the gap between these two management styles. For example, a practitioner of the second management style will achieve the same results as in the first style if the practitioner also sells a European call and buys a European put on the average spot rate, where each option has one year to maturity, a strike price equal to the average forward rate, and involves a notional amount of FX equal to ¥100 times the number of days in a year.

Average-rate options may be priced by reference to European options. The salient features are the following.

1. Relative to a European option, the volatility of an average-rate option (ARO) decreases linearly with time. To see this, consider a European option with yearly volatility v, and with 1 day to expiration ($T=1/365$). The expression $v\sqrt{T}$ in the European option formula becomes $v\sqrt{1/365}$. This represents the 1-day volatility of the spot rate S. By contrast, consider an ARO with an initial maturity of one year, where the average-rate calculation is updated at the end of each day. With 1 day to expiration, the average rate for 364 of the 365 days has already been determined, so the current value of the average rate A can be written as $A = (364/365)\overline{A} + (1/365)S$. The $\overline{A}$ part of A is nonstochastic; the only part of A that is random is the last day's spot value S. Thus the yearly volatility of A is currently $(1/365)v$ instead of v, and the 1-day volatility of the average rate is $(1/365)v\sqrt{1/365}$, instead of $v\sqrt{1/365}$ as in the European option.

2. Relative to a European option, the spot delta of an ARO decreases linearly with time. Again, with T days to expiration, the average rate A in an ARO with an initial maturity of 365 days may be written as $A = (365-T)/365\,\overline{A} + (T/365)S$. Let D be the delta of the ARO with respect to A. Hence its delta with respect to S is $D(\Delta A/\Delta S) = D(T/365)$. The delta goes to zero as $T \to 0$.

3. At the beginning of its life, the volatility of an average-rate option is between 100 percent and 57.77 percent of the volatility of the corresponding European option. The exact relationship depends on the frequency with which the average is calculated (monthly, weekly, daily, etc.). Suppose the average is calculated from daily observations. For the first day of its life, no observations will have yet been made, so no part of the average will be locked in. The volatility of the spot rate S for this day will be $v\sqrt{1/365}$ and the variance will be $v^2(1/365)$. At the end of the first day the spot rate will be observed, and this will serve as the first point to calculate the average. On the second day the random variable will be no longer S, but rather $(364/365)S$, with a variance of $(364/365)^2 v^2(1/365)$. The average daily variance over

the life (365 days) of the option will be therefore $(1/365) [1+(364/365)^2 + (363/365)^2 + \ldots + (2/365)^2 + (1/365)^2] v^2(1/365) = .3347 \, v^2(1/365)$.

The daily option volatility, or standard deviation, is the square root of this number, or $.5785 \, v\sqrt{1/365}$. The ARO volatility is 57.85 percent of the corresponding European option volatility when the observations are daily.

BARRIER OPTIONS

A *down-and-out option* (DAOO) is like an ordinary option, American or European, except that the option automatically expires worthless if the spot rate reaches some level specified in the option contract. That is, the option privileges held by the buyer are *extinguished* if the spot rate crosses a given barrier (spot rate level) during the life of the option. The probability of doing so is called a first-passage probability in probability theory. (We encountered a first-passage probability in Chapter 5 as the probability of futures margin falling to a predetermined level. See also the appendix to this chapter with respect to *first-passage options*.) For example, one might have a one-year European call on the DM with a strike of DM1.60/U.S. dollar, with the additional feature that the option automatically becomes worthless if the value of the DM falls to DM1.70/U.S. dollar during the one-year life of the option.

Variations on the DAOO are a *down-and-in option* (DAIO) in which the option feature is *activated* only if some barrier is crossed prior to option expiration. For example, one might have a one-year European put on the DM with a strike of DM1.60/U.S. dollar, but with the additional stipulation that the put feature will not be activated unless the DM falls to DM1.65/U.S. dollar at least once during the one-year period prior to option maturity. (Depending on how you measure exchange rate direction, of course, the DAOO may become an "up-and-out" option, and the DAIO an "up-and-in" option.)

Example 6.7 (in the appendix to this chapter) illustrates one way to price down-and-out options.

OPTIONS ON OPTIONS

An *option on an option* is an option that, when exercised, pays off the value of another option. A call on a call (a *cacall*) would have a value at maturity of $\max(0, c-X)$, where c is the value of the underlying call, and X is the cacall strike price. A call on a put (*caput*), by contrast, would pay off $\max(0, p-X)$, where p is the underlying put price. A company that is bidding on a contract that involves potential foreign exchange exposure might prefer to buy an option on an option instead of an option. The premium of the option on the option is lower than the option premium itself. Hence the company saves money if the contract is not received. If, however, the contract is received, the total cost to the company will normally be higher if an option on an option were purchased rather than the underlying option itself. Example 6.6 illustrates the evaluation of a cacall.

OPTIONS AND FUTURES: A BRIEF HISTORICAL PERSPECTIVE

The history of options is interconnected with that of futures. Neither contract is a recent development. The Osaka rice market in eighteenth-century Japan provides an early example of an organized exchange that included standardized spot and futures contracts and the settlement of trades through a clearinghouse. In the United States, the first spot commodity exchange was established in New York City in 1691. Exchanges provided a common meeting place to collect information as well as to trade commodities. Trade was facilitated because exchange members could agree on commercial standards and on rules for handling disputes.

Futures contracts grew out of delayed delivery contracts in the commodities markets. These delayed delivery contracts were actually forward contracts. A cotton grower in the southern United States might ship cotton to New York in return for a price that was fixed in advance. The cotton buyer faced the risk that the market price might change before the cotton arrived in New York. This risk could be transferred if the cotton buyer made a separate forward contract to sell the cotton to another party. But the chain of transfer could only terminate when someone voluntarily bore the price risk. To reduce the costs of arranging such risk transfer as well as the costs of obtaining credit information on counterparties to a contract, trading in futures contracts was organized on exchanges in a manner similar to spot commodities. Trading in grain futures began at the Chicago Board of Trade (CBT) around the time of the Civil War, while cotton futures began a few years later with the New York Cotton Exchange.

Clearinghouses were originally bookkeeping organizations. They confirmed trades but did not guarantee each side of a contract. Clearinghouses became guarantors, however, toward the end of the century and began to require the marking to market of open positions. Margin requirements were first imposed on clearing members and later extended to retail customers. Marking to market created a clear distinction between futures and forward contracts.

Option contracts arose in connection with futures. Members of the CBT would sometimes protect a futures position by taking out an option to make or take delivery of grain. But options were not universally accepted. Some said that options disrupted the futures market. When grain markets collapsed in the Great Depression of the 1930s, commodity options trading was prohibited by the Commodity Exchange Act (1936). Option trading had also appeared in connection with the stock market, and the Securities Exchange Act of 1934 placed exchange-based stock option trading under the jurisdiction of the SEC. Stock options, however, continued to trade only in an over-the-counter market until February 1973, when the Chicago Board Options Exchange (CBOE) opened.

The advent of financial futures trading began about the same time, in 1972, when contracts on several foreign currencies were listed at the IMM. In 1974, the Commodities Futures Trading Commission Act created the CFTC. This act gave the CFTC jurisdiction over futures contracts generally, including foreign currency futures. The act continued to ban agricultural options (the ban was lifted in 1982), but the CFTC was given discretion to allow options trading on other commodities and financial instruments. Trading in stock index futures and options on certain debt securities resulted in a jurisdictional dispute between the SEC and CFTC. This was resolved by an accord between the two agencies in 1981. One provision of the accord was that options on foreign currency traded on a national securities exchange would be regulated by the SEC, while the CFTC would have jurisdiction over options on foreign currency not traded on a securities exchange as well as over options on foreign currency futures. The accord was enacted into law by Congress a year later, and the SEC approved FX options trading at the PHLX in December 1982. [An overview of the accord, as well as of U.S. regulation generally, can be found in Board of Governors et al. (1984).]

PROBLEMS FOR CHAPTER 6

1. Suppose you had purchased 2 March DM PHLX calls with a 38 strike ($.38/DM) at the price shown in the following *Wall Street Journal* excerpt.

FOREIGN CURRENCY OPTIONS

Friday, November 29, 1985

Philadelphia Exchange

Option & Underlying	Strike Price	Calls Last			Puts – Last		
		Dec	Jan	Mar	Dec	Jan	Mar
12,500 British Pounds-cents per unit							
BPound	115	33.60	s	r	r	s	r
148.98	.130	18.70	r	18.90	r	r	0.25
148.98	.140	8.70	r	8.80	r	0.25	1.35
148.98	145	3.80	r	5.50	0.30	1.10	2.80
148.98	.150	0.55	1.50	3.10	1.70	3.10	r
148.98	.155	r	r	1.70	r	r	r
50,000 Canadian Dollars-cents per unit.							
CDollr	...72	0.33	r	r	0.18	0.43	0.73
72.24	.73	r	r	0.32	0.55	0.72	r
72.24	.74	r	r	r	r	r	2.05
62,500 West German Marks-cents per unit.							
DMark	.. 35	4.85	r	5.00	r	r	r
39.80	...36	3.80	r	4.12	r	r	0.10
39.80	.. 37	2.84	2.92	3.27	r	r	0.18
39.80	...38	1.84	1.90	2.44	0.01	r	0.35
39.80	...39	0.86	1.21	1.77	0.07*	r	r
39.80	... 40	0.24	0.62	1.23	0.40	0.69	r
125,000 French Francs-10ths of a cent per unit.							
FFranc	.120	r	r	r	r	r	0.80
130.45	.125	r	r	6.60	r	r	1.65
130.45	.130	r	r	3.85	r	r	r
6,250,000 Japanese Yen-100ths of a cent per unit.							
JYen	... 39	10.40	s	r	r	s	r
49.44	...42	7.38	r	r	r	r	r
49.44	...46	r	r	3.42	r	r	0.08
49.44	...47	r	r	2.66	r	r	r
49.44	...48	1.46	1.62	r	r	r	0.32
49.44	...49	0.74	0.90	1.26	0.12	0.39	0.75
49.44	...50	0.15	0.39	0.69	0.60	r	r
49.44	...51	0.06	s	s	r	s	r
62,500 Swiss Francs-cents per unit.							
SFranc	...40	8.00	s	r	r	s	0.02
48.03	...41	6.98	s	r	r	s	r
48.03	...42	6.10	s	r	r	s	r
48.03	...44	4.03	r	4.65	r	r	0.14
48.03	...45	3.03	r	r	r	r	r
48.03	...46	r	r	3.04	r	r	r
48.03	...47	1.24	1.55	2.27	r	r	0.75
48.03	...48	0.43	0.88	1.75	0.30	r	r

		Feb	May	Aug	Feb	May	Aug
62,500 West German Marks-cents per unit.							
DMark	41	0.52	s	s	r	s	s
62,500 Swiss Francs-cents per unit.							
SFranc	49	0.94	s	s	r	s	s
Total call vol.	19,587		Call open int.	211,409			
Total put vol.	7,523		Put open int.	168,078			

r – Not traded.   s – No option offered.
Last is premium (purchase price).

[Chicago Mercantile Exchange]

BRITISH POUND (CME) 25,000 pounds; cents per pound

Strike	Calls – Settle			Puts – Settle		
Price	Dec-C	Mar-C	Jun-C	Dec-P	Mar-P	Jun-P
1425	6.40	7.05	7.75	0.05	2.00	3.65
1450	3.95	5.55	6.35	0.10	2.85	4.60
1475	1.65	4.20	5.15	0.35	4.00	5.80
1500	0.50	3.20	4.20	1.65	....	....
1525	....	....	....			
1550	....	....	....			

Est. vol. 747, Wed.; vol. 1,019 calls, 598 puts
Open interest Wed.; 12,094 calls, 14,841 puts

W. GERMAN MARK (CME) 125,000 marks, cents per mark

Strike	Calls – Settle			Puts – Settle		
Price	Dec-C	Mar-C	Jun-C	Dec-P	Mar-P	Jun-P
38	1.86	2.51	3.06	.0008	0.33	0.62
39	0.88	1.79	2.40	0.02	0.60	0.94
40	0.19	1.22	1.84	0.33	1.02	1.32
41	0.02	0.82	1.37	1.16	1.58	1.81
42	....	0.52	1.00			
43	....	....	....			

Est. vol. 6,885, Wed.; vol. 4,985 calls, 1,851 puts
Open interest Wed.; 42,333 calls, 37,633 puts

SWISS FRANC (CME) 125,000 francs; cents per franc

Strike	Calls – Settle			Puts – Settle		
Price	Dec-P	Mar-P	Jun-P	Dec-P	Mar-P	Jun-P
46	2.19	3.05	3.79	.0008	0.40	0.70
47	1.20	2.32	3.10	0.01	0.67	0.99
48	0.36	1.71	2.49	0.17	1.02	1.35
49	0.06	1.23	1.98	0.87	1.52	1.80
50	....	0.86	1.56	....	2.14	2.34
51	....	....	....			

Est. vol. 1,439, Wed.; vol. 770 calls, 995 puts
Open interest Wed.; 12,972 calls, 15,357 puts

Source: The *Wall Street Journal*, Friday, November 29, 1985.

(a) What dollar amount (ignoring broker fees) would you have paid?

(b) What approximate ceiling cost of DM125,000 would you have locked in?

(c) Suppose you had held the two options for 30 days, and then sold them for "2.60" (U.S. cents per DM). What was the net dollar profit, assuming entry costs of $4/option, exit costs of $4/option, and a dollar interest opportunity cost of 9 percent per annum (360 days) on the premium?

2. Suppose you had purchased 1 June DM 41 IMM futures put at the price shown in the *Wall Street Journal* excerpt for Problem 1.

   (a) What dollar amount would you have paid?

   (b) Explain exactly what would take place if you exercised the put at a time when the futures price was $.4021/DM.

   (c) Compare the prices of PHLX options on spot exchange for Friday, November 29, with the prices of equivalent (same strike and maturity) options on IMM futures. What do you think accounts for the differences in prices between the two types of options?

3. A Japanese company buys a European call on ¥200,000,000 with a strike price of ¥240/$, and pays a premium of ¥4/$. The company's interest opportunity cost is 10 percent per year. There are no additional fees.

   (a) What is the minimal end-of-year dollar cost of the yen that would result in a net positive payoff on this insurance?

   (b) What range of end-of-year exchange rates would result in exercise of the option (assuming no exercise fees)?

   (c) Suppose the one-year forward rate were ¥238/$. For what range of end-of-year spot exchange values would the option contract prove more advantageous than the forward contract? For what range would it prove less advantageous?

4. Verify the numbers in Table 6.2. That is, given the option prices and assumptions, derive the sets of terminal spot-rate ranges that would make (after the fact) each decision the optimal one.

5. Explain why American FX calls and puts generally have values larger than European FX calls and puts. Under what circumstances would an American FX call *not* have a value larger than a European FX call? Answer the same question for FX puts.

6. Explain why futures-style FX calls and puts on spot generally have values larger than ordinary calls or puts on spot. Under what circumstances would a futures-style option have the same value as the corresponding ordinary option?

7. A trader buys a "bear spread" on the British pound that consists of a long PHLX 130 March put and a short PHLX 125 March put.

   (a) If the price of the 130 put is $.055/£ while the price of the 125 put is $.022/£, what is the net dollar amount paid for the bear spread?

   (b) What is the maximum amount the trader can make if the British pound depreciates with respect to the U.S. dollar?

   (c) Answer similar questions for a "bull spread" that consists of a long PHLX 125 March call priced at $.043/£ and a short PHLX 130 call priced at $.015/£. What is the trader's maximum profit? Maximum loss?

8. The spot price of pounds is $1.25/£, the eurodollar interest rate is 10 percent, and the eurosterling interest rate is 8 percent. Given only this information, determine the minimum value an American FX call option could rationally trade for in the market, if the exercise price of the option is $1.25/£ and there are ninety days until expiration.

9. Using the European FX call formula and a table of the normal distribution, calculate the value of an FX call on the DM, given a strike of $.30, a spot rate of $.2950, a eurodollar rate of 8.75 percent, a euro-DM rate of 5.5 percent, a term-to-expiration of ninety days, and a volatility parameter (yearly standard deviation rate) of .15.

10. Explain in what sense being long an FX futures call and short an FX futures put is similar to being long an FX futures contract.

11. Show that an American futures-style option on spot always has a larger value than an American futures-style option on futures.

12. Show that American and European futures-style options on futures have equal values.

13. Explain how to set up a delta-neutral position, being long calls and short spot exchange, whose dollar value will remain essentially unchanged for small movements in the exchange rate. What would be the preferred gamma of such a position? The preferred theta?

14. A U.S. multinational has annual cash flows of £100,000,000. The company believes the pound may either depreciate slightly or remain at the current exchange rate with respect to the U.S. dollar. The company wishes to increase the immediate dollar value of its pound sterling cash flow, and in order to obtain this the company is willing to forgo the possibility of exchange rate gains if the pound were to appreciate strongly against the dollar.
   (a) Explain why the company can meet its objectives by writing call options on the British pound (with a U.S. dollar strike price).
   (b) How is the trade-off between up-front cash inflow and forgone exchange rate gains affected by the choice of strike price in the calls that the company writes?

15. Explain the gamma/theta trade-off. Why is it not possible to be simultaneously delta neutral, long gamma, and theta positive?

16. The risk manager for a bank sets position limits for its FX options traders based on delta, gamma, and theta. In what way are these position limits insufficient with respect to the bank's risk position?

17. A trader notices that the market volatility curve (option volatilities across maturities) is steeply upward sloping, and believes that the curve will soon flatten. Devise a trading strategy that can be used to generate profits if the curve flattens, but that will be essentially neutral to market changes other than to twists in the volatility curve.

18. Derive the delta of a forward contract directly from the interest parity relationship.

19. A company buys a DM put with a strike of DM1.50/$ and writes a DM call with a strike of DM1.45/$. Interpret this position as a range forward. What happens if at option expiration the spot rate is DM1.55/$?

20. What is the advantage to the long side of a participating forward? What does one give up (relative to an ordinary forward) in order to obtain this advantage?

21. What is the advantage to the long side of a conditional forward? What does one give up (relative to an ordinary forward) in order to obtain this advantage?

22. Under what circumstances would one prefer a conditional forward to a participating forward?

23. In an average-rate option with an original maturity of one year (fifty-two weeks), the spot rate is sampled once a week. Calculate the volatility of the average-rate option, relative to an equivalent European option, after sixteen weeks have passed.

24. Derive a put-call parity relationship for average-rate options.

25.   For the calculations leading to A3, in the chapter appendix, explain the case $r^* = 0$. Interpret your answer. Explain and interpret the case $r = 0$.

26.   Repeat the option evaluation steps in Example 6.5 (see the chapter appendix), letting $X = 35$, but keeping the other variables the same.

27.   Repeat the cacall evaluation steps in Example 6.6, but with the cacall strike price $X2 = 1.2$ and $T2 = 2/3$.

28.   In Example 6.7, change the down-and-out price to $U = 32$. What is the value of the option?

29.   Why does the look-back call of Example 6.8 have a value larger than the American call of Example 6.5? Is this relationship general?

30.   Calculate the value of the look-back call in Example 6.8 using the same pricing assumptions as before, but changing the number of time steps to 5 (i.e., the option is evaluated at $T = 0$, $T = 1/5$, $T = 2/5$, $T = 3/5$, $T = 4/5$, and $T = 1$).

APPENDIX TO CHAPTER 6

CALCULATING AMERICAN FX OPTION VALUES

Perpetual American Options

We begin by considering the special case of a *perpetual* American FX option, which is an option that never matures. Its solution will provide some additional insight into American FX options generally and will be obtained from the pricing equation for another option type, a *first-passage option*.

First-passage options are neither American nor European. Consider an FX contract of the following form. Company A and company B trade currencies at a current spot rate of $1.50/British pound. The reverse trade at the same rate will take place at some future date. In the meanwhile, in the event the spot rate rises to $1.65/British pound, company A will immediately pay company B $.15/British pound. What is the value of company A's contingent obligation to pay $.15/British pound to company B? Consider an option contract with a strike price X, and which pays off an amount $Z_u - X$ at the time of the first occurrence of $S = Z_u$, provided this event takes place prior to option maturity; otherwise, the option pays nothing and expires worthless. We will designate such an option contract a *first-passage call*. In our example, company A's obligation to company B can be priced as a first-passage call with $X = \$1.50$ and $Z_u = \$1.65$. A *first-passage put* is similar, except that it pays $X - Z_d$ at the time of the first occurrence of $S = Z_d$, provided this event occurs prior to maturity.

Let the value of a first passage call be designated by $c^\wedge$, and let r and r^* be, respectively, continuously compounded nonstochastic domestic and foreign interest rates. Then the formula for $c^\wedge$ is derived in Grabbe (1985, 1987) as

$$c^\wedge = [Z_u - X] \left[\frac{Z_u}{S}\right]^{\frac{m}{v^2}} \left[\left[\frac{Z_u}{S}\right]^\Theta N(d_1) + \left[\frac{Z_u}{S}\right]^{-\Theta} N(d_2) \right], \qquad \text{(A1)}$$

where

$$d_1 = \frac{ln[S/Z_u] - v^2\Theta T}{v\sqrt{T}}, \qquad \Theta = \frac{\sqrt{m^2 + 2rv^2}}{v^2},$$

$$d_2 = \frac{ln[S/Z_u] + v^2\Theta T}{v\sqrt{T}}, \qquad m = r - r^* - 1/2\, v^2.$$

Letting $T \to \infty$, the value of a *perpetual* first-passage call becomes

$$c_\infty^\wedge = [Z_u - X]\left[\frac{Z_u}{S}\right]^{\frac{m}{v^2} - \Theta}. \tag{A2}$$

Equation (A2) corresponds to the value of an FX option that never matures, and which will be exercised when and only when $S = Z_u$. This perpetual first-passage call differs from a perpetual American FX call on spot only in that in the latter case the optimal exercise level Z_u may be freely chosen. Thus the value of a perpetual American FX call may be obtained by maximizing $c^\wedge$ over Z_u. Applying this procedure to equation (A2), we discover that the maximum is obtained at $Z_u = \infty$, for $(m/v^2) - \Theta \geq -1$. In that case, the value of the perpetual American FX call on spot (C_∞) is $C_\infty = S$. For $(m/v^2) - \Theta < -1$,

$$C_\infty = [Z_u^* - X]\left[\frac{Z_u^*}{S}\right]^{\frac{r - r^* - \frac{1}{2}v^2 - \sqrt{(r - r^*)^2 + v^2(r + r^*) + \frac{1}{4}v^4}}{v^2}} \tag{A3}$$

where

$$Z_u^* = X\left[\frac{(r^* + \sqrt{(r - r^*)^2 + v^2(r + r^*) + \frac{1}{4}v^4}) - (r - \frac{1}{2}v^2)}{(r^* + \sqrt{(r - r^*)^2 + v^2(r + r^*) + \frac{1}{4}v^4}) - (r + \frac{1}{2}v^2)}\right].$$

Sample values of perpetual American FX options are given in Table 6.9, for $S = X = 35$ and $v = .12$. We see that for $r = r^* = .10$, the values of the perpetual American call and put are equal: $C_\infty = P_\infty = 3.434$. The call will be exercised at the critical level $Z_u^* = 45.736$, while the put will be exercised at $Z_d^* = 26.784$. If the foreign interest rate falls to .01, the value of the call rises to $C_\infty = 24.909$ and the critical level for call exercise rises to 377.772, while the value of the put falls to $P_\infty = 0.983$ and the critical level for put exercise rises to 32.427. These results highlight the impact of the interest differential on the critical exercise level.

TABLE 6.9
Perpetual American FX Option Values

$S = 35$		$X = 35$		$v = .12$	
r	r^*	C_∞	Z_u^*	P_∞	Z_d^*
.10	.10	3.434	45.736	3.434	26.784
.10	.05	10.208	79.045	1.564	30.995
.10	.01	24.909	377.772	0.983	32.427
.05	.10	1.564	39.522	10.208	15.498
.01	.10	0.983	37.777	24.909	3.243

Binomial Pricing Procedure

The previous section showed that explicit pricing equations may be given for perpetual American options. The lack of an integral solution in the other cases requires a numerical approach for generating prices. An approach due to Cox, Ross, and Rubinstein (1979) values American options under the assumption of a multiplicative binomial process. Their approach can be treated either as an alternative probability assumption or as a discrete time approximation to the continuous time Wiener-Levy process. Here we will derive the relevant evaluation equations for the different types of American FX options.

Let S represent the level of the spot rate in the current time interval, while F is the price of forward exchange for delivery in the following time interval. Assume that the spot rate follows a binomial process with proportional jumps between time intervals of u or $d = 1/u$. Given the current spot value of S, at the next time interval the value will be Su with probability q, or Sd with probability $1 - q$. The current value of an American option on spot is C. If the option is exercised immediately it will have a value $C = S - X$. If the option is held until the next time interval, the value will be C_u corresponding to Su, or C_d, corresponding to Sd.

We may determine the value of the American option C by creating a portfolio whose net payoff duplicates the net payoff to the option. For an option purchased this period and sold next period, the net payoff is $C_u - C$ with probability q, or $C_d - C$ with probability $1 - q$.

Consider a purchase of a units of forward exchange at the price F, along with an investment of b units of domestic currency at the one-period rate of interest r. The payoff to this portfolio in the next time period will be $a[Su - F] + rb$, with probability q, or $a[Sd - F] + rb$, with probability $1 - q$. For these payoffs to duplicate those available from the purchase of an option, it is necessary that

$$C_u - C = a[Su - F] + rb$$
$$C_d - C = a[Sd - F] + rb.$$

Solutions of these equations shows that a and b must be chosen such that

$$a = [C_u - C_d]/S(u - d)$$
$$b = [C_u - C]/r - [C_u - C_d][u - F/S]/r(u - d).$$

Since investment in the strategy has the same net payoff as holding the option for another period, the value of retaining the option for another period is equal to the domestic currency amount invested in the portfolio. But the total domestic currency amount investment in the portfolio is b. Hence

$$C = \max[b, \ S - X].$$

Substituting this relation into the previous equation, and solving for C, we obtain

$$C = \max[[C_u([F/S - d]/[u - d]) + C_d([u - F/S]/[u - d])]/(1 + r), \ S - X].$$

This last equation may be written in the simplified form

$$C = \max[[kC_u + (1 - k)C_d]/(1 + r), \ S - X] \tag{A4}$$

where

$$k = (F/S - d)/(u - d) \tag{A5}$$

The variable k may be interpreted as a probability, since $0 < k < 1$. However, it is important to keep in mind that this interpretation is solely for convenience. The real probabilities were given by q and $1 - q$, while k and $1 - k$ are only "as if" probabilities that arise from the duplicating portfolio. They are sometimes called "risk-neutral" probabilities because they have the property that

$$F = kSu + (1 - k)Sd.$$

With probabilities k and $1 - k$, the forward rate is the expected value of next period's spot rate. There is, however, no assumption that the same is true with respect to the actual probabilities q and $1 - q$.

Notice that this procedure gives us a way of valuing the American option prior to expiration. At expiration $C_u = \max[Su - X, 0]$ and $C_d = \max[Sd - X, 0]$. Hence we may explicitly solve for C at the time period prior to expiration. Given values of C for the time period prior to expiration, we may solve for C two time periods prior to expiration, and so on, working backwards in a dynamic programming fashion.

For options on futures, C^*, a similar argument to that above leads to equations (A4) and (A5) being replaced with

$$C^* = \max[[kC_u + (1 - k)C_d]/(1 + r), F - X] \tag{A6}$$
$$k = (1 - d)/(u - d). \tag{A7}$$

For futures-style options on spot, the equation becomes

$$C^{**} = \max[[kC_u + (1 - k)C_d], S - X], \tag{A8}$$

where k is given by equation (A5). Finally, for futures-style options on futures, the pricing equations are (A7) and

$$C^{**} = \max[[kC_u + (1 - k)C_d], F - X]. \tag{A9}$$

American FX puts are priced in an analogous manner, the value of the put at each stage being the maximum of the immediate exercise value of the put or the amount b invested in the duplicating portfolio. Therefore

$$P = \max[b, X - S],$$

and so on for the other equations.

In practice, this procedure requires that the actual time interval to option expiration be broken into discreet pieces. If we divide the time interval T into n smaller pieces, each with length T/n, then u and d may be written in terms of a volatility parameter v as

$$u = \exp(v\sqrt{T/n}), d = 1/u.$$

Cox, Ross, and Rubinstein (1979) show that as n goes to infinity, the value of an option following a multiplicative binomial process will converge to the value of a similar option following a Wiener-Levy process.

EXAMPLE 6.5

The binomial procedure can be illustrated by the following. Let $S = 35$, $X = 34$, $r = .10$, and $F = 34.60$. The volatility is $v = .12$ or 12 percent, and $T = 1$. Consider an American call on the spot rate S.

Suppose we divide the year into $n = 3$ parts. The up jump u may then be calculated as $u = \exp(.12 \sqrt{1/3}) = 1.071738$. The down jump $d = 1/u$ is $d = .933063$. Since $r = .10$ for $T = 1$, for $T = 1/3$, $(1 + r)^{1/3} = 1.03228$. Similarly, the ratio of F to S for $T = 1/3$ is $(F/S)^{1/3} = .99618$.

We now calculate the probabilities k and $1 - k$ for the up and down jumps: $k = (.99618 - .933063)/(1.071738 - .933063) = .45510$, and $1 - k = .54490$.

We start at option expiration, $T = 0$, and work backwards. At option expiration there will be four possible values for the terminal spot rate S^*:

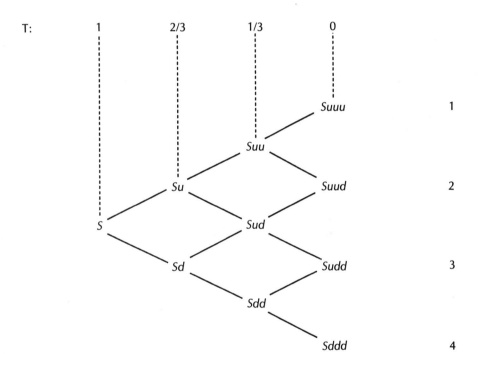

The values of the option at expiration ($T = 0$) are given in the following table:

	S^*	$S^* - X$	Option Value
1	43.086	9.086	9.086
2	37.511	3.511	3.511
3	32.657	−1.343	0
4	28.432	−5.568	0

The first value for $S*$ corresponds to $S* = Suuu$, and so on. At $T = 1/3$, we add one column to the table:

	$S*$	$S* - X$	Discounted Value	Option Value
1	40.202	6.202	5.859	6.202
2	35	1.000	1.548	1.548
3	30.471	−3.529	0	0

Note how these values are constructed. The first value for $S*$ corresponds to $S* = Suu = 40.202$. At Suu we can exercise immediately and receive $S* - X = 6.202$. Or we can hold the option for its value next period (at $Suuu$ or $Suud$). Hence the discounted future payoff from holding until the next step is:

$$[.45510(9.086) + (.54490)(3.511)]/1.03228 = 5.859.$$

By contrast, from Sdd the exercise value is negative $(−3.529)$, and holding until next period will not allow the option to acquire positive value. So the option value at $S* = Sdd$ is 0.

At $T = 2/3$,

	$S*$	$S* - X$	Discounted Value	Option Value
1	37.511	3.511	3.551	3.551
2	32.657	−1.343	.682	.682

At $T = 1$,

	$S*$	$S* - X$	Discounted Value	Option Value
1	35	1.000	1.926	1.926.

Thus the value of the call is 1.926 today at $T = 1$. It will not be exercised because the exercise value is only 1.000. If $S \to Su$ next period, the option will have a value of 3.551. But if $S \to Sd$ next period, the value will be .682. And so on.

In Example 6.5 we calculated the option value at each node of the binomial tree. We can use the same procedure to calculate the value of an option on an option.

EXAMPLE 6.6

Consider an American cacall, an American call option on the option of Example 6.5. The underlying option will be called the *back* option. Suppose the strike price of the cacall is $X2 = 1$, and the cacall has a term to maturity of $T2 = 1/3$.

We can evaluate the cacall value at $T2 = 0$ by looking at the possible back option values at $T = 2/3$:

	$S*$	Back Option	Back Option $- X2$	Cacall
1	37.511	3.551	2.551	2.551
2	32.657	.682	$-.318$	0

The first two columns were calculated in Example 6.5. The third column subtracts out the cacall exercise price ($X2 = 1$) from the value of the back option. Since the cacall will be exercised only if this number is positive, the cacall value is the maximum of its exercise value or zero. At $S* = Su$ the value is 2.551, while at $S* = Sd$ it is 0.

The value of the cacall at $T2 = 1/3$ (or $T = 1$) is then simply the maximum of its immediate exercise value or the discounted value of its two possible payoffs at $T2 = 0$. The discounted value is, using the probabilities and discount factors calculated in Example 6.5:

$$[.45510 (2.551) + .54490 (0)]/1.03228 = 1.125.$$

The exercise value of the cacall is simply the final back option value calculated in Example 6.5 minus the strike price, or $1.926 - 1 = .926$. The maximum of (1.125, .926) is 1.125, the value of the American cacall.

Consider now a down-and-out American option. This option differs from the ordinary American option in Example 6.5 in that the option value becomes zero at any node of the binomial tree that is under the down-and-out price U.

EXAMPLE 6.7

Consider an American down-and-out option with $U = 33$. The other variables are the same as in Example 6.5.

Since $Sd = 32.657$, the option value is zero at any node $< S = 35$. For $T = 0$ and $T = 1/3$, the option values are the same as those previously calculated in Example 6.5. At $T = 2/3$, however, the values become

	$S*$	Ordinary Option Value	Down-and-Out Value
1	37.511	3.551	3.551
2	32.657	.682	0

The option value becomes 0 instead of .682 at $Sd = 32.657$, because $Sd \leq U$, the down-and-out price.

At $T = 1$, the discounted down-and-out price becomes

$$[.45510 (3.551) + .54490 (0)]/1.03228 = 1.566.$$

The immediate exercise value is $S - X = 35 - 34 = 1.0$ (as previously seen in Example 6.5). Therefore the value of the down-and-out option is max (1.566, 1.0) = 1.566.

As a final example of the versatility of the binomial approach, consider a *look-back* call option (see Glossary). Since the holder of the option can set the exercise price at any level reached by the spot rate during the option life, the holder will choose the lowest node in the binomial tree reached prior to maturity.

EXAMPLE 6.8

Consider a European look-back call, using the pricing assumptions of Example 6.5. To find the option value at $T = 0$, we have to take account of the possible paths by which each outcome was reached.

	S*	X	Option Value	# Paths	Probability
1	43.086	35.000	8.086	1	.094258
2	37.511	35.000	2.511	2	.112858
		32.657	4.854	1	.112858
3	32.657	32.657	0	2	.135127
		30.471	2.186	1	.135127
4	28.432	28.432	0	1	.161790

Starting from $S = 35$, there is only one way to reach $S* = Suuu = 43.086$. The payoff at $Suuu$ is $43.086 - 35.00 = 8.086$. The probability is $(.45510)^3$. By contrast, there are three ways to reach $Suud$. Two of the paths never reach a node lower than $S = 35$, in which case the payoff is $37.511 - 35.00 = 2.511$. The probability is $(.45510)^2 (.54490) = .112858$. But the path that goes $S \rightarrow Sd \rightarrow Sud \rightarrow Suud$ has as its lowest node $Sd = 32.657$. So the payoff is $37.511 - 32.657 = 4.854$. And so on.

The probable payoff is $(8.086)(.094258) + 2(2.511)(.112858) + (4.854)(.112858) + (2.186)(.135127) = 2.1721$. The discounted expected payoff is thus $2.1721/1.10 = 1.9747$, the value of the look-back option.

THE DETERMINATION OF EXCHANGE RATES

EXPECTATIONS, INFORMATION, AND EXCHANGE RATE SPECULATION

In Chapter 3 we saw that only a small percentage of foreign exchange trading represents commercial business. The majority of transactions arise from an endless round of purchases and sales among marketmakers. We saw that FX marketmakers are a special category of inventory specialists who make the market by their willingness to deal at two-way prices and to become the counterparty to either a purchase or a sale of foreign exchange. In the absence of marketmakers, the random flow of buy and sell orders would result in large fluctuations in the exchange rate. The marketmaker provides a price-smoothing service by his willingness to buy or sell at a stated price. In the process the marketmaker acquires (if only temporarily) net long or short exchange positions.

But is all the trading that actually occurs really necessary to make the market? For each commercial transaction handled, the marketmaker may do six additional trades with other marketmakers. What is going on? The answer is that foreign currency traders have become *information dealers*. The bulk of their trading is related to the ebb and flow of economic and political events. In the words of Walter Wriston, "The information standard has replaced . . . the system invented at Bretton Woods." Each new piece of information may bring with it a shift in trader expectations. For example, "The words of a prime minister or a president appear on the screens of the trading rooms all over the world in minutes, and are reflected in the currency cross-rate immediately" (Wriston, 1984).

Much of the discussion of the FX spot, forward, futures, and option markets in Part II was concerned with arbitrage—the simultaneous buying and selling of the same or equivalent assets at two different prices. But an important additional force at work in the market is deliberate risk-taking: the acquiring of an open long or short position in foreign currency with the expectation of a profit. Some risk-taking is unavoidable. We saw in Chapter 5 that speculators are required in order to bear the risks that hedgers are trying to avoid. But of equal importance is the close connection between speculation and marketmaking itself. They differ only by degree, since the same decision process is at work in either activity. The marketmaker's ability to make a profit relies on closing out a long position (short position) at a net price that is higher (lower) than that at which the position was acquired. How long a short or long position is retained, or how often a marketmaker adjusts the bid and asked prices, depends on the marketmaker's view as to whether the current state of FX supply and demand is temporary or permanent. So whether the trader is "just marketmaking" or engaged in active speculation, his expectations are a key determinant in how he manages his position. And what expectations he has will in turn depend on the available information.

An interbank trader is not allowed the luxury of ignoring the news. Since most FX supply and demand comes from the interbank market itself, the trader knows that any news event may bring about a reaction on the part of other traders. And, perceiving an impending shift in the market, he must immediately adjust his own position according to how he thinks other traders will react. Traders are like the judges in the Keynesian beauty contest (Keynes, 1936) who, rather than voting for the girl they thought was most beautiful, instead voted for the girl they thought the other judges would think was the most beautiful. Market equilibrium will depend in part on what traders think other traders think about equilibrium.

The interplay of expectations and information in the process of bringing about market equilibrium is the subject of this chapter. In the course of the discussion, we will introduce a number of concepts that will be used throughout Part III.

EXPECTATIONS AS A FUNCTION OF INFORMATION

The fact that news moves exchange rates can hardly be taken as cause for alarm. Suppose the contrary were true. If no one bothered to become informed, for example, news events might have little immediate impact on the market. Such would hardly be a rosy state of affairs. Few companies would contemplate seeking financial advice from a bank that employed sleepy traders. When people complain about the fact that news moves exchange rates, what they really mean is that they wish the bad news (to them) would go away. Even the European Monetary System, formed "to provide a zone of monetary stability in Europe" requires the existence of well-informed exchange traders. The system is implicitly built around the notion that the exchange rate mirrors the economy. (The "community average," as we saw in Chapter 2, is based on the market value of the ECU, which represents an average of community exchange rates.)

A trader's buy and sell decisions are based on the trader's expectations or forecasts—his or her view of the future movement of the exchange rate. The direction of spot rate movement that a trader foresees is a function of what the trader knows—his or her *information set*. Information includes not only "facts" but also the technology or human capital required to evaluate facts. A shorthand way of denoting a trader's information set at time t is by the symbol

$I(t)$. Then, a simple way of writing "the expected exchange rate for the next period, given information at time t" is:

$E[S(t + 1)|I(t)]$.

Traders trade because they have different information and hence different expectations. No one who does not earn an economic reward for the effort is going to bother to collect information in the first place. If uninformed people could get along as well in the market as informed people, there would be no incentive for anyone to incur the expense of reading the news media, watching the Telerate monitor, doing research, employing a stable of econometricians and technical analysts, talking to policymakers, or hiring Wharton or Stanford MBAs. Information equilibrium requires market participants to collect information only up to the point where the benefit of additional information no longer justifies the cost. Therefore the market will always be composed of different groups who have different information sets. The information sets of group i at time t will be denoted by $I(i,t)$.

EXAMPLE 7.1

You are an interbank FX trader, and your bank has the best available forecasting model, purchased from Nostradamus, Inc. It predicts FX rates better than anything else on the market. Should you use this model to make speculative bets? In order for you to make a profit, it would have to be the case that some other FX traders were not in possession of the same model (the same information). Other traders would have to have expectations different from your own before they would take speculative positions against you, thus allowing you to win a profit when they are proved wrong. This means that they would have to be less informed than you. On the other hand, if the use of the model allowed one to earn excess profits, other people would attempt to acquire the same model. If more people began to form their expectations on the basis of the model, the advantage of using the model would diminish. Eventually market participants would become indifferent between having or not having the model, since the advantage of having the model would be no greater than the additional expense. We will call this the *Model Theorem:* Good models generate their own obsolescence. A different way of stating the same thing: Good models become bad. They lose their usefulness.

☐

An interesting question arises as to whether people who have less information can learn what informed people know just by watching their trading decisions. If one FX trader knows that another FX trader is better informed, the first trader would never be willing to take a long or short position against the second trader. If others reacted the same way, the second, informed trader would never find anyone to trade with. Hence the value of his information would be useless. As a result, neither he nor anyone else would have an incentive to acquire information. This apparent paradox is solved by Grossman and Stiglitz (1980), who show that under conditions of market uncertainty, informed traders will still retain an advantage over uninformed traders, but the value of the informed trader's information will vary inversely with the number of other traders who acquire the same information. As a result, additional traders will continue to acquire information only up to the point at which the marginal benefit is equal to the marginal cost.   ∎

EXPECTATIONAL EQUILIBRIUM

In the introduction to this chapter, we mentioned the Keynesian beauty contest: the notion that market equilibrium depends on what traders think other traders think about equilibrium. How is the market equilibrium exchange rate determined by the simultaneous actions of many traders with diverse expectations? Here we will focus on the aggregate point of view—on the "market" information set $I(M,t)$. We can think of the market information set as embodying the sum total of the different sets $I(i,t)$ of individual traders.

One notion of expectational equilibrium is the concept of *rational* expectations. Rational expectations are expectations that are *self-fulfilling* on average. That is, expectations are rational if by holding and acting on the basis of these expectations, traders would bring about an economic equilibrium that confirms their original expectations. Clearly, expectations that were not self-fulfilling could not represent an expectational equilibrium. If traders did not on average find their expectations concerning the exchange rate fulfilled, they would have an incentive to change them. If they changed their expectations, they would change their trading decisions. A change in their trading decisions would result in a change in the market rate. Hence the market could not have been originally in equilibrium. Only if expectations are self-fulfilling on average will market participants have no incentive to alter their behavior.

This process is most easily illustrated by a simple numerical example. Suppose the foreign exchange market operated according to the following natural law:

$$S(t + 1) = .6\, E[S(t + 1)|I(M,t)] + .4\, S(t) + e(t + 1), \tag{7.1}$$

where $e(t + 1)$ is a random error term with

$$E[e(t + 1)|I(M,t)] = 0.$$

This equation says that next period's spot rate will be equal to a weighted average (with weights .6 and .4) of the market's expected spot rate for next period,

$$E[S(t + 1)|I(M,t)],$$

and today's actual spot rate, $S(t)$, plus an error term. The equation implies that today's expectation for next period is an important variable determining next period's actual spot rate.

Suppose now that the market has the following expectation:

$$E[S(t + 1)|I(M,t)] = 1.1\, S(t). \tag{7.2}$$

Substituting this expectation into equation (7.1), we get that

$$S(t + 1) = .6\, [1.1\, S(t)] + .4\, S(t) + e(t + 1) = 1.06\, S(t) + e(t + 1).$$

The market expectation in this case would be wrong on average, since on average $S(t + 1)$ would be equal to $1.06\, S(t)$, and not $1.1\, S(t)$. Hence the expectation in equation (7.2) would not be rational since it is not self-fulfilling.

On the other hand, if people *lowered* their expectation to some number between $1.1\, S(t)$ and $1.06\, S(t)$, then equation (7.1) will yield a value for $S(t + 1)$

that is on average *less* than 1.06 $S(t)$, but that is still not self-fulfilling. (Try it and see. For example, substitute

$$E[S(t + 1)|I(M,t)] = 1.07\ S(t)$$

into equation (7.1).) Some experimentation will show that the only value for $E[S(t + 1)|I(M,t)]$ that *is* self-fulfilling on average is

$$E[S(t + 1)|I(M,t)] = S(t).$$

This value is the rational expectations solution to equation (7.1).

$\square$

The rational expectations approach to expectational equilibrium is credited to John Muth (1961), who assumed that "expectations, since they are informed predictions of future events, are essentially the same as the predictions of the relevant economic theory." This approach implies that if a particular model is used to explain market behavior, it should also be assumed that the market formed its expectations on the basis of the same model. For example, if a trader really thought that equation (7.1) was the correct equation governing the spot exchange rate, this approach says he ought to credit other informed people with the same knowledge. That is, equation (7.1) is itself part of the market information set $I(M,t)$ and would be used in the process of forming the expectation

$$E[S(t + 1)|I(M,t)].$$

This approach yields a straightforward way of generating solutions to equations like (7.1).

EXAMPLE 7.2

Suppose a trader believed that equation (7.1) was the best available equation for forecasting next period's spot rate. In order to use the equation, some number must be inserted for

$$E[S(t + 1)|I(M,t)].$$

If she adopts the rational expectations approach, this trader would assume that other people in the FX market formed their expectations using equation (7.1). To solve for

$$E[S(t + 1)|I(M,t)],$$

then, the trader first takes the conditional mathematical expectation of both sides of equation (7.1) with respect to $I(M,t)$:

$$E[S(t + 1)|I(M,t)] = E[.6\ E[S(t + 1)|I(M,t)]|I(M,t)] + E[.4\ S(t)|I(M,t)] \\ + E[e(t + 1)|I(M,t)]. \tag{7.3}$$

As noted previously, we have

$$E[e(t + 1)|I(M,t)] = 0.$$

Since $S(t)$ is part of one's information set at time t, we have

$$E[.4\ S(t)|I(M,t)] = .4\ E[S(t)|I(M,t)] = .4\ S(t).$$

Finally, the term

$$E[.6\, E[S(t + 1)\,|\,I(M,t)]\,|\,I(M,t)] = .6\, E[S(t + 1)\,|\,I(M,t)]$$

because the expectation of an expectation, conditional on the same information, is just the original expectation. Substituting these results back into equation (7.3), we obtain

$$E[S(t + 1)\,|\,I(M,t)] = .6\, E[S(t + 1)\,|\,I(M,t)] + .4\, S(t). \tag{7.4}$$

Finally, solving for $E[S(t + 1)\,|\,I(M,t)]$ in equation (7.4), we obtain

$$E[S(t + 1)\,|\,I(M,t)] = S(t). \tag{7.5}$$

That is, applying the rational expectations approach to the original equation (7.1), we get that the expected spot rate for next period, conditional on $I(M,t)$, is just the current spot rate. Having reached this conclusion on the basis of rational expectations, we can now substitute the conclusion (7.5) back into the original equation (7.1) to obtain:

$$\begin{aligned} S(t + 1) &= .6\, S(t) + .4\, S(t) + e(t + 1) \\ &= S(t) + e(t + 1). \end{aligned} \tag{7.6}$$

In this case, the two assumptions (a) that equation (7.1) describes the movement of exchange rates and (b) that expectations are rational leads to the conclusion that next period's spot rate will not differ in any systematic way from the current spot rate. Next period's spot rate will be this period's spot rate plus a random error term.

■

THE SPECULATIVE EFFICIENCY HYPOTHESIS

One appealing view of the world is the notion that there may be market variables that embody the sum total of the market's information about the future. Suppose that there are N different groups in the market, each with a corresponding information set $I(i,t)$, for $i = 1, 2, \ldots, N$. Meanwhile, the sum total of their information is contained in a "market" information set $I(M,t)$. If there existed market variables that reflected all of $I(M,t)$, then by observing these variables each group would be able to ensure that its information set was identical to the market's total information set: $I(i,t) = I(M,t)$ for all i. For example, suppose it were the case that the forward price $F(t,T)$ was, conditional on the current market information set $I(M,t)$, an unbiased predictor of the spot price that would occur at time $t + T$:

$$F(t,T) = E[(S(t +T)\,|\,I(M,t)]. \tag{7.7}$$

Then by observing $F(t,T)$ everyone could ensure that his private expectation

$$E[S(t +T)\,|\,I(i,t)]$$

was identical to that conditional on having the largest information set $I(M,t)$. As a result, everyone would have the same information concerning the future spot rate; everyone would be fully informed.

In particular, because forward contracts involve transactions that will take place at some time in the future, forward prices are often taken to be implicit forecasts. Is it rational to form expectations of future spot rates on the basis of forward rates? The notion that forward (or, alternatively, futures) prices represent expected spot rates relies on the belief that if the current forward rate is less than the expected spot rate,

$$F(t,T) < E[S(t + T)|I(M,t)],$$

speculators will buy forward exchange in unlimited amounts now, in the expectation of making a profit at time $t + T$ by taking delivery of exchange at the forward rate and turning around and selling at the higher spot rate at that time. This process of buying forward exchange will bid up its price until

$$F(t,T) = E[S(t +T)|I(M,t)].$$

A similar story can be told if

$$F(t,T) > E[S(t + T)|I(M,t)].$$

Speculators will sell unlimited amounts of forward exchange until

$$F(t,T) = E[S(t +T)|I(M,t)].$$

Equation (7.7) has been termed the *speculative efficiency hypothesis* (SEH). The SEH is the proposition that the T-period forward rate is the best unbiased predictor of the spot rate T periods in the future. For example, it asserts that the six-month forward exchange rate is the best unbiased predictor of what the spot exchange rate will be on the day the six-month forward rate matures. (If this six-month period is $T = 182$ days, it says that this forward rate is the best unbiased predictor of the spot rate in 182 days.) Alternative propositions to the SEH are that

$$F(t,T) > E[S(t + T)|I(M,t)]$$

(a condition referred to as *contango*), or that

$$F(t,T) < E[S(t + T)|I(M,t)]$$

(*normal backwardation*).

□
Equation (7.7) has also been termed the "efficient market" hypothesis, a term avoided here because it is ambiguous and misleading (LeRoy, 1982). ∎

We will dwell on the SEH at some length because it is an important empirical proposition. First, if it is true, it implies that all market participants have the same information set. Second, there are many corporations that hedge FX risk using the forward market, and thus any systematic divergences between the forward rate and the eventual spot rate would give an estimate of the cost of this hedging procedure. Third, many people subscribe to forecasting services. Since it does not cost anything to observe the forward rate, one would certainly expect that a forecasting service that had a non-zero cost would predict as well as (or not worse than) the forward rate did.

If we subtract the spot rate $S(t)$ from both sides of equation (7.7) and then divide both sides by $S(t)$, we obtain

$$\frac{F(t,T) - S(t)}{S(t)} = \frac{E[S(t + T)|I(M,t)] - S(t)}{S(t)}. \tag{7.8}$$

Written in this form, the SEH says that the forward premium is an unbiased forecast of appreciation of the spot foreign currency. To test for unbiasedness we can run the regression equation

$$a + b \, \frac{F(t,T) - S(t)}{S(t)} + e(t + T) = \frac{S(t + T) - S(t)}{S(t)}, \qquad (7.9)$$

where a and b are the coefficients to be estimated and e is an error term. If the SEH is correct, then a should be statistically indistinguishable from 0, while b should be statistically indistinguishable from 1. (A brief review of hypothesis testing with the simple linear regression model is given in the appendix to this chapter.) If the error terms e are drawings from a normal distribution, then the coefficient estimates of a and b, $\hat{a}$ and $\hat{b}$, can—for sufficiently large sample sizes—be treated as drawings from a normal distribution. Thus we can assign a probability of obtaining $\hat{a}$ and $\hat{b}$, given that the SEH is true. If this probability is sufficiently low, we may elect to reject the SEH.

□

There are a number of alternative formulations of the SEH. Some formulations assume a constant liquidity premium, and so do not require that $a = 0$, but do require that $b = 1$.   ■

In a sophisticated multicurrency test of equation (7.9), Bilson (1981) obtained the values $\hat{a} = 3.123 \, (\pm 1.18)$ and $\hat{b} = .178 \, (\pm.18)$, where the numbers in parentheses are the standard errors. This result, which involved weekly observations on nine currencies, enabled him to reject the hypothesis $b = 1$ with a high degree of confidence. That is, it is highly improbable that this estimated value would have occurred if the SEH were empirically true.

On the other hand, he could not—with the same regression results—reject the hypothesis that $b = 0$. That is, he could not rule out the proposition that the percentage discount or premium on forward exchange is entirely unrelated to future changes in the spot exchange rate. This implies that the forward rate $F(t,T)$ does not give any additional information about the future spot rate $S(t + T)$ that is not already contained in the current spot rate $S(t)$, at least for the forward rates that Bilson investigated.

On the basis of these results, Bilson reasoned that one might want to distinguish between discounts or premiums that are "large" (he defined "large" as a discount or premium greater than 10 percent when converted to a yearly rate) and ones that are "small" ("small" was defined as a discount or premium less than 10 percent when converted at a yearly rate). He found evidence that, once the large/small distinction was made, the forward premium or discount did give useful information. In this case, large discounts or premiums went in the wrong direction, suggesting that—if the discount or premium is greater than 10 percent per annum—one should on average bet against the forward rate getting even the direction of exchange rate change correct. For small discounts/premiums, the indicated change was in the right direction, but on average the subsequent depreciation in the spot rate was only about 25 percent of the magnitude of the forward premium.

Similar rejections of the SEH have been found by Hansen and Hodrick (1980), Hodrick and Srivastava (1984), Huang (1984), Korajczyk (1985), and

Longworth (1981). The forward exchange market is characterized by contango or normal backwardation and not by speculative efficiency. Thus the forward rate appears to be a generally biased estimate of the future spot rate. What does this rejection tell us about exchange market speculators?

SPECULATOR CHARACTERISTICS

The failure of the forward exchange rate to equal the expected spot rate would appear to be rooted in three speculator characteristics: Speculators are not risk-neutral; the information set of speculators is not identical with the full market information set; and speculators do not have unlimited wealth. Let us examine each of these characteristics in turn.

Risk Neutrality

Are people willing to take fair bets involving large amounts of money? During the eighteenth century, mathematician Daniel Bernoulli observed that people wouldn't and suggested the reason for this was that an amount of money won was worth less to an individual than the same amount of money lost. For example, suppose that you can—for a fee—participate in the following bet. A fair coin will be flipped. If it comes up heads, you win $20,000. If it comes up tails, you win $0. How much would you pay to enter into the bet? Since the probability of heads is equal to that of tails, the expected winning is .5($20,000) + .5($0) = $10,000. Thus a mathematically fair entry fee to take part in the bet is $10,000, because the expected profit becomes $0 after paying an entry fee of $10,000. Most people, however, will not pay $10,000 to enter into this bet. They may be willing to pay, for example, only $3000. Such behavior is termed *risk-averse*.

If participants in the market are risk-averse there is no reason to expect the forward rate to be equal to the expected spot rate. The forward rate will adjust to clear the market between sellers and buyers of forward exchange, but could differ from the expected spot rate by an amount dependent on market risk aversion. Since there are two sides to an exchange contract, the risk aversions of both the buyers and the sellers of forward contracts would be important. Thus the "risk premium" (the difference between $F(t,T)$ and $E[S(t + T)|I(M,t)]$) could be either positive or negative. In addition, it might change over time. Thus a market participant's information set $I(i,t)$ could include knowledge of the forward rate $F(t,T)$, but it would not be true that $F(t,T) = E[(S(t + T|I(M,t)]$.

Full Information

Even if speculators were not risk-averse, their actions will not drive the forward rate to equality with $E[S(t + T)|I(M,t)]$ if the information set of speculators is not the total market information set $I(M,t)$. As we saw in the preceding section, becoming informed usually involves incurring a cost of acquiring information. Certainly speculators can't just observe the forward rate $F(t,T)$, because—in the story—it is up to them to determine whether $F(t,T)$ is greater than or less than the expected spot rate. So speculators will have to acquire information at a cost. They will do this only up to the point at which the expected cost of further information is equal to the expected benefit.

Wealth Constraints and Ultimate Ruin

In the real world, speculators do not have infinite wealth. Wealth limitations impose an important constraint. Even if a speculator is not risk-averse, and even if he has sufficient information to know a fair bet when he sees one, a knowledge of probability will tell him that playing a fair betting game can lead to ultimate ruin if his wealth is limited. As explained in Chapter 5, a game may be fair when viewed as a single coin flip, yet not fair when viewed as a series of coin flips with a stochastic termination point. The probabilities of the game depend on the speculator's capital, among other variables.

Suppose we consider a betting process in which you will win $1 with probability p and lose $1 with probability q (where $q = 1 - p$). You start off with an amount of W. If your money drops to zero, the game stops. Your betting partner—the person on the other side of your bet who wins when you lose and loses when you win—has an amount of money R. What is the probability you will eventually lose all of your wealth W, given p and R? From probability theory the answer is (Feller, 1968):

$$\text{Ruin probability} = \frac{(q/p)^{W+R} - (q/p)^W}{(q/p)^{W+R} - 1}, \text{ for } p \neq q$$

$$\text{Ruin probability} = 1 - (W/(W + R)), \text{ for } p = q = .5. \tag{7.10}$$

EXAMPLE 7.3

You have $10 and your friend has $100. You flip a fair coin. If heads comes up, he pays you $1. If tails comes up, you pay him $1. The game ends when either player runs out of money. What is the probability your friend will end up with all of your money? From the second equation (7.10), we have $p = q = .5$, $W = \$10$, and $R = \$100$. Thus the probability of your losing everything is:

$$1 - (10/(10 + 100)) = .909.$$

You will lose all of your money with 91 percent probability in this supposedly "fair" game.

For the same reason, if speculators have limited wealth, they may only be willing to take speculative positions in the forward market when they view the odds sufficiently in their favor. This may require large divergences of $F(t,T)$ from $E[S(t + T)|I(M,t)]$.

THE MARTINGALE CHARACTER OF SPOT RATES

If next period's exchange rate is expected to be a constant multiple $(1 + k)$ of this period's exchange rate, given $I(M,t)$,

$$E[S(t + 1)|I(M,t)] = (1 + k) S(t) \tag{7.11}$$

then the exchange rate $S(t)$ is said to be a martingale with drift k.

The notion of a martingale is an important one. There is considerable empirical evidence suggesting that for the major currencies and over short time horizons, spot exchange rates follow a martingale. (See Bilson (1981), Huang

(1984), Meese and Rogoff (1983), and Mussa (1979).) Thus, one of the contributions of foreign exchange traders is that, having established a trend k, they proceed to eliminate any predictable variations of the spot exchange rate around this trend.

□

The same is not true for the forward rate. Samuelson (1972) has shown that if the forward rate were equal to the conditional expected spot rate at maturity (that is, if the SEH were true), then the forward rate would be a martingale. The failure of the SEH allows for predictable divergences between forward rates and realized spot rates. ■

□

APPENDIX TO CHAPTER 7

SIMPLE LINEAR REGRESSION AND STATISTICAL INFERENCE

The simple linear regression equation can be written as

$$y(t) = a + b\, x(t) + u(t).$$

It is assumed that the error terms $u(t)$ are independently normally distributed with mean 0 and variance v. The sample size is n.

Let $SXY = \Sigma(x(t) - \bar{x})(y(t) - \bar{y})$, $SXX = \Sigma(x(t) - \bar{x})^2$, $SYY = \Sigma(y(t) - \bar{y})^2$, where $\bar{x}$ and $\bar{y}$ are the sample means of x and y. Then the coefficient estimators for a and b are:

$$\hat{b} = SXY/SXX \qquad \hat{a} = \bar{y} - \hat{b}\bar{x}.$$

Let $RSS = \Sigma(y(t) - \hat{a} - \hat{b}x(t))^2 = SYY - (SXY)^2/(SXX)$.

1. Then $\hat{a}$ has a normal distribution with mean a and variance

$$\operatorname{var}(\hat{a}) = v((1/n) + (\bar{x}^2/SXX)).$$

2. Then $\hat{b}$ has a normal distribution with mean b and variance $\operatorname{var}(\hat{b}) = v/SXX$.
3. Then RSS/v has a chi-squared distribution with $n - 2$ degrees of freedom, and $\hat{v} = RSS/(n - 2)$ is an unbiased estimator for v.
4. The standard errors (SE) for $\hat{a}$ and $\hat{b}$ are the same as the standard deviations of $\hat{a}$ and $\hat{b}$, except that $\hat{v}$ is substituted for v (which is unknown):

$$SE(\hat{a}) = \sqrt{\hat{v}((1/n) + (\bar{x}^2/SXX))}, \; SE(\hat{b}) = \sqrt{\hat{v}/SXX}.$$

5. Then $(\hat{a} - a)/SE(\hat{a})$ and $(\hat{b} - b)/SE(\hat{b})$ have a t-distribution with $n - 2$ degrees of freedom. For large values of n (such as $n > 32$), the t-distribution is approximately the normal distribution. Therefore the probability of the estimators $\hat{a}$ and $\hat{b}$ being within 1, 2, or 3 standard errors of the mean values of a and b are:

	Probability	
$\hat{a} \in (a \pm 1\, SE(\hat{a}))$	.6826	$\hat{b} \in (b \pm 1\, SE(\hat{b}))$
$\hat{a} \in (a \pm 2\, SE(\hat{a}))$	.9544	$\hat{b} \in (b \pm 2\, SE(\hat{b}))$
$\hat{a} \in (a \pm 3\, SE(\hat{a}))$	.9974	$\hat{b} \in (b \pm 3\, SE(\hat{b}))$

6. In hypothesis testing (for example, to test the hypothesis $a = 0$, $b = 1$) we substitute our hypothesized values for a, b in the intervals just listed and evaluate the probability of having obtained the current sample for these values.   ∎

PROBLEMS FOR CHAPTER 7

1. Assume an exchange rate evolves according to the equation

$$S(t + 1) = .5\ E[S(t + 1)|I(M,t)] + .4\ S(t) + e(t + 1).$$

   (a) Assuming expectations are rational, determine $E[S(t + 1)|I(M,t)]$.
   (b) Determine the equation by which the exchange rate evolves (that is, the equation written without expectational terms).
   (c) If the market expectation were

   $$E[S(t + 1)|I(M,t)] = S(t),$$

   why would this expectation not be sustained?
   (d) If over three successive time periods we have

   $$e(t + 1) = .05\ S(t),\ e(t + 2) = -.1\ S(t),\ e(t + 3) = .02\ S(t + 2),$$

   determine the market exchange rate for each of these periods using your answer in (b).

2. A regression equation testing speculative efficiency for a particular currency yields the result

   $$S(t + 1) = .08 + .90\ F(t,1) + e(t + 1)$$
   $$(.04)\ (.02),$$

   where standard errors are in parentheses. Assume that requirements are met so that we may interpret the coefficient estimates $\hat{a} = .08$, $\hat{b} = .90$ as drawings from a normal distribution and interpret the standard errors as standard deviations.
   (a) Could we reject the hypothesis $b = 1$? Under what probability criterion?
   (b) If we assume domestic and foreign interest rates are the same, what does the above regression imply about the drift term k in equation (7.11)?

3. The value of a tick (.0001) on a DM IMM futures contract is $12.50. Suppose initial margin is $1500 and maintenance margin is $1200. You take a long position in one futures contract and plan to hold the contract until your account balance falls from $1500 to $1200 or until the account balance rises to $3000, whichever comes first.
   (a) If the probability of an upward tick is .6 and that of a downward tick is .4, what is the probability that you will end up with $3000? [*Hint:* Pretend you are playing against "the market" and assume the market's initial wealth is $3000 − $1500 = $1500, while your initial wealth is $1500 − $1200 = $300. Translate the dollar amounts into the number of betting units (ticks), and use equation (7.10).]
   (b) Answer the same question if the probability of upward and downward ticks are equal.
   (c) Assume the same values as in (a) but assume that tick values are $300. Calculate the probability of ending up with $3000.
   (d) Comparing your answers in (a) and (c), what conclusions would you draw in general for risk taking (exposure) in FX risk management? (Consider the limited capital of the firm compared to the size of FX risk exposure.)

PURCHASING POWER PARITY

INTRODUCTION

What determines the level of the spot exchange rate? We just saw in Chapter 3 that marketmakers in the interbank market will keep adjusting the level of their bid and asked prices in such a way that they are being hit in equal proportions on their bid and asked sides, except to the extent they may choose deliberately to take speculative positions (Chapter 7) by becoming long or short in their holdings of a particular currency. If a marketmaker's customers are hitting him equally at his current bid and asked prices, the marketmaker's own market is in equilibrium. The supply of foreign currency is equal to the demand for foreign currency at the trader's current prices. Thus the quick answer to our question is: The spot exchange rate is the rate that brings about equality between the supply of and the demand for spot exchange as seen by marketmakers.

But what are the fundamental economic factors that ultimately give rise to this supply and demand, and why do supply and demand factors change over time? To answer this question, we now turn to the different facets of foreign commerce. Foreign commerce includes transactions in goods, services, bank deposits, bonds, and equity between domestic residents and foreigners. Most countries maintain a record of all such transactions they know about. This record is referred to as the *balance on international transactions* or the balance of payments (BOP). The total accounting record that makes up the balance of payments can be viewed as a list of factors giving rise to demand and supply in the FX market.

It is traditional to separate out two general categories of FX supply and demand: factors relating to goods and services (the current account), and those relating to financial assets and ownership (the capital account). This chapter will focus on the first of these two categories. In particular, we will explore the relation between international trade in goods and services and the level of the spot exchange rate. As we shall see, it is a two-sided relationship. The exchange rate influences the level of trade, and the level of trade influences the exchange rate.

Consider the following chimpanzee economy. In circulation in the chimpanzee economy are blue plastic chips the chimpanzees know can be exchanged for bananas from gullible psychologists. Because of this, the otherwise uninteresting plastic chips are prized in the chimpanzee economy. Prudent chimps hoard chips by carefully concealing them under hemp mats which serve as bedding. Other chimps give chips as gifts to desirable companions in return for various favors. Such an economy is similar to one created by brain researcher Karl Pribram in experiments with chimpanzees during the 1950s. One can draw the obvious conclusion: Any chimpanzee knows that the value of money is found in what you can trade it for.

Suppose we extend this economy a bit and do an experiment Karl Pribram didn't do. We introduce two types of plastic chips: small blue ones that trade for one banana, and big red ones that trade for two bananas. Clever chimps, if they think like the economist Gustav Cassel, will reason as follows: Two blue chips give me the same number of bananas as one red chip, namely two bananas. Therefore two blue chips have the same value as one red chip. Therefore the exchange rate between blue chips and red chips should be 2 blue chips = 1 red chip. Certainly a clever chimp would never accept less than two blues for each red, since she knows that a gullible psychologist will give her two bananas for each red chip, but only one for each blue chip. Only dumber, unevolved chimps will fail to make the proper calculations.

Chimpanzees acting in this manner will have created purchasing power parity (PPP). The basic idea of the purchasing power parity, in its different formulations, is that different currencies represent purchasing power over goods and services. The exchange rate adjusts to keep purchasing power constant. This adjustment will occur through commodity arbitrage. If, for example, the market will only give a chimp 1.9 blue chips for one red chip, the chimp will trade a red chip directly for two bananas and then buy two blue chips, paying one banana each. With the blue chips, the chimp will now buy cheap red chips at a market exchange rate of 1.9 blue chips = 1 red chip, and repeat the process, all with the help of the gullible psychologist. With each transaction the chimp gains .1 blue chip, and if the market exchange rate does not change, the chimp will eventually own all chips in the economy. Presumably other primates will catch on before that happens and change the exchange rate.

There is, of course, an alternative to exchange rate adjustment that would prevent the chimp from becoming a millionaire before the age of four. The gullible psychologist could have wised up and started giving out only 1.9 bananas for each red chip. If so, this would be an example in which prices adjusted to the exchange rate rather than vice versa. PPP does not necessarily imply any direction of causality between price adjustments and exchange rate adjustments. It could happen either way.

□

The causality issue here is important. It is sometimes stated on the basis of purchasing power concepts that an exchange rate is "over-" or "under-valued." A priori, such statements have no more validity than the assertion that domestic or foreign prices are "too high" or "too low." ∎

THE LAW OF ONE PRICE

The simplest concept of PPP is the so-called *law of one price,* which says that bananas will cost the same whether purchased directly with red chips or whether the red chips are first converted to blue chips at the going rate of exchange and the blue chips then used to purchase bananas. Let $S(t)$ be the current exchange rate (the domestic currency price of foreign exchange), and $P(i,t)$ and $P^*(i,t)$ the current domestic and foreign (*) currency prices of commodity i. Then the law of one price says

$$P(i,t) = S(t)\, P^*(i,t), \text{ for any commodity } i. \tag{8.1}$$

EXAMPLE 8.1

Gold in New York is trading for $400 per ounce, while in London the price is £250 per ounce. Then the law of one price implies that

$400 = S(t)\, £250$

or that

$S(t) = \$1.60/£.$

This proposition has strong intuitive appeal. It also involves a lot of hidden assumptions that make it somewhat less than a law of nature or even sufficiently well defined to be easily testable empirically.

1. The first assumption is that there are no transactions costs involved in buying a commodity in one market and selling it in another. This, of course, is not true in the real world. So for the law of one price (LOP) to have any empirical content, it must be adjusted to say that (8.1) holds within a margin given by transactions costs. For some commodities, say for similar futures contracts available simultaneously at the IMM in Chicago and LIFFE in London, the transactions costs are so small that the proposition still holds considerable theoretical interest once we modify it to include transactions costs. That is, the transactions costs are not so large that arbitrage would be ruled out over all reasonable ranges of price deviation. On the other hand, in cases where transactions costs are large, the LOP may be meaningless as an empirical proposition. For illustration, recall that the interest parity theorem holds up well empirically because interbank traders use it to set the forward rate. They do so because if they did not set prices according to the interest parity theorem, other banks could arbitrage against them if their prices deviated from parity more than the small amount allowable by bid/asked spreads. On the other hand, if the zloty price of coal in Poland multiplied by the cruzeiro price of zlotys differs from the cruzeiro price of coal in Brazil, there is an arbitrage possibility only after the costs of shipping coal from Poland to Brazil (or vice versa) have been taken into account. Coal, unlike money, does not exist as an accounting entry in a computerized data bank, and so cannot be transferred electronically at the speed of light and at very low cost. If transactions costs are very large in

comparison to the value of the underlying commodity, then it makes little sense to appeal to a "law" of one price. One might just as well appeal to a law of large transactions costs.

2. A second condition for the LOP to hold in a rational market is that there be no barriers to trade. This would include prohibitions on trade (for example, certain countries may be blacklisted by the local government, or trade in certain items—ranging from machine guns to laser technology—may be proscribed); tariffs, taxes, and quotas that may apply differentially to a good in different countries; and exchange controls of all sorts that might prevent the exchange rate from adjusting to the market price that would prevail under free exchange. To the extent that such barriers could be quantified, (8.1) would have to be adjusted to include their effects wherever they exist.

3. A third, perhaps obvious, point is that we must be comparing homogeneous goods. There is no reason to expect (8.1) to hold if $P^*(i,t)$ is the price of a barrel of Saudi Arabian light crude while $P(i,t)$ is the price of a barrel of West Texas intermediate crude. They both represent barrels of oil, but not homogeneous goods.

THE ABSOLUTE VERSION OF PURCHASING POWER PARITY

The *absolute* version of PPP postulates a relationship similar to (8.1), except that it uses price levels instead of particular commodity prices. Let $w(i)$ be the weight of good i in the domestic economy, and let $w^*(i)$ be the weight of good i in the foreign economy. The *price levels* of the domestic and foreign countries are, respectively, defined as

$$P(t) = \sum_i w(i) \, P(i,t)$$

$$P^*(t) = \sum_i w^*(i) \, P^*(i,t).$$

Note that $P(t)$ and $P^*(t)$ are price levels, and *not* price indexes. Each domestic price $P(i,t)$ is measured in, say, dollar terms, so $P(t)$ is measured in dollars. Each price $P^*(i,t)$ of a foreign good is measured in, say, French franc terms, so $P^*(t)$ is measured in French francs. Then the absolute version of purchasing power parity states:

$$P(t) = S(t) \, P^*(t). \tag{8.2}$$

EXAMPLE 8.2

Suppose the average price of a good in the U.S. economy is $3000. That is, $P(t) = \$3000$. Meanwhile, the average price of a good in the French economy is FF24,000. $P^*(t) = FF24,000$. Then, according to absolute PPP,

$3000 = S(t)$ FF24,000

or

$S(t) = \$.125/FF$.

What are the conditions necessary for absolute PPP to hold? We can see by comparing (8.2) with (8.1) that *if the law of one price holds for each good i, then absolute PPP holds if the weights of each good in the domestic and foreign economies are the same:* i.e., if $w(i) = w^*(i)$, for all goods i. This means that if weights are not the same for all goods, then absolute PPP may not hold, even if the LOP holds for each good individually.

EXAMPLE 8.3

Consider the following two hypothetical economies:

Economy A		Economy B	
Goods (units)	*Price ($/unit)*	*Goods (units)*	*Price (¥/unit)*
4 gold	1	20 gold	200
20 wheat	2	11 wheat	400
6 oil	2	1 oil	400

The current exchange rate is ¥200 = $1. Does the absolute version of PPP hold between these economies?

First notice that the LOP holds for each of the three goods, since the ratio of prices in each case is equal to the exchange rate. The exchange rate is ¥200/$ and also

$$¥200/\$1 = ¥400/\$2 = ¥400/\$2 = ¥200/\$.$$

In order to check absolute PPP, we must first calculate the price levels for each economy. In order to calculate the price level, we weight the price of each good by its share in the economy. The dollar value of the goods in Economy A is

$$4(\$1) + 20(\$2) + 6(\$2) = \$56.$$

The share of gold in Economy A is 4($1)/$56. The share of wheat is 20($2)/$56. The share of oil is 6($2)/$56. Thus the price level in Economy A is

$$P(A) = (4(\$1)/\$56)(\$1) + (20(\$2)/\$56)(\$2) + (6(\$2)/\$56)(\$2) = \$1.928.$$

In a similar fashion, we calculate the price level of Economy B as

$$P(B) = (20(¥200)/¥8800)(¥200) + (11(¥400)/¥8800)(¥400)$$
$$+ (1(¥400)/¥8800)(¥400) = ¥309.09.$$

Given the price levels $P(A) = \$1.928$ and $P(B) = ¥309.09$, we then use equation (8.2) to obtain

$$P(B)/P(A) = ¥309.09/\$1.928 = ¥160.32/\$1,$$

which is *not* equal to the exchange rate ¥200/$1. Hence absolute PPP does not hold, due to the fact that the two economies have a different composition of goods, even though the LOP holds for each of these goods individually.

RELATIVE VERSION OF PURCHASING POWER PARITY

As a practical consideration, price levels are seldom, if ever, calculated. Calculation of a price level would require observation of all prices and all quantities in the economy—a very costly endeavor. Countries therefore typically calculate a variety of price *indexes*. Instead of taking the prices of all goods and services in the economy and calculating a weighted average, a country will take a sampling of the prices of a small subset of the economy's goods. Then an index—such as the GNP deflator or the consumer price index (CPI)—is calculated based on the sample. This index number has no meaning in itself. It is not, for example, denominated in terms of the domestic currency. Rather, the index number is measured as a pure number relative to a base year, and the base-year number is usually set at 100 for the year in which the current list of goods to be sampled was first chosen. If the representative bundle of goods costs $10.43 in the base year while it costs $11.06 in the second year, then the first year's index is 100 while the second year's index is

($11.06/$10.43) 100 = 106.04.

For the same reasons that price indexes, not price levels, are tabulated in practice, in practice people do not make absolute PPP calculations, but instead appeal to *relative purchasing power parity*. Relative PPP involves looking at price index ratios.

Let us extend our use of $P(t)$ and $P^*(t)$ at this point to denote price indexes as well as price levels. The difference will be that $P(t)$ as a price level will be in units of the domestic currency and include all goods and services while $P(t)$ as an index will be a pure number and include only a subset of all goods and services. Then *relative* PPP postulates:

$$\frac{P(t + T)}{P(t)} = \frac{S(t + T)}{S(t)} \frac{P^*(t + T)}{P^*(t)}, \tag{8.3}$$

where t is one date and $t + T$ is a later date.

EXAMPLE 8.4

Between the end of December 1978 and the end of December 1979, the dollar price of DM went from $.53217/DM to $.57671/DM. Meanwhile the U.S. CPI went from 195.4 to 217.4 and the German CPI went from 160.2 to 166.6. Suppose we postulate that relative PPP holds when consumer price indexes are used in equation (8.3). Then using five of these variables, we can substitute into equation (8.3) and solve for the sixth. If we solve for $S(t + T)$, then, since

$$S(t + T) = S(t) \frac{P(t + T)/P(t)}{P^*(t + T)/P^*(t)}$$

we have

$$S(t + T) = \$.53217/DM \frac{217.4/195.4}{166.6/160.2} = \$.56934/DM.$$

The calculated rate of $.56934/DM is somewhat less than the actual market rate of $.57671/DM. In this case, however, the calculated value for $S(t + T)$ is in the right direction, and it is of the same order of magnitude as the calculated value from relative PPP.

Relative PPP may hold in circumstances where absolute PPP does not. For example, the formulation of equation (8.3) compensates for the fact that two economies may not have the same composition of goods.

EXAMPLE 8.5

In Example 8.3 we saw a case where absolute PPP did not hold between Economy A and Economy B. Suppose that all prices double in the two economies of Example 8.3 but the spot exchange rate remains unchanged. Does relative PPP hold?

Recalculating the price levels of Economies A and B with doubled prices for all goods yields $P(A) = \$3.856$ and $P(B) = ¥618.18$. In terms of an index, if the price index in Economy A was at 100 in the original time period, it is now at 200. Or, what is equivalent, if the original index was at 1.928, it is now at 3.856. Similarly, in Economy B the index goes from 309.09 to 618.18. Thus equation (8.3) implies that

$$S(t + T)/S(t) = (3.856/1.928)/(618.18/309.09) = 1,$$

or that $S(t + T) = S(t)$. Since the actual exchange rate is also still at its original level, relative PPP holds.

On the other hand, relative PPP cannot be expected to hold, even if the LOP holds, if *relative* prices change. This is illustrated in the following example.

EXAMPLE 8.6

Let the prices in Economy A and Economy B at time t be those originally given in Example 8.3, while at time $t + T$ the price for oil has increased to \$3 in Economy A and to ¥600 in Economy B. (That is, oil has become more expensive in terms of gold and wheat.) Does relative PPP hold, assuming the exchange rate remains unchanged at ¥200/\$?

The original price levels at time t were previously calculated to be $P(A) = \$1.928$ and $P(B) = ¥309.09$. The new price levels with the changed oil price are:

$P(A) = (4(\$1)/\$62)(\$1) + (20(\$2)/\$62)(\$2) + (6(\$3)/\$62)(\$3) = \$2.226;$
$P(B) = (20(¥200)/¥9000)(¥200) + (11(¥400)/¥9000)(¥400)$
$\quad + (1(¥600)/¥9000)(¥600) = ¥324.44.$

Dropping the currencies of denomination, the price levels here correspond to price indexes, so we have for relative PPP:

$$S(t + T)/S(t) = (2.226/1.928)/(324.44/309.09) = 1.10.$$

Hence relative PPP implies

$$S(t + T) = (1.10)S(t) = (1.10)(\$1/¥200) = \$.0055/¥ \text{ or } ¥181.82/\$.$$

Since the actual exchange rate is ¥200/$, relative PPP does not hold, even though LOP holds for each good. This is a consequence of the relative increase in the price of oil in terms of wheat and gold.

RELATIVE RATES OF INFLATION

Relative PPP can be converted into a version using inflation rates. Let μ be the rate of inflation in the domestic country and μ^* the rate of inflation in the foreign country. These rates of inflation are for the time period extending between t and $t + T$. Then, observing that

$$P(t + T)/P(t) = 1 + \mu, P^*(t + T)/P^*(t) = 1 + \mu^*,$$

we have from equation (8.3):

$$\frac{S(t + T)}{S(t)} = \frac{1 + \mu}{1 + \mu^*}$$

or, rewritten,

$$\frac{S(t + T) - S(t)}{S(t)} = \frac{\mu - \mu^*}{1 + \mu^*} \tag{8.4}$$

The last equation says that the proportional appreciation or depreciation of the foreign currency depends on whether inflation is higher in, respectively, the domestic or the foreign country.

EXAMPLE 8.7

Suppose that there is inflation in Germany over the course of a year in the amount of 6 percent while there is inflation in France in the amount of 13 percent. Then, interpreting $S(t)$ as the DM price of the FF, we would expect to find on the basis of relative PPP:

$$\frac{S(t + T) - S(t)}{S(t)} = \frac{.06 - .13}{1 + .13} = -.0619.$$

The DM price of the French franc would fall. Over the course of the year the French franc would become 6.19 percent cheaper in terms of the DM.

The above equation should be modified slightly if inflation is not constant or not exactly predictable. In that case, μ and μ^* should be interpreted to be *expected* inflation rates derived from *expected* changes in price levels. This different interpretation is primarily important when an inflation rate is random with a large variation. In that case, expected and actual inflation may differ by significant amounts.

☐

Equation (8.4) is sometimes combined with interest parity in the following manner. The difference in interest rates is said to equal the difference in inflation (or expected inflation) rates, because "real" interest rates are the same everywhere. That is, (nominal) interest rates are divided up by the *Fisher equation* into the sum of the rate of inflation (μ,μ^*) and a "real" component (β,β^*) that represents the return to capital in the absence of inflation:

$$i = \beta + \mu$$
$$i^* = \beta^* + \mu^*$$

The difference between the (nominal) interest rate and *expected* inflation is referred to as the *ex ante* real rate, while the difference between the (nominal) interest rate and *actual* inflation is called the *ex post* real interest rate.

If the real interest rate is the same in both the domestic and foreign country, $\beta = \beta^*$, it follows that $\mu - \mu^*$ in equation (8.4) is the same as $i - i^*$. That is, the rate of depreciation of the domestic currency is roughly equal to the difference in interest rates. (If all variables are measured in continuous time, this approximate equality can be converted to an exact equality.) Furthermore, since the premium on forward exchange is approximately equal (exactly equal in continuous time) to the difference in interest rates by interest parity, it follows that the premium on forward exchange represents the expected rate of depreciation of the domestic currency.

This combination of concepts is objectionable on several grounds. First, it combines a well-defined market arbitrage relationship (interest parity) with a crude macroeconomic simplification (purchasing power parity). Second, it requires the assumption that the real return to capital (the real interest rate) is everywhere the same. Most current evidence contradicts that assumption. Theoretical models indicate that real interest rates should vary across countries and across time. [See Dornbusch (1983), Fama and Farber (1979), Hansen and Hodrick (1983), Solnik (1973), and Stulz (1981).] Empirical tests constructed so that their power is high have also rejected the hypothesized equality of real eurocurrency rates across countries. [See Cumby and Obstfeld (1981) and Mishkin (1984).] ∎

THE REAL EXCHANGE RATE

Does empirical violation of PPP matter? It may matter a great deal to those engaged in international commerce. Consider, for example, the case of an industrial plant whose energy supply comes from imported oil. Oil will usually be priced in U.S. dollar terms. Suppose the dollar appreciates in value 10 percent with respect to the local currency. The industrial plant's fuel bill has now increased 10 percent in local currency terms. What are the plant's options? The plant may wish to pass its cost increase on to its final customers, by increasing the price of its product. There may be obstacles, however. If the final price of the plant's product is changed, it may alter demand for the product and reduce the total revenue the plant receives. Alternatively, the plant may attempt to compensate by cutting other costs. Wage costs may be fixed, however, as the plant's workers may have long-term contracts. The plant may wish to substitute other sources of energy, but to do so may take time and may involve fixed investment in equipment of a new technological vintage.

The law of one price, (8.1), implies that either the price of the plant's product will be adjusted or else the exchange rate will adjust back in the other direction, all in such a way that the LOP will be preserved. However, as indicated in the previous paragraph, a complex set of circumstances may dictate that such does not happen. The exchange rate may have moved 10 percent without the local currency price moving at all. If the price of the product in the foreign country has not changed, then the LOP has been violated. And there may be nothing the plant—or anyone else—can do about it in the short run. The change in the exchange rate has had a *real* impact on the industrial plant's profits. Its net income has fallen as a result of the exchange rate–induced rise in energy costs.

Similarly, consider the situation of a U.S. equipment manufacturer who exports to Germany. The supply of and demand for the dollar with respect to the DM in the foreign exchange market is related to a great many more factors than U.S. equipment exports to Germany, so the exchange rate may change in ways totally unrelated to equipment prices in the United States and Germany. If so, the competitiveness of the exporter in foreign markets will be affected. The *nominal* changes in the exchange rate may be accompanied by *real* changes, because prices do not adjust in such a way as to totally offset these exchange rate changes.

A Bolivian tin mine in the hyperinflationary summer of 1985 will serve as a final example. U.S. dollars obtained by the sale of tin were supposed to be turned over to the Bolivian government at an official exchange rate of $1 = Bolivian pesos 75,000. But the mine's wage costs were tied to the black-market exchange rate. In the black market (the free trade environment of city streets), the exchange ratio was 850,000 pesos per dollar and rising. A comparison of the price of tin in Bolivia and in world markets did not yield the official exchange rate. The tin mine manager was understandably concerned at this violation of PPP.

The *real exchange rate* is a variable defined to represent cases where purchasing power parity does not hold. We will designate the real exchange rate by $R(t)$. There are, in practice, two different ways of quoting real exchange rates, so you must interpret them in line with the source you are using. We will define $R(t)$ in such a way that the following interpretations are appropriate:

$R(t) < 1$: The relative purchasing power of domestic currency over foreign goods has fallen; there has been an improvement in export competitiveness.

$R(t) > 1$: The relative purchasing power of domestic currency over foreign goods has risen; there has been a loss of export competitiveness.

By analogy with (8.2), we may define, for price *levels:*

$$R(t) = P(t)/[S(t)P^*(t)], \tag{8.5}$$

while for price *indexes:*

$$R(t + T) = \frac{P(t + T)/P(t)}{[S(t + T)/S(t)][P^*(t + T)/P^*(t)]} \tag{8.6}$$

If, respectively, absolute and relative PPP hold for the price variables under consideration, then the real exchange rate $R(t) = 1$. Roughly speaking, if the

domestic currency depreciates less rapidly than the differential between domestic and foreign inflation, then the real exchange rate will rise, $R(t) > 1$. If
the domestic currency depreciates more rapidly than the differential between
domestic and foreign inflation, the real exchange rate will fall, $R(t) < 1$.

EXAMPLE 8.8

Using the data from Example 8.4, we can calculate the change in the real exchange rate of
the dollar with respect to the DM over the period December 1978 to December 1979.
Using equation (8.6),

$$R(t) = \frac{217.4/195.4}{(.57671/.53217)(166.6/160.2)} = .9872.$$

The value $R(t) = .9872$ implies that the dollar, once converted through the FX market,
would not buy as much of a basket of German goods in December 1979 as in December
1978. On the other hand, U.S. consumer goods were cheaper to DM holders in December
1979 than in December 1978, and exporters of such goods to Germany may have seen an
increase in their export competitiveness. This interpretation, on the basis of the calculations, assumes of course that it was not changes in *relative* prices of goods (as illustrated in
Example 8.6) that caused relative PPP not to hold.

Two final terms involve an extension from the concept of bilateral (two-
country) index measures to multilateral (many-country) index measures. The
nominal effective exchange rate refers to a weighted average of bilateral
nominal exchange rates. An index is constructed by weighting each foreign
currency by the country's share in the domestic country's foreign trade. For
example, if trade with Japan represents 25 percent of U.S. foreign trade, then
the exchange rate for the yen is weighted by .25. Thus the nominal effective
exchange rate represents how much of a basket of foreign currencies you can
get for one unit of the domestic currency. A bigger number, measured relative
to a base year, implies that you will get a bigger basket of foreign currency than
in the base year. The data given in Table 8.1 are taken from Morgan Guaranty's
World Financial Markets.

Morgan Guaranty's index is set at 100 for the 1980–1982 base period. For
example, the nominal effective exchange rate for Japan is at 172.8 in 1989.
Compared to the base-period index of 100, this number indicates that the
Japanese yen would buy 72.8 percent more foreign currency in 1989 than in the
base period of 1980–1982.

The *real effective exchange rate* is just a multilateral version of the real
exchange rate. Changes in bilateral real exchange rates are weighted by a
foreign country's share of trade with the domestic country. So the real effective exchange rate measures how much of a basket of foreign goods you can get
for one unit of domestic currency. A bigger number relative to a base year
implies you will get a bigger basket of foreign goods with the domestic currency
than in the base year. For example, as measured in Table 8.1, the real effective
exchange rate for the Japanese yen in 1989 was 118.2. This indicates that the
yen would buy 18.2 percent more foreign goods than in the base period. That

TABLE 8.1
Real and Nominal Effective Exchange Rates

	United States	Canada	Japan	France	Germany	United Kingdom	Switzerland
	Nominal Effective Exchange Rates[a]						
1980	90.7	100.4	95.5	106.5	100.0	99.8	95.4
1981	99.5	100.2	105.8	100.4	97.2	102.1	98.3
1982	109.8	99.4	98.6	93.1	102.8	98.1	106.3
1983	114.2	100.8	107.8	87.3	107.6	91.6	111.5
1984	122.4	97.3	113.0	84.4	107.4	88.1	110.5
1985	127.0	92.8	115.9	85.5	107.8	88.2	109.5
1986	106.0	87.6	150.1	87.4	116.1	80.7	118.1
1987	94.1	89.6	164.4	87.1	122.0	79.0	123.1
1988	88.0	95.6	181.6	85.7	121.8	83.8	121.9
1989	91.3	100.5	172.8	84.9	121.0	81.3	115.8
	Real Effective Exchange Rates[b]						
1980	89.4	99.6	103.0	102.1	103.5	99.8	98.7
1981	100.6	100.0	104.6	100.2	97.3	102.3	98.8
1982	109.9	100.4	92.3	97.7	99.2	97.9	102.6
1983	112.6	103.1	96.6	95.9	99.3	92.0	105.3
1984	118.1	101.2	97.6	96.4	96.5	89.2	102.0
1985	122.3	96.4	97.0	100.5	96.7	92.9	98.0
1986	102.4	93.6	115.4	103.5	103.4	87.4	106.0
1987	91.8	96.8	119.6	104.8	106.9	87.5	110.1
1988	87.4	104.7	125.9	102.2	106.2	94.4	107.1
1989	91.8	108.1	118.2	100.2	104.7	93.6	100.3

Source: Morgan Guaranty, *World Financial Markets.*

[a] Index numbers, 1980–1982 average = 100. Each index shows a currency's trade-weighted appreciation or depreciation measured against fifteen other currencies, using averages of daily noon spot exchange rates in New York and bilateral trade weights based on 1980 trade in manufactures. Annual figures are calendar-year averages.

[b] Index numbers, 1980–1982 average = 100. Each index is the corresponding nominal effective exchange rate adjusted for differential inflation in wholesale prices of nonfood manufacturers. Underlying price data are partly estimated.

is, you would get 72.8 percent more foreign currency in 1989 but that foreign currency would only buy 18.2 percent more foreign goods.

An alternative measure of nominal and real effective exchange rate changes is given in Figure 8.1, which is taken from the 1985 *Economic Report of the President.* The chart indicates that from 1980 to the end of 1984, the U.S. dollar's real effective exchange rate rose by approximately 60 percent. This was only slightly less than the increase in the nominal effective exchange rate. That is, a change in the dollar's nominal exchange rate translated almost one-for-one into a change in the real exchange rate. Hence, for some economic units, a change in the dollar's nominal exchange rate translated directly into a change in competitiveness.

EMPIRICAL EVIDENCE AND THEORETICAL REFORMULATION

PPP calculations are widely used in policy formation. Central banks have relied on PPP calculations in establishing par values for their currencies. Others may appeal to PPP to pronounce even market-determined rates as

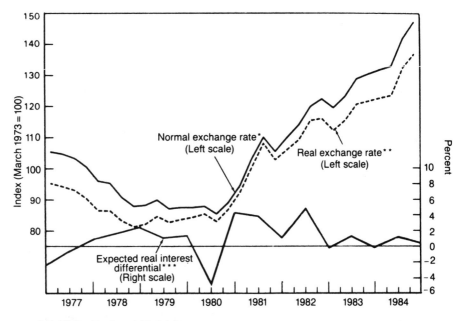

* Multilateral trade-weighted dollar.
** Nominal exchange rate adjusted by relative consumer prices.
*** U.S. interest rate (three-month) minus trade-weighted average interest rate (also three-month) for six industrial countries adjusted by corresponding OECD inflation forecasts.

FIGURE 8.1
Nominal and real effective exchange rates as calculated by the U.S. Council of Economic Advisors. (*Source: Economic Report of the President, 1985.*)

"overvalued" or "undervalued." For example, throughout the year 1983, many observers declared that the U.S. dollar was overvalued and that it would soon fall in the FX market. Apparently these observers were not in the market selling dollars, for the dollar continued to rise in value. But what they *said* was based largely on calculations such as those embodied in (8.6). They assumed that there should be a tendency for $R(t)$ to return to $R(t) = 1$. One of the arguments is that barriers to trade tend to erode over time, as individuals and companies find ways to get around them. But the argument is flawed to the extent that it assumes that all LOP deviations are the result of trade barriers.

Few people would argue with the fact that international trade does take place in the real world. In order for trade to flow from one destination to another, there has to be a price differential sufficient to pay shipping, capital, insurance, and other costs. That means that the "law of one price" can never hold in unidirectional trade from one location to another. Price differentials must exist in order to motivate trade, and they must *persist* in order for unidirectional trade to persist. These price differentials are consistent both with commodity market equilibrium and with the absence of commodity arbitrage opportunities. The shipment of oil from the Middle East to Japan implies that delivered oil in Japan commands a higher price than does the same oil at Kharg Island in the Persian Gulf. This higher price compensates the shipper and allows the shipper to earn a normal economic profit. There is no necessary reason the price of oil in Japan should *ever* equal the price at Kharg Island. Nor should we expect a "long-run" tendency for prices to adjust between the two locations. Thus it is not surprising that studies such as Isard (1977), Kravis and Lipsey (1978), Protopapadakis and Stoll (1982), and Richardson (1978) find large and persistent deviations from the "law" of one price, which is the least problematical version of PPP. As customarily formulated, PPP is not a necessary consequence of economic rationality.

Roll (1979) has indicated, however, that normal economic maximizing behavior implies that the real exchange rate $R(t)$ [see (8.6)] is a martingale without drift:

$$E[R(t + T)|I(M,t)] = R(t). \tag{8.7}$$

Given the current market information set $I(M,t)$, real exchange rate changes should not be predictable if the available information is used efficiently. For example, referring back to Table 8.1, if we assume that the real effective exchange rate changes for the U.S. dollar are not simply the product of measurement error or statistical jerry-rigging, then what is implied by (8.7) is that the change in the index from 1982 to 1983 (114.2 − 109.8 = 3.4) was not predictable based on the information that was available in 1982. The intuition behind equation (8.7) is that the current level of the real exchange rate $R(t)$ embodies the costs of trade and does not imply commodity arbitrage possibilities. But if real exchange rate *changes* were predictable, one could engage in successful commodity speculation.

☐

As noted in Chapter 7, however, there may be costs to acquiring information, which would induce a modification in (8.7). Since the collection of information is a costly enterprise, those who invest in information should also find occasional speculative opportunities sufficient to justify the cost of their research. Be that as it may, there is a good bit of evidence that says that real exchange rates, as commonly measured, are martingales. See Adler and Lehmann (1982), Darby (1982), Rogalski and Vinso (1977), and Roll (1979). Further discussion can be found in Shapiro (1983) and Adler and Dumas (1983). ■

Empirical tests of (8.7) have been generally supportive (see references just listed). On the other hand, tests of (8.1)–(8.4) have generally rejected PPP as formulated in those equations except over long-run time horizons. Most people will not find the empirical rejection of equations (8.1)–(8.4) surprising, since they may have experienced "bargain countries" as tourists as well as "expensive countries." The purchasing power of their currency was found to vary from place to place over time. In this context, equation (8.7) may be formulated as the *Tourist Theorem:* The best forecast of next season's bargain country is this season's bargain country. The usefulness of this theorem depends on the variance of the forecast errors $e(t + T)$, where

$$e(t + T) = R(t + T) - R(t) \tag{8.8}$$

and

$$E[e(t + T)|I(M,t)] = 0.$$

That is, if the error variance were large, then even if we correctly expected no change in the real exchange rate, there would be considerable risk that we could be wrong.

The implication of this evidence is that, under freely floating exchange rates, the current real exchange rate should be taken to represent long-run market equilibrium, given current information. From (8.7), a change in the real exchange rate at time t would *not* imply a change in the opposite direction at time $t + 1$. Meanwhile, if empirical data show that any of equations (8.1)–(8.4) are violated, then the size of the violation could be used as a guide indicating the magnitude of transactions or transport costs, the degree of uncertainty, the presence of barriers to trade, or the existence of measurement or statistical error.

Current deviations from the LOP (equation (8.1)) can be used by producers as a forecast of future deviations, since by (8.7) these deviations would not be expected to change. Hence, deviations from the LOP could be used as a guide to plant location, based on differences in local costs of inputs to the production process. There will be risk, however, depending on the variance of the errors in (8.8).

EXAMPLE 8.9

The following excerpt from *Business Week* reports on a company decision that reflects an application of (8.7):

Beckman Instruments Inc., a medical and laboratory-equipment subsidiary of Smith-Kline Beckman Corp., recently moved the production of two product lines sold overseas from the U.S. to plants in Europe. "With a strong dollar today, it makes absolute sense to have overseas manufacturing," says Mr. Michael T. O'Neill, director of international operations for Beckman's bioanalytical-systems group. "We're looking to expand operations in Ireland and Scotland." He has good reason: Some of the parts Beckman buys from suppliers in Europe cost 33 percent less than what U.S. suppliers charge for the same parts. Says O'Neill: "It is a permanent shift."

—October 8, 1984

PROBLEMS FOR CHAPTER 8

1. Suppose the inflation version of relative PPP holds true in terms of the U.S. dollar price of EMS currencies.
   (a) Explain the proportional change in the U.S.$/ECU rate in terms of the proportional change in the U.S. dollar prices of the individual EMS currencies.
   (b) Answer the same question for the French franc/ECU exchange rate. Why do the two answers differ?

2. For this problem and the next, assume that the stated price indexes are truly representative of purchasing power (i.e., transactions costs do not bias the calculations, and there are no changes in the relative prices of the individual goods that compose the index). Between the end of the first quarter and the end of the fourth quarter in 1979, the U.S. price index went from 207.0 to 227.6, while the Japanese

price index went from 254.0 to 267.6. Meanwhile, the U.S. dollar price of the yen went from .0048470 to .0041613. Explain what the impact was on
(a) U.S. exporters to Japan and
(b) Japanese consumers of U.S. goods.

3. Below are data from the United States and Chile for the years 1975–1980.

	1975	1976	1977	1978	1979	1980
Peso/dollar	8.5	17.4	28.0	34.0	39.0	39.0
Chile CPI	100	312	599	838	1118	1511
U.S. CPI	161.2	170.5	181.5	195.4	217.4	257.0

(a) Based on these data, would you argue that the peso is over- or undervalued at the end of 1980?
(b) What would you guess concerning Chile's current account?

4. The expected yearly inflation rate is 4 percent in the United States and 2 percent in Switzerland. The current exchange rate is SF2.3/$. Assuming that the inflation version of relative purchasing power parity holds, what is the expected exchange rate in one year?

5. Two countries, A and B, have economies with the following compositions of goods and prices:

Economy A		Economy B	
Units	Price/Unit	Units	Price/Unit
1.5 oil	$20	3 oil	DM80
1 wheat	$10	4 wheat	DM60

The market exchange rate is DM4/$1.
(a) Does the law of one price hold?
(b) Does absolute purchasing power parity hold?
(c) If all prices double in Economy A, and the exchange rate moves to DM2/$1, does relative purchasing parity hold?

6. Evidence that real exchange rates are a martingale without drift suggests all of the following *except* [choose one]:
a. The best forecast of next year's bargain country is this year's bargain country.
b. The elimination or lessening of barriers to trade is a process that is not generally forecastable.
c. Real exchange rate changes do not typically imply opportunities for commodity arbitrage.
d. If real exchange rates are measured with statistical error, such measurement errors are not generally forecastable.
e. There is a natural tendency for the real exchange rate to return to its initial value.

FOREIGN EXCHANGE RATES AND THE BALANCE OF PAYMENTS

THE BALANCE ON INTERNATIONAL TRANSACTIONS

In Chapter 8 we looked at possible relationships between the prices of goods and the foreign exchange rate. The notion of commodity arbitrage, even though it provides some intuitive insight, does not succeed in clarifying the relation of foreign exchange supply and demand to more fundamental economic forces. In particular, government policy, national consumption and savings, and the accumulation and allocation of financial assets are all variables having a direct impact on the exchange rate. It would seem desirable to deal with these variables explicitly and not just through their implicit impact on commodity prices. This consideration leads us to the balance of payments.

The accounting record of all of a country's commercial transactions with respect to the rest of the world is called *the balance on international transactions* or, more commonly, *the balance of payments*. The balance of payments (BOP) is divided into two principal divisions: the *current account*, which is the record of all purchases and sales of goods and services with respect to the rest of the world, and the *capital account*, which represents the flows of financial assets—either bought and sold outright, or in payment for goods and services. Many, but not all, of these transactions involve the foreign exchange market. Imported or exported goods will usually be priced in terms of a foreign currency on at least one side of the transaction, and sometimes the currency of denomination of trade will be foreign to both countries. (*Countertrade,* the direct barter of goods between countries, is a notable exception that circumvents the financial markets altogether.) Similarly, foreign currency transactions are involved when financial assets are bought and sold, or borrowed and lent, across national boundaries.

The term "balance of payments" is commonly abused in conversation, financial publications, and newspapers. Sometimes the term will be used to refer to the entire accounting balance sheet, and sometimes it will be used in reference to a particular item on the balance sheet, such as the current account balance or capital account balance or reserves balance. In addition, it will appear often in phrases like "balance of payments problems"—which could be construed to mean a variety of things, including the possibility the speaker or writer does not know what he's talking about and is just throwing out political or economic buzzwords. One should take care to determine what, if anything, is actually meant in a particular context.

Items recorded on the BOP balance sheet are classified into *accounts* according to the *type* of transaction. A typical balance sheet will have accounts for the yearly flow of goods and services, and yearly flow of capital, and the yearly changes in official reserves. In addition, transactions within each account will be given plus signs if they represent ways of getting money ("sources of funds") or minus signs if they represent ways of spending money ("uses of funds"). Sources of funds include exports of goods and services, sales of financial assets to foreigners, and foreign borrowing. Uses of funds include importing goods and services, purchases of financial assets, and foreign lending. By the principles of double-entry bookkeeping, sources and uses always match. The dollar amount of plus items equals the dollar amount of minus items. The sum of all items is thus zero. In order to get a non-zero amount (a "surplus" or a "deficit"), you have to leave something out.

THE CURRENT ACCOUNT

Let us begin our discussion with the *balance on current account (CA)*. This is an accounting measure of the total domestic currency value of exports of goods and services (X) over a period of time, minus the total domestic currency value of imports of goods and services (M) over the same time period:

$$CA = X - M. \tag{9.1}$$

The current account is typically divided into three subcategories: the merchandise trade balance, the services balance, and the balance on unilateral transfers. *Merchandise trade* refers to physical goods like automobiles, oil, machinery, coffee, and beef. *Services* include interest payments, shipping and insurance, tourism, dividends, and military expenditures. Unilateral transfers are gifts, such as foreign or military aid, or money sent by immigrant workers in the host country to the folks back home. In each of these three categories, items will be given a plus sign if they are sources of funds (export of goods, provision of tourist services, receipt of transfer payments from abroad), or a minus sign if they are uses of funds (imports of goods, taking foreign trips, sending money home). The sum of all plus and minus items in a category is the "balance," which will be positive if the amount of plus items is greater than that of minus items, and negative otherwise. The sum of the merchandise trade balance, the services balance, and the unilateral transfers balance is the current account balance.

Table 9.1 gives current account balances for the United States, Japan, and Germany for several recent years. We see that the United States has large deficits on its merchandise trade balance ($-$113.2 billion in 1989), while Japan and Germany have large surpluses ($76.9 billion and $75.4 billion, respectively). The United States had a small surplus on services other than investment income, while Japan had a large deficit and Germany a small deficit ($20.6 billion vs. $-$38.9 billion and $-$7.9 billion). Overall the U.S. deficit was

TABLE 9.1
Current Account Balances—United States, Japan, Germany (in billions of U.S. dollars)

	1986	1987	1988	1989
United States				
Current account (*CA*)	−143.9	−160.2	−125.5	−103.7
Trade balance	−145.1	−159.5	−127.2	−113.2
Net investment income	11.0	5.7	3.2	3.2
Other services	5.9	7.7	13.1	20.6
Transfers	−15.7	−14.2	−14.6	−14.3
Japan				
Current account (*CA*)	85.8	87.0	79.6	57.2
Trade balance	92.8	96.4	95.0	76.9
Net investment income	9.5	16.7	21.0	23.4
Other services	−14.4	−22.4	−32.3	−38.9
Transfers	−2.1	−3.7	−4.1	−4.2
Germany				
Current account (*CA*)	40.1	46.0	50.4	55.5
Trade balance	54.6	68.3	77.9	75.4
Net investment income	4.2	4.1	5.1	11.8
Other services	−3.4	−6.7	−9.8	−7.9
Transfers	−15.3	−19.7	−22.8	−23.8

Source: Bank for International Settlements.

approximately matched by the total Japanese and German surpluses (−$103.7 billion vs. $57.2 billion plus $55.5 billion).

It is important to keep in mind that the merchandise trade balance has no unique implication for the foreign exchange rate. The merchandise trade balance is widely reported in the media in the United States and is frequently referred to as the "trade balance." But actually merchandise trade is only part of total trade. A dollar's worth of foreign exchange earned in exporting goods is no different from a dollar's worth of foreign exchange earned in the provision of services. In terms of supply and demand for foreign exchange, merchandise trade is no more important than any other kind of trade.

As we saw in the last chapter, export competitiveness, as well as the purchasing power of the domestic currency over imported goods, is affected by the real exchange rate $R(t)$. Therefore we can write the CA flow at any particular time as a function of the real exchange rate at that time:

$$CA = CA[R(t)]. \tag{9.2}$$

Generally speaking—looking at the feedback of exchange rate influences on the current account—with a higher real exchange rate we would expect fewer exports and more imports, while a lower real exchange rate would imply more exports and fewer imports. Conversely—looking at the feedback of the current account on the exchange rate—if the CA is negative (a deficit), adjustment of the balance to zero would usually require the real exchange rate to fall, while if the CA is positive (a surplus), adjustment of the balance to zero would usually require the real exchange rate to rise. Whether there is any tendency for the CA to adjust to zero depends on other factors (such as the desire to accumulate or sell foreign assets, discussed later).

The explanation in the previous paragraph focused on the relation between the real exchange rate and competitiveness in international trade in goods and services. By broadening our focus somewhat, we can see that the real exchange rate will in turn depend on the underlying savings and investment behavior of the national population. Consider the standard GNP identity

$$Y = C + I + G + CA[R(t)] \tag{9.3}$$

where Y is national income, C is consumption spending, I is private investment spending, and G is government spending. Rewriting and subtracting total national taxes T from each side of the equation, we obtain

$$Y - C - T = I + G - T + CA[R(t)].$$

The expression $Y - C - T$ represents total *after-tax private savings*. Denote this by S. The expression $G - T$ is the *government deficit*. Thus, as a GNP accounting identity,

$$CA[R(t)] = S - [I + (G - T)]. \tag{9.4}$$

This is an identity, so it will always hold in equilibrium. That is, in ex post economic equilibrium, *the current account balance will identically equal the excess of private after-tax savings over the sum of private investment spending and the government deficit*. This shows that the level of the real exchange rate $R(t)$ is related to the consumption/savings decision, and the desire to invest. If, in economic equilibrium, after-tax savings is not sufficient to finance both private investment and the government deficit, then the current account will be in deficit. Conversely, to *reduce a current account deficit* (or to cause a fall in $R(t)$), one of the following must occur in equilibrium:

1. For a given level of I and $G - T$, private after-tax savings S must be increased.
2. For a given level of S and $G - T$, private investment must fall.
3. For a given level of S and I, the government deficit $G - T$ must be reduced.

Since all of these variables will influence the equilibrium value of the current account $CA[R(t)]$, it follows that they will influence, and be influenced by, the real exchange rate $R(t)$. The real exchange rate in turn will change as the nominal exchange rate $S(t)$ changes, to the extent that economic equilibrium does not imply completely offsetting price changes.

THE CAPITAL ACCOUNT

The *capital account* is an accounting measure of the total domestic currency value of financial transactions between domestic residents and the rest of the world over a period of time. It includes financial transactions associated with international trade as well as flows associated with portfolio shifts involving the purchase of foreign stocks, bonds, and bank deposits. Leaving aside countertrade, every international transaction that gives rise to a current account entry also gives rise to a capital account entry. For example, a payment for $10,000,000 of Brazilian steel will involve a minus item of $10,000,000 being recorded in the merchandise trade part of the U.S. current account, while a plus item of $10,000,000 ("capital inflow") will be recorded in the capital account to represent the transfer of a $10,000,000 bank deposit to Brazil.

However, there may be additional transactions that take place independently of the current account. For example, a purchase of $50,000,000 of Swiss franc bonds will involve two U.S. capital account entries of $50,000,000—a negative one to represent the domestic purchase of foreign bonds ("capital outflow") and a positive one to represent the foreign acquisition of the domestic bank deposits that were used to pay for the bonds ("capital inflow").

Since the sum of all plus items and all minus items is zero, it follows that the sum of current account and capital account transactions (leaving nothing out) is zero. A current account surplus equals a capital account deficit. A current account deficit equals a capital account surplus. This means that the *current account surplus or deficit represents a net change in the ownership of foreign assets*. For example, in 1974, Saudi Arabia was running a current account surplus. Saudi Arabia was earning much more on its oil exports than it was spending on imports. Since it was earning more than it was spending, it was accumulating foreign IOUs, or financial assets, in the form of bank deposits in New York and other places. These bank deposits might, in turn, be transformed into U.S. Treasury bills or eurocurrency deposits in London or real estate in Beverly Hills.

Let *FA* denote a country's ownership of foreign assets. Since the current account flow over the year gives rise to a positive or negative change in the value of these foreign assets, we may write

$$CA[R(t)] = \Delta FA. \tag{9.5}$$

If the current account is in deficit, $CA < 0$, then the country is either accumulating debt or else running down its current stock of foreign assets. If the current account is in surplus, then the country is either repaying debt or building up its stock of foreign assets. A country that already has a large stock of foreign-asset-denominated wealth can run a current account deficit and draw down its stock of foreign assets without the need for any protracted macroeconomic adjustment. On the other hand, a country that is financing its current account deficit by foreign borrowing can only continue to do so as long as creditors are willing to extend loans to the country.

EXAMPLE 9.1

In 1984, the United States ran a large current account deficit, and yet the United States dollar remained very strong in the FX markets. How was this possible? It was easily possible as long as foreigners wished to continue to accumulate dollar assets given the current exchange rate. In fact, foreigners wished to accumulate dollar assets at a rate even faster than represented by the U.S. current account deficit. As a result, the dollar improved in value in the FX markets as foreigners switched directly out of domestic assets and into U.S. dollar assets.

EXAMPLE 9.2

As a country, Japan has a high savings rate relative to the rest of the world. Referring back to equation (9.4), this fact implies a large value for after-tax savings S relative to Japan's national income Y. National after-tax savings will be absorbed either in private domestic investment I, or by a government deficit $G - T$, or by a current account surplus $CA > 0$. Thus, depending on I and $G - T$, Japan may run a current account surplus without any change in the real yen exchange rate. That is, one should not necessarily expect to see the value of the yen rise in the FX market and the CA surplus eliminated at an early date. As long as Japan maintains a high savings rate relative to the rest of the world, the current account surplus need not ever be eliminated through exchange rate adjustment. The Japanese desire to save corresponds to a desire to accumulate financial assets. If all saving were done in the form of domestic assets, then risk-adjusted rates of return would be driven down in Japan. Thus, to keep risk-adjusted rates of return equalized, some of the Japanese savings will take the form of the accumulation of foreign assets. A current account surplus would thus correspond to the desire to add to the stock of financial wealth. (On the other hand, Chapter 2 indicated that the rate of return on Japanese domestic assets was in the past kept at an artificially low rate through interest-rate ceilings, a feature apparently stemming from the government's desire to borrow at cheap interest rates. This in turn gives rise to an excess demand for foreign assets.)

THE CAPITAL ACCOUNT AND CENTRAL BANK INTERVENTION

As we saw in Chapter 2, most nations of the world fix or peg their exchange rates to one or more of the major currencies such as the U.S. dollar, the French franc, or the currencies that make up the SDR. In addition, major European currencies are pegged within the bands of the parity grid system of the EMS. And even for currencies like the U.S. dollar, the Japanese yen, and the Swiss franc—which are not pegged to any other currency or set of indicators—there is occasional or frequent central bank intervention to influence the market exchange rate.

Central bank intervention creates a link between the BOP balance sheet and the balance sheet of the central bank. Since this link has important implications for the domestic money supply, a common way of dividing up the capital account in the BOP is to separate out those items that involve the central bank (or monetary authority). Let $\Delta FACB$ denote the change in the foreign asset position of the central bank and ΔFAO denote all other items not involving the central bank:

$$CA[R(t)] = \Delta FA = \Delta FACB + \Delta FAO. \tag{9.6}$$

It follows from this identity that

$$CA - \Delta FAO - \Delta FACB = 0.$$

Previously, we treated both $-\Delta FAO$ and $-\Delta FACB$ as parts of the capital account. Let us now change terminology and call $-\Delta FAO$ the capital account and $-\Delta FACB$ the reserves account. They would appear on the BOP balance sheets as:

Balance of Payments

CA	Current account
$-\Delta FAO$	Capital account
$-\Delta FACB$	Reserves account

Of course, the total sum of items on the BOP balance sheet will sum to zero, just as before. Since, however, the amount of intervention the central bank has to undertake to peg or to influence the FX value of the domestic currency is a variable of considerable interest, one may wish to separate out this item by placing it "below the line"—which means that we draw an arbitrary line on the balance sheet and calculate a "balance" that leaves out what is below the line:

Balance of Payments

CA	Current account
$-\Delta FAO$	Capital account

$-\Delta FACB$	Reserves account

The line could have been drawn anywhere. Drawn at another point, it would imply a different "balance" on the BOP, but we will not concern ourselves here with alternative concepts.

Notice that the absolute value of the numbers above the line and below the line are equal (since they sum to zero). Thus an economic explanation of the balance below the line cannot be different from the economic explanation of the balance above the line. There is, however, a difference in the focus of attention. Looking at the current account and the capital account above the line, we are led to think about competitiveness in international trade (current account) and the portfolio determinates of capital flows (capital account). Looking at the reserves account below the line, we are led to think about central bank policy. The following discussion will focus on central bank behavior in order to explore the relationship among the central bank's intervention policy, domestic monetary policy, and the exchange rate.

Table 9.2 gives a rough measure of ΔFAO and $\Delta FACB$ for the United States, Japan, and Germany in the late 1980s. In 1989, the United States lost $121.7 billion in its foreign asset position ($\Delta FAO = -\$121.7$ billion) through the capital account, while Japan and Germany had large gains. Japan's large investments in foreign securities ($101.4 billion in 1986) have been increasingly supplanted by direct investment ($45.2 billion in 1989). Central bank intervention was heavy during the years 1986–1989. The change in the reserves account in Japan in 1989 ($\Delta FACB = -\$24.7$ billion) reflects the heavy sales of foreign currency (dollars) in support of the yen. In the United States, the Federal Reserve increased its holding of foreign exchange (such as yen and DM) by $25 billion in 1989. However, other foreign official liabilities (not shown) increased by about $7 billion, leaving a net position increase of $18 billion ($\Delta FACB = \$18.0$ billion).

Let us now connect the balance sheet of the BOP to the balance sheet of the central bank. We saw in Chapter 1 that the major items on a central bank balance sheet were:

Central Bank

Assets	Liabilities
DA	H
FACB	

TABLE 9.2
Flows in Foreign Assets—United States, Japan, Germany

	1986	1987	1988	1989
United States				
Capital account ($- \Delta FAO$)	110.1	103.3	88.9	121.7
Direct investment	18.4	19.3	39.9	26.9
Securities	70.5	29.2	38.7	47.1
Banks, other than above	19.8	46.9	14.3	10.8
Statistical discrepancy	11.3	1.9	−10.6	34.9
Reserves account ($- \Delta FACB$)	33.8	56.9	36.6	−18.0
Japan				
Capital account ($- \Delta FAO$)	−72.1	−44.7	−64.1	−81.9
Direct investment	−14.3	−18.4	−34.7	−45.2
Securities	−101.4	−93.8	−66.6	−28.1
Banks, other than above	58.5	71.8	44.5	8.6
Statistical discrepancy	2.5	−3.9	2.8	−22.0
Reserves account ($- \Delta FACB$)	−13.7	−42.3	−15.5	24.7
Germany				
Capital account ($- \Delta FAO$)	−37.0	−22.6	−69.6	−65.5
Direct investment	−8.9	−7.2	−10.0	−7.5
Securities	22.0	−2.6	−43.8	−4.2
Banks, other than above	−27.9	−3.9	−10.3	−30.3
Statistical discrepancy	−25.1	−5.5	−12.8	−23.5
Reserves account ($- \Delta FACB$)	−3.1	−23.4	19.2	10.0

Source: Bank for International Settlements.

where DA are domestic assets such as government bonds, $FACB$ are foreign assets such as foreign exchange, gold, and SDRs, and H is the domestic high-powered money base, which includes items like commercial banks' reserve deposits with the central bank and printed currency. (There may be, in addition, other types of central bank liabilities. This will not, however, materially affect the following discussion.)

Central bank monetary and FX policies can be characterized according to the changes they give rise to on the balance sheet of the central bank. Common central bank policies for some (not all) countries are *open-market operations* and *foreign exchange intervention*. Open-market operations involve changing the monetary base by buying and selling some domestic asset such as government bonds, bills of exchange, or even corporate stock:

$$\Delta DA = \Delta H.$$

The change in the monetary base, ΔH, will in turn lead to a change in the domestic money supply ($M1$), which is a multiple of ΔH. Similarly, when the central bank does foreign exchange intervention, it changes the monetary base by buying or selling foreign exchange:

$$\Delta FACB = \Delta H.$$

In general, then, the change in the monetary base over any period of time can be viewed as stemming from either domestic or foreign operations:

$$\Delta H = \Delta DA + \Delta FACB \tag{9.7}$$

Since the change in the monetary base gives rise to a change in the domestic money supply, it is natural to organize the above facts in terms of the supply of, and demand for, money, denoted respectively by *MS* and *MD*. Let's begin with the money market in equilibrium at the current real exchange rate $R(t)$:

$$MS = MD[R(t)]. \tag{9.8A}$$

Of course money demand is a function of more than just the real exchange rate, but we write it this way because $R(t)$ is the variable in which we are primarily interested. The supply of money can be written in terms of the monetary base H and the money multiplier m as:

$$MS = m H. \tag{9.8B}$$

Thus

$$MD[R(t)] = m H \tag{9.8C}$$

Then, from a position of equilibrium at time $t + T$, we can calculate:

$$MD[R(t + T)] - MD[R(t)] = m \, \Delta H$$
$$\Delta MD = m \, \Delta H$$
$$\Delta MD = m \, (\Delta DA + \Delta FACB)$$

or, rewriting,

$$[(1/m) \, \Delta MD] - \Delta DA = \Delta FACB. \tag{9.9}$$

Let's analyze the last equation. The expression $[(1/m) \, \Delta MD]$ is the change in the demand for the monetary base, which is a function of the real exchange rate at t and $t + T$. The expression ΔDA is the amount of monetary base supplied by the central bank in the form of domestic assets. The expression $\Delta FACB$ is the amount of monetary base supplied by the central bank in the form of foreign assets. The real exchange rate $R(t)$ adjusts until supply and demand are equal to $R(t + T)$.

We can now summarize the implications of (9.9) under three different central bank policy regimes:

Case 1

First, consider the case where there is no central bank intervention in the FX market. Exchange rates float freely. Since there is no intervention, $\Delta FACB = 0$. (This assumes, of course, that foreign exchange is valued at historical rates and the central bank takes no action to offset valuation changes in its reserves position that might result from the divergence of market rates from the historical rates at which the central bank intervened.) With no foreign exchange intervention,

$$[(1/m) \, \Delta MD] = \Delta DA.$$

The real exchange rate adjusts so that supply and demand for the monetary base ("high-powered money") are equal. If, for example, the central bank supplies too much of the monetary base, at the margin the public will use the increased supply of money to buy foreign currency, or domestic goods, or foreign goods. This will cause a depreciation of the domestic currency in the foreign exchange market (the nominal domestic currency price of foreign exchange, $S(t)$, will rise), and this depreciation will continue until foreign currency and foreign goods become sufficiently expensive that the demand for the monetary base is equal to the supply. While the nominal exchange rate $S(t)$ will rise, the real exchange rate $R(t)$ may or may not change. What happens to $R(t)$ depends on what relative prices do.

Case 2

Second, consider a regime of completely fixed exchange rates. The nominal exchange rate is fixed at some level by central bank intervention $S(t) = S^*$. Since the nominal exchange rate is not free to change to bring about an adjustment in monetary demand (and hence the demand for foreign exchange) all adjustment must occur through relative price changes. That is, $R(t)$ can only adjust through domestic and foreign price level adjustments, and not through the adjustment of $S(t)$. Thus we see that fixed exchange rate systems, by constraining the adjustments of $S(t)$, require greater price-level adjustments than do floating exchange rates.

In addition, equation (9.9), along with fixed exchange rates, implies that the central bank will not be able to conduct a domestic monetary policy (in the form of open market operations ΔDA) independent of its foreign exchange policy (foreign exchange intervention $\Delta FACB$). That is, $\Delta FACB$ will be determined by the need to intervene in the foreign exchange market. Thus from (9.9) we see that the central bank will have to adjust its position in DA in order to make up any resulting difference between supply and demand for the monetary base.

Countries that fix the exchange rate $[(S(t) = S^*]$ and also engage in inflationary policies (via large values of ΔDA from year to year) will have chronic deficits on their reserve accounts. The central bank will have a "shortage" of foreign currency. If ΔDA is large relative to $[(1/m) \Delta MD]$, it follows that

$$\Delta FACB = [(1/m) \Delta MD] - \Delta DA$$

will be negative, and will remain negative unless either a devaluation of the domestic currency takes place (S^* is increased) or else the rate of growth of the money supply is curtailed (ΔDA takes place at a less rapid rate). Countries that do not have large reserve positions will not be able to maintain fixed nominal exchange rates and also indulge in inflationary domestic policies. As we saw in Chapter 3, if the current nominal exchange rate S^* overvalues the domestic currency (undervalues foreign currency), then everyone will want to buy foreign currency from the central bank and no one will want to sell foreign currency to the central bank. Thus, to avoid running out of foreign exchange reserves, the central bank will have to change S^* or else impose a system of quotas and exchange controls. The latter "solution" will only lead to a black or free market that will take place outside official channels. In the summer of 1985, for example, Bolivia supposedly had a "fixed" rate of 75,000 pesos = $1. But virtually no foreign exchange transactions took place at this rate; the Bolivian peso was actually floating, since almost all transactions took place at privately negotiated rates.

The task of an exchange rate forecaster is simplified under fixed exchange rates. The exchange rate will remain unchanged unless there is a devaluation or revaluation of the current fixed rate. The forecaster's task becomes one of evaluating the consistency of policy goals to evaluate the timing and magnitude of devaluations or revaluations, using as his or her data the level of central bank reserves, the availability of credit lines, the political probability the central bank will change monetary policy, the size of the black-market premium on foreign currencies such as the U.S. dollar (if there are exchange controls), and so on. There should be no problem in getting the *direction of change* correct. That is why commercial banks and corporations made a lot of money betting against central banks in the last years of the Bretton Woods system.

Case 3

A third case involves countries that engage in "dirty floating." That is, they do some intervention ($\Delta FACB \neq 0$) to influence the exchange rate $S(t)$ but do not attempt to peg the rate at a fixed level or keep it within a fixed band. In this case, equation (9.9) implies that greater foreign exchange intervention implies less freedom to conduct an independent domestic policy (make changes in DA), while greater independence in domestic policy implies less freedom to intervene in the FX market. The less $S(t)$ is allowed to adjust to bring about market equilibrium, the greater must be the adjustment in relative prices. And so on. This third case is intermediate between cases 1 and 2.

If central bank policy is predictable, then central bank actions are part of the market information set $I(M, t)$. For example, it has been claimed that 55 to 70 percent of German central bank intervention can be explained on the basis of a statistically estimated "policy reaction function" (Neumann, 1984). It was indicated in Chapter 8 that rational economic decision making should yield the result that

$$E[R(t + T)|I(M, t)] = R(t).$$

If central bank behavior is part of the market information set, then central bank intervention should not result in predictable real exchange rates changes.

SELECTIVE CENTRAL BANK INTERVENTION IN THE FX MARKET

The third case we examined, that of "dirty floating," raises some interesting issues. Central banks have continued to intervene on a massive scale despite floating exchange rates. The Bundesbank, for example, which averaged DM4.5 billion in yearly foreign exchange purchases over the 1949–1973 Bretton Woods period, purchased a net total of DM20.1 billion in FX in 1978, while it sold DM27.6 billion in foreign assets in 1980 (Neumann, 1984). Why should central banks choose to intervene selectively in the foreign exchange market? And what does this imply for equilibrium in the FX market?

If central bankers allow rates to float, one assumes that they believe that rates determined in the market are better than fixed exchange rates. A freely floating exchange rate has the property that it is the price at which the exchange market clears when all buy and sell decisions are being made in a context of utility maximization. But if the central bank intervenes in the market for other reasons, the resulting equilibrium price that emerges as a result may represent a signal whose interpretation is uncertain. The uncertainty comes from the fact that the central bank's actions may not be predictable or consistent. If central bank policy is not a part of the market information set $I(M,t)$, the central bank is a source of random noise. Tomorrow's equilibrium exchange rate will depend in part on a future random intervention by the central bank. The uncertainty over central bank action could increase exchange rate uncertainty, volatility, and risk. The prediction error

$$e(t + T) = R(t + T) - E[R(t + T)|I(M,t)]$$

in the real exchange rate (review Chapter 8) could have a greater variance than it would without central bank intervention.

So why do central banks intervene? Surprisingly, many central banks intervene because, they say, exchange markets are too volatile. Hence, they intervene to "smooth out" such volatility. The Bundesbank, for example, has said in the past that it intervened "not only to prevent erratic variations in the rate from day-to-day but also to smooth unduly large fluctuations in the rate of the deutschemark against the dollar over longer periods" (*Annual Report,* 1974). If the domestic currency has depreciated "too much" with respect to a foreign currency, the central bank will buy up domestic currency (using the relevant foreign currency to make the purchase) in order to increase the value of the domestic currency in the FX market by decreasing its supply. If the domestic currency is appreciating too rapidly, the central bank will sell domestic currency (purchasing the relevant foreign currency in the process) in the FX market to depress the value of the domestic currency by increasing its supply.

☐

A more esoteric policy is "sterilized intervention," which involves offsetting transactions in foreign and domestic assets so that the monetary base is left unchanged. For example, a purchase of $1 billion of DM by the Federal Reserve (which would increase the monetary base by $1 billion) would be accompanied by a sale of $1 billion of U.S. government securities (which would decrease the monetary base by $1 billion). Since the monetary base is not altered, any impact of this operation would rely on the fact that dollar bonds in the hands of the public are now larger by $1 billion, while DM assets are fewer by $1 billion. If dollar assets and DM assets are not perfect substitutes, there could be some impact on the exchange rate. Recent Federal Reserve staff studies conclude there is little long-run impact from sterilized intervention (Federal Reserve, 1983).   ∎

Is there a rational argument that would justify such actions to correct "disequilibrium" exchange rates? It is difficult to construct one. Here is what the notion of "overvalued" or "undervalued" market exchange rates implies. First, *it implies that the central bank will realize a profit from foreign exchange intervention* (Friedman, 1953). Because the central bank is selling foreign currency when it is "overvalued" and buying foreign currency when it is "undervalued," the central bank will realize a profit as the exchange rate returns to its "proper" value. The central bank sells at a high price and buys back at a low price. The profit is the difference in the two prices multiplied by the volume of intervention.

But if the central bank can earn a speculative profit this way, why can't private market speculators perform the same role? The argument for central bank intervention needs more than a simple statement that exchange rates are over- or undervalued. For example, here are two alternative additional arguments one could make.

(1) One could argue that there is insufficient private market speculation. As noted in Chapter 7, individual speculators with limited wealth face ultimate ruin unless the odds are very much in their favor. Thus, if there is market failure due to insufficient speculation, the central bank might fill the gap to ensure the optimal degree of speculation. McKinnon (1979) has suggested that private FX speculation may be insufficient. Most central banks are, however, unwilling to argue that there is insufficient speculation in the FX market. They would prefer to believe there is too much.

(2) A different argument for central bank intervention—the one used most frequently—is that the central bank has an informational advantage. The information set of the central bank, the argument goes, is greater than that of other market participants. Thus the central bank is better able to know what the "right" exchange rate ought to be. If $I(CB,t)$ is the central bank's information set, then the forecast error

$$c(t + T) = R(t + T) - E[R(t + T)|I(CB,t)]$$

has smaller variance than the forecast errors of other exchange market participants. In addition, the notion of "over-" or "under-" valuation would seem to imply that the forecasts of other market participants are biased.

The intervention issue, then, hinges on empirical questions. The evidence cited in Chapter 8 that the real exchange rate is a martingale would seem to imply there is no meaningful sense in which free market exchange rates are over- or undervalued. Is this empirical state of affairs a result of past central bank intervention on the basis of superior information? (Have central banks made money?) The evidence suggests otherwise. Not only have central banks not "smoothed out" exchange rate movements, but over the floating rate years of the 1970s they have increased exchange rate volatility by buying foreign exchange when it is already overpriced and selling foreign exchange when it is underpriced. If you buy when the price is too high and sell when the price is too low, you lose money. Table 9.3 indicates the billions of dollars that central banks have lost in the process of central bank intervention. Of the central banks examined by Taylor (1982), only the Bank of France failed to lose money in U.S. dollar terms. (And in DM terms, which Taylor argues is more relevant for the French case, the Bank of France also lost money.) The empirical evidence does not justify the argument that central banks have superior information.

It is doubtful that much has changed since the period investigated by Taylor (although the Bundesbank, for one, undoubtedly made a large profit on its dollar sales in 1980). Since participating banks in the European Monetary System continue to intervene on a daily basis to maintain the parity grid (see Chapter 2), this intervention should prove a source of FX trader profit with respect to European currency cross rates, especially if neither national economic policy nor parity grid par values are altered rapidly whenever the market exchange rate moves close to parity bands. Neumann (1984) notes: "As a

TABLE 9.3
Profits and Losses from Official Intervention in the Foreign Exchange Market

Country	Period beginning	Period ending	Profit or loss (−) ($ millions)
Canada	June 1970	December 1979	−82
France*	April 1973	December 1979	1,035
			(−2,003)
Germany	April 1973	December 1979	−3,423
Italy	March 1973	December 1979	−3,724
Japan	March 1973	December 1979	−331
Spain	February 1974	December 1979	−1,367
Switzerland	February 1973	December 1979	−1,209
United Kingdom	July 1972	December 1979	−2,147
United States	April 1973	January 1980	−2,351

Source: Dean Taylor, "Official Intervention in the Foreign Exchange Market, or, Bet Against the Central Bank," *Journal of Political Economy,* April 1982.

* For France, the profit or loss is calculated assuming intervention is done in dollars and in deutschemarks. A profit is shown for the dollar figure and a dollar equivalent loss is shown in parentheses for the deutschemark figure.

rule realignments in the EMS are delayed. The main reason seems to be that any realignment of the currencies requires first a politically feasible realignment of the subsidization of the agricultural sectors of the European economies." Hence the agricultural subsidy may translate into an FX trader subsidy.

PROBLEMS FOR CHAPTER 9

1. Which of the following items would receive plus signs on the U.S. balance on international transactions, and which would receive minus signs if carried out by a domestic citizen or entity?
   a. Export of 15,000 Bruce Springsteen records.
   b. Payment for consulting services received from a Japanese securities firm in Tokyo.
   c. Receipt of $1,000,000 from relatives in Beirut as recorded under unilateral transfers.
   d. A sale by Exxon of $100,000,000 of eurobonds in London.
   e. A new issue of common stock in the London market.

2. (a) In what way is the current account balance relevant to the repayment of foreign debt?
   (b) If a debtor country has a current account deficit, how is the long-run growth of the country affected by the manner in which the country may choose to reduce that deficit? (Refer to the savings, investment, government-deficit equation.)

3. Country X had a government deficit of $40 billion in 1982. In addition, private investment exceeded private after-tax saving by $10 billion.
   (a) What can you conclude concerning Country X's current account?
   (b) If, relative to GNP, a country has a high proportion of after-tax savings, an average proportion of investment expenditures, and an average government deficit, will the country tend to have current account deficits or surpluses?

4. The following data are for Mexico for the year 1981:

   Government deficit   782.7 billion pesos
   Current account   −108.0 billion pesos

   Using the analysis of the preceding question, explain Mexico's foreign debt problem in terms of consumption and savings.

5. Comment on this statement:

   When demand for money grows faster than the supply of money would have grown due to domestic sources alone, international reserves tend to accumulate and to bring actual growth in the money stock closer to desired growth.

   Under what type of exchange regime would this statement be true?

6. Comment on this statement:

   The attempts of central banks to maintain an exchange rate when there is a change in their equilibrium level explains the consistent losses from foreign exchange intervention. They are able to influence the exchange rate for a period of time. However, market forces eventually force an adjustment and the central bank realizes a loss.

7. Assume the statement in Problem 6 is accurate. Is the following conclusion then justified?

   Counterspeculation by exchange traders dampens the destabilizing effect of central bank intervention. To the extent that speculators bet against central banks, resource misallocation is reduced and central bank losses become a subsidy to foreign exchange traders.

   The following information should be used in answering the questions in Problems 8 and 9.

   Money demand in Erewhon is fixed at 400 billion wawas. The high-powered money base in Erewhon is currently 100 billion wawas and the money multiplier has a constant value of 5. The central bank of Erewhon pegs the value of the wawa to the bancor, which is a foreign currency used throughout the rest of the world. The central bank of Erewhon has two policy instruments: foreign exchange intervention and domestic open-market operations.

8. If the central bank of Erewhon does not engage in any domestic open-market operations, then—in economic equilibrium—it will be forced to intervene in the foreign exchange market and, in the process [choose the correct answer]:
   a. Sell bancors in an amount equal to 20 billion wawas.
   b. Buy bancors in an amount equal to 20 billion wawas.
   c. Sell wawas in an amount equal to 100 billion bancors.
   d. Buy bancors in an amount equal to 100 billion wawas.
   e. Sell bancors in an amount equal to 100 billion wawas.

9. If the central bank of Erewhon wishes to maintain the pegged rate but wants to avoid any loss of foreign exchange reserves, then in economic equilibrium the central bank of Erewhon will engage in the following domestic open-market operation [choose the correct answer]:
   a. Sell government securities in the amount of 20 billion wawas.
   b. Buy governnment securities in the amount of 20 billion wawas.
   c. Sell government securities in the amount of 100 billion wawas.
   d. Buy government securities in the amount of 100 billion wawas.
   e. Sell government securities in the amount of 100 billion bancors.

10. Holding other things constant, all of the following would intend to increase the value of the Japanese yen against the U.S. dollar *except* [choose one]:

a. A tax on foreign-held U.S. dollar assets.

b. An increase in the U.S. GNP real growth rate.

c. An increase in the U.S. money supply growth rate.

d. An income tax reduction in Japan.

e. A reduction in the Japanese money supply growth rate.

FOREIGN EXCHANGE FORECASTING

In previous chapters we have looked at some of the macroeconomic variables that influence and are influenced by the exchange rate. These have included relative prices, consumption and savings, money supply and demand, central bank intervention, and capital flows (which will receive further attention in Chapter 11 in the context of portfolio theory). We can envision a "true" model of the economy that includes all of these variables and more, and that, in the context of economic maximization and random events (such as the weather), generates the time path of foreign nominal and real exchange rates. Chapter 7 indicated that some of the important variables in this model would be people's expectations. The expectations of foreign exchange marketmakers would be a crucial factor influencing the nominal exchange rate, and expectations in general would be an important influence in price determination.

Forecasting can be thought of as the formal process of generating expectations. One's expectations of future economic variables, however derived, are implicit forecasts. Such expectations can be generated in various ways: through casual reading of the newspaper or the book of Revelation, from dreams and visions, or by subscribing to an economic forecasting service. The rational expectations criterion discussed in Chapter 7 says that people form expectations of future values of the exchange rate and other variables in the same fashion that the "true" model of the economy actually generates those variables. It implies that expectations cannot be taken as arbitrary, but rather must—in expectational equilibrium—be formed in such a manner that they are self-fulfilling. One way to picture this process is to conceive of people making a model of the economy. The model will include known and expected values of different variables. To get the required expected values in the model, the model itself will be used as a forecasting device. The forecasted values will then be inserted back into the original model in place of "expected" values. Rational expectations equilibrium occurs if the final model outcome generates values for economic variables, such as the exchange rate, that are on average the same as the expected values (review Chapter 7 for an example). If expectations are self-fulfilling in this way, no one has any incentive for revising expectations or revising the way in which expectations are formed. By contrast, if expectations were *not* self-fulfilling (not rational), they cannot be expected to endure.

As a practical matter, this process seems to be pretty much the way the real world works. While most people do not engage in the formal construction of economic models, they may subscribe to the output of such models or read newspaper reports giving the projections of economic forecasters. People take these forecasts into account when they make economic decisions. These decisions then influence the direction in which the economy actually moves. (Even dreams and visions may be rational if they are a way of accessing the "true" model of the economy.)

One strong qualification is in order, however. People may not really know the "true" model of the economy. As a consequence, they are not quite sure how to react when their expectations are wrong. Suppose the current real exchange rate is $R(t + T)$ and that it is related to the expected real exchange rate by the equation

$$R(t + T) = E[R(t + T)|I(i,t)] + e(t + T).$$

In general, there will be forecasting or expectational errors $e(t + T)$. Errors result even if the "true" model of the economy is known, because actual outcomes will depend on future random events. But if errors occur, they could also be due to the fact that people may not know the true model of the economy. For example, many people did not anticipate the high real U.S. interest rates of the early 1980s. As high real interest rates emerged, economists and others asked themselves: Are these high rates simply the result of unforeseeable events that could not have been incorporated into our previous forecasts? Or were our previous forecasts wrong because our view of how the economy works was wrong? Thus, in the absence of certainty that one knows the "true" model of the economy, rational expectations cannot be expected to prevail while people are in the process of learning. Eventually, however, people can be expected to learn what the true economic model is, assuming it stays fixed. But if the true model is itself undergoing random changes in structure the learning process will be permanent, and thus expectations would never be completely rational.

And, in reality, people are always in a process of revising their perception of how the economy works. For example, the metatheory of rational expectations itself entered the economics profession as one such revision.

APPROACHES TO FX FORECASTING

The idea of forecasting is to construct a methodology that will optimally extract indications of the future FX rate from today's available set of data. No forecasting method works very well, so one should not become terribly arrogant about the "correct" way to do it. However, two main approaches are used.

The fundamental approach attempts to process a wide range of data regarding fundamental economic variables in order to determine the future course of the exchange rate. Included may be such variables as consumption, investment, savings, trade, money supplies, inflation rates, productivity indices, opinion surveys, stock prices, and the like. The methodology used to process the data may be *econometric* (information processing through mathematical equations derived from economic theory, utilizing coefficients that are usually related to historical relationships) or it may be *judgmental* (direct processing through the human biocomputer). In the latter case, a person may be employed to spend the working day looking at economic data and then come to some opinion about what will happen to exchange rates. This procedure frequently seems to work about as well as the more formal econometric methodology, at least for short-run forecasting.

The technical approach focuses on a smaller subset of the available data. For example, a technical model may look only at the past history of several exchange rate series, including both spot and forward exchange rates. This may involve "eyeballing" charts of price series or it may involve statistical procedures. Examples of technical models using statistical methodology are "momentum" models based on the relation of short-run moving averages to long-run moving averages and vector autoregressive models, which involve a simultaneous regression of several exchange rate (and possibly other) variables on a time series of observations of past values of these same variables.

In past years there has been, and perhaps there still is, strong academic bias against the use of technical models. However, the distinction between fundamental and technical analysis is not as great as many people assume. One thing is clear: The use of a smaller information set could never improve forecasting accuracy. Thus one might think that the fundamental approach is a priori the better way to do forecasting. But there are other considerations. The use of greater information implies a greater cost of collecting and processing it, and the benefits must justify this additional cost. In addition, it is not entirely clear that the fundamental approach always uses a greater information set. For example, many fundamental models use GNP data, which is only available with a considerable time lag. By the time the data become available, they may no longer be useful. In addition, such "information" is subject to considerable measurement error. By contrast, the variables generally used in technical models—interest rates, exchange rates, futures prices, and so on—are available with almost no delay and with little measurement error. Finally, it should be noted that major banks, exchange dealers, and forecasters have not only continued to use technical models, but many organizations that previously used fundamental models have also switched to technical models or added the output of a technical model to their forecasting portfolio. Why? If we grant that market participants are rational people who act in their own self-interest, then we should grant that such decisions were made on the basis of a cost-benefit analysis. Many people have come to the conclusion that, for *short-term* forecasting, good technical models outperform good fundamental models.

The Model Theorem for Chapter 7 applies equally to fundamental and technical forecasting models. Models, if they are good, should become bad. They will set in operation the events that will ensure that their use will not generate excess returns.

INFORMATION, EFFICIENCY, AND MODEL EVALUATION

A consistent record of better forecasting requires *superior information*. Superior information implies either knowing greater amounts of data or else having the ability to process data more efficiently. One type of superior information resulting from greater amounts of data would be "insider" information. The employee of a central bank, for example, may have better data concerning projected central bank intervention in the FX market than a private banker would. As an example of superior information from superior processing, consider the case of two individuals reading the *Wall Street Journal*. They have available the same facts, but one might be able to extract more information from those facts. In this case, the superior information would lie within an individual: A person who doesn't know how to read the futures page cannot gain much information from the numbers presented.

Whichever type of superior information one may possess, it will be difficult to maintain this informational superiority and at the same time earn an excess return as a result of that information. If an "insider" engages in market transactions on the basis of superior information, others may be able to deduce what the insider knows by observing his or her market transactions. Thus the "inside" information will become public if it is used. Similarly, if a forecasting firm with superior technological expertise publishes its forecasts, so as to earn a profit from its services, the forecasts can become known to everyone— whether or not they have a good forecasting model.

EVALUATION OF FUNDAMENTAL FORECASTERS

We now turn to some of the evidence on the expertise of fundamental forecasters. The results come from Richard Levich of New York University, who has made comparisons of forecasting performance for the magazine *Euromoney*.

One test Levich does is to compare the forecasting performance of various services to the forward rate. This measure of performance is in terms of *mean absolute error*. The mean absolute error is the average absolute deviation of a series of forecasts from a series of actual outcomes. Let $p(i)$ denote a forecasting service's prediction for a particular exchange rate at a particular time and let $a(i)$ be the actual value for the spot exchange rate at that time. Let $f(i)$ denote the forward rate for the same time period. Then, to calculate the mean absolute percentage error for the service as well as the forward rate over n observations we need to compute two totals:

Forecasting service	*Forward rate*
$\lvert p(1) - a(1) \rvert / a(1)$	$\lvert f(1) - a(1) \rvert / a(1)$
$\lvert p(2) - a(2) \rvert / a(2)$	$\lvert f(2) - a(2) \rvert / a(2)$
$\cdots$	$\cdots$
$\lvert p(n) - a(n) \rvert / a(n)$	$\lvert f(n) - a(n) \rvert / a(n)$
Service total	Forward total

Then the mean absolute error MA in each case is calculated as

$$MA(s) = \frac{\text{Service total}}{n}, \quad MA(f) = \frac{\text{Forward total}}{n}.$$

Finally, if the forecasting service shows a better record than the forward rate for the sample considered, then $MA(s) < MA(f)$.

For the sample period 1977–1980 and for twelve major forecasting services, Levich compared the percentage of times the services did better than the forward rate, based on the mean absolute error criterion. He looked at performance over time horizons of one month, three months, six months, and a year. The results were:

Time Horizon	Percentage of Observations with $MA(s) < MA(f)$
1 month	28.8%
3 months	24.0%
6 months	28.8%
12 months	32.7%

In terms of mean absolute error, on average the forecasting services performed worse than the forward rate more than two-thirds of the time. Since observation of the forward rate is virtually costless, and since—as noted in Chapter 7—the forward rate is not necessarily even an unbiased forecast of the future spot rate, these results suggest that paying large amounts of money to a forecasting service may be an unjustifiable expense. Forecasting services also provide other types of sage advice and commentary, however. One cannot get that from the forward rate. The forward rate just speaks for itself.

A different method of computing forecasting expertise used by Levich is in terms of the percentage of times a forecast is on the "correct side" of the forward rate. A forecast is on the correct side if the forecast diverges from the forward rate in the same direction as does the actual realized spot rate. For example, suppose the three-month forward rate is $.4205/DM and the forecast is $.4275/DM. If the actual spot rate turns out to be $.4225/DM, the forecast was "correct" in diverging from the forward rate in the same direction as the actual spot rate. On the other hand, if the forecast had been $.4200/DM, the forecast was "incorrect" because it diverged from the forward rate in the opposite direction from the actual realized spot rate.

A possible justification for this way of judging "correct" and "incorrect" forecasts has to do with the rewards from hedging or speculation. Suppose you bought foreign exchange forward because your forecast told you that the forward price was less than what the actual spot price would turn out to be. Then, as long as the spot rate turned out to be higher than the forward rate, you would have made the correct decision—regardless of how much higher the actual spot rate was. You may not have made (or saved) the exact amount indicated by your forecast, but you will not have lost money either.

EXAMPLE 10.1

Suppose the current three-month forward rate is $.4205/DM, while the forecast is $.4275/DM. A speculator who made decisions on the basis of the forecast would buy forward DM, with the intention of making a speculative profit by selling the DM received on the forward contract at the higher spot price he expects to prevail when the contract matures. If the spot rate in three months turned out to be $.4225/DM, the speculator will have made

$.4225/DM − $.4205/DM = $.0020/DM.

To be sure, this will be smaller than the amount the speculator expected to receive. His forecast indicated an earning of

$.4275/DM − $.4205/DM = $.0070/DM.

However, he will not have lost money on the transaction. Similarly, a hedger who made decisions on the basis of the forecast will have purchased DM at the forward rate of $.4205/DM and will have avoided the higher cost of $.4225/DM he would have had to pay if he had waited and purchased at the spot rate.

According to the "correct" or "incorrect" criterion, if a forecaster had *no* expertise, he should be right about half the time. Anyone could flip a coin to determine whether to make a forecast above the forward rate or below, and then choose an arbitrary number in the right direction. Or different levels of the forward rate could be painted on the wall and a monkey could throw darts. So, at the extreme case of no expertise, we can assume that the probability of a right forecast is $p = .5$. Let r be the number of right forecasts and n the total number of forecasts. Then, for a sufficiently large n, the variable

$$z = (r/n - .5)(\sqrt{n}/.5) \qquad (10.1)$$

has approximately a normal distribution. Let $N(z)$ be the cumulative normal distribution evaluated at z. Then $1 - N(z)$ gives the probability that the proportion of "correct" forecasts r/n occurred purely by chance. Only if this probability is small can we be reasonably certain that we are true witnesses to forecasting expertise.

EXAMPLE 10.2

Suppose that out of 100 total forecasts, 65 are "correct." Then

$$z = (65/100 - .5)(\sqrt{100}/.5) = 3.0.$$

Looking up z in a table of the standard normal probability distribution, we see that for

$z = 3.0$, $N(z) = .9987$.

Hence the probability of a purely random occurrence of this value for z is

$1 - N(z) = 1 - .9987 = .0013$,

or .13%. That is, if we assume that $p = .5$ (which implies no forecasting expertise), we can still expect to see 65 correct guesses out of 100 about .13 percent of the time. Since this probability is very small, we can say that the probability the forecasters record occurred purely by chance is small. We may then choose to believe the forecaster has demonstrated expertise in forecasting.

In terms of the percentage of times on the correct side of the forward rate, Levich concluded that over the period 1977–1980 the forecasters he studied showed expertise. For some currencies, the better forecasters got the "correct" side of the forward rate between 60 and 70 percent of the time. However, when he updated his data to include the years 1981 and 1982, he concluded that there is no statistically significant record of forecasting expertise for the dozen major services he investigated. This "Case of the Disappearing Expertise" is pretty much what one would expect on the basis of the Model Theorem.

EVALUATION OF TECHNICAL FORECASTERS

An evaluation of technical forecasting services has been made by Stephen Goodman of the Singer Company. Technical models give very short-term forecasts, and Goodman has claimed that over short-term time horizons all of the major technical forecasting services have a better forecasting record than any econometric service. Unfortunately, it is difficult to compare Goodman's results with Levich's, since Goodman uses a different evaluation procedure. Goodman uses two different criteria for evaluating forecasts: *return on capital at risk* and *return on selective hedging*.

Goodman claims that "return on capital at risk is the most relevant performance measure for a speculator, portfolio investor, or a multicurrency borrower, and it is the best single measure of overall forecasting performance." Technical services generate "signals" that tell the user when to buy a currency and when to sell the currency. Return on capital at risk is calculated by assuming that the user of the service buys a currency three months forward (and closes any outstanding forward contract to sell the currency) whenever the service gives a buy signal. The user sells a currency three months forward whenever the service gives a sell signal. If there is no change in the signal during the three-month life of the contract, the contract is rolled over at maturity. The "capital at risk" is considered to be the initial dollar value of the amount of currency bought or sold forward. The "return on capital at risk" is the capital gain or loss on the foreign currency position minus the U.S. dollar interest rate. The dollar interest rate is subtracted to give the return over and above what could be earned without taking risk. The *total return* on the portfolio is then equal to the sum of the return on capital at risk and the dollar interest rate.

Notice that "capital at risk" defined this way is not the same as the amount of money invested in the foreign currency portfolio. There may be no money actually invested in a forward contract. A sufficiently large bank or company may have no forward contract margin requirement. Others may have a 5 percent margin requirement. If there is, the return to the actual amount of money invested in the foreign currency would be twenty times the total return.

Below are Goodman's results comparing the average return on capital at risk for three major technical services over the period January 1977 to December 1980 for six major currencies. The average return from using the technical services is compared to the average return over the same time period and for the same currencies that would have resulted from a simple buy-and-hold strategy. Finally, both results are compared with those that would have resulted from using one of the fundamental econometric services that had one of the best forecasting records.

	Technical Services	Buy-and-Hold Strategy	Econometric Service
Average return on capital at risk	12.1%	3.4%	2.1%
Eurodollar interest rate	8.5%	8.5%	8.5%
Total return	20.6%	11.9%	10.6%

The second form of evaluation is the return on selective hedging. The return on selective hedging, according to Goodman, "is probably the most relevant performance measure for a corporate treasurer who has some flexibility in managing his company's foreign currency exposure." In order to calculate this return, two cases are distinguished. It is assumed that a company may have a "natural short" or a "natural long" position. A natural short position would arise if the ordinary business operations of the company generated foreign currency payables or debt. A natural long position would arise if ordinary business operations generated foreign currency receipts or assets. A company that is hedging will only use the service as a guide whether to cover (decrease) its foreign currency exposure, but will not take action to increase its natural exposure as a result of the service's forecasts.

Below are the average returns on selective hedging that would have resulted from using the three technical services. Results are given for both naturally long and naturally short positions. The time period and currencies involved are the same as those mentioned previously. The results are also compared to the return on selective hedging that would have resulted from using the econometric service, as well as to a hedging policy of always covering foreign currency exposures in the forward market.

	Technical Services	Econometric Service	Always Cover Forward
Natural short position	2.5%	−1.7%	−1.7%
Natural long position	9.7%	3.8%	1.7%

At face value these results are impressive. There may, however, be considerable sample selection bias in that the results for technical services as a whole were not given. The average performance for all services could be less impressive than for the three presented. If we assume that sample selection bias was not the reason for the results, then it would be of further interest to see if the *same* forecasting services can maintain the same performance record over a period of years. The Model Theorem suggests that this would not happen. This year's good performers should, if a lot of people are attracted to the service, become bad performers.

PROBLEMS FOR CHAPTER 10

1. Suppose that out of 100 forecasts I got 55 "correct" in the sense that my predictions were on the same side of the forward rate as the realized spot rate. If we agree that I would guess right half the time if I had no forecasting skill at all, then what is the

probability that my track record of 55 "correct" forecasts was purely due to chance?

2. The central bank of Surlandia pegs its currency at an exchange rate of 125 pesos/dollar. In addition, it has a scheduled weekly devaluation of the peso in the amount of 1 peso/dollar. A currency prognosticator is forecasting the Surlandian peso/dollar rate for one year ahead. He estimates that there is a probability of .7 that the schedule of devaluations will be adhered to exactly, and a probability of .3 that there will be an additional maxidevaluation in the amount of 10 percent of the exchange rate six months from now. In the event of a maxidevaluation, he assumes that the weekly devaluation schedule of 1 peso/dollar will be resumed after the maxi.

   (a) What is his point forecast for the exchange rate?
   (b) What is the standard deviation of this forecast, given the forecaster's assumptions?

3. Using daily data for the past one year, a researcher calculates values for s and f, where

   $$s = [S(t) - S(t - 1)]/S(t - 1)$$

   and

   $$f = [F(t) - F(t - 1)]/F(t - 1).$$

   Here S is the spot dollar price of DM, F is the thirty-day forward price of DM, and t corresponds to a time period of one day. The researcher assumes that s and f are drawings from a normal distribution, and finds that in the sample s and f each have a mean $m = 0$, and each have a daily standard deviation $v = .003$. The correlation coefficient between s and f is .8. Finally, the two most recent values (not in the researcher's sample) for $S(t)$ and $F(t)$ are $S(t) = \$.3950/DM$ and $F(t) = \$.4030/DM$.

   (a) Given this information, and assuming that future values of s and f will be drawings from the same probability distribution as in the sample, calculate a 68 percent probability interval for $S(t + 1)$, the next day's value of S.
   (b) What, according to the speculative efficiency hypothesis, is the best forecast for the spot rate in thirty days, $S(t + 30)$?
   (c) Suppose that, between day 1 and day 2, the spot rate S increased by 3.2 percent. On day 1, a speculator sold DM forward (the speculator sold a thirty-day forward contract) in an amount with an initial value of $1,000,000. Then, given the researcher's sample information and assumptions, what is the researcher's best guess about the change in the value of the speculator's forward contract between day 1 and day 2?

4. According to the Model Theorem [choose one of the following]:
   a. Technical models should perform better than fundamental models.
   b. Fundamental models should perform better than technical models.
   c. No fundamental or technical model should be able to maintain a good forecasting record long-term.
   d. The proof of the pudding is in the eating.
   e. The best forecast of next year's cheap vacation is this year's cheap vacation.

PORTFOLIO CHOICE AND FOREIGN EXCHANGE

FORECASTING ERRORS AND RISK

Expectations are not always borne out. In September 1983, a number of leading forecasters made exchange rate predictions for July 31, 1984, for the magazine *Euromoney* ("Why the Dollar Will Fall," October 1983). These bank economists and corporate treasurers had widely different views of what would happen to the spot exchange rate. Despite that fact, they all managed to be badly mistaken on the actual course of events. The range of their forecasts compared with realized spot rates are given in the table on the next page.

In previous chapters we have considered some of the macroeconomic influences on exchange rates, and in Chapter 10 forecasting was presented in this regard as the process of generating expectations, given available information. For many people, the future level of the real exchange rate will be of interest. For an individual with the information set $I(i,t)$, there is uncertainty associated with the magnitude of his or her forecast error

$$e(t + T) = R(t + T) - E[R(t + T)|I(i,t)].$$

But even though future real exchange rates are uncertain, financial decisions have to be made today. The outcome of these decisions will depend on the forecasting or expectational mistakes $e(t + 1)$, $e(t + 2)$, $e(t + 3)$, . . . , $e(t + T)$. There may be unexpected gains or losses from borrowing and lending in foreign currencies, purchasing or selling foreign-currency-denominated assets, or investing in projects that generate foreign currency cash flows. Few people would be willing to make a decision without allowing for the possibility of being wrong. The uncertainty inherent in one's expectation or forecast thus implies risk. And the risk of making what may turn out to be an undesirable FX decision is related to the size of the expectational mistake $e(t + T)$.

The foregoing argument implies that financial decision making involves at least a two-dimensional variable. One may have in mind an expected value—or forecast—of the exchange rate, but allowance will be made for the uncer-

	Spot rate on September 1, 1983	Range of forecasts for July 31, 1984	Actual spot rate on July 31, 1984
Pound	$1.50/£	$1.50/£–$1.89/£	$1.31/£
Deutschemark	DM2.69/$	DM2.57/$–DM2.10/$	DM2.91/$
Swiss franc	SF2.18/$	SF2.05/$–SF1.70/$	SF2.47/$
Yen	¥245/$	¥240/$–¥205/$	¥245/$

tainty inherent in the forecast. For example, one may believe that the exchange rate in six months will be ¥205/$, as a point forecast, but this number is so uncertain that one may at the same time believe that there is only a 50 percent probability that the exchange rate will lie between ¥200/$ and ¥210/$. If one is borrowing in terms of yen and calculating profits in terms of dollars, a rate of ¥200/$ will result in a dollar loss relative to the point forecast of ¥205/$. Thus it is common in financial decision making to measure risk in terms of probability. We may view future, as-yet-unknown exchange rates as drawings from a probability distribution and may measure uncertainty or risk by the dispersion of probability around a central (expected) value.

EXAMPLE 11.1

A decision maker views the logarithm of the spot exchange rate that will occur in six months as a random drawing from a normal probability distribution. In particular, it is assumed that the mean and standard deviation are:

Mean = log(¥205/$)
S.D. = .0145

Since

log(205) = 5.323

there is a probability of 68 percent that the logarithm of the exchange rate in six months will lie between

5.323 − .0145 = 5.3085 and 5.323 + .0145 = 5.3375.

This means there is a probability of 68 percent that the actual level of the exchange rate will lie between

¥202.05/$ and ¥207.99/$.

Where do people get their subjective probabilities concerning the distribution of variables like the exchange rate? If expectations are rational, then the amount of uncertainty that people will assume to be present when they make decisions will correspond to the actual uncertainty inherent in the "true" model by which the economy functions. If expectations are rational, then the amount of error or uncertainty as reflected in $var(e(t + T))$ will be on average the amount that was expected given available information:

$$var(e(t + T)) = E[var(e(t + T))|I(i,t)] + m(t + T),$$

where $E[m(t + T)|I(i,t)] = 0$. Expectations regarding risk will be self-fulfilling. In the long run, people will not act as though there is either more risk or less risk than actually exists in the economy. Their subjective probabilities will correspond to objective probabilities. We may formulate this as the *Poker Player's Theorem:* The poker player takes, as his subjective probability that another player has drawn a particular set of cards, the objective mathematical probability that that set of cards occurred. If the probabilities do not jibe in repeated play, he knows that the deck is stacked and revises his probabilities and decisions accordingly.

PORTFOLIO CHOICE IN AN INTERNATIONAL CONTEXT

How one chooses to deal with uncertainty, and hence risk, may vary according to the context. But there are many circumstances in which it would seem reasonable to assume *risk-averse behavior,* which can be defined as willingness to make a trade-off between expected return and risk (uncertainty). Three situations can be distinguished.

1. Given a choice of two different investment opportunities that yield the same expected return, but with different levels of associated risk, a risk-averter would prefer the one with smaller risk.
2. Given a choice of two different investment opportunities that have equivalent levels of associated risk, but different levels of expected return, a risk-averter would prefer the one with higher expected return.
3. A risk-averter will trade off risk with expected return in the sense that if there were only two investment assets, one with both a higher expected return and a higher risk than the other, he or she would end up placing some portion of wealth in both assets. That is, an investor could conceivably choose as a total portfolio only the low expected return, low-risk asset. The purchase of some portion of the high expected return, high-risk asset increases both the expected return and the risk of the total portfolio. Thus the willingness to buy some of the high expected return, high-risk asset would indicate a willingness to trade off risk with expected return.

Portfolio choice arises in international financial decision making in a number of contexts. Here are some examples.

1. Trust funds managed by commercial and investment banks involve international assets whose value is measured in hundreds of billions of dollars. These assets are spread around the world, and shifts in the location and type of assets are made according to changing perceptions in terms of risk and expected return. If the value of the U.S. dollar is expected to fall relative to the value of the DM, wealth may be shifted from dollar-denominated bank accounts, Treasury bills, and shares of common stock in U.S. companies to DM-denominated bank accounts, eurobonds, and shares of common stock in German companies. Similar shifts may occur as results of a change in economic risk (such as increased variability in the inflation rate) or a change in political risk (such as the impending Chinese takeover of Hong Kong, a war in the Persian Gulf, or the threat of capital controls in the United Kingdom).

2. So-called "cocktail currencies" like the ECU and the SDR, are themselves portfolios of currencies. Depending on the expected return and risk associated with each of the component currencies in the portfolio, an expected return and risk are associated with the total portfolio. The final portfolio—the ECU or the SDR—may give a better risk-return trade-off than does any individual component currency. On the other hand, the ECU or the SDR could be an inefficient portfolio: The dollar or the French franc component may be too large or the yen component too small.

3. A corporation that does not have cash inflows or outflows matched 100 percent in foreign currency terms is subject to foreign exchange risk in terms of the domestic currency. The corporation may set up a foreign finance subsidiary whose job it is to keep track of these foreign currency cash flows for the company as a whole and to make hedging decisions based on forecasted exchange rates as well as on some measure of the risk of unexpected currency valuation changes.

PORTFOLIO CHOICE AND THE BALANCE OF PAYMENTS

International portfolio choice implies acquiring or selling foreign assets or debt. In Chapter 9 we saw that such activities were recorded in the balance on international transactions (balance of payments) accounting record either as pure capital flows (switching between domestic and foreign assets) or as capital flows associated with a current account surplus or deficit.

If portfolio decisions lead to switching between domestic and foreign financial or other assets, only capital account transactions are involved. These transactions can have a strong impact on the exchange rate. For example, if DM-denominated eurobonds are sold in order to purchase dollar-denominated U.S. Treasury bonds, the ensuing sales of DM for dollars may drive down the dollar price of DM. This purely capital account transaction may also have an indirect impact on the current account. This indirect impact would occur if there were changes in the real exchange rate brought about in the process of switching between DM assets and $ assets.

A current account deficit or surplus is also related to the desired portfolio composition. As noted in Chapter 9, the current account balance is identical to the net change in foreign assets, $CA = \Delta FA$. Whether this accumulation of assets is desired or not depends on the expected return and risk associated with holding those assets, as compared to the expected return and risk associated with holding alternative assets.

Suppose that newly acquired information leads portfolio managers to make a general shift out of DM assets and into dollar assets. This shift will drive down the value of the DM relative to the dollar, until at the margin the *risk-adjusted* real return on DM and dollar assets is equalized. That is, the real return on DM and dollar assets need not be the same in equilibrium. For example, the real return on dollar assets may be higher. But, if so, the risk (which can in some cases be measured by forecasting uncertainty) of holding dollar assets must be correspondingly larger, so that at the margin portfolio managers are indifferent between holding DM assets and holding dollar assets.

In addition, in portfolio equilibrium, the rate of accumulation (or loss) of foreign assets through the current account balance must be such that it maintains the desired share of foreign assets in the total asset portfolio, given comparative real returns and risks. If a country such as Japan desires as a whole to accumulate foreign assets through a yearly flow, there will be a current account surplus. If portfolio equilibrium requires a flow reduction in foreign assets (or a flow increase in foreign borrowing) by the country as a whole, there will be a current account deficit.

For example, during the year 1984, foreigners were accumulating U.S. dollar assets at the rate of $100 billion a year, corresponding to the U.S. current account deficit. As long as this rate of addition of dollar assets to foreign portfolios was desired, there would be little pressure for any adjustment in the current account. On the other hand, if the dollar accumulation was not desired, portfolio managers would sell off their dollar assets. This would drive down the nominal and real exchange rate, which would in turn make U.S. exports more competitive and imports more expensive. A reduction in the current account deficit would in turn diminish the dollar flow into foreign portfolios.

This discussion distinguishes between *stocks of assets* (the total outstanding amounts) and *flows of assets* (the changes in those stocks over a period of time). Asset market equilibrium based on expected real return and risk says that shifts between the stocks of assets will be made up to the point risk-adjusted real rates of return are equalized between the assets denominated in different currencies. Even in stock equilibrium, however, flows will continue to take place, since total financial wealth will in general be changing. In equilibrium, the asset flow associated with the current account balance should be at a level such that the flow leaves the desired proportion of foreign assets in the total asset portfolio unchanged. [A survey of portfolio approaches to the exchange rate in macroeconomics may be found in Dornbush (1980:I).]

CALCULATING RETURNS WITH A FOREIGN
EXCHANGE COMPONENT

The return on an asset held in a foreign currency contains an exchange rate component. Consider three general types of assets: money market assets (or bonds held to maturity); bonds (not held to maturity); and equity.

The *nominal* return on foreign money market assets will be the nominal interest rate plus the gain or loss from any change in exchange rates. Suppose a foreign currency pure discount bond is purchased at a domestic currency price of $S(t)B(t,T)$ and matures at time $t + T$, when the spot exchange rate is $S(t + T)$. At that time $B(t + T, 0) = 1$, so the total return on the bond is

$$\frac{S(t + T)B(t + T, 0)}{S(t)B(t,T)} = \frac{S(t + T)}{S(t)B(t,T)}. \tag{11.1}$$

If the exchange rate remains unchanged, the nominal return on this discount bond (or money market asset) is just one plus the interest rate. The real return is the nominal return adjusted for changes in purchasing power.

For discount bonds not held to maturity, the nominal return may contain a capital gain or loss component, since the terminal value of the bond is uncertain. If the bond is sold at time $t + x$, with a remaining time to maturity of $T - x$, the nominal return on the bond may be written as

$$\frac{S(t + x)B(t + x, T - x)}{S(t)B(t,T)}. \tag{11.2}$$

For bonds that pay periodic coupons, such as a payment of C units of currency at intervals of y units of time, (11.2) must be adjusted to include the coupon yield. Assuming that the bond is bought at the beginning of a coupon period and sold at the end of a coupon period, at time $t + y$, the return to the bond would be

$$\frac{S(t + y) [B(t + y, T - y) + C(t + y)]}{S(t)B(t,T)}. \tag{11.3}$$

Again, the real return to the bond would be the nominal return adjusted for inflation.

Finally, the nominal return to equity would take the form of (11.2) if there were no dividend payments, or (11.3) if there were dividends. Just substitute the stock price in place of the bond price and the amount of the dividend in place of the coupon amount.

EXAMPLE 11.2

A DM bond with a face value of DM5000 and a 7 percent annual coupon is bought at a price of DM4960 when the spot exchange rate is \$.36/DM and sold a year later at a price of DM5010, when the spot exchange rate is \$.34/DM. What is the nominal return on the bond, assuming that the year holding period corresponds to the coupon period?

The annual coupon payment on the bond is (.07)(DM5000) = DM350. From equation (11.3), the return is

$$\frac{(\$.34/DM) [DM5010 + DM350]}{(\$.36/DM)(DM4960)} = 1.02.$$

The total nominal return on \$1 is \$1.02, corresponding to a nominal interest rate of 2 percent. Notice that three components went into this nominal return: a coupon payment, a capital gain on the price of the bond, and an exchange rate loss.

To adjust nominal returns to real returns, the change in the price level must be taken into account. If the beginning domestic price level is $P(t)$ and the ending price level is $P(t + y)$, then (11.3) becomes, for the real return to bond holdings sold at time $t + y$,

$$\frac{P(t)S(t + y) [B(t + y, T - y) + C(t + y)]}{P(t + y)S(t)B(t,T)}. \tag{11.4}$$

This represents the return measured in terms of purchasing power in the domestic country. Portfolio decisions depend on the expected value of this real return as well as the dispersion of the real return around its expected value.

EXPECTED REAL RETURNS AND THE RISE OF THE U.S. DOLLAR

The increase in the value of the U.S. dollar from 1980 to February 1985 "rivals the oil shocks of the 1970s as the most dramatic relative price change in the post–World War II world economy" (Frankel, 1985). Most of this increased value can probably be attributed to portfolio shifts in U.S. dollar assets as a result of increased expected real returns relative to assets denominated in other currencies. Table 11.1 shows that in 1980 real interest rates paid on long-term U.S. government bonds were about two percentage points *below* those paid on a weighted average of similar securities among U.S. trading partners. (The measure of "real" interest rates depends on the method used to calculate expected inflation. Three different methods used here include taking as expected inflation either one-year lagged inflation, three-year distributed lagged inflation, or the three-year inflation forecast of a private forecasting firm (DRI)). By February 1985, the real interest rate on U.S. bonds was about three percentage points *above* that on bonds of U.S. trading partners. This ongoing shift of five percentage points in favor of dollar securities led investors to switch into dollar-denominated assets until such time as *expected* risk-adjusted real returns were equal.

□

The more problematical macroeconomic question of why U.S. real interest rates rose so dramatically over this period is outside the scope of this book. The 1985 *Economic Report of the President* cites two reasons:

1. "The 1979 change to a tighter U.S. monetary stance" led to a drop in actual and expected inflation, and
2. "The Economic Recovery and Tax Act of 1981, together with reduced inflation, significantly raised the after-tax rate of return on new business investment."

Additional factors that have been cited include the large U.S. government deficit, which reduced the supply of savings relative to the demand for investment. The policy mix of easy "fiscal policy" and restrictive monetary policy is discussed in Sachs (1985).   ▪

TABLE 11.1
Real Interest Rate Differential Between Long-Term Government Bonds in the United States and a Weighted Average of U.S. Trading Partners

Item	United States	U.S. Trade Partners	Differential
Long-term government bond rate			
1980	11.39	11.34	.05
1985 (February)	11.70	9.33	2.37
Real interest rate I[a]			
1980	−2.16	−0.05	−2.11
1985 (February)	8.16	5.25	2.90
Real interest rate II[b]			
1980	−0.28	1.99	−2.27
1985 (February)	7.87	4.41	3.46
Real interest rate III[c]			
1980	1.55	2.71	−1.16
1985 (February)	7.54	4.84	2.70

Source: Jeffrey A. Frankel, "The Dazzling Dollar," *Brookings Papers on Economic Activity* I (1985).
[a] Measured as difference between the government bond rate and one-year lagged inflation.
[b] Same with three-year distributed lagged inflation.
[c] Same with DRI forecasted inflation.

BENEFITS OF FOREIGN CURRENCY DIVERSIFICATION

For simplicity, let us consider nominal returns. (Assume that governments of the world have not discovered the miracle of inflation.) Suppose a bank, a company, or an individual will have the following pattern of monthly cash flows over the immediate future

U.S. dollar	Swiss franc	DM
1,000,000	−600,000	800,000

where the current exchange rates are $.42/DM and $.50/SF. What is the magnitude of the exchange risk in nominal dollar terms? Converting the above amounts to dollars, we have

Unexposed	Exposed in SF	Exposed in DM
$1,000,000	−$300,000	$336,000

The next exposure, in nominal dollar terms, depends on how the dollar price of SF moves compared to the dollar price of the DM. For example, suppose that percentage changes in the dollar prices of SF and DM were always equal. Then long and short positions would automatically offset each other, so the net dollar exposure would be

$$-\$300,000 + \$336,000 = \$36,000,$$

a small net exposure. But suppose, at the other extreme, percentage changes in the dollar prices of SF and DM always had the opposite sign but were equal in magnitude. Then the next FX exposure would be

$$\$300,000 + \$336,000 = \$636,000$$

in nominal dollar terms. We can see that the magnitude of exchange risk depends on how currencies fluctuate with respect to each other. Thus portfolio risk depends on the *covariance* of exchange returns. If we only had one foreign asset, we might need only consider the variance of the dollar return on one foreign currency. But with several foreign assets, covariances are important in addition to variances.

CALCULATION OF PORTFOLIO EXPECTED RETURN AND VARIANCE

Consider the three foreign assets listed below.

	Expected Monthly Dollar Return
DM asset	− .500%(= − .00500)
Yen asset	.670%(= .00670)
£ asset	.872%(= .00872)

A portfolio is, by definition, an allocation of weights to each of these assets. The weights $w(i)$ are the fractions of each unit of wealth (here, each U.S. dollar) to be invested in each asset. For example, if $10 million is allocated as $5 million in DM, $3 million in yen, and $2 million in pounds sterling, the respective weights are

$w(1) = \frac{5}{10} = .5$ in DM,
$w(2) = \frac{3}{10} = .3$ in yen, and
$w(3) = \frac{2}{10} = .2$ in the £.

Three possible portfolios are:

	$w(1)$	$w(2)$	$w(3)$	Sum of Weights
Portfolio A	$\frac{1}{3}$	$\frac{1}{3}$	$\frac{1}{3}$	1
Portfolio B	$\frac{1}{4}$	$\frac{1}{4}$	$\frac{1}{2}$	1
Portfolio C	$-\frac{1}{3}$	$\frac{2}{3}$	$\frac{2}{3}$	1

The expected return on each of these portfolios is

$E(R) - A = \quad (\frac{1}{3})(-.500) + (\frac{1}{3})(.670) + (\frac{1}{3})(.872) = \quad .347\%$
$E(R) - B = \quad (\frac{1}{4})(-.500) + (\frac{1}{4})(.670) + (\frac{1}{2})(.872) = \quad .480\%$
$E(R) - C = -(\frac{1}{3})(-.500) + (\frac{2}{3})(.670) + (\frac{2}{3})(.872) = 1.195\%$

Portfolio C has the highest return, but we do not know whether to prefer it over either A or B until we have taken the relative risks of each portfolio into account. Notice that a negative weight, such as $w(1) = -\frac{1}{3}$, implies borrowing in, having an account payable in, or otherwise being short, a foreign currency.

Suppose the expected returns among the three assets have the following covariance matrix:

$$\begin{array}{c} \\ \text{DM} \\ \text{Yen} \\ \text{£} \end{array} \begin{array}{ccc} \text{DM} & \text{Yen} & \text{£} \\ \left[\begin{array}{ccc} 7.70 & 5.75 & 4.82 \\ 5.75 & 15.82 & 5.03 \\ 4.82 & 5.03 & 4.01 \end{array} \right. \end{array} \left] \times \frac{1}{10,000} \right.$$

The variance of the monthly expected return on the DM is .00077. The covariance of the expected return on the DM with the expected return on the yen is .000575. And so on.

In order to calculate the variance of a portfolio, using the covariance matrix, write the weights of the portfolio across the top and down the side of the covariance matrix:

$$\begin{array}{c} \\ w(1) \\ w(2) \\ w(3) \end{array} \begin{array}{ccc} w(1) & w(2) & w(3) \\ \left[\begin{array}{ccc} 7.70 & 5.75 & 4.82 \\ 5.75 & 15.82 & 5.03 \\ 4.82 & 5.03 & 4.01 \end{array} \right. \end{array} \left] \times \frac{1}{10,000} \right.$$

Then add together every number of the matrix multiplied by the weights in the corresponding row and column:

$$7.70 \; w(1) \; w(1) + \; 5.75 \; w(1) \; w(2) + 4.82 \; w(1) \; w(3)$$
$$+5.75 \; w(2) \; w(1) + 15.82 \; w(2) \; w(2) + 5.03 \; w(2) \; w(3)$$
$$+4.82 \; w(3) \; w(1) + \; 5.03 \; w(3) \; w(2) + 4.01 \; w(3) \; w(3)$$

Substituting the values for $w(1)$, $w(2)$, and $w(3)$, for each of portfolios A, B, and C, we obtain the portfolio variances:

Variance of return on portfolio A ($\times$ 10,000) = 6.53.
Variance of return on portfolio B ($\times$ 10,000) = 5.65.
Variance of return on portfolio C ($\times$ 10,000) = 9.44.

Thus we discover that portfolio B dominates (is preferred to) portfolio A, since B has both a higher expected return and a lower risk as measured by the variance. On the other hand, portfolio C has a higher expected return than B, but it also has a higher variance.

Note the probability interpretation of portfolio C, assuming that returns have a normal distribution. The expected return, $E(R) - C = .01195$, while the standard deviation is

$$\sqrt{(9.44)/(10,000)} = .03072.$$

This means that there is a 68 percent probability that R will lie between

.01195 + .03072 and .01195 − .03072,

a 95 percent probability that R will lie between

.01195 + 2 (.03072) and .01195 − 2 (.03072),

and a 99 pecent probability that R will lie between

.01195 + 3 (.03072) and .01195 − 3 (.03072):

Range for R	Probability
(.04267, − .01877)	.68
(.07339, − .04949)	.95
(.10411, − .08021)	.99

If we let R be the incremental return to $1,000,000 invested in portfolio C, the expected value of the investment at the end of one month is $1,011,950. The corresponding intervals and their probabilities are:

Range of Value	Probability
($1,042,760, $981,230)	.68
($1,073,390, $950,510)	.95
($1,104,110, $919,790)	.99

Even though the expected value is $1,011,950, there is only a 68 percent probability that the actual value will lie somewhere between $1,042,760 and $981,230.

OPTIMAL ALLOCATION OF PORTFOLIO SHARES

The example in the previous section shows that different choices of portfolio weights give differing amounts of expected return and variance. The basic idea of portfolio theory is to choose weights so that you get an optimal tradeoff. How do you do this? First, determine your attitude toward risk. At what rate are you willing to trade off expected return for variance? Second, gather together your forecast returns for the available assets, along with expected variances and covariances. Finally, using as inputs your risk attitude and the expected variances and covariances, calculate weights that will give an optimal trade-off. This optimal trade-off is a function of your attitude toward risk, and is also a function of your information.

In order to do these calculations, a number of additional assumptions, such as one concerning the probability distribution of returns, will need to be employed. Given standard assumptions, however, a variety of computer programs that will calculate portfolio weights are available.

☐

A number of studies have indicated that international portfolio diversification is one of the most effective avenues for risk reduction. See for example, Solnik (1974) and Lessard (1983). The amount of risk reduction available by diversifying internationally rather than restricting oneself to domestic assets is, however, difficult to measure. As noted by Adler and Dumas (1983), "The availability of risk reduction will depend upon which one [model of portfolio selection] is true. This point should put an end to all further attempts to base measures of such quantities as 'risk reduction' or 'diversifiable risk' on sample estimates of the means and variances of and correlations among market or industry indices."

Models of international portfolio selection can be found in Solnik (1973) and Sercu (1980). Adler and Dumas (1983) give a comprehensive survey of these and other models.   ■

PORTFOLIO SHARES OF OFFICIAL RESERVE ASSETS

Little useful empirical work exists testing whether capital movements in fact correspond to the implications of portfolio theory. The main problem is that data on currencies in private holdings of foreign assets are not generally available. However, it is clear that asset managers employed by investment banks, commercial banks, insurance companies, and pension and trust funds do regularly use portfolio theory in deciding where and how to invest their funds. Therefore a good guess is that actual capital movements between the major currencies are similar to the implications of the theory.

Good data exist on the currency composition of official reserve assets. The amount of these assets is small compared to private holdings of assets; and, in the past, it probably would not have been a good assumption to suppose that official reserve assets were deployed in the direction of the greatest risk-adjusted return. However, in more recent years central banks and monetary authorities have begun to manage assets more aggressively along the lines of comparative risk and return. Official reserve assets are held mostly in the form of either foreign currencies or gold.

TABLE 11.2
Currency Distribution in Official Reserve Portfolios

Year end	Total Foreign Exchange and Gold Reserves (SDR Billions)			
	1973	1978	1983	1989
Foreign exchange	102.7	224.2	310.1	542.2
Gold (valued at London market price)	95.0	179.9	344.6	286.5
Gold (millions of ounces)	1022	1037	946	939

	Currency Shares of Official Reserve Portfolio (Percent of Total Foreign Currency Holdings)			
	Beginning 1973	End 1978	End 1983	End 1989
U.S. dollar	78.4	75.6	71.4	60.2
Deutschemark	5.5	11.0	11.8	19.3
Japanese yen	—	3.2	5.0	7.9
Swiss franc	1.1	2.3	2.4	1.7
Pound sterling	6.5	1.7	2.5	2.7
French franc	0.9	1.2	0.8	1.3
Dutch guilder	0.3	0.9	0.8	1.1
Unspecified currencies	7.3	4.2	5.3	5.7

Source: International Monetary Fund, *Annual Report.*

Table 11.2 shows the changing composition of official reserve assets since the breakdown of Bretton Woods. We see that the U.S. dollar share changed little until the formation of the European Monetary System after 1978. The DM has risen from 5.5 percent (1973) to 19.3 percent (1989) of the FX component of official reserves, while the £ has fallen from 6.5 percent to 2.7 percent. The role of the yen has increased slightly, but—as noted in Chapter 2—has been hindered by Japanese capital controls. Looking at the top section of Table 11.2, we see that the major portion of official reserve assets at the end of 1983 was held in the form of gold. The rise in the market value of gold was responsible, as the stock of physical gold had been decreased slightly to 946 million ounces from 1022 million ounces. By 1989, however, gold had dropped to one-third total reserve assets.

PROBLEMS FOR CHAPTER 11

1. Suppose we have two assets, one denominated in DM and one in £, whose dollar returns have a joint normal distribution with the following expected values and covariances:

	Expected Return		Covariance Matrix	
			DM	£
DM asset	.08	DM	.0064	.0020
£ asset	.06	£	.0020	.0052

Portfolio A contains the DM asset with a weight of .5 and the £ asset with a weight of .5. Portfolio B has the DM asset with a weight of .3 and the £ asset with a weight of .7.

(a) Calculate the expected return and standard deviation of portfolios A and B.

(b) Interpret your results in terms of probability.

(c) Would a risk-averse individual prefer A over B, B over A, or can you tell from the given information?

2. Under what circumstances would one buy an asset with zero expected real return?

3. Comment on the following observation: There is no reason to believe that variance of forecast errors or correlations will remain constant over time. The high correlation between the DM and the French franc would, for example, be drastically reduced if the EMS broke up.

PART IV

EUROCURRENCY MARKETS

12

EUROBANKING AND EUROCURRENCY CENTERS

THE BUSINESS OF EUROBANKING

Most eurobank activity involves the borrowing or lending of time deposits in transaction amounts varying from one to several million dollars. Deposits will be accepted over the phone from banks or corporations, and loans will be made in the same manner to banks or to corporations according to individually established credit lines. Chapter 1 showed how such transactions look in terms of balance sheet changes. A eurobank issues a eurodollar deposit to a customer when it receives in return a demand deposit balance at some domestic U.S. bank. Similarly, a company would make a eurodeposit in Dutch guilders by turning over to a eurobank a guilder deposit at a bank in the Netherlands. Loans are made in the same manner. A eurobank in London will make a $1,000,000 loan by transferring to the borrowing party a $1,000,000 deposit at a U.S. bank.

To consider a typical transaction in more detail, suppose Citibank London, a eurobank with respect to its dollar lending activities, makes a $1 million loan to United Global, a U.S. company. Citibank London issues United Global a check drawn on Citibank New York. United Global deposits the check in its account at Morgan Guaranty in New York. Morgan Guaranty increases United Global's demand deposit balance by $1 million, and meanwhile deposits the check in Morgan Guaranty's reserve account at the Federal Reserve Bank of New York. The Federal Reserve increases Morgan Guaranty's reserve balance by $1 million, and at the same time decreases the reserve balance of Citibank New York by $1 million. When notified of this action, Citibank New York decreases the demand deposit ("due to") balance owed by it to Citibank London by $1 million. To summarize the result for each participant:

Citibank London: a) has lost $1 million from its demand deposit ("due from") account it holds at Citibank New York; b) has increased its loan assets by $1 million.

Morgan Guaranty:	a) has increased its demand deposit liabilities to United Global by $1 million; b) has increased its reserve assets at the Federal Reserve by $1 million.
Federal Reserve:	a) has increased its reserve liabilities to Morgan Guaranty by $1 million; b) has decreased its reserve liabilities to Citibank New York by $1 million.
Citibank New York:	a) has lost $1 million from its reserve account at the Federal Reserve; b) has reduced the demand deposit balance due to Citibank London by $1 million.
United Global:	a) has increased its outstanding loan liabilities by $1 million; b) has increased its assets by the $1 million deposit held at Morgan Guaranty.

In Chapter 1 we saw that eurobanking and the eurocurrency market grew up in competition with noncompetitive domestic financial intermediaries. We traced the origin to the sterling crisis of late 1956 and early 1957. British authorities banned the use of sterling to finance trade between non-sterling countries. So British banks began making trade loans in dollars. That is, they created a market for the U.S. dollar outside the geographical and legal boundaries of the United States. Involved in this were British overseas banks and merchant banks. Later in the 1960s, bursts of growth occurred in 1966 and 1968–1969 when market interest rates (interest rates on Treasury bills and commercial paper) rose above the maximum rates U.S. commercial banks could pay as allowed by the Federal Reserve's Regulation Q. Eurobanks, again, were able to capture deposits by their ability to offer competitive market interest rates, since they were not subject to Federal Reserve restrictions.

With the breakdown of the Bretton Woods system of par values for currencies with respect to the U.S. dollar, the restrictions associated with the Interest Equalization Tax and Foreign Credit Restraint Program were removed. But the euromarket continued to thrive even without the artificial advantage granted by U.S. or other domestic regulatory restrictions. In particular, the euromarkets played an important role in the 1970s in funneling savings from OPEC current account surplus countries to LDC current account deficit countries.

The balance sheet of a typical eurobank is illustrated here. Eurobanks have as liabilities call money, time deposits, floating-rate notes, and negotiable CDs (certificates of deposit), while their assets include loans to banks and loans to companies and governments. The liabilities side of the balance sheet is, by definition, made up of eurocurrencies. If denominated in dollars, these liabilities are called eurodollars, while if denominated in DM they are called euro-DM. The criterion that designates the liability as "euro" is that the bank be located outside the country where the currency is issued as legal tender. Sometimes other regional terms are used (Asian dollars, for example), but here we will simply use "eurocurrency" to refer to all external currency funds.

Call money is money that is left on deposit without any specific maturity date. The money is repaid when the depositor—usually a corporation or a sovereign depositor like the Saudi Arabian Monetary Authority—gives notice for repayment. Depending on the type of account, repayment value may be for the same day, or require two or seven days notice. A time deposit has a fixed maturity date on which the bank's obligation is repayable with interest. Time deposits are by far the largest liability category. Certificates of deposit (CDs) differ from ordinary time deposits in that there exists a secondary market. If a CD owner wants the money back prior to maturity, the CD can be sold on the secondary market for its current value in that market. A floating-rate note differs from ordinary time deposits and short-term CDs in that it pays interest at periodic intervals, not just at maturity. The interest payments will be at a markup or spread above some reference rate (see the following). Floating-rate notes typically have longer maturities than other liabilities, and a secondary market exists for these notes.

On the asset side of the balance sheet are the eurobank's loans. "Loans to banks" will usually be to other eurobanks or to money-center banks in major financial centers. These loans arise from the interbank market in eurocurrency deposits. Eurocurrency borrowing and lending between major banks is done over the phone in a fashion similar to trading in foreign currencies. A eurocurrency trader will quote bid and asked interest rates. The bid interest rate is the rate at which the eurobank will accept deposits from other banks (which will increase the eurobank's time-deposit liabilities), and the asked interest rate is the rate at which the eurobank will lend to other banks (which will increase the eurobank's loan assets). The bank's objective is to make a profit on the spread between the bid and asked prices. (The interbank market is covered in Chapter 13.)

Eurobanks

Assets	Liabilities
Loans to banks	Call money
Loans to companies	Time deposits
and governments	CDs
	Floating-rate notes

Deposits denominated in about fifteen eurocurrencies are regularly traded in the London interbank market. These currencies include the Austrian shilling, Belgian franc, Canadian dollar, Danish krone, French franc, German mark, Italian lira, Japanese yen, Netherlands guilder, Norwegian krone, Spanish peseta, Swedish krona, Swiss franc, UK pound sterling, and U.S. dollar. Some other eurocurrencies exist in special regional markets. Banks in Bahrain trade deposits denominated in Saudi riyals, for example. A typical bid/asked spread for traded eurocurrency deposits is $\frac{1}{8}$ of 1 percent for the U.S. dollar, German mark, Swiss franc, and Netherlands guilder. The other currencies usually have equivalent bid/asked spreads, but a spread may widen in thin market trading. Table 12.1 gives interest rates on eurodeposits for September 7, 1990. (Note that, as is customary in London, the asked or lending rate is listed first.)

The other eurobank asset category, "loans to companies and governments," arises from the eurocredits market. Loans in this market are generally

TABLE 12.1
Eurocurrency Interest Rates, September 7, 1990

September 7	Eurocurrency Interest Rates					
	Short Term	**Seven Days Notice**	**One Month**	**Three Months**	**Six Months**	**One Year**
Sterling	$15-14\frac{7}{8}$	$15-14\frac{7}{8}$	$15\frac{1}{16}-15$	$14\frac{15}{16}-14\frac{7}{8}$	$14\frac{13}{16}-14\frac{3}{4}$	$14\frac{9}{16}-14\frac{7}{16}$
U.S. Dollar	$8\frac{1}{16}-7\frac{13}{16}$	$8\frac{1}{16}-7\frac{13}{16}$	$8\frac{1}{16}-7\frac{13}{16}$	$8\frac{1}{16}-7\frac{13}{16}$	$8\frac{1}{8}-8$	$8\frac{1}{4}-8\frac{1}{8}$
Can. Dollar	$12\frac{3}{8}-12\frac{1}{4}$	$12\frac{3}{8}-12\frac{1}{4}$	$12\frac{9}{16}-12\frac{5}{8}$	$12\frac{9}{16}-12\frac{5}{8}$	$12\frac{1}{4}-12$	$12-11\frac{3}{4}$
D. Guilder	$8\frac{3}{8}-8\frac{1}{4}$	$8\frac{3}{8}-8\frac{1}{4}$	$8\frac{3}{8}-8\frac{1}{4}$	$8\frac{9}{16}-8\frac{7}{16}$	$8\frac{3}{4}-8\frac{5}{8}$	$9-8\frac{7}{8}$
Sw. Franc	$8-7\frac{7}{8}$	$8-7\frac{7}{8}$	$8\frac{1}{8}-8$	$8\frac{7}{16}-8\frac{1}{16}$	$8\frac{5}{8}-8\frac{1}{2}$	$8\frac{5}{8}-8\frac{1}{2}$
Deutschmark	$8\frac{1}{8}-8$	$8\frac{1}{8}-8$	$8\frac{5}{16}-8\frac{3}{16}$	$8\frac{11}{16}-8\frac{9}{16}$	$8\frac{13}{16}-8\frac{11}{16}$	$9-8\frac{1}{4}$
Fr. Franc	$10\frac{1}{8}-10$	$10\frac{1}{8}-10$	$10\frac{1}{8}-10$	$10\frac{3}{8}-10\frac{1}{4}$	$10\frac{7}{16}-10\frac{5}{16}$	$10\frac{13}{16}-10\frac{11}{16}$
Italian Lira	$13-11$	$7\frac{3}{4}-6\frac{3}{4}$	$9\frac{7}{8}-9\frac{3}{8}$	$10\frac{5}{8}-10\frac{3}{8}$	$11\frac{1}{2}-11\frac{1}{8}$	$12\frac{1}{16}-11\frac{15}{16}$
Belgian Franc	$9\frac{1}{8}-9$	$9\frac{1}{8}-9$	$9\frac{3}{16}-9\frac{1}{16}$	$9\frac{1}{4}-9\frac{1}{8}$	$9\frac{1}{2}-9\frac{3}{8}$	$9\frac{13}{16}-9\frac{11}{16}$
Yen	$7\frac{11}{16}-7\frac{7}{8}$	$7\frac{3}{4}-7\frac{11}{16}$	$8\frac{5}{8}-8\frac{1}{4}$	$8\frac{3}{8}-8\frac{1}{4}$	$8\frac{5}{8}-8\frac{9}{16}$	$8\frac{3}{4}-8\frac{11}{16}$
D. Krone	$9\frac{7}{8}-9\frac{3}{4}$	$10\frac{1}{8}-10$	$10\frac{3}{4}-10\frac{5}{8}$	$10\frac{3}{4}-10\frac{5}{8}$	$10\frac{13}{16}-10\frac{11}{16}$	$10\frac{15}{16}-10\frac{13}{16}$
Asian \$Sing	$8\frac{1}{8}-8$	$8\frac{1}{8}-8$	$8\frac{1}{16}-7\frac{15}{16}$	$8\frac{1}{16}-7\frac{13}{16}$	$8\frac{1}{16}-7\frac{13}{16}$	$8\frac{3}{16}-8\frac{1}{16}$

Source: Financial Times, September 10, 1990.

longer term and entail a greater possibility of default by the borrower. Therefore the spread the bank charges over its cost of funds is higher than in the interbank market. In addition, the concept of rollover pricing was created so eurobanks could avoid the possibility of paying higher interest rates on the bank's liabilities than the bank was receiving on its eurocredits. A credit extended through rollover pricing involves a succession of short-term loans that are periodically rolled over at a different interest rate. The interest rate on the loan is fixed for the duration of an interest period but updated at the beginning of the next interest rate period. If a new interest period begins at time t, then the interest rate $i(t)$ will be set according to a market reference rate $r(t)$ by the formula:

$$i(t) = r(t) + \text{Lending margin.}$$

The reference rate $r(t)$ is chosen in such a way that it will move up and down in step with the rates the bank pays on its liabilities. Thus, if the cost of funds to the bank has gone up or down when the bank funds its loan for a new interest rate period, the interest rate $i(t)$ on the rollover credit will rise or fall.

EXAMPLE 12.1

In 1969, Minos Zombanakis of the London merchant bank Manufacturers Hanover Ltd. organized one of the earliest rollover credits in the eurodollar market when he assembled a group of twenty-two banks to make a $200 million loan to the government of Italy. The interest rate was set at .75 percent above the six-month LIBOR, the London Interbank Offered Rate—the rate at which eurobanks in London offer to lend to other banks. In this case, LIBOR was the chosen reference rate. As an interbank offer rate, LIBOR would move up and down in conjunction with bid rates, so LIBOR was tied to a London eurobank's cost of funds. The lending margin was .75 percent. The interest rate on the loan was to be revised every six months. That meant eurobanks could fund themselves with new six-month eurodollar deposits at the beginning of each interest period, and thus lock in a profit of .75 percent plus the spread between bid and asked prices in the interbank market. (This profit was locked in, of course, only if the borrower did not default on the loan. Thus the size of the margin had to be adjusted for default risk.)

Usually, the reference rate used in rollover pricing is one of the IBORs, or Interbank Offered Rates, the rates at which eurobanks will lend to other eurobanks in the interbank market. In addition to LIBOR, other frequently used reference rates include:

BIBOR	(Bahrain Interbank Offered Rate)
BRIBOR	(Brussels Interbank Offered Rate)
DIBOR	(Dublin Interbank Offered Rate)
HIBOR	(Hong Kong Interbank Offered Rate)
LUXIBOR	(Luxembourg Interbank Offered Rate)
MIBOR	(Madrid Interbank Offered Rate)
PIBOR	(Paris Interbank Offered Rate)
SIBOR	(Singapore Interbank Offered Rate)
JLTP	(Japan Long-Term Prime Rate)

ECU Interbank Offered Rate
U.S. Prime Rate
U.S. Banker's Acceptance Rate
Sterling Acceptances Commission
Canadian Prime Rate

Of course, not all these reference rates are eurocurrency interest rates. Domestic reference rates sometimes appear in eurocredits because international loans often involve groups of banks, some of which may be lending from domestic sources and others of which may be eurobanks. The final reference rate may represent a compromise between domestic and eurocurrency funding.

LIBOR is also a frequently used reference rate for floating-rate notes, as are LIMEAN (the mean of the bid and offer rate) and LIBID (the London Interbank Bid Rate).

The *lending margin* is the fixed spread borrowers agree to pay above the reference rate. Since the loan rate on a eurocredit is adjusted according to the bank's cost of funds, the lending margin (along with any fees) represents the bank's profit in the event of no default. The bank will set the margin according to credit conditions and the perceived riskiness of the loan. Sometimes the lending margin is a floating margin. An example of a floating margin is a lending margin that is set at .3 percent above the six-month LIBOR for the first three years of the loan but 1 percent above the six-month LIBOR for the remaining life of the loan.

There are two general types of eurocredits as seen from the point of view of when and how the borrower gets the money involved in the loan: term credits and revolving credits. A *term credit* has a set time schedule during which the principal in the loan gradually becomes available to the borrower, a period of grace during which the full amount of the loan is available to the borrower, and then a schedule of repayments of the principal. Interest is paid at set time intervals, usually on a rollover basis, but occasionally at a fixed interest rate. In *revolving credit,* the borrower has a certain maximum line of credit that he can use or not use as he wishes. In either a term credit or a revolving credit, interest is paid by the borrower only on the amount of the credit actually in use, but there is a commitment fee paid by the borrower on the unused portion. In revolving credit, the amount not used is at the borrower's discretion; in term credit, the amount not used is partly determined by the time schedule.

Since 1963, the Basel-based Bank for International Settlements (BIS), which serves as a clearinghouse among central banks, has collected data on the eurocurrency market. The balance sheet below, constructed from BIS data, adds together eurocurrency market figures with those for dollars at U.S. IBFs and yen in the Japan Offshore Market (JOM). The numbers show that most eurobanking business is with other banks. That is, the interbank market, which involves borrowing and lending interbank deposits at a small bid/asked spread, accounts for most eurobank activity. Loans to banks were $4018 billion, while deposits from other banks were $4486 billion. The most important category, from the point of view of its importance to economic activity, is the category "claims on nonbanks," which represents the eurocredits market. As of end 1989, that amount was estimated to be $1255 billion. Liabilities to nonbanks were $788 billion. Thus, the amount of economic resources being funneled from ultimate savers to ultimate borrowers by the eurobanking sector at this time was probably in the neighborhood of $1 trillion. (The residual category "domestic deposits" is used to describe the matching of eurocurrency assets by domestic currency liabilities.)

Eurobanks, End 1989

Assets (billions)		Liabilities (billions)	
$4800.9	Eurocurrency claims	$4803.6	Eurocurrency deposits
289.6	IBFs	334.0	IBFs
183.0	JOM	117.0	JOM
		18.9	Domestic deposits
$5273.5	Total assets	$5273.5	Total liabilities
	Of which:		Of which:
$1255.3	Claims on nonbanks	$ 787.7	Owed to nonbanks
$4018.2	Claims on banks	$4485.8	Owed to banks

EUROCURRENCY CENTERS

A eurocurrency "center" refers to a place where there is a concentration of eurobanks. A number of factors are associated with the rise of a eurocurrency center. There should be political stability: an absence of coups d'état, the threat of foreign takeover, or fear of adverse government policy changes. There should be a favorable political environment in which to conduct international finance: favorable tax treatment of banking conducted in foreign currencies, an absence of exchange and credit controls for such business, and a respect for financial privacy. There may be other advantages such as good telecommunication links with other financial centers or a favorable time zone in terms of the geographic location of the center.

Eurocurrency centers can be categorized into five geographical areas: Western Europe, including London, Zurich, Paris and the Channel Islands; the Caribbean and Central America, including the Cayman Islands and the Bahamas; the Middle East, including Bahrain; Asia, including Singapore, Hong Kong, and Tokyo; and the United States, including various states that have provided for the establishment of International Banking Facilities. A few institutional and historical details will be of interest.

Western Europe

London was historically the first, and still the foremost, eurocurrency center. No other center approaches the diversity of its business conducted in over a dozen foreign currencies. This preeminence is an outgrowth not only of London's history of continual fixed investment in financial expertise, dating from the trade financing days of the British Empire, but also of UK regulations that have differentiated between banking conducted in sterling and banking conducted in other currencies. The Bank of England does not impose reserve requirements on eurocurrency deposits or capital requirements on the branches of foreign banks. The London-based eurocurrency market is dominated therefore not by British banks but by U.S. and Japanese overseas banks. It was a U.S. bank, Citibank, that pioneered London dollar CDs in 1966. But in recent years Japanese banks have become the largest issuers of CDs. At the end of 1988, Japanese banks in the United Kingdom had liabilities of $391.6 billion in currencies other than sterling. Of this amount, $67.4 billion was CDs (*Federal Reserve Bulletin*, February 1990). In terms of eurocurrency assets, London is the principal center for medium-term eurocredit lending, so that LIBOR is the most widely used reference rate in rollover credits.

Caribbean and Central America

The Cayman Islands is one of the most favored locations for establishing a shell branch for U.S. banks. These shell branches are legally incorporated in the Cayman Islands, but the actual "bank" is a separate set of books in the headquarters office in New York or elsewhere. Operational decisions for the Caribbean eurobank are made by traders in the bank's New York trading office. This arrangement avoids the high profit taxes that London banks, including branches of foreign banks, must pay. As of April 1990, foreign branches of U.S. banks in the Bahamas and Caymans had $146.3 billion in eurodollar liabilities, compared with only $109.7 billion at branches in the United Kingdom (*Federal Reserve Bulletin*, August 1990).

It is not difficult for a large international bank to open a branch in the Cayman Islands. The minimum capital requirement can be met using the capital of the parent bank. There are no lending, interest, or reserve requirements for eurocurrency operations. The language is English and telecommunication facilities are good. Business hours are the same as those of New York. It is perhaps not surprising that this small group of islands with fewer than 20,000 inhabitants is host to more than 350 banks and trust companies.

The Middle East

Bahrain is the center of the Middle East market for both foreign exchange and eurocurrency trading. This has been partly a function of the war in Lebanon, which destroyed Beirut's role as the traditional financial center of the Middle East, and partly a function of Bahrain's close proximity to Saudi Arabia. Bahrain is the center of euro–Saudi riyal trading, and eurocredits have been extended based on BIBOR rates for both the U.S. dollar and the Saudi riyal.

The United States

Eurocurrency operations within the geographical area of the United States were legalized on December 3, 1981, through the creation of International Banking Facilities (IBFs). IBFs are a set of books kept at U.S. banks, or at branches and agencies of foreign banks in the United States or at Edge Act corporations. There are no reserve requirements or interest ceilings on deposits booked at IBFs. However, there is a minimum maturity of two business days for nonbank deposits, and nonbank transactions can be in minimum amounts of $100,000. Loan and deposit customers of IBFs are only allowed to be foreign residents, other IBFs, or the IBF's parent. If an IBF makes loans to its parent, the parent bank is subject to the normal reserve requirement that applies to bank liabilities stemming from eurocurrency borrowing. A number of states have passed laws exempting IBFs from state and local tax. IBFs are, however, subject to federal tax. Finally, and perhaps most importantly, IBFs cannot issue negotiable instruments such as CDs or get FDIC insurance.

The prohibition on issuing negotiable instruments was intended to keep them out of the hands of U.S. residents. If IBFs were allowed to issue CDs, it was reasoned, then—even if IBFs did not issue deposits directly to U.S. residents—it would be difficult to prevent U.S. residents from purchasing the CDs of IBFs on the secondary market. This prohibition on issuing negotiable instruments originally tended to diminish the attraction of IBFs for many U.S. banks. Many banks preferred to open (or keep) a Caribbean shell branch that did not suffer from the no-CD restriction. As a consequence, the biggest enthusiasm for IBFs was initially exhibited by U.S.-based Japanese and Italian banks. Domestic legal restrictions had prevented either of these groups of banks from opening shell branches in the Caribbean, but did not prohibit them from operating IBFs in the United States. The more recent collapse of the U.S. CD market has diminished the relevancy of the no-C.D. restriction.

Asia

Singapore is the center of the eurocurrency ("Asian dollar") market in Asia. Eurobanking began in October 1968 when Bank of America, Singapore, received permission to open an international banking facility (called an Asian Currency Unit). Asian Currency Units were allowed to accept foreign deposits from nonresidents and to make foreign loans outside a restricted area. One of the immediate impetuses for the creation of the market seems to have been large area holdings of dollars acquired as a result of the Vietnam War without a concomitant outlet in a convenient time zone. SIBOR is now the commonly used reference rate for Asian dollar loans. In 1986, the Japanese Ministry of Finance allowed for the establishment of international banking facilities by Japanese domestic banks. The Japan Offshore Market (JOM) has since grown rapidly, and Tokyo has begun to rival Singapore as a eurocurrency center.

EURODEPOSITS AND SOVEREIGN RISK

Eurobanks and eurodeposits are subject to all the risks normal to banks and banking deposits generally. In addition, the borrowing and lending of currencies across national boundaries implies the additional risk that might stem from government actions to restrict the movement of capital or to impose controls on foreign currency transactions. For example, in October 1983, the Philippine government imposed controls limiting the transfer of foreign currency funds from Philippine banks. As a result, Citibank of New York froze several hundreds of millions of eurodollars deposited in its Manila branch. According to the *Wall Street Journal*, Citibank said "it had no choice but to freeze the deposits when the cash-strapped Philippine government imposed controls banning foreign-exchange outflows" (February 23, 1984). This news was not welcomed by Wells Fargo Asia Ltd., a Singapore-based subsidiary of Wells Fargo Bank of San Francisco. Wells Fargo Asia had placed two $1 million deposits with Citibank Manila in June 1983, one of which was to mature on December 9 and the other on December 12. Wells Fargo Asia expected the deposits to be repaid upon maturity at Citibank New York. When repayment did not occur, Wells Fargo Asia sued Citibank New York in a New York federal court. Japanese banks, with the largest amounts of frozen deposits, were not happy either.

Because of sovereign risks like those just illustrated, eurodeposits generally pay a premium above comparable domestic deposits. This premium is usually in the neighborhood of twenty-five basis points. (Citibank Manila was in addition reportedly paying seventy-five basis points—.75 percent—above the normal eurodollar rate.) The probability of events like the "thrilla in Manila" may be small but is nonetheless real.

Most U.S. international banking takes place through bank branches. Branches differ from subsidiaries. In U.S. law, the parent bank is responsible (liable) for deposits placed in branches. A subsidiary, by contrast, is legally independent of the parent, and the depositor has no legal recourse if the subsidiary fails to pay up. (Good business practice, however, would usually dictate that the parent pay up on its subsidiary's deposits also in the event the subsidiary failed.)

Since, for example, Citibank Manila was a foreign branch, most banks with dollar deposits there expected Citibank New York to make good on them, regardless of the actions of the Philippine government. Citibank, however, claimed an exemption on the basis that the imposition of exchange controls was an "act of state." The act-of-state doctrine in U.S. law essentially implies that since a foreign branch is under foreign jurisdiction, the parent U.S. bank will not normally be held responsible for the failure of its branch to repay if this failure is due to actions of a sovereign government. This means that, to a depositor, a dollar in Manila is not quite the same as a dollar in New York, even if the headquarters bank is the same.

REGULATION OF THE EUROCURRENCY MARKETS

The eurocurrency markets represent a type of regulatory arbitrage. Eurobanking is a managed financial package that combines the currency of one country (one regulatory environment) with the banking regulations and competitive efficiencies of another country. This repackaging was made possible by improvements in worldwide communication links and information technology. If the regulatory burden becomes too high in one area of the world, the bundle of eurobanking services can be reassembled in another. Hence, national regulators must compete to maintain their respective shares of the eurocurrency business. Competition with respect to lending quotas, reserve requirements, capital requirements, deposit insurance, the taxing and reporting of interest payments, and the taxing of profits, dividends, and capital gains, all measured against any perceived positive benefits of local regulation, governs the geographical distribution of eurocurrency market shares.

Banking regulations may operate on a country (territorial) basis or a management control (domiciliary) basis. A country's banking authorities *could* impose uniform regulations with respect to banks in its territory, regardless of whether the bank is domestic- or foreign-owned. This would be an example of uniform regulation on a territorial basis. But, as noted earlier, eurobanking exists because present regulations allow domestic- and foreign-owned banks different freedoms, or allow for foreign currency business to be treated differently from business conducted in the local currency.

On the other hand, regulatory authorities in the place of location of a bank's headquarters may impose worldwide rules that apply also to the bank's subsidiaries and offshore branches. This would be regulation on a domiciliary basis. Central banks acting through the BIS have tended in a domiciliary direction. In the Basel Concordat of 1975, revised in 1983, central banks agreed that in the event of a solvency crisis involving a eurobank, it would be the responsibility of the central bank in the country of the eurobank's headquarters to act as the lender of last resort if the eurobank was a foreign branch, but the central bank in the country of the eurobank's location would have joint responsibility if the eurobank was a foreign subsidiary. In 1980, central bank members of the BIS began requiring commercial banks in each member country to consolidate their worldwide accounts.

One current focus of central bank regulation is to stimulate banks to maintain "adequate" capital. A bank's capital is the cushion that allows it to absorb unforeseen losses and continue to remain in business. A bank can suffer losses due to changes in market variables (market risk), such as changes in the interest spread between its assets and liabilities. Or it can suffer losses from the failure of counterparties to perform on contracts (credit risk). A risk-based capital framework addressing primarily credit risk was announced in July 1988 by the BIS central bank representatives who comprised the Basel Committee on Banking Regulations and Supervisory Practices. The framework was intended to unify capital standards, and hence prevent regulatory arbitrage on a territorial basis.

The Basel standard requires a certain ratio of capital to bank assets. First, it defines what items count as "capital." Second, it discriminates among assets. Assets are weighted (multiplied by a number from 0 to 1) before being added together. Capital is then required as a percentage of risk-adjusted assets.

Under the Basel standard there are two types of capital: core (Tier 1) and supplemental (Tier 2). Core capital includes common stock valued at par, perpetual preferred stock, surplus, minority interest in consolidated subsidiaries, and retained earnings, *minus* treasury stock and goodwill. Supplemental capital includes limited-life preferred stock and related surplus, loan-loss reserves, perpetual debt, mandatory convertible securities, and subordinated debt with an original maturity of not less than five years.

Balance sheet and off-balance sheet assets are assigned one of four risk weights, either 0, .2, .5, or 1.0 (see Table 12.2). An asset with a weight of 0 doesn't use any capital, while each $1 of an asset with a weight of .5 is treated like 50 cents in the risk-adjusted asset calculation. Off-balance sheet items are assigned a further credit-conversion factor (or else a credit equivalent amount) *before* being multiplied by the risk weight (Table 12.3). The effective weight is thus the product of the credit conversion factor and the risk weight. One dollar of an off-balance sheet asset with a credit conversion factor of .5 and a risk weight of .5 has an effective weight of $.5 \times .5 \times \$1 = \$0.25$.

Next, the Basel standard called for a minimum of 7.25 percent capital (of which 3.625 percent should represent core or Tier 1 capital) against risk-adjusted assets by year-end 1990, and a minimum of 8.00 percent capital (of which 4.0 percent should represent core capital) by year-end 1992. Exceptions to the general framework were allowed over the 1990–1992 phasing-in period.

An example of calculation of risk-adjusted assets and capital usage might be

TABLE 12.2
Risk Weights Applied Against Bank Assets

Category 1: Weight = 0
—Cash
—Balances due from central banks in OECD countries
—OECD country government-guaranteed claims
—Gold bullion

Category 2: Weight = .2
—Cash items in process of collection
—Claims on, or guaranteed by, OECD banks
—Claims under one year guaranteed by non-OECD banks
—Claims on local governments in OECD countries.
—Claims on official multilateral lending institutions or regional development banks
—Claims collateralized by cash or OECD government securities or securities of official
    multilateral institutions
—Shares in funds holding only securities with weights of 0 or .2

Category 3: Weight = .5
—Loans secured by residential real estate
—Revenue bonds
—Credit equivalent amounts of interest rate and FX contracts (not falling into Categories
    1 or 2)

Category 4: Weight = 1.0
—Other claims on private obligors
—Other claims on non-OECD governments and banks
—Fixed assets and real estate
—Claims on state enterprises

Source: Federal Reserve System, *Risk-Based Capital Guidelines,* January 19, 1989.

helpful. Consider a three-month forward contract of $1 million. The forward contract was made some time ago, and the exchange rate has since moved in the bank's favor. It has a mark-to-market gain of $15,000. The bank's credit risk is the potential loss of the mark-to-market gain. How much capital does this contract use? From Table 12.3, we see that the credit equivalent amount for FX contracts less than one year is the replacement cost plus 1 percent. Adding together the replacement cost of $15,000 with 1 percent of $1 million yields a credit equivalent amount of $15,000 + $10,000 = $25,000. Then, from Table 12.2, we see that the weight applied to this contract would be .2, if the forward contract was made with another OECD bank, or .5 if the contract was with a company. Assuming the forward contract was made with a commercial firm, the adjusted asset amount is .5 × $25,000 = $12,500. The capital requirement is then 8 percent (after 1992) of this amount, or $1000. On the other hand, if the exchange rate had moved against the bank, so that there was a mark-to-market loss on the forward contract, the replacement cost would be treated as zero (it isn't allowed to be negative). Hence the adjusted asset amount would be .5 × .01 × $1 million = $5000. And the capital charge would be .08 × $5000 = $400.

Notice from Table 12.3 that a two-year interest rate swap (see Chapter 19) in a single currency would have a credit equivalent amount of .5 percent plus the swap's mark-to-market replacement value (if positive). A two-year cross-currency interest rate swap would be treated as an FX contract, and would have a credit equivalent amount of 5.0 percent plus the swap's mark-to-market replacement value (if positive).

Finally, all exchange-traded contracts requiring daily payment of variation margin are assigned a zero credit equivalent amount and hence cost zero capital. Since the bank has already received any accumulated positive value on

TABLE 12.3
Credit Conversion Factors for Off-Balance Sheet Items

Conversion Factor = 1.0:
—Direct credit substitutes such as standby letters of credit backing financial obligations
—Sale and repurchase agreements and assets sold with recourse
—Forward agreements to purchase on which drawdown is certain

Conversion Factor = 0.5:
—Transactions-related contingencies such as performance bonds and warranties, and standby letters of credit for nonfinancial obligations
—Revolving underwriting agreements (RUFs) and Note issue facilities (NIFs)

Conversion Factor = 0.2:
—Short-term, self-liquidating trade-related contingencies, such as commercial letters of credit

Conversion Factor = 0:
—Unused portions of commitments under one year that can be unconditionally cancelled

Conversion of Interest Rate and FX Contracts:
—The credit equivalent amount equals the total replacement (mark-to-market) cost of the contract (a minimum of zero) *plus*
  0.5% of interest rate contracts with > one-year maturity
  1.0% of FX contracts with ≤ one-year maturity (0% if original maturity is under fourteen days)
  5.0% of FX contracts with > one-year maturity

Source: Federal Reserve System, *Risk-Based Capital Guidelines,* January 19, 1989.

the contract (via variation margin), the Basel standards treat the credit risk as zero. This gives banks a strong incentive to manage their interest rate exposures through the use of exchange-traded financial futures, such as the three-month eurodollar contract at the IMM.

PROBLEMS FOR CHAPTER 12

1. Comment on the following statement: "Regulatory arbitrage is the chief source of eurobanking profits."

2. Comment on the following statement: "The fact that non-EEC centers (e.g., Singapore, Hong Kong) have not taken over the Euro-dollar market suggests that these centers have pushed their regulatory competition to the limit."

3. Comment on the following statement: " 'Booking' branches of international banks proliferated in offshore centers offering tax concessions, freedom from regulation, tight secrecy laws, and a geographic position that facilitated the service of money escaping neighboring jurisdictions. For if anonymity was what the original euro-dollar market offered the USSR, that same anonymity served asset strippers, drug peddlers, private arms dealers, tax evaders, and national intelligence agencies, not to speak of 'ordinary' citizens concerned with economic security in their declining years free from the smell of the favela or the scent of the secret police."

4. An OECD bank has a six-year, $10 million interest rate swap with a mark-to-market gain of $124,000. The counterparty is another OECD bank. What is the capital requirement under Basel standards?

5. Comment on the following statement: "The Basel capital standards are irrational because they require more capital for profitable currency and interest rate swaps than for ones that are losing money."

6. Do the Basel capital standards imply that OECD banks are a better credit risk than OECD companies? Do you agree?

DEPOSIT DEALING AND THE TERM STRUCTURE OF EUROCURRENCY RATES

THE INTERBANK MARKET

The interbank market in eurocurrencies, particularly eurodollars, is a complex market involving the interaction of time deposit rates, foreign exchanges rates, FRAs, and eurocurrency futures. The interbank eurodollar market, for example, is most liquid between 8:20 A.M. and 3:00 P.M. New York time, when the eurodollar futures contract at the IMM in Chicago is open for trading. The basis of the market remains, however, the borrowing (taking) and lending (placing) of time deposits.

Settlement dates for eurocurrency deposit trades were covered in Chapter 4 in connection with forward exchange rates. Most trades made today will be good two business days later. Standard maturities are for one, two, three, six, nine, and twelve months. In addition, there are deposits with a maturity of one day ("spot next"), one week ("spot week"), and two weeks ("spot fortnight"). Deposits can also be traded that are settled (good) on the same day the trade takes place and mature the following day. These are called "overnight" deposits. A similar type of deposit, called "tomorrow next," is settled on the day following the trading day, and matures one day later (on the second day after the trade).

As with foreign exchange, eurocurrencies are traded both through direct dealing and through brokers. Marketmakers will quote two-way prices with a bid/offer spread. (See Table 13.1.) The bid rate is the rate the trader will pay on deposits, while the offer rate is the rate that will be charged on loans. The size of this spread is usually .125 percent (12.5 basis points) for eurodollar trades. If a broker is used, the broker will receive a brokerage commission of perhaps .02 percent (2.0 basis points) from each of the two parties that are matched through the broker.

Since eurocurrency deposits are borrowed and lent in the form of domestic demand deposits, they are often close substitutes for domestic deposits. The substitution is not perfect: We saw in Chapter 12 that the threat of exchange or capital controls is an additional source of risk for eurocurrency deposits. To

TABLE 13.1
London Eurodollar Deposits,
August 29, 1990

Category	Bid	Offer
Overnight	$7\frac{7}{8}$	$8\frac{1}{16}$
Tomorrow next	$7\frac{7}{8}$	8
Spot next	$7\frac{15}{16}$	$8\frac{1}{16}$
1 Week	$7\frac{15}{16}$	$8\frac{1}{16}$
1 Month	8	$8\frac{1}{8}$
2 Months	$8\frac{1}{16}$	$8\frac{3}{16}$
3 Months	$8\frac{1}{16}$	$8\frac{3}{16}$
6 Months	$8\frac{1}{8}$	$8\frac{1}{4}$
9 Months	$8\frac{3}{16}$	$8\frac{5}{16}$
1 Year	$8\frac{1}{4}$	$8\frac{3}{8}$

Source: Reuters Money Service.

compete with domestic deposits, eurobanks must often pay a higher interest rate to compensate the depositor for this risk. Over the period 1980–1989, three-month LIBOR averaged a premium of 52.6 basis points over the rate on three-month U.S. CDs. If we allow 12.5 basis points for the difference between LIBOR and LIBID, the net spread between borrowing in the euromarket and domestic market was about 40 basis points. During 1989, the LIBOR-CD spread fell to an average of 16.2 basis points, with a standard deviation (of monthly averages) of only 2.2 basis points. There were (in 1989) no reserve requirement differences between the two types of deposits: Regulation D of the Federal Reserve set a uniform 3 percent reserve ratio. However, costs of FDIC insurance were about 8 basis points on CDs versus zero on eurodeposits. This narrowing of spreads can be generally attributed to deregulation in the U.S. domestic market, which made the instruments closer substitutes, and the drying up of the U.S. CD market, which pushed up relative CD yields.

The interest rate on overnight eurodollar deposits tracks closely the U.S. interest rate on federal funds and repos (repurchase agreements—a form of secured lending between banks involving the short-term purchase and resale of U.S. government securities.) LIBOR spreads against U.S. domestic rates are illustrated in Table 13.2 for some recent years. Similarly, the rate on euroyen deposits closely tracks the gensaki (repo) rate in the Japanese domestic market. For some currencies, such as the French franc prior to the lifting of intra-EEC capital constraints, the existence of a complex set of controls has in the past ensured that there is no close substitute in the domestic market for the eurocurrency deposit.

The risks faced by eurobanks and eurocurrency dealers can be divided into three types. First, there will be foreign exchange risk if the currency denomination of assets does not match the currency denomination of liabilities. The nature of foreign exchange risk was covered in detail in Part II. Eurobanks will allow some position taking by their traders but will place overall limits on the amount of currency mismatching that can take place. Some of the currency mismatching arises in connection with the interest parity theorem covered in

TABLE 13.2
Eurodollar Rates Compared to Domestic U.S. Rates (monthly averages)

	Fed Funds	3-mo. LIBOR	3-mo. LIBOR minus 3-mo. CD	3-mo. LIBOR minus 3-mo. Comm. Paper	3-mo. LIBOR minus 3-mo. T-bill
1980–1989 av.	9.97	10.42	0.53	0.47	1.37
Minimum	5.85	5.96	0.07	− 0.03	0.55
Maximum	19.10	19.61	1.75	1.62	4.23
S.D.	3.38	3.51	0.34	0.37	0.75
1989 av.	9.22	9.25	0.16	0.05	0.97
Minimum	8.45	8.47	0.14	0.00	0.69
Maximum	9.85	10.27	0.21	0.12	1.31
S.D.	0.48	0.61	0.02	0.04	0.20

Source: Citicorp Data Base Services.

Chapter 4. Just as eurocurrency deposits can be used to create an artificial forward rate, so spot and forward exchange markets can be used in connection with one eurocurrency to create artificial deposits and loans in another eurocurrency. For example, one may borrow eurodollars, buy Austrian shillings spot, and lend them for three months. Meanwhile, the shillings can be sold forward to cover the exchange risk. Thus one has created a loan of euro-Austrian shillings using the exchange markets in connection with the eurodollar market. Euro-Spanish pesetas are another example where this operation has been used. (See Problem 1.)

A second type of risk is interest rate risk to the extent the maturity of assets and liabilities is not matched. Only if maturities are perfectly matched can a bank be sure that a loan at one interest rate is funded by a deposit at a lower interest rate. Eurobanks typically engage in only small amounts of maturity transformation (maturity mismatching) in the interbank market, but a good bit more in the eurocredits market. Interest risk is considered in more detail below in connection with the term structure of interest rate. Traders will have overall position limits on the amount of interest rate betting they can practice but will be free to take positions within the overall guidelines established by bank management. Finally there is credit risk, which refers to the possibility that someone may not perform on a contract. A loan may not be repaid. This risk is dealt with in the interbank market by establishing limits on the amount of dealing with a bank according to the bank's overall reputation in the market, as well as its geographic location. For retail customers such as companies, credit limits will be established after a careful individual credit evaluation.

THE TERM STRUCTURE

The profitability of lending and borrowing across maturities depends not only on the existence of spreads between bid and asked rates in the interbank market and margins in the eurocredits market, but also on the term structure of interest rates. The term structure of interest rates is a graph of the interest rate (i) seen as a function of the term to maturity (T) of an asset or liability. For example, the current rates on eurodollars may be the following:

T (days)	i (per annum)
32	.0987
60	.1000
91	.1013
182	.1038
367	.1065

Here interest rates (measured at an annual rate) are increasing with term to maturity. This is referred to as an "upward-sloping" term structure. If rates decrease with term to maturity, the term structure is "downward-sloping." If interest rates (measured at a common annual rate) are the same across maturities, the term structure is "flat." Other shapes are also possible. For example, rates may rise over earlier maturities, then fall over later ones. The slope of the term structure is not independent of the way in which rates are quoted. Since eurocurrency rates are quoted at an annual rate for a 360-day year, it is better to forego common interpretations of the slope and instead pay attention to the implied forward rates, which will now be discussed.

For convenience, let us assume there is no bid/asked spread between borrowing and lending rates. (This is done only in order to avoid writing separate bid and asked rates in the following equations.) Consider two deposits at time t, one of which bears an interest rate $i(t,n)$ and matures at time $t + n$ and the other of which bears an interest rate $i(t,T)$ and matures at time $t + T$, with $n < T$. We can conceive of a third interest rate $f(t + n, T - n)$, a *break-even* or *implied forward rate*, such that if the earlier-maturing deposit were reinvested at the interest rate $f(t + n, T - n)$ at time $t + n$ for maturity at time $t + T$, the final yield would be the same as the yield on the deposit of longer maturity:

$$1 + i(t,T)\frac{T}{360} = \left[1 + i(t, n)\frac{n}{360}\right]\left[1 + f(t + n, T - n)\left(\frac{T - n}{360}\right)\right].(13.1)$$

Solving for $f(t + n, T - n)$, we obtain

$$f(t + n, T - n)\left(\frac{T - n}{360}\right) = \frac{1 + i(t, T)(T/360)}{1 + i(t, n)(n/360)} - 1. \tag{13.2}$$

Recognizing that $1/[1 + i(t,T)(T/360)]$ is just the price of a discount bond $B(t,T)$, equation (13.1) may be written in the simple reciprocal form

$$B(t, T) = B(t, n)H(t + n, T - n) \tag{13.3}$$

where

$$H(t + n, T - n) = 1/[1 + f(t + n, T - n)((T - n)/360)]$$

is the implied forward bond price.

EXAMPLE 13.1

Consider interest rates and maturities as follows:

T (days)	i (per annum)	B
182	.1038	.9501
367	.1050	.9033

From equation (13.3), the implied forward bond price $H(t + 182, 185)$ is:

$$(.9033) = (.9501) H(t + 182, 185)$$

or

$$H(t + 182, 185) = .9507.$$

Alternatively, the implied forward interest rate may be calculated from equation (13.1) as:

$$1 + (.1050)(367/360) = [1 + (.1038)(182/360)][1 + f(t + 182, 185)(185/360)]$$

or

$$f(t + 182, 185) = .1009.$$

The implied forward rate is easily interpreted. In Example 13.1, the implied forward rate was .1009, or 10.09 percent. This means that if you invested in 182-day deposits at a rate of 10.38 percent and then reinvested the deposit with interest for another 185 days at the implied forward rate of 10.09 percent, your final return at the end of 367 days would be the same as if you invested at the 367-day rate of 10.50 percent. Alternatively, if you borrowed for 367 days at a rate of 10.50 percent, invested the money for 182 days at a rate of 10.38 percent, and then reinvested again for 185 days at a rate of 10.09 percent, you would break even. This shows that *if you borrow long and lend short, you will break even if the loan is rolled over at the implied forward rate*. The same is true if you borrow short and lend long: *If you borrow short and lend long, you will break even if you refund the loan by borrowing again at the implied forward rate*.

On the other hand, if market interest rates at time $t + n$, for maturity at time $t + T$, were *different* from the implied forward rate, then borrowing short and lending long will earn a profit or a loss. If you were borrowing short and lending long, you would earn a profit if you refunded the loan at a rate below the implied forward rate and a loss if you refunded the loan at a rate above the implied forward rate. If you were borrowing long and lending short, you would earn a profit if you rolled over the loan at a rate above the implied forward rate and a loss if you rolled over the loan at a rate below the implied forward rate.

We see that the interest risk associated with maturity transformation is a consequence of the fact that actual short-term market rates may be different from implied forward rates. We can thus characterize maturity transformation in the form of a bet on interest rates. *Borrowing short and lending long represents a bet that actual short-term market rates will turn out to be below the implied forward rate.* Similarly, *borrowing long and lending short represents a bet that actual short-term market rates will turn out to be above the implied forward rate.* The nature of these bets suggests that implied forward interest rates should be related to interest rate expectations.

It is tempting to equate the implied forward rate $f(t + n, T - n)$ with the expected short-term interest rate that will prevail at time $t + n$. That is, if $I(M,t)$ is the market information set at time t, one possibility is that

$$f(t + n, T - n) = E[i(t + n, T - n)|I(M, t)]. \tag{13.4}$$

Equation (13.4) represents the *expectations theory of the term structure*. The expectations theory should be considered a purely empirical proposition, in the same way that the speculative efficiency hypothesis discussed in Chapter 7 is a purely empirical proposition. That is, equation (13.4) is not necessarily a consequence of economic maximization or of rational behavior, for reasons similar to those that allow the forward exchange rate to diverge from the expected spot rate. However, equation (13.4) is a useful reference case for thinking about interest risk in eurobanking. To the extent that maturity transformation can be considered as a pure gamble on interest rates, equation (13.4) defines a condition of zero expected profit.

In certain circumstances, the implied forward rates can be used as a basis for pure arbitrage transactions. If an actual forward rate can be locked in in such a way that there is a total net profit on the borrowing or lending transaction, there will be no risk or gamble associated with the unknown market interest rate that will occur in the future. Two ways in which it may be possible to establish a locked-in forward interest rate are through eurodollar futures contracts (discussed in the next chapter) or through forward rate agreements (FRAs).

FORWARD RATE AGREEMENTS (FRAs)

Under a forward rate agreement, two parties—one the buyer and the other the seller—contract whereby the seller will pay the buyer the increased interest cost on a nominal sum of money if interest rates rise above the agreed rate, but the buyer will pay the seller the increased interest cost if interest rates fall below the agreed rate. For example, it might be an agreement on a three-month interest rate for a three-month period beginning six months from the present and terminating nine months from the present. Such an agreement, if made today, would be called "six against nine." The contract would be settled in cash at the beginning of the FRA period.

Let A = the agreed rate (expressed as a decimal), S = settlement rate,

N = nominal contract amount, dtm = days in the FRA period, and $year$ = year basis (360 or 365). Then if $S > A$, the seller pays the buyer:

$$\frac{N \times (S - A) \times dtm/year}{1 + S \times dtm/year}. \tag{13.5}$$

If $S < A$, then the buyer pays the seller the absolute value of the above amount. Note that because cash settlement is made at the beginning of the FRA period, the denominator discounts the payment back to that point.

To summarize: An FRA is a cash-settled interbank forward contract on the interest rate.

EXAMPLE 13.2

A bank buys a "three against six" FRA for $2,000,000 for a three-month period, beginning three months from now and ending six months from now, at an interest rate of 7.5 percent. There are actually ninety-one days in the FRA period.

Three months from now, at the beginning of the FRA period, the interest rate is 9 percent. The bank receives *cash* at the *beginning* of the FRA-period from the selling party in the amount of

$$\$2,000,000 \times \frac{(.09 - .075)(91/360)}{1 + .09(91/360)} = \$7414.65.$$

Note that the cash payment is discounted by the market interest rate (9 percent) for ninety-one days because that is the length of the FRA period.

The bank's net borrowing cost on $2,000,000 at the *end* of the FRA period is therefore:

$$
\begin{array}{lll}
 & \$2,000,000 \times .09 \times 91/360 & = \$45,500.00 \\
\text{minus} & \$\ \ 7414.65 \times (1 + .09 \times 91/360) & = -\ 7,583.33 \\
 & \text{Net borrowing cost} & = \$37,916.67.
\end{array}
$$

The net borrowing cost is equivalent to borrowing $2,000,000 at 7.5 percent since

$$\$2,000,000 \times .075 \times 91/360 = \$37,916.67.$$

FRAs are usually traded for dates between one of the standard eurodeposit maturities, such as three, six, nine, and twelve months, but nonstandard dates are available. FRAs are off-balance sheet items and have smaller capital requirements than interbank loans. Hence FRAs are regularly used to close maturity gaps in a eurobank's balance sheet.

An FRA is an interbank-traded equivalent of the implied forward rate calculated in equation (13.2). To see this, consider how one would construct FRA bid and asked rates by reference to interbank bid and asked rates on eurocurrency deposits. To construct a quote to lend (sell) a "three against six" FRA, conceptually borrow interbank for six months at the six-month asked rate, lend interbank for three months at the three-month bid rate, and contract to lend again by selling (lending) an FRA for the second three-month period. The FRA lending (selling) rate has to be high enough to yield a profit on the total transaction. It has to be higher than the implied forward rate calculated from the six-month asked rate and the three-month bid rate.

To construct a quote to borrow (buy) "three against six" FRA, conceptually lend interbank for six months at the six-month bid rate. Fund the loan by borrowing for three months at the three-month asked rate, and contract to borrow (buy) again via the FRA for the second three-month period. Your FRA borrowing (buying) rate has to be low enough to yield a profit on the total transaction. It has to be lower than the implied forward rate constructed from the six-month bid rate and the three-month asked rate.

EXAMPLE 13.3

On September 24, a eurobanker wants $100 million of six-month deposits but is only offered $100 million of nine-month deposits by a customer at the bank's bid rate. At the current market, the other rates are these:

	Cash			FRA	
	bid	asked		bid	asked
6 months	$10\frac{7}{16}$	$10\frac{9}{16}$	6 against 9	10.48	10.58
9 months	$10\frac{9}{16}$	$10\frac{11}{16}$			

What decision does the eurobanker make?

The banker converts the nine-month deposit to a six-month deposit by selling a six against nine FRA. That is, he sells off (lends) the last three months of the deposit in the FRA market. The built-in profit spread on this transaction, assuming it was done at the market rates above, will be as follows.

There are 273 days from settlement of the deposit on September 26 to maturity on June 26. The three-month FRA period is 92 days from March 26 to June 26. The interest paid at the end of nine months to the depositor is:

$100 million $\times$ $(.10\frac{9}{16})$ $\times$ (273/360) = $8,009,895.83.

Interest earned on lending for six months in the interbank market, then another three months at the FRA rate is:

$100 million $\times$ [(1 + $(.10\frac{7}{16})$ $\times$ (181/360)) $\times$
(1 + .1048 $\times$ (92/360)) − 1] = $8,066,511.50.

There is thus a net profit of $56,615.67 at the end of nine months. Note that this profit is possible because the bank was offered a nine-month deposit at the bank's *bid* rate of $10\frac{9}{16}$ percent. Arbitrage is not, however, possible at the given market rates, because the bank would ordinarily have to borrow for nine months in the interbank market at $10\frac{11}{16}$ percent. In that case the interest paid on the deposit would be $8,104,687.50, and the bank would incur a loss.

THE STRIP YIELD CURVE

Suppose we take a piece of time and divide it into parts. For example, divide a year into months. To each month assign an interest rate to be paid over that month. Then, to compute the interest to be paid over a three-month period—

say August, September, October—compound the monthly rates for those months. To compute the interest to be paid over a year, compound the twelve monthly rates. To compute the term structure for month m, compound the first m terms. Then the monthly segments, along with the associated monthly yields, would be known as a *strip yield curve*. We can also construct a strip yield curve from other length segments.

The strips in the strip yield curve may be compounded to give the term structure of interest rates. We can also work backwards: Given a term structure, we can solve for the strip yield curve that underlies it. The strip yield for month 3, for example, is just the implied forward rate calculated from the yields on two- and three-month deposits.

EXAMPLE 13.4

Consider the following interest rates:

three-month cash deposits	8.0%
three against six FRA	8.0%
six against nine FRA	8.25%
nine against twelve FRA	8.25%

These rates constitute a strip yield curve, where the strips are each three months in length. For example, if we (fictitiously) assume each time interval is ninety days, then the rate for the first six months is

$$(360/180) \times [(1 + .08 \times 90/360) (1 + .08 \times 90/360) - 1] = .0808 = 8.08\%.$$

This example shows that FRAs may be hooked end-to-end to form pieces of a strip yield curve. In the next chapter we will see that three-month eurodollar futures constitute a strip yield curve for March–June, June–September, September–December, December–March. Hence there is an intimate association between dollar FRAs and eurodollar futures prices. The latter are the benchmark to which interbank FRAs trade.

PROBLEMS FOR CHAPTER 13

1. The central bank of Erewhon makes a forward market for Erewhon's currency, the wawa. The current bid/asked quote for 360-day forward wawas is $4.10–$4.30/wawa, while the spot wawa is $4.35–$4.45/wawa. A trader decides to create a loan of eurowawas. The trader observes that the current bid/asked quote for eurodollars is $9\frac{1}{2}$–$9\frac{5}{8}$. Given this information—and assuming no default risk on the part of the borrower—the trader will be willing to loan 360-day eurowawas at any interest rate above what level?

2. If 183-day eurodollar deposits bear an interest rate of $10\frac{3}{8}$ percent and 270-day eurodollar deposits bear an interest rate of $10\frac{1}{2}$ percent, what is the implied forward rate? What is the significance of this implied forward rate for a bank that is borrowing short and lending long in the interbank market?

3. A bank sells a "three against twelve" FRA for $1 million at a rate of 8 percent. In three months the FRA settles at 8.47 percent. There are 273 days in the FRA period.

How much cash does the bank pay or receive? What is the bank's effective lending rate for the 273-day period?

4. If the bid/asked rate on six-month (183-day) deposits is $10\frac{1}{4}$–$10\frac{3}{8}$ percent, while it is $10\frac{1}{2}$–$10\frac{5}{8}$ percent on nine-month (270-day) deposits, give the profitable ranges of bid or asked prices that the bank could quote its customers for a six against nine FRA.

EUROCURRENCY FUTURES AND OPTIONS

Eurocurrency futures contracts are traded at exchanges around the world. In the early 1990s, contracts included DIBOR (at the Irish Futures and Options Exchange in Dublin), PIBOR (at MATIF in Paris), the euromark (at MATIF and at LIFFE in London), HIBOR (at the Hong Kong Futures Exchange), euroyen (at the Tokyo International Financial Futures Exchange, TIFFE, and the Singapore International Monetary Exchange, SIMEX), MIBOR (at the Mercado Español de Futuros Financieros, MEFF, in Barcelona), eurosterling (at LIFFE, the London International Financial Futures Exchange), eurodollars (at the Chicago Mercantile Exchange, LIFFE, SIMEX, and TIFFE), and the ECU (at LIFFE). Table 14.1 lists the principal contracts ranked by volume of trading.

In this chapter we will focus on the three-month eurodollar future at the International Money Market (IMM) of the Chicago Mercantile Exchange (CME) in Chicago. This market provides some of the key reference rates for worldwide interbank trading in eurodollars. The principles illustrated apply also to other eurocurrency contracts. Eurodollar futures contracts are like currency and other futures contracts (see Chapter 5) in that the contract, considered by itself in isolation from other assets, is a pure bet. In this case, the bet concerns the direction of movements of a futures price related to the interest paid on eurodollar deposits. As with other futures contracts, there are two sides to the bet. If the price goes up, the *long* side wins and the *short* side loses. The reverse happens if the price goes down.

The eurodollar futures price is based on three-month LIBOR, the offered interest rate for three-month eurodollar deposits (for forward delivery) with a face value of $1,000,000. The interest rate on a (forward) three-month eurodollar deposit is, like all eurodollar deposit rates, quoted at an annual rate. The eurodollar futures price is defined to be:

100 − (the interest rate, in percentage terms, of a three-month eurodollar deposit for forward delivery).

TABLE 14.1
Principal Eurocurrency Contracts in 1990

Interest Rate	Exchange	Location	Volume, Jan.–June 1990
Eurodollar	CME	Chicago	16,601,033
Euroyen	TIFFE	Tokyo	12,311,388
Eurosterling	LIFFE	London	4,221,741
Eurodollar	SIMEX	Singapore	1,545,866
Euromark	LIFFE	London	1,465,008
Eurofranc	MATIF	Paris	1,077,603
Eurodollar	LIFFE	London	658,973
Euromark	MATIF	Paris	359,730
Euroyen	SIMEX	Singapore	305,645

Source: Futures and Options World.

For example, if the interest rate on the forward three-month deposit is 10.36 percent, the eurodollar futures price is

$$100 - 10.36 = 89.64.$$

Notice what this means. If *interest rates go up,* the eurodollar *futures price goes down,* so the short side of the futures contract makes money. If *interest rates go down,* the eurodollar *futures price goes up,* so the long side of the futures contract makes money. Thus a speculator would go long futures if he or she was betting that interest rates would fall and short if he or she was betting that rates would rise.

Since the face value of the contract is $1,000,000, one basis point (.01 percent) has a value of $100 for a 360-day deposit. For a three-month deposit, the value of one basis point is thus logically $25, and the futures exchanges define a one-basis-point move in the price in terms of a $25 transfer between the long and the short position. For example, if the futures price drops from 88.15 to 88.13, then the short side gains $50 (2 × $25), while the long side loses $50. The futures price is determined in the market minute by minute as the price at which the number of people (measured by contracts) who want to go long is equal to the number of people who want to go short.

At all exchanges eurodollar futures are traded for delivery in March, June, September, and December. That is, if one were to take delivery on a March eurodollar futures contract, then the three-month period for the deposit would begin counting from the day of delivery in March. Delivery at the IMM is hypothetically made on the third Wednesday of the month. The last day of trading is two business days prior to the third Wednesday.

In eurodollar (as well as other eurocurrency) contracts, delivery is only "in cash." What this means is that no eurodollar deposit is actually delivered on the IMM (or any other) eurodollar futures contract. Instead, at the end of the final day of trading on the second business day prior to the third Wednesday there occurs the usual daily cash flow, based on the movement of the futures price. After that, nothing happens. The futures contract ceases to exist and no further transfers, of cash or anything else, take place.

The IMM forces the eurodollar futures price to converge to the spot price by the way the exchange determines the settlement price on the final day of trading. The IMM keeps a list of at least twenty London banks that deal in eurodollar deposits. On the last day of trading for a particular contract, they take a sample of twelve of these banks and obtain their quotations for three-month LIBOR. The two highest and two lowest quotations are thrown out, and the other eight quotations are averaged to obtain the three-month offered rate. This sampling of twelve banks is done twice: once at 3:30 P.M. London time and also at a random time interval in the last ninety minutes of trading. The two samplings yield two values for the three-month offered rate (each value an average of eight bank quotations). The arithmetic average of these two values is the final settlement price on the final day of trading.

The following are prices on the December 1990 IMM eurodollar futures contract as quoted in the *Wall Street Journal* on September 4, 1990.

	Open	High	Low	Settle	Change	Yield
December	92.08	92.11	92.05	92.08	+.07	7.92

The "open" price of 92.08 was the market-determined price at which a contract traded (someone going long, someone going short) when the market opened at the beginning of the day. Sometime during the day a trade took place at 92.11, and this was the high price of the day. Similarly, the low price at which a trade took place was 92.05. The final settlement price for the day was 92.08, which was seven basis points higher ("change" = + .07) than the previous day's settlement price. That is, between the close of each of the two days, those with long positions had their account balances increased by (credited with) \$175 (7 × \$25), while those with short positions had their account balances decreased (debited) by \$175. The "yield" is an unnecessary column, since the 7.92 percent interest rate on three-month eurodollars can be obtained as

$$100 - 92.08 = 7.92.$$

THE EURODOLLAR STRIP YIELD CURVE AND THE IMM SWAP

Successive eurodollar futures give rise to a strip yield curve. The March future involves a three-month rate of interest that begins in March and ends in June. The June future involves a three-month rate of interest that begins in June and ends in September. And so on. To be sure, there are some holes in the curve so defined: Between the third Wednesday of March and the third Wednesday of June there will be 91 or 98 days (multiples of 7). But the eurodollar futures only cover 90 of these days. Hence one eurodollar future does not quite hedge \$1 million for the complete three months. However, the approximation is close.

If we compound the interest rates for four successive eurodollar contracts, we define a one-year rate composed from the four three-month rates. Obviously the one-year rate so constructed cannot differ much from the implied forward rate for the same period (say the implied forward rate from March of one year to March of the next) without giving rise to arbitrage opportunities.

In Chapter 19 we will discuss interest rate swaps, which involve a trade of fixed-rate interest for floating-rate interest. An "IMM swap" involves a trade whereby one party receives one-year fixed interest and makes floating payments of three-months LIBOR. The payment dates in an IMM swap correspond to the eurodollar futures expiration dates. Thus, on August 15, one might do a September–September swap. The floating-rate payer would make payments on the third Wednesday in December (at the three-month rate effective from the third Wednesday of the previous September), as well as on the third Wednesdays of the following March, June, and September. The fixed-rate payer would make a single payment on the last of these dates. The IMM swap does not involve futures contracts. However, because the floating payment dates correspond to IMM settlement dates, arbitrage ensures that the one-year fixed rate of interest in the IMM swap does not diverge materially from the one-year rate constructed from the eurodollar strip yield curve. Some divergence, however, is mandated by the fact that the actual number of days in each strip differs from the ninety days assumed in the eurodollar futures contract.

HEDGING WITH EURODOLLAR FUTURES

Several factors must always be kept in mind when hedging with eurodollar or other interest-rate futures.

Amount: A eurodollar futures contract involves a face amount of $1 million. Thus to hedge a $10 million dollar borrowing for three months, we would need ten futures contracts.

Duration: Duration measures the time at which cash flows take place. For money market instruments, all cash flows generally take place at the maturity of the instrument, so duration is synonymous with time-to-maturity. A six-month deposit has approximately twice the duration of a three-month deposit. The value of one basis point (.0001) paid on $1 million for three months is approximately $25, while the value of a basis point for six months is approximately $50. Thus one would need two eurodollar contracts to hedge a six-month deposit. One could hedge a $1 million six-month deposit beginning in March with two March eurodollar futures. This would be an example of a *stack hedge*. One could also hedge a $1 million six-month deposit beginning in March with one March eurodollar future and one June eurodollar future. The latter would be a *strip hedge*.

Slope: Eurodollar contracts may be used to hedge other interest rate assets and liabilities, such as T-bills, commercial paper, banker's acceptances, etc. The rates on these instruments may not be expected to change one-for-one with eurodollar interest rates. If we define f as the interest rate in a eurodollar futures contract, then

$$\text{slope} = \frac{\Delta \text{ underlying interest rate}}{\Delta f}.$$

Thus if the rate of change of T-bill rates with respect to eurodollar rates is .9 (slope = .9), then we would only need nine eurodollar futures contracts to hedge $10 million of three-month T-bills.

Let F_A and D_A be the face amount and duration in days of the underlying asset to be hedged. Then the number n of eurodollar futures needed to hedge is

$$n = \frac{F_A}{1,000,000} \times \frac{D_A}{90} \times \text{slope}.$$

To hedge $10 million of 270-day commercial paper with a slope of .935 would require approximately twenty-eight contracts ($n = 10 \times (270/90) \times .935$).

Margin: Eurodollar futures require a deposit of initial margin. In September 1990, this was typically around $800 per contract, while maintenance margin was $600. There is an interest charge associated with the use of initial margin. In addition, hedges that generate positive cash flows on the eurodollar futures hedge will benefit through the extra interest that can be earned on the reinvestment of the variation margin. Hedges generating negative cash flows have a corresponding additional interest charge.

Variation margin flows confer an advantage to the hedger who is short eurodollar futures. If interest rates rise there is a positive variation margin flow on the short futures position, and in addition the variation margin may be *invested* overnight at a *higher* interest rate. If interest rates fall, there is a negative variation margin flow, but the variation margin may be *financed* at a *lower* interest rate.

With these basics in mind, we now consider the use of eurodollar futures to hedge *gap* risk. Gap risk arises in eurobanking when assets and liabilities have different maturities. Such gaps tend to be managed with futures, FRAs, and interest rate swaps because these use less capital than do time deposits.

EXAMPLE 14.1

On June 12 a bank observes a rate of 10 percent on three-month eurodollar deposits in the interbank market. If a $1,000,000 deposit is borrowed today, the value date will be June 16, and the deposit will mature on September 16, a total of ninety-two days. The bank also observes that it can lend a six-month eurodollar deposit at $10\frac{13}{16}$ percent. If lent today, the value date will be June 16, and the deposit will mature on December 16, a total of 183 days. Meanwhile, September eurodollar futures are trading at 89.23 (10.77 percent). Taken together, these prices imply the bank can lend a six-month deposit, funding this loan by a sequence of two three-month deposits, and be assured of a profit for the six months.

Consider the bank's problem. If it lends for six months, it will receive interest at an annual rate of $10\frac{13}{16}$ percent. But for the first three months it will only pay interest on its borrowed three-month deposit at an annual rate of 10 percent. However, there is the risk that when the three-month deposit is rolled over after three months, the market interest rate on three-month deposits will have risen. Let us first calculate the implied forward rate f, as this is the rate the bank can afford to pay on the second three-month deposit and still break even on the total transaction:

$$1 + (.10\tfrac{13}{16})(183/360) = (1 + .10(92/360))(1 + f(91/360))$$

or

$$f = 11.34\%$$

Thus, as long as the bank can ensure that it will pay a rate *less* than 11.34 percent for the second three-month period, the bank will make a profit. But September eurodollar futures are at 10.77 percent. So by going *short* one September contract at 89.23 (10.77 percent), the bank will ensure that, if interest rates rise, the bank will have a positive cash flow that will offset the cost of borrowing above 10.77 percent for the second three months. Since the bank will make money at any rate less than 11.34 percent, it will ensure a profit on the six-month loan through the futures hedge.

More realistically, Example 14.1 can be taken as a quasi-arbitrage opportunity in that a bank that deals in the interbank market may assign a trader to arbitrage between the eurodollar deposit market and the eurodollar futures market. The trader will then be continually comparing rates in the interbank market with rates on eurodollar futures and will be looking for opportunities like the one given in Example 14.1. To do this correctly, he must make the calculations more exact than those in Example 14.1.

In the previous chapter, we saw that the cash flow in an FRA was discounted by the length of the FRA period, because the cash flow was paid at the beginning of the period. In addition, the FRA period has the same number of days as there are between settlement dates for eurodollar deposits. The number of days may be eighty-nine, ninety, ninety-one, ninety-two, etc., between three- and six-month deposits. But a eurodollar future's cash flow is based on exactly ninety days and is not discounted to the beginning of the period. For these reasons, the interest rate on eurodollar futures cannot be identified with the implied forward rate used to calculate break-even loan costs. The FRA rate, by contrast, is the same as the implied forward rate. For hedging purposes, therefore, we must calculate a hedge ratio for eurodollar futures against FRA's. (For simplicity, we will omit the interest opportunity cost associated with the daily cash flows on the futures contract. Example 5.1 and (14.3a) show the additional adjustment required when the timing of the cash flows on the future and the forward differ.)

The cash flow (ΔV) to the buyer of a dollar FRA is given by the equation (review 13.5):

$$\Delta V = \frac{N(S - A)(dtm/360)}{1 + S(dtm/360)}. \tag{14.1}$$

If we let $A = 1 - .01Z(t)$ also denote the forward interest rate at which a eurodollar future was opened (e.g., 0.09 for a futures price of 91.00), and let $S = 1 - .01Z(t + 1)$ also denote the forward interest rate at which the eurodollar futures price was closed out, then

$$
\begin{aligned}
S - A &= (1 - .01Z(t + 1)) - (1 - .01Z(t)) \\
&= .01(Z(t) - Z(t + 1)) \\
&= - .01\Delta Z.
\end{aligned}
$$

Therefore the corresponding cash flow on a eurodollar futures contract (where $N = 1,000,000$, $dtm = 90$) is

$$
\begin{aligned}
\Delta V &= - 1,000,000(.01\Delta Z)(90/360) \\
&= - 2500\Delta Z.
\end{aligned} \tag{14.2}
$$

Therefore the number of eurodollar futures contracts b needed to hedge an FRA or the implied forward rate is the ratio of (14.1) to (14.2):

$$
\begin{aligned}
b &= \frac{N}{250,000(S + 360/dtm)} \\
&= \frac{N}{250,000(1 + 360/dtm - .01Z(t + 1))}.
\end{aligned} \tag{14.3}
$$

The hedge ratio depends on the current eurodollar futures price $Z(t + 1)$. Note that if the forward interest rate were zero ($Z(t + 1) = 100$) and if the days in the FRA period were 90 ($dtm = 90$), and if the dollar amount of the FRA were $N = 1,000,000$, then $b = 1$. The number of eurodollar futures contracts needed to hedge an FRA goes down as the discount rate S increases (as the current futures price $Z(t + 1)$ decreases).

EXAMPLE 14.2

There are ninety-one days in an FRA period beginning at the expiration of a eurodollar contract. The current price of the futures is 92.00. What amount of the FRA hedges a short position in 100 eurodollar contracts?

In this example, the eurodollar hedge ratio b is prespecified as $b = -100$. Therefore we only need to calculate N from equation (14.3):

$$N = -100 \times 250,000(1 + 360/91 - .01(92.00))$$
$$= -\$100,901,099.$$

Against the short position of 100 eurodollar futures contracts, the trader should *sell* an FRA in the amount of \$100,901,099. To verify this answer, suppose that interest rates fall by 1 basis point (.0001). Then, since rates go from 8.00 to 7.99, the cash flow to the seller of the FRA is

$$\Delta V = \frac{\$100,901,099(.0001)(91/360)}{1 + .0799(91/360)} = \$2500.$$

The cash flow on the short eurodollar futures position is

$$\Delta V = 100 \times 2500(92.00 - 92.01) = -\$2500.$$

For these value changes to remain equal and offsetting, however, the amount of the FRA would have to be continually adjusted because b changes with the current futures price. For example, suppose b were left unchanged in the original position. Then for a drop of 1 percent (100 basis points) from 8.00 to 7.00, the cash flow to the FRA seller is:

$$\Delta V = \frac{\$100,901,099(.01)(91/360)}{1 + .07(91/360)} = \$250,621.$$

The cash flow on the short futures position is:

$$\Delta V = 100 \times \$2500(92.00 - 93.00) = -\$250,000.$$

The total position has a net gain of \$621. For the same reason, if interest rates rise by 1 percent (100 basis points) from 8.00 to 9.00, the FRA seller has a cash flow of

$$\Delta V = \frac{\$100,901,099(-.01)(91/360)}{1 + .09(91/360)} = -\$249,382.$$

while on the short futures position

$$\Delta V = 100 \times \$2500(92.00 - 91.00) = \$250,000.$$

The total position has a net gain of \$618. Thus the position of being short eurodollar futures and selling FRAs, at the fixed ratio b, makes money for interest rate moves in either direction. In Chapter 6 we characterized such a position in terms of options as a delta-neutral, long-gamma position. It is partially equivalent to being long eurodollar straddles. (A straddle is a long call and a long put on the interest rate or on the eurodollar futures price.)

EXAMPLE 14.3

In Example 14.1 we compared the implied forward rate to the eurodollar futures price, and determined that the eurobank could hedge its funding gap in the futures market at a profit. Suppose the bank wants to hedge $50,000,000. How many futures contracts should it go short?

Since the futures price is $Z(t + 1) = 89.23$, the number of contracts to sell is given by equation (14.3) as

$$b = \frac{50,000,000}{250,000(1 + 360/91 - .01(89.23))} \cong 49.$$

To verify this answer, suppose that when the three-month deposit is rolled over, three-month rates have risen to 12 percent. Then the bank's repayment at the end of the six-month period is

$50,000,000(1 + .10(92/360))(1 + .12(91/360)) = \$52,833,203.75.$

The bank will receive on its six-month loan

$50,000,000(1 + .10\frac{13}{18}(183/360)) = \$52,748,177.10.$

The cash flow on the short eurodollar futures position will be, once it is reinvested for ninety-one days at 12 percent:

$49 \times \$2500 \times (89.23 - 88) \times (1 + .12(91/360)) = \$155,245.48.$

The bank will thus pay out as interest $2,833,203.75 and receive in return $2,748,177.10 + $155,245.48 = $2,903,422.58.

On the other hand, if rates have fallen to 10 percent when the three-month deposit is rolled over, the bank's repayment will be

$50,000,000(1 + .10(92/360))(1 + .10(91/360)) = \$52,573,966.05.$

The cash flow on the short eurodollar futures position will be, along with the interest charge for an additional ninety-one days at 10 percent:

$49 \times \$2500 \times (89.23 - 90)(1 + .10(91/360)) = -\$96,709.33.$

The bank will, in this case, pay out as interest $2,573,966.05 and receive in return $2,748,177.10 - $96,709.33 = $2,651,467.78.

At the end of the period, the bank makes approximately $77,000 if rates fall to 10 percent, or approximately $70,000 if rates rise to 12 percent.

As noted previously, the hedge ratio b given by (14.3) does not take into consideration the variation margin flows on the eurodollar contract. Since variation margin must be paid in cash, there is in most circumstances an interest cost associated with the need to borrow negative variation margin flows, or an interest profit to be earned on positive variation margin flows. To adjust the futures position for this interest rate effect (a process called *tailing*), we discount the cash flows on the FRA from now to the *beginning* of the FRA period. That is, we present value the FRA cash flows to make them comparable to the eurodollar futures cash flows.

Let i be the relevant discount rate from now to the beginning of the FRA period, which occurs in T days. (In Examples 14.1 and 14.3, $i = 10$ percent and

$T = 92$ days.) Then, from (14.3), the adjusted futures hedge ratio (b^*) is

$$b^* = \frac{1}{1 + i(T/360)}\, b. \tag{14.3a}$$

Then as $T \to 0$, $b^* \to b$. In Example 14.3, this adjustment implies an initial position of approximately 48 contracts, which would be increased to 49 contracts as $T \to 0$.

The calculations associated with the FRA/eurodollar hedge ratio become more complicated once we allow for the general case that the FRA periods and eurodollar futures periods do not correspond. Because the eurodollar futures market is more liquid than the FRA market, an FRA period that overlaps two or more eurodollar futures periods would result in the FRA rate being calculated by an interpolation of the rates implied in the futures contracts. In addition, the hedge for the FRA would be split up among the eurodollar futures used in the interpolation.

INTEREST RATE AND EURODOLLAR FUTURES OPTIONS

Options on eurodollar futures are traded at the IMM, LIFFE, and SIMEX. An IMM eurodollar futures *call* gives the buyer the right to go long an IMM eurodollar futures contract, while a eurodollar futures *put* gives the buyer the right to go short. More specifically, an IMM eurodollar put is a contract between a buyer and a writer whereby the put buyer pays a price (the put premium) to the writer in order to acquire the right, but not the obligation, to go short one IMM eurodollar futures contract at the opening price given by the put's strike price. If the put buyer exercises the right to go short, the put writer must go long the eurodollar contract. Once option trades have cleared, the IMM Clearing House becomes the writer to every other option buyer, and the buyer to every other option writer. The options are American and expire on the last trade date for the futures contract. What this means is, since the futures contract is settled in cash, the option on futures is also settled in cash if it is exercised on the last trade date. Prior to this date, however, exercise results in a long or short futures position.

Eurodollar futures option premium quotations are in percentage points, with each basis point representing $25. For example, a price of .68 would represent $25 \times 68 = \$1700$. Strike prices are in intervals of .25 in terms of the IMM index. Thus, one may buy a put on March eurodollar futures with a strike of 89.75. If exercised, it gives the right to go short one IMM eurodollar futures contract at an opening price of 89.75.

EXAMPLE 14.4

A trader goes short a June eurodollar future at a price $Z = 93.99$, simultaneously buying a June call with a strike $X = 93.75$. The premium on the call is $C = .50$. Calculate the payoffs on the last day of trading, thirty days from today, for each of the following possible prices for the expiring future: 93.00, 93.75, 94.50, 95.00. (Assume a spot interest rate of 6 percent.)

The call premium paid today is $25 \times 50 = \$1250$. Adding the 6 percent carrying charge for thirty days gives $\$1250(1 + .06(30/360)) = \$1256.25$ at option expiration. If the future expires at 93.00, the payoff will be 93.99 − 93.00 = .99 or $2475. The call will expire worthless, so the net payoff on the position is $2475 − $1256.25 = $1218.75.

More quickly, if we ignore the carrying charge of $6.25 on the option premium, the net payoff in percent is 93.99 − 93.00 − .50 = .49, for a value of $25 × 49 = $1225. This table ignores the carrying charge:

Futures Price	Futures Payoff	Call Payoff	Option Cost	Total	$ Total
93.00	.99	0	.50	.49	$1225
93.75	.24	0	.50	− .26	− $ 650
94.50	− .51	.75	.50	− .26	− $ 650
95.00	− 1.01	1.25	.50	− .26	− $ 650

By buying the call, the trader has limited his possible loss on the future to 26 basis points or $650. This amount can be calculated as $Z − X − C = 93.99 − 93.75 − .50 = − .26$.

How should eurodollar futures options be priced? The key lies with the forward interest rate f embodied in the futures price. In Chapter 6, we introduced an option-pricing model for foreign exchange rates under the assumption the spot or forward rate was lognormally distributed (i.e., the log of the rate had a normal distribution). We can make a similar assumption for the forward interest rate involved in a eurodollar future or in an FRA. (As with foreign exchange rates, this assumption is a convenient simplifying fiction, because interest rates, like exchange rates, exhibit leptokurtosis: There are too many small changes and very large changes relative to intermediate size changes for interest rates to really have a true normal distribution.)

Thus if we substitute the forward interest (or FRA) rate f for the forward exchange rate F, then equations (6.22) and (6.13) give us the value of a European call on the forward interest rate f:

$$c(t) = B(t,T)[fN(d1) − XN(d2)], \qquad (14.4)$$

$$d1 = \frac{ln(f/X) + .5v^2T}{v \sqrt{T}}$$

$$d2 = \frac{ln(f/X) − .5v^2T}{v \sqrt{T}}.$$

TABLE 14.2
Value of European Options on Forward Interest Rates

		Calls			Puts		
	f:	7.5	8.0	8.5	7.5	8.0	8.5
X:	7.0	.541	.988	1.471	.051	.008	.001
	7.5	.218	.551	.992	.218	.060	.011
	8.0	.060	.233	.561	.551	.233	.071
	8.5	.011	.071	.248	.992	.561	.248
	9.0	.001	.015	.081	1.472	.995	.571

Assumptions: $v = .15$, $T = 90/365$, discount rate = 8 percent ($B = 98.039$), the option premium is paid today, and the cash value of the option payoff is paid at option expiration.

The European put price is obtained from the put-call conversion equation (6.19):

$$p = c + B[X - f]. \tag{14.5}$$

The latter equation shows the European put and call will have equal values when the forward interest (or FRA) rate is equal to the strike price. Table 14.2 gives some sample values for European options on interest rates. The following example shows how the values should be interpreted.

EXAMPLE 14.5

Consider the option in Table 14.2 with strike $X = 7.0$ and forward interest rate $f = 7.5$. It has a value of $c = .541$. What does this number mean?

Since X and f are in percent, the price c is also stated in percent. In order to translate this price to a dollar amount, we have to know the option size and the duration in days of the forward interest period. Suppose the option is based on three-month LIBOR and involves a nominal amount of $10 million. Suppose also there are ninety-two days in the three-month period. Then the dollar cost of the option is

$$.541 \times (1/100) \times (92/360) \times \$10 \text{ million} = \$13,825.56.$$

The values in Table 14.2 also assume that the option *premium* is paid *today*, and that the cash in the option *payoff* is received at option *expiration*, which is the *beginning* of the forward interest or FRA period. If either of these assumptions is false, there will have to be a further interest adjustment.

For example, suppose the cash in the option payoff will not be received until the *end* of the forward interest period (ninety-two days). Then the table value (for $X = 7.0$, $f = 7.5$) must be discounted by the forward interest rate $f = 7.5$ for ninety-two days:

$$.541/(1 + .075(92/360)) = .5308258.$$

This corresponds to an option premium of $13,565.55.

We now proceed to price options on eurodollar futures. Since the price of a eurodollar future Z may be written as

$$Z = 100 - f$$

we obtain, upon solving for f:

$$f = 100 - Z.$$

Note that

$$f \geq X \Rightarrow Z \leq 100 - X. \tag{14.6}$$

Thus a call on f, which pays off when $f > X$, is equivalent to a put on Z, which pays off when $Z < 100 - X$. For example, let $X = 6$. Then a call on the interest rate f has a positive exercise value when $f > 6$. But this is equivalent to the condition the eurodollar futures price $Z < 100 - 6 = 94$. So the value of a interest rate call with strike price 6 is equal to the value of a eurodollar futures put with strike price 94. To summarize:

The value of a call on the forward interest rate f with strike price X is equal to the value of a put on the eurodollar future $Z = 100 - f$ with strike price $100 - X$.

By similar reasoning:

The value of a put on the forward interest rate f with strike price X is equal to the value of a call on the eurodollar future $Z = 100 - f$ with strike price $100 - X$.

At the IMM, eurodollar options are American in style, so to price IMM eurodollar options we need to use the American counterparts to equations (14.4) and (14.5), which allow for early exercise of the option.

EXAMPLE 14.6

The eurodollar future is at 92.18. To obtain the value of a futures call with strike price of 92.25, we calculate $100 - 92.18 = 7.82$ and $100 - 92.25 = 7.75$. Thus the value of the eurodollar futures call is the value of an American put on the forward rate $f = 7.82$ with a strike price of $X = 7.75$.

Table 14.3 is the same as Table 14.2, except that eurodollar futures prices and strikes have been substituted for their interest rate equivalents, and the options are American instead of European. Thus the call value .541, corresponding to $X = 7.0$ and $f = 7.5$ in Table 14.2, should be compared to the put value .545, corresponding to $X = 93.0$ and $Z = 92.50$ in Table 14.3. The two numbers differ because .541 is the European value while .545 is the corresponding American value.

We assumed that f had a lognormal distribution. Hence f cannot be negative. This is plausible, since negative interest rates would imply you could receive interest for borrowing money—not a likely proposition. We could not, however, have made the same assumption about the eurodollar futures price Z. To assume Z was lognormal would imply that Z could take values greater than 100. But $Z > 100 \Rightarrow f < 0$. Hence the assumption that interest rates cannot be negative precludes the assumption that Z is lognormal. Therefore, we priced eurodollar futures options based on the distribution of f, not Z.

CAPS, FLOORS, AND COLLARS

Many financial contracts in the international money and capital markets are based on periodic, but variable or "floating," interest payments, such as six-month LIBOR. Parties to these contracts are at risk (as borrowers) if this

TABLE 14.3
Value of Eurodollar Futures Options

		Calls			Puts		
	Z:	91.50	92.00	92.50	91.50	92.00	92.50
X:	91.00	.575	1.007	1.500	.081	.015	.001
	91.50	.248	.564	1.004	.248	.071	.011
	92.00	.071	.233	.555	.564	.233	.061
	92.50	.011	.061	.219	1.004	.555	.219
	93.00	.001	.008	.051	1.500	1.002	.545

Assumptions: $v = .15$, $T = 90/365$, discount rate $= 8\%$ ($B = 98.039$).

series of interest payments rises dramatically. They might wish to "cap" interest rates so they do not rise above some tolerable ceiling (or *cap*) level. Others are at risk (as lenders) if the level of interest payments falls. The second group might wish to place a *floor* under interest rates, so they do not fall too low. Finally, both sides may together negotiate a *collar*, which is an arrangement involving both a long cap and a short floor (or vice versa). They may agree to cap six-month LIBOR at 9 percent, while placing a floor at 7.5 percent. If the cap level is low enough (say 8.25 percent) and the floor level is high enough (say also 8.25 percent), one is left with a fixed-rate contract. Caps, floors, and collars often arise in connection with interest rate swaps, covered in Chapter 19. Table 19.8 gives the sample terms of one interest rate collar.

Suppose a LIBOR borrower buys an interest rate cap of 9 percent on six-month LIBOR. The buyer of the cap might pay an up-front price for the cap, or negotiate other payment terms. Subsequently, when six-month LIBOR rises above 9 percent in any loan period, the cap buyer will be compensated for the increased interest cost. The interest cost is based on a nominal sum of money, say $10 million, which must be specified in the cap contract. Cap payments are made at the same time as interest payments would normally be made. For example, suppose the cap is for three years, with six-month LIBOR payments on January 30 and July 30. The market interest rate on the first six-month interval, from January 30 to July 30, is already known, and is typically excluded from the cap. But a new six-month interval will begin on July 30 and extend to the following January 30. The interest rate for this period will be fixed on July 30, but interest will be paid on the following January 30. If six-month LIBOR is fixed at 9.5 percent on July 30, then on the following January 30 (184 days later) the cap writer will pay the cap buyer.

$10 million × (9.5 − 9)/100 × (184/360) = $25,555.56.

The reader can easily see that a cap is a series of European call options on the interest rate, where the call strike price is the cap rate. The first option begins at the beginning of the cap period and expires on the first interest reset date. In the example of the previous paragraph, the first option begins on January 30 and expires on July 30 (a total of 181 days). The underlying variable in the option is the six-month implied forward (or FRA) rate from July 30 to the following January 30. The option expires on July 30 because the rate is set or determined on that date. But the cash value of the option will not be received for another 184 days (on the following January 30):

A floor is similarly a series of European put options on the interest rate, where the put strike price is the interest floor. A collar is a combination of calls and puts. If one is *long* the calls (cap) and *short* the puts (floor), then one has a series of range forward contracts (see Chapter 6). Hence a collar is a series of range forwards. If the strike prices are equal, one is left with a series of regular forwards or FRAs with the strike price as the agreed rate. If one is *long* the calls and *long* the puts, then one has a series of option "strangles" that profit from interest rate variation in either direction.

The following example shows how to value a cap as a series of options.

EXAMPLE 14.7

Consider a three-year interest rate cap of 8 percent on six-month LIBOR. The cap amount is $10 million. The cap trades on January 28 for effect on January 30. The LIBOR reset rates are determined on each July 28 and January 28, and take effect on July 30 and January 30. There are 181 days from January 30 to July 30 (182 on leap year) and 184 days from July 30 to January 30. At the time the cap is purchased, offered rates on time deposits are:

Period	Offered Rate
6 month	8
1 year	8.5
2 year	8.75
3 year	9

How should the cap be valued?

There are five options in the cap. The first six months' rate of interest is already determined at 8 percent. Option #1 is thus written on the second six-month period, and is an option on the implied forward or FRA rate between the six-month rate of 8 percent and the one-year rate of 8.5 percent. Calculating the implied forward rate from the formula $(1 + .08(181/360)) (1 + f (184/360)) = 1 + .085 (365/360)$ yields a value of $f = .08644$ or 8.644 percent. The option expires in six months, but does not settle (the cash flows are not made) until the end of the second six-month period, which is one year from today. So the discount rate on the option is 8.5 percent, the one-year interest. This gives a discount factor of $1 + .085(365/360) = 1.08618$.

The other forward (FRA) rates and discount factors may be calculated in a similar way.

Option #	Implied Forward Rate	Discount Factor
1	8.644	1.08618
2	8.803	1.13425
3	8.806	1.18530
4	9.281	1.24061
5	9.285	1.29949

The next step is to impute volatilities to each time period. Based on recent activity in the market for caps, these are assumed to rise over time to maturity from 15 to 17 percent.

We now have the information needed to price each option:

Option #	T · 365	f	X	v	B (adjusted)	Call Value	$ Amount
1	181	8.644	9	.150	1/1.08618	.203	$10,375.56
2	365	8.803	9	.155	1/1.13425	.403	$20,261.94
3	546	8.806	9	.160	1/1.18530	.507	$25,913.33
4	730	9.281	9	.165	1/1.24061	.804	$40,423.33
5	911	9.285	9	.170	1/1.29949	.866	$44,262.22
						Total:	$141,236.38

The first call has a value of .203. Since there are $365 - 181 = 184$ days in the interest period, this corresponds to a dollar amount of $(.203/100) \times (184/360) \times \$10$ million $= \$10,375.56$.

The total cost of this cap is $\$141,236.38$ or 1.41 percent of the $10 million nominal amount.

LIBOR OPTIONS AND FRAS

In Example 14.7, we made an interest adjustment to the price of the zero-coupon or discount bond price B to reflect the fact that each one of the series of call options involved in the interest rate cap expired at the beginning of the interest period, but the option payoff was only received at the end of the period. If the number of days in the period is dtm, then in the option formula (14.4) we replaced $B(t,T)$ with $B(t,T + dtm)$. Thus at option expiration, time $t + T$,

$$B(t + T, dtm) = \frac{1}{1 + f(dtm/360)} \qquad (14.7)$$

where f is the interest rate (here expressed as a decimal) fixed at time $t + T$. Thus if $f > X$, the call payoff, from (14.4), is

$$\frac{1}{1 + f(dtm/360)}(f - X). \qquad (14.8)$$

If we compare the payoff (14.8) with the value of an FRA, equation (13.5), we see they are the same, provided the option strike price X is the rate agreed (A) in the FRA. (Recall that the option payoff (14.8) will, as explained in Example 14.5, be adjusted for size (N) and the length of the interest period (dtm)). Similarly, if $f < X$, the call payoff will be zero, but the absolute value of (14.8) will be the payoff to the corresponding put.

Thus for LIBOR options involved in a cap, floor, or collar, we may replace equations (14.4), (14.5), with

$$c(t) = B(t, T + dtm)\,[fN(d1) - XN(d2)] \qquad (14.9)$$

and

$$p(t) = c(t) + B(t, T + dtm)\,[X - f] \qquad (14.10)$$

(The values of $d1$ and $d2$ remain unchanged.) Then if I go long a call and short a put, $c(t) - p(t)$, each with strike price X corresponding to the agreed rate in an FRA, the payoff at option expiration will be, by (14.7) and (14.10),

$$c(t) - p(t) = \frac{f - X}{1 + f(dtm/360)},$$

which is the payoff to the buyer of an FRA. To summarize:

Long a LIBOR call + Short a LIBOR put = FRA bought. $\qquad (14.12)$

Similarly,

Short a LIBOR call + Long a LIBOR put = FRA sold. $\qquad (14.13)$

Note that the equivalence is in terms of *value*. But the cash flow on an FRA is received at the beginning of the FRA period, whereas the cash flow for the options is received at the end of the FRA period. (Any two parties to a contract might, however, agree to alter the timing of these cash flows, making appropriate discounting adjustments).

PROBLEMS FOR CHAPTER 14

1. You buy a June eurodollar IMM contract at 89.42 and three weeks later close out the contract when the price is 90.12. Explain your cash flow on the futures contract.

2. A borrower takes out a one-year $10,000,000 loan at a .625 percent margin over six-month LIBOR and sells twenty IMM eurodollar futures contracts at a price of 89.05. The total amount of the loan is drawn down immediately. For the initial period, LIBOR is determined from the reference banks to be 10.5 percent. For the second period, LIBOR is determined to be 11.75 percent. At that time the borrower closes out his futures contracts at 88.0. What is the borrower's increased borrowing cost minus his futures profit?

3. Explain what happens if the owner of a put option on a June IMM eurodollar contract exercises the option when the futures price is 89.77. (The strike price of the option is 90.00.) If a call option on eurodollar futures is quoted in the WSJ with a price of .62, what is the dollar amount you would pay for such an option (ignoring brokerage fees)?

4. A trader has a long eurodollar futures contract and writes a eurodollar futures call option on the same contract. The futures position was opened at 89.3 and the call—with a strike price of 89.75—was written at a price of .32. Later the call is exercised when the futures price is 89.96. What is the net cash flow to the trader, ignoring any fees on the total transaction? What maximum profit would have been possible?

5. Calculate the number of June eurodollar futures contracts needed to hedge a long position in a July to October $15,000,000 FRA (with ninety-two days in the FRA period). The June futures price is 92.37. Verify your answer by calculating the profit or loss on the hedged position for a move of 100 basis points in either direction.

6. How is your answer in Problem 5 affected if you also know there are 180 days to the beginning of the FRA period, and the six-month interest rate is 7.25 percent?

7. Explain how to create a synthetic long FRA using LIBOR calls and puts. Explain how to create a synthetic FRA put using an FRA and a LIBOR call.

SYNDICATED EUROCREDITS

BANKING SYNDICATES

Much eurocredit lending takes place through large groups of banks, called syndicates, that band together to loan amounts of money that are too large for any one particular bank. In this chapter we shall see how syndicates are organized and loans priced. The syndication procedure is widely used in international bank lending, whether the loans come from eurobanks or are financed partly or entirely by domestic banks.

There are several parts to a banking syndicate. The *lead manager* (there may be more than one) is the bank with the primary responsibility for organizing a syndicated loan. The lead manager has the main responsibility for agreeing on the terms and conditions of the loan with the borrower, for arranging for other banks to take up a portion of the loan, and for evaluating market conditions. Other banks who are invited to take part in the lending and accept are known as *participating banks*. A special category among the participating banks is *managing banks,* usually distinguished from other participating banks in that they have a larger share in the loan and may assist or advise the lead bank. Although various other subcategories among the participating banks may be established (such as comanagers and so on), the titles usually don't mean much except that banks who lend more money get a more impressive title. Finally, there will be an *agent bank* appointed to oversee the loan. The agent bank (which is often one of the lead managers) collects payments on the loan from the borrower and disburses the payments to the other banks according to their share in the loan.

Borrowers usually select a particular lead manager on the basis that they already have a relationship with that bank. Well-known borrowers will nevertheless shop around, and banks themselves will approach potential customers. If approached by a creditworthy borrower, the lead manager will begin to assemble a small group of managing banks, who—with the lead manager—may supply a large part of the total loan. On the basis of demand for the loan, the lead manager will negotiate with the borrower (or potential borrower) the amount of the loan, the interest rate or rates on the loan, other banking fees, and details concerning how other banks will be invited to participate in the loan.

When there seems to be preliminary agreement on details, the lead manager will prepare a *placement memorandum*. The placement memorandum will describe the borrower, including the borrower's financial condition, and give details about the proposed loan. The lead manager will then invite other banks to participate in the loan. Prospective participating banks are usually invited by fax. Invitation faxes may be sent to several hundred banks, who will also be provided with a copy of the placement memorandum.

If demand by other banks to take part in the loan is good, then the amount of the loan may be increased if the borrower wishes. On the other hand, if there is insufficient demand, the managing banks (with the lead manager) may have to make up the difference. If the managing banks have previously guaranteed to the borrower the full amount of the proposed loan, the credit is said to be "fully underwritten." On the other hand, if the credit is on a "best efforts" basis, the managing banks have only promised to try their best. If there is not sufficient demand in the latter case, the size of the loan may be scaled down or the terms changed.

In 1989, announced new syndicated credit facilities were $152 billion, a large increase (53 percent) over 1988. Most credits (80 percent) were extended to corporations, especially to U.S. and UK companies involved in mergers and acquisitions. M&A-related credits amounted to $56 billion, according to BIS figures, including one facility for $13.6 billion and another for $11 billion.

LOAN COSTS

There are several types of costs to the borrower in addition to the obligation to repay the loan principal. These may be divided into *periodic costs* and *up-front costs*. Periodic costs include the interest paid on the amount of the credit actually in use. If the interest agreement was six-month LIBOR plus a 1 percent margin, then the borrower will make periodic interest payments on the amount of the credit drawn (the amount of the loan the borrower has actually received). The interest rate in this example will be the new six-month LIBOR rate established at the beginning of the current six-month period, plus 1 percent. In addition, there will be a commitment fee (probably in the range of .25 percent to .75 percent) to be paid periodically on the unused portion of the credit. In a revolving credit, the unused portion of the credit may be anywhere from 0 percent to 100 percent of the total amount of the credit, depending on the wishes of the borrower. In a term credit, the amount of the undrawn portion of the total amount will depend on the time schedule that has been previously agreed on for drawing down and paying back the principal. During the grace period of a term credit, 100 percent of the credit will be available, so there will be no commitment fee if the total credit line has been drawn down. Finally, there will usually be a small *agent fee* paid to the agent bank for its services. In summary:

Periodic costs = (Amount of total credit drawn)
          × (Reference rate + margin)
          + (Amount of total credit not drawn)
          × (Commitment fee) + Agent fee

The up-front cost is conceptually a .5-to-2.5 percent one-time fee on the total amount of the credit, which is paid to the lead manager and managing banks for organizing and managing the loan. In practice, the managing banks will pass along a portion of this fee to the participating banks, so that we may divide up-front costs into *management fees* and *participation fees*. The lead manager will usually receive a *praecipium,* which means that the lead bank will get a bigger share in the total management fees than will the other managing banks. On a $100,000,000 credit, a typical division of a 1.5 percent total amount of fees ($1,500,000) might be 25 percent to the lead manager ($375,000), 25 percent to be split among the managing banks ($375,000), and 50 percent to be split among the participating banks ($750,000). If, for example, there are fifty participating banks, each of which loans the same amount of money, each will receive $750,000/50 = $15,000 up front when the syndicated credit is extended.

In recent years, many of the larger banks have specialized in managing loans as middlemen. That is, they manage syndicated loans in order to receive up-front fees for their management services; afterward, they will sell off much of their share in the loan to other smaller banks or thrift institutions. This practice has stemmed not only from the comparative advantage of some banks in providing management services but also from new regulatory guidelines. In the summer of 1983, U.S. regulators ordered the nation's seventeen largest multinational banking organizations to maintain a ratio of primary capital to assets of at least 5 percent. Some of these banks did not subsequently have sufficient capital themselves to provide large amounts of new funds. The Basel Committee standards announced in 1988 (Chapter 12) added further pressure. Loan participations are discussed later.

The amount of margin added to the reference rate in a syndicated credit is related to relative risks, given the overall ratio of desired borrowing to desired lending. Risk exists whether the lending is to companies or to sovereign borrowers. It is futile to apply the usual fiction, often raised in a domestic context, that lending to governments is default-free. Governments that borrow in terms of foreign currencies do not have the power to create foreign currency by fiat, and they cannot acquire foreign currency by taxing foreign citizens. In addition, an attempt simply to produce more domestic currency and exchange it in the FX market for the required foreign exchange will normally be self-defeating, since the purchasing power of the domestic currency over foreign currency will fall correspondingly. (The effort may succeed in part, however, to the extent the government is successful in extracting real resources from the domestic economy through domestic inflation. These real resources can be used to generate foreign exchange.) Table 15.1 gives the average spread over LIBOR that governments paid in syndicated eurocredits in 1983, the year following the Mexican debt moratorium. As the different margins indicate, some governments were seen as more risky than others. Latin American countries, in particular, paid high spreads.

LOAN AGREEMENTS AND THE RISKS OF LENDING

Getting a borrower to sign a legal document will never turn a bad credit risk into a good one. Nevertheless, syndicated loan contracts are revealing in other ways. The provisions of typical loan agreements are important for our pur-

TABLE 15.1
Spread Over LIBOR Paid by Sovereign Borrowers in the Syndicated Eurocredits Market in 1983

Country	Average Weighted Spread (%)	Average Maturity (Years)	Country	Average Weighted Spread	Average Maturity (Years)
New Zealand	.25	2.00	Portugal	.73	6.48
Finland	.34	7.00	Norway	.76	1.66
Taiwan	.37	9.25	Philippines	.76	8.00
Austria	.38	8.00	Nigeria	.83	8.21
Thailand	.38	8.00	Pakistan	.88	3.30
Republic of Palau	.44	6.95	USSR	.91	1.87
France	.47	7.96	Turkey	.95	5.97
Belgium	.47	7.00	Iraq	.99	5.00
India	.48	7.84	East Germany	1.00	5.00
Indonesia	.49	8.12	Ivory Coast	1.00	0.51
Sweden	.49	7.21	Czechoslovakia	1.13	4.00
Malaysia	.50	9.91	Hungary	1.21	3.60
Jordan	.51	7.00	Nepal	1.25	7.00
Tunisia	.54	8.00	Morocco	1.26	4.18
Abu Dhabi	.56	10.00	Columbia	1.41	6.04
Ireland	.57	7.29	Trinidad & Tobago	1.45	7.00
Denmark	.58	7.00	Jamaica	1.50	10.00
Italy	.59	7.20	Egypt	1.50	10.00
Algeria	.59	7.93	Zambia	1.50	1.00
Sri Lanka	.59	7.82	Cameroons	1.63	6.00
Australia	.59	13.97	Argentina	1.75	3.00
Oman	.59	7.00	Venezuela	1.85	5.86
Iceland	.61	6.47	Congo	1.97	4.97
Greece	.65	6.96	Panama	2.00	7.00
Spain	.69	7.16	Brazil	2.11	5.44
Papua New Guinea	.72	8.00	Paraguay	2.41	8.00
Korea	.72	8.09			
Average, all countries	.76	7.04			

Source: Euromoney, *Annual Financing Report,* 1984.

poses because they give us an indication of the various economic and other risks lenders take into account before lending money. They define the rules of the game each side expects the other to live up to.

PROVISIONS FOR INTEREST RATE RISK

Recall that the concept of rollover pricing was created so that eurobanks (and other banks in syndicated lending) could avoid the problem of funding long-term loans with short-term liabilities. If, for example, a bank funded a five-year 8 percent fixed-rate loan by issuing six-month time deposits, then if short-term interest rates (the rate on six-month deposits) rose sharply, the bank might end up paying, say, 9 percent on its deposits while it was still receiving only 8 percent on the loan. That is, there is interest risk that arises because the maturity of assets (loans) may differ from the maturity of liabilities (deposits).

To be sure, all financial intermediaries engage in some maturity transformation: They issue short-term liabilities that are used to fund long-term assets.

Since long-term interest rates (received on loans) are generally higher than short-term interest rates (paid on deposits), the financial intermediary (the bank) will make a profit based on the difference between long-term and short-term interest rates. (This process is called "riding the yield curve.") That is, the bank is rewarded for assuming interest rate risk. But, as syndicated lending grew in the early 1970s, it was felt this risk was too great. Eurobanks were accepting great amounts of thirty- and ninety-day time deposits but being asked for five- and seven-year loans. So, to reduce the amount of maturity transformation they had to undertake, banks began to do part of their lending on a rollover basis, which reduced the amount of interest rate risk stemming directly from maturity transformation.

Rollover pricing is accomplished by setting a margin over a reference rate, so loan agreements have to spell out the manner in which this reference rate is calculated. If six-month LIBOR is the reference rate, then, since it is a market interest rate, six-month LIBOR will change from minute to minute, and at any one time will differ from bank to bank. The loan agreement will specify the reference banks, the banks whose offered prices in the interbank market are used to determine the "London" interbank offered rate. In addition, the agreement will specify the day and the time of day this determination is to be made. Since interbank deposits are traded at prices that are determined in the market today but are for delivery two days later, the loan agreement will usually specify that LIBOR is to be determined two days prior to the new interest rate period, at, say, 10:30 A.M. London time.

While such provisions shield the bank from interest risk due to maturity transformation, they do not shield the bank from all consequences of interest rate changes. In the early 1980s, it became apparent that some banks, by using rollover pricing, had simply *transformed interest rate risk into credit risk*. To see why, consider the situation of the borrower. Suppose a borrower like PEMEX, the Mexican state-owned oil company, has borrowed when LIBOR is 10 percent, paying a 1 percent margin above LIBOR, and LIBOR subsequently rises to 15 percent. If the dollar price of PEMEX's product, Maya or Isthmus crude, does not rise commensurately (when adjusted for demand and cost factors), then the real dollar borrowing rate as seen by PEMEX has risen. Faced with higher real borrowing costs, PEMEX may now be a higher credit risk: There may be a higher probability that PEMEX cannot repay the loan. But the bank may have supposed that the 1 percent margin charged on the loan was sufficient compensation for the credit risk involved, while falsely assuming that rollover pricing eliminated interest rate risk. But, in this case, the bank will not really have eliminated the interest risk due to changes in LIBOR, because changes in LIBOR are correlated with changes in credit risk.

PROVISIONS FOR THE RISK OF GOVERNMENT INTERVENTION

Standard loan agreements signed with company borrowers include various provisions that attempt to ensure that government action will not directly diminish the value of the lending margin. Payments must be made free of withholding taxes or other charges. In practice, this means that if, for example, the borrower's government imposes withholding taxes on the borrower's interest payments, the borrower will have to increase its payments sufficiently to meet the requirement of the loan agreement. If a 20 percent withholding tax is imposed, then the borrower will have to make payments of 10 percent interest in order to pay 8 percent to the lending banks $(.10 - .10(.20) = .08)$.

These provisions also include actions on the part of the lending bank's government. If the lender's central bank alters reserve or deposit requirements in such a way that it is more costly for the lending bank to fund the loan, the loan agreement usually requires the borrower to pay the additional cost. The borrower may also be required to pay for the lender's increased cost if the government alters tax laws in a way that affects the lender's net income.

Governmental action may also affect the way the bank funds its loans. For example, there may be a disruption of the interbank market or the euro-CD market. In such a case, loan agreements usually allow the lender to substitute a new reference rate, or way of calculating interest rates, that reflects the bank's cost of funds. Otherwise the borrower usually has the option of prepaying the loan.

PROVISIONS RELATED TO BORROWER CREDIT RISK

Loan agreements will be based on information about the financial state of the borrower at the time the loan is made as well as an understanding about how the borrower will conduct its financial affairs over the life of the loan. Statements made by a eurocredit borrower about its financial state at the time the credit is being sought are referred to as *representations* or *warranties*. Promises the borrower makes about its *future* behavior are referred to as *covenants*. A company, for example, may promise to maintain a certain asset-to-liability ratio over the life of the loan or to limit total debt service and dividends in some stipulated way. A government might promise to adhere to an IMF program, or promise that it will not give new creditors security (liens) without offering the existing creditors the same security. A promise of this latter type, a promise to *not* do something, is referred to as a *negative pledge*.

A *pari passu* covenant, like a negative pledge, is a covenant used to ensure that the lending banks will be treated equally with other creditors in the event a borrower becomes insolvent and is subsequently liquidated. Most international loans are unsecured, and *pari passu* provisions prevent the subordination of the lending banks to other *unsecured* creditors (Negative pledges prevent the subordination of lending banks to *secured* creditors.) A *cross-default clause* gives the lending banks the right to accelerate the outstanding balance of the loan in the event the borrower defaults on another indebtedness. This may include any other indebtedness or may only include certain types of indebtedness, such as foreign debt. Cross-default clauses allow the banks to accelerate the loan in the event default on the current loan is anticipated as a result of default on other loans.

RULES OF THE GAME FOR SETTLING DISPUTES

In connection with any loan, events can arise about which there was no prior agreement. Therefore loan agreements usually involve an agreement about the rules for settling disputes, such as: Which country's laws shall govern in the dispute? If the borrower is a government, is sovereign immunity waived? If judgment is rendered in a foreign court in a currency other than the lending currency, is the lender protected against currency fluctuations?

THE SECONDARY MARKET FOR EUROCREDITS

Recently various secondary markets for eurocredits have emerged. While not large, these markets may grow and consequently improve the efficiency of risk sharing in the eurocredits market. One serious impediment to the growth of the secondary market has been the Glass-Steagall Act in the United States, which prohibits banks from dealing in securities (and hence prevents loans from being traded like securities in a secondary market). Another has been growth in nonperforming loans, making bankers reluctant to have market prices reveal the true values of loan portfolios.

LOAN PARTICIPATIONS

Banks that have not taken part in a particular syndicated loan may buy shares in the loan from one of the original managing or participating banks. That is, if the agreement with the borrower allows, a bank that has taken part in a syndicated loan may later transfer its obligation—or part of its obligation—to another bank. The banks who arranged the loan may sell participations because they have a special expertise in managing loans (and hence earning management fees), or have the general goal to become investment banks, or have the need to make room on their balance sheets in order to take part in, and manage, new loans. Selling participations hinges less on capital and more on placing power or distribution.

For New York banks, New York law allows three ways to dispose of a loan asset—novation, assignment, and subparticipation. A *novation* is the discharge of one obligation and the creation of an entirely new one. The original bank lender is relieved entirely of its obligations with respect to the original loan. With the borrower's consent, a new bank creditor takes over the old creditor's rights and obligations. An *assignment,* by contrast, usually involves the transfer to another bank of the right to receive principal and interest from the borrower. The second bank now has a direct claim on the borrower but may not be able to sue the borrower under its own name. A *subparticipation* is the partial assignment of the right to receive principal or interest to another bank, but the debtor/creditor relationship between the original bank and the borrower remains unchanged. The bank buying the subparticipation typically has no recourse either to the debtor or to the bank from which the subparticipation was purchased. Subparticipations usually bear an interest payment that is $\frac{1}{8}$ to $\frac{1}{4}$ percent lower than the original participation in the eurocredit. So, in effect, the original bank continues to collect interest from the borrower and passes this to the subparticipating bank after extracting a fraction of 1 percent. Various banks, including Citicorp, Chase, Morgan, SecPac, and Bankers Trust have set up divisions to sell subparticipations.

SWAPS

Swaps are another type of secondary market activity. Loan or debt swaps between banks may take place for many reasons: differences in the perceived riskiness of the debt of different borrowers; differences in individual bank exposures; differences in disclosure requirements; preferences for public sector or private sector debt; preferences for loans with tax receipts; differences in the ability to influence different borrowers; differences in writedowns on loans from a particular borrower; differences in the need for liquidity (if cash is involved in the swap). (See Guttentag and Herring [1985].)

Asset-for-Asset Swaps

This type of swap might entail two creditor banks exchanging loans from different countries. A cash payment is sometimes used to make up the difference if the loans have different values. For example, in 1983 Bankers Trust gave the Brazilian bank Banco Real $100 million of Brazilian loans and $90 million in cash in return for $190 million of Banco Real's loans to Mexico.

In general, the debt of different borrowerrs may be discounted, so the exchange ratio in a loan swap will not be one-for-one. For example, four dollars of Polish debt may trade for three dollars of Mexican debt. In 1983–1984 the discounts on p. 294 were applied at one time or another in sovereign loans swaps. Figure 15.1 shows that such discounts have increased over time.

A different type of asset-for-asset swap is the exchange of debt for real property. In 1985, for example, foreigners who wished to invest in Argentina could redeem any holdings of government paper for its full face value. Since the paper could be acquired in the market at 70 to 75 percent of face value, the government's redemption of the paper at 100 percent of face value could be viewed as a risk premium paid by the government to attract foreign investment.

It is not clear that all swap activity represents optimizing behavior. In 1983, the SEC enacted the requirement that banks with publicly traded stock disclose their holdings of country loans if aggregate exposure for the country exceeded the lesser of 1 percent of total assets or 20 percent of primary capital. Annual reports had to list the debtor country, the aggregate exposure, and a breakdown of exposure by public, private, and banking sectors and by maturity. In addition, individual country exposures in excess of .75 percent of assets or 15 percent of primary capital had to be reported (but not broken down). Some banks subsequently engaged in swaps simply to manipulate their reported exposure levels.

Country	Discount %
Poland	40
Argentina	30
Philippines	25
Brazil	25–28
Venezuela	22
Mexico	16–17

Secondary Market Prices for Developing Country Loans, 1986–April 1990[1]
(In percent of face value)

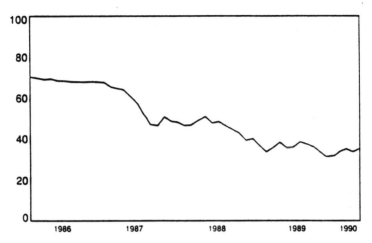

Source: Salomon Brothers, IMF.
[1] Weighted average for fifteen heavily indebted countries.

FIGURE 15.1
Secondary Market Prices of Developing Country Debt

Asset-for-Debt Swaps

This transaction typically involves Bank A paying off its debt liability to Bank B by turning over one of its own loan assets to Bank B. Bank B in effect replaces its original loan to Bank A with a different loan that it acquired from Bank A.

Asset Sales for Cash

One regional bank traded $2 million in Brazilian government debt for $1.6 million in cash and $400,000 of notes from Grupo Alfa in Mexico. " 'When we get the Alfa, we'll just write it off as worthless,' says an official of that bank, pointing out that the transaction in effect amounts to a 20 percent discount for Brazilian government debt" (*Wall Street Journal*, November 27, 1984).

By 1989, secondary debt market transactions amounted to about $70 billion per year. Some of the activity involved countries paying cash to repurchase their own debt at a discount: In 1988, Bolivia bought about one-half of its own debt, paying 6 percent of face value. The existence of the secondary market has changed the character of debt renegotiations. In 1990, the Phillipines repurchased bank claims for 50 percent of face value, their approximate price in the secondary market, while Costa Rica repurchased past-due principle and interest at 16 cents on the dollar.

EURONOTES AND EUROCOMMERCIAL PAPER

Euronotes are short-term, tradable debt instruments (IOUs) that are sold by the borrower at a discount to face value, but that promise to pay back the full amount of the face value of the note, plus add-on interest, in (usually) three to six months. Euronotes are similar to bank CDs, but were created as a substitute for syndicated loans. An enterprising investment banker faced the problems mentioned previously: If you make a syndicated loan, it is hard to get rid of it. There is no secondary market to trade it in, so it just sits on your books and eats up capital. In fact, your comparative advantage may not be lending at a spread, such as happens in a rollover credit, but in arranging loans for a fee. But your fee-earning capacity is larger than your capital. So how are you going to make the big money? Well, consider what the bank will do in order to fund such a syndicated loan: It might issue three- and six-month time deposits, or else issue tradable liabilities, such as euro-CDs. There are fund managers, corporations, and other banks who like to park money in (buy) short-term instruments. If they'll buy tradable CDs from the bank, they'll buy tradable euronotes from someone else. Why not skip the syndicated loan (rollover credit) bit, and let the borrower sell three- to six-month IOUs directly to lenders? Lenders who would buy CDs at LIBID or lower would certainly be happy to buy euronotes at a spread over LIBOR.

In a euronote facility, a group of banks may commit themselves to purchase the borrower's notes at a predetermined rate or at a maximum spread over LIBOR, if the notes can't be sold at a lower rate. In that case the notes are said to be *underwritten*. Since the notes are issued at periodic intervals, the facility may be called a *revolving underwriting facility* or RUF. A bank willing to make a revolving loan would certainly be willing to underwrite euronotes, since its financial commitment is similar. Banks earn a commitment fee *plus*—if they have to buy the notes—the predetermined spread at which the notes are underwritten. But euronotes are not necessarily underwritten; if not, they are usually called *eurocommercial paper*. The term *note issue facility* or NIF has been applied both to facilities that are underwritten and to those that are not, but the term usually implies an underwritten facility.

In addition to the underwriting banks (if any) are the dealers and brokers who form the *tender panel*. The role of the tender panel is to bid on the notes at the time of issue. They may keep the notes or resell them to investors at a small profit. If the price of the notes is not bid high enough (rate low enough) by the tender panel, the underwriters (if any) then take over and buy the notes at the agreed maximum interest rate. A less formal arrangement than the tender panel is a *placing agent,* a single bank that agrees to bid for the notes or attempt to distribute (sell) them to final investors.

The borrower faces three kinds of costs in a euronote issue: a one-time fee paid to the bank that arranges the euronote facility; quarterly or semiannual commitment fees paid retrospectively (at the end of the period) to the underwriters; and the lending margin plus the reference rate (usually LIBOR or LIBID) paid to the note buyers, whether tender panel members or final investors.

EXAMPLE 15.1

Global Commodity Corp. (GCC) arranges a $150 million euronote facility for issuing six-month notes. The agreement is signed on July 1, 1991, and will expire on June 30, 2001. Each $500,000 note will pay add-on interest equal to the current market LIBID at the time of issue. The notes will generally be sold at a discount to par. However, if the market discount would result in an effective yield greater than LIBOR + 0.15625%, a group of underwriting banks will purchase the notes at the maximum yield of LIBOR + 0.15625%. GCC will pay the underwriting banks an underwriting fee of 0.125 percent p.a., this fee to be paid semiannually in arrears. Finally, GCC pays the bank arranging the facility an up-front fee of 0.30 percent of the $150 million facility (a fee of $450,000) on July 1, 1991, the day the agreement is signed. GCC also pays the arranging bank's legal, advertising, and printing expenses.

LIBID at the time of issue is 8.25 percent, and the notes are placed at LIBOR + 0.03125% (or 8.40625%). This means that, since there are 184 days in the first interest period, each note will be repaid at maturity in the amount of $500,000 (1 + .0825 (184/360)) = $521,083.33, which is the sum of the face value of the note and the add-on LIBID interest. Since the notes are placed (sold) at a yield of 8.40625 percent, the amount the borrower receives for each note sold on July 1 is $521,083.33/(1 + .0840625(184/360)) = $499,617.14, or 99.923 percent of par.

The shift in the pattern of commercial bank intermediation from direct eurocredit lending to euronotes began in 1984. While underwritten euronote facilities were originally important, these peaked at $29.0 billion in 1987. By 1989, RUFs amounted to only $4.3 billion, compared to $47.2 billion in euro-commercial paper (Table 15.2).

PROBLEMS FOR CHAPTER 15

1. A London bank makes a term loan at a margin of 1 percent over six-month LIBOR. The credit is for $1 million, of which half is drawn down at the beginning of the first year, and the remaining half at the beginning of the second year. Principal repayments do not begin until the beginning of the third year. There is a commitment fee of .25 percent per annum. The six-month LIBOR reference rates for the first two years are 10, 10, 11, and 11 percent. Assuming 360-day years, what are the amounts of periodic interest and fees the bank receives during the first two years?

TABLE 15.2
Euronote Borrowing Facilities (U.S. $ billions)

	1987	1988	1989
Revolving underwriting facilities	29.0	14.4	4.3
Other committed facilities	2.2	2.2	2.5
Eurocommercial paper	55.8	57.1	47.2
Other Nonunderwritten facilities	15.2	19.5	18.1
Total	102.2	93.2	72.1

Source: OECD, *Financial Market Trends*, May 1990.

2. In order to obtain a syndicated loan from commercial banks, a country promises to limit its rate or expansion of central bank credit to a maximum of 25 percent per annum. This promise is an example of a [choose one]:
    a. representation
    b. covenant
    c. warranty
    d. praecipium
    e. cross-default clause

3. In what way could the secondary market trading of eurocredits prove useful ᵢ evaluating political risk?

4. A $500,000 euronote which matures in eighty-seven days is yielding 7.32 percent. The note pays six-month LIBOR minus .125 percent. Six-month LIBOR has been fixed at 7.75 percent. What is the current dollar value of the note?

INTERNATIONAL
BOND MARKETS

INTRODUCTION TO THE INTERNATIONAL BOND MARKETS

There is no unified international bond "market" in the same sense that there is a foreign exchange market or a eurocurrency market. In the case of foreign exchange, common trading of the major convertible currencies against the U.S. dollar takes place in an environment that is sufficiently free of controls and regulatory restrictions, and that has sufficiently small transactions costs, as to create a broad united market. It thus makes sense to speak of a foreign exchange "market," in the singular. The same could be said of the eurocurrency "market": Most eurocurrencies, when viewed in the context of spot and forward exchange markets, can be easily interchanged, making it natural in many contexts to treat them as a basket of similar, fairly substitutable items. But trading in international bonds is more usefully considered as taking place in a set of loosely connected individual markets. Each of these individual markets is usually more closely tied to a corresponding domestic bond market than to another one of the international bond markets.

The international bond markets may be divided into two broad groups: foreign bonds and eurobonds. *Foreign bonds* are bonds that are issued by foreign borrowers in a nation's domestic capital market and are denominated in the nation's domestic currency. What makes foreign bonds different from ordinary domestic bonds is that countries typically make legal distinctions between bonds issued by domestic residents and bonds issued by foreigners. These distinctions may include different tax laws, different regulations on the timing or amount of bonds that may be issued, different requirements as to the type or amount of information that the borrower has to disclose prior to the bond issue, different registration requirements, and different restrictions on who can buy the bonds.

The most important foreign bond markets are in Zurich, New York, Tokyo, Frankfurt, London, and Amsterdam. Some foreign bond markets have common names that are widely used in international finance. For example, foreign bonds issued in the U.S. are referred to as Yankee bonds, and the corresponding market is the "Yankee bond market." Foreign bonds issued in Japan are called samurai bonds. Foreign bonds issued in the Netherlands are called Rembrandt bonds. And foreign bonds issued in London are bulldog bonds. Foreign bonds can also be taken to include *foreign-currency*-denominated issues by foreigners in the domestic bond market. Examples include shogun bonds—foreign currency bonds issued in Tokyo—and Yankee ECU bonds issued in New York.

Eurobonds differ from foreign bonds in that eurobonds denominated in a particular currency are usually issued simultaneously in the capital markets of several nations. They differ from foreign bonds in that most nations do not have preoffering registration or disclosure requirements for eurobond issues. Neither do they have restrictions on the timing or amount of such issues if the issue is denominated in a foreign currency. Some countries—such as Germany, Japan, and France—will, however, regulate the timing or amount of a eurobond issue if the issue is denominated in the country's domestic currency. The United States and Canada, by contrast, do not make any attempt to regulate the issuing of eurobonds denominated in, respectively, the U.S. dollar or the Canadian dollar. The predominant currency used in the eurobond market is the U.S. dollar, but there are also smaller and important markets for eurobonds denominated in the DM, ECU (European Currency Unit), British pound, Canadian dollar, and Dutch guilder. Financial deregulation in 1986 in Japan made the Japanese yen eurobond market the leading nondollar market.

FEATURES OF EUROBONDS

Most eurobonds are *bearer* bonds. Your ownership of the bond is evidenced by the fact that you have the bond, just as your ownership of a U.S. dollar bill is evidenced by the fact that you have the dollar bill in your pocket. Bearer bonds contrast with registered bonds. Registered bonds have an ownership name assigned to the bond's serial number, and the bond can be transferred to a new owner only through a formal transfer of the registered name. For example, Yankee bonds are registered. The fact that eurobonds are bearer bonds and not registered means that they are attractive investment assets for people who wish to remain anonymous—because they are avoiding taxes or for any other reason.

Interest paid on eurobonds is usually free of all tax. In the event that a nation may impose withholding taxes on the borrower's interest payments, bond convenants specify that the interest payments must be increased enough that, after the tax is applied, the net interest payment is the same as before. For example, if an interest coupon is $100 payable annually, and a 20 percent withholding tax is imposed, the borrower has to pay coupons of $125. Thus the net payments to the bondholder will be

$$\$125 - .2(\$125) = \$100,$$

the same as previously.

Eurobonds differ from eurocredits in that buyers of the bonds do not get involved in the financial affairs of the borrower. In a eurocredit loan agreement, a borrower may commit itself to maintain a certain capital/asset ratio or adhere to an IMF agreement, and if it does not do so, the borrower can be in technical default whether or not the borrower is still making payment on the

TABLE 16.1
New International Bond Issues by Nationality of Issuer

	1986	1987	1988	1989
		(billions of U.S. dollars)		
Japan	31.8	42.7	50.8	96.7
United States	41.6	22.5	16.6	16.4
Canada	17.9	9.0	13.1	13.3
United Kingdom	20.2	11.2	26.3	23.0
France	13.4	8.5	16.5	13.5
Other developed countries	74.8	60.5	77.0	68.2
Developing countries	3.0	2.2	3.9	2.6
Eastern Europe	0.6	0.6	1.2	2.0
International organizations	19.1	19.9	20.6	23.1
Total	222.4	177.0	226.0	258.7

Source: BIS, *Annual Report,* 1990.

loan. But with eurobonds, since investors don't have any say about how the borrower conducts its financial affairs, default clauses say default occurs only if there is nonpayment of interest or principal. This means, of course, that investors will not buy the bonds of entities whose financial affairs they worry about. Eurobond issues are thus limited to borrowers who are considered as low credit risks. This simple fact of life can be seen in Table 16.1, showing international bond issues identified by the country location of the borrower. During 1989, for example, borrowers in Japan issued a total of $96.7 billion in the international bond markets, while UK borrowers issued $23 billion. International organizations such as the World Bank borrowed $23.1 billion. By contrast, the total amount of issues from developing countries was $2.6 billion.

The details of issuing new eurobonds are covered in the next chapter. Briefly, however, there may be several stages to the process. The borrower, after negotiation, sells its bonds to a group of managing banks. Managing banks in turn sell the bonds to other banks, who are divided into underwriters and sellers. The underwriting and selling banks in turn sell the bonds to dealers and final investors. Underwriting banks are distinguished from ordinary sellers in that they are committed to buy the bonds at a preagreed minimum price even if the bonds cannot be sold at a higher price on the market. The managing banks themselves also act as underwriters and sellers.

Eurobonds appear in a number of basic guises. Straight bonds pay a fixed interest rate at periodic intervals, usually annually. The choice of annual payments, as opposed to the more common interval of six months in domestic issues, is a simple reaction to the higher cost of disbursing interest payments to investors around the world.

EXAMPLE 16.1

The first eurobond issue that was widely recognized as such took place in July 1963. The Italian autostrada issued 60,000 bonds with a face value of $250 each. Each bond paid a fixed coupon of 5.5 percent ($13.75) annually on July 15. The issue was managed by

London merchant bankers S. G. Warburg & Co., with Banque de Bruxelles SA, Deutsche Bank AG, and Rotterdamsche Bank NV as comanagers. The bond was listed on the London Stock Exchange. This eurobond issue coincided with the proposal (and retroactive imposition) of the Interest Equalization Tax (IET) on Yankee bonds by U.S. president Kennedy on July 18, 1963. The IET was a flat tax of 15 percent of the purchase price of long maturity bonds, which increased the costs to European borrowers coming to New York by about 1 percent. [Background information on the autostrada issue is given in Kerr (1984).]

Floating-rate notes (FRNs), by contrast, have more frequent payments—usually every six months. The interest rate on floating-rate notes is stated in terms of a spread over some reference rate—usually LIBOR—appropriate for the currency. The rollover pricing feature of floating-rate notes is, of course, a reaction to interest rate uncertainty. The more frequently the interest rate is updated, the more the interest payment on the note will reflect current money market rates. The first floating-rate notes appeared in 1969 and 1970, during a period of rising interest rates. Most FRNs are dollar-denominated: Japanese yen and German mark FRNs did not appear until 1985.

EXAMPLE 16.2

In February 1984, Sweden made an offering of $500 million of floating-rate notes in the U.S. dollar eurobond market. The notes mature in March 2024 and bear semiannual interest of $\frac{1}{8}$ percent over six-month LIBOR. At the time the notes were offered, six-month LIBOR was $10\frac{7}{16}$ percent. So for the first six months Sweden paid an interest at an annual rate of

$$10\frac{7}{16}\% + \frac{1}{8}\% = 10\frac{9}{16}\%.$$

Afterward, at the end of each six-month period, the interest rates on the notes are updated to reflect the current six-month LIBOR rate for dollars. The forty-year maturity (1984–2024) was at the time of offering the longest in eurobond history. (Shortly afterward, however, National Westminister Bank issued perpetual floating-rate notes. That is, NatWest's FRNs never mature.)

EXAMPLE 16.3

LIBOR is not always the reference rate used. In February 1984, the World Bank offered $250 million of ten-year floating-rate notes, which pay quarterly interest at a rate of thirty-five basis points above the money market yield on certain ninety-one-day U.S. Treasury bills. The World Bank's total interest of about 9.65 percent for the first three-month period was approximately thirty basis points (.3 percent) *below* three-month LIBOR. The low interest the World Bank was required to pay reflects the fact that the World Bank was, at the time, considered a very low-risk borrower.

Zero-coupon bonds is the curious name given to bonds that don't pay any coupons. (Treasury bills and commercial paper don't pay coupons either, but are not referred to as "zero-coupon.") These are pure discount securities that are either sold at a fraction of their face value and redeemed at face value, or sold at face value and redeemed at a premium. The return is the difference between the purchase price and the repayment price. Zero-coupon bonds proved very popular with Japanese investors, because the increase in the bond's price as the bonds matured was treated in Japan as capital gain and was not taxed.

EXAMPLE 16.4

In June 1981, Pepsico Overseas issued three-year zero-coupon eurobonds at an issue price of 67.25 percent of face value. Since the bonds would be repaid in three years at 100 percent of face value, the compounded annual interest yield was

$$(100/67.25)^{1/3} - 1 = 14.14\%$$

By contrast, Deutsche Bank Finance N.V. issued zeros at face value in 1985. They redeem in 1995 at 287% of face value.

Convertible bonds are another fairly frequent type of bond offered in the eurobond markets. Japanese companies in particular have issued a great many convertible U.S. dollar eurobonds. A bond is convertible if, in addition to making the usual interest payments, the bond can be exchanged for some other type of asset. A common type of conversion feature is one that allows the bond to be exchanged at its face value for shares of common stock in the company issuing the bonds. Bonds have also been issued that allow conversion into other assets such as gold or oil or into other bonds with differing payment characteristics (such as bonds paying floating-rate interest being convertible, under certain circumstances, into bonds paying fixed-rate interest—or vice versa). Some bonds have allowed payments in principal or interest to be received, at the borrower's option, in one of two alternative currencies. That is, the bond has allowed conversion from one currency to another at a pre-agreed fixed exchange rate. Most conversion features, of whatever type, can be considered as options, and their value can be formally established in the same way we value foreign exchange or stock options. Chapter 20 will look further at option features on bonds.

EXAMPLE 16.5

A Canadian company issued 8 percent eurobonds, each with a face value of $1000. The bond principal was convertible at maturity, at the option of the bondholder, into common stock of the parent company at a conversion price per share of Can$23⅛, where each U.S. $1 of face value would be converted to Canadian dollars at a fixed exchange rate of 1.2007 Canadian dollars = 1 U.S. dollar.

EXAMPLE 16.6

In May 1983, CEPME issued £35 million of fixed-rate bonds convertible to floating-rate notes. Each £1000, twelve-year bond paid a fixed coupon of 11.25 percent but was convertible at the bondholder's option into one $1550, twelve-year floating-rate note paying semiannual dollar interest equal to six-month LIBOR.

A new and interesting guise in which eurobonds began appearing in 1984 was in the form of *mortgage-backed* eurobonds. Such bonds are backed by a pool of mortgages, trust deeds, or other bonds. Since mostly only borrowers perceived to have low credit risk have thus far been successful in issuing eurobonds, certain institutions, such as regional thrift institutions, would normally be excluded from the eurobond market. Mortgage-backed U.S. dollar eurobonds are a way in which some U.S. thrift institutions have created the equivalent of bonds guaranteed by the U.S. government. One way this has been done is that the financial institution puts up as security against the eurobond issue other bonds that are guaranteed by the (U.S.) Government National Mortgage Association (Ginnie Mae).

EXAMPLE 16.7

In March 1984, American Savings & Loan Association issued $125 million of eurobonds through a group of investment banks led by Salomon Brothers. To back the eurobonds, American Savings & Loan placed in escrow $187.5 million in AAA-rated debt of the Government National Mortgage Association. The Ginnie Mae debt, owned by American Savings & Loan, would be used to pay off eurobond holders in the event American Savings & Loan defaulted on its eurobonds. Aside from the mortgage backing, the eurobonds themselves were straight eurodollar bonds paying a fixed coupon of 12 percent. The importance of the Ginnie Mae credit enhancement was emphasized when American Savings subsequently became insolvent.

Dual-currency bonds are bonds that are purchased in terms of one currency but pay coupons or repay principal at maturity in terms of a second currency. As explained in Chapter 4, these bonds represent a combination of an ordinary bond combined with one or more forward contracts.

EXAMPLE 16.8

In August 1985, the Federal National Mortgage Association, a U.S. government-sponsored, privately owned corporation, issued dual-currency yen-denominated euro-bonds. The bonds were to be purchased in yen, and the 8 percent annual coupon was to be paid in yen. At maturity, however, repayment would be made in U.S. dollars. The yen face amount of the bond would be exchanged for dollars at an exchange rate of ¥ 208/$. The same year, Mobil Corporation issued eurobonds with a face value of $2475, but paying interest coupons of SF350. The bonds were to be redeemed in dollars.

Table 16.2 shows that in 1989, of the $258.7 billion in international bond issues, $150.1 billion were straight fixed-rate (plain vanilla) bonds. Equity-related issues were $85.2 billion, and floating-rate notes were $23.4 billion. About one-half of all these issues were denominated in the U.S. dollar. Equity-related issues were denominated primarily in the U.S. dollar and Swiss franc,

TABLE 16.2
New International Bond Issues by Bond Type

	1986	1987	1988	1989
		(billions of U.S. dollars)		
Straight fixed-rate issues	147.4	121.3	161.3	150.1
Floating-rate notes	47.7	12.1	22.6	23.4
Equity-related issues	27.4	43.7	42.1	85.2
Total	222.4	177.0	226.0	258.7

Source: BIS, *Annual Report,* 1990.

while floating-rate notes were in the U.S. dollar and British pound. By contrast, plain vanilla bonds were denominated in a wide range of currencies (Table 16.3).

U.S. LEGAL ASPECTS OF EURODOLLAR BOND ISSUES

As we saw in Table 16.3, many eurobonds are dollar-denominated. (Dollar-denominated eurobonds are usually referred to as eurodollar bonds. The name is shorthand, and does not imply any association with the eurocurrency market.) It will be worthwhile to look at some of the specific factors that give this important market its character.

First of all, the U.S. authorities make no special attempt to control the issuing of dollar-denominated eurobonds by foreigners. There are, however, a number of U.S. regulations that affect the management and sale of dollar

TABLE 16.3
New International Bond Issues by Currency

	1986	1987	1988	1989
		(percentage of type)		
Straight fixed-rate issues	100	100	100	100
U.S. dollar	46	25	29	36
Yen	15	18	12	15
Swiss franc	11	14	11	4
Deutschemark	8	11	13	6
ECU	4	6	7	8
British pound	4	8	7	8
Other	12	18	21	23
Floating-rate notes	100	100	100	100
U.S. dollar	80	32	29	35
British pound	11	18	45	31
Other	9	50	26	34
Equity-related issues	100	100	100	100
U.S. dollar	61	68	69	76
Swiss franc	22	16	20	16
Other	17	16	11	8
All issues	100	100	100	100
U.S. dollar	55	36	37	49
Other	45	64	63	51

Source: BIS, *Annual Report,* 1990

eurobonds. The outdated Glass-Steagall Act prohibits U.S. commercial banks from underwriting securities. Therefore, among U.S. firms only investment banks, or merchant banking subsidiaries of U.S. commercial banks, get involved in dollar eurobond issues. In addition, there are several important legal restrictions that apply either to the purchase of eurodollar bonds by U.S. citizens, to the issuing of eurobonds by U.S. companies, or to the involvement of U.S. firms in unregistered bond offerings. Three points in particular are important: sales prohibitions, private placement exemption, and withholding tax on bearer bonds.

PROHIBITION ON SALES

The U.S. Securities Act of 1933 requires public issues of new securities in the United States to be registered with the U.S. Securities and Exchange Commission (SEC). Therefore, dollar eurobonds (or other currency eurobonds), or any foreign bonds not registered in the United States, cannot be sold to U.S. citizens at the time of initial distribution. U.S. citizens can only purchase such bonds after the bonds have been seasoned in the secondary market for ninety days.

In addition, the 1933 act would appear to prohibit U.S. investment banks from even taking part in an unregistered eurobond or foreign bond issue, even if the issue were taking place in London and the bonds were being sold to non-U.S. nationals. Nevertheless, U.S. investment banks have lead-managed a great many dollar eurobond issues since the inception of the market in the early 1960s. They are allowed to do so because the SEC granted a release on July 9, 1964, which states that a public offering of securities does not have to be registered with the SEC if it "is made under circumstances reasonably designed to preclude distribution or redistribution of the securities within, or to the nationals of, the United States."

Meeting the requirements of the 1964 release presents investment bankers with a straightforward practical problem: How do you keep bearer bonds out of the hands of U.S. citizens at the time of initial distribution? The way this is typically handled in a new issue is as follows. First, members of the selling group sign an agreement not to sell bonds to U.S. nationals. Second, at the time money is actually paid and credit is received for bonds bought, the individual bonds themselves are not yet distributed. Instead, the borrower issues a *global bond,* which is a bond certificate representing the total amount of the issue. Those who have bought bonds have ownership shares in the global bond but they do not yet have the individual bearer bonds of $1000 (or so) denomination. After a ninety-day waiting period, individual investors can, if they wish, pick up from the office of a paying agent the bearer bonds they have purchased. At that time, they must present evidence they are not U.S. citizens, and must in addition sign a statement that they were not acting on behalf of U.S. citizens in purchasing the bonds. These procedures are called *lock-up* procedures and get investment bankers off the hook with respect to the SEC.

PRIVATE PLACEMENT EXEMPTION

If a eurobond offering is structured to fall under the "private placement" exemption of the Securities Act of 1933, then it can be sold to U.S. nationals— such as foreign branches of U.S. banks—during the period of initial distribution, even though the bonds are not registered with the SEC. The private placement exemption applies when the purchasers of the bonds have the following characteristics:

1. They are limited in number.
2. They are "sophisticated."
3. They are able to bear the loss if the bond issuer defaults.
4. They purchase bonds as principals (i.e., not for resale).
5. They have access to information similar to that which would be contained in a registered offering prospectus.

WITHHOLDING TAX AND BEARER BONDS

As a result of U.S. regulatory changes in the summer of 1984, there is currently no U.S. withholding tax on payments to foreigners who hold U.S. government or corporate bonds. In addition, U.S. corporations are allowed to issue bearer bonds directly to non-U.S. residents. These new changes promise to reduce significantly the distinction between domestic bonds in the United States and eurodollar bonds issued by U.S. nationals. Prior to the summer of 1984, many U.S. companies had borrowed in the eurobond market at interest rates lower than the U.S. government's borrowing rate. This will probably no longer be possible, and the net effect of the recent changes will increase corporate borrowing rates relative to that of the U.S. government. The importance of these changes can be seen if we compare the previous regime.

Prior to July 1984, whenever U.S. corporations issued bonds in the U.S. domestic market, the United States imposed a 30 percent withholding tax on interest payments to nonresidents. The same applied when U.S. companies issued eurobonds: Under normal circumstances there was a 30 percent withholding tax (since purchasers were normally nonresidents) that was applied to coupon payments. In practice, this meant that U.S. companies who issued eurobonds from the United States had to pay a higher rate of interest than other borrowers in the eurodollar bond market, because foreign borrowers who issued dollar eurobonds would not face the same 30 percent U.S. withholding tax. However, there were two ways for U.S. companies to avoid the necessity of withholding the 30 percent tax on interest payments.

1. No withholding tax was required if the bonds were issued by a domestic finance subsidiary that met the "80/20" test of the Internal Revenue Code (section 861). A company's domestic finance subsidiary would meet this test if it derived less than 20 percent of its gross income from U.S. sources. However, most U.S. parent companies did not have such a domestic finance subsidiary.
2. No withholding tax was required if the bonds were issued by a foreign finance subsidiary. For U.S. companies issuing dollar eurobonds, this foreign finance subsidiary was usually located in the Netherlands Antilles. The reason had to do with a U.S.-Netherlands tax treaty that allowed parent companies to write off on their U.S. taxes most tax payments made in the Netherlands Antilles. That is, a company would not only be exempt from withholding the tax on coupon payments to foreigners but would also be able to write off on its U.S. taxes those taxes it paid in the Netherlands Antilles. In order for a foreign finance subsidiary to meet requirements of

the tax code, the subsidiary had to be "independent" (i.e., it could not be a shell company) with its own separate books, and it could not be "thinly capitalized." The meaning of the latter phrase was not clear, but foreign finance subsidiaries with a debt/equity ratio as large as 2.5/1 had made eurobond offerings without stirring up any complaint.

In 1984, the tax treaty with the Netherlands Antilles was not renewed. In addition, the 30 percent U.S. withholding tax was removed and it became permissible for corporations to issue bearer bonds directly to foreigners. These actions removed much, but not all, of the incentive for U.S. corporations to utilize foreign finance subsidiaries. In addition, the changes worked in favor of those investment banking and brokerage firms that specialized in domestic U.S. investment banking, as some of what had previously been eurobond business could now become domestic business. The objective of the U.S. Treasury in sponsoring the changes was to reduce overall borrowing costs for the U.S. government: It was believed the net interest reduction from the increase in the demand for U.S. government debt would more than offset the loss of withholding tax. By the same token, costs to corporate dollar bond issuers in the United States and elsewhere rose, since bond purchasers now found U.S. government securities, without the 30 percent withholding tax, more attractive relative to corporate debt than they had previously.

Differences still remain, however. Congress did not approve the issuing of U.S. government bonds in bearer form. In addition, skepticism remained on the part of some traditional eurobond buyers (such as Swiss banks) whether the tax removal was permanent: What the U.S. government gives, the U.S. government can take away. As a consequence, domestic and eurobonds had become closer substitutes from a foreign purchaser's point of view, but they were not identical. The long-run effect of the change will result in a closer integration of the eurodollar and domestic dollar bond markets, and will also tend to make the U.S. government borrowing rate a floor level for borrowing rates in the eurodollar bond market.

YANKEE BONDS

For years the Yankee bond market was the largest and most important foreign bond market. In recent years, however, it has been surpassed by the Swiss franc foreign bond market. The growth of the Yankee bond market was impeded by the U.S. Interest Equalization Tax that was in force during the 1963–1974 period. This tax effectively cut off European borrowers from the Yankee bond market by making them pay higher-than-market interest rates in order to issue bonds in New York. (Other foreign borrowers were, however, exempt from the tax: Canadian borrowers; international organizations, such as the World Bank; and developing countries like Brazil and Mexico.)

Yankee bonds must be registered under the Securities Act of 1933, which involves meeting the disclosure requirements of the U.S. Securities and Exchange Commission. If the bonds are listed (usually on the New York Stock Exchange), they must also be registered under the Securities Exchange Act of 1934. The ordinarily long four-week registration period can be speeded up by *shelf registration*. In shelf registration, the borrower files a prospectus that covers all anticipated borrowings within the coming year. Then at the time of a new issue, the borrower only has to add a prospectus supplement, which takes only a week to clear.

Yankee issues are customarily rated by a bond rating agency such as Standard and Poor's Corporation or Moody's Investors Services, Inc. A rating is necessary if the bonds are to be sold to certain U.S. institutional investors. Use of the Yankee bond market has tended to be restricted to borrowers with AAA credit ratings. There is no withholding tax on coupon payments to foreigners who purchase Yankee bonds. Coupons are usually paid semiannually.

The secondary market for Yankee bonds is more liquid than that for dollar eurobonds and bid/asked spreads are smaller. New issue costs are smaller than for eurobonds (about $\frac{7}{8}$ percent versus 2 percent for eurobonds). The fact of smaller issue costs, combined with more frequent coupon payments, means one should be cautious in comparing interest rates in the Yankee market with rates in the dollar eurobond market. The semiannual coupon payments on Yankee bonds are equivalent to a slightly higher annual coupon on a eurobond. Conversely, the higher up-front fees on eurobonds increases the true borrowing rate on eurobonds proportionately more than the up-front fees on Yankee bonds increase the true Yankee bond borrowing rate.

DM EUROBONDS AND DM FOREIGN BONDS

In Germany there is no separation between investment banking and commercial banking, as there is in the United States, and the international DM bond market is dominated by the major German commercial banks. Prior to October 1984, eurobonds and foreign bonds were legally distinguished from German domestic bonds in that there was a 25 percent coupon tax to nonresidents who purchased German domestic bonds, while the coupon tax did not apply if nonresidents purchased DM eurobonds or DM foreign bonds. This meant foreigners would arbitrage between domestic DM bonds and international DM bonds only if price differences were sufficient to make up the tax differential. For some foreign investors taking advantage of double-taxation agreements there was, however, little tax distinction. German residents are similarly subject to the same tax on interest payments from either type of bond. In effect, this means both bonds are tax-free to German residents, as no coupon tax is withheld; there is no reporting requirement for coupon payments; and domestic bonds are usually issued in bearer form. After the U.S. removed its 30 percent withholding tax to foreigners on U.S. domestic bonds in the summer of 1984, German authorities responded by removing the withholding tax on German domestic bonds.

A DM eurobond is not legally different from a DM foreign bond. If the banking syndicate selling international DM bonds is composed of only German banks, the bonds are classified as DM "foreign" bonds, while if the syndicate includes non-German banks, the bonds are called DM "eurobonds." By an agreement between the Bundesbank and the major German commercial banks, the lead manager in DM eurobond issues was always a German bank prior to 1985. Since DM eurobonds and foreign bonds have no differing economic characteristics, a DM bond will essentially trade at the same price whether it is issued as a foreign bond or a eurobond.

DM eurobonds originated in 1964 when the 25 percent coupon tax was imposed. (Note that a coupon tax is different from the U.S. IET of the time, as the IET was calculated as a percentage of the *purchase price* of a bond.) Foreigners were buying German bonds as a way of speculating against the U.S. dollar (that is, they were anticipating a DM appreciation). The tax was imposed to discourage foreign purchases of DM domestic bonds ("capital inflows"), so international DM bonds were created to avoid the tax.

Prior to 1985, the total volume and the timing of issue of DM eurobonds and foreign bonds was regulated by the Subcommittee for Foreign Issues of the (German) Central Capital Market Committee, which was composed of six German banks and had the central Bundesbank as an observer. These six banks set issue quotas, which they allocated among themselves. The purpose of this cartel arrangement seems to have been an attempt to control the domestic cost of capital by regulating the amount of foreign competition for funds. In 1985, issuing quotas were eliminated, and subsidiaries of foreign underwriters were allowed to lead manage new issues. International DM bonds are issued in cities outside Germany but are listed on German stock exchanges and are cleared through the Effektengiro system, a special clearing system in Frankfurt. (Clearing is explained in Chapter 18.)

Floating-rate notes only recently emerged in the DM eurobond market because of Bundesbank opposition. The central bank was attempting to segment the money market and the capital market by prohibiting bond coupon rates being tied to short-term interest rates. Pressure for financial deregulation led to the removal of official opposition in 1985, and German commercial banks reached a consensus on the creation of an FRN reference rate: the Frankfurt Interbank Offered Rate (FIBOR). Twelve banks report their three- and six-months offered rates each day between 11:00 and 11:30 A.M. to Privat-Diskont-bank, which eliminates the lowest and highest quotes and publishes an average of the remainder as FIBOR.

SAMURAI BONDS AND YEN EUROBONDS

Japan's domestic bond market is already the second largest in the world, and with its large domestic savings base, Japan easily has the potential to make Tokyo a leading international capital market. For years, however, foreigners have had only limited access to Japan's bond market. The first yen eurobond (by the European Investment Bank) did not appear until 1977, and strict regulations prevented much subsequent growth. The samurai market began earlier, at the end of 1970, but access was limited mostly to international organizations and foreign governments. The first issue by a foreign corporation (Sears, Roebuck) did not occur until 1979. Restricted access to the bond market extended even to Japanese corporations, who were effectively shut out by the tradition that corporate bond issues had to be fully collateralized with company assets. Most domestic bond issues were made either by government, by one of the long-term credit banks (Nippon Credit Bank, Long Term Credit Bank of Japan, Industrial Bank of Japan), by the trust banks, or by the Bank of Tokyo, which has special status as a commercial bank. (The various banks mentioned here in turn provided working capital and plant and equipment loans to Japanese industry.)

Prior to 1984, the Japanese securities firms, under Ministry of Finance guidelines, allowed only four to six international issues per year, each with a maximum amount of ¥15 billion (¥20 billion for the World Bank) and a maximum maturity of ten years. Euroyen issues could be made only by supranationals who had previously made at least one samurai issue, or by government borrowers who had made three previous samurai issues and who were also rated AAA by a U.S. rating agency. A new bond issue had to be lead managed by one of the Japanese securities houses. As a consequence, over the period 1977–1984 only eleven government and international financial borrowers entered the euroyen market—the most frequent borrowers being the World Bank (IBRD), the Asian Development Bank, and the European Investment Bank.

In the beginning, borrowers in the samurai market had to convert the yen they obtained into foreign currency. Since many samurai bonds were also purchased by foreigners (at least on the secondary market), in effect yen was just the unit used to denominate the value of the bonds. The amount of a bond issue itself did not necessarily represent net lending by Japanese savers.

To see why this is true, suppose an American company borrows by issuing yen-denominated bonds for a total of ¥2 billion, and suppose the issue is purchased by investors from the United States. Then the net effect is that U.S. investors are lending to U.S. borrowers. The equivalent transaction could have been done in New York. The borrower could have issued bonds worth ¥2 billion in New York, specifying that yen is only the currency of denomination (just like the ECU or SDR). Borrowers would buy the yen bonds by paying dollars, and as coupon payments came due would receive the current dollar value of the yen coupons. For example, if at the time the bonds were offered the exchange rate were ¥200 = $1, then a ¥200,000 bond could be purchased for $1000. If each bond had a 5 percent coupon, paid semiannually, then there would be a payment worth ¥5000 every six months. If the exchange rate were ¥210 = $1 at the time of the first coupon, then the payment in dollars would be $23.81. And so on. The value of such a bond to a U.S. consumer would be equivalent to the value of an ordinary dollar bond, plus the value of a series of forward contracts corresponding to the coupon payment dates and the principal repayment date. The "forward rate" in these contracts would be the spot rate at the time the bond was purchased. Then if, at the time of each coupon payment, the spot rate has changed from its initial value, there will be an opportunity gain or loss, in the same manner that there would be an opportunity gain or loss on a forward contract if the spot rate in the market were different from the forward rate at the time the forward contract matured. If the value of the yen had increased with respect to the dollar, then the nominal dollar value of the bond to the bondholder would have increased. Similarly, the borrower's nominal dollar liability would also have increased. That is, the nominal dollar value of the bond would fluctuate according to the dollar/yen exchange rate, but no direct Japanese lending or borrowing would be involved. (Technically, only 25 percent of a samurai issue could be purchased by foreign investors at the time of offering, but there was no restriction on purchases on the secondary market. As a consequence, foreign buying of samurai issues was usually higher than the 25 percent figure suggested.)

A similar process took place when Japanese corporations issued eurodollar bonds. Japanese life insurance companies were allowed by the Ministry of Finance a maximum of 10 percent of foreign securities in their portfolios, but dollar bonds issued by Japanese companies were not categorized as foreign. Hence, dollar bonds issued by Japanese companies and purchased by Japanese life insurance firms (sushi bonds) represented a strictly Japanese savings flow, with the U.S. dollar serving only as the currency of denomination.

In May 1984, the United States and Japan announced, as part of the general agreement on Japanese financial deregulation, a lessening in restrictions on euroyen financing. The euroyen market would be expanded to allow, for the first time, both Japanese and non-Japanese corporations to make public euro-yen issues, and foreign banks would be allowed to serve as lead managers. The market was opened to issues by foreign banks in 1985, and dual-currency, zero-coupon, and FRNs were also approved. Although many complex restrictions remained, the consequences of deregulation were immediately apparent, with the amount of yen eurobonds surpassing DM eurobonds in the first half of 1985. Euroyen bonds are usually listed in Luxembourg or London while samurai bonds are listed on the Tokyo Stock Exchange.

SWISS FRANC INTERNATIONAL BONDS

It may seem surprising that a country as small as Switzerland, with only six million inhabitants, would have the largest foreign bond market in the world. We saw the principle involved, however, in the previous section on Japanese yen bonds. When Swiss-franc-denominated bonds are issued in Switzerland, it is not necessarily the domestic savings of Swiss citizens that is being borrowed. More often than not, foreign (to Switzerland) savers are lending to foreign borrowers, with the amount of the debt obligation fixed in terms of Swiss francs. The Swiss franc is chosen as a unit of account with relatively stable purchasing power, while Swiss banks act as politically neutral international financial intermediaries.

The Swiss National Bank regulated the volume of Swiss franc issues prior to 1984, when the issuing calendar was abandoned. Bonds are usually lead managed by one of the "big three": Swiss Bank Corporation, Union Bank of Switzerland, or Credit Suisse. A certain percentage of the Swiss francs received by the borrower have to be converted to other currencies. While nonresidents are subject to a 35 percent withholding tax on Swiss franc domestic bonds, they are exempt from withholding on Swiss franc foreign bonds. Swiss franc foreign bonds are bearer bonds, have annual coupons, and have a minimum denomination of SF5000. Foreign bonds are usually listed and traded on one of the Swiss stock exchanges.

After an initial Swiss franc eurobond issue by the city of Copenhagen in 1963, the Swiss franc eurobond market was "closed" from 1963 to 1982. That is, Swiss authorities prohibited the issuing of Swiss franc eurobonds. Legally, of course, there is no way that Switzerland could have stopped foreigners from issuing Swiss-franc-denominated eurobonds. But, as a practical matter, there is a heavy cost involved in incurring the displeasure of a major central bank—Swiss franc payments must be channeled through the Swiss commercial banking system—so no one is willing to issue eurobonds without the explicit consent of the authorities in the country whose currency would be used to denominate the bonds.

PROBLEMS FOR CHAPTER 16

1. It has been stated that the Japanese Ministry of Finance opposed development of a euroyen market because, among other reasons,

   . . . competition was not wanted between the euroyen bond market and the domestic yen (samurai) bond market. Euroyen bonds do not create the politically important capital outflows needed to offset Japanese current amount surpluses and thus ease international tensions.

   Criticize this statement. Did it really make a difference, with respect to capital flows, whether bonds were issued in the euroyen market or the samurai market?

2. Explain how a foreign currency coupon bond issue is, in terms of its cash flow implications for a domestic issuer, equivalent to a domestic currency coupon bond issue plus a series of forward exchange contracts. How then could a foreign currency coupon bond issue be completely hedged against foreign exchange risk?

3. Extending your answer in Problem 2, explain how a Japanese company could have issued the equivalent of a euroyen bond even prior to May 1984. [This secret was discovered by Japan Air Lines, Japan Development Bank, All Nippon Airways, and Chubu Electric Power Company.]

NEW ISSUE PROCEDURES IN THE EUROBOND MARKET

Arranging and selling a new eurobond issue has traditionally been a complicated procedure. Recently, competitive pressures brought about a simplified structure, "the bought deal," which is still standard in the eurobond market. More recently, thin profit margins lead to the "fixed price reoffer." In order to gain a perspective on this evolutionary process, we will first review the traditional structure as a background to recent changes.

ORGANIZATION OF A TRADITIONAL EUROBOND SYNDICATE

Eurobonds are issued and sold through underwriting syndicates. Participants in these syndicates are investment banks, merchant banks, and the merchant banking subsidiaries of commercial banks. The parts of a traditional eurobond syndicate are shown in Figure 17.1. A prospective borrower—a company, a bank, an international organization, or a government—will approach an investment bank and invite it to become the *lead manager* of a eurobond issue on the borrower's behalf. The lead manager may then invite a small additional group of banks to assist it in negotiating terms with the borrower, in assessing the market, and in organizing and managing the new issue. This small group, including the lead manager, is the *managing group*. In addition, two other categories of banks—*underwriters* and the selling group—will be invited to participate in bringing the bonds to market. The different syndicate categories reflect the multistage process by which the bonds are sold.

The borrower sells the bonds to the managing group. In turn—depending on the form of syndicate organization—the managing group either sells the bonds directly to both the underwriters and the selling group or else sells the bonds to the underwriters, who in turn sell bonds to the selling group. Members of the selling group, in turn, sell to final investors. Underwriters differ from pure sellers in that underwriters commit themselves ahead of time to buy the bonds at a set minimum price from the managers even if the bonds cannot be resold to sellers or end investors for a price greater than this preagreed minimum. (As

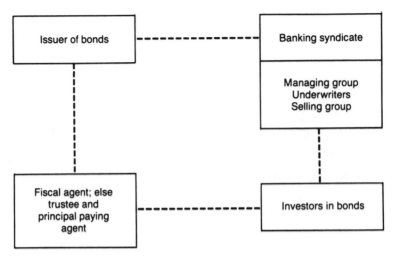

FIGURE 17.1
Role players in a new eurobond issue.

will be explained later, the term "underwriter" in the eurobond market often differs from its sense as used in a domestic context.) Roles in a eurobond syndicate are nested: Managers are also underwriters and sellers, and underwriters are usually also sellers.

The *principal paying agent* in a eurobond issue is the bank that has the responsibility for receiving interest and principal payments from the borrower and disbursing them to end investors. When a *fiscal agent* is used in a new issue, the fiscal agent and the principal paying agent are the same. A fiscal agent is a bank appointed to act on behalf of the borrower, one that takes care of the mechanics of bond authentication and distribution to investors as well as acting as principal paying agent. An alternative to a fiscal agent is a trustee. A trustee acts not on behalf of the borrower, as does a fiscal agent, but rather in the interest of investors. A trustee acts as the representative of all bondholders in any legal action stemming from bond covenant defaults. If a trustee is used for a new eurobond issue, then a separate principal paying agent will be appointed to act on behalf of the bond issuer.

Table 17.1 gives the identity of the top lead managers of eurobond issues for some recent years, where the ranking is according to the percentage dollar amount brought to market. The table shows that perennial eurobond leaders such as CSFB and Deutsche have been increasingly challenged by the Japanese securities firms of Nomura, Daiwa, Yamaichi, and Nikko. The latter have dominated with respect to equity-linked eurobond issues.

FEE STRUCTURE FOR NEW EUROBOND ISSUES

In the eurobond market, fees are extracted by discounts on the prices at which bonds are provided to syndicate members. Suppose, for example, that $1000 bonds are issued at 100, which means that the issue price for the bonds is 100 percent of face value. (If the bonds are issued at 100 percent of face value, they are said to be issued at "par." An issue price of 99.5, by contrast, is "below

TABLE 17.1
Top Lead Managers of Eurobond Issues

Rank	1985 Firm	%	1986 Firm	%	1987 Firm	%	1988 Firm	%	1989 Firm	%
1	CSFB	14.3	CSFB	11.4	Nomura	13.0	Nomura	9.9	Nomura	15.4
2	Merrill Lynch	6.0	Nomura	8.0	CSFB	7.0	CSFB	7.8	Yamaichi	7.8
3	Morgan Guaranty	5.9	Deutsche	6.6	Deutsche	6.0	Deutsche	6.7	Daiwa	7.7
4	Salomon	5.8	Morgan Guaranty	5.4	Nikko	5.7	Daiwa	5.3	Nikko	7.1
5	Deutsche	5.7	Daiwa	4.9	Yamaichi	5.2	Yamaichi	4.3	Deutsche	4.7
6	Morgan Stanley	5.0	Morgan Stanley	4.9	Daiwa	5.1	Nikko	4.0	CSFB	4.4
7	Goldman Sachs	4.1	Salomon	4.3	Morgan Stanley	3.6	Paribas	3.4	JP Morgan	3.5
8	Nomura	3.8	Paribas	4.0	Morgan Guaranty	3.4	Merrill Lynch	3.4	Morgan Stanley	3.3
9	UBS	2.8	Merrill Lynch	3.2	Salomon	3.1	JP Morgan	3.3	Banque Paribas	3.1
10	Paribas	2.5	Nikko	2.9	Paribas	3.0	IBJ	3.2	Merrill Lynch	3.0

Source: Securities Data Company.

par.'' And so on.) The amount the borrower gets, however, is not related to the issue price. For example, the managing group may have agreed to pay the borrower $975 for each $1000 bond. The $25 discount, which is 2.5 percent of the $1000 issue price of an individual bond, would be referred to as a "flotation cost" or "investment banking spread" of 2.5 percent.

However, syndicate members really receive the full 2.5 percent, or $25 per bond, only if the bonds are actually sold to retail customers at the issue price of 100 ($1000). Such may not happen. Once the bonds are in the hands of the underwriters or sellers (after the signing of final terms), there is no enforceable contract to make them sell the bonds in the market at their issue price or better. Consequently, any amount by which the bonds are sold at less than 100 reduces the overall portion of the "spread" that is received by the syndicate and increases the true yield on the bond from the bond-buyer's point of view.

In the U.S. domestic market, by contrast, underwriters are obligated to maintain the market price of the bonds at a level equal to the issue price or higher until the bond syndicate is disbanded. This obligation is enforceable because domestic bonds are registered and hence the identity of parties making particular transactions can be traced. Originally, the term "underwriter" in the eurobond market was intended to have the same meaning as in the domestic market. But legal contracts to maintain the issue price turned out to be nonenforceable, since members who wished to sell unregistered bearer bonds at a lower price could do so through third parties without the transaction being traceable to the original syndicate member. Therefore any or all of a fee may be passed along to the buyer of a bond, depending on the price the bank charges. Also by contrast to the U.S. domestic market, there is considerable price discrimination in sales to final investors. Given that selling members may pass along a part of their fee to the end investor in the form of a discount from the issue price, it follows that different investors may buy bonds at different prices. Institutions with "buying power"—such as insurance companies and banks that administer large trust and fiduciary funds—get considerable discounts.

Here is a typical structure of fees for a eurobond issue with a 2.5 percent total investment banking spread, along with terms used to refer to various parts of the fee.

Lead manager pays borrower $975 per $1000 bond.
Lead manager makes bonds available to underwriters at $980.
Lead manager makes bonds available to sellers at $985.

$1000 − $975 = $25	"Flotation cost" or "spread"	(100% of spread)
$1000 − $985 = $15	"Selling concession"	(60% of spread)
$ 985 − $980 = $ 5	"Underwriting allowance"	(20% of spread)
$ 980 − $975 = $ 5	"Management fee"	(20% of spread)

We see that for ordinary sellers, the bonds may be sold for any amount greater than $985, and there will be a marginal profit (before selling expenses are paid). An underwriter is largely just a privileged seller who gets bonds at a lower price than an ordinary member of the selling group. Underwriters who are also sellers get both an underwriting allowance and a selling concession, and managers who are also underwriters and sellers get all three fees.

In this example, total flotation costs of 2.5 percent were assumed. For U.S. dollar eurobonds, 2 percent is the typical notional spread, before discounting, for issues of ten years or longer. Shorter maturities have smaller spreads. Typical spreads for some of the foreign bond markets are these: Yankee bonds, .5 to 1 percent; samurai bonds and DM foreign bonds, 2 to 2.5 percent; Rembrandt bonds, 2.5 percent; and Swiss franc foreign bonds, 2.5 to 3 percent. (The unusually large spread for Swiss franc foreign bonds appears to stem from the oligopsony buying power of the three largest Swiss banks, who purchase the greater portion of any Swiss franc foreign bond issue.)

TRADITIONAL TIME SCHEDULE FOR A NEW OFFERING

The key dates in the traditional time schedule for a new dollar eurobond offering are shown in Figure 17.2. Here is a summary of the process. Starting perhaps two weeks before the announcement day shown at the top of Figure 17.2, the lead manager and the borrower will meet for preliminary discussions. They will discuss terms (coupon, amount, offering price) of the bond issue. Except in the case of a bought deal (discussed later), these terms will remain provisional until the formal offering day. A fiscal agent or trustee and principal paying agent will be selected, and if the issue is to be listed on a stock exchange (usually Luxembourg or London), a listing agent as well. Preparation will begin on various legal documents that will be signed between syndicate members and the borrower, and among syndicate members. Work will also begin on the offering circular or prospectus, which in its preliminary form is called a red herring. The prospectus will describe the borrower and its history. For a corporate borrower, audited financial statements will be included in the prospectus, while for a government borrower there will be relevant GNP and

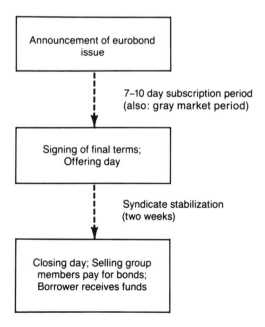

FIGURE 17.2
Time schedule of new eurobond offering, prior to the bought deal.

central bank data. The prospectus will also include a statement of the preliminary terms of the bond offering.

The lead manager will begin to organize a management group to assist in the administration of the bond issue and will compile a list of potential syndicate members who will be invited to take part either as underwriters or as sellers. On the announcement day (see top of Figure 17.2) there will be a press release announcing the new issue, and invitation faxes will be sent out inviting other banks to participate in the syndicate. Potential participants will have a week to ten days to respond (the offering period or subscription period). Potential underwriters and sellers will be sent a copy of the preliminary offering circular, a timetable of the bond offering, and relevant legal documents that they will sign if they take part in the issue. If the borrower is not well known, the borrower may at this point begin a tour, or "road show," in major financial centers in order to spread information about itself to potential investors.

The lead manager, meanwhile, will keep a *syndicate book* in which a record of the total demand for the bond issue is recorded. As interest in the bond issue is expressed, the lead manager will begin to make preliminary allotments of bonds among syndicate members, while waiting to receive signed underwriting and selling group agreements. Selling group members who cannot sell their entire allotment will later be able to return unsold bonds to the managers, while underwriters will be legally obligated to buy any unsold bonds at a preagreed minimum price. Even though underwriters may face a good deal of risk of a change in market conditions, the underwriting agreement they sign will usually give the managers considerable discretionary control over the issue. The managing group will decide final bond pricing terms with the borrower, and these terms may or may not be subject to an underwriter's approval before the underwriting agreement goes into effect. In addition, the managers will usually have considerable freedom in the number of bonds they decide to allocate to each underwriter and seller, subject to a maximal amount for which an underwriter is liable.

At the end of the subscription period, final bond pricing terms are decided upon between the managing banks and the borrower. Underwriters usually then have a day within which to accept or reject these terms, assuming they have the right of prior approval. Then the bonds are formally offered (the offering day) when the borrower and managing banks sign a subscription agreement setting out the final terms of the bond issue. At this point, the syndicate has in effect purchased the bonds from the borrower at an agreed price, though the borrower will not actually receive the funds until the closing day. A final offering circular is printed, and the lead manager notifies the underwriters and sellers of their bond allotments. The lead manager may either over- or underallocate the number of available bonds (see Stabilization, later). Sellers then have a number of days, after which they must notify the managers whether their allotments are sold. In the meantime, the newly offered bonds are bought and sold over the counter, though no money (or bonds) yet changes hands.

At the end of the stabilization period (closing day), syndicate members pay for the bonds they have purchased by depositing money into a bank account opened by the lead manager. Final investors at this point also receive book-entry credit for the bonds they have purchased (although they do not yet receive the individual bearer bonds). The borrower is paid in accordance with the terms of the subscription agreement, and the syndicate disbands. A tombstone, or advertisement, of the bond issue will later be published in a financial newspaper or journal.

For those who want them, the individual bearer bonds can usually be picked up from an office of the paying agent after ninety days have passed. In the meantime, there is a global bond, a temporary debt certificate representing the entire bond issue. Global bonds are used for U.S. dollar eurobond issues so U.S. investment banks can show that they have exercised due diligence in keeping new bonds out of the hands of U.S. citizens (for reasons explained in Chapter 16).

THE GRAY MARKET

During the subscription period, while potential sellers and underwriters are indicating their willingness to accept an allocation of bonds from the managing banks, there is uncertainty about the final terms of the bond issue, as well about how market conditions may change between the time an allocation of bonds is agreed to and the time the bonds are sold. If a seller knows he or she will receive an allocation of bonds from the lead manager (the amount of the allocation not yet certain) and knows that he will get a 1.5 percent discount from the issue price of the bonds, he or she might reason as follows: "I am getting a discount of 1.5 percent on a certain number of bonds. If I could sell these immediately for a smaller discount, say a discount of 1 percent, I would lock in a .5 percent profit and could thus avoid the risk that interest rates (and hence bond prices) will change." The bonds themselves, however, are not yet in formal existence: Final terms have not been established, and documents pertaining to the issue have not been signed. Nevertheless, there is nothing to prevent a forward market from emerging in which people make contractual commitments to trade these bonds at agreed prices once the bonds officially exist. Such a market in eurobond new issues emerged around 1977. It is referred to as the gray market or premarket. Gray market trading begins on the announcement day of a new issue. Bonds are traded in the gray market at a percentage discount on the future, as-yet-unknown issue price. A price of "less 1," for example, would mean a price of 98.75 if the bonds are issued at 99.75. A $1000 bond would then be exchanged between the two parties for 98.75 percent of its face value, or for $987.50.

The existence of the gray market raises an interesting practical question. If bonds could be bought on the gray market, say at "less 1.5," why would any final investor pay a higher price than this to a member of the selling group? And, if no one would pay higher than gray market prices, then—at the end of the subscription period when the borrower and the lead manager agree on final terms for the bond issue—gray market prices would dictate what final bond terms would be. In fact, there would be no reason to appeal to the lead manager's expertise in canvassing the market to determine the appropriate bond-pricing terms: The bonds would have been de facto priced by the market through gray market trading.

The pricing of new eurobonds issued according to the traditional timetable is, in fact, heavily influenced by gray market prices. As this market continues to develop, the gray market—or forward—price will come to represent the price at which potential demand is brought into equilibrium with potential supply. It is easy to foresee that in the future evolution of the eurobond market the traditional role of the lead manager will continue to be downgraded and new issues will come to be priced by more efficient market techniques. Until recently, however, information has flowed asymmetrically through the bond market. An investment banker named Stanley Ross began putting gray market prices on the Reuters screen in 1978, but access was limited to those members of the Association of International Bond Dealers (AIBD) registered as market-makers. But in 1982 the bond-brokering firm of Guy Butler began making prices more generally available (Anderson, 1982). Such market-oriented approaches will undoubtedly continue, despite the hostility of a number of lead managers.

Sometimes gray market trading in a new bond issue has begun even before the announcement date. That is, not only have final terms not been decided, but even the existence of the prospective bond issue has not yet been announced. Jumping the gun in this fashion has its dangers. In October 1983, based on reports that Canada and the World Bank were to offer $700 million worth of eurobonds, the securities firms of Ross and Partners (Securities) Ltd. and Guy Butler International Ltd. posted bid and asked prices for these nonexistent bonds and traded them for a day before it was realized that no such issues were in the works.

STABILIZATION

Stabilization refers to efforts by the lead manager to influence the market price of a bond during the time between the offering day and the closing day. The lead manager will put together a small group from the syndicate who will stand ready to buy up bonds to support their price if necessary. The rule of thumb typically followed is that the price of the bond in the market will not be allowed to fall below the amount of the selling concession (which is usually about 1.5 percent of the issue price of the bond). The price at which the managing group bids for bonds is referred to as the "syndicate bid." There seem to be several motives for stabilization. One has to do with the prestige of the lead manager. If the price of the bond rises immediately after terms have been signed, it will show that the lead manager didn't do a good job of assessing the market, since the borrower could have borrowed at a lower interest rate. The borrower might be upset and choose a different lead manager the next time around. Conversely, investors who buy bonds at or near their issue price will be upset if the price of the bonds drops immediately in the secondary market.

If interest rates rise over the course of the selling period, bond prices will have a tendency to fall, so the lead manager will be in the position of buying up bonds on the market in order to stabilize their price. If interest rates fall over the course of the selling period, bond prices will have a tendency to rise, so more bonds could be sold without depressing the price. Thus, for example, if the lead manager believes that interest rates will be rising during the stabilization period, the manager may, at the time terms are signed for a new issue, allocate to sellers a total of more bonds than actually exist. This is referred to as a syndicate short. The lead manager will then be obligated to buy back some of these bonds prior to closing, so as to have the required number of bonds available at the time money and bonds actually change hands. The action of the lead manager in buying back bonds on the market will support their price. Alternatively, if interest rates are expected to fall, the lead manager could engage in a syndicate long, which involves underallocating the number of available bonds.

VARIATIONS ON ISSUING PROCEDURE

A number of variations in the traditional procedure for making new eurobond issues exist. These variations represent responses to competitive pressures and interest rate risk. The bought deal is the primary example, as it has become the new standard for eurobond issues. In the bought deal, the lead manager buys the entire bond issue from the borrower at set terms—amount, coupon, issue price—prior to its announcement. Preset prices arise because of competition between individual investment banks to win mandates. They compete by quoting the borrower a package deal up front. An early bought deal was that of CSFB, who bought an entire $100 million issue overnight from General Motors Acceptance Corporation in April 1980. Only afterward did CSFB arrange a syndication. Such postsyndications result in a diminished role for selling group members and underwriters. Whether a bought deal actually involves more interest rate risk than is involved in the traditional issuing procedure is hard to say. Final terms are set without a subscription period for canvassing demand. However, the total time it takes to bring the issue to market is shortened. Hence some investment bankers use the bought deal to take advantage of windows—a "window" being essentially a stochastic drop in interest rates (or a stochastic rise in bond demand) that is perceived to be of short duration. Given these expectations, an investment banker might view the shorter time frame needed to bring a bought deal to market as implying an overall lower risk in terms of rising interest rates. In any case, the prefixed terms of the offering lead to brisk gray market trading as syndicate members hedge their interest risk by selling forward.

Yield pricing is another way of handling the possible discrepancy between the terms indicated on announcement day and the final terms signed at the end of the subscription period. In yield pricing, no preliminary terms are indicated. Instead, the coupon and the issue price of the bond, and the amount of commissions, are fixed toward the end of the subscription period, and prices are set in line with similar issues in the secondary market. Yield pricing is widely used in the U.S. domestic bond market, but has been used in the eurobond market only in recent years.

A different approach is the *auction issue,* in which the borrower announces the maturity and the coupon rate of a new bond issue and invites investors to submit bids. Interested investors—who may be brokerage firms or banks who expect to resell the bonds—submit a bid price as a percentage of par such as 99.3, along with a statement of the amount they are willing to take at this price. The borrower then sells the bonds, starting with the highest bidder and working down until all bonds have been allotted. The auction system is widely used in domestic contexts. U.S. government securities, for example, are sold through an auction system. The auction system eliminates management fees and the costs of syndication and has served well certain widely known borrowers in the eurobond market such as the European Investment Bank. For less well known borrowers, however, part of the job of an investment banking syndicate is to spread information about the borrower and the borrower's proposed bond issue. Such borrowers will find it necessary to pay the cost of a bond syndicate's marketing expertise.

Under a *fixed price reoffer*, the lead manager (book runner) and comanagers sign a contract legally obligating them not to discount fees through selling concessions. They are thus virtually guaranteed a *marginal* return on each bond sold, since institutional buyers are not able to buy bonds at a discount to the issue price. It is equivalent to the way bonds are underwritten in the U.S. domestic market. The fixed price reoffer (FPRO) method was introduced by Morgan Stanley International in a eurobond issue for the World Bank in 1989 as a reaction to the low or negative returns being realized on new eurobond issues. More than 20 percent of new eurobonds were subsequently issued under FPRO terms in the first three quarters of 1990. Typical spreads in a FPRO are $\frac{5}{16}$ to $\frac{3}{8}$ percent instead of 2 percent.

The future of the FPRO was uncertain, however. Working in its favor was the basic economic fact that firms who never earned a profit would eventually abandon the eurobond business. Working against the FPRO was its dependence on a cartel agreement among major banks, since any major player could otherwise choose to issue eurobonds under terms that would allow discounting to favored buyers.

PROBLEMS FOR CHAPTER 17

1. An investment banking syndicate follows the following table of flotation costs.

Maturity	Management fee (%)	Underwriting Allowance (%)	Selling Concession (%)	Total (%)
≤5 yrs.	$\frac{3}{8}$	$\frac{3}{8}$	$1\frac{1}{4}$	2
5–8 yrs.	$\frac{3}{8}$	$\frac{3}{8}$	$1\frac{1}{2}$	$2\frac{1}{4}$
> 8 yrs.	$\frac{1}{2}$	$\frac{1}{2}$	$1\frac{1}{2}$	$2\frac{1}{2}$

The syndicate launches a $80 million seven-year eurobond issue. The syndicate is composed of a lead manager, who takes half of the management fee, and five comanagers who split the remainder. The issue is underwritten by the six managing banks (who underwrite a total of 30 percent of the issue), fifty major underwriters (who underwrite 50 percent of the issue), and forty minor underwriters (who underwrite the rest). The underwriting allowance is split up according to the amount underwritten. The issue is sold by the six managers ($36 million total, divided equally), fifty major underwriters ($20 million total), forty minor underwriters ($12 million total), and 100 additional selling banks ($12 million total). The selling concession is split according to the amount sold. Calculate the dollar amount of total fees going to
(a)   The lead manager.
(b)   Each of the comanagers.
(c)   Each of the major underwriters.

    (d) Each of the minor underwriters.
    (e) Each of the selling banks, *assuming all bonds are sold at the issue price of 100.*
    (f) The company.

2. Assume you were the lead manager for a new eurobond issue. Explain how and under what circumstances the gray market could be helpful to you. Explain how and under what circumstances the gray market could hinder you.

3. Make the same explanations as in Problem 2, but from the point of view of a life insurance company portfolio manager.

4. Is the fixed price reoffer a positive development? From whose point of view?

CHAPTER 18

EUROBOND VALUATION AND HEDGING

Once new eurobonds have been formally offered on offering day, the bonds begin to trade in the secondary market. In our discussion of the secondary market, we want to distinguish between trading, which is the buying and selling of bonds at negotiated prices, and clearing, which is the process of transferring ownership of the bonds between parties after the bonds are traded. Trading and clearing are separate functions in the eurobond market.

TRADING

The principal center of eurobond trading is the over-the-counter market in London, although other centers such as Frankfurt, Amsterdam, and Zurich are also important. An over-the-counter market means that traders do not gather together in one physical location to trade bonds—as in a stock exchange or a futures exchange. Rather, the market is formed through a telecommunications linkage of U.S. brokerage firms, U.S. multinational banks, and major European and Japanese banks. (DM eurobonds are an exception: Most secondary market trading takes place on the German stock exchanges.)

Orders to buy or sell bonds can be placed through market participants, who can be divided into brokers and marketmakers. Brokers accept orders to buy or sell bonds and try to find a matching party for the other side of the bond transaction. They typically charge a fee of .0625 percent to the party who initiated the transaction. Brokers in the eurobond market may, in addition, buy and sell for their own account. But brokers do not in general stand ready to quote two-way prices. Nor do they typically deal with retail customers. Instead, they act as intermediaries between marketmakers. Marketmakers, by contrast, will quote two-way (bid and offer) prices to retail customers and stand ready to deal in either direction. Marketmakers invest their own capital in a bond inventory and can themselves serve as the matching party in transactions by selling bonds out of their own portfolio or adding bonds to their portfolio.

Except for a brokered transaction, no commissions are charged between participants in the secondary market. A marketmaker's reward for making the market comes through the bid/asked spread between buying and selling prices. Of course, like the marketmakers in the foreign exchange market, discussed in Chapter 3, a marketmaker actually only earns the bid/asked spread to the extent he or she is adept at adjusting prices so that the number of bid orders is matched with the number of asked orders. Bond prices are quoted as a percentage of face value. Thus a bid/asked quotation of 95.5–96 would indicate a bid price of $955 and an asked price of $960 for a bond with a face value of $1000. The typical spread on fixed rate bonds is .5 percent ($5 on a bond with a face value of $1000), but there will be a range of spreads depending on market conditions. In the first few days following a new bond issue, when trading is heaviest, spreads may be as low as .125 percent, while at other times thinly traded bonds may have spreads of 1.5 percent. The standard-size transaction is 100 bonds (or $100,000 face value), and quoted prices usually are good only for a standard-size transaction. Floating-rate notes are more liquid and enjoy a much smaller spread than fixed-rate or convertible issues.

When a trade is made, the price involved in the trade has been established, but money and bonds will not change hands until the value date, which is usually set so as to take place one week after the actual trade. Thus if a lot of 100 bonds is traded on Monday, July 23, then the purchaser will actually pay cash, and receive bonds, on Monday, July 30.

Eurobonds are bought or sold in the secondary market "cum coupon." The bond buyer will compensate the bond seller for the amount of interest that has accumulated since the last coupon payment. The calculation of accrued interest is a function of the manner in which time is calculated in the bond markets. This topic is covered in the following section.

TIME MEASURES IN THE INTEREST RATE MARKETS

As noted in Chapter 4, interest rates are always quoted at a yearly rate: the interest payment per currency unit per year. There are different conventions, however, in counting days and measuring years. These are illustrated here.

Actual/360: This year basis is used in the U.S. money markets and the eurodollar market. Interest is calculated using the literal number of calendar days between two dates, divided by 360. Interest of 10 percent between February 15, 1995, and March 15, 1995, would be paid over 28 calendar days:

$.10 \times 28/360 = .007778.$

Actual/365: This year basis is used in the UK and Australian money and bond markets and the eurosterling market. The literal number of calendar days is divided by 365. Interest of 10 percent between February 15, 1995, and March 15, 1995, would be calculated as:

$.10 \times 28/365 = .0076712.$

30/360: This year basis is used in the markets for most eurobonds and U.S. corporate bonds. Each month is considered as having 30 days. There are 30 days between February 15 and March 15. There are 31 days between February 15 and March 16. Interest of 10 percent between February 15 and March 15 would be calculated as

$.10 \times 30/360 = .0083333.$

There are some further conventions for this day count basis. *These differ in the euromarkets from the U.S. domestic market.*

U.S. market: If the *beginning* date is on the 31st, change it to the 30th. Since there are 15 days from January 30 to February 15, there are therefore also 15 days from January 31 to February 15. But if the *ending* date is on the 31st, leave it at 31, except when the beginning date is 30 or 31 (in which case change the end date to 30). Following this second rule, we count 16 days from January 15 to January 31, 30 days from December 30 to January 31, and 30 days from December 31 to January 31.

Euromarket: In these markets the AIBD rules apply, which changes a 31st date to the 30th, regardless of whether the date is a beginning or an ending date. Thus there are 15 days from January 15 to January 30, and also 15 days from January 15 to January 31.

If we alter the dates according to the rules listed above, then the number of days between date 1 (year1, month1, day1) and date 2 (year2, month2, day2) is:

$$\#\text{days} = (\text{year2} - \text{year1}) \times 360 + (\text{month2} - \text{month1}) \times 30 + (\text{day2} - \text{day1}).$$

Actual/Actual: This day count basis is used in the U.S. and Australian government security markets. It divides the literal number of calendar days between two dates by the literal number of days in a year (or, possibly, year fraction). Between August 13, 1995, and August 13, 1996, there are 366 calendar days. Interest on a single yearly coupon of 10 percent between these two dates would be calculated as

$.10 \times 366/366 = .10.$

The year basis will not, however, always be 365 or 366 under this way of counting. If a 10 percent coupon bond pays twice yearly, each coupon represents a payment of 5 percent. During each half-yearly coupon payment, interest accrues at a rate determined by the actual days in a half-year. For example, between July 1, 1996, and January 1, 1997, there are 184 days. Then, if coupons are paid on July 1 and January 1, the accrued interest from July 1 to August 1 would be calculated as:

$.05 \times 31/184 = .0084239.$

Note that in terms of the original 10 percent coupon, this can be considered a 368-day year basis:

$.10 \times 31/368 = .0084239.$

To summarize: The actual/actual uses literal calendar days for the day count, but the year basis varies according to the number of days in the fraction of a year between coupon payments:

# of Yearly Coupons	# of Days Between Coupons	Year Basis
1	365	365
1	366	366
2	181	362
2	182	364
2	184	368

EXAMPLE 18.1

On September 14, 1995, a trader buys 100 eurobonds with a face value of $1000 each, bearing a coupon of 12 percent, at a secondary market price of 93. The bonds pay annual coupons on February 10. What is the trader's total dollar payment?

The bonds settle on September 21. There are $(9 - 2) \times 30 + (21 - 10) = 221$ days of accrued interest, calculated on a 30/360 year basis. Hence the accrued interest is

$$100 \times \$1000 \times .12 \times (221/360) = \$7,366.67.$$

The payment net of accrued interest is

$$100 \times \$1000 \times .93 = \$93,000.$$

The total payment is therefore $\$93,000 + \$7,366.67 = \$100,366.67$.

CLEARING

The primary goal in clearing procedures is to reduce the costs associated with bond transactions. That means that actual physical bonds should be moved around as little as possible. By analogy, think about how foreign exchange or eurocurrency deposits are traded internationally. Money—a deposit—is simply a number stored in a data bank along with a record of ownership. Thus trading money internationally is very simple. If a $1,000,000 deposit is to be transferred from Party A to Party B, the bank simply removes Party A's name and attaches Party B's name. It costs very little to send electronic signals between New York and London. Imagine what the cost would be, by contrast, if in order to get a $1 million deposit from New York to London a large suitcase had to be stuffed with $20 bills and a courier had to go to Kennedy airport, fly to Heathrow in England, and then cart the suitcase off to the appropriate London bank. This principle applies where bonds are concerned. The costs of clearing will be low only if the bonds are put away in a vault somewhere and ownership of the bonds is simply transferred through bookkeeping entries.

Most eurobonds are cleared through one of two major clearing systems: Euroclear and Cedel. Euroclear Clearance System Limited is a clearing system located in Brussels. It is owned by a group but continues to be operated by Morgan Guaranty, which founded the system in 1968. Cedel S.A. is a clearing system located in Luxemborg. It was founded in 1971 by a group of European banks. Euroclear handles about two-thirds of the volume of bonds cleared through the two systems, Cedel one-third. Annual turnover through the clearing systems is over $1 trillion. Each of the systems has a group of depository or custodian banks in which physical bonds are stored. Members of a clearing system will maintain bond and cash accounts with the system. When bonds are purchased or sold, book-entry settlements will be made, transferring the ownership of bonds or cash between the two members. The bonds themselves are seldom, if ever, moved. Both Euroclear and Cedel have an approved list of securities that can be cleared through their operations. (In the U.S. a similar system exists for clearing U.S. government securities, which are also traded over the counter. Government bonds are stored in Federal Reserve vaults, and traders in government securities make title and money transfers via

FedWire. Treasury bills are even simpler: They exist *only* in the form of accounting entries, hence storage costs are minimal.)

Euroclear and Cedel can also be used to distribute new eurobonds from the borrower issuing the bonds to syndicate members and final investors who have purchased bonds. The printed bond certificates are delivered in bulk to the clearing system. The clearing system then collects the subscription payments, gives book-entry credits to the new owners of the bonds, and remits the funds to the eurobond underwriting syndicate. Similarly, a clearing system can be used to distribute coupon payments from a borrower. The borrower pays funds into the clearing system and the clearing system makes the appropriate payments into the accounts of members credited with the ownership of the borrower's bonds.

While most eurobonds are cleared through Euroclear or Cedel, DM eurobonds are an exception. German banks are large dealers in DM eurobonds, and they usually prefer to store bonds in a domestic group of depository banks, the Kassenvereine, and to clear bonds through the associated securities clearing system, the Effektengiro system.

The large reduction in transactions costs that comes about from the use of a clearing system can be seen in the following list of Euroclear transactions fees that was in effect in the summer of 1982. Transactions are distinguished according to whether they are simple book-entry settlements between Euroclear members or transactions with another clearing system (Cedel or the Frankfurter Kassenverein), or whether they involve physical movement of the securities. A "transaction" is a single order to transfer bonds, independent of the number of bonds.

Schedule for Euroclear Transactions Fees, Summer 1982	
Transfer of securities between Euroclear participants	$1.00
Transfer of securities against payment between Euroclear participants	$1.50
Bridge clearing of securities against payment with Cedel	$4.00
Transfer of securities via Frankfurter Kassenverein	$8.00
Deposit of securities into Euroclear system	Free
Removal of securities from Euroclear system	$12.50
Removal of securities against payment from Euroclear system	$15.00

In addition to transactions fees, there are custody fees for keeping the securities in the vault. These fees are charged according to the volume of bond turnover in a participant's account and are zero for high turnover.

Thus we can see that, except for transactions involving physical removal of securities, clearing costs are trivially small. For 100 bonds priced at 80 that are cleared against payment participants, the charge of $1.50 for $80,000 of bonds is .001875 percent of the value of the bonds.

INTEREST RATES AND COUPON BOND PRICES

Coupon bonds can be priced by reference to pure discount (zero-coupon) bonds. Let the current year be t and consider a coupon bond $P(t,T)$ that has coupon payments at times $t + 1$, $t + 2$, . . . , $t + T$, in dollar (or other currency) amounts of $C(t,1), C(t,2), \ldots, C(t,T)$. If the coupon payments are all the same, then $C(t,n) = C$, for all n. (For example, $C(t,n) = \$100$ for a 10 percent coupon on a \$1000 face-value bond.) The bond also repays the principal $K(t,T)$ at time $t + T$.

Suppose that the coupons are stripped from the bond and each of the coupons and the principal repayment are sold separately. (This is a common practice with U.S. Treasury securities. For example, CATS—certificates of accrual on Treasury securities—are composed of stripped coupons or principal for a particular maturity date.) Since a coupon $C(t,n)$ involves no cash flows prior to time $t + n$, the current value of the coupon is $B(t,n)C(t,n)$, where $B(t,n)$ is the current price of a discount bond that pays \$1 (or one unit of other currency) at time $t + n$. Because the coupon will involve a payment of $C(t,n)$ dollars, it has a value of $C(t,n)$ of these \$1 discount bonds, or a value of $B(t,n)C(t,n)$.

The value of the entire coupon bond $P(t,T)$ is therefore

$$P(t,T) = B(t,1)C(t,1) + B(t,2)C(t,2) + \ldots + B(t,T)C(t,T)$$
$$+ B(t,T)K(t,T) \tag{18.1}$$

Equation (18.1) relates the value of the coupon bond $P(t,T)$ to discount bonds of equal or shorter maturity, $B(t,1), \ldots, B(t,T)$. If all coupon payments $C(t,n)$ have the same value, $C(t,n) = C$, for all n, equation (18.1) simplifies to

$$P(t,T) = C[B(t,1) + B(t,2) + \ldots + B(t,T)] + B(t,T)K(t,T). \tag{18.2}$$

There are several ways to refer to an interest rate in connection with the price of a coupon bond. One way is the coupon yield, which is the ratio of the coupon to the principal repayment:

$$\text{Coupon yield} = C/K(t,T). \tag{18.3}$$

Another rate is the current yield, which is the ratio of the coupon to the current bond price:

$$\text{Current yield} = C/P(t,T). \tag{18.4}$$

For example, if a 10 percent coupon bond with a \$1000 face value is currently selling for \$975, the current yield is \$100/\$975 $= 10.26$ percent.

Finally, there is the yield-to-maturity, which applies a uniform discount rate to each future time period. To calculate yield-to-maturity for annual coupons, let B be a fictional bond price such that, when it is raised to powers $1, 2, \ldots, T$:

$$P(t,T) = C[B + B^2 + \ldots + B^T] + B^T K(t,T). \tag{18.5}$$

Then the yield-to-maturity (measured as a fraction) is defined as

$$\text{Yield-to-maturity} = (1/B) - 1. \tag{18.6}$$

For example, if a 10 percent annual coupon bond with a face value of \$1000 and with five years remaining to maturity has a yield-to-maturity of 11.11 percent (i.e., $B = 1/1.1111 = .9$), the current price $P(t,5)$ is:

$$P(t,5) = \$100 [.9 + .9^2 + .9^3 + .9^4 + .9^5] + .9^5(\$1000)$$
$$= \$100 [3.6856] + .59(\$1000)$$
$$= \$368.56 + \$590.00 = \$958.56.$$

The yield-to-maturity of 11.11 percent is higher than the current yield of $100/$958.56 = 10.43 percent.

Any one of these rates has a clear economic interpretation only in special circumstances. The coupon rate only indicates the size of the coupon payments, though it usually also represents the market interest rate on bonds in the present bond's risk class at the time the bond was first issued, assuming the bond was issued at par. The current yield would represent the return on a bond if it were bought at its present market value now and sold at the same price a year later, following a single coupon payment. The yield-to-maturity is relevant to individuals or institutions who apply uniform discount rates to the future, since in that case a bond with a higher yield-to-maturity is a more attractive asset than one with a lower yield-to-maturity. For an individual or institution that applies nonuniform discount rates to the future, the yield-to-maturity is a misleading method of ranking bond investments.

The yield-to-maturity does, however, have the attractive feature that there is a one-to-one relationship between a bond's price and its associated yield. Given a yield, we can calculate the price, and vice versa. Hence bonds are frequently quoted in terms of their yield. The price that is to be associated with a given yield is, however, a function of the day count basis—which affects accrued interest and the way the cash flows are discounted—and the individual market where a bond trades. Consider an 8 percent coupon bond that pays coupons on March 15 and September 15, and which matures on March 15, 2001. Then a yield of 9.403 percent would imply the following prices on January 3, 1995:

Market	Day Count	Price
U.S. corporate	30/360	93.497
U.S. government	actual/actual	93.500927
Eurobond	30/360	93.497782
UK government	actual/365	93.535118
Australian government	actual/actual	93.501

Note that in addition to different discounting conventions, there are also different rounding or truncation conventions.

EUROBOND VALUATION

Eurobonds are intermediate to long-term assets, and their valuation depends on the relation between short-term interest rates and bond coupon rates. Interest rates in today's market, combined with a market participant's expectations of future interest rates, give rise to a number of different trading strategies whose execution influences bond prices. Here are some examples.

Arbitrage

As bonds mature, there may be straightforward profit opportunities based on borrowing or lending short-term and buying or selling bonds. If a profit can be locked in with certainty, then this is a form of arbitrage. (If the bonds are denominated in a foreign currency, then there must also be an exchange rate transaction in order to fix with certainty the domestic currency value of the entire operation.) The process of arbitrage will bring about price adjustments so that arbitrage opportunities are eliminated. The absence of arbitrage opportunities will thus define a relation between bond prices and short-term interest rates.

EXAMPLE 18.2

A trader in the over-the-counter market in London observes a DM1000 eurobond with a 4 percent coupon and with one year to maturity quoted with a bid/asked price of 95.5–96. He has access to the interbank market, and observes that one-year eurodollar deposits are available at 10.5–10.625 percent, that spot rates are quoted at DM2.4783–2.4798/$, while one-year forward rates are DM2.3954–2.3981/$. If he buys any number of bonds, clearing charges through Euroclear will be $1.50. Given these prices, will the trader buy the DM eurobond?

In one year the DM bond will pay DM1000 principal plus a coupon of DM40. The DM return on the bond is $1040/960 = 1.0833$ or 8.33 percent. DM can be purchased spot for DM2.4783/$ and sold forward for DM2.3981/$, so the dollar return is

$$(1.0833)(2.4783/2.3981) = 1.1195$$

or 11.95 percent. This is greater than the trader's borrowing rate of 10.625 percent, so the trader will buy the bond. For a lot of 100 bonds, the trader will need to pay DM96,000. This implies that he must borrow

$$\$38,736 = (DM96,000)/(DM2.4783/\$)$$

and pay back in one year

$$\$42,851.70 = (\$38,736)(1.10625).$$

If he sells forward today the DM he will receive in one year, he will sell forward DM104,000 for

$$\$43,368 = (DM104,000)/(DM2.3981/\$).$$

The profit at the end of one year will be $516.30, from which should be subtracted the Euroclear fee of $1.50 plus about $.16 in interest, the interest being the opportunity cost of paying the $1.50 fee one year in advance. Alternatively, the value of the profit discounted to the present time when the transaction is made would be:

$$\$516.30/1.10625 - \$1.50 = \$465.21.$$

Of course, in practice the procedure in the example would be simplified. Exchange exposure, if it existed, would be dealt with in the context of the total bond portfolio, not on the basis of individual transactions. An arbitrager might buy the bond if the total return, calculated in terms of DM, were greater than the arbitrager's DM borrowing rate.

Riding the Yield Curve

If the term structure of interest rates is upward-sloping—that is, if short-term interest rates are lower than long-term interest rates—then this strategy involves borrowing at short term in order to finance a bond portfolio. If the level of coupon payments on the bonds is greater than the level of interest payments on the borrowing by an amount sufficient to cover management expenses, this strategy will yield a profit. The risk is, of course, that short-term rates may rise above long-term rates. If the yield curve becomes inverted in this fashion, the cost of financing the portfolio will exceed the income from coupon payments and principal repayments on the bonds in the portfolio. Moreover, the bond portfolio could not in that case easily be liquidated without incurring a large capital loss, since bond prices will have fallen with the rise in short-term interest rates. If a eurobond futures market existed, this risk of capital loss could be more easily managed. Unfortunately, no such futures market currently exists (see, however, Bond Futures, later).

Most eurobond dealers finance their bond portfolios by borrowing through the clearing systems—Euroclear and Cedel. A clearing system will loan a dealer up to 90 percent of the value of bonds the dealer has deposited within the clearing system, so that only a small portion of the bond portfolio must be financed using the dealer's own capital.

Speculation on Capital Gains and Losses

As short-term interest rates rise and fall, bond prices fall and rise (refer back to equation (18.1)). Bond investors discount future coupon payments according to current and expected future short-term interest rates. A change in current short-term interest rates usually entails also a change in expected future interest rates. As a result, when the new present and expected future interest rates are used to discount the future coupon and principal payments on a bond, the bond's value—and market price—will change.

The speculator's strategy in this case is to sell bonds short if the speculator expects interest rates to rise since—if the expectations prove accurate—the price of a bond when it is sold will be greater than the price of a bond when it is repurchased. If the speculator expects interest rates to fall, the strategy is to be long bonds now, with an anticipation of selling bonds after interest rates have fallen and bond prices risen. The execution of these strategies is made easier by recent institutional innovations. The two clearing systems have bond borrowing and lending facilities. This makes possible short-selling, since bonds may be borrowed from the system at a preagreed interest rate for a preagreed period of time and sold.

THE FORWARD PRICE OF A COUPON BOND

In Chapter 4 we saw that forward foreign exchange prices were determined by reference to spot prices and short-term interest rates. In a similar way we may determine the forward value of a coupon bond. For simplicity we will here ignore bid/asked spreads. Also for simplicity we will limit the number of bond coupons paid within the term-to-maturity of the forward to one. The analysis is easily intended to include multiple coupon payments.

Consider the following transaction: Borrow short-term for T_2 days at an interest rate r_2, buy a coupon bond at a price P plus accrued interest $A1$, receive a coupon C at the end of T_1 days, and sell the bond at the end of T_2 days at the forward price F, receiving also accrued interest $A2$.

$$
\begin{array}{ccc}
P + A1 & C & F + A2 \\
\vdash\! & \top & \!\dashv \\
0 & T_1 & T_2
\end{array}
$$

The borrower will have to pay interest on $P + A1$ for T_2 days, but will receive interest on C for $T_2 - T_1$ days. If the interest rate for T_1 days is r_1, then there is an implied forward rate f for lending the cash received on the coupon payment:

$$
1 + f\frac{(T_2 - T_1)}{360} = \frac{1 + r_2 T_2/360}{1 + r_1 T_1/360}.
$$

To avoid an arbitrage profit, the borrower must end up at time T_2 with less cash than he paid out. Hence

$$
(P + A1)(1 + r_2 T_2/360) - C\frac{(1 + r_2 T_2/360)}{1 + r_1 T_1/360} \geq F + A2.
$$

F must be low enough to avoid arbitrage. But if F is too low, a bondholder can sell the bond, invest the cash at short-term interest rates, and buy the bond back forward at a profit. So F must be high enough to avoid this reverse arbitrage. Thus, ignoring bid/asked spreads, we conclude that the forward bond price F is:

$$
F = (P + A1)(1 + r_2 T_2/360) - C\frac{(1 + r_2 T_2/360)}{1 + r_1 T_1/360} - A2. \tag{18.7}
$$

EXAMPLE 18.3

A Treasury bond is trading at a price of 84 '17 (that is, $84\frac{17}{32}$), and has an 11 percent coupon payable on July 15 and January 15. Short-term interest rates as of May 23 are 8 percent for two months or less and $8\frac{1}{4}$ percent for three months. What is the forward price of the bond calculated to August 23?

In this example, $T_2 = 92$ days (May 23 to August 23), $T_1 = 53$ days (May 23 to July 15). There are 128 days of accrued interest as of May 23, which calculated on an actual/actual basis is:

$$
\frac{11\%}{2} \times \frac{128}{181} = 3.8895\%.
$$

As of August 23 there will be 39 days of accrued interest (July 15 to August 23), which, calculated on an actual/actual basis, is

$$
\frac{11\%}{2} \times \frac{39}{184} = 1.16576\%.
$$

Therefore, converting the bond price 84 '17 to its decimal equivalent of 84.53125%, we calculate the forward price as

$$
F = (84.53125 + 3.8895)(1 + .0825 \times 92/360)
$$

$$
- 5.5\frac{(1 + .0825 \times 92/360)}{(1 + .08 \times 53/360)} - 1.16576 = 83.5686.
$$

This corresponds to an approximate forward price of 83 '18. Note that in this calculation the semiannual coupon payment of $5\frac{1}{2}$ percent has been reinvested at the forward interest rate.

BOND FUTURES

Bond dealers regularly utilize futures contracts to manage the risks on their bond portfolios. How this is done depends on the particular future. Not all bond futures are alike. We will discuss three types: notional, cheapest-to-deliver, and index-based.

Notional Bond Futures: A notional bond future represents a hypothetical bond of fixed principal, coupon, and maturity. For example, a futures contract could be based on a $100,000 government bond with an 8 percent coupon, paid semiannually, and maturing in twenty years. There may, in fact, be no such actual cash bond in existence. But such a bond could be priced by reference to other bonds trading in the market, and a futures contract on this notional bond could be used to hedge currently traded cash bonds.

Notional government bonds trade at the MATIF in Paris, the Deutsche Terminborse in Frankfurt, the FTA in Amsterdam, the MEFF in Barcelona, and LIFFE in London.

Cheapest-to-Deliver Bond Futures: The most widely traded bond and note futures contracts, such as those at the CBOT in Chicago and the Tokyo Stock Exchange, allow for actual delivery of one of a number of bonds against the futures contract. The short side of the bond futures contract makes the choice of which bond to deliver. Some of the bonds on the list will, at a given moment, cost less than others. The seller of the futures contract will choose the issue that costs the least amount of money. Because bond futures traders know this, the futures price will move in conjunction with the cash bond issue that is cheapest to deliver.

CBOT futures contracts have a face value of $100,000 and different contracts trade for delivery in March, June, September, and December. The price is quoted as a fraction of face value, expressed in percent and $\frac{1}{32}$ percent. A price of 61 '07, for example, would denote $61\frac{7}{32}$ percent of par. If the price moved from 61 '07 to 61 '08, the long side of the T-bond futures contract would make

$$\tfrac{1}{32} \times .01 \times \$100,000 = \$31.25,$$

while the short side would lose $31.25. If the price went from 61 '07 to 60 '31, the long side would lose

$$\tfrac{8}{32} \times .01 \times \$100,000 = \$250$$

on each contract, while the short side would gain $250 on each contract.

Dealers in the U.S. government securities market can hedge the risk of capital losses on their bond portfolios that would result from rising interest rates by going short T-bond futures. If interest rates rise, the price of T-bond futures will fall, and any profit on the futures position will offset capital loss on the portfolio. A short cash bond position can be hedged by going long T-bond futures. The precision of this hedge will depend on the change in value of the T-bond futures contract compared with the change in value of the position in government securities. If the two value changes are not exactly offsetting, the hedge will not be perfect. Nevertheless, such valuation changes are sufficiently predictable that T-bond futures prove in practice to be a useful way to hedge.

There is no unique price-to-yield relationship in a cheapest-to-deliver bond future like there is in a notional bond future. Instead, the price-to-yield futures relationship depends on the price-to-yield relationship of the particular cash bond that is currently cheapest to deliver.

At the CBOT, deliverable bonds against the T-bond futures contract are U.S. Treasury bonds with a maturity of at least fifteen years if not callable or, if callable, with at least fifteen years remaining from the first day of the delivery month to the first call date. Delivery may be initiated by the seller of the bond futures contract on any business day of the delivery month, or on the last two business days of the previous month. The delivery process takes three days. On the third day, delivery day, the buyer (long side) pays the seller for the bonds, and in return receives book-entry Treasury bonds that are transferred to him via the Federal Reserve wire transfer system. While cash bond deliveries may take place until the end of the month, the deliverable futures contract itself stops trading on the eighth to last day of the delivery month.

What is the equilibrium price for a deliverable T-bond future? During the delivery month, traders will continually compare the value of a deliverable cash bond in the cash market to its equivalent in the futures market. When the long side of the bond futures contract takes delivery, he pays an invoice price (I), representing the cash price as a percentage of face value, and also pays accrued interest on the cash bond. The invoice price is the futures price (Z), multiplied by an exchange conversion factor (cf):

$$I = Z \times cf.$$

The same bond in the cash market may be purchased at the current market price (P), plus accrued interest. Equating the two ways of obtaining the cash bond, we conclude

$$P = Z \times cf. \tag{18.8}$$

The exchange conversion factor (cf) at the CBOT is calculated by setting the yield to maturity (or to first call, if callable) on the bond to be delivered equal to 8 percent, and dividing the resulting price by 100. In doing this calculation the maturity of the bond is rounded down to the nearest quarter, as calculated from the first day of the delivery month. For example, in March 1995, the U.S. Treasury 7.5 percent coupon bonds maturing on November 15, 2016, have twenty-one years and eight months to maturity. Rounding down to the nearest quarter, we obtain a maturity of twenty-one years and six months. Setting the yield-to-maturity on the bond equal to 8 percent results in a (decimal) price of 94.91 percent. Dividing by 100 gives a conversion factor of $cf = .9491$. Thus, if the futures price were 75, the invoice price would be

$$I = 75 \times .9491 = 71.1825\%.$$

This price applies to a principal amount of $100,000, so actual cash payment is $71,182.50.

The reader may at this point be wondering why any deliverable cash bond should be "cheaper" than any other. Prices and yields of cash bonds should adjust so that in equilibrium there are no arbitrage opportunities, and hence no "cheaper" bonds. The answer lies in the exchange conversion factor. The conversion factor (cf) values bonds as though each yields 8 percent to maturity or first call. But in the cash market the deliverable bonds will be in equilibrium at generally different yields, depending on coupon and maturity. The futures conversion factor, by forcing all bonds to a yield of 8 percent, creates a divergence between the bonds' conversion values relative to their market values.

Suppose yields are in equilibrium at 9 percent. By lowering the yield to 8 percent, the conversion factor will increase the conversion value of low-coupon, long-maturity bonds more than it will high-coupon, short-maturity bonds. Hence the low-coupon, long-maturity bonds will be cheaper to deliver because they will have high conversion values relative to their cash market values. For similar reasons, if market yields are below 8 percent, then high-coupon, short-maturity bonds will be cheaper to deliver.

Cheapest-to-deliver futures may trade at a discount to the cash market even during the delivery month because of option features associated with the delivery process. One is the *delivery option*, associated with the fact that the short side of the bond futures contract has a choice of which of the available cash bonds (those meeting the Exchange's deliverable grade criteria) it will deliver against the contract. Another is the *wild card option*, associated in the case of the CBOT with the fact that the futures market closes at 2 P.M. (Chicago time), which locks in that day's futures settlement price, while the short side has until 8 P.M. to declare an intention to deliver. Because the cash market continues to trade for six hours, the cash price P will continue to adjust, even though the futures invoice price I is already fixed.

The delivery option gives an advantage to a dealer who is long deliverable cash bonds and short bond futures. To see why, assume he is completely hedged with position V:

$$V = P - Z \times cf = 0.$$

If yields change, some other bond may become cheaper to deliver. The short futures contract will compensate the dealer for any loss of value associated with the change. Meanwhile the dealer can realize a profit by selling his relatively expensive cash bond and replacing it with the deliverable bond that has become cheaper.

The wild card option is a six-hour put option. The strike price of the put is the invoice price fixed by the 2 P.M. futures settlement. In the event the cash bond price has fallen below the invoice price by 8 P.M., the short side of the bond futures contract can exercise this put and receive the higher invoice price.

Both the delivery option and the wild card option have positive value. Thus, in market equilibrium the futures price should be bid down by the value of these options:

$$Z = P/cf - \text{option values.}$$

So, in general, in a cheapest-to-deliver bond futures market we will observe:

$$P > Z \times cf. \tag{18.9}$$

The bond in the cash market will be trading at a higher price than its futures equivalent, but this would only imply arbitrage opportunities during the delivery month if the futures discount were greater than the value of the options.

The difference between the cash price of a bond and its futures equivalent is referred to as the *basis*:

$$\text{basis} = P - cf \times Z \tag{18.10}$$

Equation (18.8) indicates that the basis should be zero during the delivery month, except for embedded option features. Equation (18.9), which includes the effect of the options, indicates that the basis should be positive even during the delivery month.

What about during the period prior to the delivery month? In this case, traders cannot buy a case bond and make immediate delivery. Instead they would have to finance the cash bond until delivery were possible. Therefore they would compare, not the current cash bond price to its futures equivalent, but instead the forward price (F) of the bond to its futures equivalent. The forward bond price takes into account the impact of the short-term borrowing cost, and also the coupon interest that will be earned on the cash bond. Define the *basis after carry* (BAC) as

$$\text{BAC} = F - cf \times Z. \tag{18.11}$$

The BAC indicates the cost, in terms of forward dollars, of buying a cash bond and delivering it against the futures contract. A trader will want to minimize this cost in terms of each futures contract he is short, so we can characterize the cheapest-to-deliver bond as that bond with the smallest BAC.

EXAMPLE 18.4

Tables 18.1 and 18.2 give the relevant calculations for determining which Treasury bond is cheapest to deliver against the June 1990 CBOT bond futures contract. The calculations are made on April 16 with respect to June 1, the first available delivery day. From Table 18.2, we see that the $7\frac{1}{2}$ maturing November 15, 2016, has the smallest BAC (0.21962) and hence is cheapest to deliver among those bonds shown, if we assume an 8 percent short rate.

Let's go through most of the relevant calculations for one of these bonds. Take the first bond listed, with a coupon of 14 percent. Even though this bond actually matures in 2011, the bond may be called from November 15, 2006. Hence, as of June 1, 1990, there will be a little over sixteen years and five months to call. To get the exchange conversion factor, we round down to the nearest quarter, and therefore calculate the price of the bond from August 15, 1990. Setting the yield-to-call equal to 8 percent gives a price of 154.00, so the exchange conversion factor is 1.5400.

The June future is at 92 '03 or 92.09375. The invoice price is therefore

92.09375 × 1.5400 = 141.82438.

The price in the cash market, meanwhile, is 143 '15 or 143.46875. As of April 16, accrued interest from November 15 is calculated as

$A1 = 14/2 \times 152/181 = 5.87845.$

TABLE 18.1
Conversion Value of Selected Deliverable T-Bonds, April 16, 1990

Maturity (or 1st Call)	Coupon (%)	Conversion Factor (cf)	June Future (Z)	Invoice Price (Z × cf)
Nov. 15, 2006	14	1.5400	92 '03	141.82438
Aug. 15, 2015	10⅝	1.2820	92 '03	118.06419
Nov. 15, 2016	7½	0.9453	92 '03	87.05622
May 15, 2016	7¼	0.9185	92 '03	84.58811

TABLE 18.2
Forward Value of Deliverable Treasury Bonds, Calculated from April 16 to June 1 with a
Short Rate of 8 Percent

Maturity (or 1st Call)	Price (P)	Accrued Interest (April 16)	Coupon (May 15)	Accrued Interest (June 1)	Forward Price (June 1)	BAC
Nov. 15, 2006	143 '15	5.87845	7.0000	0.64674	143.20085	1.37647
Aug. 15, 2015	118 '13	1.76105	0	3.11119	118.28449	0.22030
Nov. 15, 2016	87 '10	3.14917	3.7500	0.34647	87.27584	0.21962
May 15, 2016	84 '27	3.04420	3.6250	0.33492	84.81283	0.22472

On June 1, there will be seventeen days of accrued interest from May 15:

$$A2 = 14/2 \times 17/184 = 0.64674.$$

Assuming an 8 percent short rate, the 7 percent coupon that will be paid on May 15 may be reinvested at the forward interest rate f given by

$$1 + f \times 17/360 = \frac{1 + .08 \times 46/360}{1 + .08 \times 29/360}.$$

Applying equation (18.7) for the forward bond price, we get

$$F = (143.46875 + 5.87845)(1 + .08 \times 46/360)$$

$$- 7.0 \times \frac{1 + .08 \times 46/360}{1 + .08 \times 29/360} - 0.64674$$

$$= 143.20085.$$

Applying equation (18.11), we get the basis after carry:

$$BAC = 143.20085 - 141.82438 = 1.37647.$$

The calculations are similar for the other bonds. Note that the issue maturing on August 15, 2015, is the only one not having a coupon payment on May 15.

Index-Based Futures: A variety of bond futures contracts fall into this category. A future may be based on an index constructed from an average of cash bond prices. Or it may be based on yield-to-maturity (YTM). The ten- and three-year Australian government bond contracts at the Sydney Futures Exchange are quoted in terms of an index "price" Q defined as:

$$Q = 100 - \text{YTM}.$$

A quotation of 87 thus corresponds to a yield-to-maturity of 13 percent. Given the YTM, the contract works like a purely notional bond future, for there is a one-to-one relationship between the YTM and the price Z of a notional bond expressed as a percentage of face value. The Australian ten-year future is based on a 12 percent government bond, paying two coupons a year, with a face value of Aus\$100,000. Let $B = 1/(1 + \text{YTM}/200)$. Then the price Z as a percentage of face value is

$$Z = 6 \times (1 - B^{20})/(\text{YTM}/200) + 100 \times B^{20}.$$

For YTM $= 12$, $Z = 100$. For YTM $= 13$, $Z = 94.4907$. Thus the value change between $Q = 88$ and $Q = 87$ is approximately Aus\$5,509.

HEDGING WITH BOND FUTURES

Hedging with bond futures relies on the notion of *basis point value* (*bpv*). The basis point value of a bond is the change in the bond's price for a one basis point movement in yield. It is easy to calculate this value for a cash bond or for a notional bond that underlies a notional bond future. For cheapest-to-deliver bond futures, we can calculate the basis point value of the future by first calculating the basis point value of the cheapest-to-deliver bond, and then (see equation (18.8)) dividing by the exchange conversion factor:

$$bpv_{\text{future}} = bpv_{\text{ctd}}/cf. \tag{18.12}$$

Suppose we have two bonds, one with a $bpv = 2$ and the other with a $bpv = 1$. Assume that the yields on the bond will move in a parallel fashion. That is, the spread between the yields is constant. Then to create a hedged position, it is clear that for each dollar we have long in the bond with $bpv = 2$, we will need to be short two dollars of the bond with $bpv = 1$. For a basis point rise in yields, the price of the long bond will fall by 2, while the price of the short bond will fall by 1. So we would need twice as many units of the short bond to have a value change of zero.

If we define the *hedge ratio* of bond A as the number of units of bond A needed to create a hedged position against another bond, B, then

$$\text{hedge ratio A} = -\frac{bpv_B}{bpv_A}. \tag{18.13}$$

Similarly, the hedge ratio of a bond future (the number of futures contracts needed to establish a hedged position) is

$$\text{hedge ratio future} = -\frac{bpv_{\text{bond}}}{bpv_{\text{future}}}. \tag{18.14}$$

Comparing equations (18.12) and (18.14), we see that the hedge ratio for a cheapest-to-deliver (CTD) future is

$$\text{hedge ratio CTD future} = \frac{-bpv_{\text{bond}}}{bpv_{\text{ctd}}} \times cf. \tag{18.15}$$

Each of these equations assumes that yield spreads remain constant. If we change this assumption and estimate a coefficient k such that

change in yield $B = k \times$ change in yield A

then 18.13 should be modified to read

$$\text{hedge ratio A} = \frac{-k \times bpv_B}{bpv_A} \tag{18.16}$$

EXAMPLE 18.5

The *bpv*s of the deliverable bonds in Tables 18.1 and 18.2 are as follows:

Bond	Coupon	bpv
Nov. 15, 2006	14	.1133
Aug. 15, 2015	10⅜	.1162
Nov. 15, 2016	7½	.0919
May 15, 2016	7¼	.0894

Notice what this means. If yields drop 10 basis points, the price of the 14 percent of November 15, 2006, will rise by 1.133 percent, from 143.469 to 144.602. Alternatively, a basis point value of .1133 means that $100,000 face value of these bonds will change in market value by $113.30 for a one basis point move.

Consider a eurobond with a *bpv* = .145. Then, from equation (18.15), the number of CBOT T-bond futures contracts needed to hedge $100,000 in face value of this bond was, on April 16, 1990:

$$\text{hedge ratio} = -\frac{.145}{.0919} \times 0.9453 = -1.4915.$$

Thus to hedge $10,000,000 of the given bond, one would go short 149 T-bond futures. If the August 15, 2015, bond subsequently became cheapest to deliver, one would need to sell approximately eleven more futures contracts.

The amount of risk reduction that can be obtained from hedging a eurobond portfolio using T-bond futures is less than would be possible if there existed a eurobond futures contract based on a standardized eurobond. Eurobond futures contracts are being considered at some futures exchanges. In the meantime, some market participants have created the equivalent to a eurobond futures contract through private forward contracting.

In October 1983, Weyerhaeuser Capital Corporation issued $60 million in seven-year eurobonds bearing a coupon of 11.5 percent. At the same time, it took out a side bet with the investment banking firm of Morgan Stanley concerning the direction of movement of interest rates over the next seven months. If eurobond interest rates fell within the next seven months, Morgan Stanley was to pay Weyerhaeuser a cash amount such that Weyerhaeuser's borrowing cost would be reduced to the equivalent of borrowing the $60 million at the reduced interest rate. Conversely, if eurobond interest rates rose, Weyerhaeuser's borrowing cost would be increased to the equivalent of borrowing the $60 million at the increased interest rate.

The way to view this deal between Weyerhaeuser and Morgan Stanley is as a eurobond forward contract, with Morgan Stanley on one side of the contract going short, while Weyerhaeuser was on the other side going long. If interest rates fell, the value of the long side of the eurobond forward contract would rise, and the short side of the contract would pay the long side. The converse transaction would occur if interest rates rose.

It was reported at the time (*Business Week*, November 28, 1983) that Morgan Stanley simultaneously offset its risk on the contract with Weyerhaeuser by taking a position in T-bond futures. If so, it would be logical for Morgan Stanley, which was short a eurobond forward contract, to have gone long T-bond futures. Then if interest rates fell, the gain on the T-bond futures would be used to offset the loss on the eurobond forward contract, while if interest rates rose, the loss on T-bond futures would be offset by the gain on the eurobond forward contract with Weyerhaeuser. Of course Morgan Stanley would still face the risk that the gain or loss on the T-bond futures contract might not match the gain or loss on the forward contract. That would depend on the effectiveness of its hedge.

PROBLEMS FOR CHAPTER 18

1. Calculate the dollar amount of interest paid on $100 between March 15, 1995, and April 15, 1995, assuming (a) an actual/360 day basis, (b) an actual/365 day basis, when the quoted rate is 8.75 percent.

2. Calculate the dollar amount of accrued interest on a $1000, 8.75 percent coupon bond between March 15, 1995, and April 15, 1995, assuming (a) annual coupons on a 30/360 basis; (b) semiannual coupons on a 30/360 basis; (c) annual coupons on an actual/actual basis; (d) semiannual coupons on an actual/actual basis.

3. Comment on this statement: "Arbitrage opportunities in the bond markets are revealed by bond prices, not by bond yields."

4. A trader buys 100 eurobonds in the secondary market at a price of 84, each bond with a face value of $1000 and bearing an annual coupon of 12 percent. As of the value date for the trade, 112 days will have passed since the last coupon. What is the trader's total dollar payment for the bonds?

5. A French franc bond with a market price of FF8765 and a face value of FF10,000 pays annual coupons of FF700 and matures in one year. Calculate the coupon yield, the current yield, and the yield to maturity. Interpret each number.

6. A eurobond with a face value of $1000 and an annual coupon of $115 is purchased when the current yield is 10 percent. A year later the bond is sold for $995. What is the capital gain or loss on the purchase/resale?

7. A U.S. Treasury bond is trading at a price of 96 '29, and has a 7.5 percent coupon payable on May 15 and November 15. Short-term interest rates as of September 15 are 6.5 percent for one month, 6.75 percent for two months, and 7.0 percent for three months. What is the forward price of the bond calculated to December 15?

8. During the subscription period of a eurodollar bond issue, a member of the managing group sells short 100 T-bond futures at the CBOT at an average price of 70 '12. Later the futures position is closed out at an average price of 71 '01. What was the net gain or loss on the futures position?

9. A marketmaker with a long position of $346,500 in eurobonds at a current price of 99 goes short three CBOT T-bond futures contracts at 71 '16. Rising interest rates cause the price of the eurobonds to fall to $97\frac{1}{2}$, while the price of T-bond futures falls to 69 '04. What is the change in the total value of the marketmaker's position?

10. Calculate the CBOT conversion factor for the $10\frac{5}{8}$ percent U.S. Treasury bond maturing August 15, 2015, as of June 1, 1995.

11. What is the invoice price of the bond in Problem 10, assuming a futures settlement price of 103 '02? What is the amount of the accrued interest?

12. Both answers in Problem 11 were calculated without any information on the market yield-to-maturity of the bond. Is the market yield-to-maturity therefore irrelevant?

13. Calculate the hedge ratio for a short bond with a *bpv* value of .12, which is hedged with a CBOT bond future with a conversion factor of 1.1 and a cheapest-to-deliver *bpv* of .095.

INTEREST RATE AND CURRENCY SWAPS

The subject of this chapter should not be confused with that of Chapter 4. In Chapter 4 we saw that in the FX interbank market, a swap contract involved a spot sale or purchase of currency combined with a forward purchase or sale of the same currency. In this chapter, the term "swap" will have a somewhat different meaning. A *swap* is a contract between two parties to deliver one sum of money against another sum of money at periodic intervals. The two sums exchanged may be denominated in different currencies (*currency swap*), or in the same currency where one is a fixed sum and the other a variable or "floating" sum (*interest rate swap*), or in two different currencies where one currency payment is fixed and the other is variable (*cross-currency interest rate swap*). Also possible are fixed-for-fixed or floating-for-floating swaps, either in the same or different currencies.

Currency swaps differ from ordinary interest rate swaps not only in that interest payments are in different currencies, but also in that principal amounts are exchanged. In a currency swap the two parties initially exchange a principal amount in one currency for the same amount converted to another currency at the prevailing spot rate. Interest payments are then made in the respective currencies at interest payment dates, and the principal amounts are re-exchanged at maturity.

ECONOMIC MOTIVES FOR SWAPS

Most currency and interest rate swaps can be economically interpreted in one of three ways: risk sharing, arbitrage, or market completions. Many currency and interest rate swaps represent simple risk sharing. A company (or other party) has unmatched cash flows in terms of foreign currencies, or in terms of the proportion of variable-rate assets matched by variable-rate liabilities. The company finds a second party with a complementary mismatch and arranges a swap in such a way that its foreign currency cash flows are now more closely matched (currency swap), or that its variable-interest-rate asset and liability flows are now more closely matched (interest rate swap). In some cases, however, currency or interest rate swaps can be interpreted either as arbitrage or as market completions. Swaps may take place because arbitrage opportunities exist. These arbitrage opportunities may arise from exchange or capital controls, tax regulations, or simple inconsistencies in market pricing of fixed-versus floating-rate debt or debt denominated in different currencies. Finally, swaps could be termed "market completions" if they represent the emergence of new markets for risk sharing, giving rise to beneficial transactions that were not economically possible given the previously available markets and the associated costs of transacting in those markets.

The fact that some currency and interest rate swaps involve arbitrage is obvious. Suppose a Japanese company wanted debt denominated in Japanese yen. There are at least two ways to get yen debt:

1. Issue yen debt.
2. Issue dollar debt and swap it for yen debt.

Why might a company take the second route of issuing dollar debt? Answer: Issuing dollar debt and swapping may be a cheaper way of getting yen debt than would a direct issue of yen debt. If so, the Japanese company is taking advantage of an arbitrage opportunity. A few Japanese companies have, through swaps, borrowed at yen interest rates lower than the concurrent borrowing rate paid by the Japanese government.

In the same way, it may in some circumstances be cheaper to get fixed-rate debt by issuing floating-rate debt first and then swapping it for fixed-rate debt. For example, the market might be pricing the fixed-rate debt of one company relative to the fixed-rate debt of another company at a ratio that is inconsistent with the ratio at which the market is pricing the floating-rate debt of each company. In that case, both companies can arrange a debt swap that will exploit the inconsistencies in current market pricing. If these inconsistencies are large enough to pay a bank to put the two companies in touch with each other so that the bank makes a profit, then a debt swap can take place.

Swaps in some cases represent market completions. A company that wishes to issue French franc debt may not have access to the French market. As a result, it may make a deal with a second company that has French franc debt and assume the second company's obligation to pay coupons and principal denominated in French francs in return for the second company's taking on of the obligation to pay coupons and principal of a different currency. Often the two companies will not be known to each other. A banking intermediary may arrange the deal, and may guarantee both sides of the swap transaction.

TYPES OF CURRENCY SWAPS

The term "swap" is currently used in a fairly broad sense to denote a trade of one sort or another. The following types of transactions are generally considered examples of currency swaps.

Long-Term Forward Contracts

These contracts are not any different from the FX forward contracts in the interbank market. However, forward contracts for certain less-traded currencies are not available in the interbank market, and even for widely traded currencies forward contract maturities are fairly short. There is a market failure for forward trade in certain currencies and certain maturities. A long-term forward contract is thus essentially a barter transaction. A company or institution seeks out a counterparty with which it arranges a contract to exchange two currencies at some time in the future, the exchange to take place at a price that is agreed to today. The market failure in this case may be only one of degree. Commercial or investment banks may act as brokers who find a matching party on behalf of a company. They will keep careful (and carefully guarded) lists of particular institutions who are potential matching parties for particular transactions. There is a sense in which this collective set of institutions constitutes a market through the broker's intermediation.

Straight Currency Swap

A straight currency swap is the exchange of two currencies at the current exchange rate with an agreement to reverse the trade—at the same exchange rate—at some set date in the future. One of the parties will pay the other annual interest payments. These interest payments are usually agreed to on the basis of the interest parity relation. If interest rates on assets denominated in currency A are higher than in currency B, then the party who receives currency A in exchange for currency B will pay the interest differential to the other party. For example, if $1,000,000 is swapped for ¥180,000,000 and dollars pay 5 percent higher interest than yen, then the party getting dollars might pay the other party annual interest in the amount of $50,000.

Back-to-Back and Parallel Loans

Back-to-back loans are loans between two companies in different countries, each of which makes the other a loan in its respective currency. Parallel loans involve two companies in different countries, each of which has a subsidiary in the other's country. Each company makes a loan to the other company's subsidiary. For example, a U.S. company might loan dollars to a Brazilian company's U.S. subsidiary, while the Brazilian company would loan cruzeiros to the U.S. company's subsidiary in Brazil. Parallel loans got started for the same reason the eurodollar market get started: Bank of England regulations. At one time, if UK companies went through the London FX market, they had to pay a premium over the market rate for U.S. dollars in order to finance their foreign subsidiaries. To avoid this tax on dollar purchases, they arranged for their foreign subsidiaries to get dollar loans from U.S. companies, while the UK companies in turn loaned sterling to the subsidiaries of the U.S. companies in the United Kingdom.

The periodic payments of interest on each loan in a parallel loan transaction, and the repayment of principal, are usually timed to coincide in the two countries, and each company has the right to deduct payments not received in one country from payments due in the other country. Often the loan agreement includes a quasi-futures contract: If one currency depreciates in value relative to the other currency, the lender of the depreciated currency has to increase its loan to offset the changes in the loan's value due to exchange rate changes. The typical futures contract in this case, however, does not involve a cash flow for every small change in the exchange rate. Rather, it is a step function: Only if the exchange rate moves beyond certain limit points (for example, above $1.60/£ or below $1.40/£) will additional lending or repayment take place. Hence the contract is a first passage option (see the appendix to Chapter 6).

Swap of Debt Payments

In this type of currency swap, each company (or other party) issues fixed-rate debt in a currency that is available to it; then the two companies swap the proceeds of the debt issue and also assume each other's obligation to make interest and principal payments. One company may issue debt in the amount of $10,000,000, while the other issues debt in the amount of FF80,000,000. The two companies then swap currencies and in addition assume each other's obligation to make interest payments and principal repayments. The dollar-issuing company will make periodic French franc coupon payments, while the French franc issuing company will make periodic dollar payments. The coupon payment dates are set so that they coincide. The payments may be made directly between the two companies, or the payments may be made to a commercial or investment banking intermediary that passes the payment to the other company. The intermediary may, or may not, skim off part of a payment before passing it along. When the French-franc-issuing company receives the coupon payments from the other company, it then passes these along to its debt-holders. Similarly, when the dollar-issuing company receives dollar coupon payments from its counterparty, it then pays the owners of the dollar debt. The debt-holders of either company are not usually aware of the currency swap arrangement.

One early example of a swap of debt payments in different currencies was the one that took place between IBM and the World Bank in August 1981, with Salomon Brothers as the intermediary. In previous years IBM had borrowed in the capital markets of West Germany and Switzerland, acquiring fixed-interest-rate debt in DM and in Swiss francs. When the dollar appreciated sharply against these two currencies during 1981, IBM enjoyed a capital gain from the reduced dollar value of its foreign debt liabilities. The DM, for example, fell in value from DM1.93/$ in March 1980 to DM2.52/$ in August 1981. Thus a coupon payment of DM100 had fallen in dollar cost from $51.81 to $36.68. By swapping its foreign interest payment obligations for dollar obligations, IBM could realize this capital gain immediately. This is similar to closing out an FX forward contract after a profit has accumulated. IBM chose to get out of the implicit bet regarding the direction of exchange rate movements. The swap took place when the World Bank made two dollar eurobond issues, one that matched the maturity of IBM's DM debt and one that matched the maturity of IBM's Swiss franc debt. The World Bank agreed to pay all future interest and principal payments on IBM's DM and Swiss franc debt, while IBM in turn agreed to pay future interest and principal payments on the World Bank's dollar debt.

INTEREST RATE SWAPS

In a typical interest rate swap, one party issues fixed-rate debt while another issues floating-rate debt, and the two parties swap interest payment obligations based on a notional principal amount. For example, a bank might want floating-rate dollar debt while a company wants fixed-rate dollar debt. Assume the bank can borrow at 11.5 percent fixed or at LIBOR. The company can borrow at 14 percent fixed or at 1 percent above LIBOR. The bank and the company enter into an interest rate swap agreement that involves the following provisions. The bank issues $50,000,000 of fixed-rate debt at 11.5 percent while the company issues $50,000,000 of floating-rate debt at 1 percent above LIBOR. The company subsequently makes coupon payments to the bank in the amount of 12 percent, while the bank makes LIBOR payments to the company. (See Figure 19.1.) The company's net interest cost on its debt is:

$$(LIBOR + 1\%) + (12\%) - (LIBOR) = 13\%.$$

The bank's net interest cost is:

$$(11.5\%) - (12\%) + (LIBOR) = (LIBOR - .5\%).$$

Each party has reduced its borrowing cost: The bank gets floating-rate funds at $(LIBOR - .5\%)$ instead of LIBOR; the company gets fixed-rate funds at 13 percent instead of 14 percent.

There may be no magic in this transaction. The bank, for example, could be in a riskier position than if it just borrowed at LIBOR, because if the company were to default on its payments (in which case the bank would also halt interest payments to the company), the bank would be left with 11.5 percent fixed-rate debt. In that case, the bank would not have the floating-rate debt it had wanted. Thus, the reduction in the bank's cost of funds from LIBOR to $(LIBOR - .5\%)$ may only compensate it for the greater funding risk. Only if the .5 percent reduction in funding cost were greater than the amount sufficient to compensate it for the greater risk involved would the bank be unambiguously better off. That is, for the transaction to be an arbitrage transaction, it would have to be the case that the risk premium on the company's fixed-rate debt (relative to the bank's debt) was not consistent with the risk premium on the company's floating-rate debt.

In Chapter 18, we saw that changes in interest rates and interest rate expectations could bring about capital gains and losses on assets such as long-term bonds. The same is true from the point of view of a debt-issuer: If interest rates rise, the market value of a company's debt falls. Hence the company can realize a capital gain by getting rid of its current debt obligation at current market prices. One way to do this is for the company to buy up its own

FIGURE 19.1
Reduction of Borrowing Costs through an Interest Rate Swap

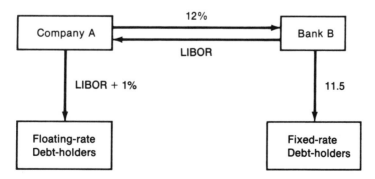

debt in the secondary market. Another way is to swap its coupon and/or principal obligations to another party.

As just noted, a cross-currency interest rate swap involves the swap of floating-rate debt denominated in one currency for fixed-rate debt denominated in another currency. One such swap took place between Renault, the French automotive company, and Yamaichi, the Japanese securities firm. Renault wanted to issue fixed-rate yen debt, but faced regulatory barriers that prevented it from issuing fixed-rate yen debt directly in the international capital markets. A swap arranged by Bankers Trust Company had the following components. Yamaichi purchased dollar floating-rate notes, and passed the dollar payments (interest and principal) from the notes to Renault via Bankers Trust. Renault used the dollar payments to make payments on its own floating-rate dollar debt. In return for the floating-rate payments, Renault made yen fixed-rate interest and principal payments to Yamaichi via Bankers Trust. Thus Renault had turned its floating-rate dollar payment obligations into fixed-rate yen obligations. Yamaichi had acquired dollar assets but had subsequently hedged its exchange risk, as it now received payments in yen from Renault.

THE SWAP MARKET

The market for swaps is organized by marketmakers, usually large commercial banks, who take the opposite side of any reasonable swap transaction. Swaps done on one side will be warehoused until they can be done on the other. Prices are quoted with respect to a standard, or generic, swap. The terms of a generic interest rate swap are illustrated in Table 19.1. Interest payments are made on the basis of a *notional principal amount,* which is itself not paid or received.

TABLE 19.1
Terms of a Generic U.S. Dollar Interest Rate Swap

General terms:	
Maturity:	1 to 15 years.
Effective date:	5 business days after trade date, corresponding to the beginning of new fixed and floating coupon periods.
All-in-cost:	The value of a swap, quoted as the semiannual yield to maturity of the fixed coupons versus the floating index flat.
Fixed side:	
Fixed coupon:	Current market rate, quoted as a credit or "swap" spread over Treasury rate.
Payment frequency:	Semiannual or annual.
Day count:	30/360.
Floating side:	
Floating index:	LIBOR, Treasury bills, commercial paper, federal funds, or prime.
Spread:	None.
Quote source:	A publicly quoted source.
Payment frequency:	The term of the floating index.
Day count:	Actual/360 (actual/actual for Treasury bills).
Reset frequency:	Same as term of floating index (except weekly for Treasury bills).
First coupon:	Current market rate for index.

On the *trade* date the two parties agree to a swap, and interest begins accruing on the *effective* date. (There is also a *settlement* date when any net cash payments for entering into the swap take place between the two parties. It is usually the same as the effective date).

The price of the swap, its *all-in-cost,* is quoted as the rate the fixed-rate payer will pay to the floating-rate payer. It is quoted on a semiannual basis, either as an absolute level (such as "9.00 percent fixed against six-month LIBOR flat") or as a basis-point spread over the U.S. Treasury yield curve ("the Treasury yield plus 57 basis points against six-month LIBOR flat").

The fixed-rate payer receives floating interest, and is said to be "long" or to have "bought" the swap. The long side has conceptually purchased a floating-rate note (because he receives floating interest) and issued a coupon bond (because he pays out fixed interest at periodic intervals).

The floating-rate payer is said to be "short" or to have "sold" the swap. The short side has conceptually purchased a coupon bond (because he receives fixed interest) and issued a floating-rate note (because he pays floating interest).

Swaps are quoted with a bid/asked spread in terms of yield. A quote of "74 bid 79 offered" means that fixed payers (the potential long sides) are willing to pay 74 basis points (or lower) over Treasuries against receiving the floating index, while fixed receivers (the potential short sides) are willing to receive 79 basis points (or higher) over Treasuries against paying the floating index. A swap dealer will attempt to sell a swap to receive the offered spread of 79 and buy it back to pay the bid spread of 74. He will thus earn the difference of 5 basis points for the firm.

Swaps are also arranged through brokers. A broker will match a party willing to pay 76 over Treasuries with another willing to receive 76 over Treasuries. The broker then collects 1 basis point per annum from each side of the swap. All of the brokerage fee is paid up front.

Table 19.2 gives a picture of the interest rate swap market at the end of 1988. The majority (over 70 percent) involved U.S. dollar interest payments, based on a notional principal value of $728.2 billion. Of this amount, $243.9 billion were interdealer swaps, while the rest involved retail users. There were also significant interest swap volumes done in yeri, deutschemark, and British pounds. The market for currency swaps can be seen in Table 19.3 Eighty-five percent of these were against the U.S. dollar, with the yen and Swiss franc comprising the principle countercurrencies. About 58 percent ($183 billion) of

TABLE 19.2
Interest Rate Swaps, Year-End 1988

Currency	Notional Principal Value	End-User	Interbank
	(billions of U.S. dollars)		
U.S. dollar	728.2	484.3	243.9
Yen	78.5	35.5	43.0
Deutschemark	56.5	39.3	17.2
British pound	52.3	34.7	17.6
Other	94.7	75.1	19.6
Total	1010.2	668.9	341.3

Source: International Swap Dealers Association.

TABLE 19.3
Currency Swaps, Year-End 1988

Currency	Notional Amount	Fixed-to- Float	End-User	Against U.S. Dollar
		(billions of U.S. dollars)		
Yen	131.0	74.9	93.9	103.5
Swiss franc	74.0	23.6	43.2	39.5
Deutschemark	34.0	17.5	28.0	25.1
Australian dollar	32.6	20.0	24.3	29.0
Canadian dollar	29.3	17.9	24.2	23.7
ECU	24.5	15.6	20.8	17.2
Other	38.7	21.7	33.2	31.5
Cross-currency doublecounting	(47.3)	(8.2)	(33.1)	—
Total	316.8	183.0	234.5	269.5

Source: International Swap Dealers Association.

currency swaps were cross-currency interest rate swaps, involving fixed for floating payments.

The documentation of a single-currency interest rate swap is similar to that of a syndicated loan, but is not nearly so elaborate, since the risk involved is only related to the interest payments and not to the principal. But many of the issues are the same. There has to be agreement on the manner in which the floating rate is calculated, the circumstances under which another reference rate can be substituted, when and how interest payments are to be made, and the governing law to be used in the event disputes arise. Standard swap documentation has been created by the British Bankers Association (BBA) and the International Swap Dealers Association (ISDA).

VALUING SWAPS

The fixed-rate payer, or long side, of a swap has conceptually issued a coupon bond and purchased a floating-rate note. If the swap is closed out prior to maturity, the fixed-rate payer reverses this transaction: He or she sells the floating-rate note and repurchases the coupon bond. Thus the value of the swap in the secondary market is, to the fixed-rate payer, the value of the floating-rate note minus the value of the coupon bond. If the floating-rate note is more valuable than the coupon bond, the swap long side receives the difference in value from the short side. If the floating-rate note is less valuable than the coupon bond, the long side pays the short side the difference.

The value of the floating-rate note is equal to the present value of future payments. (However, see below for treatment of the spread.)

EXAMPLE 19.1

The swap of Table 19.4 is closed out on July 1, 1990, as shown in Table 19.5. Since the floating index was fixed at 8.75 percent for the current coupon period, but the market rate

TABLE 19.4
Example of a U.S. Dollar Interest Rate Swap

General terms	
Notional principal amount:	$10,000,000
Trade date:	June 8, 1990
Effective date:	June 15, 1990
Maturity:	June 15, 1995
All-in-cost:	9.00%
Fixed side	
Fixed coupon:	9.00%
Payment frequency:	Semiannual
Day count:	30/360
Floating side	
Floating index:	6-month LIBOR
Spread:	−0.25%
Quote source:	Reuter's Money Rate Service
Payment frequency:	Semiannual
Day count:	Actual/360
Reset frequency:	Semiannual
First coupon:	8.75%

is now 8.65 percent, the present value of future payments (to be received in 167 days) is

$$\frac{1 + (.0875)(183/360)}{1 + (.0865)(167/360)} (\$10,000,000) = \$10,041,848.55.$$

There are sixteen days accrued interest, so the accrued interest portion of this amount is

$$(.0875)(16/360)(\$10,000,000) = \$38,888.89.$$

Thus the value of the floating-rate note can be divided into two parts: $38,888.89 in accrued interest; and $10,002,959.66, which represents the present value of the floating payment exclusive of accrued interest.

TABLE 19.5
Value of Swap in Table 19.4 If Closed Out on July 1, 1990, When All-in-Cost = 9.25 Percent and 5.5-month LIBOR = 8.65 Percent

Present value of fixed payments (including notional "repayment"):	$ 9,901,500.00
Accrued interest on fixed side:	$ 40,000.00
Present value of adjustment flows:	$ 100,134.97
Total fixed payment value:	$10,041,634.97
Present value of floating payments (including notional "repayment"):	$10,002,959.66
Accrued interest on floating side:	$ 38,888.89
Total floating payment value:	$10,041,848.55
Net amount payable by long side (negative sign denotes a payment from short side to long side):	$ −213.58

The coupon bond, or fixed-rate, portion of the swap is valued like the bonds discussed in Chapter 18. There are, however, some additional conventions relating to the swap market. First, the all-in-cost (AIC) of the swap is always quoted at a semiannual rate. If the fixed payments are not semiannual, this quotation must be converted to correspond to the annual number of payments (N) of the fixed bond, giving an adjusted yield-to-maturity (YTM):

$$\text{YTM} = [(1 + \text{AIC}/200)^{2/N} - 1] (100) (N). \tag{19.1}$$

EXAMPLE 19.2

If the AIC were quoted in the market at 8.75 percent, then the equivalent yield-to-maturity for valuing annual ($N = 1$) fixed-rate coupon payments would be 8.941406 percent.

Secondly, the AIC is always quoted against the floating index flat. In the example of Table 19.4, however, there is a spread under LIBOR of 0.25 percent. It is market practice to calculate adjustment flows in order to alter the floating side to the index flat, using the formula

$$\sum_{i=1}^{n} \frac{(\text{spread}) (D_i/360)}{[1 + \text{AIC}/(100 \times N)]^{P_i}} \tag{19.2}$$

where n = the number of floating coupon payments from the current date to maturity, D_i = the actual number of days in the ith floating-rate period, and P_i = the number of whole and fractional coupon periods from the current date to the ith coupon payment date.

EXAMPLE 19.3

In the swap of Table 19.4, the present value of the adjustment flows on July 1, 1990, can be calculated as:

$$\frac{0.25(183/360)}{(1 + 9.25/200)^{164/180}} + \frac{0.25(182/360)}{(1 + 9.25/200)^{1 + 164/180}}$$
$$+ \ldots + \frac{0.25(182/360)}{(1 + 9.25/200)^{9 + 164/180}} = 1.0013496\%.$$

This is, in dollar terms,

$$(1.0013496/100) (\$10,000,000) = \$100,134.96.$$

Because 16 days have passed in the floating period, the accrued interest portion of the adjustment flows can be calculated as

$$(16/360) (.25/100) (\$10,000,000) = \$1,111.11.$$

With these adjustments we can easily value a swap like that of Table 19.4. If the all-in-cost, or yield-to-maturity, of the coupon bond (fixed payments) were

9.25 percent on July 1, 1990, this would imply a price of 99.015 percent, or a value of $9,901,500.00. In addition, there would be

$$(16/360) \ (9/100) \ (\$10,000,000) = \$40,000$$

accrued interest. The total value of the fixed payments would thus be the value of the bond, including accrued interest, plus the value of the adjustment flows, or $10,041,634.97 (see Table 19.5). Since this is lower than the value of the floating-rate note, the fixed-rate payer (long side)—who is now "selling" the floating-rate note by closing out the swap—will receive $213.58 in payment from the floating-rate payer (short side).

These calculations are not greatly complicated if we add currency factors.

EXAMPLE 19.4

The cross-currency interest rate swap detailed in Table 19.6 represents a swap of fixed-rate Swiss francs for floating-rate dollars. The fixed-rate payer has committed to make annual Swiss franc coupon payments, and at maturity a principal payment of SF15,000,000. The floating-rate payer has committed to make semiannual U.S. dollar payments, and at maturity a principal payment of $10,000,000. We value the fixed-rate side the same way we did in the previous examples, obtaining a present value in terms of Swiss francs. The dollar value is just the Swiss franc value converted at the current spot rate (see Table 19.7, where the spot rate is SF1.47/U.S.$1). Comparing this to the dollar value of floating-rate payments, we see that the dollar floating-rate note is less valuable than the Swiss franc coupon bond. Thus, in order to close out the swap, the long side of the swap (the fixed-rate SF payer, who is short the bond and long the floating-rate note) would have to pay the value difference to the short side of the swap. With the assumptions given in Table 19.7, the long side would pay $59,308.26—or the equivalent in Swiss francs.

TABLE 19.6
Example of a Cross-Currency Interest Rate Swap

General terms	
Trade date:	June 8, 1990
Effective date:	June 15, 1990
Maturity:	June 15, 1995
All-in-cost:	6.00%
Exchange rate:	SF1.50/U.S.$1
Fixed side	
Principal amount:	SF15,000,000
Fixed coupon:	6.00%
Pay frequency:	Annual
Day count:	30/360
Floating side	
Principal amount:	$10,000,000
Floating index:	Six-month LIBOR
Payment frequency:	Semiannual
Day count:	Actual/360
First coupon:	8.375%

TABLE 19.7
Value of Swap in Table 19.6 If Closed Out on August 15, 1990, When All-in-Cost = 7.00 Percent, 5.5-month LIBOR = 8.5 Percent, and Exchange Rate is SF1.47/U.S.$1

Present value of fixed payments:	SF	14,833,500.00
Accrued interest on fixed side:	SF	150,000.00
Total fixed payment SF value:	SF	14,983,500.00
Total fixed payment U.S.$ value:	$	10,192,857.14
Present value of floating payments:	$	9,991,909.16
Accrued interest on floating side:	$	141,909.72
Total floating payment value:	$	10,133,818.88
Net amount payable by long side:	$	59,038.26
	(or SF	86,786.24)

CAPS, FLOORS, AND COLLARS

In Chapter 14 we saw that a cap was a series of European call options on the interest rate, a floor was a series of European put options, and a collar was a series of range forwards—involving a long cap at one strike price and a short floor at a lower strike price. Table 19.9 indicates that at the end of 1989 there were $253 billion of outstanding caps, $86 billion of floors, and $18 billion of collars.

EXAMPLE 19.5

In the interest rate collar of Table 19.8, the bank is short a cap and long a floor, while the company is long a cap and short a floor. In this case the index in question is a floating index, which is monitored once a month. If the interest rate were fixed at 9.25 percent on December 24, 1991, then on January 24, 1992, the bank would pay the company

$$\$165,000,000 \times (9.25 - 9.00)/100 \times 31/360 = \$35,520.83.$$

Notice that in this case the cap is a *series* of European call options, having maturities of 1 month, 2 months, . . . , 2 years and 11 months. Each of these European calls has a strike rate of 9 percent. Similarly, the floor can be viewed as a series of European put options, each with a strike rate of 7.65 percent. At the time the collar was initiated, the values of the cap and the floor were equal; hence the net premium amount on the collar was zero.

TABLE 19.8
Example of an Interest Rate Collar

Notional principal amount:	$165,000,000
Cap seller:	New York Bank
Floor seller:	U.S. Company
Cap buyer:	U.S. Company
Floor buyer:	New York Bank
Effective date:	July 24, 1989
Maturity date:	July 24, 1992
Cap strike rate:	9.00%

TABLE 19.8 (*Continued*)

Floor strike rate:	7.65%
Collar index:	Daily average one-month commercial paper (converted to money market yield) determined by Fed H-15
Collar premium amount:	$0.0
Rate fixing dates:	24th of each month
Collar payment dates:	24th of each month in arrears
Mechanics of cap:	If collar index at any rate fixing date exceeds the cap strike rate, then New York Bank pays U.S. Company the difference between the collar index and cap strike rate on an actual/360 day basis.
Mechanics of floor:	If collar index at any reference date falls below the floor strike rate, then U.S. Company pays New York Bank the difference between the collar index and the floor strike rate on an actual/360 day basis.

A cap pays off at any interest reset date when the floating index is above the rate fixed in the cap strike price. A floor pays off at any interest reset date when the floating index is below the rate fixed in the floor strike price. Notice the analogy of these option payoffs with the swap itself: The fixed-rate payer (long) side of a swap gains in any reset period when the floating index is above the fixed rate, and loses in any reset period when the floating index is below the fixed rate. That is, the long side of the swap is long a cap and short a floor, where the strike price of the cap and floor is set equal to the fixed rate at which the swap is done:

$$\text{Long swap at fixed rate } X = \text{Long cap at strike } X + \text{Short floor at strike } X. \quad (19.3)$$

The floating-rate payer (short) side of a swap gains in any reset period when the long loses, and vice versa. Hence:

$$\text{Short swap at fixed rate } X = \text{Short cap at strike } X + \text{Long floor at strike } X. \quad (19.4)$$

SWAPTIONS

Options associated with swaps are often termed *swaptions*. Swaption contracts give the right to enter into a swap agreement, or to exit out of a swap, under specified terms and conditions. Table 19.9 indicates there were $72 billion in outstanding swaptions at the end of 1989.

A *swaption call* gives the buyer the right (but not the obligation) to *receive* fixed payments based on a fixed interest rate X (the call strike price) and to pay floating. That is, the swaption call gives the buyer the right to go *short* a swap, as the short side or seller of a swap receives fixed interest payments. Denoting this contract as a "call" may seem confusing, but the name comes from the bond markets. A call on a bond gives the right to buy a bond at a strike price P, which is a function of the yield to maturity X. If you buy a bond, you receive fixed coupon payments. If you consider financing or carrying the bond by

TABLE 19.9
Composition of Swap-Related Markets for Derivative Products at End-1989
(Amounts Outstanding, in Billions of US Dollars)

Counterparty and Transaction Type	U.S. Dollar	Other Currencies	Total
	Caps		
End-user			
Bought...	34.0	23.2	57.2
Sold..	80.9	18.5	99.4
Interbank (ISDA member)[1]	37.3	33.0	70.3
Unidentified	24.3	2.1	26.4
Total..	176.5	76.8	253.3
	Floors		
End-user			
Bought...	17.2	11.9	29.1
Sold..	13.7	5.7	19.4
Interbank (ISDA member)[1]	15.8	13.1	28.9
Unidentified	7.2	1.5	8.7
Total..	53.9	32.2	86.1
	Collars and other combinations[2]		
End-user			
Bought...	3.2	0.2	3.4
Sold..	5.1	1.4	6.5
Interbank (ISDA member)[1]	2.7	0.4	3.1
Unidentified	3.6	1.6	5.2
Total..	14.6	3.6	18.2
	Unallocated		
	20.5	—	20.5
	Swaptions		
End-user			
Bought...	25.9	14.4	40.3
Sold..	4.6	2.4	7.0
Interbank (ISDA member)[1]	11.1	2.4	13.5
Unidentified	9.4	1.9	11.3
Total..	51.0	21.1	72.1

[1] Adjusted for double-counting by taking only the higher amount of either "bought" or "sold" contracts reported as having an ISDA member counterparty.

[2] Including participation options on caps and floors.

Source: BIS, *International Banking and Financial Market Developments,* August 1990.

borrowing at short-term intervals corresponding to the bond coupon payments, then buying the bond is effectively equivalent to entering into a swap to receive fixed and pay floating. We may summarize:

Swaption call with strike price X (19.5)
      = Right to receive fixed payments at rate X
      = Right to go short a swap at fixed rate X
      = Call on a coupon bond with strike price $P = P(X)$
      = Right to lend long term by borrowing short term.

The writer of the swaption call has the obligation to go long the swap if the call buyer exercises. If a swaption can be exercised at any time prior to option expiration, it is *American,* or if only at expiration, it is *European.* A swaption typically expires at the beginning of the swap period, but not necessarily. The option may expire at other times, even at the expiration date for the underlying swap.

A *swaption put* gives the put buyer the right, but not the obligation, to pay a fixed rate and receive floating, i.e. the right to go long a swap. This situation is similar to that of a coupon bond issuer (seller) who makes fixed coupon payments. We can hypothetically view these payments as financed by lending the money received from the bond issue for short-term periods, rolling over the loan after each coupon payment date. Thus we conclude:

Swaption put with strike price X (19.6)
    = Right to make payments at fixed rate X
    = Right to go long a swap at fixed rate X
    = Put on a coupon bond with strike price $P = P(X)$
    = Right to lend short term by borrowing long term.

Let I denote the current swap market fixed rate or all-in-cost. Let i denote the current market floating rate. Denote the current value of a swap to the long side as $Q(I,i,t)$. Since the long side (fixed-rate payer) of the swap has conceptually issued a coupon bond and purchased a floating-rate note, we may write

$$Q(I,i,t) = F(i,i^*,t) - B(I,I^*,t) \qquad (19.7)$$

where $F(i,i^*,t)$ is the value of a floating-rate note paying a coupon i^* during the current floating-rate period, and $B(I,I^*,t)$ is the value of a bond paying the fixed coupon I^*. Equation (19.7) may be simplified if we assume that the floating rate i is always set in such a way as to make the value of the floating-rate note F equal to par. This assumption is correct if the current date is prior to the beginning date for the swap, or if the current date corresponds to a reset date for the floating interest rate i (in which case i^* would be reset to the current value of i). Then, expressing Q, F, and B as percentages, and setting $F = 100$, we get

$$Q(I,i,t) = 100 - B(I,I^*,t) \qquad (19.8)$$

Note that

$$\Delta Q/\Delta I = - \Delta B/\Delta I > 0. \qquad (19.9)$$

The bond value falls with rising I, and hence the change in swap value, which has the reverse sign, is positive. The swap long side continues to make fixed payments at the rate I^* even while I rises, and this privilege has positive value.

Now consider the American swaption call $C(t)$ with strike price X. When exercised, it gives a *short* position in a swap at the fixed coupon rate $I^* = X$. Hence, from equation (19.8), the value of $C(t)$ at the time of exercise is

$$C(t) = B(I,X,t) - 100. \qquad (19.10)$$

Note that $C(t) > 0$ as long as $I < X$, because if $I < X$, the right to receive at the higher fixed rate X must have positive value. The swaption call will be exercised only if the current market yield on the bond (I) is less than the bond coupon rate (call strike price X). This implies that the swaption call delta with respect to yield is negative. This delta at the time of exercise is

$$\Delta C/\Delta I = \Delta B/\Delta I < 0. \tag{19.11}$$

Similarly,

$$\Delta C/\Delta X = \Delta B/\Delta X > 0. \tag{19.12}$$

The last equation simply says that the right to receive fixed payments is an increasing function of the fixed coupon rate or strike price X.

For swaption puts at the time of exercise, the equations are similar to (19.10)–(19.12), but with the signs reversed:

$$P(t) = 100 - B(I,X,t). \tag{19.13}$$
$$\Delta P/\Delta I = - \Delta B/\Delta I > 0. \tag{19.14}$$
$$\Delta P/\Delta X = - \Delta B/\Delta X < 0. \tag{19.15}$$

Since the premium on a swaption is paid up front, there is an interest opportunity cost. Suppose a call buyer pays C^* for a call, and exercises it at time t, after incurring an interest cost of rC^* on the call premium. Then the payoff on the total transaction will be positive if

$$C^*(1 + r) > B(I,X,t) - 100. \tag{19.16}$$

That is, for a swaption call buyer to realize a net profit, I must drop sufficiently below X to pay the interest opportunity cost on the call premium also.

There are different ways a call buyer can realize the exercise value of the call. The call can be sold back to the writer for a cash payment of $C(t)$. Or the call buyer can exercise the call, thereby going short the swap, and then transfer the short side of the swap to another counterparty for a cash payment of $C(t)$. Or the call buyer can exercise the call, thereby going short the swap and receiving at a fixed rate of X, and then go long an equivalent swap and pay a current market fixed rate of I. The value of the swap would in this case be received as a series of cash payments (as an annuity) over time, representing the difference $X - I > 0$ in the fixed interest rates between the two swaps.

A swaption call gives the right to receive at a fixed level X and pay floating, so, once exercised, it will confer an advantage to the owner in any subsequent interest period when the floating rate i is less than X. This makes a swaption call similar to a floor with a strike price of X, because a floor pays off if the floating rate fixed for the current interest period is below the strike level X. There is, however, a difference between a swaption call and a floor. As we saw in Chapter 14, a floor is a series or portfolio of European put options on the interest rate. Any one of these options will be exercised (the floor will pay off) only if it expires at the beginning of an interest period when the floating rate set for the period is less than the strike price X. By contrast to a floor, a swaption call can only be exercised once and for all. Thus, even if the swaption call pays off in the current interest period, there is no guarantee it will pay off in future interest periods. This implies that for equivalent strike prices, the value of the swaption call is less than the value of the equivalent floor:

$$\text{Value of swaption call} \leqslant \text{Value of floor.} \tag{19.17}$$

A put swaption gives the right to pay at a fixed rate X, and hence if exercised conveys advantage in any interest period when the floating rate i is above X. So a put swaption is similar to a cap (which is a portfolio of European calls) except that the put swaption also can be exercised only once:

Value of swaption put $\leq$ Value of cap.   (19.18)

In short, a cap allows you to do anything you can do with a swaption put, and in addition gives you more alternatives. So as long as the probability of using one of these additional alternatives is positive, the cap is more valuable. Exercising a swaption put is equivalent to exercising all the European call options in the cap, even though some of the call options may have a negative value if exercised rather than disgarded.

Another type of swaption is an option that gives the holder the *right to terminate* a swap. It typically arises in conjunction with callable bonds. Suppose a company issues coupon bonds with a call feature. If yields fall and the price of the bonds rises above some ceiling level, the call feature allows the company to recall the bonds—to repay the principle at an early date. Suppose also the company sold a swap when it made the bond issue. In the swap the company receives fixed payments (which it passes along to the bondholders) and pays floating. The company now has the equivalent of floating-rate debt. But if yields fall in such a way that the company would choose to exercise the call feature on its fixed-rate bonds, it would also probably want to terminate the matching fixed payments it receives from the swap. So what the company does is sell the buyer or long side of the swap an option to terminate the swap. Then if the long side exercises the option, terminating fixed payments to the company, the company exercises the call feature on its bonds, and terminates fixed payments to the bond holders. Instead of actually receiving fixed payments, as in a swaption call, here exercise results in an end to the obligation to make fixed payments.

This type of swaption, then, is equivalent to a call feature on coupon bonds. A party who buys a swap and also buys callable bonds to hedge (the fixed payments cancel out) will want to buy a swaption right-to-terminate to protect himself against the event the bonds are called. (A swap combined with this type of option is referred to as a *putable swap,* alluding to the fact the long side has the right to cancel (sell) the swap without paying an exit cost. But, in our terminology, this feature is analogous to a swaption call.)

VALUING SWAPTIONS

As noted in (19.5) and (19.6), a swaption call is a call on a coupon bond, while a swaption put is a put on a coupon bond. The swaption call gives the right to buy a bond, or receive fixed payments, by issuing a floating-rate note. If the floating rate i is chosen in such a way that the floating-rate note is valued at par ($F = 100$), then the swaption call can be viewed as giving the right to buy the bond at a price of 100 (review (19.10)). Hence the swaption call is a call on a coupon bond with a strike (in terms of bond price) equal to 100:

Value of swaption call = Value of call on a coupon bond
with the strike set at par.   (19.19)

Similarly, a swaption put gives the right to sell or issue a bond in exchange for paying the value of (purchasing) the floating-rate note. Thus, valuing the floating-rate note at par:

Value of swaption put = Value of put on a coupon bond
with the strike set at par.   (19.20)

The valuation of options on coupon bonds is covered briefly in Chapter 20. Many of the principles relating to such options, however, can be ascertained by following arguments similar to those of Chapter 6. For example, a long position in a European swaption call and a short position in a European swaption put is equivalent to a long position in a forward bond, where the forward bond was purchased at a price of 100. (The forward price for a bond is given in (18.7), or the equivalent for multiple coupon payments).

RISKS IN SWAP ARRANGEMENTS

Swaps involve both market risks and credit risks. The *market risk* to a swap dealer (or similar party) is the possibility that exchange rates or interest rates may move in a direction such that the value of the swap becomes negative to the dealer. The dealer would in that case have to pay a positive amount if it chose to get out of the swap in the secondary market. The *credit risk* to a dealer is the possibility the dealer's counterparty may default when the value of the swap to the dealer is positive. The dealer could then lose part or all of the swap's accumulated positive value. In one sense these risks are mirrors to each other. A dealer will incur credit risk if the market moves in the dealer's favor. If the market moves against the dealer, then the dealer's counterparty incurs credit risk.

If interest rates fall, the fixed-rate payer (long side) incurs a loss as the value of his bond liability rises. The fixed-rate payer becomes a credit risk to the floating-rate payer. If interest rates rise, the fixed-rate payer has a capital gain as the value of the bond liability falls. (The fixed side gains by having the ability to pay at the same fixed rate even though market rates have risen.) The fixed-rate payer in that case faces credit risk from the floating-rate payer. So from the dealer's perspective:

falling interest rates ⟹ parties paying fixed to the dealer become sources of credit risk.

rising interest rates ⟹ parties paying floating to the dealer become sources of credit risk.

Credit risk therefore hinges first on the volatility of interest rates, because the probability interest rates will rise or fall corresponds to the probability swap values will become positive or negative. Secondly, once a swap, swap A, has acquired positive value, credit risk is a function of the probability that the counterparty to swap A will default in that interest rate environment.

Let the probability of the fixed interest rate going to state i be denoted by $p(i)$, swap values (to the dealer) in state i by $Q(i)$, and the probability the counterparty to swap A defaults in state i by $pA(i)$. Then counterparty A's credit risk to the dealer is measured as

$$\text{credit risk } A = \sum_i p(i)\, pA(i)\, \max[Q(i),0].$$

An estimate of swap risk can be obtained by procedures like that leading to Table 19.10. Suppose fixed interest rates have a lognormal distribution, with yearly volatilities (standard deviations in log changes) for time horizons of one, three, five, seven, and ten years of .195, .166, .160, .148, and .142, respectively. Consider a dealer who has matched pairs of swaps. That is, for each swap in which the dealer pays fixed at a certain rate and receives floating, there

TABLE 19.10
Average Lifetime Credit Exposures on a Matched Pair of Swaps as a Percentage of Notional Principal[a]

Swap Maturity Confidence Limit	10-Year	7-Year	5-Year	3-Year	1-Year
99%	12.99	9.46	7.18	3.92	.780
95%	9.54	6.99	5.21	2.78	.010
90%	8.01	5.81	4.31	2.29	.005
75%	5.66	4.14	3.01	1.61	.003
50%	3.80	2.78	2.04	1.08	.002
Mean Expected Lifetime Exposure $\bar{R}(j)$	4.50	3.27	2.41	1.27	.002

Source: Katerina Simons, "Measuring Credit Risk in Interest Rate Swaps," *New England Economic Review,* Federal Reserve Bank of Boston, November/December 1989.
[a] Calculated from simulations at an interest rate of 9 percent.

is a corresponding swap in which the dealer receives fixed at that rate and pays floating. Then the dealer is only exposed to credit risk to one member of this swap pair at any one time. Finally, assume the initial fixed rate is 9 percent. Using these assumptions, we generate probabilities $p(i,j)$ for time horizons of j = one, three, five, seven, and ten years, and calculate the variable R:

$$R(j) = \sum_i p(i,j) \, |Q(i,j)|, \text{ for year } j.$$

Note that R differs slightly from the previous definition of credit exposure. First, we assigned $pA(i,j) = 1$. Secondly, since we are considering matched swap pairs, there is always credit exposure on one side whether interest rates rise or fall. Hence, we take the absolute value of Q for each state i. The value of $R(j)$ for any year depends, of course, on the actual probabilities $p(i,j)$. Since we don't know what these will be, we simulate an interest rate N times for each year j (using the assumptions just given), and calculate $Q(i,j)$ for each of the N times. We sort them in order, from $|Q(i,j)| = 0$ to the largest value for $|Q(i,j)|$. We also take as our expected $R(j)$ the average

$$\bar{R}(j) = \sum_{i=1}^{N} |Q(i,j)|/N.$$

In Table 19.10, N = 5000 for each year j. We see, for example, a seven-year swap has a 90 percent confidence limit of 5.81, where 5.81 is measured as a percentage of the notional principal amount of the swap. What this means is that, in the simulated drawings from a lognormal distribution, using the volatility assumptions above, for 90 percent of the 5000 drawings (i.e., in 4500 of the drawings) the swap credit exposure (the value of $|Q(i,7)|$) did not exceed 5.81 percent of the notional swap value. For the other 10 percent of the drawings (500 of them), swaps acquired a value to the dealer greater than 5.81 percent of the notional principal amount. Hence there would be a loss greater than 5.81 percent of the notional principal amount if the counterparty (the relevant member of the matched pair) defaulted. The expected loss, however, which assumes the probability of default $(pA(i))$ is certain, is given by the average of the $|Q(i,7)|$. This number is $\bar{R}(7)$ = 3.27 percent of the notional value of one of the matched pair of swaps.

PROBLEMS FOR CHAPTER 19

1. Calculate the value of the floating payments in the swap of Table 19.4, assuming it is closed out on July 15, 1990, at a floating index of 8.70 percent. Calculate the accrued interest portion of this value. Why might it be important to divide up the value in this way (so that one part is accrued interest)?

2. Why, in Example 19.1, is the floating spread of $-.25$ percent not subtracted from the floating index before the calculation is made? (*Comment:* There are alternative calculation procedures that give approximately the same answers. In the procedure used here, the floating spread is accounted for separately, as illustrated in Example 19.2.)

3. The AIC of a swap is quoted at 9.0 percent. What is the corresponding yield-to-maturity for a bond making fixed quarterly payments? For annual payments?

4. In what sense is calculation of the adjustment flows by equation (19.2) just the calculation of the value of a bond with variable coupon payments? (*Hint:* Note that the "coupons" in this case vary because the number of days in each floating period varies.)

5. In Chapter 18, equation (18.1), we saw that ordinary coupon bonds could be valued through a strip of pure discount (zero-coupon) bonds. A bond's yield-to-maturity is a market-quoted rate that leads to the same valuation by applying a uniform discount rate to each coupon period. In what way would swap valuation by a zero-coupon methodology differ from valuation by the AIC?

6. Relate the forward value of a coupon bond (Chapter 18, equation (18.7)) to the position of a lender who is borrowing short and lending long.

7. Relate your answer in Problem 6 to the circumstances in which one would exercise a swaption call.

8. In equation (19.7), giving the value of a swap, which of the two terms is more volatile (i.e., fluctuates in value more), F or B?

9. Comment on this statement: "The volatility of a swaption call or put can be approximated by the volatility of the yield to maturity of the corresponding coupon bond."

10. Suppose you own a banking license, but have no deposits or loan portfolio. In what sense are you long an at-the-money swaption straddle (long a swaption call and a swaption put)?

11. Explain in words why a swaption put is a decreasing function of the swaption fixed coupon rate or strike price X.

12. Give a simple numerical example showing why an interest rate cap has a greater value than the corresponding swaption put.

13. Write equations (19.19) and (19.20) in a more general form that allows the value of the floating-rate note to differ from par. Show that the value of a swaption is the value of an option to exchange one interest-bearing asset for another.

14. In Table 19.10 interpret the number "3.80" under the 10-year column. Interpret the number "4.50" in the same column.

PRICING OPTION FEATURES IN INTERNATIONAL BONDS

Bond covenants in international bond issues often contain creative contingency provisions that distinguish them from ordinary bonds. Many of these contractural features can be identified as options. Since most types of options can be given explicit values in terms of other market assets, it follows that such contingency features in a bond convenant can be given an explicit value. Thus the total value of the bond will not be determined in the usual way. The value of a coupon bond with an option feature, for example, is no longer given by the arbitrage relation of equation (18.1) in Chapter 18. Equation (18.1) expresses the current value of a coupon bond in terms of the discounted value of its future coupon and principal payments (where the market price of pure discount bonds for maturity at the coupon payment dates acts as the discount factor). But if the bond covenant has option features in addition to coupon and principal payments, the option features have to be treated explicitly. Options may also be found in domestic bond contracts, but historically they have been more prevalent in international bonds.

In this chapter we will look at some examples in which a bond can be priced in two parts as the sum of (1) the value of an ordinary bond with cash flow features, and (2) the value of one or more options. That is, many bonds with option features can split into two distinct pieces. One part is just an ordinary bond X. The other part is an option (or options) Y. Each of these is priced separately. Since the bond covenant includes both parts, the value W of the bond is the sum of the values of its two parts:

$$W = X + Y.$$

(Not all bonds can be valued this simply. In some cases, the ordinary cash flows are contingent on whether the option is exercised. In such a case, the value of the bond W is not a simple sum of two independent parts but has a more complex structure.

$$W = W(X, Y),$$

where $W(X, Y)$ denotes a general function of X and Y.)

IDENTIFYING OPTION FEATURES IN BONDS

Before attempting actually to price a bond with an option feature, we will first acquire some practice in identifying exactly what the option feature is. After the option feature has been identified, valuing the option feature is made easy through the use of standard formulas.

Attached Options

The most obvious case of an option feature on a bond is one explicitly labeled "option [warrant] attached." Warrant is the name given to an option contract issued by a company. Next are two examples of stock options, the second of which involves a foreign exchange factor (but not a foreign exchange option) from the point of view of the option buyer.

EXAMPLE 20.1

In November 1983, Prudential Overseas Funding Corporation NV issued $150 million worth of U.S. dollar bonds. Each 10⅛ percent ten-year note had attached to it seven warrants. These warrants gave the holder the right to purchase ten shares of the (reorganized) American Telephone & Telegraph Company, plus one share each of the seven new regional U.S. telephone companies. The strike price at which the warrants could be exercised was fixed at a premium over the market price of the stock at the time the bonds were issued.

The fair value of one bond thus depended on (1) the fair value of the ten-year stream of 10⅛ percent coupon payments and principal repayment, plus (2) the fair value of the seven warrants. Each of the warrants represented an American call option on stock. They were *call* options because they gave the right to *purchase* stock at a prefixed strike price. They were *American* call options because they could be exercised at any time.

EXAMPLE 20.2

On February 19, 1982, BASF Overzee NV issued $165 million worth of six-year 11 percent coupon bonds at par, each with three warrants (which could be detached and traded separately as of April 19) to subscribe to, respectively, one, nine, and ten bearer shares of BASF at DM136 per share.

The fair value of each $1000 bond was the sum of (1) the value of an ordinary $1000, six-year 11 percent coupon issued at par, plus (2) the value of the three warrants. Each of the three warrants had a value that was different from the others. It is easy to see that the warrant on nine shares of stock had a value that was nine times the value of the warrant on one share, while the warrant on ten shares of stock had a value that was ten times the value of the warrant on one share.

Consider the value of the warrant to purchase one share of BASF for DM136. Seen from the point of view of a German consumer, this is just the current DM value of an American call option on one share of BASF with a strike price of DM136. This can be priced by means of an option formula for stock options. Denote this value by $V(t)$. The same option, seen from the point of view of a consumer in the United States, who—not being a member of the jet set—is interested only in U.S. dollar consumption, has the current value $S(t)V(t)$, where $S(t)$ is the spot U.S. dollar price of DM1. For example, if

$V(t) = DM5$ and $S(t) = \$.42/DM$,

then

$S(t)V(t) = (\$.42/DM)(DM5) = \$2.10.$

Then, on the same assumption, the value of the warrant to buy nine shares would be

$(9)(\$2.10) = \$18.90,$

while the value of the warrant to buy ten shares would be

$(10)(\$2.10) = \$21.00.$

Bonds with Options on the Principal Repayment

We now look at some bonds that have the characteristic that the principal repayment can, at the choice of the bondholder, be valued in one of two ways. The bondholder, in choosing one value, will be giving up the other. Thus the choice of two alternative methods of valuation represents a European call option. The choice is a call option, because it gives the right to "purchase" one value of the bond by "paying" (giving up) the other value. It represents a *European* call option, because the exchange—if it occurs—only takes place at the maturity of the bond. (The same valuation feature could also be represented as a put option, but we will not pursue that representation here.)

EXAMPLE 20.3

In 1980, at a time when Nelson Bunker Hunt had bid up the market price of silver, a happy company called Sunshine Mining issued fifteen-year 8½ percent bonds. Each $1000 bond was to be redeemed at maturity (1995) at par or at the market price of 50 ounces of silver, whichever was higher.

The option to receive the market price of silver (and forgo $1000) was equivalent to a European call option on 50 ounces of silver, with an exercise price $X = \$1000$. The option will end up "in the money" in 1995 if the market value of the silver at that time is greater than $20 per ounce, because in that case the value of 50 ounces would be greater than (50 ounces) ($20/ounce) = $1000. The maturity T of this European option is $T = 15$ years, because the option cannot be used prior to the time the bond is redeemed.

Thus the value of one of Sunshine Mining's bonds was the value of an ordinary fifteen-year 8½ percent bond in the same risk class as Sunshine Mining, plus the value of a European call option on 50 ounces of silver with a strike price of $X = \$1000$ and a maturity of $T = 15$ years.

EXAMPLE 20.4

A Japanese company issues $1000 bonds at par in the eurobond market. The coupon rate is 12 percent payable annually in U.S. dollars, and the bonds mature in May 1990. At maturity the bonds may be redeemed, at the owner's discretion, for dollars or for yen at an exchange rate of ¥200/$. What value would one place on this bond?

Assuming the bond owner is interested in U.S. dollar consumption, he or she would clearly opt for repayment of principal in yen if the number of yen per dollar were less than

¥200 in May 1990. For example, if the exchange rate were ¥166.67/$, the bondholder could redeem the bond for

($1000)(¥200/$) = ¥200,000,

and then sell the yen for

(¥200,000)/(¥166.67/$) = $1200.

Thus the value of this eurobond can be viewed as the sum of (1) the value of an ordinary $1000 bond with a 12 percent coupon, and (2) the value of a European call option on ¥200,000, with an exercise price $X = \$1000$, and with an expiration date in May 1990. If, in May 1990, the number of yen per dollar is 200 or greater the option is worthless, so it will not be exercised. The bondholder will simply take the $1000. But if the number of yen per dollar is less than 200, the owner will exercise the option by giving up the right to receive $1000 and instead take payment of ¥200,000.

EXAMPLE 20.5

A company issues $1000 8 percent bonds, the principal of which is convertible into common stock of the parent company at maturity at a fixed exchange rate of Can$ 1.2007/$. The conversion price per share is Can$23⅛. How should the bond be valued?

The first thing to note is that the combination of a fixed conversion price and a fixed exchange rate to be used for the conversion implies that the bond is exchangeable for a fixed number of shares. Namely, the bond is convertible into

($1000)(Can$1.2007/$)/(Can$23⅛) = 51.92 shares.

Suppose, for example, that at maturity the market price of the shares were Can$25 per share, and the market exchange rate were $.80/Can$. Then the Canadian dollar value of the shares would be

(Can$25)(51.92) = Can$1298.05.

The U.S. dollar value of the shares (the conversion value) would in that case be

($.80/Can$)(Can$1298.05) = $1038.44.

Hence, for that share price and exchange rate it would be to the bondholder's advantage to convert the bond into shares rather than to simply take repayment of the $1000 principal. For that share price and exchange rate, the conversion option would expire in the money.

In general, the bond has as its value the sum of (1) an ordinary 8 percent bond, plus (2) a European call option on the U.S. dollar value of 51.92 shares of stock in the parent company. The exercise price of the option is $1000, and the expiration date of the option corresponds to the maturity date of the bond.

Coupon Options

In the following example, payment of coupons as well as principal can be taken in a choice of two alternative currencies, where the conversion of one currency into another is made at a prefixed exchange rate. As a result, there is a European FX option feature associated with each coupon payment as well as the principal repayment. Since the coupon payments all take place at different times, the expiration dates of the associated options differ in each case.

EXAMPLE 20.6

A British company issues five-year $1000 bonds with 10 percent annual coupons. The holder of a bond has the right to receive payment of coupons or principal in either dollars or pounds. If the option to take pounds is chosen, the dollar payment will be converted to pounds at a fixed exchange rate of $1.50/£. How is the bond to be valued?

Each annual coupon payment of $100 can be converted to pounds at a fixed exchange rate of $1.50/£, which implies that the bondholder can take payment of

$$(\$100)/(\$1.50/£) = £66\tfrac{2}{3}$$

in place of $100. At maturity, the bondholder has the option to take repayment of principal in the amount of

$$(\$1000)/(\$1.50/£) = £666\tfrac{2}{3}$$

in place of $1000. Thus we can value the conversion feature as the value of six FX options:

	Exercise Price	Time to Maturity	No. of £s
Option 1	$ 100	1 year	66⅔
Option 2	$ 100	2 years	66⅔
Option 3	$ 100	3 years	66⅔
Option 4	$ 100	4 years	66⅔
Option 5	$ 100	5 years	66⅔
Option 6	$1000	5 years	666⅔

The total value of the bond is thus the sum of an ordinary bond without the privilege to convert to pounds, plus the value of the six FX options. Notice that each of the options may be valued separately from the others, because the decision to exercise any one of the options does not affect the decision to exercise (or not exercise) any of the remaining options with a later maturity. On the other hand, since Options 5 and 6 have the same maturity—and since Option 5 will be exercised if and only if Option 6 is exercised—they could be considered as a single option. If Option 5 and Option 6 are combined this way, then the exercise price of the combined option is

$$\$100 + \$1000 = \$1100.$$

The number of £s on which the combined option is written would be

$$£66\tfrac{2}{3} + £666\tfrac{2}{3} = £733\tfrac{1}{3}.$$

The value of the combined option would have a value identical to the sum of the values of Option 5 and Option 6.

PRICING BONDS WITH OPTION FEATURES—
NUMERICAL EXAMPLES

Up to this point we have practiced dividing up bonds into their ordinary cash flow features and their option features, but we have not yet formally priced any option features themselves. The following numerical examples will show how this is done. One example involves European FX options and the other involves European stock options. An explanation will be given on how to convert the FX European option formula into a formula for European stock options.

EXAMPLE 20.7

A British company offers five-year $1000 bonds with an annual coupon rate of 8 percent. It also offers bondholders the option to take payment of coupons or the principal repayment in £s or dollars at a fixed exchange rate of $1.60/£. The current spot exchange rate is $1.55/£ and the forward rates for years one through five are $1.6275/£, $1.6926/£, $1.7434/£, $1.7782/£, and $1.7960/£. Over the past five years, the yearly average instantaneous standard deviation rate of the logarithm of the forward exchange rate (v) has been $v = .15$, and there is no reason to expect the next five years to be different. The term structure of dollar interest rates on pure discount securities is flat at 9 percent per annum for years one through five. What is the fair value of each $1000 bond?

Each coupon and the principal repayment can be priced separately as a European FX option (compare Example 20.6). Coupon payments are either $80 or £50, and the principal repayment is either $1000 or £625. The pricing formula for a European FX option was given in equation (6.22) of Chapter 6. The pricing formula for a European call option on one unit of foreign exchange (here one British pound) uses as inputs X, $F(t,T)$, $B(t,T)$, T, and v. Applying this formula to the data in the present problem we obtain:

X	F(t,T)	B(t,T)	T	v	No. of £s	Value of Call on 1£	Total Call Value
$1.60	$1.6275/£	1/(1.09)	1	.15	50	$.1017	$ 5.09
$1.60	$1.6926/£	1/(1.09)²	2	.15	50	$.1601	$ 8.01
$1.60	$1.7434/£	1/(1.09)³	3	.15	50	$.1960	$ 9.80
$1.60	$1.7782/£	1/(1.09)⁴	4	.15	50	$.2145	$ 10.73
$1.60	$1.7960/£	1/(1.09)⁵	5	.15	675	$.2193	$148.03
Total option value							$181.66

The value of the options in the bond contract is $181.66. To this we must add the value of the ordinary cash flows. Discounting by the discount bond prices $B(t,T)$ given in this table, we get that the present value of the coupons is

Year	1	2	3	4	5
Cash flow	$80	$80	$80	$80	$1080
Present value	$73.39	$67.33	$61.77	$56.67	$701.93
Total present value of cash flows: $961.08.					

Therefore the value of a $1000 8 percent coupon bond with the FX option features is $961.08 + $181.66 = $1142.74.

Example 20.7 valued a bond with the coupon rate fixed at 8 percent. In practice, most companies would wish to choose a coupon so that the bond would sell at par at the time the bond is issued. In the previous example, this would require an adjustment of one or more of the contractural features of the bond. For example, the exercise price of the FX option could be changed, or the coupon rate could be changed. The following example shows how to adjust the coupon—leaving the other features unchanged—so that the fair value of the bond in Example 20.7 would be the par value of $1000.

EXAMPLE 20.8

In Example 20.7, what is the appropriate coupon rate such that the bond will sell at par? Let the unknown coupon payments be $Q. The present value of the cash flows on the bond is then

Year	1	2	3	4	5
Cash flow	$Q	$Q	$Q	$Q	$Q + $1000
Present value	$Q/(1.09)	$Q/(1.09)^2	$Q/(1.09)^3	$Q/(1.09)^4	($Q + $1000)/(1.09)^5

The value of the FX call options can be calculated as:

No. of £s	Value of Call on 1£	Total Call Value
Q/1.6	$.1017	$.1017(Q/1.6)
Q/1.6	$.1601	$.1601(Q/1.6)
Q/1.6	$.1960	$.1960(Q/1.6)
Q/1.6	$.2145	$.2145(Q/1.6)
(Q + 1000)/1.6	$.2193	$.2193(Q + 1000)/1.6

The value of the bond is the sum of the cash flow value and the value of the five call options. We want this total bond value to equal $1000, so that the bond will sell at par. Thus *we set the sum of the above amounts equal to $1000, and solve for the unknown Q.*

$$\$1000 = \$Q[(1/1.09) + (1/1.09)^2 + (1/1.09)^3 + (1/1.09)^4 + (1/1.09)^5$$
$$+ \$1000(1/1.09)^5] + (\$Q/1.6)(.1017 + .1601 + .1960 + .2145 + .2193)$$
$$+ (\$1000/1.6)(.2193)$$

Solving for Q, we obtain $Q = $47.90. Coupon payments of $47.90 correspond to a coupon rate of 4.79 percent. Hence the coupon on the bond should be lowered to 4.79 percent for the bond to sell at par. If this coupon seems too low, an alternative adjustment so that the bond is fairly priced at par is to change the exercise price of the option.

The next example will involve an option on stock. To convert the European FX option-pricing formula given in equation (6.22) to a European stock option-pricing formula, we need to change our interpretation slightly. The symbol $S(t)$ will now be used to denote the price of one share of stock in domestic currency terms. For example, $S(t) = \$40/\text{share}$. If the stock is that of a foreign company, then the foreign currency price will need to be converted to domestic currency terms using the spot exchange rate. $B^*(t,T)$ will no longer represent the price of a foreign bond. Rather, interpret $B^*(t,T)$ as the current price of a bond that pays \$1 at maturity, and *whose average yield is the same as the average dividend yield on the stock*. For example, if a \$40 stock pays an annual dividend of \$2, the dividend yield is $\$2/\$40 = .05$. This corresponds to a value for $B^*(t,1)$ of

$$B^*(t,1) = 1/(1.05) = .95238.$$

The same annual dividend yield corresponds to a value for $B^*(t,2)$ of

$$B^*(t,2) = 1/(1.05)^2 = .90703.$$

And so on. The other variables are the same. X is the exercise price, v is the average instantaneous standard deviation of log $F(t,T)$ [where

$$F(t,T) = S(t)B^*(t,T)/B(t,T),$$

as reinterpreted], and $B(t,T)$ is the market price of a discount bond that pays one unit of domestic currency at maturity.

EXAMPLE 20.9

A Canadian company issues seven-year 6 percent annual coupon \$1000 bonds, the principal of which is convertible into common stock of the parent company at maturity at a fixed exchange rate of Can\$1.2007/\$. The conversion price per share is Can\$23⅛. The current spot rate is \$.80/Can\$, and the current market price of the stock is Can\$18. The current annual yield on discount dollar bonds is 8 percent for years one to seven. No dividends are paid on the stock. What is the fair value of one of these bonds, if the yearly standard deviation rate for the *U.S. dollar value of the shares* is $v = .25/\text{year}$? (Note that the value of v calculated from changes in the U.S. dollar value of the stock would be different from the value of v calculated from the Canadian dollar value of the stock because the volatility in U.S. dollar terms includes the volatility of the Can\$/U.S.\$ exchange rate.)

The bond is convertible into

$$\$1000(\text{Can}\$1.2007/\$)/(\text{Can}\$23⅛) = 51.92 \text{ shares of stock.}$$

The current dollar value of 51.92 shares of stock is

$$S(t) = (51.92)(\text{Can}\$18)(\$.80/\text{Can}\$) = \$747.648.$$

The value for $B^*(t,T) = 1.00$, as the stock pays no dividends. The exercise price of the option to buy 51.92 shares is $X = \$1000$, the face value of the bond. The maturity $T = 7$ years, while $v = .25/\text{year}$. Thus the price of a call is:

$$c(t) = S(t)B^*(t,T)N(d1) - XB(t,T)N(d2)$$
$$= (\$747.648)(1.00)N(d1) - (\$1000)(1/1.08)^7)N(d2).$$
$$= (\$747.648)N(d1) - (\$583.49)N(d2).$$

Solving for $d1$ and $d2$, we get

$$d1 = .70552 \text{ and } d2 = .04408.$$

Thus

$N(d1) = .75974$ and $N(d2) = .51759$.

Hence

$c(t) = (\$747.648)(.75974) - (\$583.49)(.51759)$
$= \$266.01.$

The value of the cash flows is

Year	1	2	3	4	5	6	7
Cash flow	$60	$60	$60	$60	$60	$60	$1070
Present value	$55.56	$51.44	$47.63	$44.10	$40.83	$37.81	$618.50

The total present value of the cash flows is $895.87. Thus the bond has a value of $895.87 + $266.01 = $1161.88.

OPTIONS ON CASH BONDS

In Chapter 14 we saw that any assumption that a eurodollar futures price was lognormally distributed was unwarranted, because it would imply a positive probability that the price could take values greater than 100, meaning interest rates could take negative values. Similar probability distribution issues arise in connection with options on cash bonds.

Cash bond prices face three boundary constraints: a lower bound that holds at all times; an upper bound that holds at all times; and a convergence point that holds at bond maturity.

1. The lower bound for a bond price is zero. In this respect the bond price is no different from foreign exchange and stock prices.
2. The upper bound of a bond price is the one occurring when the yield-to-maturity on the bond falls to zero. If the yield-to-maturity (ytm) falls to zero, future cash flows are no longer discounted. For example, a ten-year $1000 face value bond that makes annual coupon payments of $100 would have a value of $1000 + 10 ($100) = $2000 if the YTM were zero. So in this case the bond value must at all times trade in the range from $0 to $2000 (its price must trade in the range 0 to 200.) Note, however, that the range (0, 200) for bond prices corresponds to the range (infinity, 0) for bond YTM. Hence the boundary restrictions on the bond price do not preclude YTM being lognormally distributed.
3. At maturity the price of a bond goes to par. Par is usually set at 100, except for some zero-coupon issues. The price at bond maturity is thus a single point, namely 100, with probability 1.0. In Chapter 6, we priced European FX options under assumptions that implied the spot rate at option expiration had a lognormal distribution. Clearly the same assumption would make no sense for a European option on a cash bond, if the option expired at bond maturity. A European call with a strike of 100 would expire at the money,

and hence would always be worthless. The same would apply to a European put with a strike of 100. A European call with a strike of 95 would expire with a value of $100 - 95 = 5$, and hence the current value of this option would be 5 discounted back to the present by the relevant interest rate.

Once again, however, the point distribution at bond maturity does not preclude the assumption that YTM is lognormal. Suppose we have a cash bond with less than six months remaining to maturity. We may (ignoring differences in market conventions) denote its price as $P = 100/(1 + \text{YTM} \times T/360)$, where T is the number of days remaining to maturity, and YTM is measured as a decimal. As $T \to 0$, $P \to 100$, regardless of the distribution of YTM.

The implication of these three points is that if we wish to use an option-pricing model in which the underlying random variable is taken to be the *price* P of the bond, we have to pay careful attention to the boundary constraints. But if YTM is taken as the random variable, with the price P calculated from the realized value for YTM, we may use the standard approximating assumption that YTM has a lognormal distribution.

In particular, if we take P as the underlying random variable, it is clear that the variation of P will diminish as P approaches maturity, since it cannot depart very far from 100. This approach is followed by Shaefer and Schwartz (1987), who adjust the bond return volatility by the bond's duration (by the time average of the bond's cash flows from now to bond maturity). Alternatively, we may constrain the bond price movements by the current term structure of interest rates (as in Ho and Lee, 1986).

If a European option written on the zero-coupon, or pure discount, bond $B(t,T)$ will expire at time $t + n$ when the bond price will be $B(t + n, T - n)$ it can be considered an option on today's forward value of $B(t + n, T - n)$; that is, an option on the forward bond price $H(t + n, T - n)$ defined by equation (13.3). Since H is a forward price, we obtain, upon substituting H for f into equation (14.4) and making the adjustment for option maturity at time $t + n$ instead of $t + T$:

$$c(t,n) = B(t,n) \left[H(t + n, T - n) N(d1) - X N(d2) \right] \qquad (20.1)$$

$$\text{where } d1 = \frac{ln(H/X) + .5\, v^2 n}{v\sqrt{n}}, \; d2 = d1 - v\sqrt{n}.$$

Because the forward bond price H is constrained to converge to par (here defined to be $H = 1$ or 100 percent) as $n \to T$, the mean drift m per unit time in the expression $ln[H(t + n, T - n)] - ln[H(t + n - 1, T - n + 1)]$ is a random variable, even though the variance v per unit time can be treated as constant. H is said to follow a *Brownian bridge process*. (The same is true for the discount bond prices B and B^* here and in the option formulas of Chapter 6.) A detailed explanation of the Brownian bridge process can be found in Ball and Torus (1983).

EXAMPLE 20.10

What, according to equation (20.1), is the value of a three-year European call option written on a three-year zero-coupon bond?

In this case $n = T$, and $H(t + T,0) = 1$ (or 100 percent of par). Since H is constant, necessarily $v = 0$. If $X > H = 1$, then $d1$, $d2 = -\infty$, and $N(d1) = N(d2) = 0$. Hence $c(t,n) = 0$. The call has no value if the strike price is above par. On the other hand, if $X < H$, then $N(d1) = N(d2) = 1$, and $c(t,n) = c(t,T) = B(t,T)\ [1 - X]$. The call value is simply the discounted difference between the bond's par value and the strike price of the call.

Example 20.10 considered the extreme case where the maturity of the option was equal to the maturity of a zero-coupon bond. But for a two-year call option on a three-year zero-coupon bond, H would be a random variable, and its volatility v would be greater than zero. Hence the call value would be greater than the discounted difference between the bond's par value and the call strike price.

OPTIONS ON BOND FUTURES

AT the CBOT, options are traded on the CBOT Treasury bond and Treasury note contracts. On bonds, options are struck at two-point increments (84, 86, 88, 90, etc.) and on notes at one-point increments (89, 90, 91, 92, etc.). A call gives the call buyer the right to go long one futures contract, while a put gives the put buyer the right to go short one futures contract. These options are American and expire prior to the futures delivery date. For example, between September 23, 1991, and October 18, 1991, there will be four Treasury options trading: a November 1991 option on the December 1991 future, a December 1991 option on the December 1991 future, a March 1992 option on the March 1992 future, and a June 1992 option on the June 1992 future. The November 1991 option will begin trading on September 23 and cease trading on October 18. The December 1991 option will begin trading on February 18, 1991, and cease trading in November 1991 five business days before the first notice day for the December future.

As noted in Chapter 18, the futures are cheapest-to-deliver (CTD) futures. Since the futures contracts trade to the bond that is CTD, the volatility of the futures contract will change if a different cash bond becomes CTD. Hence the volatility in the option on futures is a weighted average of the volatilities of the underlying deliverable bonds. The weights depend on conversion factors and probabilities. If there is low probability that a particular cash bond on the deliverable list will become CTD, then the volatility of that bond will not affect the option volatility much. By contrast, the volatility of the cash bond that is currently CTD will have a strong impact on the option volatility.

CALLABLE BONDS

A callable bond is one issued under a legal contract (indenture) with a provision allowing the bond issuer to repurchase (retire) the bonds prior to their maturity date. The price at which a bond can be retired early is usually set at a premium to the bond's redemption value at maturity. That is, the bond will ordinarily be callable by the issuer at a price above par, such as a price of 102.5.

If the call price is 102.5, the issuer will call the bond only if the bond has a market price of 102.5 or higher. For if the market price were less than 102.5, it would be cheaper for the company to simply repurchase the bond in the market rather than to call it. The right the company has to call the bond is thus a call option on the underlying cash bond, with a strike price of 102.5. The bondholder has effectively written this call to the company, so the bond's value (V) to the bondholder is the value (P) of an ordinary (plain vanilla) cash bond without call features minus the value (Call) of the bond call option:

$$V = P - \text{Call}.$$

Let's make this relationship more explicit. Let $V(n,T)$ denote the value of a T-year bond that is callable in n years ($n < T$). Let the prices of ordinary bonds that mature in n and T years be denoted by $P(n)$ and $P(T)$, respectively. Finally, let $\text{Call}(n,T)$ and $\text{Put}(n,T)$ represent the prices of a European call and a European put on a T-year bond, where the options expire in n years, and which have strike prices equal to the call price (we assume there is just one call price). These instruments are related by the equations:

$$P(T) - \text{Call}(n,T) = P(n) - \text{Put}(n,T) = V(n,T) \tag{20.2a}$$

$$\begin{aligned} P(T) - P(n) &= \text{Call}(n,T) - \text{Put}(n,T) \\ &= V(n,T) - P(n) + \text{Call}(n,T) \end{aligned} \tag{20.2b}$$

$$\begin{aligned} P(T) + \text{Put}(n,T) &= P(n) + \text{Call}(n,T) \\ &= V(n,T) + \text{Call}(n,T) + \text{Put}(n,T) \end{aligned} \tag{20.2c}$$

The first equation, (20.2a), simply says that the value of a callable bond can be expressed as the value of an ordinary bond minus a call (where the ordinary bond expires at the same time as the callable bond) or an ordinary bond minus a put (where the ordinary bond expires at the call date). The other two equations are variations of the first. For example, the second equation says that the difference in prices between bonds of two different maturities can be expressed as the difference between the values of two options: namely, a call and a put written on the bond with longer maturity, but expiring at the same time as the bond with shorter maturity.

Why do these relationships hold? Consider the relationship $V(n,T) = P(T) - \text{Call}(n,T)$. Suppose an owner of bond $P(T)$ has written a call on it, where the call expires in n years. At the end of n years, interest rates may have risen or fallen. If they have fallen, the bond P has risen in value, and the holder of the call option will exercise it and buy the bond P from the call writer. Hence the combination of the T-year bond and written call resulted in the bond being held for only n years when interest rates fell. But the same would have happened with the callable bond V, since if interest rates had fallen by year n, and its price had risen above the call price, the company issuing it would call it at the call price.

On the other hand, suppose interest rates had risen by year n. Then bond prices would have fallen and the call option $\text{Call}(n,T)$ would have expired worthless. So the owner of P would hold the bond for the entire T years. But the same would have happened with the callable bond V. The bond would have fallen in value and the company would not call it, hence its owner would continue to hold it for T years.

PROBLEMS FOR CHAPTER 20

1. PEMEX issues $1000 bonds, with the bondholder having the right to take repayment of principal at maturity either as a payment of $1000 *or* forty barrels of Maya crude *or* the dollar value (at market exchange rates) of sixty-five cases of Dos Equis. Then the option feature on these bonds can be described as [choose one]:
    a. Forty European call options, each on one barrel of Maya crude, each with a strike price of $25 per barrel;
    b. One European call option on sixty-five cases of Dos Equis, each with a strike price of $1000;
    c. Forty European call options, each on 1.625 cases of Dos Equis, each with a strike price of one barrel of crude;
    d. Sixty-five European call options, each on one case of Dos Equis, each with a strike price of $15.3846 per case;
    e. Forty European call options, each on the maximum of the value of one barrel of Maya crude or 1.625 cases of Dos Equis, each with a strike price of $25.

2. A Japanese company, Toshiba Corp., issued fifteen-year eurodollar bonds, each bond convertible into shares of common stock at ¥198 per share, at a fixed exchange rate of ¥226.45/$. That is, each $1000 (face value) bond was convertible into $(1000)(226.45/198) = 1143+$ shares of stock. Explain how this conversion feature is an option whose value depends on both the yen value of the stock and the yen/dollar exchange rate. [*Hint:* As an example, do the following calculations. Suppose the market exchange rate were ¥245/$. What would the yen share price have to be for the option to be "at the money" if the market price of the bond is $1000? For what range of share prices would the option then be "in the money"? Alternatively, suppose the share price were ¥270/share. What would the exchange rate have to be for the option to be "at the money" if the market price of the bond is $1000? For what range of exchange rates would the option then be "in the money"?]

3. Available are European call and put options on the British pound, each with a strike price of $1.20/£, and with a maturity of one year. Then if I wish to purchase the equivalent of the current dollar value of a one-year discount (zero-coupon) British pound bond, I can do so by [choose one]:
    a. buying the put, writing the call, and buying 1.2 dollar discount bonds.
    b. buying the call, writing the put, and buying 1.2 dollar discount bonds.
    c. buying the put, buying the call, and buying 1.2 dollar discount bonds.
    d. writing the put, writing the call, and issuing 1.2 dollar discount bonds.
    e. buying the put, writing the call, and buying 1.2 dollar discount bonds.

4. A one-year zero-coupon bond with a face value of $1000 is issued at a price of $97\frac{1}{2}$. Bondholders have the option of taking repayment of principal in the form of $1000 or £800. The yield-to-maturity on similar zeros without option features is 10 percent. Assuming the zero with the option is fairly priced at the time of issue, what is the fair value of a one-year European call option on one British pound with a strike price of $1.25/£?

5. A company is issuing a two-year $1000 eurobond with options to take payment of the annual coupons and principal in either of two currencies at a prefixed exchange rate. Zero-coupon bonds for one- and two-year maturity are yielding 10 percent and 11 percent, respectively. The value of the option on the first coupon is determined to be $5, while the value of the option on the second coupon and principal is determined to be worth $27. It is desired that the bond sell at par when

issued. Given current market interest rates, at what value should the coupon on the bond be set?

6. A company issues dollar-denominated zero-coupon bonds at an interest rate of 11 percent, which corresponds to the current market rate on dollar instruments. The bonds mature in 360 days. At expiration, a bondholder may redeem each bond for either $1000 or SF2500. The current spot rate is $.40/SF and the 360-day Swiss interest rate is 6 percent. If a potential bond buyer assumes a yearly standard deviation rate of .12 (for a 365-day year) for the logarithm of the $/SF forward exchange rate, what would be the value of each bond?

7. The three-year rate of interest is 8 percent per annum. Calculate the value of a three-year European call option, with a strike of 90, on a three-year zero-coupon bond. Calculate the value of the corresponding European put.

8. Would American options have different values than the European options of Problem 7?

9. In Example 20.10, analyze the case $X = H$.

10. The implied volatility of a CBOT option on bond futures is found to be precisely the average of two deliverable bonds. Under what circumstances would you expect this relationship to hold?

11. Explain, in words, the meaning of Equation (20.2c).

SELECTED BIBLIOGRAPHY

Adler, Michael, and Bernard Dumas, International Portfolio Choice and Corporation Finance: A Synthesis, *Journal of Finance,* 38 (June 1983), 925–984.

Adler, Michael, and B. Lehmann, Deviations in PPP in the Long Run: A Random Walk?, Columbia University Working Paper, 1982.

Aliber, Robert Z., The Interest Parity Theorem: A Reinterpretation, *Journal of Political Economy,* 81 (November 1973), 1451–1459.

Anderson, Tim, Stop. You're Broking My Bonds, *Euromoney,* December 1982.

Andrews, Michael D., Recent Trends in the U.S. Foreign Exchange Market, *Quarterly Review,* Federal Reserve Bank of New York, Summer 1984.

Antl, Boris, ed., *Swap Financing Techniques,* Euromoney Publications, London, 1983.

Antl, Boris, and Richard Ensor, eds., *The Management of Foreign Exchange Risk,* Euromoney Publications, London, 1982.

Bahmani-Oskooee, Mohsen, and Satya P. Das, Transactions Costs and the Interest Parity Theorem, *Journal of Political Economy* 93 (August 1985), 793–799.

Ball, C. A., and W. Torus, Bond Price Dynamics and Options, *Journal of Financial and Quantitative Analysis,* 18 (December 1983), 517–531.

Bandow, Doug, What's Still Wrong with the World Bank? *Orbis,* Winter 1989.

Bank of England, The London Gold Market, *Quarterly Bulletin,* March 1964.

Bank of England, Intervention Arrangements in the European Monetary System, *Quarterly Bulletin,* June 1979.

Bank of England, The Effects of Exchange Control Abolition on Capital Flows, *Quarterly Bulletin,* September 1981.

Bank for International Settlements, *Payments Systems in Eleven Developed Countries,* Bank Administration Institute, May 1985.

Bank for International Settlements, *Annual Report,* Basel, various years.

Bank for International Settlements, *Large Value Funds Transfer Systems in the Group of Ten Countries,* May 1990.

Bank for International Settlements, *Survey of Foreign Exchange Market Activity,* February 1990.

Bank for International Settlements, Committee on Banking Regulations and Supervisory Practices, *International Convergence of Capital Measurement and Capital Standards,* Basel, July 1988.

Barnett, Richard J., *The Alliance—America, Europe, Japan,* Simon and Schuster, New York, 1983.

Baughn, William H., and Donald R. Mandich, eds., *The International Banking Handbook,* Dow-Jones-Irwin, Homewood, Ill., 1983.

Bilson, John F. O., The "Speculative Efficiency" Hypothesis, *Journal of Business,* 54 (July 1981), 435–451.

Black, Fischer, and Myron Scholes, The Pricing of Options and Corporate Liabilities, *Journal of Political Economy,* 81 (May 1973), 637–659.

Board of Governors of the Federal Reserve System, Commodities Futures Trading Commission, Securities and Exchange Commission, *A Study of the Effects on the Economy of Trading in Futures [and] Options,* December 1984.

Bodner, David E., The Major Foreign Exchange Markets, in *The International Banking Handbook. See* Baughn and Mandich, 1983.

Bodurtha, Jr., James N., and Georges R. Courtadon, Empirical Tests of the Philadelphia Stock Exchange Foreign Currency Options Market, The Ohio State University, August 1984.

Brennen, Michael J., and Eduardo S. Schwartz, The Valuation of American Put Options, *Journal of Finance,* 32 (May 1977), 449–462.

Brown, Bowman, ed., *International Banking Centers,* Euromoney Publications, London, 1982.

Bunge, Frederica M., ed., *Japan: A Country Study,* 4th ed., U.S. Government Printing Office, Washington, D.C., 1983.

Chicago Mercantile Exchange, *Clearing House Manual,* mimeographed, 1985.

Coninx, Raymond G. F., *Foreign Exchange Dealer's Handbook,* Woodhead-Faulkner, Cambridge, 1982.

Cornell, Bradford, and J. K. Dietrich, The Efficiency of the Market for Foreign Exchange Under Floating Exchange Rates, *Review of Economics and Statistics,* 60 (February 1978), 111–120.

Cornell, Bradford, and Marc R. Reinganum, Forward and Futures Prices: Evidence from the Foreign Exchange Markets, *The Journal of Finance,* 36 (December 1981), 1035–1045.

Cox, J. C., J. E. Ingersoll, and S. A. Ross, The Relationship Between Forward and Futures Prices, *Journal of Financial Economics,* 9 (December 1981), 321–346.

Cox, J. C., Stephen A. Ross, and Mark Rubinstein, Option Pricing: A Simplified Approach, *Journal of Financial Economics,* 7 (September 1979), 229–263.

Culbertson, W. P., The Welfare Costs of Exchange Control Systems, *Southern Economic Journal* (April 1977).

Cumby, R. E., and M. Obstfeld, A Note on Exchange Rate Expectations and Nominal Interest Differentials: A Test of the Fisher Hypothesis, *Journal of Finance,* 36 (June 1981), 697–704.

Darby, M. R., Does Purchasing Power Parity Work? *Proceedings of Fifth West Coast Academic/Federal Reserve Economic Research Seminar,* Federal Reserve Bank of San Francisco, 1982.

Deardorff, Alan V., One-Way Arbitrage and Its Implications for the Foreign Exchange Market, *Journal of Political Economy,* 87 (April 1979), 351–364.

Dooley, M. P., and P. Isard, Capital Controls, Political Risk, and Deviations from Interest Rate Parity, *Journal of Political Economy,* 88 (April 1980), 370–384.

Dornbusch, Rudiger, *Open Economy Macroeconomics,* Basic Books, New York, 1980a.

Dornbusch, Rudiger, Exchange Rate Economics: Where Do We Stand? *Brookings Papers on Economic Activity,* 1980:I, 143–185.

Dornbusch, Rudiger, Exchange Rate Risk and the Macroeconomics of Exchange Rate Determination, *Research in International Business and Finance,* 3 (1983), 3–27.

Economic Report of the President, various years.

Einsig, Paul, *The Theory of Forward Exchange,* Macmillan, London, 1937.

Einsig, Paul, *The Euro-dollar System,* 4th ed., Macmillan, New York, 1970.

Fama, E., and A. Farber, Money, Bonds, and Foreign Exchange, *American Economic Review,* 69 (September 1979), 639–649.

Federal Reserve, Intervention in Foreign Exchange Markets: A Summary of Ten Staff Studies, *Federal Reserve Bulletin,* November 1983.

Feller, William, *An Introduction to Probability Theory and Its Applications,* Vol. I, 3rd ed., John Wiley & Sons, New York, 1968.

Fisher, Frederick G. III, *International Bonds,* Euromoney Publications, London, 1981.

Fitzgerald, M. Desmond, *Financial Futures,* Euromoney Publications, London, 1983.

Frankel, Jeffrey A., The Dazzling Dollar, *Brookings Papers on Economic Activity,* I (1985), 199–217.

Fratianni, Michele, The European Monetary System: How Well Has It Worked?, *The Cato Journal,* (Fall 1988), 477–501.

Frenkel, J., ed., *Exchange Rates and International Macroeconomics,* University of Chicago Press, Chicago, 1983.

Frenkel, J. A., and R. M. Levich, Covered Interest Arbitrage: Unexploited Profits? *Journal of Political Economy,* 83 (April 1975), 325–338.

Frenkel, J. A., and R. M. Levich, Transaction Costs and Interest Arbitrage: Tranquil Versus Turbulent Periods, *Journal of Political Economy,* 85 (November 1977), 1209–1226.

Friedman, Milton, The Case for Flexible Exchange Rates, *Essays in Positive Economics,* University of Chicago Press, Chicago, 1953.

Garman, Mark B., and Steven W. Kohlhagen, Foreign Currency Option Values, *Journal of International Money and Finance,* 2 (December 1983), 231–237.

George, Abraham, and Ian Giddy, ed., *International Finance Handbook,* 2 vols., John Wiley & Sons, New York, 1983.

Geske, R., and H. Johnson, The American Put Valued Analytically, *Journal of Finance,* 39 (December 1984), 1511–1524.

Giddy, I. H., Measuring the World Foreign Exchange Market, *Columbia Journal of World Business,* Winter 1979.

Goodman, Stephen, Evaluating the Performance of the Technical Analysts, in *The Management of Foreign Exchange Risk. See* Antl and Ensor, 1982.

Grabbe, J. Orlin, Liquidity Creation and Maturity Transformation in the Eurodollar Market, *Journal of Monetary Economics,* 9 (July 1982), 39–72.

Grabbe, J. Orlin, The Pricing of Call and Put Options on Foreign Exchange, *Journal of International Money and Finance,* 2 (December 1983), 239–253.

Grabbe, J. Orlin, The Pricing of First-Passage and Perpetual American Options, Department of Finance, The Wharton School, January 1985.

Grabbe, J. Orlin, Foreign Currency Options: A Survey, in *Recent Developments in International Banking and Finance. See* Khoury and Ghosh, 1987.

Gray, Roger W., Risk Management in Commodities and Financial Markets, *American Journal of Agricultural Economics,* May 1976, 280–285, 296–304.

Green, Timothy, *The Prospect for Gold,* Walker and Company, New York, 1987.

Green, Timothy, *The New World of Gold,* Walker and Company, New York, 1981.

Grossman, S., and J. Stiglitz, On the Impossibility of Informationally Efficient Markets, *American Economic Review,* 70 (June 1980), 393–408.

Guttentag, Jack M., and Richard J. Herring, Financial Innovations to Stimulate Credit Flows to Developing Countries, Wharton Program in International Banking and Finance, Working Paper, April 1985.

Guttentag, Jack M., and Richard J. Herring, The Current Crisis in International Lending, *Studies in International Economics,* January 1985.

Hansen, L. P., and R. J. Hodrick, Forward Exchange Rates as Optimal Predictors of Future Spot Rates: An Econometric Analysis, *Journal of Political Economy,* 88 (October 1980), 829–853.

Hansen, L. P., and R. J. Hodrick, Risk Averse Speculation in the Foreign Exchange Market: An Econometric Analysis, in *Exchange Rates and International Macroeconomics. See* Frenkel, 1983.

Herring, R. J., and R. C. Marston, The Forward Market and Interest Rates in the Eurocurrency and National Money Markets, in *Eurocurrencies and the International Monetary System. See* Stein, Makin, and Logue, 1976.

Hilley, J. R., C. R. Beidleman, and J. A. Greenleaf, Why There Is No Long Forward Market in Foreign Exchange, *Euromoney,* January 1981.

Ho, Thomas S. Y., and S. B. Lee, Term Structure Movements and Pricing Interest Rate Contingent Claims, *Journal of Finance,* 41 (December 1986), 1011–1029.

Hodrick, Robert J., and Sanjay Srivastava, An Investigation of Risk and Return in Forward Foreign Exchange, *Journal of International Money and Finance,* 3 (April 1984), 5–30.

Houthakker, Hendrik, The Breakdown of Bretton Woods, in *Economic Advice and Executive Policy. See* Sichel, 1978.

Huang, Roger D., Some Alternative Tests of Forward Exchange Rates as Predictors of Future Spot Rates, *Journal of International Money and Finance,* 3 (August 1984), 153–167.

Hudson, Nigel R. L., *Money and Exchange Dealing in International Banking,* John Wiley & Sons, New York, 1979.

International Monetary Fund, *Annual Report,* various issues.

International Monetary Fund, *World Economic Outlook,* various issues.

Isard, P., How Far Can We Push the Law of One Price? *American Economic Review,* 67 (December 1977), 942–948.

Joint Economic Committee, *The European Monetary System,* U.S. Government Printing Office, Washington, D.C., 1979.

Kane, Alex, and Alan J. Marcus, Valuation and Optimal Exercise of the Wild Card Option in the Treasury Bond Futures Market, *Journal of Finance,* 41 (March 1986), 195–207.

Kerr, Ian M., *A History of the Eurobond Market: The First 21 Years,* Euromoney Publications, London, 1984.

Keynes, John Maynard, *The Economic Consequences of the Peace,* 1919.

Keynes, John Maynard, *A Tract on Monetary Reform,* 1923.

Keynes, John Maynard, *General Theory of Employment, Interest, and Money,* Harcourt, Brace, and World, New York, 1936.

Khoury, Sarkis J., and Alo Ghosh, *Recent Developments in International Banking and Finance,* Vol. 1, D.C. Heath and Company, 1987.

Korajczyk, Robert A., The Pricing of Forward Contracts for Foreign Exchange, *Journal of Political Economy,* 93 (April 1985), 346–368.

Kravis, I. B., and R. E. Lipsey, Price Behavior in the Light of Balance of Payments Theory, *Journal of International Economics,* 8 (May 1978), 193–246.

Krueger, A. O., Some Economic Costs of Exchange Controls: The Turkish Case, *Journal of Political Economy,* October 1966.

Kuberek, Robert C., and Norman G. Pefley, Hedging Corporate Debt with U.S. Treasury Bond Futures, *The Journal of Futures Markets,* 3 (1983), 345–353.

LeRoy, Stephen F., Expectations Models of Asset Prices: A Survey of Theory, *Journal of Finance,* 37 (March 1982), 185–217.

Lessard, Donald, Principles of International Portfolio Diversification, in *International Finance Handbook. See* George and Giddy, 1983.

Levich, Richard, Evaluating the Performance of the Forecasters, in *The Management of Foreign Exchange Risk. See* Antl and Ensor, 1982.

Levich, Richard, and Ingo Walter, The Regulation of Global Financial Markets, in *New York's Financial Markets. See* Noyelle, 1988.

Levy, M. D., Taxation and "Abnormal" International Capital Flows, *Journal of Political Economy,* 85 (1977), 635–646.

Arthur D. Little, Inc., *Report on the Payments System* to the Association of Reserve City Bankers, April 1982.

Longworth, D., Testing the Efficiency of the Canadian-U.S. Exchange Market Under the Assumption of No Risk Premium, *Journal of Finance,* 36 (March 1981), 43–49.

Maddala, G. S., *Econometrics,* McGraw-Hill, New York, 1977.

Mandelbrot, B., The Variation of Certain Speculative Prices, *Journal of Business,* 36 (October 1963), 394–419.

McCulloch, J. Huston, Foreign Exchange Option Pricing with Log-Stable Uncertainty, in *Recent Developments in International Banking and Finance. See* Khoury and Ghosh, 1987.

McFarland, James W., Richardson Pettit, and Sam K. Sung, The Distribution of Foreign Exchange Prices Changes: Trading Day Effects and Risk Measurement, *Journal of Finance,* 37 (June 1982), 693–715.

McKinnon, Ronald I., *Money in International Exchange,* Oxford University Press, Oxford, 1979.

Meese, R. A., and K. Rogoff, Empirical Exchange Rate Models in the Seventies: Do They Fit Out of Sample? *Journal of International Economics,* 14 (February 1983), 3–24.

Merton, Robert C., Theory of Rational Option Pricing, *Bell Journal of Economics and Management Science,* 4 (Spring 1973), 141–183.

Monnet, Jean, *Memoirs,* Doubleday, Garden City, New York, 1978.

Morgan Guaranty, *World Financial Markets,* various issues.

Mussa, M., Empirical Regularities in the Behavior of Exchange Rates and Theories of the Foreign Exchange Markets, *Carnegie-Rochester Conference Series on Public Policy,* 11 (Autumn 1979), 9–57.

Muth, John F., Rational Expectations and the Theory of Price Movements, *Econometrica,* 29 (July 1961), 315–335.

Neumann, Manfred J. M., Intervention in the Mark/Dollar Market: The Authorities' Reaction Function, *Journal of International Money and Finance,* 3 (August 1984), 223–240.

Noyelle, T., ed., *New York's Financial Markets,* Westview Press, Boulder, 1988.

OECD, *Financial Market Trends,* various issues.

Parkinson, Michael, Option Pricing: The American Put, *Journal of Business,* 50 (January 1977), 21–36.

Protopapadakis, Aris, and H. R. Stoll, Spot and Futures Prices and the Law of One Price, Federal Reserve Bank of Philadelphia Working Paper No. 82–4, April 1982.

Revey, P., Evolution and Growth of the U.S. Foreign Exchange Market, *Quarterly Review,* Federal Reserve Bank of New York, Autumn 1981.

Richardson, J. D., Some Empirical Evidence on Commodity Arbitrage and the Law of One Price, *Journal of International Economics,* 8 (May 1978), 341–352.

Riley, David H., "Foreign Exchange and International Money Broking," in *The International Banking Handbook. See* Baughn and Mandich, 1983.

Rogalski, R. J., and J. D. Vinso, Price Level Variations as Predictors of Flexible Exchange Rates, *Journal of International Business Studies,* 8 (Summer 1977), 71–81.

Roll, Richard, Violations of Purchasing Power Parity and Their Implications for Efficient International Commodity Markets, in *International Finance and Trade. See* Sarnat and Szego, 1979.

Roll, Richard, A Simple Implicit Measure of the Effective Bid-Ask Spread in an Efficient Market, *Journal of Finance,* 39 (September 1984), 1127–1139.

Ross, Stephen A., Options and Efficiency, *Quarterly Journal of Economics,* 90 (February 1976), 75–89.

Sachs, Jeffrey D., The Dollar and the Policy Mix: 1985, *Brookings Papers on Economic Activity* I (1985), 117–185.

Salomon Brothers Inc., *The Interest Rate Swap Market: Yield Mathematics, Terminology, and Conventions,* June 1985.

Samuelson, P. A., Proof That Properly Anticipated Prices Fluctuate Randomly, in *Collected Scientific Papers of Paul A. Samuelson,* Vol. 3, MIT Press, Cambridge, 1972, 782–790.

Sarnat, M., and G. P. Szego, eds., International Finance and Trade, Vol. I, Ballinger Publishing Co., Cambridge, 1979.

Schulze-Gaevernitz, Gerhard von, *Volkswirtschaftliche Studien aus Russland,* Duncker und Humblot, Leipzig, 1899.

Seidel, Andrew D., and Philip M. Ginsburg, *Commodities Trading Foundations, Analysis, and Operations,* Prentice-Hall, Englewood Cliffs, N.J., 1983.

Sercu, P., A Generalization of the International Asset Pricing Model, *Revue de l'Association Française de Finance,* 1 (June 1980), 91–135.

Shaefer, Steve M., and E. S. Schwartz, Time Dependent Variance and the Pricing of Bond Options, *Journal of Finance,* 42 (December 1987), 1113–1128.

Shapiro, Alan C., What Does Purchasing Power Parity Mean? *Journal of International Money and Finance,* 2 (December 1983), 295–318.

Shastri, Kuldeep, and Kishore Tandon, Valuation of American Options on Foreign Currency, Graduate School of Business Working Paper #579, University of Pittsburgh, February 1985.

Sheffrin, Steven M., *Rational Expectations,* Cambridge University Press, Cambridge, 1983.

Sichel, Werner, ed., *Economic Advice and Executive Policy,* Praeger Special Studies, New York, 1978.

Silber, William L., Marketmaker Behavior in an Auction Market: An Analysis of Scalpers in Futures Markets, *Journal of Finance,* 39 (September 1984), 937–953.

Simons, Katerina, Measuring Credit Risk in Interest Rate Swaps, *New England Economic Review,* Federal Reserve Bank of Boston, November/December 1989.

So, Jackie, The Sub-Gaussian Distribution of Currency Futures: Stable Paretian or Non-Stationary, *Review of Economics and Statistics,* 1987, 100–107.

Solomon, Robert, *The International Monetary System, 1945–1981,* Harper & Row, New York, 1982.

Solnik, Bruno, *European Capital Markets: Toward a General Theory of International Investment,* Lexington Books, Lexington, Mass., 1973.

Solnik, Bruno, Why Not Diversify Internationally Rather than Domestically, *Financial Analysis Journal* 30 (July 1974), 48–54.

Stein, Carl H., John H. Makin, and Dennis E. Logue, eds., *Eurocurrencies and the International Monetary System,* American Enterprise Institute, Washington, 1976.

Stein, Jerome L., Mark Rzepczynski, and Robert Selvaggio, A Theoretical Explanation of the Empirical Studies of Futures Markets in Foreign Exchange and Financial Instruments, *Financial Review,* 18 (February 1983), 1–32.

Stigler, George, The Economics of Information, *Journal of Political Economy,* 68 (June 1961), 213–235.

Stulz, Rene, A Model of International Asset Pricing, *Journal of Financial Economics,* 9 (December 1981), 383–406.

Taylor, Dean, Official Intervention in the Foreign Exchange Market, or Bet Against the Central Bank, *Journal of Political Economy,* April 1982.

Tobin, James, and William C. Brainard, Financial Intermediaries and the Effectiveness of Monetary Controls, *American Economic Review,* 53 (July 1963), 383–400.

Tousey, Mark J., Secondary Markets for Restructured Debt, Advanced Study Project, The Wharton School, April 1985.

Uchino, Tatsuro, *Sengo Nihon keizaishi,* 1978. Translated by Mark A. Harbison as *Japan's Postwar Economy,* Kodansha International Ltd., Tokyo, 1983.

Van Dormael, Armand, *Bretton Woods: Birth of a Monetary System,* Holmes & Meier, New York, 1978.

Walmsley, Julian, *The Foreign Exchange Handbook: A User's Guide,* John Wiley & Sons, New York, 1983.

Westerfield, Janice Moulton, An Examination of Foreign Exchange Risk Under Fixed and Floating Rate Regimes, *Journal of International Economics,* 7 (May 1977), 181–200.

Working, Holbrook, Futures Trading and Hedging, *American Economic Review,* 56 (June 1953), 314–343.

Wriston, Walter, The Information Standard, *Euromoney,* October 1984.

Yeager, Leland, *International Monetary Relations: Theory, History, and Policy,* 2d ed., Harper & Row, New York, 1976.

GLOSSARY

Agent Bank A bank appointed in a syndicated credit to oversee the loan.

AIBD (Association of International Bond Dealers) A private organization founded in Zurich, Switzerland, in April 1969 to establish uniform issuing and trading procedures in the international bond markets.

Allotment The number or amount of bonds in a new bond issue set aside by the lead manager for sale by a member of the issuing syndicate.

Announcement Day The day on which a new issue of bonds is publicly announced, with invitation faxes sent out to prospective underwriters and sellers.

Appreciation An increase in the market value of a currency with respect to a second currency or a real asset. The term is used in reference to a *market* price as opposed to an official price or par value.

Arbitrage The simultaneous purchase and sale or lending and borrowing of two assets or two groups of equivalent assets in order to profit from a price disparity.

Asian option Average-rate option.

Asked Price The price at which a marketmaker in an asset will sell the asset; the price sought by any prospective seller.

Assignment The transfer from one bank to another of the right to receive loan principal and interest from a borrower.

At the Money A term used to refer to a call option or a put option whose strike price is equal (or virtually equal) to the current price of the asset on which the option is written.

Average-Rate Option Option on foreign exchange or commodity prices that pays off the difference between the option strike price and the average price of the underlying asset, this average calculated over the life of the option.

Backwardation A relationship in which spot or cash prices are higher than futures (or forward) prices.

Balance of Payments An accounting record of all officially recorded economic transactions between residents of one country and residents of other countries over a stated period of time. Sources of funds (such as exports, sales of assets, and foreign borrowing) are recorded with a plus sign, while uses of funds (such as imports, purchases of foreign assets, and foreign lending) are recorded with a minus sign. Transactions are recorded in the form of double-entry bookkeeping so that plus and minus items always match (the total balance is zero). A positive or negative balance can only be obtained by restricting attention to a subset of total transactions (such as the current account, the capital account, or the reserves account).

Barrier option An otherwise ordinary American or European option with the added feature that the right of the option buyer to exercise is either activated or extinguished when the market price of the underlying asset reaches a level specified in the contract.

Barter An exchange of goods or services directly between two parties without the use of financial instruments such as currency or credit.

Basis The cash or spot price minus the futures price.

Basis Point One-hundredth of a percentage point (.0001).

Bearer Bonds Bonds on which the coupon and principal is payable to whoever has possession of the bond certificate.

Bid Price The price at which a marketmaker in an asset will buy the asset; the price sought by any prospective buyer.

BIS (Bank for International Settlements) An international bank located in Basel, Switzerland, which serves as a forum for monetary cooperation among the major central banks of Europe, the United States, and Japan. It monitors and collects data on international banking activity and serves as a clearing agent for the European Monetary System. The bank was originally founded in 1930 to handle the payment of German reparations after World War I.

Black Market Any private market that operates in contravention of government restrictions. For example, such a market may involve the exchange of currencies or goods at prices that are outside government-mandated levels, the trading of prohibited goods, or trading between individuals and/or institutions that are not approved by the government.

Bond A security issued by a corporation or official borrower which promises to pay a fixed terminal or redemption amount at maturity, and which usually also promises to pay fixed or variable amounts of interest at stated times prior to maturity.

Bought Deal A procedure for a new bond issue whereby the lead manager or managers buy the entire issue from the borrower on previously agreed fixed terms, including coupon level and issue price.

Bretton Woods Agreement Agreement signed by forty-four nations at Bretton Woods, New Hampshire, in July 1944; basis of the post–World War II monetary system. Each participating nation declared a par value for its currency and agreed to intervene in foreign exchange markets to maintain the exchange rate with respect to the U.S. dollar within plus or minus 1 percent of the par value. The United States agreed to the obligation to convert dollars to gold at $35 per ounce.

Broker An individual who matches buy and sell orders in return for a commission. A broker, by contrast to a marketmaker, does not buy or sell for his or her own account and hence does not ordinarily risk the firm's capital in order to stand behind a price quotation.

Bulldog Bonds British pound sterling-denominated foreign bonds issued in London.

Call Option A contract giving the purchaser the right, but not the obligation, to buy an asset at a stated strike price on or before a stated date.

Cap A contract on a short-term interest rate under which the writer of the cap pays the cap buyer the increased borrowing cost for any interest period (occurring prior to cap expiration) in which the short-term rate is fixed at a level above the ceiling rate specified in the cap.

Capital Account Those items in the balance of payments showing net changes in the domestic private sector's holdings of foreign financial assets or in foreign holdings of domestic financial assets.

Capital Controls Governmental restrictions (such as prohibitions, taxes, quotas) on the acquisition of foreign assets or foreign liabilities by domestic citizens, or the acquisition of domestic assets or domestic liabilities by foreigners.

Caption An option on a cap.

Cedel One of two main clearing systems in the eurobond market. Cedel S.A. is based in Luxembourg and began operations in January 1971.

Certificates of Deposit (CDs) Negotiable instruments issued by a bank and payable to the bearer. CDs pay a stated amount of interest and mature on a stated date, but may be bought and sold daily in a secondary market.

CFTC (Commodities Futures Trading Commission) A U.S. regulatory body that regulates all exchange-based futures trading in the

United States. Established by the Commodity Futures Trading Commission Act of 1974.

Clearing Corporation A clearinghouse that exists as an independent corporation rather than as a subdivision of an exchange.

Clearinghouse A department of an exchange or an independent corporation through which all trades must be confirmed, matched, and settled daily until offset.

Clearing Member A firm qualified to clear trades through a clearinghouse or clearing corporation.

Clearing System An institutional arrangement for transferring securities and payment between sellers and buyers subsequent to the establishment of a trading price.

Closing Day The day on which new bonds from the borrower are delivered against payment by members of a bond-issuing syndicate.

CME (Chicago Mercantile Exchange) Futures exchange where eurodollar and foreign currency options on futures are traded. See IMM.

Collar A contract that involves being long a cap and short a floor (or vice versa).

Comanager A bank ranking just below that of lead manager in a syndicated eurocredit or an international bond issue. The status of comanager usually indicates a larger share in the loan or a larger bond allotment, and a larger share in the fees, than banks of lower rank. Comanagers may also assist the lead managers in assessing the market or deciding borrower terms.

Commercial Paper A short-term, unsecured debt instrument issued by a corporation and sold at a discount from its maturity value.

Commitment Fee A fee paid on the unused portion of a credit line.

Common Market See *EEC.*

Contango A relationship in which spot or cash prices are lower than futures (or forward) prices.

Convertibility Freedom to exchange a currency, under certain circumstances, without government restrictions or controls. Originally the term meant the ability to be exchanged for gold. *Current account* convertibility connotes the freedom to buy and sell foreign exchange in relation to trade in goods and services. *Capital account* con-

vertibility connotes a similar freedom in relation to direct investment or trade in financial assets.

Coupon The periodic interest payment on a bond. Many bond certificates come with literally detachable coupons that must be removed and presented for payment usually annually or semiannually.

Coupon Yield The interest yield on a bond when calculated as the annual amount of money paid on coupons, divided by the face value of the bond.

Covenant Agreement in a syndicated loan or bond contract concerning the borrower's future conduct. Such a convenant may involve, for example, the agreement to maintain a given balance sheet ratio in the future, or the agreement to adhere to an IMF program.

Cross-default Term used to describe a clause in a syndicated loan or bond contract that gives the lender the right to accelerate repayment of the loan if the borrower defaults on another loan.

Cross-hedging The hedging of an asset with a futures contract of a different asset.

Cross Rate An exchange rate between two currencies neither of which is the U.S. dollar. A cross rate is usually constructed from the individual exchange rates of the two currencies with respect to the U.S. dollar.

Currency Swap A contractual obligation entered into by two parties to deliver a sum of money in one currency against a sum of money in another currency at stated intervals (or a stated interval) or according to stated circumstances. In the interbank FX market, see *Swap.*

Current Account Those items in the balance of payments involving imports and exports of goods and services as well as unilateral transfers (gifts).

Current Yield The interest yield on a bond when calculated as the annual amount of money paid on coupons, divided by the current market price of the bond.

Delivery The offset of an obligation to buy or sell an asset by the actual transfer of title to the asset at a preagreed price. In the futures market, the transfer or receipt of a cash instrument against a short or long futures contract.

Delivery Month In the futures market, the calendar month during which delivery can be made or taken on a futures contract.

Delta *Option Delta* is the ratio of a change in the option price to a small change in the price of the asset on which the option is written. The partial derivative of the option price with respect to the price of the underlying asset. *Futures Delta* is the ratio of a change in the futures price to a small change in the spot price.

Depreciation A decrease in the market value of a currency with respect to a second currency or a real asset. The term is used in reference to a *market* price as opposed to an official price or par value.

Devaluation A decrease in the official value of a currency with respect to a second currency or a real asset. The term is used in reference to an *official* price, such as a fixed exchange rate or a declared par value, as opposed to a market price.

Disintermediation A process in which savers withdraw deposits from financial intermediaries (like commercial banks and thrift institutions) and lend directly to investors and consumers by purchasing debt instruments such as commercial paper, bonds, and Treasury bills.

Divergence Indicator System One aspect of the European Monetary System that measures the departure of a country's economic policies from the European Economic Community "average." The measure of divergence is based exclusively on the movement of a country's exchange rate with respect to the ECU, which represents the community average exchange rate. In the event of excessive divergence (see Chapter 2), the country is expected to alter economic policy to conform with the EEC average.

Down-and-in Option Barrier option that is activated only if, during the life of the option, the spot rate falls to some level specified in the option contract.

Down-and-out Option Barrier option that becomes worthless if, during the life of the option, the spot rate falls to some specified level.

Dual Trader A floor broker on a futures exchange who trades for his or her own account in addition to executing customer orders.

ECU (European Currency Unit) A portfolio currency used in the European Monetary System as a community "average" exchange rate, and used in the private market as a means of payment and as a currency of denomination of lending, borrowing, and trade.

Edge Corporations Specialized banking institutions, chartered by the Federal Reserve Board in the United States, which are allowed to engage in transactions that have a foreign or international character, and that are not subject to any restrictions on interstate banking. U.S. banks chartered outside New York, for example, may conduct foreign exchange trading in New York City through an edge corporation.

EEC (European Economic Community) An economic association of European countries founded by the Treaty of Rome in 1957. The goals of the EEC were the removal of trade barriers among member countries, the formation of a common commercial policy toward non-EEC countries, and the removal of barriers restricting competition and the free mobility of factors of production. Original members were West Germany, France, Belgium, Luxembourg, the Netherlands, and Italy. The United Kingdom, Ireland, and Denmark joined the EEC in 1973, and Greece was added in 1981. Spain and Portugal became members in 1986.

Elasticity The percentage change in an option price that results from a 1 percent change in the price of the asset on which the option is written.

Eurobank A bank that regularly accepts foreign currency denominated deposits and makes foreign currency loans.

Eurobonds Bonds that are issued simultaneously in the capital markets of several nations and that are issued outside the normal regulatory restrictions that apply to domestic issues in each of those capital markets.

Euroclear One of two main clearing systems in the eurobond market. Euroclear Clearance System Limited began operations in December 1968. It is located in Brussels and managed by Morgan Guaranty.

Eurocredits Intermediate-term loans of eurocurrencies made by banking syndicates to corporate and government borrowers.

Eurocurrency Market The money market for borrowing and lending currencies that are held in the form of deposits in banks located outside the countries in which those currencies are issued as legal tender.

Eurodollar A dollar-denominated deposit in a bank outside the United States or at International Banking Facilities (IBFs) in the United States.

Eurodollar Bonds Eurobonds denominated in U.S. dollars.

European Monetary System An exchange arrangement formed on March 13, 1979, that involves the currencies of EEC member countries. Included in the arrangement are a parity grid and a divergence indicator system.

Exchange Controls Governmental restrictions (such as prohibitions, taxes, quotas, or government-set prices) on the purchase of foreign currencies by domestic citizens or on the purchase of the local domestic currency by foreigners.

Exercise The use of the right given by an option: purchase (if a call) or sale (if a put) of an asset at the strike price stated in the option contract.

Exercise Price See *Strike Price*.

Expiration Date The last day on which an option may be exercised.

Face Value The monetary amount paid on a bond at redemption (excluding any terminal coupon payment). The face value is printed on the bond certificate.

Federal Funds Market Federal funds are deposits held by commercial banks at the Federal Reserve System. The federal funds market is the interbank market for borrowing and lending these deposits. Since reserve requirements of commercial banks are satisfied by federal funds, banks with deposits in excess of required reserves will lend the excess deposits to banks with a reserve shortage at a market-determined interest rate, the federal funds rate.

Federal Reserve System The central bank of the United States, created by the Federal Reserve Act of 1913, consisting of a board of governors in Washington, D.C., and twelve regional Federal Reserve banks. The Federal Reserve has monopoly control over the monetary base and has the power to set reserve requirements, to conduct open-market operations, and to lend directly to commercial banks.

Floating Exchange Rate An exchange rate whose value is not constrained by central bank intervention to remain within a fixed range.

Floating-Rate Notes Bonds that pay interest at an agreed margin above a market reference rate. The interest rate varies according to variations in the market reference rate.

Floor A contract on a short-term interest rate under which the writer of the floor pays the floor buyer the increased borrowing cost for any interest period (occurring prior to floor expiration) in which the short-term rate is fixed at a level below the floor rate specified in the cap.

Floor Broker In the futures market, an exchange member who executes orders on the floor of the exchange for the account of one or more clearing members and who is licensed by the CFTC.

Floortion An option on a floor.

Floor Trader In the futures market, an exchange member who is qualified to trade on the exchange floor and who primarily trades for his or her own account or for accounts he or she controls.

Foreign Bonds Bonds issued by nonresidents in a country's domestic capital market. Such bonds are subject to domestic regulations and are underwritten primarily by banks registered in the country where the issue is made.

Foreign Exchange Market The market in which the currencies of different nations are bought and sold (in the form of bank deposits) with respect to each other. Most trading takes place with respect to the U.S. dollar.

(At a) Forward Discount Phrase used to describe a currency whose forward price is cheaper than its spot price.

Forward Exchange Foreign currency traded for settlement beyond two working or business days from today.

Forward Option A forward exchange contract (as opposed to an option contract) that differs from an ordinary forward contract only in that it has a variable, instead of a fixed, maturity date. The buyer of a forward option may, for example, be entitled to take delivery of a currency at any time during a given month, as opposed to a specific day.

(At a) Forward Premium Phrase used to describe a currency whose forward price is more expensive than its spot price.

Forward Rate Agreement (FRA) A cash-settled interbank forward contract on interest rates. The seller pays the buyer the difference if the interest rate has risen above the agreed rate. In the reverse case, the buyer pays the seller.

Fundamental Forecasting Forecasting that is primarily based on processing information about ultimate supply and demand factors.

Fungible Securities Securities that are not individually designated by serial number as belonging to a particular owner. Instead, a clearing system or depository institution credits owners with a given number of a particular bond issue (or other security issue). The owner has title to, say, fifty bonds, but not to fifty specific bonds with designated serial numbers.

Futures Commission Merchant (FCM) A firm that is registered with the CFTC and legally authorized to solicit or accept orders from the public for the purchase or sale of futures contracts. Acts as an intermediary between a public customer and a floor broker.

Futures Contract An obligation incurred pursuant to the rules of a futures exchange that results in daily cash flows that occur with changes in the futures price. If held until expiration, the futures contract may involve accepting (if long) or delivering (if short) the asset on which the futures price is based.

Gambler's Ruin Problem A problem in probability theory that shows that, for players with limited capital, the odds of winning or losing a repeated series of similar bets are different from the odds of winning or losing any one of the individual bets.

Gamma The ratio of a change in the option delta to a small change in the price of the asset on which the option is written. The second partial derivative of the option price with respect to the price of the underlying asset.

Global Bond A temporary debt certificate issued by a eurobond borrower, representing the borrower's total indebtedness. The global bond will subsequently be replaced by the individual bearer bonds.

Gray Market A forward market for newly issued bonds that takes the form of forward contracting between market participants during the period between the announcement day of a new issue and the day final terms of the bond issue are signed. Bonds are traded at prices stated at a discount or premium to the (now unknown) issue price.

Hedging The process of reducing the variation in the value (from price fluctuations) of a total portfolio. Hedging is accomplished by adding to an original portfolio items such as spot assets or liabilities, forward contracts, futures contracts, or options contracts in such a way that the total variation of the new portfolio is smaller than that of the original portfolio.

High-powered Money See *Monetary Base*.

IBF (International Banking Facility) An IBF is a division of an existing U.S. banking operation that is allowed to conduct eurocurrency business but (unlike a Caribbean eurobank branch) is prohibited from issuing negotiable certificates of deposit. IBFs were allowed by the Federal Reserve Board beginning December 1981, and have since become popular with U.S.-based Japanese and Italian banks.

IBOR (Interbank Offered Rate) The rate at which banks will lend to other banks for a particular currency at a particular location. Examples include BIBOR, BRIBOR, DIBOR, PIBOR, LIBOR, LUXIBOR, MIBOR, and SIBOR, defined in Chapter 12.

IBRD (International Bank for Reconstruction and Development) See *World Bank*.

IMF (International Monetary Fund) Organization founded at Bretton Woods in July 1944, and located in Washington, D.C., with the goal of overseeing exchange arrangements and lending foreign currency reserves to members. Members were pledged to eliminate exchange controls; they agreed not to alter the exchange values of their currencies without IMF approval, except once by an amount not greater than 10 percent; members could borrow reserves from the IMF, subject to conditions imposed by the IMF; the IMF obtained funds to lend through member subscriptions usually paid 25 percent in gold and U.S. dollars and 75 percent in the member's own currency.

IMM (The International Money Market of the Chicago Mercantile Exchange) The IMM is the world's largest market for foreign currency and eurodollar futures trading.

Implied Forward Rate The rate of interest at which a borrowing or a lending transaction of a shorter maturity may be rolled over to yield an equivalent interest rate with a borrowing or a lending transaction of longer maturity.

Initial Margin The minimum deposit a futures exchange requires from customers for each futures contract in which a customer has a net long or short position.

Interest Equalization Tax (IET) A measure proposed in July 1963 by U.S. president John Kennedy which levied a 15 percent tax on the purchase price of foreign bonds issued by European and Asian borrowers in New York. The tax was extended to certain bank loans in early 1964 and was repealed as of the beginning of 1974.

Interest Parity An equilibrium condition under which a borrower (lender) is indifferent between borrowing (lending) in the domestic currency or in the foreign currency, taking into account the need to convert currency now through the spot market, with exchange risk covered by a reverse transaction through the forward market. A restatement of the interest parity condition yields the forward exchange rate as a function of the spot rate and the interest rates on the two currencies.

Interest Rate Swap A contractual obligation entered into by two parties to deliver a fixed sum of money against a variable sum of money at periodic intervals. Typically involves an exchange of payments on fixed- and floating-rate debt. If the sums involved are in different currencies, the swap is simultaneously an interest rate swap and a currency swap.

International Bonds Collective term referring to both eurobonds and foreign bonds.

In the Money A term used to refer to a call option whose strike price is below, or to a put option whose strike is above, the current price of the asset on which the option is written.

Issue Price The price, stated as a percentage of face value, at which a new eurobond is announced. It is used as a basis for calculating investment banking fees, but does not necessarily represent the actual price paid by any investor.

Lambda The ratio of a change in the option price to a small change in the option volatility. The partial derivative of the option price with respect to the option volatility.

Last Trading Day The final day on a futures or options exchange when trading may occur in a given futures contract month or in a given option series. Futures contracts that are still open at the end of the last trading day must be settled by making (if short) or taking (if long) delivery of the underlying asset (e.g., foreign currency futures), except for cash-settled contracts (e.g., eurodollar futures).

Lead Manager The commercial or investment bank with the primary responsibility for organizing a syndicated bank credit or bond issue. This includes the recruitment of additional lending or underwriting banks, the negotiation of terms with the borrower, and the assessment of market conditions.

Lending Margin The fixed percentage above the reference rate paid by a borrower in a rollover credit or on a floating-rate note.

LIBOR (London Interbank Offered Rate) The rate at which banks in London will lend eurocurrencies in the interbank market.

LIFFE (London International Financial Futures Exchange) A London exchange where eurodollar futures are traded as well as futures-style options.

Limit Order An order given to an exchange, bank, or other agency to make a transaction at a given price or better. A purchase order is not to be executed above, and a sale order is not to be executed below, the stated price.

Listing The formal process required in order to have the price of a bond or other security regularly quoted on a stock exchange. Eurobonds are usually listed so that they can be purchased by those institutional investors who are constrained to invest in listed securities.

Lock-up Term used to refer to procedures followed in a eurobond issue to prevent the sale of securities to U.S. investors during the period of initial distribution.

Long A term used to describe a position that involves an excess of foreign currency purchases over sales, an excess of foreign currency assets over liabilities, or an excess of purchases of a particular futures contract over sales of the same contract.

Lookback Option An option that allows the buyer to choose as the option strike price any price of the underlying asset that has occurred during the life of the option. If a call, the buyer will choose the minimal price that has occurred during the option's life, whereas if a put, the buyer will choose the maximal price.

M1 A measure of the money supply that is composed of demand deposits at commercial banks and currency in circulation.

Maintenance Margin The minimum equity a futures exchange requires in a customer's account for each futures contract subsequent to deposit of the initial margin. If equity drops below the maintenance level, funds must be added to the account to bring the equity up to the initial level.

Management Fee The portion of total investment banking fees accruing to the managing banks in a bond issue. In a syndicated credit, the fee paid to the managing bank or banks for organizing the loan.

Margin The amount of money and/or securities that must be posted as a security bond to ensure performance on a contract. In the futures market, both short and long positions post margin. This ensures that the side with a daily cash flow loss will meet its payment obligation. See also *Initial Margin* and *Maintenance Margin.*

Marketmaker An individual who quotes both buying and selling prices and who stands ready to commit the firm's capital in order to complete buying or selling transactions at the prices quoted.

Market Order An order that is to be executed immediately at the best available price in the market.

Mark to Market The revaluation of a futures contract or a security to reflect the most recently available market price.

Marshall Plan The European Recovery Program proposed by U.S. Secretary of State George C. Marshall in June 1947. The program was intended to rebuild the economies of Europe in order to create political stability and to inhibit the spread of communism. Led to an accumulation of foreign exchange (U.S. dollar) reserves on the part of European countries. The absence of such reserves had been used as an excuse to prohibit free trading in foreign exchange throughout post–World War II Europe.

Martingale A price series forms a martingale with drift k if, conditional on today's information, the expected price for next period is equal to $1 + k$ times the current price.

Maturity Transformation Long-term lending financed by short-term borrowing in such a way that interest costs on borrowings will be updated to reflect market rates more frequently than will interest earnings from loans.

Maxidevaluation (Maxi) A large, unscheduled devaluation of a currency that normally follows a minidevaluation schedule.

Minidevaluation (Mini) A small devaluation of a currency that takes place at scheduled intervals. The amount of the devaluation may be equal to a fixed number or may vary according to a known set of indicators.

Monetary Base The amount of central bank liabilities that will potentially serve to satisfy the required reserves of the commercial banking system. In the United States, the monetary base consists of deposits at the Federal Reserve and currency in circulation.

Money Multiplier The number of units of the money supply (M1) that will be created by the banking system from one unit of the monetary base. The size of the money multiplier depends on reserve requirements and the public's portfolio choice among different depository assets.

Negative Pledge A contractual promise by a borrower in a syndicated loan or a bond issue not to undertake some future action. One typical negative pledge is that future new creditors will not be given rights that existing creditors do not have.

Novation The discharge of one obligation in a debtor/creditor relationship and the creation of an entirely new one.

OECD (Organization for Economic Cooperation and Development) Founded in 1961 as a successor organization to the Organization for European Economic Cooperation (OEEC). The OEEC had been set up in 1948 to administer Marshall Plan aid. The goals of the successor OECD were to stimulate world trade, economic growth, and economic development. Members included Austria, Belgium, Canada, Denmark, Finland, France, the Federal Republic of Germany (West Germany), Greece, Iceland, Ireland, Italy, Japan, Luxembourg, the Netherlands, Norway, Portugal, Spain, Sweden, Switzerland, Turkey, the United Kingdom, and the United States.

Offering Circular A document giving a description of a new securities issue, as well as a description of the firm or entity making the issue.

Offering Day The day on which final terms of a bond issue are signed between the managing banks and the borrower.

Offer Price See *Asked Price*.

OPEC Organization of the Petroleum Exporting Countries, a federation of country oil exporters formed in 1960 as a response to the unilateral reduction in posted oil prices by major oil companies the previous year. OPEC resolved to restore oil prices to previous levels and to unify petroleum policies for member countries. Founding members were Iran, Iraq, Kuwait, Saudi Arabia, and Venezuela. Subsequently admitted were Qatar (1961), Libya and Indonesia (1962), Abu Dhabi (1967), Algeria (1969), Nigeria (1971), Ecuador (1973), and Gabon (1975).

Open Interest The total number of futures contracts for a particular asset that have not been liquidated by an offsetting trade or that have not been fulfilled by delivery.

Open-Market Operations Purchases or sales of securities or other assets by the central bank. Such actions change the monetary base. Usually the term is restricted to purchases and sales of domestic assets (such as government bonds), while purchases and sales of foreign exchange are called "foreign exchange intervention." Either activity changes the monetary base in a similar way.

Open Position A net long or short foreign currency or futures position whose value will change with a change in the foreign exchange rate or futures prices.

Option An exchange-traded contract giving the purchaser the right, but not the obligation, to buy (call option) or to sell (put option) an asset at a stated price (strike or exercise price) on a stated date (European option) or at any time before a stated date (American option). Any nonexchange-traded contract with similar economic characteristics to an exchange-traded option.

Options Clearing Corporation (OCC) A Delaware corporation that is owned equally by the Chicago Board Options Exchange, the American Stock Exchange, the Philadelphia Stock Exchange, the Pacific Stock Exchange, and the Midwest Stock Exchange. The OCC clears all options, including foreign currency options, traded at a U.S. securities exchange.

Out of the Money A term used to refer to a call option whose strike price is above, or to a put option whose strike price is below, the current price of the asset on which the option is written.

Overnight In the foreign exchange market, term used to describe a swap transaction for value today with the reverse transaction taking place the next business day. In the eurocurrency market, term used to describe a loan or deposit for value today with maturity on the next business day.

Parity Grid The system of fixed bilateral par values in the European Monetary System. The central banks of both countries whose currencies are involved in an exchange rate are supposed to intervene in the foreign exchange market to maintain market rates within a range defined by an upper and a lower bank around the par value. The upper (lower) band is obtained by multiplying (dividing) the par value by 1.022753 except for par values involving the British pound, where the multiplier (divisor) is 1.061798.

Participation The act of taking part in a syndicated credit or a bond issue. In a syndicated credit, participation may involve membership in the original group of lending banks, or may involve lending later via a participation certificate. In a eurobond issue, a participation refers to the size of the underwriting commitment.

Participation Fees The portion of total fees in a syndicated credit that go to the participating banks.

Paying Agent One or a syndicate of banks responsible for paying the interest and principal of a bond issue to bondholders on behalf of the bond issuer.

PHLX (Philadelphia Stock Exchange) A securities exchange where American and European foreign currency options on spot exchange are traded.

Placement Memorandum A document in a syndicated eurocredit that sets out details of the proposed loan and that gives information about the borrower.

Point The last (fourth) decimal place of a foreign currency price quotation.

Premarket See *Gray Market*.

Premium The price of an option agreed upon between the buyer and writer or their agents in a transaction on the floor of an exchange.

Prospectus See *Offering Circular*.

Purchasing Power (of a currency) The value of a currency expressed in terms of its exchange value against a basket of goods and services.

Purchasing Power Parity (PPP) The notion that in equilibrium the market exchange rate for any two currencies will exactly reflect the relative purchasing powers of the two currencies.

Put Option A contract giving the purchaser the right, but not the obligation, to sell a particular asset at a stated strike price on or before a stated date.

Rating A letter grade given to a bond by a rating agency (such as Moody's or Standard and Poor's) signifying the amount of credit risk on the bond.

Real Interest Rate The market interest rate as commonly quoted (nominal interest rate) minus the rate of inflation of the price level. The ex ante real rate is calculated by subtracting expected inflation, while the ex post real rate is calculated by subtracting actual inflation.

Redemption Discharge of a bond obligation by the issuer by payment of the bond's face value to the bondholder. Redemption may occur at bond maturity or earlier, under conditions stated in the bond contract.

Red Herring A preliminary prospectus (offering circular) giving the expected, but not final, details of a forthcoming securities offering.

Reference Banks The group of banks surveyed in order to determine a reference rate.

Reference Rate A market interest rate that is periodically monitored in connection with a rollover credit or a floating rate note in order to determine the subsequent interest payment by the borrower.

Registered Term used to refer to bonds that are recorded in the bond issuer's books in the name of the bond owner. Ownership of such bonds can only be transferred by a formal transfer of the ownership name in the issuer's books.

Rembrandt Bonds Dutch-guilder-denominated foreign bonds issued in Amsterdam.

REPO (Repurchase Agreement) An agreement by one party to sell a security with an agreement to buy it back at a specified price on a specified date. The seller gets immediate cash, for the use of which he will in return pay the difference between the repurchase price and the sale price. If the buyer takes possession of the security in the meantime, a repo represents a form of secured lending from the buyer's standpoint, since if the seller defaults on the repurchase, the buyer still has the security.

Representations Statements made by a borrower in a syndicated credit or bond issue describing the borrower's current state of affairs, such as the borrower's financial condition.

Reserve Account Those items in the balance of payments measuring changes in the central bank's holdings of foreign assets (such as gold, convertible currencies, or SDRs).

Reserve Currency A foreign currency held by a central bank (or exchange authority) for the purposes of exchange intervention and the settlement of intergovernmental claims.

Reserve Requirements Obligations imposed on commercial banks to maintain a certain percentage of deposits with the central bank or in the form of central bank liabilities.

Revolving Credit A line of bank credit that may be used or not used at the borrower's discretion. Interest is paid on the amount of credit actually in use, while a commitment fee is paid on the unused portion.

Risk-averse Term used to describe any decision maker who would prefer a known amount of wealth to a fair bet (a bet with the same amount of wealth as its expected value).

Rollover Credit A bank loan whose interest rate is periodically updated to reflect market interest rates. The interest rate in the loan for each subperiod is specified as the sum of a reference rate and a lending margin.

Samurai Bonds Yen-denominated foreign bonds issued in Tokyo.

SDR (Special Drawing Right) An artificial reserve asset created and held on the books of the IMF. At the time of first issue on January 1, 1970, the SDR was defined as having a value equal to $\frac{1}{35}$ ounce of gold. The definition was altered in 1974 to specify the value in terms of a portfolio of sixteen currencies. Since 1981, the SDR has been defined in terms of the U.S. dollar, German mark, French franc, Japanese yen, and British pound.

Seasoned Securities Securities that have traded in the secondary market for more than ninety days.

SEC (Securities and Exchange Commission) A U.S. regulatory agency established in 1934 to regulate the issuing and trading of securities.

Secondary Market A market in which securities, such as bonds, are traded following the time of their original issue.

Selling Concession The share of total investment banking fees accruing to the selling group.

Selling Group All banks involved in selling or marketing a new issue of bonds. Sometimes the term is used in reference to dealers acting only as sellers, and is intended to exclude reference to underwriters or managers.

Selling Period A period following the signing of terms of a new bond issue during which bonds are bought and sold (in the form of price agreements) prior to actual payment for, and distribution of, the bonds themselves.

Settlement Day The day on which the actual transfer of two currencies, or the transfer

of money for an asset, takes place at a previously arranged price.

Settlement Price The official daily closing price for any futures or option contract. This price is established and used by a clearinghouse or clearing corporation to determine each clearing firm's settlement variation.

Settlement Variation The sum of all changes in dollar (or local currency) amount for each of a firm's futures or options positions as calculated from each day's settlement price. This amount is paid to, or received from, the clearinghouse or clearing corporation each day based on the previous day's trading.

Shogun Bonds Foreign bonds issued in Tokyo and denominated in currencies other than the Japanese yen. The usual denomination is the U.S. dollar.

Short A term used to describe a position that involves an excess of foreign currency sales over purchases, an excess of foreign currency liabilities over assets, or an excess of sales of a particular futures contract over purchases of the same contract.

Smithsonian Agreement A revision to the Bretton Woods system that was signed at the Smithsonian Institution in Washington, D.C., in December 1971. Included were a new set of par values, widened bands to plus or minus 2.25 percent around par, and an increase in the official value of gold to $38/ounce.

Speculative Efficiency Hypothesis (SEH) The empirical proposition that forward or futures prices represent expected spot prices.

Speculator An individual or firm who attempts to anticipate price movements and attempts to profit from them by taking appropriate long or short positions on market-traded assets.

Spot Exchange Foreign currency traded for settlement generally two business or working days from the trade date.

Spot Month The futures contract month that is also the current calendar month.

Spot/Next In the foreign exchange market, term used to describe a swap transaction for value on the spot date with the reverse transaction taking place the next working day after the spot date. In the eurocurrency market, term used to describe a loan or deposit for value on the spot date with maturity on the next working day after the spot date.

Spread The difference between the buying and selling rates of a foreign currency or a bond, or the difference between borrowing and lending rates on eurocurrency deposits.

Stabilization The efforts by a lead manager in a bond issue to regulate the price at which bonds trade in the secondary market during the period while the bond syndicate is still in existence.

Sterilization Intervention in the foreign exchange market by a central bank where the change in the monetary base caused by the foreign exchange intervention is offset by open market operations involving domestic assets.

Straight Bonds Bonds with fixed coupon payments and without any option features (such as provisions for conversion into equity, other bonds, or other currencies).

Strike Price The price at which an option buyer may purchase (if a call option) or sell (if a put option) the asset upon which the option is written.

Subparticipation The partial assignment by one bank of the right to receive monetary sums from a borrower to another bank.

Subscription Agreement An agreement between a bond issuer and the managing banks that describes the terms and conditions of the issue and the obligation of the parties to the agreement.

Subscription Period The time period between the day on which a new bond issue is announced and the day on which the terms of the issue are signed and the bonds are formally offered for sale.

Sushi Bonds Dollar-denominated eurobonds issued by Japanese companies, managed by Japanese banks, and purchased primarily by Japanese investors. Such bonds were not subject to the Japanese Ministry of Finance prohibition of more than 10 percent foreign securities in the portfolios of life insurance companies.

Syndicate A group of banks that acts jointly, on a temporary basis, to loan money in a bank credit (syndicated credit) or to underwrite a new issue of bonds (bond issuing syndicate).

Swap In the interbank foreign exchange market, the simultaneous purchase and sale of identical amounts of a currency for different value dates. (The currency will be priced in terms of a second currency whose amounts will differ, depending on the relationship between the purchase price and the sale price of the first currency.) More generally, a swap is a contractual obligation entered into by two parties to deliver one sum of money against another sum of money at stated intervals. See also *Currency Swap* and *Interest Rate Swap*.

Swaption An option to enter a fixed for floating swap at a predetermined fixed rate.

Technical Forecasting Forecasting that is primarily based on processing price information, as opposed to the ultimate supply and demand factors that lead to a price series.

Term Credit A bank loan that is made according to a time schedule. In the initial period, increasing portions of the total loan amount become available to the borrower. In the final period the loan is repaid at scheduled intervals.

Term Structure The level of interest rates on debt instruments of a particular type viewed as a function of term-to-maturity. The interest rate level may rise or fall with increasing maturity.

Theta The ratio of a change in the option price to a small change in the option term-to-maturity. The partial derivative of the option price with respect to the option term-to-maturity.

Tombstone Advertisement placed in a newspaper or magazine by banks in a syndicated credit to record their participation in the loan, or in a bond issue to record their role in managing, underwriting, or placing the bonds.

Tomorrow/Next In the foreign exchange market: term used to describe a swap transaction for value tomorrow with the reverse transaction taking place the next working day after tomorrow. In the eurocurrency market: term used to describe a loan or deposit for value tomorrow with maturity on the next working day after tomorrow.

Treasury Bills U.S. government debt instruments that are auctioned by the Federal Reserve, and which have a maturity of three, six, or twelve months. The bills are sold at a discount from their par or face value, and repay the face value at maturity. The return on the bills is determined solely by the difference between the purchase price and the face value. Three- and six-month bills are auctioned each Monday, and twelve-month bills are auctioned once every month.

Trustee An institution or group appointed in a bond issue to look after investor interests.

Underwriting Allowance The share of total investment banking fees accruing to the underwriting group.

Underwriting Syndicate The banks, in a new bond issue, that agree to pay a minimum price to the borrower even if the bonds cannot be sold on the market at a higher price.

Unilateral Transfers Items in the current account of the balance of payments that correspond to gifts to or from foreigners. A gift of military goods to a foreign country would, for example, be recorded under exports as a plus item, but there would be no corresponding minus item in the capital account as no payment was received in turn. Hence a special category, unilateral transfers, is created. The same gift of military goods would be recorded as a minus item under unilateral transfers.

Value Date In the foreign exchange market; same as settlement date.

Vega A term used by Cretans ignorant of the Greek language. See Lambda.

Volatility The standard deviation of changes in the logarithm of an asset price, expressed at a yearly rate. The volatility is a variable that appears in option formulas. The units of this variable are such that the square of the volatility multiplied by the option term-to-maturity is a pure number (is unit-free).

Warrant An option issued by a company. A warrant differs from an exchange-traded option in that exchange-traded options are issued typically by individuals and performance on an exchange-traded option contract is guaranteed by a clearinghouse or clearing corporation.

Withholding Tax A tax deducted at source, such as a deduction prior to the payment of coupon interest or dividends.

World Bank (International Bank for Reconstruction and Development) A creation of the Bretton Woods negotiations in July 1944, the bank began operations in June 1946. The original intent of the bank was to make postwar reconstruction loans, a role soon supplanted by the Marshall Plan. The bank consequently shifted its attention to development lending. Funds for lending are obtained from the paid-in capital subscriptions of member nations, from borrowings in the world's capital markets, and from net earnings.

Writer An individual who issues an option and consequently has the obligation to sell the asset (if the option is a call) or to buy the asset (if the option is a put) on which the option is written if the option buyer exercises the option.

Yankee Bond A dollar-denominated foreign bond issued in New York.

Yield Curve See *Term Structure*.

Yield-to-Maturity The rate of interest on a bond when calculated as that rate of interest which, if applied uniformly to future time periods, sets the discounted value of future bond coupon and principal payments equal to the current market price of the bond.

Zero-coupon Bond A bond that pays no interest but that is redeemed at its face value at maturity. Such bonds are sold at a discount from their face value, and the return to the bond depends solely on the relation between the purchase price and the face value.

INDEX

A

Absolute purchasing power parity, 195
Actual/Actual, 331
Actual/360, 330
Actual/365, 330
After tax private savings, 208
Agent banks, 287
Agent fee, 288
All-in-cost price, 353
American calls on futures, value relationships with
    American calls on spot, 148
American calls on spot, 121
  value relationship with American calls on futures,
    148
American foreign currency options
  advantage of, 136
  binomial pricing procedures, 169–174
  calculation of, 167–174
  first-passage, 167
  perpetual, 167–168
  pricing of, 146–149
  value of, 136–137
American put on spot, 122
American swaption call, 361
American terms, quoted price in, 70, 71
Arbitrage, 70, *See also* Interest parity
  in currency and interest-rate swaps, 348
  eurobond valuation and, 335–336
  opportunities, detection of, interest parity and,
    89–90
  regulatory, 256
  strategy, futures and forward prices and, 106
  triangular, 70
Asia, eurocurrency operations in, 254–255
Asian Currency Units, 254
"Asian dollar," 254
Asian option, *See* Average-rate option
Asked interest rate, 249

Asked price, 67
  in foreign exchange market, 71
  quoting of, 83
Asset(s)
  accumulation of, 234
  Basle Committee on Banking Regulations and
    Supervisory Practices and, 256
  central bank, 23
  expected returns on, 239
  flows of, 235
  loan, 293
  long-term, funding of, 290–291
  official reserve, portfolio shares of, 241–242
  returns on, calculation of, exchange rate
    component and, 235–236
  risk-adjusted, 257
  stocks of, 235
  weights of, allocation of, 239
Asset-for-asset swaps, 294–295
Asset-for-debt swaps, 295
Asset sales for cash, 295
Assignment, 293
Association of International Bond Dealers (AIBD),
    35, 324
Atlantic Alliance, against Soviet Union, 13
Attached options, in international bonds, 368–369
Auction issue, 325–326
Average behavior, in EMS, 41
Average-rate (Asian) option, 160–162
  pricing of, 161
  volatility of, 161–162

B

Back-to-back loans, 349–350
Bahrain, eurocurrency operations in, 254
Baker, James, 55–56

Balance of payments (BOP), 205–220
  balance sheet, 206
    central bank intervention and, 210–212
  capital account, 208–210
    central bank intervention and, 210–215
  current account, 205, 206–208
  deficit, 8, 13
  defined, 205–206
  exchange controls for, 79
  foreign exchange market, central bank intervention
    in, 215–218
  loan, 30
  portfolio choice and, 234–235
  problems, 206
  surplus, 8
Balance of trade, deterioration in, 48
Balance sheet, balance of payments, 206
Bank
  assets, risk weights applied against, 257–258
  interest risk, provisions for, 290–291
  marketmaking, 69
  as middleman, 289
  options written by, 130
  profit, 216–217
Bank for International Settlements (BIS), 46, 124,
    252, 256
Bank of England, 16, 18, 253
  exchange controls by, 80
Bank of France, 217
Bankers Trust, 35
  interest rate swaps by, 352
Bankhaus I.D. Hersatt, 28
Banking regulations, 256–258
Banking syndicate, parts of, 287
  agent bank, 287
  lead manager, 287–288
  managing banks, 287, 288
  participating banks, 287, 288
Bankruptcy, bank, 53
Barrier options, 162
Basis after carry (BAC), 342
Basis point value (bpv), hedging with bond futures
    and, 344, 345t
Basis risk, hedging with futures and, 109
Basle Committee on Banking Regulations and
    Supervisory Practices, 256–257, 289
  types of capital, 257
Basle Concordat, 256
Bearer bonds, 302
  individual, 323
  issuing of, to non U.S. residents, 309
Behavior
  average, in EMS, 41
  optimizing, 295
Belgium, multiple exchange rates in, 80
"Benign neglect," 24
Best effort basis, credit on, 288
Bid
  in foreign exchange market, 71
  syndicate, 324
Bid/asked (bid/offer) spread, 67, 85
  future markets, 108
  interest parity with, 90–93
  profit from, 68
Bid interest rate, 249

Bid/offer spread, See Bid asked spread
Bid price, 67
  futures trading and, 107
  quoting of, 83
Bid rate, for eurocurrencies, 261
"Big Bang," 35
Binomial pricing procedure, 169–174
BIS, See Bank for International Settlements
Black market, 214
  selling of dollars on, 78–79
Bond(s)
  book-entry credit for, 322
  call on, 359
  dual-currency, 96
  fixed-rate, 330
  high-yield, 36
  international, See International bonds
  junk, 36
Bond covenants, in international bond issues, 368
Bond futures, 339–346
  cheapest-to-deliver, 339–343
  conversion values, 340–341
  hedging with, 344–346
  index-based, 343–344
  notional bond, 339
Bond issues, ECU-denominated, 47
Bond markets, international, See International bond
    markets
Bond prices
  logarithmic changes in, 143
  quoting of, 330
Bond rating agency, 311
Book-entry credit, for bonds, 322
Borrowed money, riskless profit using, 86
Borrower
  costs to, 288–289
  credit risk, provisions related to, 292
  selection of lead manager, 287–288
Borrowing
  inflation-related, 27
  long, 265, 266
  short, 265, 266
Borrowing countries, IMF and, 53–54
"Bought deal," 36, 325
Brady, Nicholas, 56
Brazil
  black market, 78–79
  borrowing by, 51–52
Bretton Woods agreement, 3–25, 36
  cold war, Marshall Plan and European integration
    and, 9–12
  basis for, 5–6
  breakdown of, 22–25, 27, 41
  dollar restrictions and origins of the eurodollar
    market, 12–18
  events leading to, 4
  fixing the price of foreign exchange and gold, 7–9
  politics of gold and the SDR, 18–22
  postwar system evolving from, 6–7
  Smithsonian Agreement, 25
  speculative positions against central banks and, 28
  timing of, 3
British Ministry of Information, 4
Broker, 69
  in eurobond market, 329

foreign currency options, 126
swaps arranged through, 353
Broker-traders, 102
Brownian bridge process, 376
Bundesbank, 12, 22, 28, 312
  assets and liabilities, 23t
  intervention in foreign exchange market, 215, 216
  profits, 217
Buyer of options, 122, 126, 134–135
  on foreign currency futures, 122
  option privileges, extinguishing of, 162
Buying, options for, 121, *See also* Calls
Buying price, in foreign exchange market, 71
Buyouts, leveraged, 36

C

Cacall, 162
Call(s), call options, 121
  American, boundary constraints on, 147–148
  on a call (*cacall*), 162
  eurodollar futures, 279
  European, 141–142, 283, 358, 369
  first-passage, 167
  foreign currency
    domestic currency on, 137
    prices of, 139–142
  on futures, 122
    prices of, 134
    value of, at expiration, 135
  look back, 174
  on a put (*caput*), 162
  on spot, 128
    defined, 138
    value of, 135, 137
Call money, 248–249
Call prices
  American foreign currency, 149
  European foreign currency, 149
Call strike price, 283
Call writers, 131
Callable bond, pricing options on, 377–378
Cap(s), 283
  interest rate, 283
  swaps and, 358–359
  swaption, 363
Cap rate, 283
Capital
  adequacy, 34, 257
  control of, 79–80
    during 1970s, 28
  core, 257
  flows, portfolio determinants of, 211
  gains and losses, speculation on, 337
  inflow 209, 312
  international flow of, 27–28
  movements, portfolio theory and, 241
  outflow, 209
    in Japan, 60
  at risk, 227
    return on, forecast evaluation with, 227–228
  supplemental, 257
  usage of, calculation of, 257
Capital account, 234
  central bank intervention and, 210–215

"Capital shortage," 11
Caribbean, eurocurrency operations in, 253
Carter, J. (Pres.), 29
"Carter bonds," 29
Cash, asset sales for, 295
Cash bonds
  ordinary (plain vanilla), 378
  prices, boundary constraints on, 375–376
  pricing option features in, 375–377
Cash call, 104
Cash flows, on futures contracts, 116–117
  compared to forwards contracts, 104–105, 106
Cash margin, foreign currency options deposits and, 130–131
Cash price, futures price and, 114
  loss, 109
Cassel, G., 189
Causality issue, purchasing power parity and, 190
Cayman Islands, eurocurrency operations in, 253
CBOT, 340
  exchange conversion factor at, 340
CDs, *See* Certificates of deposit
Cedel S.A., 35, 332, 333
Central account, 208–210
Central America, eurocurrency operations in, 253
Central banks, 7
  assets, 23
  behavior, 211
  interventions
    capital account and, 210–215
    in currency markets, 28
    in foreign exchange market, 215–218
  liabilities, 23
  pegging of prices, 8
  policies, 212–215
  regulation, 256
  shortage of foreign currency, 214
  speculation against, 28
Certificates of deposit (CDs), 248, 249
  issuers of, 253
CFTC, *See* Commodities Futures Trading Commission
Cheapest-to-deliver bonds
  basis after carry, 342
  delivery option, 341
  wild card option, 341
Cheapest-to-deliver (CTD) futures, 339–343
  pricing options on, 377
Chicago Board of Trade (CBT), 163
Chicago Mercantile Exchange (CME), 124, 272t
  FX option, 124, 125t, 126
  International Money Market, 271, *See also* International Money Market
  writing foreign currency options by, 131
Chicago Mercantile Exchange Clearing House, 126
China, 11
Churchill, W., 4, 5
Citibank, 159
  freezing of eurodollars by, 255
"Claims on nonbanks," 252
Clayton, W., 6
Clearing, in eurobond market, 329, 332–333
Clearing house, 163
  futures, 102
Clearing member, futures, 102

Closing day, *See* Stabilization period
CME, *See* Chicago Mercantile Exchange
"Cocktail currencies," 234
Cold War, Bretton Woods agreement and, 9–12
Collars, 283
  swaps and, 358–359
Comanagers, 287
Comex, 31
Commission merchant, futures, 102, 103
Commitment, fee, 288
Commodities Futures Trading Commission (CFTC),
    102, 163–164
Commodities Futures Trading Commission Act, 163
Commodity Exchange Act, 115, 163
Common Market, 12, 36, *See also* European
    Economic Community
Common stock, 233
Community average
  concept of, systems organized according to, 41
  ECU definition of, 42
Compensated value principle, 75
Competition
  eurocurrency market and, 256
  in international trade, 211
Completely fixed exchange rates, 214
Conditional forward option, 160
Conditionality, 30
Consumer price index (CPI), 194
Continuous time Wiener-Levy process, 169
Convergence, in futures markets, 113
Convertibility, restoring of, Bretton Woods
    agreement and, 10
Convertible bonds, 305–306
Core capital, 257
Corporate bonds, withholding tax on, 309
Corporation
  alteration of hedging costs, 90
  arbitrage by, 90
Council for Mutual Economic Assistance
    (COMECON), 10
Countertrade, 205
Coupon(s), payment of, 370–371
Coupon bonds
  call on, 363, *See also* Swaption call
  portion of swap, 356
  prices, 333–334
    forward price, 337–338
  valuation of options on, 364
Coupon yield, 236
Covariance, portfolio, 241
Covenants, 292
  pari passu, 292
Credit
  on best effort basis, 288
  forward contracts and, 105
  fully underwritten, 288
  revolving, 288
  syndicated, 289
  term, 351–352, 288
Credit conversion factors, for off-balance sheet
    items, 258, 258t
Credit fund, EMS countries buying into, 46
Credit risk
  borrower, 292
  for eurobanks and eurocurrency dealers, 263

in swap arrangements, 364–365
  transformation of interest risk into, 291
Creditors
  secured, 292
  unsecured, 292
Cross-currency interest rate swap, 347, 352
  two year, 258
  valuing of, 357–358t
Cross-default clauses, 292
Cross-hedging, with futures, 113–114
Cross rate, 70
  banks specializing in, 70
CSFB, 325
"Cum coupon," 330
Currency, *See also* Domestic currency;
    Eurocurrency; Foreign currency
  arrangements, as of March 31, 1990, 32t–33t
  convertibility, Bretton Woods agreement and, 7
  daily fixing of, 68
  distribution of, in official reserve portfolios, 242t,
      242
  divergence of, 44, *See also* Divergence
    market, adjusted percentage of, 44
  exchange rate for, *See also* Exchange rate
    Bretton Woods agreement and, 7
    quoting of, 70
  intervention point, 38
  overevaluation of, 48
  par value for
    Bretton Woods agreement and, 7, 10
    U.S. dollar and, 248
  as reserve asset, 21
  trading of
    for foreign currency, 77
    mechanics of, 70–72
    risks in, 28
  vehicular, 70
  volatility of, 155
Currency markets, central bank intervention in, 28
Currency reform, post World War II, 11
Currency swap, 347
  arbitrage in, 348
  back-to-back and parallel loans, 349–350
  economic motives for, 347–348
  long-term forward contracts, 348–349
  market for, 353, 354t, 354
  straight, 349
  swap of debt payments, 350
  types of, 348–350
Current account (CA)
  balance on, 205, 206–208
  deficit, 209–210, 235
    reduction of, 208
  portfolio composition and, 234
  surplus, 209, 210, 235
    OPEC countries, 48–49
Current yield, 335
Cylinder options, 158–159

D

Daily price limit, futures contracts compared with
    forward contracts, 107
de Gaulle, C. 19, 20

Debt, payments, swap of, 350
Debt crisis
    international, 47–57
    during 1980s, 27
Debt issue, junk bonds and, 36
Debt-issuer, interest rate swap and, 351–352
Debt swaps, 293–294
Decision-making, financial, portfolio choice and, 233
    international, 233
    variables involved in, 231–232
Deductible insurance, 127
Default
    cross-default, 292
    risk of, in foreign currency options, 130
Default-free discount bonds, future prices and
        forward prices and, 106
Default-free lending, 289
Deficit, jerry-rigging of, 8
Delayed delivery contracts, 163
Deliverable cash bond, cheapest-to-deliver, 339–343
Delivery, 101–102
Delivery option, cheapest-to-deliver bonds, 341
Delta factors, 151
Delta hedge, futures, 113–115, 151
Delta, option, 150–151, 153
Delta position
    negative, 151
    neutral, 151, 152
Deposits, foreign exchange, transferring of, 66
Depression of the 1930s, 3
Deregulation, 35
Derivative products, swap-related market for, 360t
Deutschemark (DM), 11
    ECU central rate for, changes in, 46–47
    undervaluation of, 22–23, 24, 58–59
Devaluation
    maxidevaluation, 30
    unscheduled, 30
Developing countries
    loans, 34
    non-OPEC, international debt of, 47–53
        repayment of, 55
Deviations, forecast of, 203
Direct dealing, 69
Direct terms, quoted price in, 70, 71
Dirty floating, 28, 215
Discount, 83
    on forward exchange, interest parity and, 84–87
    forward rates quoted in, 83
    large, 184
    quoting of, 83–84
    small, 184
Discount bond
    domestic, 138
    default-free, future prices and forward prices and,
        106
    nominal return on, 235
Disequilibrium, fundamental, 7, 9
Disequilibrium exchange rates, 216
Divergence
    adjusted market, calculation of, 44
    calculated value of, 44
    maximum
        calculation of, 44, 45
        constancy of, 45

Divergence indicator, 41–46
    calculations, 44–46
Diversification, foreign currency, benefits of,
        238
DM, See Deutschemark
Dollar (Canadian), margin requirements on, 103
Dollar (U.S.)
    accumulation of, by foreign agencies, 14
    Bretton Woods agreement and, 7
        restrictions, 12–18
    buyers of, 77
    currency trading and, 70
    depreciation of, 13
        during 1980s, 29
    interest rate swap, 355t
    market value of ECU and, 42
    overvalued, 201
    par values for currency and, 248
    as reserve asset, 20
    rise in
        expected real returns and, 236–237
        during 1980s, 29
    sellers of, 77, 78–79
    specialty market in, Great Britain, 17
Dollar-priced goods, 77
Dollar-reserve holders, 20
"Dollar shortage," 11
Domestic assets, 23
    rate of return, equality with covered foreign
        assets, 87
Domestic banks, liabilities, eurobank activity
        and, 16
Domestic bonds
    differentiated from foreign bonds, 301
    discount, related to payoff at option expiration,
        138
Domestic countries, price levels of, 192
Domestic currency, 134
    borrowing of, interest parity with bid/asked
        spreads and, 91
    excess supply of, 8
    exchange value of, pegging, of, 8
    foreign currency call option on, 137
    foreign currency put option on, 137
    at forward discount, 83
    at premium, 83
    supply
        Bretton Woods agreement and, 23
        change in, 212–213
Domestic currency assets, portfolio of, 143
Domestic currency price
    of forward exchange, 86
        ceiling price on, 128
    of spot exchange, 85–86
Domestic policies, inflationary, 214
Domestic reference rates, 251
Domiciliary basis, regulation on, 256
Down-and-in option (DAIO), 162
Down-and-out option (DAOO), 162
Drexel Burnham Lambert, 36
Dual-currency bonds
    forward contracts and, 96
    issuing of, reasons for, 96
Dual traders, 102
Dulles, J. F., 57

E

Econometric methods in forecasting, 223
Economic models
output of, 222
true, 222
Economic Report of the President (1985), 200
ECU, *See* European Currency Unit
EEC, *See* European Economic Community
Effective date, in interest rate swap, 353
Effektengiro system, 312
Einsig, P., 16, 94–95
Elasticity, of option, 153
EMS. *See* European Monetary system
Energy consumption, 48
Equilibrium, expectational, 180–182
Equilibrium market price, 68
Equities, boom in, during 1980s, 27
Equity-related issues, 306, 307t, 307
Erdman, Paul, 49
Eurobank
balance sheet, 248
asset side of, 249–250
"claims on nonbanks," 252
concentration of, 252, *See also* Eurocurrency
centers
liabilities of, 248–249
risks faced by, 262, 263
sovereign risk and, 255
Eurobanking, business of, 247–252
Eurobond(s)
bearer bonds, 302, 309–310
convertible bonds, 305–306
development of, 35
differentiated from
eurocredits, 302–303
foreign bonds, 302
DM, 311–312
dollar-denominated, *See* Eurodollar bonds
equity-related, 35
features of, 302–307
floating rate notes, 304
interest paid on, 302
international bond issues, new, by bond type,
306–307
marginal return on, 326
mortgage-backed, 306
new, issuing of, 303
private placement exemption, 308–309
prohibition of sales, 308
straight bonds, 303
Swiss franc, 314–315
underwriting risks in, 36
valuation, 335–337
arbitrage, 335–336
riding the yield curve, 336–337
speculation on capital gains and losses, 337
withholding taxes, 309–310
yen, 312–314
zero-coupon bonds, 304–305
Eurobond issues, 35
Eurobond market
clearing in, 332–333, 329
interest rates and coupon bond prices,
333–334

new issue procedures in 317–327
fee structure, 318, 320–321
Gray market, 323–324
organization of a traditional eurobond syndicate,
317–318, 318t
stabilization, 324–325
traditional time structure, 321–323
variations on, 325–326
trading in, 329–330
Euroborrowing, by non-OPEC countries, 49
Euroclear Clearance System Limited, 35, 332, 333
Eurocommercial paper, euronotes and, 295–297
Eurocredits
differentiated from eurobonds, 302–303
revolving credit, 252
syndicated, *See* Syndicated eurocredits
term credit, 251–252
Eurocurrency(ies)
borrowing and lending of, 249
contracts, delivery, 272
Eurobank deposits denominated in, 249
interbank market in, 261–262
interchanging of, 301
interest rates, 85
trader and, 88
trading of, 261
Eurocurrency centers, 252–255
Caribbean and Central America, 253
defined, 252
western Europe, 253
Eurocurrency dealers, risks faced by, 262, 263
Eurocurrency deposits, 261–262
arbitrage using, 88
interest parity and, 95–96
interest rates on, 249, 250t
OPEC, 49
settlement dates, 85, 261
sovereign risk and, 255
"tomorrow-next," 261
trading of, 85
Eurocurrency futures options, LIBOR options and
FRAs, 285–286
Eurocurrency market, 248
conventions in, 88
developments in, 31–34t
regulation of, 256–258
Eurodollar
contracts, delivery, 272
creation of, 14–15
defined, 14
Eurodollar bonds
Japanese corporations issuing, 314
U.S. legal aspects of, 307–310
Eurodollar deposits, eurobank issuing of, 247
Eurodollar futures
options
interest rate and, 279–282
price, 280–282
strike, 282
price, 34
Eurodollar market, growth of, 14
interbank, 261–262
origins of, 12–18
time measures in, 331

Euronotes
    costs in, 296
    eurocommercial paper and, 295–297
    underwriting of, 296
Europe
    currencies, margins of fluctuation, 36
    developments, in, EMS and, 47
    monetary system, snake arrangement, 36–47
European countries, trade amongst, post World
    War II, 11–12
European Currency Unit (ECU), 39, 42–46, 234
    central rate, 39, 44, 45
    composition of, 42
    issuing of, 46
    market value of, 42–44, 45
    new central values assigned to, 45
European Economic Community (EEC), 12, 30,
    36–37, See also Common Market
    bands
      narrowing of, 36
      widening of, 36
    currencies, joint float of, 37
European Free Trade Area (EFTA), 29–30
European integration, Bretton Woods agreement
    and, 9–12
European Monetary System (EMS), 30,242
    banks in, 217
    success of, 46
    main points of, 37–47
European options, 122
    advantage of, 136
    call, 369
      cap, 283, 358
      on spot, 141–142
    compared to American options, 146–147
    duplication of, 143
    on futures, 150
    pricing formula, 143
    on spot, 143
      futures-style, 146
      values of, 145t, 145
European Options Exchange (EOE), 124
European Payments Union, 11
European puts, on spot, 141–142
European Recovery Program, See Marshall Plan
European swaption, 364
    call, 361
European terms, quoted price in, 70–71
Exchange authority, 7
Exchange conversion factor, 340
Exchange for physicals (EFP) market, foreign
    exchange futures in, 115
Exchange markets, developments in, 28–31
Exchange rate
    changes, daily proportional, 74
    control of, 77–80
    current account flow and, 207–208
    disequilibrium, 216
    distribution of, 232
    fixed, 79–80
      Bretton Woods agreement and, 7–8
      completely fixed, 214
      demise of, 31
      versus flexible, 79

    floating, 37
      freely floating, 215
    forward, See Forward exchange rate
    futures contract and, 99
    futures market and, 118
    gain, 109
    loss, avoiding of, 109
    macroeconomic variables influencing, 221
    market, 38
    market equilibrium, 180
    movement, day-to-day, 69
    multiple, 80
    news and, 178
    nominal, 214
      change in, 198
      effective, 199, 200t
    purchasing power parity and, 190
    real, See Real exchange rate
    spot, 139–140, 189
    transaction, 335–336
Exchange-rate forecaster, 214–215
Exchange-rate insurance, foreign currency options
    as, 126
Exchange returns, covariance of, 238
Exchange-trade options, 126
    clearing house for, 130
Exchange value, Bretton Woods agreement
    and, 7–8
Exercise price, 121, 137
Expectations, 177–189
    errors, 222
    expectational equilibrium, 180–182
      rational, 221–222
    as function of information, 178–179
    martingale character of spot rates, 186–187
    not rational, 222
    rational, 222
    simple linear regression and statistical inference,
      187–188
    speculative efficiency hypothesis, 182–185
    speculator characteristics, 185–186
Expectations theory of the term structure, 266
Expected inflation rates, 196
Expected return, portfolio, calculation of, 238–240
Expected spot rate, 183
    forward exchange rate and, 185
Expected values, 221
Expiration date, 121
Export(s), as percentage of GNP, 58
Export sectors, noncompetitive, 48
Exporters, price controls by, 77–78

F

Fair value, of foreign currency option, 126
Federal Reserve
    Regulation D, 262
    Regulation Q, 17, 18f
Fee structures, for new eurobond issues, 318,
    320–321
FIBOR, See Frankfurt Interbank Offered Rate
First-passage call, 167
First-passage option, 162, 167

First-passage put, 167
Fiscal policy, easy, 237
Fisher equation, 197
Fixed interest rates, borrowing at, 27
Fixed price re-offer, 326
Fixed rate bonds, spread of, 330
Fixed rate debt, cheaper to get, 348
Fixed-rate payer
    interest rate swaps and, 353
    valuing swaps and, 354
Fixed-rate portion of swap, 356
Flat options, 156
Floating
    dirty, 28, 215
    managed, 28
Floating exchange rates, 37
Floating-rate debt, 348
Floating rate notes (FRNs), 35, 304, 307
    in DM eurobond market, 312
    features of, 330
    value of, 354–355
Floating rate payer, interest rate swaps and, 353
Floor(s), 283
    interest rate, 283
    swaps and, 358–359
Floor broker, 102
Floor traders, 102
Flows of assets, 235
Forecasted values, 221
Forecasting, foreign exchange, 221–229
    approaches to, 222–223
    errors and risks, 222, 231–232
    correct and incorrect, 225–227
    expertise, measurement of, 224–225
    forward rate compared to, 224–225
    fundamental forecasters, evaluation of, 224–227
    information, efficiency, and model evaluation, 224
    short-term, 223
    technical forecasters, evaluation of, 227–228
Foreign currency, at discount, 83
Foreign assets, 23
    accumulation and loss of, 234–235
    covered, domestic assets rate of return and, 87
    flows in, 212, 212t
Foreign bonds
    differentiated from
        domestic bonds, 301
        eurobonds, 302
    DM, 311–312
    domestic purchase of, 209
    markets for, 301–302
    value of, conversion into domestic currency terms, 143
Foreign capital inflows, in Japan, 60
Foreign commerce, 189
Foreign countries, price levels of, 192
Foreign Credit Restraint Program, 17, 25, 248
Foreign currency
    borrowing of, interest parity of bid/asked spreads and, 91–92
    deposits and loans denominated in, 16–17
    excess supply of, 8
    forward value of, 83
    at a premium, 83

supply and demand of, 189
    undervaluation of, 214
Foreign currency assets, portfolio of, 143
Foreign currency futures, See Futures
Foreign currency options, See Options
Foreign exchange
    fixing price of, Bretton Woods agreement and, 7–9
    forward contracts and dual-currency bonds, 96
    government access to, 10
    one unit of, option prices and, 133–134
    rationing of, 78
    reserves, preservation of, 214
    risks, for eurobanks and eurocurrency dealers, 262–263
Foreign Exchange and Foreign Trade Control Law of 1980, 60
Foreign exchange component, calculating returns with, 235–236
Foreign exchange forecasting, See Forecasting
Foreign exchange intervention, central bank and, 212
Foreign exchange market, 65–81, 301, See also International bond markets
    currencies used, 65
    description of, 65–66
    exchange controls, 77–80
    marketmakers versus Walrasian auctioneers, 66–69
    mechanics of currency trading, 70–72
    official intervention in, profits and losses from, 217, 218t
    open position in, risk from, 73–74
    participants in, 65
    settlement dates, 75–77
    trading, prices involved in, 71
    transactions in
        forward, 71
        outright forward, 71
        spot, 71
Foreign finance subsidiary, 234
Foreign securities, American purchasing of, 14
Forward bond rate, implied, 264, 265f, 265
Forward contracts, 83, 182
    daily price limit, 107
    dual-currency bonds and, 96
    futures contracts compared to, 104–107
    long-term, 348–349
    monetary exchange, 106–107
    options, foreign currency options compared to, 121
    purchase of, 105
    trading of, 106
    value of, 104
Forward exchange, 84
    domestic currency price of, 86
    percentage discount or premium on, 184
Forward-forward swaps, 83
Forward hedge, interest parity and, 93
Forward markets, 263
    historical background, 94–96
Forward maturity, 76
Forward maturity dates
    bunching of, 76
    rule for, 76
Forward options, 159–160
    conditional, 160

participating, 159–160
range forwards, 158–159
Forward price
 of coupon bond, 337–338
 interest rate and, 112
Forward rate
 artificial, 263
 equation for, 145–146
 expectations on future spot rates and, 182
 expected spot rate and, 185
 forecasting performance compared to, 224–225
 implied, interbank-traded equivalent of, 267f, 267
 outward forward, 83
 spot rate and, 87–88
Forward rate agreements (FRAs), 266–268, 276, 277, 285–286
 "six against nine," 266
 strip yield curve, 269
 "three against six," 267, 268
Forward rate quotations, 83–84
Forward trade, market failure in, 349
Forward transactions, 71
Franc (French), ECU percentage changes for, 47
Franc (Swiss)
 international bonds, 314–315
 margin requirements on futures, 103
France, See also Franc
 gold pool and, 19–20
Frankfurt Interbank Offered Rate (FIBOR), 312
Frankfurter Kassenverein, 333
Franklin National Bank, 28
FRAs, See Forward rate agreements
Free market, 214
Free trade, 6
Freely floating exchange rate, 215
Fully underwritten credit, 288
Fund(s)
 sources of, 206
 uses of, 206
Fundamental approach, to foreign exchange forecasting, 222–223
Fundamental disequilibrium, 7, 9
Fundamental forecasters, evaluation of, 224–227
Future spot rate, 184
 expectations of, 182
Futures
 bond, 339–346
  pricing option features in, 377
 eurocurrency, contracts, 271–273
 eurodollar
  amount, 274
  duration, 274
  slope, 274
  exchanges, 272
  gap risk, 275
  hedging with, 274–279
  margin, 275
  price, 34, 271–272
  strip yield curve, 273–274
  variation margin flows, 275
 European option on, 150
 foreign currency, 99–119
  American calls on, 148
  calculating the risk in a delta hedge, 113–115

contracts, See Futures contract
 delivery, 101–102
 description of, 99–101
 economic functions of foreign exchange contracts, 117–118
 European options on, 137–138
 exchange for physicals, 115
 exchange trading and marketmaking, 107–108
 foreign exchange risk management and the gambler's ruin problem, 115–116
 futures-style options compared to, 138
 hedging with, 108–112
 historical perspective, 162–164
 International Money Market (IMM), 101–102, See also International Money Market
 margin management, 116–117
 margin requirements, 102–104
 options on, 121, 122, 127, 130, 149t See also Futures-style options; Options
 size of bet, 100
 stopping of bet, 100
 trading of, 99,107
 value of calls on, at expiration, 135
 worldwide trade in, 34, 34t
Futures contract
 buying and selling of, 107
 cash flows on, 116–117
 compared with forward contracts, 104–107
 daily price limit, 107
 delta-hedging with, 151
 expiration of, 106
 netting out of, 107
 placing of orders in, 99
 price movements on, 103
 purchase of, 105
 spot month, 101
 trading of, 106
 value of, 104
Futures market
 economic functions of, 117–118
 price quotations, 107–108
Futures prices, movement of, 109, 112
Futures-style options, 121, 123–124
 compared to
  options on spot and options on futures, 149t
  ordinary options on spot or futures, 138
 eurodollar, interest rate on, 279–282
 insurance on, 127
 payoff of, 138
 terminology applied to, 139
 value of, 150
Futures-style put on spot, 124

G

Gambler's ruin problem, 115–116, 186
Gamma, option, 151–152, 153
Gamma position, long, 157
Gamma tradeoff, 156, 158

General Agreement on Trade and Tariffs (GATT),
    6, 58
General Motors Acceptance Corporation, 325
Gensaki market, 60
Gensaki (repo) rate, 262
Germany
    current account balances, 206, 207t, 207
    exchange rate control by, 79
    flows in foreign assets, 211, 212t
    hyperinflation in, 5
    Nazi, trade and exchange controls, 6
    noninflationary stance, 13
    occupation plan, 57
    occupied, currency reform in, 10–11
    parity grid system, 41
    propaganda broadcasts, Bretton Woods agreement
        and, 4
    reparations from, 4–5
Glass-Steagall act, 35, 57, 293, 308
Glossary of terms, 389–401
GNP
    exports as percentage of, 58
GNP deflator, 194
    rate of growth of, 58
Going short to offset, 122
Gold
    Bretton-Woods agreement and
        conversion to dollars, 13
        fixing price of, 7–9
        private market for, 18–22
    market value of, rise in, 242
    price fixing, 67
        British, 18–19
    pricing of
        purchasing power and, 9
        two-tier system, 20–21, 25
    purchase of, by U.S. citizens, 31
    relative price of, 9
    role of, demotion of, 31
Gold pool, 18, 19–20
    disbanding of, 21
Goodman, S., 227
Goods, weights for, 193
Governments
    bank funding of loans and, 292
    deficits, 208
    intervention, risk of, 291–292
    lending to, default-free, 289
Gray market, 323–324
    prices, 323–324
    trading in new issues, 324
Great Britain
    gold pool and, 21
    gold price fixing by, 18–19
    imperial preference system, 6
    Lend-Lease aid to, 5
    Ministry of Information, 4
    pound sterling
        Bretton Woods agreement and, 16
        devaluation of, 20
        exchange rate for, 10
    specialty market in dollars in, 17
Great Society Program, 22
Great War of 1914-1919, 3

H
Haberlier, G., 24
"Hard currencies," 11
Hedge ratio, in bond futures, 344
Hedging
    with eurodollar futures, 274–279
    with foreign exchange options, 126
    with futures, 108–112, 113, 117
        with bond futures, 339, 344–346
        cross-hedging, 113–114
        delta hedge, 113–114
    option concepts for, 149–154
    selective, return on, forecast evaluation with,
        227–228
Hedging costs
    alteration of, 90
    interest parity and, 93, 94
Hideki, T (Gen.), 57
High-yield bonds, 36
Hitler, A., 5, 57
Homogeneous goods, law of one price and, 192
Houthakker, H., 10, 58

I
IBM, swap of debt payments by, 350
IBORs, *See* Interbank offered rates
IET, *See* Interest Equalization Tax
IMF, *See* International Monetary Fund
IMM, *See* International Money Market
Implied foreward bond rate, 264, 265f, 265
Implied volatility, calculation of, 154
Import sectors, subsidizing of, 48–49
Importers, buying of dollars by, licensing for, 78
Index-based futures, 343–344
Indirect terms, quoted price in, 70–71
Individual bearer bonds, 323
Industrial countries
    floating of currencies, 30
    international debt crisis and, 55–57
Inflation
    forecasting of, 237
    -related borrowing, 27
Inflation rates
    expected, 196
    relative, 196–197
Inflationary policies, 214
Information
    of central bank, advantages in, 217
    cost of, interest parity and, 93–94
    expectations as function of, 178–179
    for forecasting, 224
    investing in, 202
Information set
    market, 181, 182
    size of, 223
    speculator's, 185
    traders 178–179
Information dealers, 177
Insider information, for forecasting, 224
Insurance
    deductible, 127
    exchange-rate, 126–130
    foreign currency, FX options as, 126–130

Inter-Allied Bank, 6, *See also* United Nations Bank
Interbank offered rates (IBORs), 251
Interbank trader, 178
Interest
    paid on eurobonds, 302
    risk, transformation into credit risk, 291
Interest Equalization Tax (IET), 14, 17, 25, 248,
        312
Interest parity, 84–94, 191
    with bid/asked spreads, 90–93
    cost of information and, 93–94
    divergences from, 89–90
    hedging with futures and, 113
    pricing models for, foreign exchange options and,
        142–143
    purchasing power parity and, 196, 197
    swaps and, 87–89
    tests of, 95
Interest payments, swap of debt payments and, 350
Interest rate(s)
    American foreign currency options pricing and,
        147, 148–149
    asked, 249
    bet on, maturity transformation and, 266
    bid, 249
    bond prices and, 324–325
    capping of, 283
    credit risk in swaps and, 364
    discount and premium, 84–85
    eurobonds, 333–334
    eurodollar futures options and, 279–282
    fixed, borrowing at, 27
    floor, 283
    futures contracts compared to forwards contracts,
        105–106
    futures prices and forward prices and, 112, 272
    historical background, 94–96
    on loans, 288
        parallel, 349–350
    long-term, 336, 337
    nominal, 197
    quoting of, 85
    real, 237, 237t
    relevant, 95
    risk
        for eurobanks and eurocurrency dealers, 263
        provisions for, 290–293
    short-term, 291, 336, 337
        change in, 337
    term structure of, 263–266
        upward-sloping, 336
    in straight currency swap, 349
Interest rate markets, time measures in, 330–332
Interest rate swap, 347, 350–352
    arbitrage in, 348
    cross-currency, *See* Cross-currency interest rate
            swap
    economic motives for, 347–348
    market for, 352–353t
        documentation of, 354
    two year, 258
Interest reset date
    caps and, 359
    floors and, 359

International bank, assets and liabilities, by
        nationality, 61t
International Bank for Reconstruction and
        Development, *See* World Bank
International Banking Facilities (IBFs), 254
    in U.S., 14
International bond(s), pricing option features in,
        367–380
    attached options, 368–369
    bond futures, 377
    bonds with options on principal repayment,
        369–370
    on callable bonds, 377–378
    on cash bonds, 375–377
    coupon options, 370–371
    identifying of 368–371
    pricing of bonds, 371–375
International bond issues, new, by currency, 307t
International bond markets, 310–315
    developments in, 35–36
    eurobonds, 301, *See also* Eurobonds
    eurodollar bond issues, U.S. legal aspects of,
        307–310
    foreign bonds, 301, *See also* foreign bonds
    Yankee bonds, 310–311
International debt crisis, 47–57
    borrowing countries governments and, 53–54
    IMF and, 54–55
    industrial countries and, 55–57
    lending banks and, 53
    World Bank and, 55–56
International Monetary and Financial Conference of
        the United and Associated Nations, 3
International Monetary Fund (IMF), 30, 31,
        54–55, 58
    balance of payments loans, 30
    borrowing countries and, 53–54
    criticism, 55
    funds for, 55
    history of, 6
    purpose of, 6–7
International Money Market (IMM), 34, 101–102,
        106, 271, 272
    eurodollar futures call, 279
    futures contract, 125
    swap, 273–274
International trade, competitiveness in, 211
International transactions, balance on, *See* Balance
        of payments
Intervention, no-fault, 3
Intervention points, in parity grid par value,
        39–41
Intrinsic value, of foreign currency options, 139
Investment banks, profits, during 1980s, 35
Italian Autostrada, 35

J
Jamaica agreement, 30
Japan, *See also* Yen
    capital controls, 59
    capital outflows, 60
    companies, issuing of dollar eurobonds, 35

Japan [*cont.*]
  current account
    balances, 206, 207t, 207
    surplus, 59
  domestic market, 262
  financial market
    deregulation, 59–60
    opening of, 57–61
  flows in foreign assets, 211, 212t
  foreign bonds issued in
    Samurai bonds, 301–302, 312–314
    yen eurobonds, 312–314
  foreign capital inflows in, 60
Japan Offshore Market (JOM), 252
Jensen's inequality, 39
Johnson, L. (Pres.), 14, 22
Joint float, 37
Judgmental methods in forecasting, 223
Junk bonds, 36

K

Kennedy, J. F. (Pres.), 13, 14, 22
Keynes, J. M., 4, 5, 94
Kissinger, H., 29
Korean War, effect on Japan's economy, 58

L

Lambda, option, 153
Lambda value, 155, 156
Law of one price (LOP), 191–192
  assumptions, 191–192
  current deviations from, 203
  preservation of, 198
  unidirectional trade and, 201
  violation of, 198
LDC debt, non-OPEC countries, 48–49, 50t, 51
Lead manager
  bank, 287
    negotiations with borrower, 287–288
  in eurobond market, 317, 318, 319t, 333
    stabilization and, 324–325
  praecipium, 289
Lend-Lease aid, 5
Lending
  default-free, 289
  long, 265, 266
  risks of, loan agreements and, 289–291
  securitization of, 31
  short, 265, 266
  through subscription, 7
Lending banks, amount and pace of lendings,
    1979–1982, 53
Lending margin, 251
Lenin, V. I., 21
Leptokurtosis, 74
Leveraged buyouts, 36
Levich, R., 224–225
Liabilities
  central bank, 23
  short-term, 290
LIBID (London Interbank Offered Rate), 251, 262

LIBOR (London Interbank Offered Rate), 31, 32, 49,
    51, 251, 262, 289
  -CD spread, 262
  three-month, 271, 272, 274
LIFFE, 279
LIMEAN, 251
"Limit moves," in futures contracts, 101
Limit orders, 107
Linear regression equation, 187–188
Lira, devaluation of, 47
Loan
  foreign exchange, transferring of, 66
  increase of, 288
  principal, repayment of, 288
  syndicated, 47, 289–293
Loan agreements, standard, 291
Loan asset, disposal of, 293
Loan costs, 288–289
  periodic, 288
  up-front, 288
Loan loss provisions, 34
Loan participations, 293
Loan swaps, 293–294
Lock-up procedures, 308
London Interbank Offered Rate, *See* LIBOR
London International Bid Rate, *See* LIBID
Long position, 73
  borrowing at, 265, 266
  in foreign currency options, 131
  in futures contract, 102, 107
  in futures pricing, 99, 100–101
  gamma, 157
  lending at, 265, 266
  natural, 228
Look-back call option, 174
Louvre Accord, 29

M

Managed floating, 28
Manager group, in eurobond syndicate, 317
Managing banks, 287, 288
  best effort credit and, 288
  fully underwritten credit and, 288
Mao Tse-tung, 11
Margin
  initial, 103
  maintenance, 103
  requirements, 163
    for foreign exchange futures, 102–104
Marginal return on bonds, 326
Marked to market daily price, of futures-style
    options, 123
Market completions, swaps representing, 348
Market-determined rates, 201
Market equilibrium, *See* Equilibrium
Market exchange rates, allowable range for, 38
Market failure, in forward trade, 349
Market information set, 181, 182
Market orders, buying or selling of futures contracts
    and, 107

Market price
  equilibrium, 68
  futures price and, 99–100
Market risk, in swap arrangements, 364
Marketmaker, 177
  in eurobond market, 329–330
  foreign exchange
    expectations of, 221, *See also* Forecasting
    trading among, 69
    versus Walrasian auctioneer, 66–69
  function of, 177
  profit margins, 178
  speculative positions, 189
  supply and demand for spot exchange and, 189
Marketmaking
  exchange trading and, 107–108
  in foreign currency options, 155–158
Marketmaking banks, 83
"Marking to market," futures contracts compared to
    forwards contracts, 104
Marshall Plan, Bretton Woods agreement and, 9–12
Martingale characteristics, 202
  of spot rates, 186–187
Maturity, amount of, reduction of, 291
Maturity date, 121
Maturity transformation, interest risk associated
    with, 265–266
Maxidevaluation, 30
McKinnon, R., 25
Mean absolute error, performance measurement by,
    224–225
Merchandise trade, 206, 207
Merchant Bank's Market, 16
Mexico
  borrowing by, 51–52
  exchange control by, 79
Middle East, eurocurrency operations in, 254
Milken, M., 36
Minimum margin, in foreign exchange futures, 103
Momental models, in forecasting, 223
Monetary base, change in, 212–213
Money market hedge, interest parity and, 93
Money supply and demand, 213
  increase, prevention of, 24
Monnet, J., 11, 12, 19
Moody's Investors Services, Inc., 311
Morgan Guaranty, 29, 35
Morgan Stanley, 345
Morgenthau, H., 5, 6
Mortgage-backed eurobonds, 306
Moscow Narodny Bank, 17, 21
Muth, J., 181

N

Nasser, G. A., 16
Natural long position, 228
Natural short position 228
Negative delta position, 151
Net speculator, 68
Netherlands, foreign bonds issued in, 302
Neutral delta position, 251, 252
"New Order," 4

"New World Order," 28
New York Stock Exchange, 310
News, exchange rates and, 178
1970s, inflationary pressures, 27
1980s, economic climate during, 27
1990s, international financial arena during, 27
Nominal exchange rate, 214
  effective, 199, 200t
Nominal returns
  adjustment to real returns, 236
  on foreign money, 235
  to equity, 236
Note issue facility (NIF), 296
Notional bond futures, 339
Notional principal amount, 352
Novation, 293
Nuclear war, 13

O

Off-balance sheet items, credit conversion factors
    for, 258, 258t
Offered price, in foreign exchange market, 71
Official reserve assets, portfolio shares of, 241–242
Offset, going short to, 122
Oil reserves, use of, 48
OPEC countries
  current account surplus, 48–49
  eurocurrency deposits, 49
  OPEC I, 48, 49
  OPEC II, 48, 55
Open-market operations, central bank and, 212
Open position, in foreign exchange, risk from, 73–74
Operation Bird Dog, 11
Opportunity cost, in futures contract, 103
Optimizing behavior, 295
Option(s), foreign currency
  American, *See* American foreign currency options
  average-rate (Asian) options, 160–162
  barrier options, 162
  classification of, 121
  concepts for hedging and risk management,
      149–154
  contracts, expiration dates on, 125
  definitions, 124
  elasticity of, 153
  exchange-traded, 126, 130
  forward options, 159–160
  on futures, 122–123
  futures-style, 123–124
  historical perspective, 162–164
  implied volatility, 154–155
  as insurance, 126–130
  market, 124–126
  marketmaking in, 155–158
  options on options, 162
  over-the-counter, 125–126
  payoff value, settlement of, 160
  premium of, 121, 122
  price change, 154
    measurement of, 150–151
  pricing models for, 142–146
  pricing principles, 133–142

Option(s), foreign currency [*cont.*]
  range forwards and cylinder options, 158–160
  relative values, 150
  foreign currency, on spot, 121–122, 124, *See also*
       Swaption
  value relationships among, 148t, 148
  worldwide trade in, 34, 34t
  writing of, 130-133
Option on an option, 162
Options Clearing corporation (OCC), 126, 130
Order, futures, 102
Organization for Economic Cooperation and
     Development (OECD), 10
Organization for European Economic Cooperation
     (OEEC), 10
Organization of Petroleum Exporting Countries, *See*
     OPEC
OTC, *See* Over-the counter
Outright forwards, 83
  transactions, 71
Over-the counter market, 65, 329
Over-the-counter options, 125–126
Over-the counter trader, 156

                         P
Par value
  Bretton Woods agreement and, 7, 10, 22
  in parity grid, 38–39
     intervention points, 39–41
  U.S. dollar and, 248
Parallel loans, 349–350
Pari passu covenant, 292
Parity
  interest, 84–94, *See also* Interest parity
  purchasing power, 189–204, *See also* Purchasing
       power parity
Parity grid, 37–38, 41, 44
  maintenance of, 217
  par values in, 38–39
     intervention points, 39–41
Participating banks, 287, 288
Participating forward option, 159–160
Peg exchange rates, 7, 8
Perfect competition, 77
Periodic costs, 288
Periodic coupons, bonds paying, 236
Perpetual American foreign currency options, 167
Perpetual floating rate notes, 35
PHLX, 124, 125t, 126
Placement memorandum, 288
Placing agent, 296
Plain vanilla cash bond, 378
Poker Player's Theorem, 233
Political equilibrium, 77
Portfolio choice, 231–243
  balance of payments and, 234–235
  benefits of foreign currency diversification, 238
  calculation of returns with foreign exchange
       component, 235–236
  domestic and foreign currency assets, 143
  expected return and variance calculation, 238–240
  expected real returns and rise of U.S. dollar,
       236–237

forecasting errors and risk and, 231–233
  international, 233–234
     implications of, 234
  optimal allocation of portfolio shares, 241
  portfolio shares of official reserve assets, 241–242
Praecipium, 289
Premarket, eurobond, *See* Gray market
Premium(s), 83
  on forward exchange, interest parity and, 84–87
  forward rates quoted in, 83
  interest parity and, 85
  large, 184
  of option, 121, 122
     payment of, in call on futures, 122
  quoting of, 84
  small, 184
Pribram, K., 190
Price
  exercise, 131, 137
  in foreign exchange market, 66–69
     agreement on, 65
     fixing of, 68
  movement
     in futures contracts, 101
     hedging with futures and, 110
     between spot rate and futures rate, 112–113
  quoted
     in American terms, 70, 71
     in European terms, 70–71
Price differentials, 201
Price fixing, Bretton Woods agreement and, 7–9
Price level
  calculation of, 194
  of domestic and foreign countries, 192
  expected changes in, 196
Price-to-yield relationship, in cheapest-to-deliver
     bond futures, 339
Pricing
  binomial, of American foreign currency options,
       169–174
  of foreign currency options, 133–149
     American, 146–149
     models for, 142–146
  rollover, 250, 251, 290, 291
  yield, 325
Pricing option features, in international bonds,
     367–380, *See also* International bonds
Pricing sheets, for exchange options, 155, 155t, 156
Principal
  payments, swap of debt payments and, 350
  repayment, bonds with options on, 369–370
Principal paying agent, in eurobond syndicate, 318
Private market speculation, 217
Probability, risk measurement and, 232
Probability distribution, 74, 241
Punt, devaluation of, 47
Purchasing power, gold price and, 9
Purchasing power parity (PPP), 189–204
  absolute, 192–193, 195
  basic idea of, 190
  causality issue and, 190
  empirical evidence and theoretical reformulation,
       200–203
  law of one price, 191–192

real exchange rate and, 197–200
relative rates of inflation and, 196–197
relative version of, 194–196
violation of, 197
Put option, 121
call on, 162
eurodollar futures, 279
first-passage, 167
foreign currency
domestic currency on, 137
future-style, prices of, 134
prices of, 139–142
on futures, 122
on spot, 128
defined, 138–139
futures-style, 124
value of, at expiration date, 135–136
Put swaption, 362
valuing of, 363
Put writers, 131
Putable swap, 363

R

Range forward contract, 158–160
Rate of return, nominal, 235
Rational expectations, 222
concept of, 180, 181
Reagan, R. (Pres.), 29, 55
Real dollar borrowing rates, 51t, 52–53
Real exchange rate
changes in, 46, 202
current account flow and, 207–208
effective, 199–200
future level of, 231
measurement of, 202
purchasing power parity and, 197–200
Real interest rates, 237, 237t
Real property, debt for, 295
Real returns
adjustment of nominal returns to, 236
expected, rise of U.S. dollar and, 236–237
risk-adjusted, 234
Reciprocal terms, quoted price in, 70–71
Reference rates, 250–251
domestic, 251
listing of, 251
setting a margin over, 291
Registered bonds, eurobonds compared to, 302
Regulatory arbitrage, 256
Reichsbank, 5
Reichsmark, printing of, by U.S. and Russia, 10–11
Relative price, change, 195
Relative purchasing power parity, 194–196
holding of, 195
Relative rates of inflation, 196–197
Rembrandt bonds, 302
Renault, interest rate swaps by, 352
Reparations, 4–5
Reserves
currency as, 21
foreign exchange, preservation of, 214
international, formal agreement on, 22

losing of, 8
official, portfolio shares of, 241–242
Returns
on capital at risk, forecast evaluation with, 227–228
to equity, nominal, 236
expected, portfolio, calculation of, 238–240
exchange, covariance of, 238
probability distribution of, 241
real, 236–237
on selective hedging, forecast evaluation with, 227–228
Revolving credit, 252, 288
Revolving underwriting facility (RUF), 296
Riding the yield curve, 291, 336–337
Risk
calculation of, in a delta hedge, 113–115
of eurobanks and eurocurrency dealers, 262, 263
forecasting, 231–232
of government intervention, 291–292
hedging with futures and, 109, 111
interest rate, 290–291
of lending, loan agreements and, 289–293
management, 115–116
option concepts for, 149–154
writing options as, 131
from open position in foreign exchange, 73–74
shifts occurring as result of, 233
sovereign, eurodeposits and, 255
speculator's neutrality, 185
in swap arrangements, 364–365
Risk-adjusted assets, calculation of, 257
Risk-adjusted real return, 234
Risk-adverse behavior, 233
Risk attitude, portfolio allocation and, 241
Risk weights, applied against bank assets, 257–258
Rockefeller, N., 49
Rollover credits, 31
Rollover pricing, 250, 290
method of, 291
reference rate used in, 251
Ross, S., 324
N. M. Rothschild Bank, 67
gold price fixing and, 18–19
Ruble, 3
Ruin probability, speculator's, 115–116, 186

S

Samurai bonds, 301–302, 312–314
foreign buying of, 313
Savings, private, after tax, 208
"Scalpers," 108
Schmidt, H., 37
SDR, *See* Special Drawing Right
Sears, Roebuck, 312
SEC, *See* U.S. Security and Exchange Commission
Second world war, financial system reconstruction following, 3, *See also* Bretton Woods agreement
Secondary debt market transactions, 295
Secondary market, 329
eurobonds bought and sold in, 330

Securities and Exchange Commission, *See* U.S.
    Securities and Exchange Commission
Securities and Exchange Law, 57
Securities Exchange Act, 163
Securities firms, profits, during 1980s, 35
Selling, options for, 121, *See also* Put option
Selling group, in eurobond syndicate, 317
Selling price, in foreign exchange market, 71
Services, defined, 206
Settlement dates
    for eurocurrency deposits, 85
    in foreign exchange market, 75–77
Settlement location, 75
Shelf registration, of Yankee bonds, 310–311
Short position, 73, 107
    borrowing at, 265, 266
    cash bond, 339
    in foreign currency options, 131
    in futures contract, 107, 122, 123
    in futures pricing, 99, 100–101
    lending at, 265, 266
    natural, 228
    swap, 359
Shuman, R., 11
SIBOR, 254
SIMEX, 254, 279
    futures contracts compared with forward
        contracts, 106–107
Singapore, eurocurrency operations in, 254–255
Single European Act, 47
"Six against nine" forward rate agreement, 266
Slope, eurodollar futures, 274
Smithsonian Agreement, 25, 30, 36
Snake arrangement, in European monetary system,
    36–47
"Snake in the lake," 37
"Snake in the tunnel," 37
Society for Worldwide Interbank Financial
    Telecommunication (SWIFT), 66
South Africa, gold pool and, 21
South African Reserve Bank, 21
Sovereign risk, eurodeposits and, 255
Soviet Foreign Trade Bank, 21
Soviet Union
    Atlantic Alliance against, 13
    marketing of gold by, 21
Special Drawing Right (SDR), 18–22, 31, 234
Speculation
    marketmakers and, 177–178
    private market, 217
Speculative efficiency hypothesis (SEH), 182–185
    formulations of, 184
    rejections of, 184–185
Speculator
    characteristics, 185–186
        full information, 185
        risk neutrality, 185
        wealth constraints and ultimate ruin, 186
    in futures market, risks, 117–118
    information set, 185
Spot, 124, 127
    buyer of options on, 122
    call option on, 128
        American, 121, 148

defined, 138
    European, 135, 141–142, 143
    value of, 135, 145t, 145
European puts on, 141–142
foreign currency options on
    compared to options of futures and futures-style
        options, 149t
    futures-style options on, 150
    futures-style put on, 124
    ordinary options on, futures-style options
        compared to, 138
    put option on, 128
        American, 122
        defined, 138–139
        European, 141–142
        value of, at expiration date, 135–136
    trader's sheet price for, 156
    writer of options on, 130
Spot delta, of average-rate option, 161
Spot exchange, 83, 84
    bid and asked currency prices of, 90–91
    foreign, domestic currency price of, 85–86
    market, 263
    options on, 121–122
    rate
        expected, 183, 185
        foreign currency option pricing and, 139–140
        level of, determinants of, 189
Spot month, 101
"Spot fortnight," 261
"Spot next," 261
Spot price, 106
    futures price and, 114
    movement of, 109, 112
Spot rate, 73–74, 83, 150
    European option price and, 139
    expected, 183, 185
    forward rate and, 87–88
    future, 182, 183
    martingale characteristics of, 186–187
Spot transactions, 71
"Spot week," 261
Stabilization, 324–325
Stabilization period (closing day), in eurobond
    market, 322
Stack hedge, 274
Standard and Poor's Corporation, 311
Standard deviation (SD), of deltas, 73–75
Statistical inference, 187–188
Statistical methodology, in forecasting, 223
Sterilization, 24
Sterilized intervention, 216
Sterling crisis, 16
    origin of, 248
Sterling loans, external, prohibition of, 16
Stock(s)
    of assets, 235
    pricing options on, 373–375
Stock-broking, fixed commissions on, 35
Straight bonds, 303
Straight currency swap, 349
Strike
    coupon bond with, call on, 363
    eurodollar futures, 282

Strike price, 121, 150
  on written option, 131–133
Strip yield curve, 268–269
  eurodollar futures, 273–274
Subparticipation, 293
Subscription
  lending through, 7
  quotas, 7
Superior information, for forecasting, 224
Supplemental capital, 257
Surplus, jerry-rigging of, 8
Swap(s), 71, 83, 293–295, 347–366
  asset-for-asset, 294–295
  asset-for-debt, 295
  asset sales for cash, 295
  caps, floors and collars, 358–359
  coupon bond portion of, 356
  currency, *See* Currency swap
  debt, 293
  defined, 347
  economic motives for, 347–348
  fixed-rate portion of, 356
  forward-forward, 83
  going short on, 359
  interest parity and, 87–89
  interest-rate, *See* Interest-rate swap
    cross-currency, 258
  loan, 293
  market for, 352–354
  options associated with, *See* Swaption
  price of, all-in-cost, 353
  right to terminate, 363
  risks in, 364–365
  valuing of, 354–358
Swap rate, 71
  bank quoting of, 89
Swaption(s), 359–364
  European, 364
  put, 362, 363
  putable swap, 363
  right to terminate swap, 363
  valuing of, 363–364
Swaption call, 359–362, 363
  delta, 361–362
  valuing of, 363
Swiss National Bank, 28, 314–315
Switzerland, *See also* Franc
  exchange rate control by, 80
  international bonds issued in, 314–315
Syndicate, eurobond
  lead manager, 317, 318, 319t
  managing group, 317
  principal paying agent in, 318
  selling group, 317
  traditional, organization of, 317–318, 318t
  underwriters, 317, 318, 320, 322
Syndicate bid, 324
Syndicate book, 322
Syndicate short, 324
Syndicated credit, reference rate in, margin added
    to, 289
Syndicated eurocredits
  banking syndicates, 287–288
  euronotes and eurocommercial paper, 295–297

loan agreements and risks of lending, 289–291
loan costs, 288–289, 290t
market for, 34
provisions for risk of government intervention,
    291–292
provisions related to borrower credit risk, 292
rules of the game for settling disputes, 292–293
secondary market for, 293–295
Syndicated loans, 47
  agreements, risk of lending and, 289–293
  bank management of, 289

T

T-bill, *See* Treasury bill
T-bond futures, *See* Treasury bond futures
Taxes, *See* Withholding taxes
Technical approach, to foreign exchange forecasting,
    223
Technical forecasters, evaluation of, 227–228
Tender panel, 296
Term credit, 251–252, 288
Term structure of eurocurrency rates, 263–266
  expectations theory of, 266
  "flat," 264
  "upward-sloping," 264
Theta, option, 152–153
Theta tradeoff, 156, 158
Theta value, 156
30/360, 330
"Three against six" forward rate agreement, 267,
    268
3-5-3 rule, 34
"Ticks," 101
Time deposits, 248, 249
  borrowing or lending of, 247
Time measures, in interest rate markets, 330–332
Time value, of foreign currency options, 139
Tokyo stock market crash, 35
"Tomorrow-next" deposits, 261
Total return, 227
Tourist Theorem, 202–203
Trade
  agreements, preferential, 30
  barriers to, 192, 201
  prohibitions on, 192
Trade balance, 207
Trade date, interest rate swap, 353
Trader
  arbitrage by, 88, 91
  buy and sell decisions, 178
  eurocurrency interest rates and, 88
  in foreign exchange market, 65, 73
    interbank, 69, 178
    as net speculator, 68
    profits, 69
  futures, 102
  information set, 178–179
  interest parity and, 86–87
  market equilibrium and, 180
Trading, in eurobond market, 329–330
Traditional time schedule, for new eurobond
    offering, 321–323

Transaction
  costs, law of one price and, 191–192
  in eurobond market, 333
Treasury bill (T-bill), 233
  margin posted as, 103–104
Treasury bond (T-bond) futures
  contract, 340
  equilibrium price for, 340
  hedging with, 345–346
  short, 339
Treaty of Rome, 47
Triangular arbitrage, 70
Trust funds, 233
"Two business days after," defined, 75–76

U

Unbiasedness, test for, 184
Uncertainty, dealing with, 233
Underwriters, in eurobond syndicate, 317, 318, 320,
  322
Underwriting, 36
  bought deal, 36
United Nations Bank, 6, See also Inter-Allied Bank
United States, See also Dollar
  assistance to Japan, 58
  domestic banks, See Domestic banks
  domestic market
    fee structure for new eurobond issues in, 320
    time measures in, 331
  domestic rates, eurodollar rates compared to, 263t
  eurocurrency operations in, 254
  flows in foreign assets, 211, 212t
  foreign bonds issued in, 301, See also Yankee
    bonds
  gold prices and, Bretton Woods agreement and,
    8–9
  international banking, 255
  International Banking Facilities in, 14
  international debt crisis and, 55–57
  involvement in Bretton Woods agreement, 4
  legal aspects of eurodollar bonds issues, 307–310
  Lend-Lease aid to Great Britain, 5
  margin requirements, 103
  money supply (M1) growth, 22
U.S. bonds
  bearer bonds
    issuing of, to non U.S. residents, 309
    withholding tax and, 309–310
  corporate bonds, withholding tax on, 309
  government bonds, 309
  real interest rate on, 237
  treasury bonds, 340, See also Treasury-bond
    futures
United States citizens, purchase of eurobonds by,
  308
U.S. Congress, Bretton Woods agreement and, 10
U.S. Council of Economic Advisors, 10
U.S. Equalization Tax, 35
U.S. Securities ACT of 1933, 308, 310
U.S. Securities and Exchange Commission (SEC),
  295, 308
U.S. Treasury, 310

U.S. Voluntary Foreign Credit Restraint Program
  (FCRP), 14
Up-front costs, 288, 289

V

Values, 286
  expected, 221
  forecasted, 221
Variance, portfolio, calculation of, 238–240, 241
Variation margin, 103
  eurodollar futures, 275, 278
Vega. See also Lambda
Vehicular currency, 70
Vietnam War, effect on Japan's economy, 58
Viner, J., 5
Vneshtorgbank, 21
Volatility, implied, 154–155

W

Wall Street Journal, The, 255
Walras, L., 67
Walrasian auctioneer, marketmakers versus, 66–69
S. G. Warburg, 35
Warrant, 368
Wealth, limitations, speculator's, 115–116, 186
Weights, 193
  portfolio, 239, 241
Wells Fargo, 255
Werner, P., 36
Western Europe, eurocurrency operations in, 253
Weyerhaeuser Capital Corporation, 345
White, H.D., 4, 5–6
Wild card option, 341
Windows, 325
Withholding taxes
  bearer bonds and, 309–310
  on loans, 291–292
World Bank (International Bank for Reconstruction
    and Development), 6
  and Baker Plan, 55–56
  swap of debt payments by, 350
Wozchod Handelsbank, 21
Wriston, W., 54
Writer of options, 122, 130–133
  on foreign currency futures, 122

Y

Yamaichi, interest rate swaps by, 352
Yankee bonds, 301
  market for, 310–311
    secondary, 311
  rating of, 311
  shelf registration, 310–311
Yen
  internationalization of, 60
  reevaluation of, 58
  undervaluation of, 22–23, 24, 58–59
Yen eurobonds, 312–314
Yield
  current, 335
  swaps quoted in terms of, 353

Yield curve, riding of, 336–337
Yield pricing, 325
Yield to maturity, 335
  in index-based futures, 343–344
Yoshida, S., 57

Z
Zaibatsu, 57
Zero-coupon bonds, 304–305, 333
Zero-sum game, 99
"Zone of monetary stability," 37